S0-BBX-821

Learning Theories

An Educational Perspective

Sixth Edition

Dale H. Schunk
The University of North Carolina at Greensboro

Boston   Columbus   Indianapolis   New York   San Francisco   Upper Saddle River
Amsterdam   Cape Town   Dubai   London   Madrid   Milan   Munich   Paris   Montreal   Toronto
Delhi   Mexico City   Sao Paulo   Sydney   Hong Kong   Seoul   Singapore   Taipei   Tokyo

Vice President/Editor in Chief: Paul Smith
Editorial Assistant: Matthew Buchholz
Marketing Manager: Joanna Sabella
Managing Editor: Central Publishing
Project Manager: Laura Messerly
Full-Service Project Management: Sudeshna Nandy/Aptara®, Inc.
Operations Specialist: Laura Messerly
Composition: Aptara®, Inc.
Photo Researcher: Annie Pickert
Design Director: Jayne Conte
Cover Designer: Suzanne Duda
Cover Image: Shutterstock
Printer/Binder: Courier/Westford
Cover Printer: Lehigh-Phoenix Color
Text Font: 10/12 Garamond

Credits and acknowledgments borrowed from other sources and reproduced, with permission, in this textbook appear on appropriate page within.

Copyright © 2012, 2008, 2004, 2000, 1996, 1991 by Pearson Education, Inc., publishing as Allyn & Bacon, 501 Boylston Street, Boston, MA, 02116. All rights reserved. Manufactured in the United States of America. This publication is protected by Copyright, and permission should be obtained from the publisher prior to any prohibited reproduction, storage in a retrieval system, or transmission in any form or by any means, electronic, mechanical, photocopying, recording, or likewise. To obtain permission(s) to use material from this work, please submit a written request to Pearson Education, Inc., Permissions Department, 501 Boylston Street, Boston, MA, 02116, or email permissionsus@pearson.com.

Library of Congress Cataloguing in Publication Data

Schunk, Dale H.
    Learning theories : an educational perspective / Dale H. Schunk.—6th ed.
        p. cm.
    Includes bibliographical references and index.
    ISBN-13: 978-0-13-707195-1
    ISBN-10: 0-13-707195-7
    1. Learning.   2. Cognition.   3. Learning, Psychology of.   I. Title.
    LB1060.S37 2012
    370.15'23—dc22

                                    2010048468

10 9 8 7 6 5 4 3 2

www.pearsonhighered.com

ISBN-10:   0-13-707195-7
ISBN-13: 978-0-13-707195-1

Dedication

To Barry Zimmerman,
mentor, colleague, and friend

Brief Contents

Contents

Preface

The study of human learning continues to develop and expand. As researchers from various theoretical traditions test their ideas and hypotheses in basic and applied settings, their research findings give rise to improvements in teaching and learning by students of all ages. Especially noteworthy is how topics once seen as not intimately connected with learning—such as motivation, technology, and self-regulation—are increasingly being addressed by researchers and practitioners.

Although the field of learning is ever changing, the primary objectives of this sixth edition remain the same as those of the previous editions: (a) to inform students of learning theoretical principles, concepts, and research findings, especially as they relate to education and (b) to provide applications of principles and concepts in settings where teaching and learning occur. The text continues to focus on cognition, although behaviorism also is discussed. This cognitive focus is consistent with the contemporary constructivist emphasis on active learners who seek, form, and modify their knowledge, skills, strategies, and beliefs.

STRUCTURE OF THIS TEXT

The text's 10 chapters are organized as follows. The introductory chapter discusses learning theory, research, and issues, as well as historical foundations of the study of learning and the relation of learning to instruction. At the end of this chapter are three scenarios involving elementary, secondary, and university settings. Throughout the text, these three settings are used to demonstrate applications of principles of learning, motivation, and self-regulation. Chapter 2 discusses the neuroscience of learning. Presenting this material early in the text is beneficial so that readers better understand subsequent links made between brain functions and cognitive and constructivist learning principles. Behaviorism, which dominated the field of learning for many years, is addressed in Chapter 3. Current cognitive and constructivist views of learning are covered in the next four chapters: social cognitive theory; information processing theory; constructivism; and cognitive learning processes. The final three chapters cover topics relevant to and closely integrated with learning theories: motivation; self-regulation; and development.

NEW TO THIS EDITION

Readers familiar with prior editions will notice many content and organizational changes in this edition, which reflect evolving theoretical and research emphases. Self-regulation, which in recent editions was covered in other chapters, now is a chapter on its own. This chapter highlights the importance of self-regulation in learning and reflects the increasing emphasis on self-regulation by researchers and practitioners. Given the prevalence of technology in schools and homes, the text includes new sections on learning from electronic media and in computer-based learning environments. In prior editions, content-area learning and instructional models were covered in separate chapters. In this sixth edition, this material is integrated into other chapters at appropriate places, which provides better coherence and connection between learning and content instruction. Some chapters have been reordered in the text, and some topics have been shifted within chapters to provide a better flow. The continued growth of research relevant to academic learning led to new terms incorporated into the glossary and to more than 140 new references.

This edition continues to provide many examples of learning concepts and principles applied to settings where learning occurs. Each chapter after the introductory chapter contains a new section on instructional applications. Chapters open with vignettes that illustrate some of the principles discussed in the chapters and also contain many informal examples and detailed applications. Many of the latter are set in the scenarios described in Chapter 1. Most of the applications in the chapters pertain to K-12 learners, but applications also address younger and older students and learning in out-of-school settings.

The text is intended for use by graduate students in education or related disciplines, as well as by upper-level undergraduates interested in education. It is assumed that most students have taken a prior course in education or psychology and currently work in an educational capacity or anticipate pursuing an educational career. In addition to courses on learning, the text is appropriate for any course that covers learning in some depth, such as courses on motivation, educational psychology, human development, and instructional design.

ACKNOWLEDGMENTS

I gratefully acknowledge several individuals for their assistance with this project. Throughout my career, many colleagues have enriched my thinking about learning processes and applications, including Albert Bandura, Curt Bonk, James Chapman, Herb Clark, Lyn Corno, Peg Ertmer, Doreen Ferko, the late Nate Gage, Marilyn Haring, Carolyn Jagacinski, Mark Lepper, Dave Lohman, Judith Meece, Sam Miller, Carol Mullen, the late John Nicholls, the late Frank Pajares, the late Paul Pintrich, Don Rice, Ellen Usher, Claire Ellen Weinstein, Allan Wigfield, Phil Winne, and Barry Zimmerman. I continue to benefit from activities with members of professional organizations, especially the Motivation in Education Special Interest Group of the American Educational Research Association, and Division 15 (Educational Psychology) of the American Psychological Association. My learning has been broadened by many outstanding students, teachers, counselors, administrators, and superintendents with whom I have worked. Sincere thanks go to graduate and undergraduate student collaborators for their assistance on research projects.

For many years, my editor at Pearson Education was Kevin Davis. I am so thankful for all the guidance and support provided by Kevin, which has served to strengthen and improve this text. With this edition, Paul Smith assumed the editorial responsibilities, and he has done a fantastic job. It has been a pleasure working with Paul. Special thanks also are due to Matt Buchholz and Cynthia Parsons at Pearson for their editorial assistance. I wish to thank the following reviewers of the fifth edition: Ronald A. Beghetto, University of Oregon; Denise Ward Hood, Northern Arizona University; and Sherri Horner, Bowling Green State University. At the University of North Carolina at Greensboro, I appreciate the assistance with administrative tasks provided by Tomi Register, Liz Meeks, and Melissa Edmonds-Kruep.

I am ever grateful for the love and encouragement from my parents, the late Mil and Al Schunk, and for the ways that friends Bill Gattis, Rob Eyman, Doug Curyea, and the late Jim Tozer have helped me keep life's priorities straight. I express deep gratitude to Caryl and Laura Schunk for their understanding, support, encouragement, and love since the first edition of this text appeared in 1991. Caryl assisted with many of the examples and applications based on her experiences in K-12 education. Laura, who was a baby when the first edition was published and today is poised to graduate from college, is an intelligent, motivated, and sociable young woman. The impact of learning in her life continually brings this text close to home.

1

Introduction to the Study of Learning

Russ Nyland teaches an education course for graduate students on cognitive instruction and learning. It is toward the end of the semester, and, as class finishes one day, three students approach him: Jeri Kendall, Matt Bowers, and Trisha Pascella.

Russ: What's up? Wasn't I clear today?

Jeri: Dr. Nyland, can we talk with you? We've been talking, and it's late in the course and we're still confused.

Russ: About what?

Jeri: Well, we've been studying all these theorists. It seems like they're saying different things, but maybe not. Bandura, Bruner, Anderson, Vygotsky, and the others. They make different points, but then some of what they say seems to overlap what others say.

Matt: Yeah, I'm so confused. I read these theorists and think like, yeah, I agree with that. But then it seems like I agree with everything. I thought you were supposed to have one theory, to believe one way and not others. But it seems like there's a lot of overlap between theories.

Russ: You're right Matt, there is. Most of what we've studied in this course are cognitive theories, and they are alike because they say that learning involves changes in cognitions—knowledge, skills, beliefs. Most theorists also say that learners construct their knowledge and beliefs; they don't automatically adopt what somebody tells them. So yes, there is much overlap.

Trisha: So then what are we to do? Am I supposed to be something like an information processing theorist, a social cognitive theorist, a constructivist? That's what I'm confused about.

Russ: No, you don't have to be one or the other. There may be one theory that you like better than the others, but maybe that theory doesn't address everything you want it to. So then you can borrow from other theories. For example, when I was in grad school I worked with a professor whose specialty was cognitive learning. There was another professor who did developmental research. I really liked her research, probably because I had been a teacher and was interested in development, especially the changes in kids from elementary to middle school. So I was a learning theorist who borrowed from the developmental literature and still do. It's ok to do that!

Jeri: Well that makes me feel better. But it's late in the course, and I guess I want to know what I should be doing next.

Russ: Tell you what—next class I'll spend some time on this. A good place to start is not to decide which type of theorist you are, but rather determine what you believe about learning and what types of learning you're interested in. Then you can see which theory matches up well to your beliefs and assumptions and maybe do as I did—borrow from others.

Matt: Isn't that what you call being eclectic?

Russ: Perhaps, but you may still have one preferred theory that you then adapt as needed. That's okay to do. In fact, that's how theories are improved—by incorporating ideas that weren't in them originally.

Trisha: Thanks Dr. Nyland. This is really helpful.

Learning involves acquiring and modifying knowledge, skills, strategies, beliefs, attitudes, and behaviors. People learn cognitive, linguistic, motor, and social skills, and these can take many forms. At a simple level, children learn to solve $2 + 2 = ?$, to recognize y in the word *daddy*, to tie their shoes, and to play with other children. At a more complex level, students learn to solve long-division problems, write term papers, ride a bicycle, and work cooperatively on a group project.

This book is about how human learning occurs, which factors influence it, and how learning principles apply in various educational contexts. Animal learning is de-emphasized, which is not intended to downgrade its importance because we have gained much knowledge about learning from animal research. But human learning is fundamentally different from animal learning because human learning is more complex, elaborate, rapid, and typically involves language.

This chapter provides an overview of the study of learning. Initially, learning is defined and examined in settings where it occurs. An overview is given of some important philosophical and psychological precursors of contemporary theories that helped to establish the groundwork for the application of learning theories to education. The roles of learning theory and research are discussed, and methods commonly used to assess learning are described. The links between learning theories and instruction are explained, after which critical issues in the study of learning are presented.

At the end of this chapter are three scenarios that involve learning with elementary, secondary, and college students. Background information is given about the learners, teachers, instruction, content, setting, and other features. In subsequent chapters, these scenarios will be used to exemplify the operation of learning principles. Readers will benefit from seeing how different learning principles are applied in an integrated fashion in the same settings.

The opening scenario describes a situation that happens to many students when they take a course in learning, instruction, or motivation and are exposed to different theories. Students often think that they are supposed to believe in one theory and adopt the views of those theorists. They often are confused by the perceived overlap between theories.

As Russ says, that is normal. Although theories differ in many ways, including their general assumptions and guiding principles, many rest on a common foundation. This text focuses on cognitive views of learning, which contend that learning involves changes in learners' cognitions—their thoughts, beliefs, skills, and the like. These theories differ in how they predict that learning occurs—in the processes of learning—and in what aspects of learning they stress. Thus, some theories are oriented more toward basic learning and others toward applied learning (and, within that, in different content areas); some stress the role of development, others are strongly linked with instruction; and some emphasize motivation.

Russ advises his students to examine their beliefs and assumptions about learning rather than decide which type of theorist they are. This is good advice. Once it is clear in our minds where we stand on learning in general, then the theoretical perspective or perspectives that are most relevant will emerge. As you study this text, it will help if you reflect on your beliefs and assumptions about learning and decide how these align with the theories.

This chapter should help to prepare you for an in-depth study of learning by providing a framework for understanding learning and some background material against which to view contemporary theories. When you finish studying this chapter, you should be able to do the following:

- Define learning and identify instances of learned and unlearned phenomena.

- Distinguish between rationalism and empiricism and explain the major tenets of each.

- Discuss how the work of Wundt, Ebbinghaus, the Structuralists, and the Functionalists helped to establish psychology as a science.

- Describe the major features of different research paradigms.

- Discuss the central features of different methods of assessing learning.

- State some instructional principles common to many learning theories.

- Explicate the ways that learning theory and educational practice complement and refine one another.

- Explain differences between behavioral and cognitive theories with respect to various issues in the study of learning.

LEARNING DEFINED

People agree that learning is important, but they hold different views on the causes, processes, and consequences of learning. There is no one definition of learning that is universally accepted by theorists, researchers, and practitioners (Shuell, 1986). Although people disagree about the precise nature of learning, the following is a general definition of learning that is consistent with this book's cognitive focus and that captures the criteria most educational professionals consider central to learning.

Learning is an enduring change in behavior, or in the capacity to behave in a given fashion, which results from practice or other forms of experience.

Table 1.1
Criteria of learning.

- Learning involves change
- Learning endures over time
- Learning occurs through experience

Let us examine this definition in depth to identify three criteria for learning (Table 1.1).

One criterion is that *learning involves change*—in behavior or in the capacity for behavior. People learn when they become capable of doing something differently. At the same time, we must remember that learning is inferential. We do not observe learning directly but rather its products or outcomes. Learning is assessed based on what people say, write, and do. But we also add that learning involves a changed capacity to behave in a given fashion because it is not uncommon for people to learn skills, knowledge, beliefs, or behaviors without demonstrating them at the time learning occurs (Chapter 4).

A second criterion is that *learning endures over time*. This excludes temporary behavioral changes (e.g., slurred speech) brought about by such factors as drugs, alcohol, and fatigue. Such changes are temporary because when the cause is removed, the behavior returns to its original state. But learning may not last forever because forgetting occurs. It is debatable how long changes must last to be classified as learned, but most people agree that changes of brief duration (e.g., a few seconds) do not qualify as learning.

A third criterion is that *learning occurs through experience* (e.g., practice, observation of others). This criterion excludes behavioral changes that are primarily determined by heredity, such as maturational changes in children (e.g., crawling, standing). Nonetheless, the distinction between maturation and learning often is not clear-cut. People may be genetically predisposed to act in given ways, but the actual development of the particular behaviors depends on the environment. Language offers a good example. As the human vocal apparatus matures, it becomes able to produce language; but the actual words produced are learned from interactions with others. Although genetics are critical for children's language acquisition, teaching and social interactions with parents, teachers, and peers exert a strong influence on children's language achievements (Mashburn, Justice, Downer, & Pianta, 2009). In similar fashion, with normal development children crawl and stand, but the environment must be responsive and allow these behaviors to occur. Children whose movements are forcibly restrained do not develop normally.

PRECURSORS OF MODERN LEARNING THEORIES

The roots of contemporary theories of learning extend far into the past. Many of the issues addressed and questions asked by modern researchers are not new but rather reflect a desire for people to understand themselves, others, and the world about them.

This section traces the origins of contemporary learning theories, beginning with a discussion of philosophical positions on the origin of knowledge and its relation to the environment and concluding with some early psychological views on learning. This review is selective and includes historical material relevant to learning in educational settings. Readers interested in a comprehensive discussion should consult other sources (Bower & Hilgard, 1981; Heidbreder, 1933; Hunt, 1993).

Learning Theory and Philosophy

From a philosophical perspective, learning can be discussed under the heading of *epistemology*, which refers to the study of the origin, nature, limits, and methods of knowledge. How can we know? How can we learn something new? What is the source of knowledge? The complexity of how humans learn is illustrated in this excerpt from Plato's *Meno* (427?–347? B.C.):

> I know, Meno, what you mean . . . You argue that a man cannot enquire (*sic*) either about that which he knows, or about that which he does not know; for if he knows, he has no need to enquire (*sic*); and if not, he cannot; for he does not know the very subject about which he is to enquire (*sic*). (1965, p. 16)

Two positions on the origin of knowledge and its relationship to the environment are rationalism and empiricism. These positions are recognizable in current learning theories.

Rationalism. *Rationalism* refers to the idea that knowledge derives from reason without recourse to the senses. The distinction between mind and matter, which figures prominently in rationalist views of human knowledge, can be traced to Plato, who distinguished knowledge acquired via the senses from that gained by reason. Plato believed that things (e.g., houses, trees) are revealed to people via the senses, whereas individuals acquire ideas by reasoning or thinking about what they know. People have ideas about the world, and they learn (discover) these ideas by reflecting upon them. Reason is the highest mental faculty because through reason people learn abstract ideas. The true nature of houses and trees can be known only by reflecting upon the ideas of houses and trees.

Plato escaped the dilemma in *Meno* by assuming that true knowledge, or the knowledge of ideas, is innate and is brought into awareness through reflection. Learning is recalling what exists in the mind. Information acquired with the senses by observing, listening, tasting, smelling, or touching constitutes raw materials rather than ideas. The mind is innately structured to reason and provide meaning to incoming sensory information.

The rationalist doctrine also is evident in the writings of René Descartes (1596–1650), a French philosopher and mathematician. Descartes employed doubt as a method of inquiry. By doubting, he arrived at conclusions that were absolute truths and not subject to doubt. The fact that he could doubt led him to believe that the mind (thought) exists, as reflected in his dictum, "I think, therefore I am." Through deductive reasoning from general premises to specific instances, he proved that God exists and concluded that ideas arrived at through reason must be true.

Like Plato, Descartes established a mind–matter dualism; however, for Descartes the external world was mechanical, as were the actions of animals. People are distinguished by their ability to reason. The human soul, or the capacity for thought, influences the body's mechanical actions, but the body acts on the mind by bringing in sensory experiences. Although Descartes postulated dualism, he also hypothesized mind–matter interaction.

The rationalist perspective was extended by the German philosopher Immanuel Kant (1724–1804). In his *Critique of Pure Reason* (1781), Kant addressed mind–matter dualism and noted that the external world is disordered but is perceived as orderly because order is imposed by the mind. The mind takes in the external world through the senses and alters it according to subjective, innate laws. The world never can be known as it exists but only as it is perceived. People's perceptions give the world its order. Kant reaffirmed the role of reason as a source of knowledge, but contended that reason operates within the realm of experience. Absolute knowledge untouched by the external world does not exist. Rather, knowledge is empirical in the sense that information is taken in from the world and interpreted by the mind.

In summary, rationalism is the doctrine that knowledge arises through the mind. Although there is an external world from which people acquire sensory information, ideas originate from the workings of the mind. Descartes and Kant believed that reason acts upon information acquired from the world; Plato thought that knowledge can be absolute and acquired by pure reason.

Empiricism. In contrast to rationalism, *empiricism* refers to the idea that experience is the only source of knowledge. This position derives from Aristotle (384–322 B.C.), who was Plato's student and successor. Aristotle drew no sharp distinction between mind and matter. The external world is the basis for human sense impressions, which, in turn, are interpreted as lawful (consistent, unchanging) by the mind. The laws of nature cannot be discovered through sensory impressions, but rather through reason as the mind takes in data from the environment. Unlike Plato, Aristotle believed that ideas do not exist independently of the external world. The latter is the source of all knowledge.

Aristotle contributed to psychology with his principles of association as applied to memory. The recall of an object or idea triggers recall of other objects or ideas similar to, different from, or experienced close, in time or space, to the original object or idea. The more that two objects or ideas are associated, the more likely that recall of one will trigger recall of the other. The notion of associative learning is prominent in many learning theories.

Another influential figure was British philosopher John Locke (1632–1704), who developed a school of thought that was empirical but that stopped short of being truly experimental (Heidbreder, 1933). In his *Essay Concerning Human Understanding* (1690), Locke noted that there are no innate ideas; all knowledge derives from two types of experience: sensory impressions of the external world and personal awareness. At birth the mind is a *tabula rasa* (blank tablet). Ideas are acquired from sensory impressions and personal reflections on these impressions. Nothing can be in the mind that does not originate in the senses. The mind is composed of ideas that have been combined in different ways. The mind can be understood only by breaking down ideas into simple units. This atomistic notion of thought is associationist; complex ideas are collections of simple ones.

The issues Locke raised were debated by such profound thinkers as George Berkeley (1685–1753), David Hume (1711–1776), and John Stuart Mill (1806–1873). Berkeley believed that mind is the only reality. He was an empiricist because he believed that ideas derive from experiences. Hume agreed that people never can be certain about external reality, but he also believed that people cannot be certain about their own ideas. Individuals experience external reality through their ideas, which constitute the only reality. At the same time, Hume accepted the empiricist doctrine that ideas derive from experience and become associated with one another. Mill was an empiricist and associationist, but he rejected the idea that simple ideas combine in orderly ways to form complex ones. Mill argued that simple ideas generate complex ideas, but that the latter need not be composed of the former. Simple ideas can produce a complex thought that might bear little obvious relation to the ideas of which it is composed. Mill's beliefs reflect the notion that the whole is greater than the sum of its parts, which is an integral assumption of Gestalt psychology (Chapter 5).

In summary, empiricism holds that experience is the only form of knowledge. Beginning with Aristotle, empiricists have contended that the external world serves as the basis for people's impressions. Most accept the notion that objects or ideas associate to form complex stimuli or mental patterns. Locke, Berkeley, Hume, and Mill are among the better-known philosophers who espoused empiricist views.

Although philosophical positions and learning theories do not neatly map onto one another, conditioning theories (Chapter 3) typically are empiricist whereas cognitive theories (Chapters 4–6) are more rationalistic. Overlap often is evident; for example, most theories agree that much learning occurs through association. Cognitive theories stress association between cognitions and beliefs; conditioning theories emphasize the association of stimuli with responses and consequences.

Beginnings of the Psychological Study of Learning

The formal beginning of psychology as a science is difficult to pinpoint (Mueller, 1979), although systematic psychological research began to appear in the latter part of the nineteenth century. Two persons who had a significant impact on learning theory are Wundt and Ebbinghaus.

Wundt's Psychological Laboratory. The first psychological laboratory was opened by Wilhelm Wundt (1832–1920) in Leipzig, Germany, in 1879, although William James had started a teaching laboratory at Harvard University four years earlier (Dewsbury, 2000). Wundt wanted to establish psychology as a new science. His laboratory acquired an international reputation with an impressive group of visitors, and he founded a journal to report psychological research. The first research laboratory in the United States was opened in 1883 by G. Stanley Hall (Dewsbury, 2000; see Chapter 10).

Establishing a psychological laboratory was particularly significant because it marked the transition from formal philosophical theorizing to an emphasis on experimentation and instrumentation (Evans, 2000). The laboratory was a collection of scholars who conducted research aimed at scientifically explaining phenomena (Benjamin, 2000). In his book *Principles of Physiological Psychology* (1873), Wundt contended that psychology is the study of the mind. The psychological method should be patterned after the physiological method; that is, the process being studied should be experimentally investigated in terms of controlled stimuli and measured responses.

Wundt's laboratory attracted a cadre of researchers to investigate such phenomena as sensation, perception, reaction times, verbal associations, attention, feelings, and emotions. Wundt also was a mentor for many psychologists who subsequently opened laboratories in the United States (Benjamin, Durkin, Link, Vestal, & Acord, 1992). Although Wundt's laboratory produced no great psychological discoveries or critical experiments, it established psychology as a discipline and experimentation as the method of acquiring and refining knowledge.

Ebbinghaus's Verbal Learning. Hermann Ebbinghaus (1850–1909) was a German psychologist who was not connected with Wundt's laboratory but who also helped to validate the experimental method and establish psychology as a science. Ebbinghaus investigated higher mental processes by conducting research on memory. He accepted the principles of association and believed that learning and the recall of learned information depend on the frequency of exposure to the material. Properly testing this hypothesis required using material with which participants were unfamiliar. Ebbinghaus invented *nonsense syllables*, which are three-letter consonant-vowel-consonant combinations (e.g., cew, tij).

Ebbinghaus was an avid researcher who often used himself as the subject of study. In a typical experiment, he would devise a list of nonsense syllables, look at each syllable briefly, pause, and then look at the next syllable. He determined how many times through the list (trials) it took to him learn the entire list. He made fewer errors with repeated study of the list, needed more trials to learn more syllables, forgot rapidly at first but then more gradually, and required fewer trials to relearn syllables than to learn them the first time. He also studied a list of syllables some time after original learning and calculated a *savings score*, defined as the time or trials necessary for relearning as a percentage of the time or trials required for original learning. He memorized some meaningful passages and found that meaningfulness made learning easier. Ebbinghaus compiled the results of his research in the book *Memory* (1885/1964).

Although important historically, there are concerns about this research. Ebbinghaus typically employed only one participant (himself), and it is unlikely he was unbiased or a typical learner. We also might question how well results for learning nonsense syllables generalize to meaningful learning (e.g., text passages). Nonetheless, he was a careful researcher, and many of his findings later were validated experimentally. He was a pioneer in bringing higher mental processes into the experimental laboratory.

Structuralism and Functionalism

The work by Wundt and Ebbinghaus was systematic but confined to particular locations and of limited influence on psychological theory. The turn of the century marked the beginning of more widespread schools of psychological thought. Two perspectives that emerged were structuralism and functionalism. Although neither exists as a unified doctrine today, their early proponents were influential in the history of psychology as it relates to learning.

Structuralism. Edward B. Titchener (1867–1927) was Wundt's student in Leipzig. In 1892 he became the director of the psychology laboratory at Cornell University. He imported Wundt's experimental methods into U.S. psychology.

Titchener's psychology, which eventually became known as *structuralism*, represented a combination of associationism with the experimental method. Structuralists believed that human consciousness is a legitimate area of scientific investigation, and they studied the structure or makeup of mental processes. They postulated that the mind is composed of associations of ideas and that to study the complexities of the mind, one must break down these associations into single ideas (Titchener, 1909).

The experimental method used often by Wundt, Titchener, and other structuralists was *introspection*, which is a type of self-analysis. Titchener noted that scientists rely on observation of phenomena and that introspection is a form of observation. Participants in introspection studies verbally reported their immediate experiences following exposure to objects or events. For example, if shown a table they might report their perceptions of shape, size, color, and texture. They were told not to label or report their knowledge about the object or the meanings of their perceptions. Thus, if they verbalized "table" while viewing a table, they were attending to the stimulus rather than to their conscious processes.

Introspection was a uniquely psychological process and helped to demarcate psychology from the other sciences. It was a professional method that required training in its use so that an introspectionist could determine when individuals were examining their own conscious processes rather than their interpretations of phenomena.

Unfortunately, introspection often was problematic and unreliable. It is difficult and unrealistic to expect people to ignore meanings and labels. When shown a table, it is natural that people say "table," think of uses, and draw on related knowledge. The mind is not structured to compartmentalize information so neatly, so by ignoring meanings introspectionists disregarded a central aspect of the mind. Watson (Chapter 3) decried the use of introspection, and its problems helped to rally support for an objective psychology that studied only observable behavior (Heidbreder, 1933). Edward L. Thorndike, a prominent psychologist (Chapter 3), contended that education should be based on scientific facts, not opinions (Popkewitz, 1998). The ensuing emphasis on behavioral psychology dominated U.S. psychology for the first half of the twentieth century.

Another problem was that structuralists studied associations of ideas, but they had little to say about how these associations are acquired. Further, it was not clear that introspection was the appropriate method to study such higher mental processes as reasoning and problem solving, which are removed from immediate sensation and perception.

Functionalism. While Titchener was at Cornell, developments in other locales challenged the validity of structuralism. Among these was work by the functionalists. *Functionalism* is the view that mental processes and behaviors of living organisms help them adapt to their environments (Heidbreder, 1933). This school of thought flourished at the University of Chicago with John Dewey (1867–1949) and James Angell (1869–1949). An especially prominent functionalist was William James (1842–1910). Functionalism was the dominant American psychological perspective from the 1890s until World War I (Green, 2009).

James's principal work was the two-volume series, *The Principles of Psychology* (1890), which is considered one of the greatest psychology texts ever written (Hall, 2003). An abridged version was published for classroom use (James, 1892). James was an empiricist who believed that experience is the starting point for examining thought, but he was not an associationist. He thought that simple ideas are not passive copies of environmental inputs but rather are the product of abstract thought and study (Pajares, 2003).

James (1890) postulated that consciousness is a continuous process rather than a collection of discrete bits of information. One's "stream of thought" changes as experiences change. "Consciousness, from our natal day, is of a teeming multiplicity of objects and relations, and what we call simple sensations are results of discriminative attention, pushed often to a very high degree" (Vol. I, p. 224). James described the purpose of consciousness as helping individuals adapt to their environments.

Functionalists incorporated James's ideas into their doctrine. Dewey (1896) argued that psychological processes could not be broken into discrete parts and that consciousness must be viewed holistically. "Stimulus" and "response" describe the roles played by objects or events, but these roles could not be separated from the overall reality (Bredo, 2003). Dewey cited an example from James (1890) about a baby who sees a candle burning, reaches out to grasp it, and experiences burned fingers. From a stimulus–response perspective, the sight of the candle is a stimulus and reaching is a response; getting burned (pain) is a stimulus for the response of withdrawing the hand. Dewey argued that this sequence is better viewed as one large coordinated act in which seeing and reaching influence each other.

Functionalists were influenced by Darwin's writings on evolution and studied the utility of mental processes in helping organisms adapt to their environments and survive (Bredo, 2003; Green, 2009). Functional factors were bodily structures, consciousness, and such cognitive processes as thinking, feeling, and judging. Functionalists were interested in how mental processes operate, what they accomplish, and how they vary with environmental conditions. They also saw the mind and body as interacting rather than existing separately.

Functionalists opposed the introspection method, not because it studied consciousness but rather because of how it studied consciousness. Introspection attempted to reduce consciousness to discrete elements, which functionalists believed was not possible. Studying a phenomenon in isolation does not reveal how it contributes to an organism's survival.

Dewey (1900) argued that the results of psychological experiments should be applicable to education and daily life. Although this goal was laudable, it also was problematic because the research agenda of functionalism was too broad to offer a clear focus. This weakness paved the way for the rise of behaviorism as the dominant force in U.S. psychology (Chapter 3). Behaviorism used experimental methods, and it was psychology's emphasis on experimentation and observable phenomena that helped to firmly secure its standing as a science (Asher, 2003; Tweney & Budzynski, 2000).

LEARNING THEORY AND RESEARCH

Theory and research are integral to the study of learning. This section discusses some general functions of theory, along with key aspects of the research process.

Functions of Theory

A *theory* is a scientifically acceptable set of principles offered to explain a phenomenon. Theories provide frameworks for interpreting environmental observations and serve as bridges between research and education (Suppes, 1974). Research findings can be organized and systematically linked to theories. Without theories, people could view research findings as disorganized collections of data, because researchers and practitioners would have no overarching frameworks to which the data could be linked. Even when researchers obtain findings that do not seem to be directly linked to theories, they still must attempt to make sense of data and determine whether the data support theoretical predictions.

Theories reflect environmental phenomena and generate new research through *hypotheses*, or assumptions, that can be empirically tested. Hypotheses often can be stated as if-then statements: "If I do X, then Y should occur," where X and Y might be such events as "praise students for their progress in learning" and "raise their self-confidence and achievement," respectively. Thus, we might test the hypothesis, "If we praise students when they make progress in learning, then they should display higher self-confidence and achievement than students who are not praised for their progress." A theory is strengthened when hypotheses are supported by data. Theories may require revision if data do not support hypotheses.

Researchers often explore areas where there is little theory to guide them. In that case they formulate research objectives or questions to be answered. Regardless of whether researchers are testing hypotheses or exploring questions, they need to specify the research conditions as precisely as possible. Because research forms the basis for theory development and has important implications for teaching, the next section examines types of research and the process of conducting research.

Conducting Research

To specify the research conditions, we need to answer such questions as: Who will participate? Where will the study be conducted? What procedures will be employed? What are the variables and outcomes to be assessed?

We must define precisely the phenomena we are studying. We provide conceptual definitions of phenomena and also define them *operationally*, or in terms of the operations, instruments, and procedures we use to measure the phenomena. For example, we might define *self-efficacy* (covered in Chapter 4) conceptually as one's perceived capabilities for learning or performing a task and operationally by specifying how we assess self-efficacy in our study (e.g., one's score on a 30-item questionnaire). In addition to defining operationally the phenomena we study, we also must be precise about the procedure we follow. Ideally, we specify conditions so precisely that, after reading the description, another researcher could replicate our study.

Research studies that explore learning employ various types of *paradigms* (models). The following paragraphs describe the correlational, experimental, and qualitative paradigms, followed by a discussion of laboratory and field studies (Table 1.2).

Table 1.2
Learning research paradigms.

Type	Qualities
Correlational	Examines relations between variables
Experimental	One or more variables are altered and effects on other variables are assessed
Qualitative	Concerned with description of events and interpretation of meanings
Laboratory	Project conducted in a controlled setting
Field	Project conducted in a natural setting (e.g., school, home, work)

Correlational Research. *Correlational research* deals with exploring relations that exist between variables. A researcher might hypothesize that self-efficacy is positively correlated with (related to) achievement such that the higher the students' self-efficacy, the higher they achieve. To test this relation, the researcher might measure students' self-efficacy for solving mathematical problems and then assess how well they actually solve the problems. The researcher could statistically correlate the self-efficacy and achievement scores to determine the direction of the relation (positive, negative) and its strength (high, medium, low).

Correlational research helps to clarify relations among variables. Correlational findings often suggest directions for further research. If the researcher were to obtain a high positive correlation between self-efficacy and achievement, the next study might be an experiment that attempts to raise students' self-efficacy for learning and determine whether such an increase produces higher achievement.

A limitation of correlational research is that it cannot identify cause and effect. A positive correlation between self-efficacy and achievement could mean that (a) self-efficacy influences achievement, (b) achievement influences self-efficacy, (c) self-efficacy and achievement influence each other, or (d) self-efficacy and achievement are influenced by other, nonmeasured variables (e.g., parents, teachers). To determine cause and effect, an experimental study is necessary.

Experimental Research. In *experimental research* the researcher changes one or more (independent) variables and determines the effects on other (dependent) variables. The experimental researcher could form two groups of students, systematically raise self-efficacy beliefs among students in one group and not among students in the other group, and assess achievement in the two groups. If the first group performs better, the researcher might conclude that self-efficacy influences achievement. While the researcher alters variables to determine their effects on outcomes, she or he must hold constant other variables that potentially can affect outcomes (e.g., learning conditions).

Experimental research can clarify cause-effect relations, which helps us understand the nature of learning. At the same time, experimental research often is narrow in scope. Researchers typically study only a few variables and try to minimize effects of others, which is difficult to do and often unrealistic. Classrooms and other learning settings are complex places where many factors operate at once. To say that one or two variables cause outcomes may overemphasize their importance. It is necessary to replicate experiments and examine other variables to better understand effects.

Qualitative Research. The *qualitative research* paradigm is characterized by intensive study, descriptions of events, and interpretation of meanings. The theories and methods used are referred to under various labels including qualitative, ethnographic, participant observation, phenomenological, constructivist, and interpretative (Erickson, 1986).

Qualitative research is especially useful when researchers are interested in the structure of events rather than their overall distributions, when the meanings and perspectives of individuals are important, when actual experiments are impractical or unethical, and when there is a desire to search for new potential causal linkages that have not been discovered by experimental methods (Erickson, 1986). Research is varied and can range from analyses of verbal and nonverbal interactions within single lessons to in-depth observations and interviews over longer periods. Methods may include observations, use of existing records, interviews, and think-aloud protocols (i.e., participants talk aloud while performing tasks). It is not the choice of method that characterizes this approach—all of the aforementioned methods could be used in correlational or experimental studies—but rather the depth and quality of data analysis and interpretation.

The qualitative researcher might be curious about how self-efficacy contributes to the development of skills over time. She or he might work with a small group of students for several months. Through observations, interviews, and other forms of data collection, the researcher might examine how students' self-efficacy for learning changes in relation to skill refinement in reading, writing, and mathematics.

Qualitative research yields rich sources of data, which are more intensive and thorough than those typically obtained in correlational or experimental research. This model also can raise new questions and fresh perspectives on old questions that often are missed by traditional methods. A potential limitation is that qualitative studies typically include only a few participants, who may not be representative of a larger population of students or teachers. This limits generalization of findings beyond the research context. Another limitation is that data collection, analysis, and interpretation can be time consuming and therefore impractical for students wanting to graduate and professors wanting to build their publication records! Nonetheless, as a research model, this paradigm offers a useful approach for obtaining data typically not collected with other methods.

Laboratory and Field Research. *Laboratory research* is conducted in controlled settings, whereas *field research* is conducted where participants live, work, or attend school. During the first half of the twentieth century, most learning research was conducted on animals in laboratories. Today most learning research is conducted with people, and much is done in field settings. Any of the preceding research models (experimental, correlational, qualitative) can be applied in the laboratory or the field.

Laboratories offer a high degree of control over extraneous factors that can affect results, such as phones ringing, people talking, windows to look out of, and other persons in the room who are not part of the study. Light, sound, and temperature can be regulated. Laboratories also allow researchers to leave their equipment set up over lengthy periods and have all materials at their immediate disposal.

Such control is not possible in the field. Schools are noisy, and often it is difficult to find space to work. There are numerous distractions: Students and teachers walk by, bells ring, public announcements are made, and fire drills are held. Rooms may be too bright or dark, cold or warm, and used for other purposes so researchers have to set up equipment each time they work. Interpreting results in light of these distractions can be a problem.

An advantage of field research is that results are highly generalizable to other similar settings because studies are conducted where people typically learn. In contrast, generalization of laboratory findings to the field is done with less confidence. Laboratory research has yielded many important insights on learning, and researchers often attempt to replicate laboratory findings in the field.

Whether we choose the laboratory or the field depends on such factors as the purpose of the research, availability of participants, costs, and how we will use the results. If we choose the laboratory, we gain control but lose some generalizability, and vice versa if we choose the field. In the field, researchers try to minimize extraneous influences so that they can be more confident that their results are due to the factors they are studying.

ASSESSMENT OF LEARNING

We know that learning is inferential; we do not observe it directly but rather through its products and outcomes. Researchers and practitioners who work with students may believe that students have learned, but the only way to know is to assess learning's products and outcomes.

Assessment involves "a formal attempt to determine students' status with respect to educational variables of interest" (Popham, 2008, p. 6). In school, the educational variable of interest most often is student achievement in such areas as reading, writing, mathematics, science, and social studies. Although student achievement always has been critical, its importance was underscored by the federal government's No Child Left Behind Act of 2001 (Shaul & Ganson, 2005). This act has many provisions (Popham, 2008). Among the most significant are the requirements for annual testing of students in grades 3 through 8 and again in high school in reading and mathematics and for school systems to show increases in students making adequate yearly progress in these subjects.

Two points are noteworthy with respect to this text. Although accountability often leads to testing being the means of assessment, the latter includes many measurement procedures besides testing (described below). Researchers and practitioners want to know whether learning has occurred, and there may be procedures other than testing that provide evidence of student learning. Second, students' skills in content areas often are the learning outcome assessed, but researchers and practitioners may also be interested in other forms of learning. For example, they may want to know whether students have learned new attitudes or self-regulation strategies or whether students' interests, values, self-efficacy, and motivation have changed as a result of content learning.

This section covers ways to assess the products or outcomes of learning. These methods include direct observations, written responses, oral responses, ratings by others, and self-reports (Table 1.3).

Direct Observations

Direct observations are instances of student behavior that we observe to assess whether learning has occurred. Teachers employ direct observations frequently. A chemistry teacher wants students to learn laboratory procedures. The teacher observes students in the laboratory to determine whether they are implementing the proper procedures. A physical education instructor observes students dribble a basketball to assess how well they have learned the skill. An elementary teacher gauges how well students have learned the classroom rules based on their class behavior.

Direct observations are valid indexes of learning if they are straightforward and involve little inference by observers. They work best when the behaviors can be specified and then the students can be observed to ascertain whether their behaviors match the standard.

Table 1.3
Methods of assessing learning.

Category	Definition
Direct observations	Instances of behavior that demonstrate learning
Written responses	Written performances on tests, quizzes, homework, papers, and projects
Oral responses	Verbalized questions, comments, and responses during learning
Ratings by others	Observers' judgments of learners on attributes indicative of learning
Self-reports	People's judgments of themselves
■ Questionnaires	Written ratings of items or answers to questions
■ Interviews	Oral responses to questions
■ Stimulated recalls	Recall of thoughts accompanying one's performances at given times
■ Think-alouds	Verbalizing aloud one's thoughts, actions, and feelings while performing a task
■ Dialogues	Conversations between two or more persons

A problem with direct observations is that they focus only on what can be observed and therefore bypass the cognitive and affective processes that underlie actions. For example, the chemistry teacher knows that students have learned laboratory procedures but she or he does not know what the students are thinking about while they are performing the procedures or how confident they are about performing well.

A second problem is that, although directly observing a behavior indicates that learning has occurred, the absence of appropriate behavior does not mean that learning has not occurred. Learning is not the same as performance. Many factors other than learning can affect performance. Students may not perform learned actions because they are not motivated, are ill, or are busy doing other things. We have to rule out these other factors to conclude from the absence of performance that learning has not occurred. That requires making the assumption—which at times may be unwarranted—that since students usually try to do their best, if they do not perform, they have not learned.

Written Responses

Learning often is assessed based on students' *written responses* on tests, quizzes, homework, term papers, and reports. Based on the level of mastery indicated in the responses, teachers decide whether adequate learning has taken place or whether additional instruction is needed because students do not fully comprehend the material. For example, assume that a teacher is planning a unit on the geography of Hawaii. Initially the teacher assumes that students know little about this topic. A pretest given prior to the start of instruction will support the teacher's belief if the students score poorly. The teacher retests students following the instructional unit. Gains in test scores lead the teacher to conclude that learners have acquired some knowledge.

Their relative ease of use and capacity for covering a wide variety of material makes written responses desirable indicators of learning. We assume that written responses reflect learning, but many factors can affect performance of behavior even when students have learned. Written responses require us to believe that students are trying their best and that no extraneous factors (e.g., fatigue, illness, cheating) are operating such that their written work does not represent what they have learned. We must try to identify extraneous factors that can affect performance and cloud assessments of learning.

Oral Responses

Oral responses are an integral part of the school culture. Teachers call on students to answer questions and assess learning based on what they say. Students also ask questions during lessons. If their questions indicate a lack of understanding, this is a signal that proper learning has not occurred.

Like written responses, we assume that oral responses are valid reflections of what students know, which may not always be true. Further, verbalization is a task, and there may be problems translating what one knows into its oral expression due to unfamiliar terminology, anxiety about speaking, or language difficulties. Teachers may rephrase what students say, but such rephrasing may not accurately reflect the nature of students' thoughts.

Ratings by Others

Another way to assess learning is for individuals (e.g., teachers, parents, administrators, researchers, peers) to rate students on the quantity or quality of their learning. These *ratings by others* (e.g., "How well can Timmy solve problems of the type $52 \times 36 = ?$" "How much progress has Alicia made in her printing skills in the past 6 months?") provide useful data and can help to identify students with exceptional needs (e.g., "How often does Matt need extra time to learn?" "How quickly does Jenny finish her work?").

An advantage of ratings by others is that observers may be more objective about students than students are about themselves (self-reports, discussed next). Ratings also can be made for learning processes that underlie actions (e.g., comprehension, motivation, attitudes) and thereby provide data not attainable through direct observations; for example, "How well does Seth comprehend the causes of World War II?" But ratings by others require more inference than do direct observations. It may be problematic to accurately rate students' ease of learning, depth of understanding, or attitudes. Further, ratings require observers to remember what students do and will be distorted when raters selectively remember only positive or negative behaviors.

Self-Reports

Self-reports are people's assessments of and statements about themselves. Self-reports take various forms: questionnaires, interviews, stimulated recalls, think-alouds, and dialogues.

Questionnaires present respondents with items or questions asking about their thoughts and actions. Respondents may record the types of activities they engage in, rate their perceived levels of competence, and judge how often or how long they engage in them (e.g., "How long have you been studying Spanish?" "How difficult is it for you to learn geometric theorems?"). Many self-report instruments ask respondents to record ratings on numerical scales ("On a 10-point scale, where 1 = low and 10 = high, rate how good you are at reducing fractions.").

Interviews are a type of questionnaire in which an interviewer presents the questions or points to discuss and the respondent answers orally. Interviews typically are conducted individually, although groups can be interviewed. A researcher might describe a learning context and ask students how they typically learn in that setting (e.g., "When the French teacher begins a lesson, what are your thoughts? How well do you think you will do?"). Interviewers may need to prompt respondents if replies are too brief or not forthcoming.

In the *stimulated recall* procedure, people work on a task and afterward recall their thoughts at various points during the task. Interviewers query them (e.g., "What were you thinking about when you got stuck here?"). If the performance was videotaped, respondents subsequently watch it and recollect, especially when interviewers stop the recording and ask questions. It is imperative that the recall procedure be accomplished soon after the performance so that participants do not forget their thoughts.

Think-alouds are procedures in which students verbalize their thoughts, actions, and feelings while working on a task. Verbalizations may be recorded by observers and subsequently scored for level of understanding. Think-alouds require that respondents verbalize; many students are not used to talking aloud while working in school. Talking aloud may seem awkward to some, and they may feel self-conscious or otherwise have difficulty expressing their thoughts. Investigators may have to prompt students if they do not verbalize.

Another type of self-report is the *dialogue*, which is a conversation between two or more persons while engaged in a learning task. Like think-alouds, dialogues can be recorded and analyzed for statements indicating learning and factors that seem to affect learning in the setting. Although dialogues use actual interactions while students are working on a task, their analysis requires interpretation that may go beyond the actual elements in the situation.

The choice of self-report measure should match the purpose of the assessment. Questionnaires can cover a lot of material; interviews are better for exploring a few issues in depth. Stimulated recalls ask respondents to recall their thoughts at the time actions took place; think-alouds examine present thoughts. Dialogues allow for investigation of social interaction patterns.

Self-report instruments typically are easy to develop and administer; questionnaires are usually easy to complete and score. A problem can arise when inferences have to be drawn about students' responses. It is essential to have a reliable scoring system. Other concerns about self-reports are whether students are giving socially acceptable answers that do not match their beliefs, whether self-reported information corresponds to actual behavior, and whether young children are capable of self-reporting accurately. By guaranteeing that data are confidential, researchers can help promote truthful answering. A good means of validating self-reports is to use multiple assessments (e.g., self-reports, direct observations, oral and written responses). There is evidence that beginning around the third grade self-reports are valid and reliable indicators of the beliefs and actions they are designed to assess (Assor & Connell, 1992), but researchers need to use self-reports cautiously to minimize potential problems.

RELATION OF LEARNING AND INSTRUCTION

Historical Perspective

We have seen how theories and research findings help to advance the field of learning. Their ultimate contribution, however, must be to improve teaching that promotes learning. Although it may seem odd, historically there was little overlap between the fields of learning and instruction (Shuell, 1988). One reason for this lack of integration may have been that these fields traditionally were dominated by persons with different interests. Most learning theorists and researchers have been psychologists. Much early learning research used nonhuman species. Animal research has benefits, but animals do not allow for proper exploration of instructional processes. In contrast, instruction was the domain of educators, who were primarily concerned with directly applying teaching methods to classrooms and other learning settings. This applied focus has not always lent itself well to exploring how learning processes are affected by instructional variations.

A second reason for lack of integration of learning with instruction derives from the common belief that teaching is an art and not a science like psychology. As Highet (1950) wrote: "[This book] is called *The Art of Teaching* because I believe that teaching is an art, not a science. It seems to me very dangerous to apply the aims and methods of science to human beings as individuals" (p. vii). Highet stated, however, that teaching is inseparable from learning. Good teachers continue to learn about their subject areas and ways to encourage student learning.

Gage (1978) noted that the use of "art" in reference to teaching is a metaphor. As a way to understand and improve teaching, the "art of teaching" has received inadequate attention. Teaching as an art can become the object of the same type of scrutiny and scientific investigation as any other type of art, including drawing, painting, and musical composition. Thus, teaching can be improved through scientific study.

A third possible reason stems from the idea that different theoretical principles may govern the two domains. Sternberg (1986) contended that cognition (or learning) and instruction require separate theories. This may be true for learning and instruction by themselves, but as Shuell (1988) noted: "Learning from instruction differs from traditional conceptions of learning and teaching considered separately" (p. 282). Learning from instruction involves an interaction between learners and contexts (e.g., teachers, materials, setting), whereas much psychological learning research is less context dependent. Sequencing of material, for example, affects learners' cognitive organizations and development of memory structures. In turn, how these structures develop affects what teachers do. Teachers who realize that their instruction is not being comprehended will alter their approach; conversely, when students understand material that is being presented, teachers are apt to continue with their present approach.

Fourth, traditional research methods may be inadequate to study instruction and learning simultaneously. *Process–product research* conducted in the 1970s and 1980s related changes in teaching processes (such as number and type of questions asked, amount of warmth and enthusiasm displayed) to student products or outcomes (e.g., achievement, attitudes; Pianta & Hamre, 2009). Although this research paradigm produced many useful results, it neglected the important roles of teacher and student thoughts. Thus, we might know which type of questions produce higher student achievement, but not why they do so (i.e., how questions change students' thinking). Process–product research also focused primarily on student achievement at the expense of other outcomes relevant to learning (e.g., expectations, values). In short, a process–product model is not well designed to examine how students learn.

At the same time, much learning research has used experimental methods in which some conditions are varied and changes in outcomes are determined. Teaching methods often are held constant across changes in variables, which negates the potential effects of the former.

Fortunately, the situation has changed. Researchers increasingly are viewing teaching as the creation of learning environments that assist students in executing the cognitive activities necessary to develop skills and reasoning abilities (Floden, 2001). Researchers are examining student learning by observing teaching during content instruction, especially in schools and other places where people typically learn (Pellegrino, Baxter, & Glaser, 1999; Pianta & Hamre, 2009). Researchers today are more concerned with analyzing teaching patterns rather than discrete teaching behaviors (Seidel & Shavelson, 2007). Children's learning has received increased attention (Siegler, 2000, 2005), and more research is being devoted to how what is learned in school is related to what skills are important outside of school (Anderson, Reder, & Simon, 1996). Researchers of different traditions accept the idea that instruction and learning interact and are best studied in concert. Instructional research can have a profound impact on learning theories and their applications to promote student learning (Glaser, 1990; Glaser & Bassok, 1989; Pianta & Hamre, 2009).

Instructional Commonalities

Regardless of perspective, most learning theories share principles that are predicted to enhance learning from instruction (Table 1.4). One principle is that learners progress through stages or phases of learning that can be distinguished in various ways, such as in terms of progressive skill levels: novice, advanced beginner, competent, proficient, expert (Shuell, 1990). Processes and behaviors often used in such classifications include speed and type of cognitive processing, ability to recognize problem formats, proficiency in dealing with problems that arise, organization and depth of knowledge structures, and ability to monitor performance and select strategies depending on personal and contextual factors.

Table 1.4
Instructional principles common to diverse learning theories.

- Learners progress through stages/phases
- Material should be organized and presented in small steps
- Learners require practice, feedback, and review
- Social models facilitate learning and motivation
- Motivational and contextual factors influence learning

Teaching and learning emphasize various factors as important in acquiring skills, strategies, and behaviors. These include organization of material to be taught, presentation of material in short steps (small units to be cognitively processed), opportunities for practice, provision of corrective feedback, and frequent review sessions (Rosenshine & Stevens, 1986; Shuell, 1988, 1990).

The role of practice is especially critical. Thorndike and other behaviorists believed that practice helps establish connections or associations between stimuli and responses. Cognitive views of learning stress practice as a means of building associations between concepts and propositions in memory (Anderson, 1990).

Ericsson, Krampe, and Tesch-Römer (1993) noted that deliberate practice includes activities designed to improve current performance level. The development of skill requires learners' time and energy, as well as access to instructional materials, teachers, and facilities. Parents or other adults often invest financial resources, time, and effort to raise their children's skill levels (e.g., hiring tutors, transporting children to practices and competitions).

Research shows that a regimen of deliberate practice not only raises skillful performance but also reduces memory constraints and cognitive processing limitations (Ericsson & Charness, 1994). Although abilities and natural talents are important, only extended intense training in a domain can result in expert performance.

Many young children are not inclined to put in long hours improving skills. Parental support of children's regular practice is critical (Ericsson et al., 1993). Parents and other adults can serve as models by practicing their own skills, provide children with feedback on their progress, and arrange for opportunities for children to practice and receive expert feedback (i.e., from teachers and coaches).

Most views of learning and instruction highlight the importance of learner motivational factors, including perceived value of learning, self-efficacy, positive outcome expectations, and attributions that emphasize ability, effort, and use of strategies (Stipek, 1996; Chapter 8). In addition, research shows that environmental factors affect what teachers do and how students learn (Ames, 1992a, 1992b; Shuell, 1996).

Integration of Theory and Practice

A goal of this book is to help you understand how learning theory and educational practice complement one another. Learning theory is no substitute for experience. Theory without experience can be misguided because it may underestimate the effects of situational factors. When properly used, theory provides a framework to use in making educational decisions.

Conversely, experience without theory may often be wasteful and potentially damaging. Experience without a guiding framework means that each situation is treated as unique, so decision making is based on trial and error until something works. Learning how to teach involves learning what to do in specific situations.

Theory and practice affect one another. Many theoretical developments eventually become implemented in classrooms. Contemporary educational practices—such as cooperative learning, reciprocal teaching, and differentiating instruction for individual learners—have strong theoretical underpinnings and research to support them.

Educational practice also influences theory. Experience can confirm theoretical predictions or suggest revisions. Theories are modified when research and experience present conflicting evidence or suggest additional factors to include. Early information processing theories were not directly applicable to school learning because they failed to consider factors other than those connected with the processing of knowledge. When cognitive psychologists began to study school content, theories were revised to incorporate personal and situational factors.

Educational professionals should strive to integrate theory, research, and practice. We must ask how learning principles and research findings might apply in and out of school. In turn, we should seek to advance our theoretical knowledge through results of informed teaching practice.

CRITICAL ISSUES FOR LEARNING THEORIES

Most professionals accept in principle the definition of learning given at the outset of this chapter. When we move beyond the definition, we find less agreement on many learning issues. This section presents some of these issues and sources of controversy between theoretical perspectives (Table 1.5). These issues are addressed in subsequent chapters as different theories of learning are discussed. Before considering these issues, however, some explanation of behavioral and cognitive theories will provide a background against which to frame the learning theories covered in this text and a better understanding of the concepts underlying human learning principles.

Behavioral theories view learning as a change in the rate, frequency of occurrence, or form of behavior or response, which occurs primarily as a function of environmental factors (Chapter 3). Behavioral theories contend that learning involves the formation of associations between stimuli and responses. In Skinner's (1953) view, a response to a stimulus is more likely to occur in the future as a function of the consequences of prior responding: Reinforcing consequences make the response more likely to occur, whereas punishing consequences make it less likely.

Behaviorism was a powerful force in psychology in the first half of the twentieth century, and most older theories of learning are behavioral. These theories explain learning in terms of observable phenomena. Behavioral theorists contend that explanations for learning need not include internal events (e.g., thoughts, beliefs, feelings), not because

Table 1.5
Critical issues in the study of learning.

- How does learning occur?
- What is the role of memory?
- What is the role of motivation?
- How does transfer occur?
- Which processes are involved in self-regulation?
- What are the implications for instruction?

these processes do not exist (because they do—even behavioral theorists have to think about their theories!), but rather because the causes of learning are observable environmental events.

In contrast, *cognitive theories* stress the acquisition of knowledge and skills, the formation of mental structures, and the processing of information and beliefs. The theories covered in Chapters 4 through 6 are cognitive, as are the principles discussed in later chapters. From a cognitive perspective, learning is an internal mental phenomenon inferred from what people say and do. A central theme is the mental processing of information: Its construction, acquisition, organization, coding, rehearsal, storage in memory, and retrieval or nonretrieval from memory. Although cognitive theorists stress the importance of mental processes in learning, they disagree over which processes are important.

These two conceptualizations of learning have important implications for educational practice. Behavioral theories imply that teachers should arrange the environment so that students can respond properly to stimuli. Cognitive theories emphasize making learning meaningful and taking into account learners' perceptions of themselves and their learning environments. Teachers need to consider how instruction affects students' thinking during learning.

How Does Learning Occur?

Behavioral and cognitive theories agree that differences among learners and in the environment can affect learning, but they diverge in the relative emphasis they give to these two factors. Behavioral theories stress the role of the environment—specifically, how stimuli are arranged and presented and how responses are reinforced. Behavioral theories assign less importance to learner differences than do cognitive theories. Two learner variables that behavioral theories consider are *reinforcement history* (the extent to which the individual was reinforced in the past for performing the same or similar behavior) and *developmental status* (what the individual is capable of doing given his or her present level of development). Thus, cognitive handicaps will hinder learning of complex skills, and physical disabilities may preclude acquisition of motor behaviors.

Cognitive theories acknowledge the role of environmental conditions as influences on learning. Teachers' explanations and demonstrations of concepts serve as environmental inputs for students. Student practice of skills, combined with corrective feedback as needed, promotes learning. Cognitive theories contend that instructional factors alone do not fully account for students' learning (Pintrich, Cross, Kozma, & McKeachie, 1986). What students do with information—how they attend to, rehearse, transform, code, store, and retrieve it—is critically important. The ways that learners process information determine what, when, and how they learn, as well as what use they will make of the learning.

Cognitive theories emphasize the role of learners' thoughts, beliefs, attitudes, and values. Learners who doubt their capabilities to learn may not properly attend to the task or may work halfheartedly on it, which retards learning. Such learner thoughts as "Why is this important?" or "How well am I doing?" can affect learning. Teachers need to consider students' thought processes in their lesson planning.

What Is the Role of Memory?

Learning theories differ in the role they assign to memory. Some behavioral theories conceive of memory in terms of neurological connections established as a function of behaviors being associated with external stimuli. More commonly, theorists discuss the formation of habitual ways of responding with little attention to how these behavioral patterns are retained in memory and activated by external events. Most behavioral theories view forgetting as caused by lack of responding over time.

Cognitive theories assign a prominent role to memory. Information processing theories equate learning with *encoding*, or storing knowledge in memory in an organized, meaningful fashion. Information is retrieved from memory in response to relevant cues that activate the appropriate memory structures. Forgetting is the inability to retrieve information from memory caused by interference, memory loss, or inadequate cues to access information. Memory is critical for learning, and how information is learned determines how it is stored in and retrieved from memory.

One's perspective on the role of memory has important implications for teaching. Behavioral theories posit that periodic, spaced reviews maintain the strength of responses in learners' repertoires. Cognitive theories place greater emphasis on presenting material such that learners can organize it, relate it to what they know, and remember it in a meaningful fashion.

What Is the Role of Motivation?

Motivation can affect all phases of learning and performance. Although a separate chapter is devoted to motivation (Chapter 8), its relevance to learning theories also is discussed in other chapters.

Behavioral theories define motivation as an increased rate or probability of occurrence of behavior, which results from repeating behaviors in response to stimuli or as a consequence of reinforcement. Skinner's (1968) operant conditioning theory contains no new principles to account for motivation: Motivated behavior is increased, or continued responding is produced, by reinforcement. Students display motivated behavior because they previously were reinforced for it and because effective reinforcers are present. Behavioral theories do not distinguish motivation from learning but rather use the same principles to explain all behavior.

In contrast, cognitive theories view motivation and learning as related but not identical (Schunk, 1991). One can be motivated but not learn; one can learn without being motivated to do so. Cognitive theories emphasize that motivation can help to direct attention and influence how information is processed. Although reinforcement can motivate students, its effects on behavior are not automatic but instead depend on how students interpret it. When reinforcement history (what one has been reinforced for doing in the past) conflicts with present beliefs, people are more likely to act based on their beliefs (Bandura, 1986; Brewer, 1974). Research has identified many cognitive processes that motivate students; for example, goals, social comparisons, self-efficacy, values, and interests. Teachers need to consider the motivational effects of instructional practices and classroom factors to ensure that students remain motivated to learn.

How Does Transfer Occur?

Transfer refers to knowledge and skills being applied in new ways, with new content, or in situations different from where they were acquired (Chapter 7). Transfer also explains the effect of prior learning on new learning—whether the former facilitates, hinders, or has no effect on the latter. Transfer is critical, for without it all learning would be situationally specific. Transfer lies at the heart of our system of education (Bransford & Schwartz, 1999).

Behavioral theories stress that transfer depends on identical elements or similar features (stimuli) between situations. Behaviors transfer (or *generalize*) when the old and new situations share common elements. Thus, a student who learns that $6 \times 3 = 18$ should be able to perform this multiplication in different settings (school, home) and when the same numbers appear in a similar problem format (e.g., $36 \times 23 = ?$).

Cognitive theories postulate that transfer occurs when learners understand how to apply knowledge in different settings. How information is stored in memory is important. The uses of knowledge are stored along with the knowledge itself or can be easily accessed from another memory storage location. Situations need not share common elements.

Instructional implications of these views diverge. From a behavioral view, teachers should enhance the similarity between situations and point out common elements. Cognitive theories supplement these factors by emphasizing that students' perceptions of the value of learning are critical. Teachers can address these perceptions by including in lessons information on how knowledge can be used in different settings, by teaching students rules and procedures to apply in situations to determine what knowledge will be needed, and by providing students with feedback on how skills and strategies can benefit them in different ways.

Which Processes Are Involved in Self-Regulation?

Self-regulation (or *self-regulated learning*) refers to the process whereby learners systematically direct their thoughts, feelings, and actions toward the attainment of their goals (Zimmerman & Schunk, 2001; Chapter 9). Researchers of different theoretical traditions postulate that self-regulation involves having a purpose or goal, employing goal-directed actions, and monitoring strategies and actions and adjusting them to ensure success. Theories differ in the mechanisms postulated to underlie students' use of cognitive and behavioral processes to regulate their activities.

Behavioral researchers posit that self-regulation involves setting up one's own contingencies of reinforcement; that is, the stimuli to which one responds and the consequences of one's responses. No new processes are needed to account for self-regulated behavior. Behavioral researchers focus on overt responses of learners: self-monitoring, self-instruction, self-reinforcement.

Cognitive researchers emphasize mental activities such as attention, rehearsal, use of learning strategies, and comprehension monitoring. These theorists also stress motivational beliefs about self-efficacy, outcomes, and perceived value of learning (Schunk, 2001). A key element is *choice:* For self-regulation to occur, learners must have some choice in their motives or methods for learning, time spent learning, criterion level of learning, the setting where learning occurs, and the social conditions in effect

(Zimmerman, 1994, 1998, 2000). When learners have few choices, their behaviors are largely externally regulated rather than self-regulated.

What Are the Implications for Instruction?

Theories attempt to explain various types of learning but differ in their ability to do so (Bruner, 1985). Behavioral theories emphasize the forming of associations between stimuli and responses through selective reinforcement of correct responding. Behavioral theories seem best suited to explain simpler forms of learning that involve associations, such as multiplication facts, foreign language word meanings, and state capital cities.

Cognitive theories explain learning with such factors as information processing, memory networks, and student perceptions and interpretations of classroom factors (teachers, peers, materials, organization). Cognitive theories appear to be more appropriate for explaining complex forms of learning, such as solving mathematical word problems, drawing inferences from text, and writing essays.

But commonalities often exist among different forms of learning (Bruner, 1985). Learning to read is fundamentally different from learning to play the violin, but both benefit from attention, effort, and persistence. Learning to write term papers and learning to throw the javelin may not appear to be similar, but both are promoted by goal setting, self-monitoring of progress, corrective feedback from teachers and coaches, and feelings of intrinsic motivation.

Effective teaching requires that we determine the best theoretical perspectives for the types of learning we deal with and draw on the implications of those perspectives for teaching. When reinforced practice is important for learning, then teachers should schedule it. When learning problem-solving strategies is important, then we should study the implications of information processing theory. A continuing challenge for research is to specify similarities and differences among types of learning and identify effective instructional approaches for each.

THREE LEARNING SCENARIOS

Following are three scenarios that are intended to be typical of contexts where school learning occurs. Throughout this text, these scenarios will serve to exemplify the systematic application of learning principles and demonstrate how learning can occur in a coherent fashion.

Kathy Stone's Third-Grade Class

Kathy Stone teaches one of five self-contained third-grade classes in a K–5 elementary school of 550 students. The school is located at the edge of a city near a large suburban housing community. Kathy has been a teacher in this building for 8 years and previously taught second grade in another school for 4 years. She has been active in developing curriculum and has chaired several school and systemwide committees for implementing creative programs to expand the activities incorporated into the regular program.

There are 21 students in Kathy's class. Ethnic backgrounds are varied, and about 50% of the students are middle class and most of the rest receive free or reduced-cost lunches. There are 11 boys and 10 girls ranging in age from 8 to 10. Most students are eager to learn, but some have difficulties due to learning disabilities or family or emotional problems. Six students attend resource classes, 2 are in counseling for acting-out behaviors, and 1 is in counseling because her mother has a serious illness.

Students attend from 8:15 a.m. to 2:45 p.m. each day. They remain with Kathy for the major academic content areas: reading, writing, spelling, mathematics, science, social studies, health, and computer applications. Students visit other teachers for art, music, physical education, and library time. Students have an hour for lunch and recess, at which time they are supervised by cafeteria and playground personnel. The wide range of abilities in the class presents challenges in implementing an effective curricular program.

Jim Marshall's U.S. History Class

U.S. history is a core curriculum course that is required for graduation at a small-town high school. Multiple sections are offered each semester so that all high school students are able to enroll. Jim Marshall teaches this course, as well as other courses in the history department. Jim has been teaching at this school for 14 years and has received several teaching awards and history grants.

There are 23 students in Jim's class, including 4 who failed the class last year. Ethnic backgrounds are mixed, and students primarily are middle class. Most students perform at an average or above-average level, although some are not motivated to participate in class or complete the assignments. In addition, 3 students have been identified as having a learning disability and receive help from a resource teacher.

The course meets daily for 50 minutes. The course objectives are for students to become more familiar with the major periods in U.S. history beginning with the establishment of the 13 colonies through the present. Course objectives also include analyzing those time periods and examining the impact various events had on forming and shaping the United States. Units include lectures and demonstrations, small-group discussions, student research, history projects, online assignments, and role-playing.

Gina Brown's Educational Psychology Class

EDUC 107, Educational Psychology for Teachers, is a three-credit required course in the undergraduate teacher education program at a large university. Several sections of the course are offered each semester. Gina Brown, an associate professor in the College of Education, teaches one section. Gina has been on the faculty for 7 years. Prior to completing her doctorate, she taught middle school mathematics for 10 years.

There are 30 students in the class this semester: 12 elementary majors, 10 middle grades or secondary majors, and 8 special-education majors. Ethnic backgrounds vary, and students primarily are middle class; ages range from 18 to 37 (mean = 20.7 years). The course meets 3 hours per week and includes lectures, discussions, classroom videos, and online assignments. Students take a concurrent one-credit field experience class, which Gina supervises.

The course content is standard for an educational psychology course. Topics include development, individual differences, learning, motivation, classroom management, students with exceptional needs, and assessment. Students complete projects (in conjunction with the field experience) and are tested on course content. There is a tremendous amount of material to cover, although student motivation generally is high because students believe that understanding these topics is important for their future success in teaching.

SUMMARY

The study of human learning focuses on how individuals acquire and modify their knowledge, skills, strategies, beliefs, and behaviors. Learning represents an enduring change in behavior or in the capacity to behave in a given fashion, which results from practice or other experiences. This definition excludes temporary changes in behavior due to illness, fatigue, or drugs, as well as behaviors reflecting genetic and maturational factors, although many of the latter require responsive environments to manifest themselves.

The scientific study of learning had its beginnings in writings of such early philosophers as Plato and Aristotle. Two prominent positions on how knowledge is acquired are rationalism and empiricism. The psychological study of learning began late in the nineteenth century. Structuralism and functionalism were active schools of thought at the beginning of the twentieth century with such proponents as Titchener, Dewey, and James, but these positions suffered from problems that limited widespread applicability to psychology.

Theories provide frameworks for making sense of environmental observations. Theories serve as bridges between research and educational practices and as tools to organize and translate research findings into recommendations for educational practice. Types of research include correlational, experimental, and qualitative. Research may be conducted in laboratories or in field settings. Common ways to assess learning include direct observations, written and oral responses, ratings by others, and self-reports.

Learning theory and educational practice often are viewed as distinct, but in fact they should complement one another. Neither is sufficient to ensure good teaching and learning. Theory alone may not fully capture the importance of situational factors. Practical experience without theory is situationally specific and lacks an overarching framework to organize knowledge of teaching and learning. Theory and practice help to refine one another.

Behavioral theories explain learning in terms of observable events, whereas cognitive theories also consider the cognitions, beliefs, values, and affects of learners. Theories of learning differ in how they address critical issues. Some of the more important issues concern how learning occurs, the role of memory, the role of motivation, how transfer occurs, which processes are involved in self-regulation, and the implications for instruction.

FURTHER READING

Benjamin, L. T., Jr. (2000). The psychological laboratory at the turn of the 20th century. *American Psychologist, 55,* 318–321.

Bruner, J. (1985). Models of the learner. *Educational Researcher, 14*(6), 5–8.

Glaser, R. (1990). The reemergence of learning theory within instructional research. *American Psychologist, 45,* 29–39.

Popham, W. J. (2008). *Classroom assessment: What teachers need to know* (5th ed.). Boston: Allyn & Bacon.

Shuell, T. J. (1988). The role of the student in learning from instruction. *Contemporary Educational Psychology, 13,* 276–295.

Tweney, R. D., & Budzynski, C. A. (2000). The scientific status of American psychology in 1900. *American Psychologist, 55,* 1014–1017.

Chapter

2

Neuroscience of Learning

The Tarrytown Unified School District was holding an all-day workshop for teachers and administrators on the topic of "Using Brain Research to Design Effective Instruction." During the afternoon break a group of four participants were discussing the day's session: Joe Michela, assistant principal at North Tarrytown Middle School; Claudia Orondez, principal of Templeton Elementary School; Emma Thomas, teacher at Tarrytown Central High School; and Bryan Young, teacher at South Tarrytown Middle School.

Joe: So, what do you think of this so far?

Bryan: It's really confusing. I followed pretty well this morning the part about the functions of different areas of the brain, but I'm having a hard time connecting that with what I do as a teacher.

Emma: Me, too. And the presenters are saying things that contradict what I thought. I had heard that each student has a dominant side of the brain so we should design instruction to match those preferences, but these presenters say that isn't true.

Joe: Well they're not exactly saying it isn't true. What I understood was that different parts of the brain have different primary functions but that there's a lot of crossover and that many parts of the brain have to work at once for learning to occur.

Claudia: That's what I heard too. But I agree with Bryan—it's confusing to know what a teacher is to do. If we're supposed to appeal to all parts of the brain, then isn't that what teachers try to do now? For years we've been telling teachers to teach to different learning styles, such as seeing, hearing, touching. Seems like this brain research says the same thing.

Joe: And especially seeing. I heard them say how important the visual sense is. I do work with teachers on that—don't lecture so much since that's not an effective way to learn.

Bryan: Very true, Joe. And another thing they said that threw me was how much teens' brains are developing. I thought their wacky behavior was all about hormones. I see now that I need to be helping them more to make good decisions.

Emma: I think this really is fascinating. This session has made me aware of how the brain receives and uses information. But it's so complex! For me, the challenge is to match brain functioning with how I organize and present information and the activities I design for students.

Claudia: I've got lots of questions to ask after this break. I know there's much that researchers don't know, but I'm ready to start working with my elementary teachers to use this brain research to benefit our children.

Many different learning theories and processes are discussed in subsequent chapters in this text. Conditioning theories (Chapter 3) focus on external behaviors and consequences, whereas cognitive theories—the focus of this text—posit that learning occurs internally. Cognitive processes include thoughts, beliefs, and emotions, all of which have neural representations.

This chapter addresses the *neuroscience of learning*, or the science of the relation of the nervous system to learning and behavior. Although neuroscience is not a learning theory, being familiar with neuroscience will give you a better foundation to understand the conditioning and cognitive learning chapters that follow.

The focus of this chapter is on the *central nervous system (CNS)*, which comprises the brain and spinal cord. Most of the chapter covers brain rather than spinal cord functions. The *autonomic nervous system (ANS)*, which regulates involuntary actions (e.g., respiration, secretions), is mentioned where relevant.

The role of the brain in learning and behavior is not a new topic, but it is only recently that its significance among educators has increased. Although educators always have been concerned about the brain because the business of educators is learning and the brain is where learning occurs, much brain research has investigated brain dysfunctions. To some extent, this research is relevant to education because educators

have students in their classes with handicaps. But because most students do not have brain dysfunctions, findings from brain research have not been viewed as highly applicable to typical learners.

The explosion in technology that has occurred in recent years has yielded new methods that can show how the brain functions while performing mental operations involving learning and memory. The data yielded by these new methods are highly relevant to classroom teaching and learning and suggest implications for learning, motivation, and development. Educators increasingly are showing interest in findings from neuroscience research as they seek ways to improve teaching and learning (Byrnes & Fox, 1998). This interest by educators is evident in the opening vignette.

This chapter begins by reviewing the brain's neural organization and major structures involved in learning, motivation, and development. The topics of localization and interconnections of brain structures are discussed, along with methods used to conduct brain research. The neurophysiology of learning is covered, which includes the neural organization of information processing, memory networks, and language learning. The important topic of brain development is discussed to include the influential factors on development, phases of development, critical periods of development, and language development. How motivation and emotions are represented in the brain is explained, and the chapter concludes with a discussion of the major implications of brain research for teaching and learning.

Discussions of the CNS are necessarily complex, as Emma notes in the opening scenario. Many structures are involved, there is much technical terminology, and CNS operation is complicated. The material in this chapter is presented as clearly as possible, but a certain degree of technicality is needed to preserve the accuracy of information. Readers who seek more technical descriptions of CNS structures and functions as they relate to learning, motivation, and development are referred to other sources (Bradford, 1998; Byrnes, 2001; Jensen, 2005; National Research Council, 2000; Trevarthen, 1998; Wolfe, 2001).

When you finish studying this chapter, you should be able to do the following:

- Describe the neural organization and functions of axons, dendrites, and glial cells.

- Discuss the primary functions of the major areas of the brain.

- Identify some brain functions that are highly localized in the right and left hemispheres.

- Discuss the uses of different brain research technologies.

- Explain how learning occurs from a neuroscience perspective to include the operation of consolidation and memory networks.

- Discuss how neural connections are formed and interact during language acquisition and use.

- Discuss the key changes and critical periods in brain development as a function of maturation and experience.

- Explain the role of the brain in the regulation of motivation and emotions.

- Discuss some instructional implications of brain research for teaching and learning.

ORGANIZATION AND STRUCTURES

The central nervous system (CNS) is composed of the brain and spinal cord and is the body's central mechanism for control of voluntary behavior (e.g., thinking, acting). The autonomic nervous system (ANS) regulates involuntary activities, such as those involved in digestion, respiration, and blood circulation. These systems are not entirely independent. People can, for example, learn to control their heart rates, which means that they are voluntarily controlling an involuntary activity.

The spinal cord is about 18 inches long and the width of an index finger. It runs from the base of the brain down the middle of the back. It is essentially an extension of the brain. Its primary function is to carry signals to and from the brain, making it the central messenger between the brain and the rest of the body. Its ascending pathway carries signals from body locations to the brain, and its descending pathway carries messages from the brain to the appropriate body structure (e.g., to cause movement). The spinal cord also is involved in some reactions independently of the brain (e.g., knee-jerk reflex). Damage to the spinal cord, such as from an accident, can result in symptoms ranging from numbness to total paralysis (Jensen, 2005; Wolfe, 2001).

Figure 2.1
Structure of neurons.
Source: Brain Matters: Translating Research into Classroom Practice, by P. Wolfe, p. 15, © 2001. Reprinted by permission of the Association for Supervision and Curriculum Development, Alexandria, VA.

Neural Organization

The CNS is composed of billions of cells in the brain and spinal cord. There are two major types of cells: neurons and glial cells. A depiction of neural organization is shown in Figure 2.1.

Neurons. The brain and spinal cord contain about 100 billion neurons that send and receive information across muscles and organs (Wolfe, 2001). Most of the body's neurons are found in the CNS. Neurons are different from other body cells (e.g., skin, blood) in two important ways. For one, most body cells regularly regenerate. This continual renewal is desirable; for example, when we cut ourselves, new cells regenerate to replace those that were damaged. But neurons do not regenerate in the same fashion. Brain and spinal cord cells destroyed by a stroke, disease, or accident may be permanently lost. On a positive note, however, there is evidence that neurons can show some regeneration (Kempermann & Gage, 1999), although the extent to which this occurs and the process by which it occurs are not well understood.

Neurons are also different from other body cells because they communicate with one another—by means of electrical signals and chemical reactions. They thus are organized differently than other body cells. This organization is discussed later in this section.

Glial Cells. The second type of cell in the CNS is the *glial cell.* Glial cells are far more numerous than neurons. They may be thought of as supporting cells since they support the work of the neurons. They do not transmit signals like neurons, but they assist in the process.

Glial cells perform many functions. A key one is to ensure that neurons operate in a good environment. Glial cells help to remove chemicals that may interfere with neuron operation. Glial cells also remove dead brain cells. Another important function is that glial cells put down myelin, a sheathlike wrapping around axons that help transmit brain signals (discussed in the next section). Glial cells also appear to play key functions in the development of the fetal brain (Wolfe, 2001). Thus, glial cells work in concert with neurons to ensure effective functioning of the CNS.

Synapses. Figure 2.1 shows neural organization with cell bodies, axons, and dendrites. Each neuron is composed of a cell body, thousands of short dendrites, and one axon. A *dendrite* is an elongated tissue that receives information from other cells. An *axon* is a long thread of tissue that sends messages to other cells. *Myelin sheath* surrounds the axon and facilitates the travel of signals.

Each axon ends in a branching structure. The ends of these branching structures connect with the ends of dendrites. This connection is known as a *synapse*. The interconnected structure is the key to how neurons communicate, because messages are passed among neurons at the synapses.

The process by which neurons communicate is complex. At the end of each axon are chemical *neurotransmitters*. They do not quite touch dendrites of another cell. The gap is called the *synaptic gap*. When electrical and chemical signals reach a high enough level, neurotransmitters are released into the gap. The neurotransmitters either will activate or inhibit a reaction in the contacted dendrite. Thus, the process begins as an electrical reaction in the neuron and axon, changes to a chemical reaction in the gap, and then reconverts to an electrical response in the dendrite. This process continues from neuron to neuron in lightning speed. As discussed later in this chapter, the role of the neurotransmitters in the synaptic gap is critical for learning. From a neuroscience perspective, *learning* is a change in the receptivity of cells brought about by neural connections formed, strengthened, and connected with others through use (Jensen, 2005; Wolfe, 2001).

Brain Structures

The human adult brain (*cerebrum*) weighs approximately three pounds and is about the size of a cantaloupe or large grapefruit (Tolson, 2006; Wolfe, 2001). Its outward texture has a series of folds and is wrinkly in appearance, resembling a cauliflower. Its composition is mostly water (78%), with the rest fat and protein. Its texture is generally soft. The major brain structures involved in learning are shown in Figure 2.2 (Byrnes, 2001; Jensen, 2005; Wolfe, 2001) and described below.

Cerebral Cortex. Covering the brain is the *cerebral cortex*, which is a thin layer about the thickness of an orange peel (less than $1/4$ of an inch). The cerebral cortex is the wrinkled "gray matter" of the brain. The wrinkles allow the cerebral cortex to have more surface area, which allows for more neurons and neural connections. The cerebral cortex has two hemispheres (right and left), each of which has four lobes (occipital, parietal, temporal, and frontal). The cortex is the central area involved in learning, memory, and processing of sensory information.

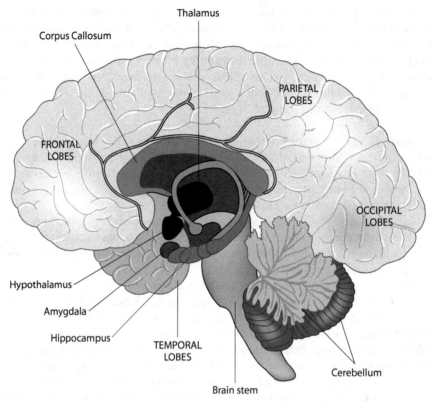

Figure 2.2
Major brain structures.
Source: Brain Matters: Translating Research into Classroom Practice, by P. Wolfe, p. 20, © 2001.
Reprinted by permission of the Association for Supervision and Curriculum Development, Alexandria, VA.

Brain Stem and Reticular Formation. At the base of the brain is the *brain stem*. The brain stem handles ANS (involuntary) functions through its *reticular formation,* which is a network of neurons and fibers that regulates control of such basic bodily functions as breathing, heart rate, blood pressure, eyeball movement, salivation, and taste. The reticular formation also is involved in awareness levels (e.g., sleep, wakefulness). For example, when you go into a quiet, dark room, the reticular formation decreases brain activation and allows you to sleep. The reticular formation also helps to control sensory inputs. Although we constantly are bombarded by multiple stimuli, the reticular formation allows us to focus on relevant stimuli. This is critical for attention and perception (Chapter 5), which are key components of the human information processing system. Finally, the reticular formation produces many of the chemical messengers for the brain.

Cerebellum. The *cerebellum* at the back of the brain regulates body balance, muscular control, movement, and body posture. Although these activities are largely under conscious control (and therefore the domain of the cortex), the cortex does not have all the equipment it needs to regulate them. It works in concert with the cerebellum to coordinate movements. The cerebellum is the key to motor skill acquisition. With practice, many motor skills become automatic (e.g., playing the piano, driving a car). This automaticity occurs because the cerebellum takes over much of the control, which allows the cortex to focus on activities requiring consciousness (e.g., thinking, problem solving).

Thalamus and Hypothalamus. Above the brain stem are two walnut-sized structures—the *thalamus* and *hypothalamus*. The thalamus acts as a bridge by sending inputs from the sense organs (except for smell) to the cortex. The hypothalamus is part of the ANS. It controls bodily functions needed to maintain homeostasis, such as body temperature, sleep, water, and food. The hypothalamus also is responsible for increased heart rate and breathing when we become frightened or stressed.

Amygdala. The *amygdala* is involved in the control of emotion and aggression. Incoming sensory inputs (except for smell, which travel straight to the cortex) go to the thalamus, which in turn relays the information to the appropriate area of the cortex and to the amygdala. The amygdala's function is to assess the harmfulness of sensory inputs. If it recognizes a potentially harmful stimulus, it signals the hypothalamus, which creates the emotional changes noted above (e.g., increased heart rate and blood pressure).

Hippocampus. The *hippocampus* is the brain structure responsible for memory of the immediate past. How long is the immediate past? As we will see in Chapter 5, there is no objective criterion for what constitutes immediate and long-term (permanent) memory. Apparently the hippocampus helps to establish information in long-term memory (which resides in the cortex), but maintains its role in activating that information as needed. Thus, the hippocampus may be involved in currently active (working) memory. Once information is fully encoded in long-term memory, the hippocampus may relinquish its role.

Corpus Callosum. Running along the brain (cerebrum) from front to back is a band of fibers known as the *corpus callosum*. It divides the cerebrum into two halves, or hemispheres, and connects them for neural processing. This is critical, because much mental processing occurs in more than one location in the brain and often involves both hemispheres.

Occipital Lobe. The *occipital lobes* of the cerebrum are primarily concerned with processing visual information. The occipital lobe also is known as the *visual cortex*. Recall that visual stimuli are first received by the thalamus, which then sends these signals to the occipital lobes. Many functions occur here that involve determining motion, color, depth, distance, and other visual features. Once these determinations have occurred, the visual stimuli are compared to what is stored in memory to determine recognition (perception). Thus, an object that matches a stored pattern is recognized. When there is no match, then a new stimulus is encoded in memory. The visual cortex must communicate with other brain systems to determine whether a visual stimulus matches a stored pattern (Gazzaniga, Ivry, & Mangun, 1998). The importance of visual processing in learning is highlighted in the opening vignette by Joe.

People can readily control their visual perception by forcing themselves to attend to certain features of the environment and to ignore others. For example, if we are searching for a friend in a crowd we can ignore thousands of visual stimuli and focus only on those stimuli (e.g., facial features) that will help us determine whether our friend is present. Teachers use this idea by asking students to pay attention to visual displays and by informing them of the lesson's objectives at the start of the lesson.

Parietal Lobe. The *parietal lobes* at the top of the brain in the cerebrum are responsible for the sense of touch, and they help to determine body position and integrate visual information. The parietal lobes have anterior (front) and posterior (rear) sections. The anterior part receives information from the body regarding touch, temperature, body position, and sensations of pain and pressure (Wolfe, 2001). Each part of the body has certain areas in the anterior part that receive its information and make identification accurate.

The posterior portion integrates tactile information to provide spatial body awareness, or knowing where the parts of your body are at all times. The parietal lobes also can increase or decrease attention to various body parts. For example, a pain in your leg will be received and identified by the parietal lobe, but if you are watching an enjoyable movie and are attending closely to that, you may "forget about" the pain in your leg.

Temporal Lobe. The *temporal lobes*, located on the side of the cerebrum, are responsible for processing auditory information. When an auditory input is received—such as a voice or other sound—that information is processed and transmitted to auditory memory to determine recognition. That recognition then can lead to action. For example, when a teacher tells students to put away their books and line up at the door, that auditory information is processed and recognized, and then leads to the appropriate action.

Located where the occipital, parietal, and temporal lobes intersect in the cortex's left hemisphere is *Wernicke's area,* which allows us to comprehend speech and to use proper syntax when speaking. This area works closely with another area in the frontal lobe of the left hemisphere known as *Broca's area,* which is necessary for speaking. Although these key language processing areas are situated in the left hemisphere (but Broca's area is in the right hemisphere for some people, as explained later), many parts of the brain work together to comprehend and produce language. Language is discussed in greater depth later in this chapter.

Frontal Lobe. As the name implies, the *frontal lobes* lie at the front of the cerebrum. The frontal lobes make up the largest part of the cortex. Their central functions are to process information relating to memory, planning, decision making, goal setting, and creativity. The frontal lobes also contain the primary motor cortex that regulates muscular movements.

It might be argued that the frontal lobes in the brain most clearly distinguish us from lower animals and even from our ancestors of generations past. The frontal lobes have evolved to assume ever more complex functions. They allow us to plan and make conscious decisions, solve problems, and converse with others. Further, these lobes provide us with consciousness of our mental processes, a form of *metacognition* (Chapter 7).

Running from the top of the brain down toward the ears is a strip of cells known as the *primary motor cortex*. This area is the area that controls the body's movements. Thus, if while dancing the "Hokey Pokey" you think "put your right foot in," it is the motor cortex that directs you to put your right foot in. Each part of the body is mapped to a particular location in the motor cortex, so that a signal from a certain part of the cortex leads to the proper movement being made.

In front of the motor cortex is *Broca's area,* which is the location governing the production of speech. This area is located in the left hemisphere for about 95% of people; for the other 5% (30% of left-handers) this area is in the right hemisphere (Wolfe, 2001). Not surprisingly, this area is linked to *Wernicke's area* in the left temporal lobe with nerve fibers. Speech is formed in Wernicke's area and then transferred to Broca's area to be produced (Wolfe, 2001).

The front part of the frontal lobe, or *prefrontal cortex*, is proportionately larger in humans than in other animals. It is here that the highest forms of mental activity occur (Ackerman, 1992). Chapter 5 discusses how cognitive information processing associations are made in the brain. The prefrontal cortex is the key area for these associations, because information received from the senses is related to information stored in memory. In short, the seat of learning appears to be in the prefrontal cortex. It also is the regulator of consciousness, allowing us to be aware of what we are thinking, feeling, and doing. As explained later, the prefrontal cortex seems to be involved in the regulation of emotions.

Table 2.1 summarizes the key functions of each of the major brain areas (Byrnes, 2001; Jensen, 2005; Wolfe, 2001). When reviewing this table, keep in mind that no part of the brain works independently. Rather, information (in the form of neural impulses) is rapidly transferred among areas of the brain. Although many brain functions are localized, different parts of the brain are involved in even simple tasks. It therefore makes little sense to label any brain function as residing in only one area, as brought out in the opening vignette by Emma.

Localization and Interconnections

We know much more about the brain's operation today than ever before, but the brain has been studied for many years. The functions of the left and right hemispheres have been the subject of continued debate. Wolfe (2001) noted that around 400 B.C. Hippocrates spoke of the duality of the brain. Cowey (1998) reported that in 1870 researchers electrically stimulated different parts of the brains of animals and soldiers with head injuries. They found that stimulation of certain parts of the brain caused movements in different parts of the body. The idea that the brain has a major hemisphere was proposed as early as 1874 (Binney & Janson, 1990).

It has been known for many years that, in general, the left hemisphere governs the right visual field and side of the body and the right hemisphere regulates the left visual field and side of the body. However, the two hemispheres are joined by bundles of fibers, the largest of which is the corpus callosum. Gazzaniga, Bogen, and Sperry (1962) demonstrated that language is controlled largely by the left hemisphere. These researchers found that when the corpus callosum was severed, patients who held an object out of sight in

Table 2.1
Key functions of areas of the brain.

Area	Key Functions
Cerebral cortex	Processes sensory information; regulates various learning and memory functions
Reticular formation	Controls bodily functions (e.g., breathing and blood pressure), arousal, sleep–wakefulness
Cerebellum	Regulates body balance, posture, muscular control, movement, motor skill acquisition
Thalamus	Sends inputs from senses (except for smell) to cortex
Hypothalamus	Controls homeostatic body functions (e.g., temperature, sleep, water, and food); increases heart rate and breathing during stress
Amygdala	Controls emotions and aggression; assesses harmfulness of sensory inputs
Hippocampus	Holds memory of immediate past and working memory; establishes information in long-term memory
Corpus callosum	Connects right and left hemispheres
Occipital lobe	Processes visual information
Parietal lobe	Processes tactile information; determines body position; integrates visual information
Temporal lobe	Processes auditory information
Frontal lobe	Processes information for memory, planning, decision making, goal setting, creativity; regulates muscular movements (primary motor cortex)
Broca's area	Controls production of speech
Wernicke's area	Comprehends speech; regulates use of proper syntax when speaking

their left hands claimed they were holding nothing. Apparently, without the visual stimulus and because the left hand communicates with the right hemisphere, when this hemisphere received the input, it could not produce a name (because language is localized in the left hemisphere) and, with a severed corpus callosum, the information could not be transferred to the left hemisphere.

Brain research also has identified other localized functions. Analytical thinking seems to be centered in the left hemisphere, whereas spatial, auditory, emotional, and artistic processing occurs in the right hemisphere (but the right hemisphere apparently processes negative emotions and the left hemisphere processes positive emotions; Ornstein, 1997). Music is processed better in the right hemisphere; directionality, in the right hemisphere; and facial recognition, the left hemisphere.

The right hemisphere also plays a critical role in interpreting contexts (Wolfe, 2001). For example, assume that someone hears a piece of news and says, "That's great!" This could mean the person thinks the news is wonderful or horrible. The context determines the correct meaning (e.g., whether the speaker is being sincere or sarcastic). Context can be gained from intonation, people's facial expressions and gestures, and knowledge of other elements in the situation. It appears that the right hemisphere is the primary location for assembling contextual information so that a proper interpretation can be made.

Because functions are localized in brain sections, it has been tempting to postulate that people who are highly verbal are dominated by their left hemisphere (left brained), whereas those who are more artistic and emotional are controlled by their right hemisphere (right brained). But this is a simplistic and misleading conclusion, as the educators in the opening scenario now realize. Although hemispheres have localized functions, they also are connected and there is much passing of information (neural impulses) between them. Very little mental processing likely occurs only in one hemisphere (Ornstein, 1997). Further, we might ask which hemisphere governs individuals who are both highly verbal and emotional (e.g., impassioned speakers).

The hemispheres work in concert; information is available to both of them at all times. Speech offers a good example. If you are having a conversation with a friend, it is your left hemisphere that allows you to produce speech but your right hemisphere that provides the context and helps you comprehend meaning.

There is much debate among cognitive neuroscientists about the extent of lateralization. Some argue that specific cognitive functions are localized in specific regions of the brain, whereas others believe that different regions have the ability to perform various tasks (Byrnes & Fox, 1998). This debate mirrors that in cognitive psychology between the traditional view that knowledge is locally coded and the parallel distributed processing view (see Chapter 5) that knowledge is coded not in one location but rather across many memory networks (Bowers, 2009).

There is research evidence to support both positions. Different parts of the brain have different functions, but functions are rarely, if ever, completely localized in one section of the brain. This is especially true for complex mental operations, which depend on several basic mental operations whose functions may be spread out in several areas. As Byrnes and Fox (1998) contended, "Nearly any task requires the participation of both hemispheres, but the hemispheres seem to process certain types of information more efficiently than others" (p. 310). Educationally speaking, therefore, the practice of teaching to different sides of the brain (right brain, left brain) is not supported by empirical research. Some applications of these points on interconnectedness and lateralization are given in Application 2.1.

Brain Research Methods

One reason why we know so much more today about the operation of the CNS than ever before is that there has been a convergence of interest in brain research among people in different fields. Historically, investigations of the brain were conducted primarily by researchers in medicine, the biological sciences, and psychology. Over the years, people in other fields have taken greater interest in brain research, believing that research findings would have implications for developments in their fields. Today we find educators, sociologists, social workers, counselors, government workers (especially those in the judicial system), and

APPLICATION 2.1
Teaching to Both Brain Hemispheres

Brain research shows that much academic content is processed primarily in the left hemisphere, but that the right hemisphere processes context. A common educational complaint is that teaching is too focused on content with little attention to context. Focusing primarily on content produces student learning that may be unconnected to life events and largely meaningless. These points suggest that to make learning meaningful—and thereby build more extensive neural connections—teachers should incorporate context as much as possible.

Kathy Stone is doing a unit on butterflies with her third-grade class. They study material in a book, and Kathy shows them pictures of different butterflies and a film. To help connect this learning with context, Kathy uses other activities. A local museum has a butterfly area, where butterflies live in a controlled environment. She takes her class to visit this so they can see the world of butterflies. A display is part of this exhibit, showing the different phases of a butterfly's life. These activities help children connect characteristics of butterflies with contextual factors involving their development and environment.

Jim Marshall knows that studying history in isolation is boring for many students. Over the years, many world leaders have sought solutions for global peace. When covering President Wilson's work to establish the League of Nations, Jim draws parallels to the United Nations and contemporary ways that governments try to eliminate aggression (e.g., nuclear disarmament) to put the League of Nations into a context. Through class discussions, Jim has students relate the goals, structures, and problems of the League of Nations to current events and discuss how the League of Nations set the precedent for the United Nations and for worldwide vigilance of aggression.

Learning about psychological processes in isolation from real situations often leaves students wondering how the processes apply to people. When Gina Brown covers Piagetian processes in child development (e.g., egocentrism), she has students in their internships document behaviors displayed by children that are indicative of those processes. She does the same thing with other units in the course to ensure that the content learning is linked with contexts (i.e., psychological processes have behavioral manifestations).

others interested in brain research. Funding for brain research also has increased, including by agencies that primarily fund non-brain–related research (e.g., education).

Another reason for our increased knowledge is that there have been tremendous advances in technology for conducting brain research. Many years ago, the only way to perform brain research was to conduct an autopsy. Although examining brains of persons who have died has yielded useful information, this type of research cannot determine how the brain functions and processes information. The latter information is needed to develop understanding about how the brain changes during learning and uses learned information to produce actions and new learning.

Table 2.2
Methods used in brain research.

Method	Description
X-rays	High-frequency electromagnetic waves used to determine abnormalities in solid structures (e.g., bones)
Computerized Axial Tomography (CAT) Scans	Enhanced images (three dimensions) used to detect body abnormalities (e.g., tumors)
Electroencephalographs (EEGs)	Measures electrical patterns caused by movement of neurons; used to investigate various brain disorders (e.g., language and sleep)
Positron Emission Tomography (PET) Scans	Assesses gamma rays produced by mental activity; provides overall picture of brain activity but limited by slow speed and participants' ingestion of radioactive material
Magnetic Resonance Imaging (MRIs)	Radio waves cause brain to produce signals that are mapped; used to detect tumors, lesions, and other abnormalities
Functional Magnetic Resonance Imaging (MRIs)	Performance of mental tasks fires neurons, causes blood flow, and changes magnetic flow; comparison with image of brain at rest shows responsible regions

Techniques that have yielded useful information are discussed below and summarized in Table 2.2. These are ordered roughly from least to most sophisticated.

X-Rays. *X-rays* are high frequency electromagnetic waves that can pass through nonmetallic objects where they are absorbed by body structures (Wolfe, 2001). The unabsorbed rays strike a photographic plate. Interpretation is based on light and dark areas (shades of gray). X-rays are two dimensional and are most useful for solid structures, such as determining whether you have broken a bone. They do not work particularly well in the brain because it is composed of soft tissue, although X-rays can determine damage to the skull (a bone structure).

CAT Scans. *CAT (computerized axial tomography) scans* were developed in the early 1970s to increase the gradations in shades of gray produced by X-rays. CAT scans use X-ray technology but enhance the images from two to three dimensions. CAT scans are used by doctors to investigate tumors and other abnormalities, but, like X-rays, they do not provide detailed information about brain functioning.

EEGs. The *EEG (electroencephalograph)* is an imaging method that measures electrical patterns created by the movements of neurons (Wolfe, 2001). Electrodes placed on the scalp detect neural impulses passing through the skull. The EEG technology magnifies the signals and records them on a monitor or paper chart (brain waves). Frequency of brain waves (oscillations) increase during mental activity and decrease during sleep. EEGs have proven useful to image certain types of brain disorders (e.g., epilepsy, language), as well as to monitor sleep disorders (Wolfe, 2001). EEGs provide valuable temporal information through *event-related potentials* (see the section, Language Development), but they cannot detect the type of spatial information (i.e., where the activity occurs) that is needed to investigate learning in depth.

PET Scans. *PET (positron emission tomography) scans* allow one to investigate brain activity while an individual performs tasks. The person is injected with a small dose of radioactive glucose, which the blood carries to the brain. While in the PET scanner the individual performs mental tasks. Those areas of the brain that become involved use more of the glucose and produce gamma rays, which are detected by the equipment. This leads to computerized color images (maps) being produced that show areas of activity.

Although PET scans represent an advance in brain imaging technology, their usefulness is limited. Because the procedure requires ingesting radioactive material, there is a limit to how many sessions one can do and how many images can be produced at one time. Also, producing the images is a relatively slow process, so the speed with which neural activity occurs cannot be fully captured. Although the PET scan gives a good idea of overall brain activity, it does not show the specific areas of activity in sufficient detail (Wolfe, 2001).

MRIs and fMRIs. *Magnetic resonance imaging (MRI),* and the newer *functional magnetic resonance imaging (fMRI),* are brain imaging techniques that address problems with PET scans. In an MRI, a beam of radio waves is fired at the brain. The brain is mostly water, which contains hydrogen atoms. The radio waves make the hydrogen atoms produce radio signals, which are detected by sensors and mapped onto a computerized image. The level of detail is superior to that of a CAT scan, and MRIs are commonly used to detect tumors, lesions and other abnormalities (Wolfe, 2001).

The fMRI works much like the MRI, except that the persons are required to perform mental or behavioral tasks. As they do, the parts of the brain responsible fire neurons, which cause more blood to flow to these regions. The blood flow changes the magnetic field so the signals become more intense. The fMRI scanner senses these changes and maps them onto a computerized image. This image can be compared to an image of the brain at rest to detect changes. The fMRI can capture brain activity as it occurs and where it occurs because the fMRI can record four images per second and because it takes about a half a second for the brain to react to a stimulus (Wolfe, 2001). There is, however, some temporal disparity because the blood flow changes can take several seconds to occur (Varma, McCandliss, & Schwartz, 2008).

Compared with other methods, the fMRI has many advantages. It does not require ingesting a radioactive substance. It works quickly and can measure activity precisely. It can record an image of a brain in a few seconds, which is much faster than other methods. And the fMRI can be repeated without problems.

An issue with brain technologies is that they must be used in artificial contexts (e.g., laboratories), which precludes their capturing learning in active classrooms. This issue can be partially addressed by giving participants learning tasks during brain experiments or by subjecting them to the technology immediately after they have experienced different classroom contexts (Varma et al., 2008). Further, the field of brain research is rapidly changing and technologies are being developed and refined. In the future, we can expect to see techniques of greater sophistication that will help us further pinpoint brain processes while learning occurs. We now turn to the neurophysiology of learning, which addresses how the brain functions to process, integrate, and use information.

NEUROPHYSIOLOGY OF LEARNING

The discussion in this section covering brain processing during learning uses as a frame of reference the information processing model discussed in Chapter 5 (see Figure 5.1). Brain processing during learning is complex (as the opening scenario shows), and what follows covers only the central elements. Readers who want detailed information about learning and memory from a neurophysiological perspective should consult other sources (Byrnes, 2001; Jensen, 2005; Rose, 1998; Wolfe, 2001).

Information Processing System

As explained in Chapter 5, the information processing system includes sensory registers, short-term (STM) or working (WM) memory, and long-term memory (LTM). The sensory registers receive input and hold it for a fraction of a second, after which the input is discarded or channeled to WM. Most sensory input is discarded, since at any given time we are bombarded with multiple sensory inputs.

Earlier in this chapter we saw that all sensory input (except for smells) goes directly to the thalamus, where at least some of it then is sent to the appropriate part of the cerebral cortex for processing (e.g., brain lobes that process the appropriate sensory information). But the input is not sent in the same form in which it was received; rather, it is sent as a neural "perception" of that input. For example, an auditory stimulus received by the thalamus will be transformed into the neural equivalent of the perception of that stimulus. This perception also is responsible for matching information to what already is stored in memory, a process known as *pattern recognition* (see Chapter 5). Thus, if the visual stimulus is the classroom teacher, the perception sent to the cortex will match the stored representation of the teacher and the stimulus will be recognized.

Part of what makes perception meaningful is that the brain's reticular activating system filters information to exclude trivial information and focus on important material (Wolfe, 2001). This process is adaptive because if we tried to attend to every input, we would never be able to focus on anything. There are several factors that influence this filtering. Perceived importance, such as teachers announcing that material is important (e.g., will be tested), is apt to command students' attention. Novelty attracts attention; the brain tends to focus on inputs that are novel or different from what might be expected. Another factor is intensity; stimuli that are louder, brighter, or more pronounced get more attention. Movement also helps to focus attention. Although these attentional systems largely operate unconsciously, it is possible to use these ideas for helping to focus students' attention in the classroom, such as by using bright and novel visual displays. Applications of these ideas to learning settings are given in Application 2.2.

APPLICATION 2.2
Arousing and Maintaining Students' Attention

Cognitive neuroscience research shows that various environmental factors can arouse and maintain people's attention. These factors include importance, novelty, intensity, and movement. As teachers plan instruction, they can determine ways to build these factors into their lessons and student activities.

Importance

Kathy Stone is teaching children to find main ideas in paragraphs. She wants children to focus on main ideas and not be distracted by interesting details. Children ask the question, "What is this story mostly about?" read the story, and ask the question again. They then pick out the sentence that best answers the question. Kathy reviews the other sentences to show how they discuss details that may support the main idea but do not state it.

A middle-grade teacher is covering a unit on the state's history. There are many details in the text, and the teacher wants students to focus on key events and persons who helped create the history. Before covering each section, the teacher gives students a list of key terms that includes events and persons. Students have to write a short explanatory sentence for each term.

Novelty

A fifth-grade teacher contacted an entomology professor at the local university who is an expert on cockroaches. The teacher took her class to his laboratory. There the students saw all types of cockroaches. The professor had various pieces of equipment that allowed students to see the activities of cockroaches firsthand, for example, how fast they can run and what types of things they eat.

A high school tennis coach obtained a ball machine that sends tennis balls out at various speeds and arcs, which players then attempt to return. Rather than have players practice repetitively returning the balls, the coach sets up each session as a match (player versus machine) without the serves. If a player can successfully return the ball sent out from the ball machine, then the player gets the point; if not, the machine earns the point. Scoring follows the standard format (love-15-30-40-game).

Intensity

Many elementary children have difficulty with regrouping in subtraction and incorrectly subtract the smaller from the larger number in each column. To help correct this error, a teacher has students draw an arrow from the top number to the bottom number in each column before they subtract. If the number on top is smaller, students first draw an arrow from the top number in the adjacent column to the top number in the column being subtracted and then perform the appropriate regrouping. The use of arrows makes the order of operations more pronounced.

Jim Marshall wants his students to memorize the Gettysburg Address and be able to recite it with emphasis in key places. Jim demonstrates the reading while being accompanied at a very low volume by an instrumental version of "The Battle Hymn of the Republic." When he comes to a key part (e.g., "of the people, by the people, for the people"), he uses body and

APPLICATION 2.2 (continued)

hand language and raises his inflection to emphasize certain words.

Movement

Studying birds and animals in books can be boring and does not capture their typical activities. An elementary teacher uses Internet sources and interactive videos to show birds and animals in their natural habitats. Students can see what their typical activities are as they hunt for food and prey, take care of their young, and move from place to place.

Gina Brown works with her interns on their movements while they are teaching and working with children. Gina has each of her students practice a lesson with other students. As they teach they are to move around and not simply stand or sit in one place at the front of the class. If they are using projected images, they are to move away from the screen. Then she teaches the students seat work monitoring, or how to move around the room effectively and check on students' progress as they are engaged in tasks individually or in small groups.

In summary, sensory inputs are processed in the sensory memories portions of the brain, and those that are retained long enough are transferred to WM. WM seems to reside in multiple parts of the brain but primarily in the prefrontal cortex of the frontal lobe (Wolfe, 2001). As we will see in Chapter 5, information is lost from WM in a few seconds unless it is rehearsed or transferred to LTM. For information to be retained there must be a neural signal to do so; that is, the information is deemed important and needs to be used.

The parts of the brain primarily involved in memory and information processing are the cortex and the medial temporal lobe (Wolfe, 2001). It appears that the brain processes and stores memories in the same structures that initially perceive and process information. At the same time, the particular parts of the brain involved in LTM vary depending on the type of information. In Chapter 5 a distinction is made between declarative memory (facts, definitions, events) and procedural memory (procedures, strategies). Different parts of the brain are involved in using declarative and procedural information.

With declarative information, the sensory registers in the cerebral cortex (e.g., visual, auditory) receive the input and transfer it to the hippocampus and the nearby medial temporal lobe. Inputs are registered in much the same format as they appear (e.g., as a visual or auditory stimulus). The hippocampus is not the ultimate storage site; it acts as a processor and conveyor of inputs. As we will see in the next section, inputs that occur more often make stronger neural connections. With multiple activations, the memories form neural networks that become strongly embedded in the frontal and temporal cortexes. LTM for declarative information, therefore, appears to reside in the frontal and temporal cortex.

Much procedural information becomes automatized such that procedures can be accomplished with little or no conscious awareness (e.g., typing, riding a bicycle). Initial procedural learning involves the prefrontal cortex, the parietal lobe, and the cerebellum, which ensure that we consciously attend to the movements or steps and that these movements or steps are assembled correctly. With practice, these areas show less activity and other brain structures, such as the motor cortex, become more involved (Wolfe, 2001).

Observational learning is covered in Chapter 4. Cognitive neuroscience supports the idea that much can be learned through observation (Bandura, 1986). Research shows that the cortical circuits involved in performing an action also respond when we observe someone else perform that action (van Gog, Paas, Marcus, Ayres, & Sweller, 2009).

With nonmotor procedures (e.g., decoding words, simple addition), the visual cortex is heavily involved. Repetition actually can change the neural structure of the visual cortex. These changes allow us to recognize visual stimuli (e.g., words, numbers) quickly without consciously having to process their meanings. As a consequence, many of these cognitive tasks become routinized. Conscious processing of information (e.g., stopping to think about what the reading passage means) requires extended activity in other parts of the brain.

But what if no meaning can be attached to an input? What if incoming information, although deemed important (such as by a teacher saying, "Pay attention"), cannot be linked with anything in memory? This situation necessitates creation of a new memory network, as discussed next.

Memory Networks

With repeated presentations of stimuli or information, neural networks can become strengthened such that the neural responses occur quickly. From a cognitive neuroscience perspective, *learning* involves forming and strengthening neural connections and networks (synaptic connections). This definition is quite similar to the definition of learning in current information processing theories (e.g., ACT-R; Chapter 5).

Hebb's Theory. The process by which these synaptic connections and networks are formed has been the study of scientific investigations for many years. Hebb (1949) formulated a neurophysiological theory of learning that highlights the role of two cortical structures: cell assemblies and phase sequences. A *cell assembly* is a structure that includes cells in the cortex and subcortical centers (Hilgard, 1956). Basically a cell assembly is a neural counterpart of a simple association and is formed through frequently repeated stimulations. When the particular stimulation occurs again, the cell assembly is aroused. Hebb believed that when the cell assembly was aroused, it would facilitate neural responses in other systems, as well as motor responses.

How do cell assemblies form? Hebb only could speculate on this, because in his time the technology for examining brain processes was limited. Hebb felt that repeated stimulations led to the growth of synaptic knobs that increased the contact between axons and dendrites (Hilgard, 1956). With repeated stimulations, the cell assembly would be activated automatically, which facilitates neural processing.

A *phase sequence* is a series of cell assemblies. Cell assemblies that are stimulated repeatedly form a pattern or sequence that imposes some organization on the process. For example, we are exposed to multiple visual stimuli when we look at the face of a friend. One can imagine multiple cell assemblies, each of which covers a particular aspect of the face (e.g., left corner of the left eye, bottom of the right ear). By repeatedly looking at the friend's face, these multiple cell assemblies are simultaneously activated and become connected to form a coordinated phase sequence that orders the parts (e.g., so we do not transpose the bottom of the right ear onto the left corner of the left eye). The phase sequence allows the coordinated whole to be meaningfully and consciously perceived.

Neural Connections. Despite Hebb's ideas being over 60 years old, they are remarkably consistent with contemporary views on how learning occurs and memories are formed. As we will see in the next section on development, we are born with a large number of neural (synaptic) connections. Our experiences then work on this system. Connections are selected or ignored, strengthened or lost. Further, connections can be added and developed through new experiences (National Research Council, 2000).

It is noteworthy that the process of forming and strengthening synaptic connections (learning) changes the physical structure of the brain and alters its functional organization (National Research Council, 2000). Learning specific tasks produces localized changes in brain areas appropriate for the task, and these changes impose new organization on the brain. We tend to think that the brain determines learning, but in fact there is a reciprocal relationship because of the "neuroplasticity" of the brain, or its capacity to change its structure and function as a result of experience (Begley, 2007).

Although brain research continues on this important topic, available information indicates that memory is not formed completely at the time initial learning occurs. Rather, memory formation is a continuous process in which neural connections are stabilized over a period of time (Wolfe, 2001). The process of stabilizing and strengthening neural (synaptic) connections is known as *consolidation*. The hippocampus appears to play a key role in consolidation, despite the fact that the hippocampus is not where memories are stored.

What factors improve consolidation? As discussed in depth in Chapter 5, organization, rehearsal, and elaboration are important because they serve to impose a structure. Research shows that the brain, far from being a passive receiver and recorder of information, plays an active role in storing and retrieving information (National Research Council, 2000).

In summary, it appears that stimuli or incoming information activates the appropriate brain portion and becomes encoded as synaptic connections. With repetition, these connections increase in number and become strengthened, which means they occur more automatically and communicate better with one another. Learning alters the specific regions of the brain involved in the tasks (National Research Council, 2000). Experiences are critical for learning, both experiences from the environment (e.g., visual and auditory stimuli) and from one's own mental activities (e.g., thoughts).

Given that the brain imposes some structure on incoming information, it is important that this structure help to facilitate memory. We might say, then, that simple consolidation and memory are not sufficient to guarantee long-term learning. Rather, instruction should play a key role by helping to impose a desirable structure on the learning, a point noted by Emma and Claudia in the opening scenario. Some applications of these ideas and suggestions for assisting learners to consolidate memories are given in Application 2.3.

APPLICATION 2.3
Teaching for Consolidation

Factors such as organization, rehearsal, and elaboration help the brain impose structure on learning and assist in the consolidation of neural connections in memory. Teachers can incorporate these ideas in various ways.

Organization

Ms. Standar's students are studying the American Revolution. Rather than ask them to learn many dates, she creates a time line of key events and explains how each event led to subsequent events. Thus, she helps students chronologically organize the key events by relating them to events that they helped to cause.

In her high school statistics course, Ms. Conwell organizes information about normally distributed data using the normal curve. On the curve she labels the mean and the standard deviations above and below the mean. She also labels the percentages of the area under portions of the curve so students can relate the mean and standard deviations to the percentages of the distribution. Using this visual organizer is more meaningful to students than is written information explaining these points.

Rehearsal

Mr. Luongo's elementary students will perform a Thanksgiving skit for parents. Students must learn their lines and also their movements. He breaks the skit into subparts and works on one part each day, then gradually merges the parts into a longer sequence. Students thus get plenty of rehearsal, including several rehearsals of the entire skit.

Mr. Gomez has his ninth grade English students rehearse with their vocabulary words. For each word list, students write the word and the definition and then write a sentence using the word. Students also write short essays every week, in which they try to incorporate at least five vocabulary words they have studied this year. This rehearsal helps to build memory networks with word spellings, meanings, and usage.

Elaboration

Elaboration is the process of expanding information to make it meaningful. Elaboration can help to build memory networks and link them with other relevant ones.

Mr. Jackson knows that students find precalculus difficult to link with other knowledge. Mr. Jackson surveys his students to determine their interests and what other courses they are taking. Then he relates precalculus concepts to these interests and courses. For example, for students taking physics he links principles of motion and gravity to conic sections (e.g., parabolas) and quadratic equations.

Ms. Kay's middle school students periodically work on a unit involving critical thinking on issues of personal responsibility. Students read vignettes and then discuss them. Rather than letting them simply agree or disagree with the story character's choices, she forces them to elaborate by addressing questions such as: How did this choice affect other people? What might have been the consequences if the character would have made a different choice? What would you have done and why?

Language Learning

The interaction of multiple brain structures and synaptic connections is seen clearly in language learning and especially in reading. Although modern technologies allow researchers to investigate real-time brain functioning as individuals acquire and use language skills, much brain research on language acquisition and use has been conducted on persons who have suffered brain injury and experienced some degree of language loss. Such research is informative of what functions are affected by injury to particular brain areas, but this research does not address language acquisition and use in children's developing brains.

Brain trauma studies have shown that the left side of the brain's cerebral cortex is central to reading and that the posterior (back) cortical association areas of the left hemisphere are critical for understanding and using language and for normal reading (Vellutino & Denckla, 1996). Reading dysfunctions often are symptoms of left posterior cortical lesions. Autopsies of brains of adolescents and young adults with a history of reading difficulties have shown structural abnormalities in the left hemispheres. Reading dysfunctions also are sometimes associated with brain lesions in the anterior (front) lobes—the area that controls speech—although the evidence much more strongly associates it with posterior lobe abnormalities. Since these results come from studies of persons who knew how to read (to varying degrees) and then lost some or all of the ability, we can conclude that the primarily left-sided areas of the brain associated with language and speech are critical for the maintenance of reading.

It is important to keep in mind, however, that there is no, one central area of the brain involved in reading. Rather, the various aspects of reading (e.g., letter and word identification, syntax, semantics) involve many localized and specialized brain structures and synaptic connections that must be coordinated to successfully read (Vellutino & Denckla, 1996). The section that follows examines how these interconnections seem to develop in normal readers and in those with reading problems. The idea is that coordinated reading requires the formation of *neural assemblies*, or collections of neural groups that have formed synaptic connections with one another (Byrnes, 2001). Neural assemblies seem conceptually akin to Hebb's cell assemblies and phase sequences.

Results from neuroscience research show that specific brain regions are associated with orthographic, phonological, semantic, and syntactic processing required for reading (Byrnes, 2001). Orthographic (e.g., letters, characters) processing depends heavily on the primary visual area. Phonological processing (e.g., phonemes, syllables) is associated with the superior (upper) temporal lobes. Semantic processing (e.g., meanings) is associated with Broca's area in the frontal lobe and areas in the medial (middle) temporal lobe in the left hemisphere. Syntactic processing (e.g., sentence structure) also seems to occur in Broca's area.

We noted earlier two key areas in the brain involved in language. Broca's area plays a major role in the production of grammatically correct speech. Wernicke's area (located in the left temporal lobe below the lateral fissure) is critical for proper word choice and elocution. Persons with deficiencies in Wernicke's area may use an incorrect word but one close in meaning (e.g., say "knife" when "fork" was intended).

Language and reading require the coordination of the various brain areas. Such coordination occurs through bundles of nerve fibers that connect the language areas to each other and to other parts of the cerebral cortex on both sides of the brain (Geschwind, 1998). The corpus callosum is the largest collection of such fibers, but there are others. Damage to or destruction of these fibers prevents the communication in the brain needed for proper language functioning, which can result in a language disorder. Brain researchers explore how dysfunctions operate and which brain functions continue in the presence of damage.

This topic is considered further in the following section, because it is intimately linked with brain development. For educators, knowing how the brain develops is important because developmental changes must be considered in planning instruction to ensure student learning.

BRAIN DEVELOPMENT

So far this chapter has focused on mature CNS functioning. Many educators, however, work with preschoolers, children, and adolescents. The topic of brain development is of interest not only in its own right, but also because the educational implications for teaching and learning vary depending on the level of brain development. In the opening scenario, Bryan notes the importance of educators understanding brain development. This section discusses influential factors on development, the course of development, critical periods in development, and the role of development in language acquisition and use.

Influential Factors

Although human brains are structurally similar, there are differences among individuals. Five influences on brain development are genetics, environmental stimulation, nutrition, steroids, and teratogens (Byrnes, 2001; Table 2.3).

Genetics. The human brain differs in size and composition from those of other animals. Although the difference between the human genome and that of our closest animal relative (the chimpanzee) is only 1.23% (Lemonick & Dorfman, 2006), that difference and other genetic variations produce a species that can design and build bridges, compose music, write novels, solve complex equations, and so forth.

Human brains have a similar genetic structure, but they nonetheless differ in size and structure. Studies of monozygotic (one-egg) twins show that they sometimes develop brains that are structurally different (Byrnes, 2001). Genetic instructions determine the size, structure, and neural connectivity of the brain. Most of the time these differences

Table 2.3
Factors affecting brain development.

- Genetics
- Environmental stimulation
- Nutrition
- Steroids
- Teratogens

yield normally functioning brains, but brain research continues to identify how certain genetic differences produce abnormalities.

Environmental Stimulation. Brain development requires stimulation from the environment. Prenatal development sets the stage for learning by developing a neural circuitry that can receive and process stimuli and experiences. Those experiences further shape the circuitry by adding and reorganizing synapses. For example, pregnant women who talk and sing to their babies may, through their speech and singing, help to establish neural connections in the babies (Wolfe, 2001). Brain development lags when experiences are missing or minimal. Although there are certain critical periods when stimulation can have profound effects (Jensen, 2005), research suggests that stimulation is important during the entire life span to ensure continued brain development.

Nutrition. Lack of good nutrition can have major effects on brain development, and the particular effects depend on when the poor nutrition occurs (Byrnes, 2001). Prenatal malnutrition, for example, slows the production and growth of neurons and glial cells. A critical period is between the 4th and 7th months of gestation when most brain cells are produced (Jensen, 2005). Later malnutrition slows how quickly cells grow in size and acquire a myelin sheath. Although the latter problem can be corrected with proper diet, the former cannot because too few cells have developed. This is why pregnant women are advised to avoid drugs, alcohol, and tobacco; maintain a good diet; and avoid stress (stress also causes problems for a developing fetus).

Steroids. *Steroids* refer to a class of hormones that affect several functions, including sexual development and stress reactions (Byrnes, 2001). Steroids can affect brain development in various ways. The brain has receptors for hormones. Such hormones as estrogen and cortisol will be absorbed and will potentially change brain structure during prenatal development. Excessive stress hormones can produce death of neurons. Rsearchers also have explored whether gender and sexual preference differences arise in part due to differences in steroids. Although the evidence on the role of steroids in brain development is less conclusive than that for nutrition, steroids have the potential to affect the brain.

Teratogens. *Teratogens* are foreign substances (e.g., alcohol, viruses) that can cause abnormalities in a developing embryo or fetus (Byrnes, 2001). A substance is considered to be a teratogen only if research shows that a not unrealistically high level can affect brain development. For example, caffeine in small amounts may not be a teratogen, but it may become one when intake is higher. Teratogens can have effects on the development and interconnections of neurons and glial cells. In extreme cases (e.g., the rubella virus), they can cause birth defects.

Phases of Development

During prenatal development, the brain grows in size and structure, as well as in number of neurons, glial cells, and neural connections (synapses). Prenatal brain development is rapid, because it occurs in nine months and most cells are produced between months 4 and 7 (Jensen, 2005). Cells travel up the neural tube, migrate to various parts of the brain, and form connections. It is estimated that at its peak, the embryo generates a quarter of a million brain cells a minute.

At birth the brain has over a million connections, which represent about 60% of the peak number of synapses that will develop over the lifetime (Jensen, 2005). Given these numbers, it is little wonder that prenatal development is so important. Changes that occur then can have far-reaching and permanent effects.

Brain development also occurs rapidly in infants. By the age of 2 years, a child will have as many synapses as an adult, and by the age of 3 years the child will have billions more than an adult. Young children's brains are dense and have many complex neural connections and more than at any other time in life (Trawick-Smith, 2003).

In fact, young children have too many synapses. About 60% of babies' energy is used by their brains; in comparison, adult brains require only 20–25% (Brunton, 2007). With development, children and adolescents lose far more brain synapses than they gain. By the time adolescents turn 18, they have lost about half of their infant synapses. Brain connections that are not used or needed simply disappear. This "use it or lose it" strategy is desirable because connections that are used will be reinforced and consolidated, whereas those not used will be permanently lost.

By the age of 5 years, the child's brain has acquired a language and developed sensory motor skills and other competencies. The rapid changes of the first years have slowed, but the brain continues to add synapses. Neural networks are becoming more complex in their linkages. This process continues throughout development.

As noted by Bryan in the opening vignette, major changes occur during the teenage years when the brain undergoes structural alterations (Jensen, 2005). The frontal lobes, which handle abstract reasoning and problem solving, are maturing, and the parietal lobes increase in size. The prefrontal cortex, which controls judgments and impulses, matures slowly (Shute, 2009). There also are changes in neurotransmitters—especially *dopamine*—that can leave the brain more sensitive to the pleasurable effects of drugs and alcohol. There is a thickening of brain cells and massive reorganizations of synapses, which makes this a key time for learning. The "use it or lose it" strategy results in brain regions becoming strengthened through practice (e.g., practicing the piano thickens neurons in the brain region controlling the fingers) (Wallis, 2004).

Given these widespread changes in their brains, it is not surprising that teenagers often make poor decisions and engage in high-risk behaviors involving drugs, alcohol, and sex. Instructional strategies need to take these changes into account. Applications of these ideas to instruction are given in Application 2.4.

Critical Periods

Many books on child rearing stress that the first two years of life represent a critical period such that if certain experiences do not occur, the child's development will suffer permanently. There is some truth to this statement, although the claim is overstated. Five aspects of brain development for which there seem to be critical periods are lan-

APPLICATION 2.4
Teaching and Learning with Teenagers

The rapid and extensive changes that occur in teenagers' brains suggest that we not view teens as smaller versions of adults (or as young children either). Some suggestions for instruction with teens based on brain research follow.

Give Simple and Straightforward Directions

Mr. Glenn, who teaches 10th grade English, knows that his students' memories may not accommodate many ideas at once. For each novel students read, they must do a literary analysis that comprises several sections (e.g., plot summary, literary devices, analysis of a major character). Mr. Glenn reviews these sections carefully. For each, he explains what it should include and shows a sample or two.

Use Models

Students process information well when it is presented in multiple modes—visual, auditory, tactile. In her chemistry class, Ms. Carchina wants to ensure that students understand laboratory procedures. She explains and demonstrates each procedure she wants students to learn, then has students work in pairs to perform the procedure. As students work, she circulates among them and offers corrective feedback as needed.

Ensure That Students Develop Competence

Motivation theory and research show that students want to avoid appearing incompetent (Chapter 8). This is especially true during the teenage years when their senses of self are developing. Ms. Patterson teaches calculus, which is difficult for some students. Through quizzes, homework, and class work she knows which students are having difficulty. Ms. Patterson holds review sessions before school every day for her students, and she makes a point to advise students having difficulty to attend those sessions.

Incorporate Decision Making

The rapid development occurring in teens' brains means that their decision making often is flawed. They may base decisions on incomplete information or what they think will please their friends and fail to think through potential consequences. Mr. Manley incorporates much decision making and discussions of consequences into his marine science classes. Students read about topics such as global warming and water pollution, and then he presents them with case studies that they discuss (e.g., a ship's captain who wants to dump garbage at sea). Teachers ask students questions that address topics such as the potential consequences of possible actions and other ways that the problem could be addressed.

guage, emotions, sensory motor development, auditory development, and vision (Jensen, 2005; Table 2.4). Language and emotions are discussed elsewhere in this chapter; the remaining three are covered next.

Sensory Motor Development. The systems associated with vision, hearing, and motor movements develop extensively through experiences during the first two years of life.

Table 2.4
Aspects of brain development
having critical periods.

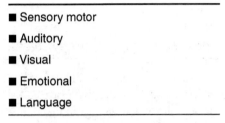

- Sensory motor
- Auditory
- Visual
- Emotional
- Language

The vestibular system in the inner ear influences the senses of movement and balance and affects other sensory systems. There is evidence that inadequate vestibular stimulation among infants and toddlers can lead to learning problems later (Jensen, 2005).

Too often, however, infants and toddlers are not in stimulating environments, especially those children who spend much time in day care centers that provide mostly caregiving. Many children also do not receive sufficient stimulation outside of those settings, because they spend too much time in car seats, walkers, or in front of televisions. Allowing youngsters movement and even rocking them provides stimulation. About 60% of infants and toddlers spend an average of one to two hours per day watching television or videos (Courage & Setliff, 2009). Although young children can learn from these media, they do not do so easily. Children's comprehension and learning are enhanced when parents watch with them and provide descriptions and explanations (Courage & Setliff, 2009).

Auditory Development. The child's first two years are critical for auditory development. By the age of 6 months, infants can discriminate most sounds in their environments (Jensen, 2005). In the first two years, children's auditory systems mature in terms of range of sounds heard and ability to discriminate among sounds. Problems in auditory development can lead to problems in learning language, because much language acquisition depends on children hearing the speech of others in their environments.

Vision. Vision develops largely during the first year of life and especially after the fourth month. Synaptic density in the visual system increases dramatically, including the neural connections regulating the perception of color, depth, movement, and hue. Proper visual development requires a visually rich environment where infants can explore objects and movements. Television and movies are poor substitutes. Although they provide color and movement, they are two dimensional and the developing brain needs depth. The action shown on television and in the movies often occurs too rapidly for infants to focus on properly (Jensen, 2005).

In short, the first two years of life are critical for proper development of the sensory motor, visual, and auditory systems, and development of these systems is aided when infants are in a rich environment that allows them to experience movements, sights, and sounds. At the same time, brain development is a lifelong process; brains need stimulation after the age of 2 years. The brain continually is adding, deleting, and reorganizing synaptic connections and changing structurally. Although researchers have shown that certain aspects of brain development occur more rapidly at certain times, individuals of all ages benefit from stimulating environments.

Language Development

Previously we saw how certain functions associated with language operate in the brain. Although researchers have explored brain processes with different types of content involving various mental abilities, a wealth of research has been conducted on language acquisition and use. This is a key aspect of cognitive development and one that has profound implications for learning.

As noted earlier, much brain research on language has been conducted on persons who have suffered brain injury and experienced some degree of language loss. Such research is informative of what functions are affected by injury to particular brain areas, but these research investigations do not address language acquisition and use in children's developing brains.

Brain studies of developing children, while less common, have offered important insights into the development of language functions. Studies often have compared normally developing children with those who have difficulties learning in school. In place of the surgical techniques often used on brain-injured or deceased patients, these studies employ less-invasive techniques such as those described earlier in this chapter. Researchers often measure *event-related potentials* (or *evoked potentials*), which are changes in brain waves that occur when individuals anticipate or engage in various tasks (Halliday, 1998).

Differences in event-related potentials reliably differentiate among below-average, average, and above-average children (Molfese et al., 2006). Children who are normally developing show extensive bilateral and anterior (front) cortical activation and accentuated left-sided activations in language and speech areas. In contrast to reading maintenance, it appears that reading development also depends on anterior activation, perhaps on both sides of the brain (Vellutino & Denckla, 1996). Other research shows that developing children who experience left-sided dysfunction apparently compensate to some extent by learning to read using the right hemisphere. The right hemisphere may be able to support and sustain an adequate level of reading, but it seems critical for this transition to occur prior to the development of language competence. Such assumption of language functions by the right hemisphere may not occur among individuals who have sustained left-hemisphere damage as adults. A critical period in language development seems to be between birth and age 5. During this time, children's brains develop most of their language capabilities. There is a rapid increase in vocabulary between the ages of 19 and 31 months (Jensen, 2005). The development of these language capabilities is enhanced when children are in language-rich environments where parents and others talk with children. This critical period for language development overlaps the critical period of auditory development between birth and age 2.

In addition to this critical period, language development also seems to be part of a natural process with a timetable. We have seen how the auditory and visual systems develop capacities to supply the input for the development of language. A parallel process may occur in language development for the capacity to perceive *phonemes*, which are the smallest units of speech sounds (e.g., the "b" and "p" sounds in "bet" and "pet"). Children learn or acquire phonemes when they are exposed to them in their environments; if phonemes are absent in their environments, then children do not acquire them. Thus, there may be a critical period in which synaptic connections are properly formed, but only if the environment provides the inputs. In short, children's brains may be "ready" ("prewired") to learn various aspects of language at different times in line with their levels of brain development (National Research Council, 2000).

Importantly for education, instruction can help to facilitate language development. Different areas of the brain must work together to learn language, such as the areas involved in seeing, hearing, speaking, and thinking (Byrnes, 2001; National Research Council, 2000). Acquiring and using language is a coordinated activity. People listen to speech and read text, think about what was said or what they read, and compose sentences to write or speak. This coordinated activity implies that language development should benefit from instruction that coordinates these functions, that is, experiences that require vision, hearing, speech, and thinking (see Application 2.5).

In summary, different areas of the brain participate in language development in normally developing children, although left-hemisphere contributions typically are more prominent than right-hemisphere ones. Over time, language functions are heavily subsumed by the left hemisphere. In particular, reading skill seems to require left-hemisphere control. But more research is needed before we fully understand the relationships between brain functions and developing language and reading competencies.

Like other aspects of brain development, language acquisition reflects the interaction between heredity and environment discussed in Chapter 1. The cultural experiences of infants and children will determine to a large extent which brain synapses they retain. If the culture stresses motor functions, then these should be strengthened; whereas if the culture stresses cognitive processes, then these will ascend. If young children are exposed to a rich linguistic environment stressing oral and written language, then their language acquisition will develop more rapidly than will the language capabilities of children in impoverished environments.

The implication for facilitating early brain development is to provide rich experiences for infants and young children, stressing perceptual, motor, and language functions. This is especially critical in the first years of life. These experiences should enhance the formation of synaptic connections and networks. There also is evidence that babies who have suffered in utero (e.g., from mothers' drug or alcohol abuse), as well as those with developmental disabilities (e.g., retardation, autism), benefit from early intervention in the first three years (Shore, 1997).

APPLICATION 2.5
Facilitating Language Development

Although the period of birth to age 5 represents a critical period for language development, language acquisition and use are lifelong activities. Teachers can work with students of all ages to help develop their language skills. It is important that instruction coordinate the component language functions of seeing, hearing, thinking, and speaking.

A kindergarten teacher works regularly with her students on learning phonemes. To help develop recognition of phonemes in "__at" words (e.g., mat, hat, pat, cat, sat), she has each of these words printed on a large piece of cardboard. The phoneme is printed in red and the "at" appears in black. She gives students practice by holding up a card, asking them to say the word, and then asking individual students to use the word in a sentence.

Kathy Stone teaches her students animal names and spellings. She has a picture of each animal and its printed name on a display board, along with two to three interesting facts about the animal (e.g., where it lives, what it eats). She has children pronounce the animal's name several times and spell it aloud, then write a short sentence using the word. This is especially helpful for animal names that are difficult to pronounce or spell (e.g., giraffe, hippopotamus).

A middle-grade mathematics teacher is working with her students on place value. Some students are having a lot of difficulty and cannot correctly order numbers from smallest to largest (e.g., .007, 7/100, seven-tenths, 7). The teacher has three large magnetic number lines, each ranging from 0 to 1 and broken into units of tenths, hundredths, and thousandths. She asked students to put a magnetic bar on the appropriate number line (e.g., put the bar on the 7 of the hundredths line for 7/100). Then she broke students into small groups and gave them problems, and asked them to use number lines or pie charts to show where numbers fell so they could properly order them. Next she worked with them to convert all numbers to a common denominator (e.g., 7/10 = 70/100) and to place the markers on the same board (e.g., thousandths) so they could see the correct order.

Students in Jim Marshall's class learn about key historical documents in U.S. history (e.g., Declaration of Independence, Constitution, Bill of Rights). To appeal to multiple senses, Jim brought facsimile copies of these documents to class. Then he had students engage in role-playing where they read selections from the documents. Students were taught how to put emphasis at appropriate places while reading to make these passages especially distinctive.

Many students in Gina Brown's educational psychology class have difficulty comprehending and correctly using psychological terms (e.g., assimilation, satiation, zone of proximal development). Where possible, she obtains films that demonstrate these concepts (e.g., child being administered Piagetian tasks). For others, she uses websites with case studies that students read and respond to, after which they discuss in class how that concept comes into play. For example, in one case study a student is repeatedly praised by a teacher. Finally the student becomes satiated with praise and tells the teacher that she does not always have to tell him that he did so well.

MOTIVATION AND EMOTIONS

Researchers have investigated how brain processes link with many different cognitive functions. But researchers also have been concerned with the brain processes involved with noncognitive functions, such as motivation and emotions. These functions are discussed in turn.

Motivation

In Chapter 8, *motivation* is defined as the process whereby goal-directed activities are instigated and sustained. Motivated actions include choice of tasks, effort (physical and mental), persistence, and achievement. Chapter 8 also discusses the various processes that have been hypothesized to affect motivation, such as goals, self-efficacy, needs, values, and perceptions of control.

Contemporary theories depict motivation largely in cognitive terms. Most motivational processes have cognitive components. *Self-efficacy*, for example, refers to perceived capabilities to learn or perform behaviors at designated levels. Self-efficacy is a cognitive belief. As such, it likely has a neural representation of the kind discussed in this chapter. Although research is lacking in this area, we might expect that self-efficacy beliefs are represented in the brain as a neural network that links the domain being studied (e.g., fractions, reading novels) with current sensory input. Other motivational processes also may be represented in synaptic networks, as might processes involved in self-regulation, such as metacognition and goals (Chapter 9). More neurophysiological research on motivation and self-regulation variables would help to bridge the gap between education and neuroscience (Byrnes & Fox, 1998).

From a cognitive neuroscience perspective, there are at least two kinds of neural counterparts of motivation. These involve rewards and motivational states.

Rewards. Rewards have a long history in motivation research. They are key components of conditioning theories, which contend that behaviors that are reinforced (rewarded) tend to be repeated in the future. Motivation represents an increase in the rate, intensity, or duration of behavior (Chapter 3).

Cognitive and constructivist theories of motivation postulate that it is the expectation of reward, rather than the reward itself, that motivates behavior. Rewards can sustain motivation when they are given contingent on competent performance or progress in learning. Motivation may decline over time when people view the rewards as controlling their behavior (i.e., they are performing a task so that they can earn a reward).

The brain seems to have a system for processing rewards (Jensen, 2005), but, like other brain functions, this one also is complex. Many brain structures are involved, including the hypothalamus, prefrontal cortex, and amygdala. The brain produces its own rewards in the form of opiates that result in a natural high. This effect suggests that the brain may be predisposed toward experiencing and sustaining pleasurable outcomes. The expectation that one may receive a reward for competent or improved performance can activate this pleasure network, which produces the neurotransmitter *dopamine*. It may be that the brain stores, as part of a neural network, the expectation of reward for performing the action. In fact, dopamine can be produced by the expectation of pleasure (anticipation of reward), as well as by the pleasure itself. Dopamine increases when there is a discrepancy between expected and realized rewards (e.g., persons expect a large reward but receive a small one). The dopamine system can help people adjust their expectations, which is a type of learning (Varma et al., 2008).

But the brain also can become satiated with rewards such that the expectation of a reward or the receipt of a reward does not produce as much pleasure as previously. It is possible that the expectation of a larger reward is needed to produce dopamine, and if that is not forthcoming, then the effect may extinguish. This point may help to explain why certain rewards lose their power to motivate over time.

Research is needed on whether other cognitive motivators—such as goals and the perception of learning progress—also trigger dopamine responses and thus have neurophysiological referents. The point to be noted, however, is that dopamine production is idiosyncratic. The same level of reward or expectation of reward will not motivate all students uniformly, which suggests that additional brain processes are involved in motivation. This point has practical implications for teaching, because it suggests that teachers who plan to use rewards must learn what motivates each student and establish a reward system that can accommodate changes in students' preferences.

Motivational States. From a cognitive neuroscience perspective, *motivational states* are complex neural connections that include emotions, cognitions, and behaviors (Jensen, 2005). States change with conditions. If it has been several hours since we have eaten, then we likely are in a hunger state. We may be in a worried state if problems are pressing on us. If things are going well, we may be in a happy state. Similarly, a motivational state may include emotions, cognitions, and behaviors geared toward learning. Like other states, a motivational state is an integrated combination of mind, body, and behavior that ultimately links with a web-like network of synaptic connections.

States are fluid; they are ever changing based on internal (e.g., thoughts) and external (e.g., environmental) events. Any given motivational state can strengthen, weaken, or change to another type of state. This changing nature of synaptic connections matches the nature of motivation (discussed in Chapter 8), that motivation is a process rather than a thing. As a process, it typically is not steady but rather waxes and wanes. The key to education and learning is to maintain motivation within an optimal range.

Teachers intuitively understand the idea of motivational states. Their goal is to have students in a motivational state for learning. At any given moment, some students will be in that state, but others will be experiencing different states, including apathy, sadness, hyperactivity, and distraction. To change these states, teachers may have to first address the present states (e.g., attend to why Kira is sad) and then attempt to focus students' attention on the task at hand.

The integration of cognition, emotion, and behavior posited by neuroscience is important. The individual components will not lead to desirable learning. For example, students who believe they want to learn and are emotionally ready to do so nonetheless will learn little if they engage in no behavior. Likewise, motivated behavior without a clear cognitive focus on learning will be wasted activity. Students who are experiencing emotional stress yet want to learn and engage in learning actions are apt to find their learning less than maximal because emotions are thwarting synaptic connections from being formed and consolidated.

Emotions

Similar to the neurophysiological evidence for motivation, the operation of emotions in the CNS is not fully understood. There are various theories to account for human emotions (Byrnes, 2001).

One theory that is consistent with the preceding view of motivation is a network theory (Halgren & Marinkovic, 1995). In this view, emotional reactions consist of four overlapping stages: orienting complex, emotional event integration, response selection, and sustained emotional context. The orienting complex is an automatic response in which individuals direct their attention toward a stimulus or event and mobilize resources to deal with it. The orienting complex produces a neural response that is sent to other stages. In the emotional event integration stage, this stimulus or event is integrated with information in WM and LTM, such as information about the definition or meaning of the stimulus or event and the context.

In the third (response selection) stage, the individual ascribes cognitive meaning to the stimulus or event, integrates this meaning with an affective component, identifies possible actions, and selects one. Finally, during the sustained emotional context stage, the individual's mood is linked with outputs of prior stages. Each stage is linked with specific neural areas. For example, sustained emotional context seems to be associated with neural firings in areas of the frontal lobe (Halgren & Marinkovic, 1995).

But emotions appear to be more complex than this analysis, because the same event has the potential to arouse different emotions. The English language reflects this potential multiple triggering, as when one says after hearing a piece of news, "I didn't know whether to laugh or cry." It also is possible that emotional activity in the brain is different for primary and culturally based emotions (Byrnes, 2001). Primary emotions (e.g., fear, anger, surprise) may have an innate neural basis centered in the right hemisphere (which regulates much ANS functioning), whereas emotions that involve cultural meanings (e.g., statements made by people that can be interpreted in different ways) may be governed more by the left hemisphere with its language functions.

Emotions can help to direct attention, which is necessary for learning (Phelps, 2006). Information from the environment goes to the thalamus, where it is relayed to the amygdala and to the frontal cortex. The amygdala determines the emotional significance of the stimulus (Wolfe, 2001). This determination is facilitative, because it tells us whether to run, seek shelter, attack, or remain neutral. The frontal cortex provides the cognitive interpretation of the stimulus, but this takes additional time. Part of what is meant by "emotional control" is not to simply react to the emotional significance (although when safety is an issue, that is desirable), but rather to delay action until the proper cognitive interpretation can be made.

In addition to their role in attention, emotions also influence learning and memory (Phelps, 2006). It appears that the hormones epinephrine and norepinephrine, which are secreted by the adrenal cortex to produce the autonomic responses involved in emotions, also enhance memory for the triggering stimulus or event in the temporal lobe of the brain (Wolfe, 2001). Conscious memory of emotional situations is consolidated better due to the actions of these hormones.

The point that emotions can enhance learning should not be interpreted as a recommendation that educators should make learning as stressful as possible. As we saw earlier, too much stress interferes with the formation and consolidation of neural networks. Rather, this

APPLICATION 2.6
Involving Emotions in Learning

Kathy Stone wants her students to enjoy school, and she knows how important it is to arouse children's emotions for learning. She always tries to link academic content to students' experiences so that their positive emotions associated with these experiences become associated with the learning. When her children read a story about a child who took a trip, she asked them to tell about when they took a trip to visit a relative, go on vacation, or so forth. When working on mathematical division, she asked children to think about something that was divided into parts (e.g., pie, cake) so that several people could enjoy it.

Jim Marshall wants his students to not only learn U.S. history but also experience the emotions involved in key events. Reading about events such as the Civil War and the Great Depression can devoid them of emotions, yet these and other events stirred strong emotions among those who lived then. Jim makes heavy use of films depicting events and role-playing with his students. He works with students to ensure that they express emotions they likely would have felt. For one role-playing on the Great Depression,

one student was a person looking for work and others played the roles of employers he visited asking for work. As each employer turned him down, the job seeker became more frustrated and finally began sobbing and saying, "All I want is a job so I can provide for my family. I hope my children never see this again in their lives!"

Gina Brown understands how some students can view educational psychology content as dry and boring. To invoke her students' emotions, each week she has her students focus on one or two concepts to address in their school internships (see Application 2.1). For example, reading about learning can be dull, but seeing a child learn is exciting. Thus, as students work with schoolchildren, they keep a log on the children's behaviors and reactions during a lesson as they are learning. Gina's students report how excited they become when they are tutoring children and the children begin to show that they are learning. As one of Gina's students reported, "I became so excited while working with Keenan when he said, 'Oh I get it,' and sure enough he did!"

point suggests that motivation and emotions can be used constructively to produce better learning. Teachers who lecture a lot engender little emotional involvement by students. But emotional interest should rise when teachers get students involved in the learning. Activities such as role-playing, discussions, and demonstrations are likely to instigate greater motivation and emotions and lead to better learning than will teacher lecturing (Application 2.6).

Increasing emotion during learning is effective only up to a point. Too much emotion (e.g., high stress) for lengthy periods is not desirable because of all the negative side effects (e.g., increased blood pressure, compromised immune system). Students in prolonged stressful situations also worry excessively, and the thoughts associated with worry thwart learning.

These negative effects brought on by stress or threats arise partly because of the hormone *cortisol*, which like epinephrine and norepinephrine is secreted by the adrenal glands

(Lemonick, 2007). Epinephrine and norepinephrine act quickly, and cortisol is a type of long-lasting backup. High amounts of cortisol in the body over long time periods can lead to deterioration of the hippocampus and a decline in cognitive functioning (Wolfe, 2001).

Cortisol also is critical during brain development. Infants bond emotionally with parents or caregivers. When babies experience stress, their levels of cortisol become elevated in their bodies. Cortisol retards brain development because it reduces the number of synapses and leaves neurons vulnerable to damage (Trawick-Smith, 2003). In contrast, when babies form attachments and maintain them over time, cortisol levels do not become elevated (Gunnar, 1996). When attachments are secure, cortisol levels do not rise to dangerous levels even under stressful conditions. Thus, it is critical that young children believe that their parents or caregivers love them and are reliable caregivers.

In summary, we can see that motivation and emotions are integrally linked with cognitive processing and neural activities. Further, the evidence summarized in this section makes it clear that when motivation and emotions are properly regulated, they can positively affect attention, learning, and memory. We now turn to the instructional applications of neuroscience for teaching and learning.

INSTRUCTIONAL APPLICATIONS

Relevance of Brain Research

There has been a surge of interest in the last several years in neurophysiological research exploring brain development and functioning. Many educators view brain research with interest, because they believe that it might suggest ways to make educational materials and instruction compatible with how children process information and learn.

Unfortunately, the history of behavioral science reflects a disconnect between brain research and learning theories. Research on the brain and behavior is not new; recall Hebb's (1949) neurophysiological theory discussed earlier in this chapter. Learning theorists in various traditions, while acknowledging the importance of brain research, have tended to formulate and test theories independently of brain research findings.

This situation clearly is changing. Educational researchers increasingly believe that understanding brain processes provides additional insights into the nature of learning and development (Byrnes & Fox, 1998). Indeed, some cognitive explanations for learning (e.g., activation of information in memory, transfer of information from WM to LTM; Chapter 5) involve CNS processes, and brain psychology has begun to explain operations involved in learning and memory. Findings from brain research actually support many results obtained in research studies on learning and memory (Byrnes, 2001; Byrnes & Fox, 1998).

It is unfortunate that some educators have overgeneralized results of brain research to make unwarranted instructional recommendations. Although brain functions are to some extent localized, there is much evidence that tasks require activity of both hemispheres and that their differences are more relative than absolute (Byrnes & Fox, 1998). The identification of "right-brained" and "left-brained" students usually is based on informal observations rather than on scientifically valid and reliable measures and instruments. The result is that some educational methods are being used with students not because of proven effects on learning, but rather because they presumably use students' assumed brain preferences.

Table 2.5
Educational issues relevant to brain research.

- Role of early education
- Complexity of cognitive processes
- Diagnosis of specific difficulties
- Multifaceted nature of learning

Educational Issues

Brain research, and CNS research in general, raises many issues relevant to education (Table 2.5). With respect to developmental changes, one issue involves the critical role of early education. The fact that children's brains are super-dense implies that more neurons are not necessarily better. There likely is an optimal state of functioning in which brains have the "right" number of neurons and synapses—neither too many nor too few. Physical, emotional, and cognitive development involves the brain approaching its optimal state. Atypical development—resulting in developmental disabilities—may occur because this paring-down process does not proceed normally.

This molding and shaping process in the brain suggests that early childhood education is critically important. The developmental periods of infancy and preschool can set the stage for the acquisition of competencies needed to be successful in school (Byrnes & Fox, 1998). Early intervention programs (e.g., Head Start) have been shown to improve children's school readiness and learning, and many states have implemented preschool education programs. Brain research justifies this emphasis on early education.

A second issue concerns the idea that instruction and learning experiences must be planned to take into account the complexities of cognitive processes such as attention and memory (Chapter 5). Neuroscience research has shown that attention is not a unitary process, but rather includes many components (e.g., alerting to a change in the current state, localizing the source of the change). Memory is similarly differentiated into types, such as declarative and procedural. The implication is that educators cannot assume that a particular instructional technique "gains students' attention" or "helps them remember." Rather, we must be more specific about what aspects of attention that instruction will appeal to and what specific type of memory is being addressed.

A third issue involves remedying students' learning difficulties. Brain research suggests that the key to correcting deficiencies in a specific subject is to determine with which aspects of the subject the learner is having difficulty and then to specifically address those. Mathematics, for example, includes many subcomponents, such as comprehension of written numbers and symbols, retrieval of facts, and the ability to write numbers. Reading comprises orthographic, phonological, semantic, and syntactic processes. To say that one is a poor reader does not diagnose where the difficulty lies. Only fine-tuned assessments can make that identification, and then a corrective procedure can be implemented that will address the specific deficiency. A general reading program that addresses all aspects of reading (e.g., word identification, word meanings) is analogous to a general antibiotic given to one who is sick; it may not be the best therapy. It seems educationally advantageous to offer corrective instruction in those areas that require correction most. For example, cognitive strategy instruction in children's weaknesses can be combined with traditional reading instruction (Katzir & Paré-Blagoev, 2006).

The final issue concerns the complexity of learning theories. Brain research has shown that multifaceted theories of learning seem to capture the actual state of affairs better than do parsimonious models. There is much redundancy in brain functions, which accounts for the common finding that when an area of the brain known to be associated with a given function is traumatized, the function may not completely disappear (another reason why the "right-brain" and "left-brain" distinctions do not hold much credibility). Over time, theories of learning have become more complex. Classical and operant conditioning theories (Chapter 3) are much simpler than social cognitive theory, cognitive information processing theory, and constructivist theory (Chapters 4–6). These latter theories better reflect brain reality. This suggests that educators should accept the complexity of school learning environments and investigate ways that the many aspects of environments can be coordinated to improve student learning.

Brain-Based Educational Practices

This chapter suggests some specific educational practices that facilitate learning and that are substantiated by brain research. Byrnes (2001) contended that brain research is relevant to psychology and education to the extent that it helps psychologists and educators develop a clearer understanding of learning, development, and motivation; that is, it is relevant when it helps to substantiate existing predictions of learning theories.

In other chapters of this text, theories and research findings are reviewed that suggest effective teaching and learning practices. Table 2.6 lists some educational practices that are derived from learning theories and supported by both learning research and brain research. In the opening vignette, we suspect that Emma and Claudia will be using these practices (among others). Application 2.7 gives examples of these applied in learning settings. These practices are discussed in turn.

Problem-Based Learning. Problem-based learning is an effective learning method (Chapter 6). Problem-based learning engages students in learning and helps to motivate them. When students work in groups, they also can improve their cooperative learning skills. Problem-based learning requires students to think creatively and bring their knowledge to bear in unique ways. It is especially useful for projects that have no one correct solution.

Table 2.6
Educational practices substantiated by brain research.

- Problem-based learning
- Simulations and role-playing
- Active discussions
- Graphics
- Positive climate

APPLICATION 2.7
Effective Educational Practices

There are many educational practices whose positive effects on learning are supported by both learning and brain research. Some important practices are problem-based learning, simulations and role-playing, active discussions, graphics, and positive climate.

Problem-Based Learning

Mr. Abernathy's eighth graders have studied their state's geography to include characteristics of the main regions and cities of the state. He divided the class into small groups to work on the following problem. A large computer company wants to open a manufacturing facility in the state. Each small student group is assigned a specific region in the state. The task for each group is to make a convincing argument for why the facility should be located in that region. Factors to be addressed include costs associated with locating in that area, accessibility to major highways and airports, availability of a labor force, quality of schools, nearness of higher education facilities, and support from the community. Students gather information from various sources (e.g., media center, Internet), prepare a poster with pictures and descriptions, and give a 10-minute presentation supporting their position. Each member of a group has responsibility for one or more aspects of the project.

Simulations and Role-Playing

Mr. Barth's fifth-grade students have read "Freedom on the Menu" by Carole Boston Weatherford. This book tells the story of the Greensboro, North Carolina lunch counter sit-ins in the 1960s as seen through the eyes of a young African American girl. Mr. Barth discusses this book with the students and probes them for how they thought it felt to these individuals to be discriminated against. He then organizes class simulations and role-plays so that students can see how discrimination can operate. For one activity, he selected the girls to be the leaders and the boys to follow their directions. For another activity, he only called on boys with blue eyes, and for a third activity he moved all students with dark hair to the front of the room. Using these activities, he hoped that students would see and feel the unfairness of treating people differently based on characteristics that they cannot change.

Active Discussions

Ms. Carring's civics class has been studying U.S. presidential elections. U.S. presidents are elected by electoral votes. There have been occasions where presidents elected by gaining the necessary electoral votes have not had a majority (50%) of the popular vote or have actually had a lower popular vote total than the losing candidate. Ms. Carring holds a class discussion on the topic, "Should U.S. presidents be elected by popular vote?" She facilitates the discussion by raising questions in response to points raised by students. For example, Candace argued that a popular vote better reflects the will of the people. Ms. Carring then asked whether, if we used only a popular vote, candidates would tend to focus on voters in large cities (e.g., New York, Chicago) and neglect voters in states with small populations (e.g., Montana, Vermont).

(continued)

APPLICATION 2.7 (continued)

Graphics

Mr. Antonelli, a high school vocational instructor, has his students design a house, which they then will help to build with help from community members. The school system owns the land, a local contractor will pour the foundation, and a builder's supply company will donate the lumber and electrical and plumbing supplies. The students use computer graphics to design different house styles and interior layouts. The class considers these and decides on an exterior and interior design plan. They then work with Mr. Antonelli and the builder's supply company to determine what supplies and equipment they will need. Several community members volunteer to help students build the house, and after they finish it the house is given to a local family selected by a community organization.

Positive Climate

Ms. Taylor teaches second grade in a school serving a high poverty neighborhood. Many of her students live in single-parent homes, and over 80% of the students receive lunch for free or at a reduced cost. Ms. Taylor does many things to create a positive climate. Her classroom ("Taylor's Nest") is warm and inviting and has cozy corners where students can go to read. Each day she talks with every student individually to learn what is happening in their lives. Ms. Taylor has a teacher's aide and an intern from a local university in her class, so students get much individual attention. She has a private space ("Taylor's Corner") where she goes to talk privately with a student about any problems or stresses the student may be experiencing. She contacts the parents or guardians of her students to invite them to come to class and assist in any way that they can.

The effectiveness of problem-based learning is substantiated by brain research. With its multiple connections, the human brain is wired to solve problems (Jensen, 2005). Students who collaborate to solve problems become aware of new ways that knowledge can be used and combined, which forms new synaptic connections. Further, problem-based learning is apt to appeal to students' motivation and engender emotional involvement, which also can create more extensive neural networks.

Simulations and Role-Playing. Simulations and role-playing have many of the same benefits as does problem-based learning. Simulations might occur via computers, in the regular class, or in special settings (e.g., museums). Role-playing is a form of modeling (Chapter 4) where students observe others. Both simulations and role-playing provide students with learning opportunities that are not ordinarily available. These methods have motivational benefits and command student attention. They allow students to engage with the material actively and invest themselves emotionally. Collectively, these benefits help to foster learning.

Active Discussions. Many topics lend themselves well to student discussions. Students who are part of a discussion are forced to participate; they cannot be passive observers. This increased level of cognitive and emotional engagement leads to better learning. Further, by participating in discussions, students are exposed to new ideas and integrate these with their current conceptions. This cognitive activity helps to build synaptic connections and new ways of using information.

Graphics. The human body is structured such that we take in more information visually than through all other senses (Wolfe, 2001). Visual displays help to foster attention, learning, and retention. The collective findings from learning and brain research support the benefits of graphics. Teachers who use graphics in their teaching and have students employ graphics (e.g., overheads, PowerPoint$^©$ presentations, demonstrations, drawings, concept maps, graphic organizers) capitalize on visual information processing and are apt to improve learning.

Positive Climate. We saw in the section on emotions that learning proceeds better when students have a positive attitude and feel emotionally secure. Conversely, learning is not facilitated when students are stressful or anxious, such as when they fear volunteering answers because the teacher becomes angry if their answers are incorrect. In Chapter 8 and elsewhere in this text we discuss how students' positive beliefs about themselves and their environments are critical for effective learning. Brain research substantiates the positive effect that emotional involvement can have on learning and the building of synaptic connections. Teachers who create a positive classroom climate will find that behavior problems are minimized and that students become more invested in learning.

SUMMARY

The neuroscience of learning is the science of the relation of the nervous system to learning and behavior. Although neuroscience research has been conducted for several years in medicine and the sciences, it recently has become of interest to educators because of the instructional implications of research findings. Neuroscience research addresses the central nervous system (CNS), which comprises the brain and spinal cord and regulates voluntary behavior, and the autonomic nervous system (ANS), which regulates involuntary actions.

The CNS is composed of billions of cells in the brain and spinal cord. There are two major types of cells: neurons and glial cells. Neurons send and receive information across muscles and organs. Each neuron is composed of a cell body, thousands of short dendrites, and one axon. Dendrites receive information from other cells; axons send messages to cells. Myelin sheath surrounds axons and facilitates the travel of signals. Axons end in branching structures (synapses) that connect with the ends of dendrites. Chemical neurotransmitters at the ends of axons activate or inhibit reactions in the contracted dendrites. This process allows signals to be sent rapidly across neural and bodily structures. Glial cells support the work of neurons by removing unneeded chemicals and dead brain cells. Glial cells also establish the myelin sheath.

The human adult brain (cerebrum) weighs about three pounds and is about the size of a cantaloupe. Its outer texture is wrinkled. Covering the brain is the cerebral cortex, a thin layer that is the wrinkled gray matter of the brain. The wrinkles allow the cortex to have more neurons and neural connections. The cortex has two hemispheres (left and right), each of which has four lobes (occipital, parietal, temporal, frontal). With some exceptions, the structure of the brain is roughly symmetrical. The cortex is the primary area involved in learning, memory, and processing of sensory information. Some other key areas of the brain are the brain stem, reticular formation, cerebellum, thalamus, hypothalamus, amygdala, hippocampus, corpus callosum, Broca's area, and Wernicke's area.

The brain's left hemisphere generally governs the right visual field, and vice versa. Many brain functions are localized to some extent. Analytical thinking seems to be centered in the left hemisphere, whereas spatial, auditory, emotional, and artistic processing occurs primarily in the right hemisphere. At the same time, many brain areas work together to process information and regulate actions. There is much crossover between the two hemispheres as they are joined by bundles of fibers, the largest of which is the corpus callosum.

The working together of multiple brain areas is seen clearly in language acquisition and use. The left side of the brain's cerebral cortex is central to reading. Specific brain regions are associated with orthographic, phonological, semantic, and syntactic processing required in reading. Wernicke's area in the left hemisphere controls speech comprehension and use of proper syntax when speaking. Wernicke's area works closely with Broca's area in the left frontal lobe, which is necessary for speaking. However, the right hemisphere is critical for interpreting context and thus the meaning of much speech.

Various technologies are used to conduct brain research. These include X-rays, CAT scans, EEGs, PET scans, MRIs, and fMRIs. The field of brain research is changing rapidly, and new technologies of greater sophistication will continue to be developed.

From a neuroscientific perspective, learning is the process of building and modifying neural (synaptic) connections and networks. Sensory inputs are processed in the sensory memories portions of the brain; those that are retained are transferred to WM, which seems to reside in multiple parts of the brain but primarily in the prefrontal cortex of the frontal lobe. Information then may be transferred to LTM. Different parts of the brain are involved in LTM depending on the type of information (e.g., declarative, procedural). With repeated presentations of stimuli or information, neural networks become strengthened such that the neural responses occur quickly. The process of stabilizing and strengthening synaptic connections is known as *consolidation*, and through consolidation the physical structure and functional organization of the brain is changed.

Influential factors on brain development are genetics, environmental stimulation, nutrition, steroids, and teratogens. During prenatal development, the brain grows in size, structure, and number of neurons, glial cells, and synapses. The brain develops rapidly in infants; young children have complex neural connections. As children lose brain synapses, those they retain depend partly on the activities they engage in. There seem to be critical periods during the first few years of life for the development of language, emotions, sensory motor functions, auditory capabilities, and vision. Early brain development benefits from rich environmental experiences and emotional bonding with parents and caregivers. Major changes also occur in teenagers' brains in size, structure, and number and organization of neurons.

Two neural counterparts of motivation involve rewards and motivational states. The brain seems to have a system for processing rewards and produces its own rewards in the form of opiates that result in a natural high. The brain may be predisposed toward experiencing and sustaining pleasurable outcomes, and the pleasure network can be activated by the expectation of reward. Motivational states are complex neural connections that include emotions, cognitions, and behaviors. The key to education is to maintain motivation for learning within an optimal range.

The operation of emotions in the CNS is complex. Emotional reactions consist of stages, such as orienting to the event, integrating the event, selecting a response, and sustaining the emotional context. Brain-linked emotional activity may differ for primary and culturally based emotions. Emotions can facilitate learning because they direct attention and influence learning and memory. Emotional involvement is desirable for learning; but when emotions become too great, cognitive learning is impeded.

Findings from brain research support many results obtained in cognitive research studies on learning and memory. But it is important not to overgeneralize brain research findings through such labeling of students as right or left brained. Most learning tasks require activity of both hemispheres, and the differences between brain functions are more relative than absolute.

Brain research suggests that early education is critical, instruction should take children's cognitive complexities into account, assessment of specific problems is necessary to plan proper interventions, and complex theories of learning capture the brain's operation better than do simpler theories. Some effective brain-based educational practices are problem-based learning, simulations and role-playing, active discussions, graphics, and a positive climate.

A summary of learning issues appears in Table 2.7.

Table 2.7
Summary of learning issues.

How Does Learning Occur?

From a cognitive neuroscience perspective, learning involves the forming and strengthening of neural connections (synapses), a process known as consolidation. Repeated experiences help to strengthen connections and make neural firings and transmissions of information more rapid. Other factors that improve consolidation are organization, rehearsal, elaboration, and emotional involvement in learning.

What Is the Role of Memory?

Memory is not a unitary phenomenon. Instead, different areas of the brain are involved in short-term (STM) and long-term (LTM) memory. Memory involves information being established so that neural connections are made and neural transmissions become automatic.

What Is the Role of Motivation?

The brain has a natural predisposition toward pleasurable outcomes and produces opiates to produce a natural high. This predisposition also seems to be triggered by the expectation of rewards. Motivational states are complex neural connections that include emotions, cognitions, and behaviors.

(continued)

Table 2.7 (*continued*)

How Does Transfer Occur?

Transfer involves using information in new ways or in new situations. From a neuroscientific perspective, this means that neural connections are formed between the learning and the new uses and situations. These connections are not made automatically. Students must learn them through experiences (e.g., teaching) or determine them on their own (e.g., through problem solving).

Which Processes Are Involved in Self-Regulation?

The processes discussed elsewhere in this text involved in self-regulation (e.g., goals, assessment of goal progress, self-efficacy; Chapter 9) are cognitions that are represented in the same way that knowledge is represented; namely, by synaptic connections in the brain. Most of these self-regulatory activities likely reside in the brain's frontal lobe. Neural connections formed between self-regulatory activities and the task students are engaged in allow learners to self-regulate their learning.

What Are the Implications for Instruction?

Brain research suggests that early childhood education is important and that instruction and remediation must be specified clearly so that interventions can be tailored to specific needs. Activities that engage learners (e.g., discussions, role playing) and command and hold their attention (e.g., graphical displays) are apt to produce better learning.

FURTHER READING

Ackerman, S. (1992). *Discovering the brain*. Washington, DC: National Academy Press.

Byrnes, J. P. (2001). *Mind, brains, and learning: Understanding the psychological and educational relevance of neuroscientific research*. New York: Guilford Press.

Byrnes, J. P., & Fox, N. A. (1998). The educational relevance of research in cognitive neuroscience. *Educational Psychology Review, 10,* 297–342.

Jensen, E. (2005). *Teaching with the brain in mind* (2nd ed.). Alexandria, VA: Association for Supervision and Curriculum Development.

Ornstein, R. (1997). *The right mind*. Orlando: Harcourt Brace.

Varma, S., McCandliss, B. D., & Schwartz, D. L. (2008). Scientific and pragmatic challenges for bridging education and neuroscience. *Educational Researcher, 37*(3), 140–152.

Wolfe, P. (2001). *Brain matters: Translating research into classroom practice*. Alexandria, VA: Association for Supervision and Curriculum Development.

3

Behaviorism

It's the end of the school day at Park Lane Elementary, and three teachers leave the building together: Leo Battaglia, Shayna Brown, and Emily Matsui. Their conversation as they walk to the parking lot is as follows:

Leo: Boy, they were wild today. I don't know what got into them. Hardly anyone earned any points today.

Emily: What points, Leo?

Leo: I give points for good behavior, which they then can exchange for privileges, such as extra free time. I take away points when they misbehave.

Emily: And it works?

Leo: Sure does. Keeps them in line most days. But not today. Maybe there was something in the water.

Shayna: Or in their heads, most likely. What do you suppose they were thinking about? Like, maybe spring break next week?

Leo: Perhaps. But that's not really my job, to see into their heads. Besides, lots of things can trigger wild behavior, and how am I supposed to know what does it? My best bet is to focus on the behavior.

Shayna: Yes, but sometimes you need to go beyond the behavior. For example, Sean's been acting out lately. If I would have just focused on his behavior, I would not have learned that his parents are getting divorced and he's blaming himself for it.

Leo: Isn't that why we have a counselor? Isn't that her job?

Shayna: Yes it is, but we have a role, too. I think you focus too much on what you see and not enough on what you don't see.

Leo: Maybe so, but at least I keep them under control with my system of rewards and punishments. I don't waste a lot of time on classroom management issues.

Emily: Or on personal issues, like their thoughts and emotions.

Psychology was an infant science at the beginning of the twentieth century. Two prominent schools of thought were structuralism and functionalism (Chapter 1), but each had problems. Structuralism used the introspection method, which placed it out of touch with important developments in science and did not incorporate Darwin's work on adaptation and evolution. Functionalism had an overly broad focus because its proponents advocated too many research directions.

Against this background, behaviorism began its rise to become the leading psychological discipline (Rachlin, 1991). John B. Watson (1878–1958), generally considered to be the founder and champion of modern behaviorism (Heidbreder, 1933; Hunt, 1993), believed that schools of thought and research methods that dealt with the mind were unscientific. If psychology were to become a science, it had to structure itself along the lines of the physical sciences, which examined observable and measurable phenomena. Behavior was the proper material for psychologists to study (Watson, 1924). Introspection was unreliable, conscious experiences were not observable, and people having such experiences could not be trusted to report them accurately (Murray, Kilgour, & Wasylkiw, 2000).

Watson (1916) thought that Pavlov's conditioning model (discussed later in this chapter) was appropriate for building a science of human behavior. He was impressed with Pavlov's precise measurement of observable behaviors. Watson believed that Pavlov's model could be extended to account for diverse forms of learning and personality characteristics. For example, newborns are capable of displaying three emotions: love, fear, and rage (Watson, 1926a). Through Pavlovian conditioning, these emotions could become attached to stimuli to produce a complex adult life. Watson expressed his belief in the power of conditioning in this famous pronouncement:

> Give me a dozen healthy infants, well-formed, and my own specified world to bring them up in and I'll guarantee to take any one at random and train him to become any type of specialist I might select—a doctor, lawyer, artist, merchant-chief and, yes, even into beggar-man and thief, regardless of his talents, penchants, tendencies, abilities, vocations and race of his ancestors. (Watson, 1926b, p. 10)

Although Watson's research has little relevance for academic learning, he spoke and wrote with conviction, and his adamant views influenced psychology from around 1920 until the early 1960s (Hunt, 1993). His emphasis on the importance of the environment is readily seen in the ensuing work of Skinner (discussed later in this chapter) (Horowitz, 1992).

This chapter covers behaviorism as expressed in conditioning theories of learning. The hallmark of conditioning theories is not that they deal with behavior (all theories do that), but rather that they explain learning in terms of environmental events. While not denying the existence of mental phenomena, these theories contend that such phenomena are not necessary to explain learning. In the opening scenario, Leo espouses a conditioning position.

The best-known *conditioning theory* is B. F. Skinner's *operant conditioning*. Before discussing this theory, some historical work in the conditioning tradition is presented to set the backdrop for Skinner's work; specifically, Thorndike's connectionism, Pavlov's classical conditioning, and Guthrie's contiguous conditioning.

When you finish studying this chapter, you should be able to do the following:

- Explain how behaviors are learned according to connectionism theory.

- Discuss some of Thorndike's contributions to educational practice.

- Explain how responses become conditioned, extinguished, and generalized, according to classical conditioning theory.

- Describe a process whereby an emotional response might become conditioned to an initially neutral object.

- Explain, using contiguous conditioning principles, how movements are combined to become an act.

- Describe Skinner's three-term contingency model of operant conditioning, and provide examples.

- Define and exemplify key operant conditioning concepts: positive and negative reinforcement, punishment, generalization,

discrimination, shaping, and Premack Principle.

- Provide a brief overview of a behaviorist model of self-regulation.

- Explain some key educational applications of operant principles to education: behavioral objectives, learning time, mastery learning, programmed instruction, and contingency contracts.

CONNECTIONISM

Edward L. Thorndike (1874–1949) was a prominent U.S. psychologist whose theory of learning—*connectionism*—was dominant in the United States during the first half of the twentieth century (Mayer, 2003). Unlike many early psychologists, he was interested in education and especially learning, transfer, individual differences, and intelligence (Hilgard, 1996; McKeachie, 1990). He applied an experimental approach when measuring students' achievement outcomes. His impact on education is reflected in the Thorndike Award, the highest honor given by the Division of Educational Psychology of the American Psychological Association for distinguished contributions to educational psychology.

Trial-and-Error Learning

Thorndike's major work is the three-volume series *Educational Psychology* (Thorndike, 1913a, 1913b, 1914). He postulated that the most fundamental type of learning involves the forming of associations (*connections*) between sensory experiences (perceptions of stimuli or events) and neural impulses (responses) that manifest themselves behaviorally. He believed that learning often occurs by *trial and error* (selecting and connecting).

Thorndike began studying learning with a series of experiments on animals (Thorndike, 1911). Animals in problem situations try to attain a goal (e.g., obtain food, reach a destination). From among the many responses they can perform, they select one, perform it, and experience the consequences. The more often they make a response to a stimulus, the more firmly that response becomes connected to that stimulus.

In a typical experimental situation, a cat is placed in a cage. The cat can open an escape hatch by pushing a stick or pulling a chain. After a series of random responses, the cat eventually escapes by making a response that opens the hatch. The cat then is put back into the cage. Over trials, the cat reaches the goal (it escaped) quicker and makes fewer errors prior to responding correctly. A typical plot of results is shown in Figure 3.1.

Trial-and-error learning occurs gradually (incrementally) as successful responses are established and unsuccessful ones are abandoned. Connections are formed mechanically through repetition; conscious awareness is not necessary. Animals do not "catch on" or "have insight." Thorndike understood that human learning is more complex because

Figure 3.1
Incremental performance over trials exemplifying Thorndike's trial-and-error learning.

people engage in other types of learning involving connecting ideas, analyzing, and reasoning (Thorndike, 1913b). Nonetheless, the similarity in research results from animal and human studies led Thorndike to explain complex learning with elementary learning principles. An educated adult possesses millions of stimulus–response connections.

Laws of Exercise and Effect

Thorndike's basic ideas about learning are embodied in the Laws of Exercise and Effect. The *Law of Exercise* has two parts: The *Law of Use*—a response to a stimulus strengthens their connection; the *Law of Disuse*—when a response is not made to a stimulus, the connection's strength is weakened (forgotten). The longer the time interval before a response is made, the greater is the decline in the connection's strength.

The *Law of Effect* is central to Thorndike's theory (Thorndike, 1913b):

> When a modifiable connection between a situation and a response is made and is accompanied or followed by a satisfying state of affairs, that connection's strength is increased: When made and accompanied or followed by an annoying state of affairs, its strength is decreased. (p. 4)

The Law of Effect emphasizes the *consequences* of behavior: Responses resulting in satisfying (rewarding) consequences are learned; responses producing annoying (punishing) consequences are not learned. This is a functional account of learning because satisfiers (responses that produce desirable outcomes) allow individuals to adapt to their environments.

The following study illustrates application of the Law of Effect (Thorndike, 1927). Participants were shown 50 strips of paper, ranging in length from 3 to 27 centimeters (cm), one at a time. Next to each strip was a second strip that participants knew was 10 cm long. They initially estimated the length of each strip without feedback. Following this pretest, the 50 strips were presented again, one at a time. After each estimate, they were told "right" or "wrong" by the experimenter. After the 50 strips were presented repeatedly over several days, they again were presented without feedback about accuracy of length judgments. Following training, participants' length estimates more closely approximated the actual lengths of the strips than had their prior estimates. Thorndike concluded that these results, which were similar to those from experiments in which animals were rewarded with food or freedom, support the idea that satisfying (correct) stimulus–response connections are strengthened and annoying (incorrect) ones are weakened.

Other Principles

Thorndike's (1913b) theory included other principles relevant to education. One principle is the *Law of Readiness,* which states that when one is prepared (ready) to act, to do so is rewarding and not to do so is punishing. If one is hungry, responses that lead to food are in a state of readiness, whereas other responses not leading to food are not in a state of readiness. If one is fatigued, it is punishing to be forced to exercise. Applying this idea to learning, we might say that when students are ready to learn a particular action (in terms of developmental level or prior skill acquisition), then behaviors that foster this learning will be rewarding. When students are not ready to learn or do not possess prerequisite skills, then attempting to learn is punishing and a waste of time.

The principle of *associative shifting* refers to a situation in which responses made to a particular stimulus eventually are made to an entirely different stimulus if, on repeated trials, there are small changes in the nature of the stimulus. For example, to teach students to divide a two-digit number into a four-digit number, we first teach them to divide a one-digit number into a one-digit number and then gradually add more digits to the divisor and dividend.

The principle of identical elements affects *transfer (generalization),* or the extent that strengthening or weakening of one connection produces a similar change in another connection (Hilgard, 1996; Thorndike, 1913b; see Chapter 7). Transfer occurs when situations have identical elements and call for similar responses. Thorndike and Woodworth (1901) found that practice or training in a skill in a specific context did not improve one's ability to execute that skill generally. Thus, training on estimating the area of rectangles does not advance learners' ability to estimate the areas of triangles, circles, and irregular figures. Skills should be taught with different types of educational content for students to understand how to apply them (Application 3.1).

Revisions to Thorndike's Theory

Thorndike revised the Laws of Exercise and Effect after other research evidence did not support them (Thorndike, 1932). Thorndike discarded the Law of Exercise when he found that simple repetition of a situation does not necessarily "stamp in" responses. In one experiment, for example, participants closed their eyes and drew lines they thought were 2, 4, 6, and 8 inches long, hundreds of times over several days, without feedback on accuracy of the lengths (Thorndike, 1932). If the Law of Exercise were correct, then the response performed most often during the first 100 or so drawings ought to become more frequent afterward; but Thorndike found no support for this idea. Rather, mean lengths changed over time; people apparently experimented with different lengths because they were unsure of the correct length. Thus, repetition of a situation may not increase the future likelihood of the same response occurring.

APPLICATION 3.1
Facilitating Transfer

Thorndike suggested that drilling students on a specific skill does not help them master it nor does it teach them how to apply the skill in different contexts.

When teachers instruct secondary students how to use map scales, they also must teach them to calculate miles from inches. Students become more proficient if they actually apply the skill on various maps and create maps of their own surroundings than if they are just given numerous problems to solve.

When elementary teachers begin working with students on liquid and dry measurement, having the students use a recipe to actually measure ingredients and create a food item is much more meaningful than using pictures, charts, or just filling cups with water or sand.

In medical school, having students actually observe and become involved in various procedures or surgeries is much more meaningful than just reading about the conditions in textbooks.

With respect to the Law of Effect, Thorndike originally thought that the effects of satisfiers (rewards) and annoyers (punishments) were opposite but comparable, but research showed this was not the case. Rather, rewards strengthened connections, but punishment did not necessarily weaken them (Thorndike, 1932). Instead, connections are weakened when alternative connections are strengthened. In one study (Thorndike, 1932), participants were presented with uncommon English words (e.g., *edacious, eidolon*). Each word was followed by five common English words, one of which was a correct synonym. On each trial, participants chose a synonym and underlined it, after which the experimenter said "right" (reward) or "wrong" (punishment). Reward improved learning, but punishment did not diminish the probability of that response occurring to that stimulus word.

Punishment suppresses responses, but they are not forgotten. Punishment is not an effective means of altering behavior because it does not teach students correct behaviors but rather informs them of what not to do. This also is true with cognitive skills. Brown and Burton (1978) found that students learn *buggy algorithms* (incorrect rules) for solving problems (e.g., subtract the smaller number from the larger, column by column, $4371 - 2748 = 2437$). When students are informed that this method is incorrect and are given corrective feedback and practice in solving problems correctly, they learn the correct method but do not forget the old way.

Thorndike and Education

As a professor of education at Teachers College, Columbia University, Thorndike wrote books that addressed topics such as educational goals, learning processes, teaching methods, curricular sequences, and techniques for assessing educational outcomes (Hilgard, 1996; Mayer, 2003; Thorndike, 1906, 1912; Thorndike & Gates, 1929). Some of Thorndike's many contributions to education are the following.

Principles of Teaching. Teachers should help students form good habits. As Thorndike (1912) noted:

- Form habits. Do not expect them to create themselves.
- Beware of forming a habit which must be broken later.
- Do not form two or more habits when one will do as well.
- Other things being equal, have a habit formed in the way in which it is to be used. (pp. 173–174)

The last principle cautions against teaching content that is removed from its applications: "Since the forms of adjectives in German or Latin are always to be used with nouns, they should be learned with nouns" (p. 174). Students need to understand how to apply knowledge and skills they acquire. Uses should be learned in conjunction with the content.

Sequence of Curricula. A skill should be introduced (Thorndike & Gates, 1929):

- At the time or just before the time when it can be used in some serviceable way
- At the time when the learner is conscious of the need for it as a means of satisfying some useful purpose
- When it is most suited in difficulty to the ability of the learner
- When it will harmonize most fully with the level and type of emotions, tastes, instinctive and volitional dispositions most active at the time
- When it is most fully facilitated by immediately preceding learnings and when it will most fully facilitate learnings which are to follow shortly. (pp. 209–210)

These principles conflict with typical content placement in schools, where content is segregated by subject (e.g., social studies, mathematics, science). But Thorndike and Gates (1929) urged that knowledge and skills be taught with different subjects. For example, forms of government are appropriate topics not only in civics and history, but also in English (how governments are reflected in literature) and foreign language (government structure in other countries). Some additional applications are shown in Application 3.2.

Mental Discipline. *Mental discipline* is the view that learning certain subjects (e.g., the classics, mathematics) enhances general mental functioning better than learning other subjects. Mental discipline was a popular view among educators during Thorndike's time. He tested this idea with 8,500 students in grades 9 to 11 (Thorndike, 1924). Students were given intelligence tests a year apart, and their programs of study that year were compared to determine whether certain courses were associated with greater intellectual gains. The results provided no support for mental discipline. Students who had greater ability to begin with made the best progress regardless of what they studied.

> If our inquiry had been carried out by a psychologist from Mars, who knew nothing of theories of mental discipline, and simply tried to answer the question, "What are the amounts of influence of sex, race, age, amounts of ability, and studies taken, upon the gain made during the year in power to think, or intellect, or whatever our stock intelligence tests measure," he might even dismiss "studies taken" with the comment, "The differences are so small and the unreliabilities are relatively so large that this factor seems unimportant." The one causal factor which he would be sure was at work would be the intellect already existent. Those who have the most to begin with gain the most during the year. (Thorndike, 1924, p. 95)

APPLICATION 3.2
Sequence of Curricula

Thorndike's views on the sequence of curricula suggest that learning should be integrated across subjects. Kathy Stone prepared a unit for her third-grade class in the fall on pumpkins. The students studied the significance of pumpkins to the American colonists (history), where pumpkins currently are grown (geography), and the varieties of pumpkins grown (agriculture). They measured and charted the various sizes of pumpkins (mathematics), carved the pumpkins (art), planted pumpkin seeds and studied their growth (science), and read and wrote stories about pumpkins (language arts). This approach provides a meaningful experience for children and "real life" learning of various skills.

In developing a history unit on the Civil War, Jim Marshall went beyond just covering factual material and incorporated comparisons from other wars, attitudes and feelings of the populace during that time period, biographies and personalities of individuals involved in the war, and the impact the war had on the United States and implications for the future. In addition, Mr. Marshall worked with other teachers in the building to expand the unit by examining the terrain of major battlefields (geography), weather conditions during major battles (science), and the emergence of literature (language arts) and creative works (art, music, drama) during that time period.

So rather than assuming that some subject areas improve students' mental abilities better than others, we should assess how different subject areas affect students' ability to think, as well as other outcomes (e.g., interests, goals). Thorndike's influential research led educators to redesign curricula away from the mental discipline idea.

CLASSICAL CONDITIONING

We have seen that events in the United States in the early twentieth century helped establish psychology as a science and learning as a legitimate field of study. At the same time, there were important developments in other countries. One of the most significant was the work of Ivan Pavlov (1849–1936), a Russian physiologist who won the Nobel Prize in 1904 for his work on digestion.

Pavlov's legacy to learning theory was his work on *classical conditioning* (Cuny, 1965; Hunt, 1993; Windholz, 1997). While Pavlov was the director of the physiological laboratory at the Institute of Experimental Medicine in Petrograd, he noticed that dogs often would salivate at the sight of the attendant bringing them food or even at the sound of the attendant's footsteps. Pavlov realized that the attendant was not a natural stimulus for the reflex of salivating; rather, the attendant acquired this power by being associated with food.

Table 3.1
Classical conditioning procedure.

Phase	Stimulus	Response
1	UCS (food powder)	UCR (salivation)
2	CS (metronome), then UCS (food powder)	UCR (salivation)
3	CS (metronome)	CR (salivation)

Basic Processes

Classical conditioning is a multistep procedure that initially involves presenting an *unconditioned stimulus (UCS)*, which elicits an *unconditioned response (UCR)*. Pavlov presented a hungry dog with meat powder (UCS), which would cause the dog to salivate (UCR). To condition the animal requires repeatedly presenting an initially neutral stimulus for a brief period before presenting the UCS. Pavlov often used a ticking metronome as the neutral stimulus. In the early trials, the ticking of the metronome produced no salivation. Eventually, the dog salivated in response to the ticking metronome prior to the presentation of the meat powder. The metronome had become a *conditioned stimulus (CS)* that elicited a *conditioned response (CR)* similar to the original UCR (Table 3.1). Repeated nonreinforced presentations of the CS (i.e., without the UCS) cause the CR to diminish in intensity and disappear, a phenomenon known as *extinction* (Larrauri & Schmajuk, 2008; Pavlov, 1932b).

Spontaneous recovery occurs after a time lapse in which the CS is not presented and the CR presumably extinguishes. If the CS then is presented and the CR returns, we say that the CR spontaneously recovered from extinction. A CR that recovers will not endure unless the CS is presented again. Pairings of the CS with the UCS restore the CR to full strength. The fact that CS–CR pairings can be instated without great difficulty suggests that extinction does not involve unlearning of the associations (Redish, Jensen, Johnson, & Kurth-Nelson, 2007).

Generalization means that the CR occurs to stimuli similar to the CS (Figure 3.2). Once a dog is conditioned to salivate in response to a metronome ticking at 70 beats per minute, it also may salivate in response to a metronome ticking faster or slower, as well as to ticking clocks or timers. The more dissimilar the new stimulus is to the CS or the fewer elements that they share, the less generalization occurs (Harris, 2006).

Discrimination is the complementary process that occurs when the dog learns to respond to the CS but not to other, similar stimuli. To train discrimination, an experimenter might pair the CS with the UCS and also present other, similar stimuli without the UCS. If the CS is a metronome ticking at 70 beats per minute, it is presented with the UCS, whereas other cadences (e.g., 50 and 90 beats per minute) are presented but not paired with the UCS.

Once a stimulus becomes conditioned, it can function as a UCS and *higher-order conditioning* can occur (Pavlov, 1927). If a dog has been conditioned to salivate at the sound of a metronome ticking at 70 beats per minute, the ticking metronome can function as a UCS for higher-order conditioning. A new neutral stimulus (such as a buzzer)

Figure 3.2
Generalization curve showing decreased magnitude of conditioned response as a function of increased dissimilarity with the conditioned stimulus.

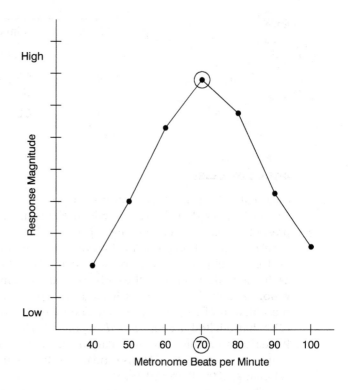

can be sounded for a few seconds, followed by the ticking metronome. If, after a few trials, the dog begins to salivate at the sound of the buzzer, the buzzer has become a second-order CS. Conditioning of the third order involves the second-order CS serving as the UCS and a new neutral stimulus being paired with it. Pavlov (1927) reported that conditioning beyond the third order is difficult.

Higher-order conditioning is a complex process that is not well understood (Rescorla, 1972). The concept is theoretically interesting and might help to explain why some social phenomena (e.g., test failure) can cause conditioned emotional reactions, such as stress and anxiety. Early in life, failure may be a neutral event. Often it becomes associated with disapproval from parents and teachers. Such disapproval may be an UCS that elicits anxiety. Through conditioning, failure can elicit anxiety. Cues associated with the situation also can become conditioned stimuli. Thus, students may feel anxious when they walk into a room where they will take a test or when a teacher passes out a test.

CSs capable of producing CRs are called *primary signals*. Unlike animals, people have the capacity for speech, which greatly expands the potential for conditioning (Windholz, 1997). Language constitutes the *second signal system*. Words or thoughts are labels denoting events or objects and can become CSs. Thus, thinking about a test or listening to the teacher discuss a forthcoming test may cause anxiety. It is not the test that makes students anxious but rather words or thoughts about the test, that is, its linguistic representation or meaning.

Informational Variables

Pavlov believed that conditioning is an automatic process that occurs with repeated CS–UCS pairings and that repeated nonpairings extinguish the CR. In humans, however, conditioning can occur rapidly, sometimes after only a single CS–UCS pairing. Repeated nonpairings of the CS and UCS may not extinguish the CR. Extinction seems highly context dependent (Bouton, Nelson, & Rosas, 1999). Reponses stay extinguished in the same context, but when the setting is changed, CRs may recur. These findings call into question Pavlov's description of conditioning.

Research subsequent to Pavlov has shown that conditioning depends less on the CS–UCS pairing and more on the extent that the CS conveys information about the likelihood of the UCS occurring (Rescorla, 1972, 1976). As an illustration, assume there are two stimuli: One is always followed by a UCS and the other is sometimes followed by it. The first stimulus should result in conditioning, because it reliably predicts the onset of the UCS. It even may not be necessary to pair the CS and UCS; conditioning can occur by simply telling people that they are related (Brewer, 1974). Likewise, repeated CS–UCS nonpairings may not be necessary for extinction; telling people the contingency is no longer in effect can reduce or extinguish the CR.

An explanation for these results is that people form *expectations* concerning the probability of the UCS occurring (Rescorla, 1987). For a stimulus to become a CS, it must convey information to the individual about the time, place, quantity, and quality of the UCS. Even when a stimulus is predictive, it may not become conditioned if another stimulus is a better predictor. Rather than conditioning being automatic, it appears to be mediated by cognitive processes. If people do not realize there is a CS–UCS link, conditioning does not occur. When no CS–UCS link exists, conditioning can occur if people believe it does. Although this contingency view of conditioning may not be entirely accurate (Papini & Bitterman, 1990), it provides a different explanation for conditioning than Pavlov's and highlights its complexity.

Biological Influences

Pavlov (1927, 1928) believed that any perceived stimulus can be conditioned to any response that can be made. Subsequent research has shown that the generality of conditioning is limited. Within any species, responses can be conditioned to some stimuli but not to others. Conditioning depends on the compatibility of the stimulus and response with species-specific reactions (Hollis, 1997). All organisms inherently possess the basic behavioral patterns that enable them to survive in their niches, but learning provides the fine-tuning necessary for successful adaptation (Garcia & Garcia y Robertson, 1985, p. 197).

An experiment by Garcia and Koelling (1966) with rats demonstrated the importance of biological factors. Some rats drank water accompanied by bright lights and noise (aversive stimulus—bright, noisy water). Rats either were shocked immediately or treated so that they became nauseous some time later. Other rats drank regular (saccharin) water and were either shocked or became nauseous later. Bright, noisy water plus shock led to a conditioned aversion to the water, but bright, noisy water plus nausea did not. Regular (saccharin) water plus nausea led to an aversion to the water, but regular water plus shock did not. The shock (an external event) was easily associated with the bright lights and noise (external cues), but not nausea (an internal event). Nausea became a CR to an internal stimulus (taste). Although the interval between drinking the water and nausea (an hour) was too long to satisfy a classical conditioning model, the results support the complexity of classical conditioning by suggesting that rats have developed an evolutionary mechanism to guard against taste aversions. In general, it appears that conditioning may occur only if stimuli somehow "belong" together, and thus the process may serve to help animals adapt to their environments (Hollis, 1997).

Conditioned Emotional Reactions

Pavlov (1932a, 1934) applied classical conditioning principles to abnormal behavior and discussed how neuroses and other pathological states might develop. His views were speculative and unsubstantiated, but classical conditioning principles have been applied by others to condition emotional reactions.

Watson claimed to demonstrate the power of emotional conditioning in the well-known Little Albert experiment (Watson & Rayner, 1920). Albert was an 11-month-old infant who showed no fear of a white rat. During conditioning, a hammer was struck against a steel bar behind Albert as he reached out for the rat. "The infant jumped violently and fell forward, burying his face in the mattress" (p. 4). This sequence was immediately repeated. One week later when the rat was presented, Albert began to reach out but then withdrew his hand. The previous week's conditioning was apparent. Tests over the next few days showed that Albert reacted emotionally to the rat's presence. There also was generalization of fear to a rabbit, dog, and fur coat. When Albert was retested a month later with the rat, he showed a mild emotional reaction.

Although this study is widely cited as showing how conditioning can produce emotional reactions, the influence of conditioning usually is not that powerful (Harris, 1979). As we saw in the preceding section, classical conditioning is a complex phenomenon; one cannot condition any response to any stimulus. Species have evolved mechanisms predisposing them to being conditioned in some ways and not in others (Hollis, 1997). Among humans, conditioning occurs when people are aware of the relation between the CS and the UCS, and information that the UCS may not follow the CS can produce extinction. Attempts to replicate Watson and Rayner's findings were not uniformly successful. Valentine (1930a), for example, found no evidence of conditioning when he used objects as the CS instead of animals.

A more reliable means of producing emotional conditioning is with *systematic desensitization*, which is often used with individuals who possess debilitating fears (Wolpe, 1958; see Application 3.3). Desensitization comprises three phases. In the first phase, the therapist and the client jointly develop an anxiety hierarchy of several situations graded from least-to-most anxiety-producing for the client. For a test-anxious student, low-anxiety situations might be hearing a test announcement in class and gathering together materials to study. Situations of moderate anxiety might be studying the night before the test and walking into class on the day of the test. High-anxiety situations could include receiving a copy of the test in class and not knowing the answer to a test question.

APPLICATION 3.3
Emotional Conditioning

Principles of classical conditioning are relevant to some dysfunctional behaviors. Children entering kindergarten or first grade may possess fears related to the new experiences. At the beginning of the school year, primary teachers might develop procedures to desensitize some of the children's fears. Visitation sessions give students the opportunity to meet their teacher and other students and to see their classroom and the seat with their name on it. On the first few days of school, the teacher might plan fun but relatively calm activities involving students getting to know their teacher, classmates, room, and school building. Students could tour the building, return to their room, and draw pictures. They might talk about what they saw. Students can be taken to offices to meet the principal, assistant principal, nurse, and counselor. They also could play name games in which they introduce themselves and then try to recall names of classmates.

These activities represent an informal desensitization procedure. For some children, cues associated with the school serve as stimuli eliciting anxiety. The fun activities elicit pleasurable feelings, which are incompatible with anxiety. Pairing fun activities with cues associated with school may cause the latter to become less anxiety producing.

Some education students may be anxious about teaching complete lessons to an entire class. Anxieties should be lessened when students spend time in classrooms and gradually assume more responsibility for instruction. Pairing classroom and teaching experiences with formal study can desensitize fears related to being responsible for children's learning.

Some drama students have extreme problems with stage fright. Drama teachers may work with students to lessen these anxieties by practicing more on the actual stage and by opening up rehearsals to allow others to watch. Exposure to performing in front of others should help diminish some of the fears.

In the second phase, the client learns to relax by imagining pleasant scenes (e.g., lying on a beach) and cuing relaxation (saying "relax"). In the third phase, the client, while relaxed, imagines the lowest (least-anxious) scene on the hierarchy. This may be repeated several times, after which the client imagines the next scene. Treatment proceeds up the hierarchy until the client can imagine the most anxiety-producing scene without feeling anxious. If the client reports anxiety while imagining a scene, the client drops back down the hierarchy to a scene that does not produce anxiety. Treatment may require several sessions.

Desensitization involves counterconditioning. The relaxing scenes that one imagines (UCS) produce relaxation (UCR). Anxiety-producing cues (CS) are paired with the relaxing scenes. Relaxation is incompatible with anxiety. By initially pairing a weak anxiety cue with relaxation and by slowly working up the hierarchy, all of the anxiety-producing cues eventually should elicit relaxation (CR).

Desensitization is an effective procedure that can be accomplished in a therapist's or counselor's office. It does not require the client to perform the activities on the hierarchy. A disadvantage is that the client must be able to imagine scenes. People differ in their ability to form mental images. Desensitization also requires the skill of a professional therapist or counselor and should not be attempted by anyone unskilled in its application.

CONTIGUOUS CONDITIONING

Another individual who advanced a behavioral perspective on learning was Edwin R. Guthrie (1886–1959), who postulated learning principles based on associations (Guthrie, 1940). For Guthrie, the key behaviors were acts and movements.

Acts and Movements

Guthrie's basic principles reflect the idea of *contiguity of stimuli and responses:*

> A combination of stimuli which has accomplished a movement will on its recurrence tend to be followed by that movement. (Guthrie, 1952, p. 23)

And alternatively,

> Stimulus patterns which are active at the time of a response tend, on being repeated, to elicit that response. (Guthrie, 1938, p. 37)

Movements are discrete behaviors that result from muscle contractions. Guthrie distinguished movements from *acts*, or large-scale classes of movements that produce an outcome. Playing the piano and using a computer are acts that include many movements. A particular act may be accompanied by a variety of movements; the act may not specify the movements precisely. In basketball, for example, shooting a basket (an act) can be accomplished with a variety of movements.

Contiguity learning implies that a behavior in a situation will be repeated when that situation recurs (Guthrie, 1959); however, contiguity learning is selective. At any given moment, a person is confronted with many stimuli, and associations cannot be made to all of them. Rather, only a small number of stimuli are selected, and associations are formed between them and responses. The contiguity principle also applies to memory. Verbal cues are associated with stimulus conditions or events at the time of learning (Guthrie, 1952). *Forgetting* involves new learning and is due to interference in which an alternative response is made to an old stimulus.

Associative Strength

Guthrie's theory contends that learning occurs through pairing of stimulus and response. Guthrie (1942) also discussed the strength of the pairing, or *associative strength:*

> A stimulus pattern gains its full associative strength on the occasion of its first pairing with a response. (p. 30)

He rejected the notion of associations through frequency, as embodied in Thorndike's original Law of Exercise (Guthrie, 1930). Although Guthrie did not suggest that people learn complex behaviors by performing them once, he believed that initially one or more movements become associated. Repetition of a situation adds movements, combines movements into acts, and establishes the act under different environmental conditions.

The Guthrie and Horton (1946) experiment with cats was interpreted as supporting this *all-or-none* principle of learning. Guthrie and Horton used a puzzle box similar to Thorndike's. Touching a post in the center triggered the mechanism that sprang open the door, allowing the cat to escape. When cats initially were placed in the box, they explored it and made a series of random movements. Eventually they made a response that released the mechanism, and they escaped. They may have hit the post with a paw; brushed against it; or backed into it. The cat's last response (hitting the pole) was successful because it opened the door, and cats repeated their last response when put back into the box. The last movement became associated with the puzzle box, because it allowed the animal to escape.

Guthrie's position does not imply that once students successfully solve a quadratic equation or write a research paper they have mastered the requisite skills. Practice links the various movements involved in the acts of solving equations and writing papers. The acts themselves may have many variations (types of equations and papers) and ideally should transfer—students should be able to solve equations and write papers in different contexts. Guthrie accepted Thorndike's notion of identical elements. To produce transfer, behaviors should be practiced in the exact situations in which they will be called for, such as at desks, in small groups, and at home.

Rewards and Punishments

Guthrie believed that responses do not need to be rewarded to be learned. The key mechanism is *contiguity*, or close pairing in time between stimulus and response. The response does not have to be satisfying; a pairing without consequences could lead to learning.

Guthrie (1952) disputed Thorndike's Law of Effect because satisfiers and annoyers are effects of actions; therefore, they cannot influence learning of previous connections but only subsequent ones. Rewards might help to prevent *unlearning* (forgetting) because they prevent new responses from being associated with stimulus cues. In the Guthrie and Horton (1946) experiment, the reward (escape from the box) took the animal out of the learning context and prevented acquisition of new associations to the box. Similarly, punishment will produce unlearning only if it causes the animal to learn something else.

Contiguity is a central feature of school learning. Flashcards help students learn arithmetic facts. Students learn to associate a stimulus (e.g., 4×4) with a response (16). Foreign-language words are associated with their English equivalents, and chemical symbols are associated with their element names.

Habit Formation and Change

Habits are learned dispositions to repeat past responses (Wood & Neal, 2007). Because habits are behaviors established to many cues, teachers who want students to behave

Table 3.2
Guthrie's methods for breaking habits.

Method	Explanation	Example
Threshold	Introduce weak stimulus. Increase stimulus, but keep it below threshold value that will produce unwanted response.	Introduce academic content in short blocks of time for children. Gradually increase session length, but not to a point where students become frustrated or bored.
Fatigue	Force child to make unwanted response repeatedly in presence of stimulus.	Give child who makes paper airplanes in class a stack of paper and have child make each sheet into a plane.
Incompatible response	In presence of stimulus, have child make response incompatible with unwanted response.	Pair cues associated with media center with reading rather than talking.

well in school should link school rules with many cues. "Treat others with respect," needs to be linked with the classroom, computer lab, halls, cafeteria, gymnasium, auditorium, and playground. By applying this rule in each of these settings, students' respectful behaviors toward others become habitual. If students believe they have to practice respect only in the classroom, respecting others will not become a habit.

The key to changing behavior is to "find the cues that initiate the action and to practice another response to these cues" (Guthrie, 1952, p. 115). Guthrie identified three methods for altering habits: threshold, fatigue, and incompatible response (Table 3.2). Although these methods have differences, they all present cues for an habitual action but arrange for it not to be performed (Application 3.4).

In the *threshold* method, the cue (stimulus) for the habit to be changed (the undesired response) is introduced at such a weak level that it does not elicit the response; it is below the threshold level of the response. Gradually the stimulus is introduced at greater intensity until it is presented at full strength. Were the stimulus introduced at its greatest intensity, the response would be the behavior that is to be changed (the habit). For example, some children react to the taste of spinach by refusing to eat it. To alter this habit, parents might introduce spinach in small bites or mixed with a food that the child enjoys. Over time, the amount of spinach the child eats can be increased.

In the *fatigue* method, the cue for engaging in the behavior is transformed into a cue for avoiding it. Here the stimulus is introduced at full strength and the individual performs the undesired response until he or she becomes exhausted. The stimulus becomes a cue for not performing the response. To alter a child's behavior of repeatedly throwing toys, parents might make the child throw toys until it is no longer fun (some limits are needed!).

APPLICATION 3.4
Breaking Habits

Guthrie's contiguity principle offers practical suggestions for how to break habits. One application of the threshold method involves the time young children spend on academic activities. Many young children have short attention spans, which limit the length of time they can sustain work on one activity. Most activities are scheduled to last no longer than 30–40 minutes. However, at the start of the school year, attention spans quickly wane and behavior problems often result. To apply Guthrie's theory, a teacher might, at the start of the year, limit activities to 15–20 minutes. Over the next few weeks the teacher could gradually increase the time students spend working on a single activity.

The threshold method also can be applied to teaching printing and handwriting. When children first learn to form letters, their movements are awkward and they lack fine motor coordination. The distances between lines on a page are purposely wide so children can fit the letters into the space. If paper with narrower lines is initially introduced, students' letters would spill over the borders and students might become frustrated. Once students can form letters within the wider lines, they can use paper with narrower lines to help them refine their skills.

Teachers need to be judicious when using the fatigue method. Jason likes to make paper airplanes and sail them across the room. His teacher might remove him from the classroom, give him a large stack of paper, and tell him to start making paper airplanes. After Jason has made several airplanes, the activity should lose its attraction and paper will no longer be a cue for him to make airplanes.

Some students like to race around the gym when they first enter their physical education class. To employ the fatigue method, the physical education teacher might just let these students keep running after the class has begun. Soon they will tire and quit running.

The incompatible response method can be used with students who talk and misbehave in the media center. Reading is incompatible with talking. The media center teacher might ask the students to find interesting books and read them while in the center. Assuming that the students find the books enjoyable, the media center will, over time, become a cue for selecting and reading books rather than for talking with other students.

A social studies teacher has some students who regularly do not pay attention in class. The teacher realized that using the board and slides while lecturing was very boring. Soon the teacher began to incorporate other elements into each lesson, such as experiments, film clips, and debates, in an attempt to involve students and raise their interest in the course.

In the *incompatible response* method, the cue for the undesired behavior is paired with a response incompatible with the undesired response; that is, the two responses cannot be performed simultaneously. The response to be paired with the cue must be more attractive to the individual than the undesired response. The stimulus becomes a cue for performing the alternate response. To stop snacking while watching TV, people should keep their hands busy (e.g., sew, paint, work crossword puzzles). Over time, watching TV becomes a cue for engaging in an activity other than snacking. Systematic desensitization (described earlier) also makes use of incompatible responses.

Punishment is ineffective in altering habits (Guthrie, 1952). Punishment following a response cannot affect the stimulus–response association. Punishment given while a behavior is being performed may disrupt or suppress the habit but not change it. Punishment does not establish an alternate response to the stimulus. The threat of punishment even can prove to be exciting and bolster the habit. It is better to alter negative habits by replacing them with desirable ones (i.e., incompatible responses).

Guthrie's theory does not include cognitive processes and thus is not considered to be a viable learning theory today. Nonetheless, its emphasis on contiguity is timely because current theories stress contiguity. In cognitive theories, a key point is that people must understand the relationship between a stimulus (situation, event) and the appropriate response. Guthrie's ideas about changing habits also are thought provoking and provide good general guidance for anyone wishing to develop better habits.

OPERANT CONDITIONING

A well-known behavioral theory is *operant conditioning*, formulated by B. F. (Burrhus Frederic) Skinner (1904–1990). Beginning in the 1930s, Skinner published a series of papers reporting results of laboratory studies with animals in which he identified the various components of operant conditioning. He summarized much of this early work in his influential book, *The Behavior of Organisms* (Skinner, 1938).

Skinner applied his ideas to human problems. Early in his career, he became interested in education and developed teaching machines and programmed instruction. *The Technology of Teaching* (Skinner, 1968) addresses instruction, motivation, discipline, and creativity. In 1948, after a difficult period in his life, he published *Walden Two*, which describes how behavioral principles can be applied to create a utopian society. Skinner (1971) addressed the problems of modern life and advocated applying a behavioral technology to the design of cultures in *Beyond Freedom and Dignity*. Skinner and others have applied operant conditioning principles to such domains as school learning and discipline, child development, language acquisition, social behaviors, mental illness, medical problems, substance abuse, and vocational training (DeGrandpre, 2000; Karoly & Harris, 1986; Morris, 2003).

As a young man, Skinner aspired to be a writer (Skinner, 1970):

> I built a small study in the attic and set to work. The results were disastrous. I frittered away my time. I read aimlessly, built model ships, played the piano, listened to the newly-invented radio, contributed to the humorous column of a local paper but wrote almost nothing else, and thought about seeing a psychiatrist. (p. 6)

He became interested in psychology after reading Pavlov's (1927) *Conditioned Reflexes* and Watson's (1924) *Behaviorism*. His subsequent career had a profound impact on the psychology of learning.

Despite his admission that "I had failed as a writer because I had had nothing important to say" (Skinner, 1970, p. 7), he was a prolific writer who channeled his literary aspirations into scientific writing that spanned six decades (Lattal, 1992). His dedication to his profession is evident in his giving an invited address at the American Psychological Association convention eight days before his death (Holland, 1992; Skinner, 1990). The association honored him with a special issue of its monthly journal, *American Psychologist* (American Psychological Association, 1992). Although his theory has been discredited by current learning theorists because it cannot adequately explain higher-order and complex forms of learning (Bargh & Ferguson, 2000), his influence continues as operant conditioning principles are commonly applied to enhance student learning and behavior (Morris, 2003). In the opening scenario, for example, Leo employs operant conditioning principles to control student misbehavior. Emily and Shayna, on the other hand, argue for the importance of cognitive factors.

Conceptual Framework

This section discusses the assumptions underlying operant conditioning, how it reflects a functional analysis of behavior, and the implications of the theory for the prediction and control of behavior. The theory and principles of operant conditioning are complex (Dragoi & Staddon, 1999); those principles most relevant to human learning are covered in this chapter.

Scientific Assumptions. Pavlov traced the locus of learning to the nervous system and viewed behavior as a manifestation of neurological functioning. Skinner (1938) did not deny that neurological functioning accompanies behavior, but he believed a psychology of behavior can be understood in its own terms without reference to neurological or other internal events.

Skinner raised similar objections to the unobservable processes and entities proposed by modern cognitive views of learning (Overskeid, 2007). *Private events*, or internal responses, are accessible only to the individual and can be studied through people's verbal reports, which are forms of behavior (Skinner, 1953). Skinner did not deny the existence of attitudes, beliefs, opinions, desires, and other forms of self-knowledge (he, after all, had them), but rather qualified their role.

People do not experience consciousness or emotions but rather their own bodies, and internal reactions are responses to internal stimuli (Skinner, 1987). A further problem with internal processes is that translating them into language is difficult, because language does not completely capture the dimensions of an internal experience (e.g., pain). Much of what is called *knowing* involves using language (verbal behavior). Thoughts are types of behavior that are brought about by other stimuli (environmental or private) and that give rise to responses (overt or covert). When private events are expressed as overt behaviors, their role in a functional analysis can be determined.

Functional Analysis of Behavior. Skinner (1953) referred to his means of examining behavior as a *functional analysis:*

> The external variables of which behavior is a function provide for what may be called a causal or functional analysis. We undertake to predict and control the behavior of the individual organism. This is our "dependent variable"—the effect for which we are to find the cause. Our

"independent variables"—the causes of behavior—are the external conditions of which behavior is a function. Relations between the two—the "cause-and-effect relationships" in behavior—are the laws of a science. A synthesis of these laws expressed in quantitative terms yields a comprehensive picture of the organism as a behaving system. (p. 35)

Learning is "the reassortment of responses in a complex situation"; *conditioning* refers to "the strengthening of behavior which results from reinforcement" (Skinner, 1953, p. 65). There are two types of conditioning: Type S and Type R. *Type S* is Pavlovian conditioning, characterized by the pairing of the reinforcing (unconditioned) stimulus with another (conditioned) stimulus. The S calls attention to the importance of the stimulus in eliciting a response from the organism. The response made to the eliciting stimulus is known as *respondent behavior.*

Although Type S conditioning may explain conditioned emotional reactions, most human behaviors are emitted in the presence of stimuli rather than automatically elicited by them. Responses are controlled by their consequences, not by antecedent stimuli. This type of behavior, which Skinner termed *Type R* to emphasize the response aspect, is *operant behavior* because it operates on the environment to produce an effect.

If the occurrence of an operant is followed by presentation of a reinforcing stimulus, the strength is increased. . . . If the occurrence of an operant already strengthened through conditioning is not followed by the reinforcing stimulus, the strength is decreased. (Skinner, 1938, p. 21)

We might think of operant behavior as "learning by doing," and in fact much learning occurs when we perform behaviors (Lesgold, 2001). Unlike respondent behavior, which prior to conditioning does not occur, the probability of occurrence of an operant is never zero because the response must be made for reinforcement to be provided. Reinforcement changes the likelihood or rate of occurrence of the response. Operant behaviors act upon their environments and become more or less likely to occur because of reinforcement.

Basic Processes

This section examines the basic processes in operant conditioning: reinforcement, extinction, primary and secondary reinforcers, the Premack Principle, punishment, schedules of reinforcement, generalization, and discrimination.

Reinforcement. *Reinforcement* is responsible for response strengthening—increasing the rate of responding or making responses more likely to occur. A reinforcer (or *reinforcing stimulus*) is any stimulus or event following a response that leads to response strengthening. Reinforcers (rewards) are defined based on their effects, which do not depend upon mental processes such as consciousness, intentions, or goals (Schultz, 2006). Because reinforcers are defined by their effects, they cannot be determined in advance.

The only way to tell whether or not a given event is reinforcing to a given organism under given conditions is to make a direct test. We observe the frequency of a selected response, then make an event contingent upon it and observe any change in frequency. If there is a change, we classify the event as reinforcing to the organism under the existing conditions. (Skinner, 1953, pp. 72–73)

Reinforcers are situationally specific: They apply to individuals at given times under given conditions. What is reinforcing to a particular student during reading now may not be during mathematics now or during reading later. Despite this specificity, stimuli or events that reinforce behavior can, to some extent, be predicted (Skinner, 1953). Students typically find reinforcing such events as teacher praise, free time, privileges, stickers, and high grades. Nonetheless, one never can know for certain whether a consequence is reinforcing until it is presented after a response and we see whether behavior changes.

The basic operant model of conditioning is the *three-term contingency:*

$$S^D \rightarrow R \rightarrow S^R$$

A *discriminative stimulus* (S^D) sets the occasion for a response (R) to be emitted, which is followed by a *reinforcing stimulus* (S^R, or *reinforcement*). The reinforcing stimulus is any stimulus (event, consequence) that increases the probability the response will be emitted in the future when the discriminative stimulus is present. In more familiar terms, we might label this the *A-B-C* model:

$$A \text{ (Antecedent)} \rightarrow B \text{ (Behavior)} \rightarrow C \text{ (Consequence)}$$

Positive reinforcement involves presenting a stimulus, or adding something to a situation, following a response, which increases the future likelihood of that response occurring in that situation. A *positive reinforcer* is a stimulus that, when presented following a response, increases the future likelihood of the response occurring in that situation. In the opening scenario, Leo uses points as positive reinforcers for good behavior (Table 3.3).

Table 3.3
Reinforcement and punishment processes.

$S^D \rightarrow$ Discriminative Stimulus	$R \rightarrow$ Response	S^R Reinforcing (Punishing) Stimulus
Positive Reinforcement (Present positive reinforcer)		
T gives independent study time	L studies*	T praises L for good work
Negative Reinforcement (Remove negative reinforcer)		
T gives independent study time	L studies	T says L does not have to do homework
Punishment (Present negative reinforcer)		
T gives independent study time	L wastes time	T gives homework
Punishment (Remove positive reinforcer)		
T gives independent study time	L wastes time	T says L will miss free time

*T refers to teacher and L to learner.

Negative reinforcement involves removing a stimulus, or taking something away from a situation following a response, which increases the future likelihood that the response will occur in that situation. A *negative reinforcer* is a stimulus that, when removed by a response, increases the future likelihood of the response occurring in that situation. Some stimuli that often function as negative reinforcers are bright lights, loud noises, criticism, annoying people, and low grades, because behaviors that remove them tend to be reinforcing. Positive and negative reinforcement have the same effect: They increase the likelihood that the response will be made in the future in the presence of the stimulus.

To illustrate these processes, assume that a teacher is holding a question-and-answer session with the class. The teacher asks a question (S^D or A), calls on a student volunteer who gives the correct answer (R or B), and praises the student (S^R or C). If volunteering by this student increases or remains at a high level, praise is a positive reinforcer and this is an example of positive reinforcement because giving the praise increased volunteering. Now assume that after a student gives the correct answer the teacher tells the student he or she does not need to do the homework assignment. If volunteering by this student increases or remains at a high level, the homework is a negative reinforcer and this is an example of negative reinforcement because removing the homework increased volunteering. Application 3.5 gives other examples of positive and negative reinforcement.

APPLICATION 3.5
Positive and Negative Reinforcement

Teachers can use positive and negative reinforcement to motivate students to master skills and spend more time on task. For example, while teaching concepts in a science unit, a teacher might ask students to complete questions at the end of the chapter. The teacher also might set up activity centers around the room that involve hands-on experiments related to the lesson. Students would circulate and complete the experiments contingent on their successfully answering the chapter questions (positive reinforcement). This contingency reflects the Premack Principle of providing the opportunity to engage in a more-valued activity (experiments) as a reinforcer for engaging in a less-valued one (completing chapter questions). Students who complete 80% of the questions correctly and who participate in a minimum of two

experiments do not have to complete homework. This would function as negative reinforcement to the extent that students perceive homework as a negative reinforcer.

A middle school counselor working with a student on improving classroom behavior could have each of the student's teachers check "yes" or "no" as it relates to class behavior for that day (acceptable, unacceptable). For each "yes," the student receives 1 minute in the computer lab to play computer games (positive reinforcement for this student). At the end of the week the student can use the earned computer time following lunch. Further, if the student earns a minimum of 15 minutes in the lab, he or she does not have to take a behavior note home to be signed by parents (this assumes the student perceives a behavior note as a negative reinforcer).

Extinction. *Extinction* involves the decline of response strength due to nonreinforcement. Students who raise their hands in class but never get called on may stop raising their hands. People who send many e-mail messages to the same individual but never receive a reply eventually may quit sending messages to that person.

How rapidly extinction occurs depends on the *reinforcement history* (Skinner, 1953). Extinction occurs quickly if few preceding responses have been reinforced. Responding is much more durable with a lengthier history of reinforcement. Extinction is not the same as *forgetting*. Responses that extinguish can be performed but are not because of lack of reinforcement. In the preceding examples, the students still know how to raise their hands and the people still know how to send e-mail messages. Forgetting involves a true loss of conditioning over time in which the opportunities for responding have not been present.

Primary and Secondary Reinforcers. Stimuli such as food, water, and shelter are called *primary reinforcers* because they are necessary for survival. *Secondary reinforcers* are stimuli that become conditioned through their association with primary reinforcers. A child's favorite milk glass becomes secondarily reinforcing through its association with milk (a primary reinforcer). A secondary reinforcer that becomes paired with more than one primary reinforcer is a *generalized reinforcer*. People work long hours to earn money (a generalized reinforcer), which they use to buy many reinforcers (e.g., food, housing, TVs, vacations).

Operant conditioning explains the development and maintenance of much social behavior with generalized reinforcers. Children may behave in ways to draw adults' attention. Attention is reinforcing because it is paired with primary reinforcers from adults (e.g., food, water, protection). Important educational generalized reinforcers are teachers' praise, high grades, privileges, honors, and degrees. These reinforcers often are paired with other generalized reinforcers, such as approval (from parents and friends) and money (a college degree leads to a good job).

Premack Principle. Recall that we label a behavioral consequence as reinforcing only after we apply it and see how it affects future behavior. It is somewhat troubling that we must use common sense or trial and error in choosing reinforcers because we cannot know for certain in advance whether a consequence will function as a reinforcer.

Premack (1962, 1971) described a means for ordering reinforcers that allows one to predict reinforcers. The *Premack Principle* says that the opportunity to engage in a more valued activity reinforces engaging in a less valued activity, where "value" is defined in terms of the amount of responding or time spent on the activity in the absence of reinforcement. If a contingency is arranged such that the value of the second (contingent) event is higher than the value of the first (instrumental) event, an increase will be expected in the probability of occurrence of the first event (the reward assumption). If the value of the second event is lower than that of the first event, the likelihood of occurrence of the first event ought to decrease (the punishment assumption).

Suppose that a child is allowed to choose between working on an art project, going to the media center, reading a book in the classroom, or working at the computer. Over the course of 10 such choices the child goes to the media center 6 times, works at the computer 3 times, works on an art project 1 time, and never reads a book in the classroom. For this child, the opportunity to go to the media center is valued the most. To apply the

Premack Principle, a teacher might say to the child, "After you finish reading this book, you can go to the media center." Considerable empirical evidence supports Premack's ideas, especially with respect to the reward assumption (Dunham, 1977).

The Premack Principle offers guidance for selecting effective reinforcers: Observe what people do when they have a choice, and order those behaviors in terms of likelihood. The order is not permanent, since the value of reinforcers can change. Any reinforcer, when applied often, can result in *satiation* and lead to decreased responding. Teachers who employ the Premack Principle need to check students' preferences periodically by observing them and asking what they like to do. Determining in advance which reinforcers are likely to be effective in a situation is critical in planning a program of behavioral change (Timberlake & Farmer-Dougan, 1991).

Punishment. *Punishment* decreases the future likelihood of responding to a stimulus. Punishment may involve withdrawing a positive reinforcer or presenting a negative reinforcer following a response, as shown in Table 3.3. Assume that during a question-and-answer session a student repeatedly bothers another student when the teacher is not watching (teacher not watching = S^D or A; misbehavior = R or B). The teacher spots the misbehavior and says, "Stop bothering him" (S^R or C). If the student quits bothering the other student, the teacher's criticism operates as a negative reinforcer and this is an example of punishment because giving the criticism decreased misbehavior. But note that from the teacher's perspective, this is an example of negative reinforcement (misbehavior = S^D or A; criticism = R or B; end of misbehavior = S^R or C). Since the teacher was negatively reinforced, the teacher is likely to continue to criticize student misbehavior.

Instead of criticizing the student, assume that the teacher says, "You'll have to stay inside during recess today." If the student's misbehavior stops, recess operates as a positive reinforcer and this is an example of punishment because the loss of recess stops the misbehavior. As before, the cessation of student misbehavior is negatively reinforcing for the teacher.

Punishment *suppresses* a response but does not eliminate it; when the threat of punishment is removed, the punished response may return. The effects of punishment are complex. Punishment often brings about responses that are incompatible with the punished behavior and that are strong enough to suppress it (Skinner, 1953). Spanking a child for misbehaving may produce guilt and fear, which can suppress misbehavior. If the child misbehaves in the future, the conditioned guilt and fear may reappear and lead the child quickly to stop misbehaving. Punishment also conditions responses that lead one to escape or avoid punishment. Students whose teacher criticizes incorrect answers soon learn to avoid volunteering answers. Punishment can condition maladaptive behaviors, because punishment does not teach how to behave more productively. Punishment can further hinder learning by creating a conflict such that the individual vacillates between responding one way or another. If the teacher sometimes criticizes students for incorrect answers and sometimes does not, students never know when criticism is forthcoming. Such variable behavior can have emotional by-products—fear, anger, crying—that interfere with learning.

Punishment is used often in schools to deal with disruptions. Common punishments are loss of privileges, removals from the classroom, in- and out-of-school suspensions, and expulsions (Maag, 2001). Yet there are several alternatives to punishment (Table 3.4). One is to *change the discriminative stimuli* for negative behavior. For example, a student

Table 3.4
Alternatives to punishment.

Alternative	Example
Change the discriminative stimuli	Move misbehaving student away from other misbehaving students.
Allow the unwanted behavior to continue	Have student who stands when he or she should be sitting continue to stand.
Extinguish the unwanted behavior	Ignore minor misbehavior so that it is not reinforced by teacher attention.
Condition an incompatible behavior	Reinforce learning progress, which occurs only when student is not misbehaving.

seated in the back of the room may misbehave often. Teachers can change the discriminative stimuli by moving the disruptive student to the front of the class. Another alternative is to *allow the unwanted behavior to continue* until the perpetrator becomes satiated, which is similar to Guthrie's fatigue method. A parent may allow a child throwing a tantrum to continue to throw it until he or she becomes fatigued. A third alternative is to *extinguish an unwanted behavior* by ignoring it. This may work well with minor misbehaviors (e.g., students whispering to one another), but when classrooms become disruptive, teachers need to act in other ways. A fourth alternative is to *condition incompatible behavior* with positive reinforcement. Teacher praise for productive work habits helps condition those habits. The primary advantage of this alternative over punishment is that it shows the student how to behave adaptively.

Schedules of Reinforcement. Schedules refer to when reinforcement is applied (Ferster & Skinner, 1957; Skinner, 1938; Zeiler, 1977). A *continuous schedule* involves reinforcement for every correct response. This may be desirable while skills are being acquired: Students receive feedback after each response concerning the accuracy of their work. Continuous reinforcement helps to ensure that incorrect responses are not learned.

An *intermittent schedule* involves reinforcing some but not all correct responses. Intermittent reinforcement is common in classrooms, because usually it is not possible for teachers to reinforce each student for every correct or desirable response. Students are not called on every time they raise their hands, are not praised after working each problem, and are not constantly told they are behaving appropriately.

Intermittent schedules are defined in terms of time or number of responses. An *interval schedule* involves reinforcing the first correct response after a specific time period. In a *fixed-interval (FI) schedule*, the time interval is constant from one reinforcement to the next. An FI5 schedule means that reinforcement is delivered for the first response made after 5 minutes. Students who receive 30 minutes of free time every Friday (contingent on good behavior during the week) are operating under a fixed-interval schedule. In a *variable-interval (VI) schedule*, the time interval varies from occasion to occasion around some average value. A VI5 schedule means that on the average, the first correct response after 5 minutes is reinforced, but the time interval varies (e.g., 2, 3, 7, or 8 minutes). Students who receive 30 minutes of free time (contingent on good behavior) on an average of once a week, but not necessarily on the same day each week, are operating under a variable-interval schedule.

A *ratio schedule* depends on the number of correct responses or rate of responding. In a *fixed-ratio (FR) schedule*, every nth correct response is reinforced, where n is constant. An FR10 schedule means that every 10th correct response receives reinforcement. In a *variable-ratio (VR) schedule*, every nth correct response is reinforced, but the value varies around an average number n. A teacher may give free time after every fifth workbook assignment is completed (FR5) or periodically around an average of five completed assignments (VR5).

Reinforcement schedules produce characteristic patterns of responding, as shown in Figure 3.3. In general, ratio schedules produce higher response rates than interval schedules. A limiting factor in ratio schedules is fatigue due to rapid responding. Fixed-interval schedules produce a scalloped pattern. Responding drops off immediately after reinforcement but picks up toward the end of the interval between reinforcements. The variable-interval schedule produces a steady rate of responding. Unannounced quizzes operate on variable-interval schedules and typically keep students studying regularly. Intermittent schedules are more resistant to extinction than continuous schedules: When reinforcement is discontinued, responding continues for a longer time if reinforcement has been intermittent rather than continuous. The durability of intermittent schedules can be seen in people's persistence at such events as playing slot machines, fishing, and shopping for bargains.

Generalization. Once a certain response occurs regularly to a given stimulus, the response also may occur to other stimuli. This is called *generalization* (Skinner, 1953).

Figure 3.3
Patterns of responding under different reinforcement schedules.
Note: VR = variable ratio; FR = fixed ratio; FI = fixed interval; VI = variable interval.

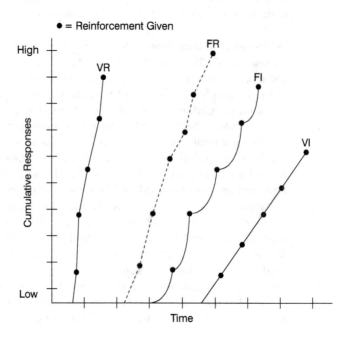

Generalization seems troublesome for operant theory, because a response should not be made in a situation in which it never has been reinforced. Skinner explained generalization by noting that people perform many behaviors that lead to the final (reinforced) response. These component behaviors are often part of the chains of behavior of different tasks and therefore are reinforced in different contexts. When people are in a new situation, they are likely to perform the component behaviors, which produce an accurate response or rapid acquisition of the correct response.

For example, students with good academic habits typically come to class, attend to and participate in the activities, take notes, do the required reading, and keep up with the assignments. These component behaviors produce high achievement and grades. When such students begin a new class, it is not necessary that the content be similar to previous classes in which they have been enrolled. Rather, the component behaviors have received repeated reinforcement and thus are likely to generalize to the new setting.

Generalization, however, does not occur automatically. O'Leary and Drabman (1971) noted that generalization "must be programmed like any other behavioral change" (p. 393). One problem with many behavior modification programs is that they change behaviors but the new behaviors do not generalize outside the training context. O'Leary and Drabman (1971) offer suggestions on ways to facilitate generalization (Table 3.5 and Application 3.6).

Discrimination. *Discrimination,* the complementary process to generalization, involves responding differently (in intensity or rate) depending on the stimulus or features of a situation (Rilling, 1977). Although teachers want students to generalize what they learn

Table 3.5
Suggestions for facilitating generalization.

Parental Involvement:	Involve parents in behavioral change programs.
High Expectations:	Convey to students that they are capable of performing well.
Self-Evaluation:	Teach students to monitor and evaluate their behaviors.
Contingencies:	Withdraw artificial contingencies (e.g., points), and replace with natural ones (privileges).
Participation:	Allow students to participate in specifying behaviors to be reinforced and reinforcement contingencies.
Academics:	Provide a good academic program because many students with behavior problems have academic deficiencies.
Benefits:	Show students how behavioral changes will benefit them by linking changes to activities of interest.
Reinforcement:	Reinforce students in different settings to reduce discrimination between reinforced and nonreinforced situations.
Consistency:	Prepare teachers in regular classes to continue to shape behaviors of students in special classes after they are mainstreamed into the regular program.

APPLICATION 3.6
Generalization

Generalization can advance skill development across subject areas. Finding main ideas is relevant to language arts, social studies, mathematics (word problems), and other content areas. A language arts teacher might provide students with a strategy for finding main ideas. Once students master this strategy, the teacher explains how to modify its use for other academic subjects and asks students to think of uses. By teaching the strategy well in one domain and facilitating potential applications in other domains, teachers save much time and effort because they do not have to teach the strategy in each content area.

Teaching expected behaviors (e.g., walking in the hall, raising a hand to speak) can also be generalized. For example, if all seventh-grade teachers decide to have students use the same format for the heading on their papers, it could be explained in one class. Then students could be asked to use the same format (with minor alterations) in each of their other classes.

to other situations, they also want them to respond discriminately. In solving mathematical word problems, teachers might want students to adopt a general problem-solving approach comprising steps such as determining the given and the needed information, drawing a picture, and generating useful formulas. Teachers also want students to learn to discriminate problem types (e.g., area, time-rate-distance, interest rate). Being able to identify quickly the type of problem enhances students' successes.

Spence (1936) proposed that to teach discrimination, desired responses should be reinforced and unwanted responses extinguished by nonreinforcement. In school, teachers point out similarities and differences among similar content and provide for periodic reviews to ensure that students discriminate properly and apply correct problem–solution methods.

Errors generally are thought to be disruptive and to produce learning of incorrect responses. This suggests that student errors should be kept to a minimum. Whether all errors need to be eliminated is debatable. Motivation research shows that students who learn to deal with errors in an adaptive manner subsequently persist longer on difficult tasks than do students who have experienced errorless learning (Dweck, 1975; see Chapter 8).

Behavioral Change

Reinforcement can be given for making correct responses only when people know what to do. Often, however, operant responses do not exist in final, polished form. If teachers wait to deliver reinforcement until learners emit the proper responses, many learners would never receive reinforcement because they never would acquire the responses. We now turn to a discussion of how behavioral change occurs in operant conditioning, which has important implications for learning.

Successive Approximations (Shaping). The basic operant conditioning method of behavioral change is *shaping*, or differential reinforcement of successive approximations to the desired form or rate of behavior (Morse & Kelleher, 1977). To shape behavior, one adheres to the following sequence:

- Identify what the student can do now (initial behavior)
- Identify the desired behavior
- Identify potential reinforcers in the student's environment
- Break the desired behavior into small substeps to be mastered sequentially
- Move the student from the initial behavior to the desired behavior by successively reinforcing each approximation to the desired behavior

Shaping is learning by doing with corrective feedback. A natural instance of shaping can be seen in a student attempting to shoot a basketball from a point on the court. The first shot falls short of the basket. The student shoots harder the second time, and the ball hits the backboard. The student does not shoot quite as hard the third time, and the ball hits the right rim and bounces off. On the fourth attempt, the student shoots as hard as the third attempt but aims left. The ball hits the left rim and bounces off. Finally, the student shoots just as hard but aims slightly to the right, and the ball goes into the basket. Gradually the shot was honed to an accurate form.

Shaping might be applied systematically with a hyperactive student who can work on a task for only a couple of minutes before becoming distracted. The goal is to shape the student's behavior so she can work uninterrupted for 30 minutes. Initially the teacher delivers a reinforcer when the student works productively for 2 minutes. After several successful 2-minute intervals, the criterion for reinforcement is raised to 3 minutes. Assuming that she works uninterrupted for several 3-minute periods, the criterion is raised to 4 minutes. This process continues to the goal of 30 minutes as long as the student reliably performs at the criterion level. If the student encounters difficulty at any point, the criterion for reinforcement decreases to a level at which she can perform successfully.

An academic skill that might be shaped is teaching a student the multiplication facts for 6. Presently he only knows $6 \times 1 = 6$ and $6 \times 2 = 12$. To earn reinforcement, he must correctly recite these two plus $6 \times 3 = 18$. After he can do this reliably, the criterion for reinforcement is raised to include $6 \times 4 = 24$. This process continues until he accurately recites all the facts up to $6 \times 10 = 60$.

Chaining. Most human actions are complex and include several three-term contingencies (A–B–C) linked successively. For example, shooting a basketball requires dribbling, turning, getting set in position, jumping, and releasing the ball. Each response alters the environment, and this altered condition serves as the stimulus for the next response. *Chaining* is the process of producing or altering some of the variables that serve as stimuli for future responses (Skinner, 1953). A chain consists of a series of operants, each of which sets the occasion for further responses.

Consider a student solving an algebraic equation (e.g., $2x - 10 = 4$). The -10 serves as the S^D, to which the student makes the appropriate response (R, add 10 to both sides of the equation). This product ($2x = 14$) is the S^R and also the S^D for the next response (divide both sides of the equation by 2) to solve the equation ($x = 7$). This stimulus serves as the S^D to move to the next equation. Operations within each equation constitute a chain, and the entire problem set constitutes a chain.

Chains are similar to Guthrie's acts, whereas individual three-term contingencies resemble movements. Some chains acquire a functional unity; the chain is an integrated sequence such that successful implementation defines a skill. When skills are well honed, execution of the chain occurs automatically. Riding a bicycle consists of several discrete acts, yet an accomplished rider executes these with little or no conscious effort. Such automaticity is often present in cognitive skills (e.g., reading, solving mathematical problems). Chaining plays a critical role in the acquisition of skills (Gollub, 1977; Skinner, 1978).

Behavior Modification

Behavior modification (or *behavior therapy*) refers to the systematic application of behavioral learning principles to facilitate adaptive behaviors (Ullmann & Krasner, 1965). Behavior modification has been employed with adults and children in such diverse contexts as classrooms, counseling settings, prisons, and mental hospitals. It has been used to treat phobias, dysfunctional language, disruptive behaviors, negative social interactions, poor child rearing, and low self-control (Ayllon & Azrin, 1968; Becker, 1971; Keller & Ribes-Inesta, 1974; Ulrich, Stachnik, & Mabry, 1966). Lovaas (1977) successfully employed behavior modification to teach language to autistic children. Classroom applications are given in Application 3.7.

APPLICATION 3.7
Behavior Modification

Behavior modification for disruptive students is difficult because such students may display few appropriate responses to be positively reinforced. A teacher might use shaping to address a specific annoying behavior. Kathy Stone has been having problems with Erik, who continually pushes and shoves other students when the class gets in line to go somewhere in the building. When the class is going only a short distance, Mrs. Stone could inform Erik that if he stays in line without pushing and shoving, he will be the line leader on the way back to the class; however, if he pushes or shoves, he immediately will be removed from the line. This procedure can be repeated until Erik can handle short distances. Mrs. Stone then can allow him to

walk with the class for progressively longer distances until he can behave in line for any distance.

Sarah, another child in Kathy Stone's class, frequently turns in messy work. Mrs. Stone might use generalized reinforcers such as special stickers (exchangeable for various privileges) to help Sarah, whose work typically is dirty, torn, and barely readable. Sarah is told if she turns in a paper that is clean, she can earn one sticker; if it is not torn, another sticker; and if the writing is neat, a third sticker. Once Sarah begins to make improvements, Mrs. Stone gradually can move the rewards to other areas for improvement (e.g., correct work, finishing work on time).

Techniques. The basic techniques of behavior modification include reinforcement of desired behaviors and extinction of undesired ones. Punishment is rarely employed but, when used, more often involves removing a positive reinforcer rather than presenting a negative reinforcer.

In deciding on a program of change, behavior modifiers typically focus on the following three issues (Ullmann & Krasner, 1965):

- Which of the individual's behaviors are maladaptive, and which should be increased (decreased)?
- What environmental contingencies currently support the individual's behaviors (either to maintain undesirable behaviors or to reduce the likelihood of performing more adaptive responses)?
- What environmental features can be altered to change the individual's behavior?

Change is most likely when modifiers and clients agree that a change is needed and jointly decide on the desired goals. The first step in establishing a program is to define the problem in behavioral terms. For example, the statement, "Keith is out of his seat too often," refers to overt behavior that can be measured: One can keep a record of the amount of time that Keith is out of his seat. General expressions referring to unobservables ("Keith has a bad attitude") do not allow for objective problem definition.

The next step is to determine the reinforcers maintaining undesirable behavior. Perhaps Keith is getting teacher attention only when he gets out of his seat and not when he is seated. A simple plan is to have the teacher attend to Keith while he is seated and engaged in academic work and to ignore him when he gets out of his seat. If the amount of times that Keith is out of his seat decreases, teacher attention is a positive reinforcer.

A behavior modification program might employ such generalized reinforcers as points that students exchange for *backup reinforcers*, such as tangible rewards, free time, or privileges. Having more than one backup ensures that at least one will be effective for each student at all times. A behavioral criterion must be established to earn reinforcement. The five-step shaping procedure (discussed previously) can be employed. The criterion is initially defined at the level of initial behavior and progresses in small increments toward the desired behavior. A point is given to the student each time the criterion is satisfied. To extinguish any undesirable behavior by Keith, the teacher should not give him too much attention if he gets out of his seat, but rather should inform him privately that because he does not satisfy the criterion, he does not earn a point.

Punishment is used infrequently but may be needed when behavior becomes so disruptive that it cannot be ignored (e.g., fighting). A common punishment is *time-out* (from reinforcement). During time-out, the student is removed from the class social context. There the student continues to engage in academic work without peer social interaction or the opportunity to earn reinforcement. Another punishment is to remove positive reinforcers (e.g., free time, recess, privileges) for misbehavior.

Critics have argued that behavior modification shapes quiet and docile behaviors (Winett & Winkler, 1972). Although a reasonable amount of quiet is needed to ensure that learning occurs, some teachers seek a quiet classroom at all times, even when some noise from social interactions would facilitate learning. The use of behavior modification is inherently neither good nor bad. It can produce a quiet classroom or promote social initiations by withdrawn children (Strain, Kerr, & Ragland, 1981). Like the techniques themselves, the goals of behavior modification need to be thought out carefully by those implementing the procedures.

Cognitive Behavior Modification. Researchers also have incorporated cognitive elements into behavior modification procedures. In *cognitive behavior modification,* learners' thoughts (when verbalized) function as discriminative and reinforcing stimuli. Thus, learners may verbally instruct themselves what to do and then perform the appropriate behavior. Cognitive behavior modification techniques often are applied with students with handicaps (Hallahan, Kneedler, & Lloyd, 1983), and used to reduce hyperactivity and aggression (Robinson, Smith, Miller, & Brownell, 1999). Meichenbaum's (1977) *self-instructional training* is an example of cognitive behavior modification (see Chapter 4).

Self-Regulation

Operant conditioning also addresses self-regulation (Mace, Belfiore, & Hutchinson, 2001; Mace, Belfiore, & Shea, 1989). This perspective is covered in depth in Chapter 9. Operant theory contends that self-regulated behavior involves choosing among alternative courses of action (Brigham, 1982), typically by deferring an immediate reinforcer in favor of a different, and usually greater, future reinforcer. For example, Trisha stays home on Friday night to study for an exam instead of going out with friends, and Kyle keeps working on an academic task despite taunting peers nearby. They are deferring immediate reinforcement for anticipated future reinforcement, as is John in the next example.

John is having difficulty studying. Despite good intentions, he spends insufficient time studying and is easily distracted. A key to changing his behavior is to establish discriminative stimuli (cues) for studying. With the assistance of his high-school counselor, John establishes a definite time and place for studying (7 P.M. to 9 P.M. in his room with one 10-minute break). To eliminate distracting cues, John agrees not to use his cell phone, CD player, computer, or TV during this period. For reinforcement, John will award himself one point for each night he successfully accomplishes his routine. When he receives 10 points, he can take a night off.

From an operant conditioning perspective, one decides which behaviors to regulate, establishes discriminative stimuli for their occurrence, evaluates performance in terms of whether it matches the standard, and administers reinforcement. As discussed in Chapter 9, the three key subprocesses are self-monitoring (deliberate attention to selected aspects of one's behavior), self-instruction (S^Ds that set the occasion for self-regulatory Rs leading to S^Rs), and self-reinforcement (reinforcing oneself for performing a correct response).

INSTRUCTIONAL APPLICATIONS

Skinner (1954, 1961, 1968, 1984) wrote extensively on how his ideas can be applied to solve educational problems. He believed that there is too much aversive control. Although students rarely receive corporal punishment, they often work on assignments not because they want to learn or because they enjoy them but rather to avoid punishments such as teacher criticism, loss of privileges, and a trip to the principal's office.

A second concern is that reinforcement occurs infrequently and often not at the proper time. Teachers attend to each student for only a few minutes each day. While students are engaged in seat work, several minutes can elapse between when they finish an assignment and when they receive teacher feedback. Consequently, students may learn incorrectly, which means that teachers must spend additional time giving corrective feedback.

A third point is that the scope and sequence of curricula do not ensure that all students acquire skills. Students do not learn at the same pace. To cover all the material, teachers may move to the next lesson before all students have mastered the previous one.

Skinner contended that these and other problems cannot be solved by paying teachers more money (although they would like that!), lengthening the school day and year, raising standards, or toughening teacher certification requirements. Rather, he recommended better use of instructional time. Since it is unrealistic to expect students to move through the curriculum at the same rate, individualizing instruction would improve efficiency.

Skinner believed that teaching required properly arranging reinforcement contingencies. No new principles were needed in applying operant conditioning to education. Instruction is more effective when (1) teachers present the material in small steps, (2) learners actively respond rather than passively listen, (3) teachers give feedback immediately following learners' responses, and (4) learners move through the material at their own pace.

The basic process of instruction involves shaping. The goal of instruction (desired behavior) and the students' initial behavior are identified. Substeps (behaviors) leading from the initial behavior to the desired behavior are formulated. Each substep represents a small modification of the preceding one. Students are moved through the sequence using various approaches including demonstrations, small-group work, and individual seat work. Students actively respond to the material and receive immediate feedback.

This instructional approach involves specifying learners' present knowledge and desired objectives in terms of what learners do. Desired behaviors often are specified as behavioral objectives, to be discussed shortly. Individual differences are taken into account by beginning instruction at learners' present performance levels and allowing them to progress at their own rates. Given the prevailing teaching methods in our educational system, these goals seem impractical: Teachers would have to begin instruction at different points and cover material at different rates for individual students. Programmed instruction circumvents these problems: Learners begin at the point in the material corresponding to their performance levels, and they progress at their own rates.

The remainder of this section describes some instructional applications that incorporate behavioristic principles. Not all of these applications are derived from Skinner's or other theories covered in this chapter, but they all reflect to some extent key ideas of behaviorism.

Behavioral Objectives

Behavioral objectives are clear statements of the intended student outcomes of instruction. Objectives can range from general to specific. General or vague objectives such as "improve student awareness" can be fulfilled by almost any kind of instruction. Conversely, objectives that are too specific and document every minute change in student behavior are time consuming to write and can cause teachers to lose sight of the most important learning outcomes. Optimal objectives fall somewhere between these extremes (Application 3.8).

APPLICATION 3.8
Behavioral Objectives

As teachers prepare lesson plans, it is important that they decide on specific behavioral objectives and plan activities to assist students in mastering these objectives. Instead of an art teacher planning a lesson with the objective, "Have students complete a pen-and-ink drawing of the front of the building," the teacher should decide on the major objective for the students to master. Is it to use pen and ink or to draw the front of the school building? The objective may be better stated as follows: "Have the students draw the major lines of the front of the building in correct perspective (materials/medium: drawing paper, pens, ink)."

A kindergarten teacher writes that she wants "Students to go to art, music, and physical education in an orderly fashion." For that age child, it would be better if the teacher would spell out the objective in more specific terms; for example, "Students should move to other classrooms by walking in a line without talking and by keeping their hands to themselves."

A behavioral objective describes what students do when demonstrating their achievements and how teachers know what students are doing (Mager, 1962). Four parts of a good objective are:

- The specific group of students
- The actual behaviors students are to perform as a consequence of instructional activities
- The conditions or contexts in which the students are to perform the behaviors
- The criteria for assessing student behaviors to determine whether objectives have been met

A sample objective with the parts identified is:

Given eight addition problems with fractions of unlike denominators (3), the fourth-grade math student (1) will write the correct sums (2) for at least seven of them (4).

Behavioral objectives can help determine the important learning outcomes, which aid in lesson planning and testing to assess learning. Formulating objectives also helps teachers decide what content students can master. Given unit-teaching objectives and a fixed amount of time to cover them, teachers can decide which objectives are important and focus on them. Although objectives for lower-level learning outcomes (knowledge, comprehension) are generally easier to specify, good behavioral objectives can be written to assess higher-order outcomes (application, analysis, synthesis, evaluation) as well.

Research shows that students given behavioral objectives have better verbatim recall of verbal information compared with students not provided with objectives (Faw & Waller, 1976; Hamilton, 1985). Objectives may cue students to process the information at the appropriate level; thus, when students are given objectives requiring recall, they engage in rehearsal and other strategies that facilitate that type of recall. Research also shows that providing students with objectives does not enhance learning of material unrelated to the objectives (Duchastel & Brown, 1974), which suggests that students may concentrate on learning material relevant to the objectives and disregard other material.

The effect of objectives on learning depends on students' prior experience with them and on how important they perceive the information to be. Training in using objectives or familiarity with criterion-based instruction leads to better learning compared to the absence of such training or familiarity. When students can determine on their own what material is important to learn, providing objectives does not facilitate learning. Informing students of the objectives seems to be more important when students do not know what material is important. Also, Muth, Glynn, Britton, and Graves (1988) found that text structure can moderate the effect of objectives on learning. Information made salient by being in a prominent position (e.g., early in a text or highlighted) is recalled well, even when objectives are not provided.

Learning Time

Operant theory predicts that environmental variables affect students' learning. One key environmental variable is learning time.

Carroll (1963, 1965) formulated a model of school learning that places primary emphasis on the instructional variable of time spent learning. Students successfully learn to the extent that they spend the amount of time they need to learn. *Time* means academically engaged time, or time spent paying attention and trying to learn. Although time is an environmental (observable) variable, this definition is cognitive because it goes beyond a simple behavioral indicator of clock time. Within this framework, Carroll postulated factors that influence how much time learning requires and how much time is actually spent learning.

Time Needed for Learning. One influence on this factor is *aptitude for learning the task.* Learning aptitude depends on the amount of prior task-relevant learning and on personal characteristics such as abilities and attitudes. A second, related factor is *ability to understand instruction.* This variable interacts with instructional method; for example, some learners comprehend verbal instruction well, whereas others benefit more from visual presentations.

Quality of instruction refers to how well the task is organized and presented to learners. Quality includes what learners are told about what they will learn and how they will learn it, the extent to which they have adequate contact with the learning materials, and how much prerequisite knowledge is acquired prior to learning the task. The lower the quality of instruction, the more time learners require to learn.

Time Spent in Learning. *Time allowed for learning* is one influence on this factor. The school curriculum includes so much content that time allotted for a particular type of learning is less than optimal for some students. When teachers present material to the entire class at once, some learners are more likely to experience difficulty grasping it and require additional instruction. When students are ability grouped, the amount of time devoted to different content varies depending on the ease with which students learn.

A second influence is *time the learner is willing to spend learning.* Even when learners are given ample time to learn, they may not spend that time working productively.

Whether due to low interest, high perceived task difficulty, or other factors, students may not be motivated to persist at a task for the amount of time they require to learn it. Carroll incorporated these factors into a formula to estimate the degree of learning for any student on a given task:

degree of learning = time spent/time needed

Ideally, students spend as much time as they need to learn (degree of learning = 1.0), but learners typically spend either more time (degree of learning > 1.0) or less time (degree of learning < 1.0) than they require.

Carroll's model highlights the importance of academic engaged time required for learning and the factors influencing time spent and time needed to learn. The model incorporates valid psychological principles, but only at a general level as instructional or motivational factors. It does not explore cognitive engagement in depth. Carroll (1989) admitted that more research was needed to complete the details. As discussed in the next section, mastery learning researchers, who have systematically investigated the time variable, have provided greater specificity.

In line with what Skinner (1968) contended, many educators have decried the way that time is misspent (Zepeda & Mayers, 2006). The time variable is central to current discussions on ways to maximize student achievement. For example, the *No Child Left Behind Act of 2001* greatly expanded the role of the federal government in elementary and secondary education (Shaul & Ganson, 2005). Although the act did not specify how much time was to be devoted to instruction, its requirements for student achievement and its accountability standards, combined with various writers calling for better use of time, have led school systems to re-examine their use of time to ensure better student learning.

One consequence is that many secondary schools have abandoned the traditional six-hour schedule in favor of *block scheduling*. Although there are variations, many use the A/B block, in which classes meet on alternate days for longer periods per day. Presumably block scheduling allows teachers and students to explore content in greater depth that often was not possible with the traditional shorter class periods (e.g., 50 minutes).

Given that block scheduling still is relatively new, there is not a lot of research assessing its effectiveness. In their review, Zepeda and Mayers (2006) found that block scheduling may improve school climate and students' grade-point averages, but studies showed inconsistent results for student attendance and scores on standardized tests. As block scheduling becomes more common, we can expect more research that may clarify these inconsistencies.

Another means for increasing time for learning is through out-of-school programs, such as after-school programs and summer school. Compared with research on block scheduling, research on the effects of out-of-school programs shows greater consistency. In their review, Lauer et al. (2006) found positive effects for such programs on students' reading and mathematics achievement; effects were larger for programs with enhancements (e.g., tutoring). Mahoney, Lord, and Carryl (2005) found benefits of after-school programs on children's academic performances and motivation; results were strongest for children rated as highly engaged in the after-school program's activities. Consistent with Carroll's model, we might conclude that out-of-school programs are successful to the extent that they focus on student learning and provide supports to encourage it.

Mastery Learning

Carroll's model predicts that if students vary in aptitude for learning a subject and if all receive the same amount and type of instruction, their achievement will differ. If the amount and type of instruction vary depending on individual differences among learners, then each student has the potential to demonstrate mastery; the positive relation between aptitude and achievement will disappear because all students will demonstrate equal achievement regardless of aptitudes.

These ideas form the basis of *mastery learning* (Anderson, 2003; Bloom, 1976; Bloom, Hastings, & Madaus, 1971). Mastery learning incorporates Carroll's ideas into a systematic instructional plan that includes defining mastery, planning for mastery, teaching for mastery, and grading for mastery (Block & Burns, 1977). Mastery learning contains cognitive elements, although its formulation seems more behavioral in nature compared with many current cognitive theories.

To *define mastery*, teachers prepare a set of objectives and a final (summative) exam. Level of mastery is established (e.g., where A students typically perform under traditional instruction). Teachers break the course into learning units mapped against course objectives.

Planning for mastery means teachers plan instructional procedures for themselves and students to include corrective feedback procedures (formative evaluation). Such evaluation typically takes the form of unit mastery tests that set mastery at a given level (e.g., 90%). Corrective instruction, which is used with students who fail to master aspects of the unit's objectives, is given in small-group study sessions, individual tutorials, and supplemental materials.

At the outset of *teaching for mastery*, teachers orient students to the mastery procedures and provide instruction using the entire class, small groups, or individual seat work activities. Teachers give the formative test and certify which students achieve mastery. Students who fall short might work in small groups reviewing troublesome material, often with the aid of peer tutors who have mastered the material. Teachers allow students time to work on remedial materials along with homework. *Grading for mastery* includes a summative (end-of-course) test. Students who score at or above the course mastery performance level receive A grades; lower scores are graded accordingly.

The emphasis on student abilities as determinants of learning may seem uninteresting given that abilities generally do not change much as a result of instructional interventions. Bloom (1976) also stressed the importance of *alterable variables* of schooling: cognitive entry behaviors (e.g., student skills and cognitive processing strategies at the outset of instruction), affective characteristics (e.g., interest, motivation), and specific factors influencing the quality of instruction (e.g., student participation, type of corrective feedback). Instructional interventions can improve these variables.

Reviews of the effect of mastery learning on student achievement are mixed. Block and Burns (1977) generally found mastery learning more effective than traditional forms of instruction. With college students, Péladeau, Forget, and Gagné (2003) obtained results showing that mastery learning improved students' achievement, long-term retention, and attitudes toward the course and subject matter. Kulik, Kulik, and Bangert-Drowns (1990) examined more than 100 evaluations of mastery learning programs and found positive effects on academic performances and course attitudes among college, high school, and upper-grade elementary school learners. They also found that mastery learning may increase the time students spend on instructional tasks. In contrast, Bangert, Kulik, and Kulik (1983) found weaker support for mastery learning programs. They noted that mastery-based instruction was more effective at the college level than at lower levels. Its effectiveness undoubtedly depends on the proper instructional conditions (e.g., planning, teaching, grading) being established (Kulik et al., 1990).

Students participating in mastery instruction often spend more time in learning compared with learners in traditional classes (Block & Burns, 1977). Given that time is at a premium in schools, much mastery work—especially remedial efforts—must be accomplished outside of regular school hours. Most studies show smaller effects of mastery instruction on affective outcomes (e.g., interest in and attitudes toward the subject matter) than on academic outcomes.

An important premise of mastery learning is that individual differences in student learning decrease over time. Anderson (1976) found that when remedial students gained experience with mastery instruction, they gradually required less extra time to attain mastery because their entry-level skills improved. These results imply cumulative benefits of mastery learning. There remains, however, the question of how much practice is enough (Péladeau et al., 2003). Too much repetitive practice might negatively affect motivation, which will not promote learning. These points require further research, but have important instructional implications. Some examples of mastery learning are given in Application 3.9.

APPLICATION 3.9
Mastery Learning

A mastery learning approach can be beneficial in certain learning environments. For example, in a remedial reading group for secondary students, a well-organized mastery learning program would allow students to progress at their own rates. Students motivated to make rapid progress are not slowed down by this type of instruction, as might happen if they are placed in a traditional learning format. A key requirement is to include a progression of activities from easier to more difficult. The program should have checkpoints at which the students interact with the teacher so that their progress is evaluated and reteaching or special assistance is provided if needed.

Young children enter school with a wide range of experiences and abilities. Mastery learning can help teachers deal effectively with the varying abilities and developmental levels. Mastery learning techniques can be implemented by using learning centers and small groups. Children can be placed in the different centers and groups according to their current levels. Then they can move through the various levels at their own rates.

Mastery learning also can build students' self-efficacy for learning (Chapter 4). As they note their progress in completing units, they are apt to believe they are capable of further learning. Enhancing self-efficacy is particularly important with remedial learners who have encountered school failures and doubt their capabilities to learn, as well as for young children with limited experiences and skills.

Programmed Instruction

Programmed instruction (PI) refers to instructional materials developed in accordance with operant conditioning principles of learning (O'Day, Kulhavy, Anderson, & Malczynski, 1971). In the 1920s, Sidney Pressey designed machines to use primarily for testing. Students were presented with multiple-choice questions, and they pressed a button corresponding to their choice. If students responded correctly, the machine presented the next choice; if they responded incorrectly, the error was recorded and they continued to respond to the item.

Skinner revived Pressey's machines in the 1950s and modified them to incorporate instruction (Skinner, 1958). These teaching machines presented students with material in small steps (frames). Each frame required learners to make an overt response. Material was carefully sequenced and broken into small units to minimize errors. Students received immediate feedback on the accuracy of each response. They moved to the next frame when their answer was correct. When it was incorrect, supplementary material was provided. Although errors occurred, the programs were designed to minimize errors and ensure that learners typically succeeded (Benjamin, 1988).

There are many benefits when students generally perform well, but as noted earlier, research suggests that preventing errors may not be desirable. Dweck (1975) found that an occasional failure increased persistence on difficult tasks more than did constant success. Further, constant success is not as informative of one's capabilities as is occasionally having difficulty because the latter highlights what one can and cannot do. This is not to suggest that teachers should let students fail, but rather that under the proper circumstances students can benefit from tasks structured so that they occasionally encounter difficulty.

PI does not require the use of a machine; a book by Holland and Skinner (1961) is an example of PI. Today, however, most PI is computerized and many computer instructional programs incorporate principles of behavioral instruction.

PI incorporates several learning principles (O'Day et al., 1971). Behavioral objectives specify what students should perform on completion of the instruction. The unit is subdivided into sequenced frames, each of which presents a small bit of information and a test item to which learners respond. Although a lot of material may be included in the program, the frame-to-frame increments are small. Learners work at their own pace and respond to questions as they work through the program. Responses may require learners to supply words, provide numerical answers, or choose which of several statements best describes the idea being presented. Feedback depends on the learner's response. If the learner is correct, the next item is given. If the learner answers incorrectly, additional remedial information is presented and the item is tested in slightly different form.

Because PI reflects shaping, performance increments are small and learners almost always respond correctly. Linear and branching programs are distinguished according to how they treat learner errors. *Linear programs* are structured in such a way that all students proceed through them in the same sequence (but not necessarily at the same rate). Regardless of whether students respond correctly or incorrectly to a frame, they move to the next frame where they receive feedback on the accuracy of their answer. Programs minimize errors by covering the same material in more than one frame and by prompting student responses (Figure 3.4).

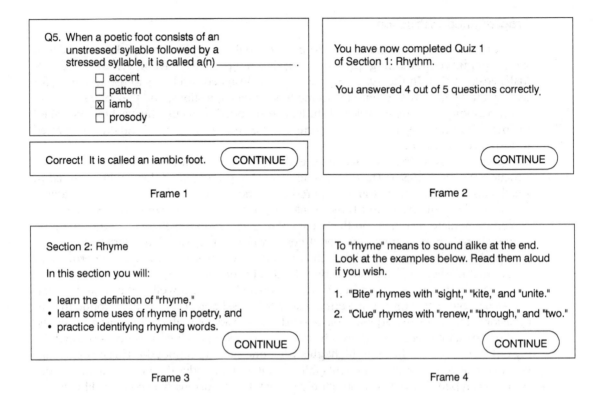

Frame 1

Q5. When a poetic foot consists of an unstressed syllable followed by a stressed syllable, it is called a(n) _____ .
- ☐ accent
- ☐ pattern
- ☒ iamb
- ☐ prosody

Correct! It is called an iambic foot.   (CONTINUE)

Frame 2

You have now completed Quiz 1 of Section 1: Rhythm.

You answered 4 out of 5 questions correctly.

(CONTINUE)

Frame 3

Section 2: Rhyme

In this section you will:

- learn the definition of "rhyme,"
- learn some uses of rhyme in poetry, and
- practice identifying rhyming words.

(CONTINUE)

Frame 4

To "rhyme" means to sound alike at the end. Look at the examples below. Read them aloud if you wish.

1. "Bite" rhymes with "sight," "kite," and "unite."
2. "Clue" rhymes with "renew," "through," and "two."

(CONTINUE)

Figure 3.4
Frames from a linear program.

Branching programs are set up so that students' movement through them depends on how they answer the questions (Figure 3.5). Students who learn quickly skip frames and bypass much of the repetition of linear programs, whereas slower learners receive additional instruction. A disadvantage is that branching programs may not provide sufficient repetition to ensure that all students learn concepts well.

Research suggests that linear and branching programs promote student learning equally well and that PI is as effective as conventional classroom teaching (Bangert et al., 1983; Lange, 1972). Whether PI is used instead of traditional instruction depends in part on how well existing programs cover the required scope and sequence of instruction. PI seems especially useful with students who demonstrate skill deficiencies; working through programs provides remedial instruction and practice. PI also is useful for independent study on a topic.

Programmed instruction in computer format is a type of *computer-based instruction (CBI)*. Until a few years ago, CBI was the most common application of computer learning in schools (Jonassen, 1996; today it is the Internet). CBI often is used for drills and tutorials. Whereas drills review information, tutorials are interactive: They present information and feedback to students and respond based on students' answers (e.g., branching programs).

Q5. When the _____ was
opened water flowed through the dam.
- ☒ upstream
- ☐ downstream
- ☐ reservoir
- ☐ spillway
- ☐ floodgate

No. "Upstream" is the direction against the flow of water in a river. The correct answer is a part of a dam.

(PLEASE TRY AGAIN)

Frame 1

Q5. When the _____ was
opened water flowed through the dam.
- ☐ downstream
- ☐ reservoir
- ☐ spillway
- ☒ floodgate

That is correct. The floodgate lets water go through the dam.

Frame 2   (CONTINUE)

You have completed
SECTION 1: VOCABULARY

What would you like to do next?

- ☐ Repeat Section 1
- ☐ See summary of Section 1
- ☐ Go on to Section 2
- ☒ MAIN MENU

Frame 3

MAIN MENU

- ☐ Section 1: VOCABULARY
- ☐ Section 2: CAUSES OF FLOODING
- ☐ Section 3: CONSEQUENCES OF FLOODING
- ☐ Section 4: FLOOD CONTROL
- ☐ Section 5: SIMULATION
- ☐ Section 6: CONSEQUENCES OF CONTROL
- ☐ QUIT

Frame 4

Figure 3.5
Frames from a branching program.

Studies investigating CBI in college courses yield beneficial effects on students' achievement and attitudes (Kulik, Kulik, & Cohen, 1980). Several CBI features are firmly grounded in learning theory and research. Computers command students' attention and provide immediate feedback, which can be of a type typically not given in class (e.g., how present performances compare with prior performances to highlight progress). Computers individualize content and rate of presentation.

Although drills and tutorials place strict limitations on how students interact with material, one advantage of CBI is that it can be personalized: Students enter information about themselves, parents, and friends, which is then included in the instructional presentation. Personalization can produce higher achievement than other formats (Anand & Ross, 1987; Ross, McCormick, Krisak, & Anand, 1985). Anand and Ross (1987) gave elementary children instruction in dividing fractions according to one of three problem formats (abstract, concrete, personalized):

> (Abstract) There are three objects. Each is cut in half. In all, how many pieces would there be?
> (Concrete) Billy had three candy bars. He cut each of them in half. In all, how many pieces of candy did Billy have?
> (Personalized for Joseph) Joseph's teacher, Mrs. Williams, surprised him on December 15 when she presented Joseph with three candy bars. Joseph cut each one of them in half so that he could share the birthday gift with his friends. In all, how many pieces of candy did Joseph have? (pp. 73–74)

The personalized format led to better learning and transfer than the abstract format and to more positive attitudes toward instruction than the concrete format.

Contingency Contracts

A *contingency contract* is an agreement between teacher and student specifying what work the student will accomplish and the expected outcome (reinforcement) for successful performance (Homme, Csanyi, Gonzales, & Rechs, 1970). A contract can be made verbally, although it usually is written. Teachers can devise the contract and ask if the student agrees with it, but it is customary for teacher and student to formulate it jointly. An advantage of joint participation is that students may feel more committed to fulfilling the contract's terms. When people participate in goal selection, they often are more committed to attaining the goal than when they are excluded from the selection process (Locke & Latham, 1990).

Contracts specify goals or expected outcomes in terms of particular behaviors to be displayed. The "contingency" is the expected outcome, which often can be reduced to, "If you do this, then you will receive that." The behaviors should be specific—for example, "I will complete pages 1–30 in my math book with at least 90% accuracy," or "I will stay in my seat during reading period." General behaviors (e.g., "I will work on my math" or "I will behave appropriately") are unacceptable. With young children, time frames should be brief; however, objectives can cover more than one time, such as successive 30-minute periods or during each social studies period for one week. Contracts may include academic and nonacademic behaviors (Application 3.10).

APPLICATION 3.10
Contingency Contracting

A contingency contract represents a systematic application of reinforcement principles to change behavior. It can be used to change any type of behavior, such as completing work, not disrupting the class, and participating in discussions. When developing a contract, a teacher should make sure that the reward is something that interests and motivates the students.

Assume that Kathy Stone has tried unsuccessfully to apply several motivational techniques to encourage James, a student in her class, to complete work in language arts. She and James might jointly develop a contract to address the inappropriate behaviors. They should discuss the problem, identify the desired behavior, and list the consequences and time frame for fulfilling the terms of the contract. A sample contract might be as follows:

Contract for the Week of January 9–13

I will complete my language arts seat work with 80% accuracy in the time allotted during class.

If I complete my seat work, I will be allowed to participate in a learning center activity.

If I do not complete my seat work, I will miss recess and complete my work at that time.

Monday:
_____ Completed   _____ Not completed
Tuesday:
_____ Completed   _____ Not completed
Wednesday:
_____ Completed   _____ Not completed
Thursday:
_____ Completed   _____ Not completed
Friday:
_____ Completed   _____ Not completed

Bonus: If I complete my work three out of five days, I will be able to work in the computer lab for 30 minutes on Friday afternoon.

_____   _____
Student   Teacher
Signature/Date   Signature/Date

Developing contracts with students and monitoring progress is time consuming. Fortunately, most learners do not require contracts to behave appropriately or accomplish work. Contracts seem especially helpful as a means of assisting students to work on assignments more productively. A lengthy, long-term assignment can be subdivided into a series of short-term goals with due dates. This type of plan helps students keep up with the work and turn in material on time.

Contracts are based on the principle that goals that are specific, temporally close at hand, and difficult but attainable will maximize performance (Schunk, 1995). Contracts also convey information to students about their progress in completing the task. Such information on progress raises student motivation and achievement (Locke & Latham, 1990). Contracts should promote achievement if they reinforce student progress in learning or in accomplishing more on-task behavior.

SUMMARY

Behaviorism—as expressed in conditioning theories—dominated the psychology of learning for the first half of the twentieth century. These theories explain learning in terms of environmental events. Mental processes are not necessary to explain the acquisition, maintenance, and generalization of behavior.

The learning theories of Thorndike, Pavlov, and Guthrie are of historical importance. Although these theories differ, each views learning as a process of forming associations between stimuli and responses. Thorndike believed that responses to stimuli are strengthened when followed by satisfying consequences. Pavlov experimentally demonstrated how stimuli could be conditioned to elicit responses by being paired with other stimuli. Guthrie hypothesized that a contiguous relation between stimulus and response established their pairing. Although these theories are no longer viable in their original form, many of their principles are evident in current theoretical perspectives. These theories and the research they generated helped to establish the psychology of learning as a legitimate area of study.

Operant conditioning—the learning theory formulated by B. F. Skinner—is based on the assumption that features of the environment (stimuli, situations, events) serve as cues for responding. Reinforcement strengthens responses and increases their future likelihood of occurring when the stimuli are present. It is not necessary to refer to underlying physiological or mental states to explain behavior.

The basic operant conditioning model is a three-term contingency involving a discriminative stimulus (antecedent), response (behavior), and reinforcing stimulus (consequence). The consequences of behaviors determine the likelihood that people will respond to environmental cues. Consequences that are reinforcing increase behavior; consequences that are punishing decrease behavior. Some other important operant conditioning concepts are extinction, generalization, discrimination, primary and secondary reinforcers, reinforcement schedules, and the Premack Principle.

Shaping is the process used to alter behavior. Shaping involves reinforcing successive approximations of the desired behavior toward its desired form or frequency of occurrence. Complex behaviors are formed by chaining together simple behaviors in successive three-term contingencies. Behavior modification programs have been commonly applied in diverse contexts to promote adaptive behaviors. Self-regulation is the process of bringing one's behaviors under self-selected stimulus and reinforcement control.

The generality of operant conditioning principles has been challenged by cognitive theorists who contend that by ignoring mental processes, operant conditioning offers an incomplete account of human learning. Stimuli and reinforcement may explain some human learning, but much research shows that to explain learning—and especially higher-order and complex learning—we must take into account people's thoughts, beliefs, and feelings.

Operant principles have been applied to many aspects of teaching and learning. These principles can be seen in applications involving behavioral objectives, learning time, mastery learning, programmed instruction, and contingency contracts. Research evidence generally shows positive effects of these applications on student achievement. Regardless of theoretical orientation, one can apply behavioral principles to facilitate student learning and achievement.

A summary of the learning issues (Chapter 1) for conditioning theories appears in Table 3.6.

Table 3.6
Summary of learning issues.

How Does Learning Occur?

The basic model of operant learning is expressed by the three-term contingency: $S^D \rightarrow R \rightarrow S^R$. A response is performed in the presence of a discriminative stimulus and is followed by a reinforcing stimulus. The likelihood of the R being performed in the future in the presence of that S^D is increased. To build complex behaviors requires shaping, which consists of chains of three-term contingencies, where gradual approximations to the desired form of behavior are successively reinforced. Factors affecting learning are developmental status and reinforcement history. For conditioning to occur, one must have the physical capabilities to perform the behaviors. The responses that one makes in given situations depend on what one has been reinforced for doing in the past.

What Is the Role of Memory?

Memory is not explicitly addressed by conditioning theories. These theories do not study internal processes. Responses to given stimuli are strengthened through repeated reinforcement. This response strengthening accounts for present behavior.

What Is the Role of Motivation?

Motivation is an increase in the quantity or rate of behavior. No internal processes are used to explain motivation. The increase in quantity or rate can be explained in terms of reinforcement history. Certain schedules of reinforcement produce higher rates of responding than others.

How Does Transfer Occur?

Transfer, or generalization, occurs when one responds in an identical or similar fashion to stimuli other than the ones that were used in conditioning. At least some of the elements in the transfer setting must be similar to those in the conditioning setting for transfer to occur.

Which Processes Are Involved in Self-Regulation?

The key processes are self-monitoring, self-instruction, and self-reinforcement. One decides which behaviors to regulate, establishes discriminative stimuli for their occurrence, participates in instruction (often in computer-based form), monitors performance and determines whether it matches the standard, and administers reinforcement.

What Are the Implications for Instruction?

Learning requires establishing responses to discriminative stimuli. Practice is needed to strengthen responses. Complex skills can be established by shaping progressive, small approximations to the desired behavior. Instruction should have clear, measurable objectives, proceed in small steps, and deliver reinforcement. Mastery learning, computer-based instruction, and contingency contracts are useful ways to promote learning.

FURTHER READING

Mager, R. (1962). *Preparing instructional objectives*. Palo Alto, CA: Fearon.

Mayer, R. E. (2003). E. L. Thorndike's enduring contributions to educational psychology. In B. J. Zimmerman & D. H. Schunk (Eds.), *Educational psychology: A century of contributions* (pp. 113–154). Mahwah, NJ: Erlbaum.

Morris, E. K. (2003). B. F. Skinner: A behavior analyst in educational psychology. In B. J. Zimmerman & D. H. Schunk (Eds.), *Educational psychology: A century of contributions* (pp. 229–250). Mahwah, NJ: Erlbaum.

Skinner, B. F. (1968). *The technology of teaching*. New York: Appleton-Century-Crofts.

Watson, J. B., & Rayner, R. (1920). Conditioned emotional reactions. *Journal of Experimental Psychology, 3,* 1–14.

Windholz, G. (1997). Ivan P. Pavlov: An overview of his life and psychological work. *American Psychologist, 52,* 941–946.

Wood, W., & Neal, D. T. (2007). A new look at habits and the habit-goal interface. *Psychological Review, 114,* 843–863.

4

Social Cognitive Theory

The girls' tennis team of Westbrook High School is practicing after school. The team has played a few matches; they are playing well, but some improvements are needed. Coach Sandra Martin is working with Donnetta Awalt, the number four singles player. Donnetta's overall game is good, but lately she has been hitting many of her backhands into the net. Coach Martin asks Donnetta to hit backhands to her as she hits balls to Donnetta.

Donnetta: This is impossible. I just can't do it.

Coach Martin: Sure you can. You've been able to hit backhands before, and you will again.

Donnetta: Then what do I do?

Coach Martin: I see that you are swinging down during your backhand. By swinging downward you're almost guaranteeing that you'll hit the ball into the net. We need for you to develop more of an upward swing. Come over here please, and I'll demonstrate (Coach Martin demonstrates Donnetta's swing and then an upward swing and points out the differences). Now you try it, slowly at first. Do you feel the difference?

Donnetta: Yes. But from where should I start my swing? How far back and how low down?

Coach Martin: Watch me again. Adjust your grip like this before hitting a backhand (Coach Martin demonstrates grip). Get into position, about like this relative to the ball (Coach Martin demonstrates). Now start your backhand like this (Coach Martin demonstrates) and bring it through like this (Coach Martin demonstrates). You see you're actually swinging upward, not downward.

Donnetta: OK, that feels better (practices). Can you hit some to me?

Coach Martin: Sure. Let's try it, slowly at first, then we'll pick up speed (they practice for several minutes). That's good. I've got a book I want you to take home and look at the section on backhands. There are some good pictures in there with explanations of what I've been teaching you this afternoon.

117

Donnetta: Thanks, I will. I really felt I couldn't do this anymore, so I've been trying to avoid hitting backhands in matches. But now I'm feeling more confident.

Coach Martin: That's good. Keep thinking like that and practicing and you may be able to move up to number three singles.

The preceding chapter focused on conditioning theories (behaviorism), which held sway in the field of learning for the first half of the twentieth century. Beginning in the late 1950s and early 1960s, these theories were challenged on many fronts. Their influence waned to the point where today the major theoretical perspectives are cognitive.

One of the major challenges to behaviorism came from studies on observational learning conducted by Albert Bandura and his colleagues. A central finding of this research was that people could learn new actions merely by observing others perform them. Observers did not have to perform the actions at the time of learning. Reinforcement was not necessary for learning to occur. These findings disputed central assumptions of conditioning theories.

This chapter covers *social cognitive theory*, which stresses the idea that much human learning occurs in a social environment. By observing others, people acquire knowledge, rules, skills, strategies, beliefs, and attitudes. Individuals also learn from models the usefulness and appropriateness of behaviors and the consequences of modeled behaviors, and they act in accordance with beliefs about their capabilities and the expected outcomes of their actions. The opening scenario portrays an instructional application of modeling.

The focus of this chapter is on Bandura's (1986, 1997, 2001) social cognitive theory. Bandura was born in Alberta, Canada, in 1925. He received his doctorate in clinical psychology from the University of Iowa, where he was influenced by Miller and Dollard's (1941) *Social Learning and Imitation* (discussed later in this chapter).

After arriving at Stanford University in the 1950s, Bandura began a research program exploring the influences on social behavior. He believed that the conditioning theories in vogue at that time offered incomplete explanations of the acquisition and performance of prosocial and deviant behaviors:

> Indeed, most prior applications of learning theory to issues concerning prosocial and deviant behavior . . . have suffered from the fact that they have relied heavily on a limited range of principles established on the basis of, and mainly supported by, studies of animal learning or human learning in one-person situations. (Bandura & Walters, 1963, p. 1)

Bandura formulated a comprehensive theory of observational learning that he has expanded to encompass acquisition and performance of diverse skills, strategies, and behaviors. Social cognitive principles have been applied to the learning of cognitive, motor, social, and self-regulation skills, as well as to the topics of violence (live, filmed), moral development, education, health, and societal values (Zimmerman & Schunk, 2003).

Bandura is a prolific writer. Beginning with the book *Social Learning and Personality Development*, written in 1963 with Richard Walters, he has authored several other books, including *Principles of Behavior Modification* (1969), *Aggression: A Social Learning Analysis* (1973), *Social Learning Theory* (1977b), and *Social Foundations of Thought and Action: A Social Cognitive Theory* (1986). With the publication of *Self-Efficacy: The Exercise of Control* (1997), Bandura extended his theory to address ways people seek control over important events of their lives through self-regulation of their thoughts and actions. The basic processes involve setting goals, judging anticipated outcomes of actions, evaluating progress toward goals, and self-regulating thoughts, emotions, and actions. As Bandura (1986) explained:

> Another distinctive feature of social cognitive theory is the central role it assigns to self-regulatory functions. People do not behave just to suit the preferences of others. Much of their behavior is motivated and regulated by internal standards and self-evaluative reactions to their own actions. After personal standards have been adopted, discrepancies between a performance and the standard against which it is measured activate evaluative self-reactions, which serve to influence subsequent behavior. An act, therefore, includes among its determinants self-produced influences. (Bandura, 1986, p. 20)

This chapter discusses the conceptual framework of social cognitive theory, along with its underlying assumptions about the nature of human learning and behavior. A significant portion of the chapter is devoted to modeling processes. The various influences on learning and performance are described, and motivational influences are discussed with special emphasis on the critical role of self-efficacy. Some instructional applications that reflect social cognitive learning principles are provided.

When you finish studying this chapter, you should be able to do the following:

- Describe and exemplify the process of triadic reciprocal causality.

- Distinguish between enactive and vicarious learning and between learning and performance.

- Explain the role of self-regulation in social cognitive theory.

- Define and exemplify three functions of modeling.

- Discuss the processes of observational learning.

- Explain the various factors that affect observational learning and performance.

- Discuss the motivational properties of goals, outcome expectations, and values.

- Define self-efficacy and explain its causes and effects in learning settings.

- Discuss how features of models (e.g., peers, multiple, coping) affect self-efficacy and learning.

- Describe some educational applications that reflect social cognitive theoretical principles.

CONCEPTUAL FRAMEWORK FOR LEARNING

Social cognitive theory makes some assumptions about learning and the performance of behaviors. These assumptions address the reciprocal interactions among persons, behaviors, and environments; enactive and vicarious learning (i.e., how learning occurs); the distinction between learning and performance; and the role of self-regulation (Zimmerman & Schunk, 2003).

Reciprocal Interactions

Bandura (1982a, 1986, 2001) discussed human behavior within a framework of *triadic reciprocality*, or reciprocal interactions among behaviors, environmental variables, and personal factors such as cognitions (Figure 4.1). These interacting determinants can be illustrated using *perceived self-efficacy*, or beliefs concerning one's capabilities to organize

Figure 4.1

Triadic reciprocality model of causality.
Source: Social Foundations of Thought and Action
by A. Bandura, © 1986. Reprinted by permission
of Pearson Education, Inc. Upper Saddle River, NJ.

and implement actions necessary to learn or perform behaviors at designated levels (Bandura, 1982b, 1986, 1997). With respect to the interaction of self-efficacy (personal factor) and behavior, research shows that self-efficacy beliefs influence such achievement behaviors as choice of tasks, persistence, effort expenditure, and skill acquisition (person → behavior; Schunk, 1991, 2001; Schunk & Pajares, 2002). Notice in the opening scenario that Donnetta's low self-efficacy led her to avoid hitting backhands in matches. In turn, students' actions modify their self-efficacy. As students work on tasks, they note their progress toward their learning goals (e.g., completing assignments, finishing sections of a term paper). Such progress indicators convey to students that they are capable of performing well and enhance their self-efficacy for continued learning (behavior → person).

Research on students with learning disabilities has demonstrated the interaction between self-efficacy and environmental factors. Many such students hold a low sense of self-efficacy for performing well (Licht & Kistner, 1986). Individuals in students' social environments may react to students based on attributes typically associated with students with learning disabilities (e.g., low self-efficacy) rather than on the individuals' actual abilities (person → environment). Some teachers, for example, judge such students less capable than students without disabilities and hold lower academic expectations for them, even in content areas where students with learning disabilities are performing adequately (Bryan & Bryan, 1983). In turn, teacher feedback can affect self-efficacy (environment → person). When a teacher tells a student, "I know you can do this," the student likely will feel more confident about succeeding.

Students' behaviors and classroom environments influence one another in many ways. Consider a typical instructional sequence in which the teacher presents information and asks students to direct their attention to the board. Environmental influence on behavior occurs when students look at the board without much conscious deliberation (environment → behavior). Students' behaviors often alter the instructional environment. If the teacher asks questions and students give the wrong answers, the teacher may reteach some points rather than continue the lesson (behavior → environment).

The model portrayed in Figure 4.1 does not imply that the directions of influence are always the same. At any given time, one factor may predominate. When environmental influences are weak, personal factors predominate. For instance, students allowed to write a report on a book of their choosing will select one they enjoy. However, a person caught in a burning house is apt to evacuate quickly; the environment dictates the behavior.

Much of the time the three factors interact. As a teacher presents a lesson to the class, students think about what the teacher is saying (environment influences cognition—a personal factor). Students who do not understand a point raise their hands to ask a question (cognition influences behavior). The teacher reviews the point (behavior influences environment). Eventually the teacher gives students work to accomplish (environment influences cognition, which influences behavior). As students work on the task, they believe they are performing it well (behavior influences cognition). They decide they like the task, ask the teacher if they can continue to work on it, and are allowed to do so (cognition influences behavior, which influences environment).

Enactive and Vicarious Learning

In social cognitive theory:

Learning is largely an information processing activity in which information about the structure of behavior and about environmental events is transformed into symbolic representations that serve as guides for action. (Bandura, 1986, p. 51)

Learning occurs either *enactively* through actual doing or *vicariously* by observing models perform (e.g., live, symbolic, portrayed electronically).

Enactive learning involves learning from the consequences of one's actions. Behaviors that result in successful consequences are retained; those that lead to failures are refined or discarded. Conditioning theories also say that people learn by doing, but social cognitive theory provides a different explanation. Skinner (1953) noted that cognitions may accompany behavioral change but do not influence it (Chapter 3). Social cognitive theory contends that behavioral consequences, rather than strengthening behaviors as postulated by conditioning theories, serve as sources of information and motivation. Consequences inform people of the accuracy or appropriateness of behavior. People who succeed at a task or are rewarded understand that they are performing well. When people fail or are punished, they know that they are doing something wrong and may try to correct the problem. Consequences also motivate people. People strive to learn behaviors they value and believe will have desirable consequences, whereas they avoid learning behaviors that are punished or otherwise not satisfying. People's cognitions, rather than consequences, affect learning.

Much human learning occurs *vicariously*, or without overt performance by the learner, at the time of learning. Common sources of vicarious learning are observing or listening to models who are live (appear in person), symbolic or nonhuman (e.g., televised talking animals, cartoon characters), electronic (e.g., television, computer, videotape, DVD), or in print (e.g., books, magazines). Vicarious sources accelerate learning over what would be possible if people had to perform every behavior for learning to occur. Vicarious sources also save people from personally experiencing negative consequences. We learn that poisonous snakes are dangerous through teaching by others, reading books, watching films, and so forth, rather than by experiencing the unpleasant consequences of their bites!

Learning complex skills typically occurs through a combination of observation and performance. Students first observe models explain and demonstrate skills, then practice them. This sequence is evident in the opening scenario, where the coach explains and demonstrates and Donnetta observes and practices. Aspiring golfers, for example, do not simply watch professionals play golf; rather, they engage in much practice and receive corrective feedback from instructors. Students observe teachers explain and demonstrate skills. Through observation, students often learn some components of a complex skill and not others. Practice gives teachers opportunities to provide corrective feedback to help students perfect their skills. As with enactive learning, response consequences from vicarious sources inform and motivate observers. Observers are more apt to learn modeled behaviors leading to successes than those resulting in failures. When people believe that modeled behaviors are useful, they attend carefully to models and mentally rehearse the behaviors.

Learning and Performance

Social cognitive theory distinguishes between new learning and performance of previously learned behaviors. Unlike conditioning theories, which contend that learning involves connecting responses to stimuli or following responses with consequences, social cognitive theory asserts that learning and performance are distinct processes. Although much learning occurs by doing, we learn a great deal by observing. Whether we ever perform what we learn depends on factors such as our motivation, interest, incentives to perform, perceived need, physical state, social pressures, and type of competing activities. Reinforcement, or the belief that it will be forthcoming, affects performance rather than learning.

Years ago, Tolman and Honzik (1930) experimentally demonstrated the learning–performance distinction. These researchers investigated *latent learning*, which is observational learning in the absence of a goal or reinforcement. Two groups of rats were allowed to wander through a maze for 10 trials. One group always was fed in the maze, whereas the other group was never fed. Rats fed in the maze quickly reduced their time and number of errors in running the maze, but time and errors for the other group remained high. Starting on the 11th trial, some rats from the nonreinforced group received food for running the maze. Both their time and number of errors quickly dropped to the levels of the group that always had been fed; the running times and error rates for rats that remained nonreinforced did not change. Rats in the nonreinforced group had learned features of the maze by wandering through it without reinforcement. When food was introduced, the latent learning quickly displayed itself.

Some school activities (e.g., review sessions) involve performance of previously learned skills, but much time is spent on learning. By observing teacher and peer models, students acquire knowledge they may not demonstrate at the time of learning. For example, students might learn in school that skimming is a useful procedure for acquiring the gist of a written passage and might learn a strategy for skimming, but may not employ that knowledge to promote learning until they are at home reading a text.

Self-Regulation

A key assumption of social cognitive theory is that people desire "to control the events that affect their lives" and to perceive themselves as agents (Bandura, 1997, p. 1). This sense of agency manifests itself in intentional acts, cognitive processes, and affective processes. *Perceived self-efficacy* (discussed later in this chapter) is a central process affecting one's sense of agency. Other key processes (also discussed in this chapter) are outcome expectations, values, goal setting, self-evaluation of goal progress, and cognitive modeling and self-instruction.

Central to this conception of personal agency is *self-regulation (self-regulated learning),* or the process whereby individuals activate and sustain behaviors, cognitions, and affects, which are systematically oriented toward the attainment of goals (Zimmerman & Schunk, 2001). By striving to self-regulate important aspects of their lives, individuals attain a greater sense of personal agency. In learning situations, self-regulation requires that learners have choices; for example, in what they do and how they do it. Choices are not always available to learners, as when teachers control many aspects by giving students an assignment and spelling out the parameters. When all or most task aspects are controlled, it is accurate to speak of external regulation or regulation by others. The potential for self-regulation varies depending on choices available to learners.

An early social cognitive perspective viewed self-regulation as comprising three processes: self-observation (or self-monitoring), self-judgment, and self-reaction (Bandura, 1986; Kanfer & Gaelick, 1986). Students enter learning activities with such goals as acquiring knowledge and problem-solving strategies, finishing workbook pages, and completing experiments. With these goals in mind, students observe, judge, and react to their perceived progress.

Zimmerman (1998, 2000) expanded this early view by proposing that self-regulation encompasses three phases: forethought, performance control, and self-reflection. The forethought phase precedes actual performance and comprises processes that set the stage for action. The performance control phase involves processes that occur during learning and affect attention and action. During the self-reflection phase, which occurs after performance, people respond behaviorally and mentally to their efforts. Zimmerman's model reflects the cyclical nature of triadic reciprocality, or the interaction of personal, behavioral, and environmental factors. It also expands the classical view, which covers task engagement, because it includes behaviors and mental processes that occur before and after engagement. The social cognitive theoretical perspective on self-regulation is covered in greater depth in Chapter 9.

MODELING PROCESSES

Modeling—a critical component in social cognitive theory—refers to behavioral, cognitive, and affective changes deriving from observing one or more models (Rosenthal & Bandura, 1978; Schunk, 1987, 1998; Zimmerman, 1977). Historically, modeling was equated with *imitation*, but modeling is a more inclusive concept. Some historical work is covered next to provide a background against which the significance of modeling research by Bandura and others can be appreciated.

Theories of Imitation

Throughout history, people have viewed imitation as an important means of transmitting behaviors (Rosenthal & Zimmerman, 1978). The ancient Greeks used the term *mimesis* to refer to learning through observation of the actions of others and of abstract models exemplifying literary and moral styles. Other perspectives on imitation relate it to instinct, development, conditioning, and instrumental behavior (Table 4.1).

Table 4.1
Theories of imitation.

View	Assumptions
Instinct	Observed actions elicit an instinctive drive to copy those actions.
Development	Children imitate actions that fit with existing cognitive structures.
Conditioning	Behaviors are imitated and reinforced through shaping. Imitation becomes a generalized response class.
Instrumental behavior	Imitation becomes a secondary drive through repeated reinforcement of responses matching those of models. Imitation results in drive reduction.

Instinct. At the beginning of the twentieth century, the dominant scientific view was that people possessed a natural instinct to imitate the actions of others (James, 1890; Tarde, 1903). James believed that imitation was largely responsible for socialization, but he did not explain the process by which imitation occurs. McDougall (1926) restricted his definition of imitation to the instinctive copying by one person of the actions of another.

Behaviorists rejected the instinct notion (and thus it became discarded) because it assumed the existence of an internal drive, and possibly a mental image, intervening between a stimulus (action of another person) and response (copying of that action). Watson (1924) believed that people's behaviors labeled "instinctive" resulted largely from training and therefore were learned.

Development. Piaget (1962) offered a different view of imitation. He believed that human development involved the acquisition of *schemes (schemas)*, or cognitive structures that underlie and make possible organized thought and action (Flavell, 1985). Thoughts and actions are not synonymous with schemes; they are overt manifestations of schemes. Schemes available to individuals determine how they react to events. Schemes reflect prior experiences and comprise one's knowledge at any given time.

Schemes presumably develop through maturation and experiences slightly more advanced than one's existing cognitive structures. Imitation is restricted to activities corresponding to existing schemes. Children may imitate actions they understand, but they should not imitate actions incongruent with their cognitive structures. Development, therefore, must precede imitation.

This view severely limits the potential of imitation to create and modify cognitive structures. Further, there is little empirical support for this developmental position (Rosenthal & Zimmerman, 1978). In an early study, Valentine (1930b) found that infants could imitate actions within their capabilities that they had not previously performed. Infants showed a strong tendency to imitate unusual actions commanding attention. The imitation was not always immediate, and actions often had to be repeated before infants would imitate them. The individual performing the original actions was important: Infants were most likely to imitate their mothers. These and results from subsequent research show that imitation is not a simple reflection of developmental level but rather may serve an important role in promoting development (Rosenthal & Zimmerman, 1978).

Conditioning. Conditioning theorists construe imitation in terms of associations. According to Humphrey (1921), imitation is a type of circular reaction in which each response serves as a stimulus for the next response. A baby may start crying (response) because of a pain (stimulus). The baby hears its own crying (auditory stimulus), which then becomes a stimulus for subsequent crying. Through conditioning, small reflex units form progressively more complex response chains.

Skinner's (1953) operant conditioning theory treats imitation as a generalized response class (Chapter 3). In the three-term contingency ($S^D \to R \to S^R$), a modeled act serves as the S^D (discriminative stimulus). Imitation occurs when an observer performs the same response (R) and receives reinforcement (S^R). This contingency becomes established early in life. For example, a parent makes a sound ("Dada"), the child imitates, and the parent delivers reinforcement (smile, hug). Once an imitative response class is established, it can be maintained on an intermittent reinforcement schedule. Children imitate the behaviors of models (parents, friends) as long as the models remain discriminative stimuli for reinforcement.

A limitation of this view is that one can imitate only those responses one can perform. In fact, much research shows that diverse types of behaviors can be acquired through observation (Rosenthal & Zimmerman, 1978). Another limitation concerns the need for reinforcement to produce and sustain imitation. Research by Bandura and others shows that observers learn from models in the absence of reinforcement to models or observers (Bandura, 1986). Reinforcement primarily affects learners' performance of previously learned responses rather than new learning.

Instrumental Behavior. Miller and Dollard (1941) proposed an elaborate theory of imitation, or *matched-dependent behavior*, which contends that imitation is instrumental learned behavior because it leads to reinforcement. Matched-dependent behavior is matched to (the same as) that of the model and depends on, or is elicited by, the model's action.

Miller and Dollard believed that initially the imitator responds to behavioral cues in trial-and-error fashion, but eventually the imitator performs the correct response and is reinforced. Responses performed by imitators previously were learned.

This conception of imitation as learned instrumental behavior was an important advance, but it has problems. Like other historical views, this theory postulates that new responses are not created through imitation; rather, imitation represents performance of learned behaviors. This position cannot account for learning through imitation, for delayed imitation (i.e., when imitators perform the matching responses some time after the actions are performed by the model), or for imitated behaviors that are not reinforced (Bandura & Walters, 1963). This narrow conception of imitation restricts its usefulness to imitative responses corresponding closely to those portrayed by models.

Functions of Modeling

Bandura (1986) distinguished three key functions of modeling: response facilitation, inhibition/disinhibition, and observational learning (Table 4.2).

Table 4.2
Functions of modeling.

Function	Underlying Process
Response facilitation	Social prompts create motivational inducements for observers to model the actions ("going along with the crowd").
Inhibition and disinhibition	Modeled behaviors create expectations in observers that they will experience similar consequences should they perform the actions.
Observational learning	Processes include attention, retention, production, and motivation.

Response Facilitation. People learn many skills and behaviors that they do not perform because they lack motivation to do so. *Response facilitation* refers to modeled actions that serve as social prompts for observers to behave accordingly. Consider an elementary teacher who has set up an attractive display in a corner of the classroom. When the first students enter in the morning, they spot the display and immediately go to look at it. When other students enter the room, they see a group in the corner, so they, too, move to the corner to see what everyone is looking at. Several students together serve as a social prompt for others to join them, even though the latter may not know why the others are gathered.

Response facilitation effects are common. Have you ever seen a group of people looking in one direction? This can serve as a cue for you to look in the same direction. Newcomers at meetings of volunteer groups may watch with interest as a basket is passed for donations. If most people put in a dollar, that serves as a signal that a dollar is an acceptable donation. Note that response facilitation does not reflect true learning because people already know how to perform the behaviors. Rather, the models serve as cues for observer's actions. Observers gain information about the appropriateness of behavior and may be motivated to perform the actions if models receive positive consequences.

Response facilitation modeling may occur without conscious awareness. Chartrand and Bargh (1999) found evidence for a *Chameleon effect,* whereby people nonconsciously mimic behaviors and mannerisms of people in their social environments. Simply perceiving behavior may trigger a response to act accordingly.

Inhibition/Disinhibition. Observing a model can strengthen or weaken inhibitions to perform behaviors previously learned. *Inhibition* occurs when models are punished for performing certain actions, which in turn stops or prevents observers from acting accordingly. *Disinhibition* occurs when models perform threatening or prohibited activities without experiencing negative consequences, which may lead observers to perform the same behaviors. Inhibitory and disinhibitory effects on behavior occur because the modeled displays convey to observers that similar consequences are probable if they perform the modeled behaviors. Such information also may affect emotions (e.g., increase or decrease anxiety) and motivation.

Teachers' actions can inhibit or disinhibit classroom misbehavior. Unpunished student misbehavior may prove disinhibiting: Students who observe modeled misbehavior not punished might start misbehaving themselves. Conversely, misbehavior in other students may be inhibited when a teacher disciplines one student for misbehaving. Observers are more likely to believe that they, too, will be disciplined if they continue to misbehave and are spotted by the teacher.

Inhibition and disinhibition are similar to response facilitation in that behaviors reflect actions people already have learned. One difference is that response facilitation generally involves behaviors that are socially acceptable, whereas inhibited and disinhibited actions often have moral or legal overtones (i.e., involve breaking rules or laws) and have accompanying emotions (e.g., fears). Looting may occur during a riot or natural disaster if looters go unpunished, which disinhibits looting (an illegal act) in some observers.

Observational Learning. Observational learning through modeling occurs when observers display new patterns of behavior that, prior to exposure to the modeled behaviors, have a zero probability of occurrence even when motivation is high (Bandura, 1969). A key mechanism is the information conveyed by models to observers of ways to produce new behaviors (Rosenthal & Zimmerman, 1978). In the opening scenario, Donnetta needed to learn (or relearn) the correct procedure for hitting a backhand. Observational learning comprises four processes: attention, retention, production, and motivation (Bandura, 1986; Table 4.3).

The first process is observer *attention* to relevant events so that they are meaningfully perceived. At any given moment one can attend to many activities. Characteristics of the model and the observer influence one's attention to models. Task features also command attention, especially unusual size, shape, color, or sound. Teachers often make modeling more distinctive with bright colors and oversized features. Attention also is influenced by perceived functional value of modeled activities. Modeled activities that observers believe

Table 4.3
Processes of observational learning.

Process	Activities
Attention	Student attention is directed by physically accentuating relevant task features, subdividing complex activities into parts, using competent models, and demonstrating usefulness of modeled behaviors.
Retention	Retention is increased by rehearsing information to be learned, coding in visual and symbolic form, and relating new material to information previously stored in memory.
Production	Behaviors produced are compared to one's conceptual (mental) representation. Feedback helps to correct deficiencies.
Motivation	Consequences of modeled behaviors inform observers of functional value and appropriateness. Consequences motivate by creating outcome expectations and raising self-efficacy.

are important and likely to lead to rewarding outcomes command greater attention. Students believe that most teacher activities are highly functional because they are intended to enhance student learning. Learners also are apt to believe that their teachers are highly competent, which enhances attention. Factors that promote the perception of model competence are modeled actions that lead to success and symbolic indicators of competence, such as one's title or position.

The second process is *retention*, which requires cognitively organizing, rehearsing, coding, and transforming modeled information for storage in memory. Observational learning postulates two modes of storing knowledge. A modeled display can be stored as an image, in verbal form, or both (Bandura, 1977b). Imaginal coding is especially important for activities not easily described in words; for example, motor skills performed so rapidly that individual movements merge into a larger organized sequence or act (e.g., golf swing). Much cognitive skill learning relies upon verbal coding of rules or procedures. (Storage of information in memory is discussed in Chapter 5.)

Rehearsal, or the mental review of information, serves a key role in the retention of knowledge (Chapter 5). Bandura and Jeffery (1973) found benefits of coding and rehearsal. Adults were presented with complex-modeled movement configurations. Some participants coded these movements at the time of presentation by assigning to them numerical or verbal designators. Other participants were not given coding instructions but were told to subdivide the movements to remember them. In addition, participants either were or were not allowed to rehearse the codes or movements following presentation. Both coding and rehearsal enhanced retention of modeled events; individuals who coded and rehearsed showed the best recall. Rehearsal without coding and coding without rehearsal were less effective.

The third observational learning process is *production*, which involves translating visual and symbolic conceptions of modeled events into overt behaviors. Many simple actions may be learned by simply observing them; subsequent production by observers indicates learning. Rarely, however, are complex behaviors learned solely through observation. Learners often will acquire a rough approximation of a complex skill by observing modeled demonstrations (Bandura, 1977b). They then refine their skills with practice, corrective feedback, and reteaching.

Problems in producing modeled behaviors arise not only because information is inadequately coded but also because learners experience difficulty translating coded information in memory into overt action. For example, a child may have a basic understanding of how to tie shoelaces but not be able to translate that knowledge into behavior. Teachers who suspect that students are having trouble demonstrating what they have learned may need to test students in different ways.

Motivation, the fourth process, influences observational learning because people are more likely to engage in the preceding three processes (attention, retention, production) for modeled actions that they feel are important. Individuals form expectations about anticipated outcomes of actions based on consequences experienced by them and models (Bandura, 1997). They perform those actions they believe will result in rewarding outcomes and avoid acting in ways they believe will be responded to negatively (Schunk, 1987). Persons also act based on their values, performing activities they value and avoiding those they find unsatisfying, regardless of the consequences to themselves or others. People forgo money, prestige, and power when they believe activities they must engage in to receive these rewards are unethical (e.g., questionable business practices).

Motivation is a critical process of observational learning that teachers promote in various ways, including making learning interesting, relating material to student interests, having students set goals and monitor goal progress, providing feedback indicating increasing competence, and stressing the value of learning. These and other factors are considered in Chapter 8.

Cognitive Skill Learning

Observational learning expands the range and rate of learning over what could occur through shaping (Chapter 3), where each response must be performed and reinforced. Modeled portrayals of cognitive skills are standard features in classrooms. In a common instructional sequence, a teacher explains and demonstrates the skills to be acquired, after which the students receive guided practice while the teacher checks for student understanding. The skills are retaught if students experience difficulty. When the teacher is satisfied that students have a basic understanding, they may engage in independent practice while the teacher periodically monitors their work. Examples of teacher modeling are given in Application 4.1.

Many features of instruction incorporate models, and there is much research evidence showing that students of various ages learn skills and strategies by observing models (Horner, 2004; Schunk, 2008). Two especially germane applications of modeling to instruction are cognitive modeling and self-instruction.

Cognitive Modeling. *Cognitive modeling* incorporates modeled explanation and demonstration with verbalization of the model's thoughts and reasons for performing given actions (Meichenbaum, 1977). Coach Martin used cognitive modeling with Donnetta. In teaching division skills, a teacher might verbalize the following in response to the problem $276 \div 4$:

> First, I have to decide what number to divide 4 into. I take 276, start on the left, and move toward the right until I have a number the same as or larger than 4. Is 2 larger than 4? No. Is 27 larger than 4? Yes. So my first division will be 4 into 27. Now I need to multiply 4 by a number that will give an answer the same as or slightly smaller than 27. How about 5? $5 \times 4 = 20$. No, too small. Let's try $6.6 \times 4 = 24$. Maybe. Let's try $7.7 \times 4 = 28$. No, too large. So 6 is correct.

Cognitive modeling can include other types of statements. Errors may be built into the modeled demonstration to show students how to recognize and cope with them. Self-reinforcing statements, such as "I'm doing well," also are useful, especially with students who encounter difficulties learning and doubt their capabilities to perform well.

Researchers have substantiated the useful role of cognitive modeling and shown that modeling combined with explanation is more effective in teaching skills than explanation alone (Rosenthal & Zimmerman, 1978). Schunk (1981) compared the effects of cognitive modeling with those of didactic instruction on children's long-division self-efficacy and achievement. Children lacking division skills received instruction and practice. In

APPLICATION 4.1
Teacher Modeling

Teachers often incorporate modeled demonstrations into lessons designed to teach students diverse skills such as solving mathematical problems, identifying main ideas in text, writing topic sentences, using power tools, and executing defensive basketball maneuvers. Modeled demonstrations can be used to teach elementary school children how to head their papers properly. In her third-grade class, Kathy Stone might draw on the board a sketch of the paper students are using. She then can review the heading procedure step by step, explaining and demonstrating how to complete it.

In his ninth-grade American history class, Jim Marshall models how to study for a test. Working through several chapters, he explains and demonstrates how to locate and summarize the major terms and points for each section.

In a middle school life skills class, students can learn how to insert a sleeve into a garment through modeled demonstrations.

The teacher might begin by describing the process and then use visual aids to portray the procedure. The teacher could conclude the presentation by demonstrating the process at a sewing machine.

Several students in Gina Brown's undergraduate class have been coming to her office after class with questions about how to present their findings from their field projects. During the next class, she uses a research project she completed to demonstrate how one might present findings to a group. She uses handouts, charts, and PowerPoint® to illustrate ways to present data.

A drama teacher can model various performance skills while working with students as they practice a play. The teacher can demonstrate desired voice inflections, mood, volume, and body movements for each character in the play. While presenting a word decoding lesson using phonics, a first-grade teacher can demonstrate sounding out each letter in a list of words.

the cognitive modeling condition, students observed an adult model explain and demonstrate division operations while applying them to sample problems. In the didactic instruction condition, students reviewed instructional material that explained and demonstrated the operations, but they were not exposed to models. Cognitive modeling enhanced children's division achievement better than did didactic instruction.

Self-Instruction. *Self-instruction* has been used to teach students to regulate their activities during learning (Meichenbaum, 1977). In an early study, Meichenbaum and Goodman (1971) incorporated cognitive modeling into self-instructional training with impulsive second graders in a special-education class. The procedure included:

- *Cognitive modeling:* Adult tells child what to do while adult performs the task.
- *Overt guidance:* Child performs under direction of adult.
- *Overt self-guidance:* Child performs while self-instructing aloud.
- *Faded overt self-guidance:* Child whispers instructions while performing task.
- *Covert self-instruction:* Child performs while guided by inner silent speech.

Self-instruction often is used to slow down children's rate of performing. An adult model used the following statements during a line-drawing task:

> Okay, what is it I have to do? You want me to copy the picture with the different lines. I have to go slow and be careful. Okay, draw the line down, down, good; then to the right, that's it; now down some more and to the left. Good, I'm doing fine so far. Remember go slow. Now back up again. No, I was supposed to go down. That's okay, just erase the line carefully. . . . Good. Even if I make an error I can go on slowly and carefully. Okay, I have to go down now. Finished. I did it. (Meichenbaum & Goodman, 1971, p. 117)

Note that the model makes a mistake and shows how to deal with it. This is an important form of learning for students with attention-deficit disorders, hyperactivity, and behavioral problems because they may become frustrated and quit easily following errors. Meichenbaum and Goodman (1971) found that cognitive modeling slowed down response times, but that the self-instructions decreased errors.

Self-instruction has been used with a variety of tasks and types of students (Fish & Pervan, 1985). It is especially useful for students with learning disabilities (Wood, Rosenberg, & Carran, 1993) and for teaching students to work strategically. In teaching reading comprehension, the preceding instructions might be modified as follows: "What is it I have to do? I have to find the topic sentence of the paragraph. The topic sentence is what the paragraph is about. I start by looking for a sentence that sums up the details or tells what the paragraph is about" (McNeil, 1987, p. 96). Statements for coping with difficulties ("I haven't found it yet, but that's all right") can be built into the modeled demonstration.

Motor Skill Learning

Social cognitive theory postulates that motor skill learning involves constructing a mental model that provides the conceptual representation of the skill for response production and serves as the standard for correcting responses subsequent to receiving feedback (Bandura, 1986; McCullagh, 1993; Weiss, Ebbeck, & Wiese-Bjornstal, 1993). The conceptual representation is formed by transforming observed sequences of behaviors into visual and symbolic codes to be cognitively rehearsed. Individuals usually have a mental model of a skill before they attempt to perform it. For example, by observing tennis players, individuals construct a mental model of such activities as the serve, volley, and backhand. These mental models are rudimentary in that they require feedback and correction to be perfected, but they allow learners to perform approximations of the skills at the outset of training. We saw this in the opening scenario where Donnetta needed to construct a mental model of a backhand. In the case of novel or complex behaviors, learners may have no prior mental model and need to observe modeled demonstrations before attempting the behaviors.

The social cognitive approach to motor skill learning differs from traditional explanations. Adams's (1971) *closed-loop theory* postulates that people develop perceptual (internal) traces of motor skill movements through practice and feedback. These traces serve as the reference for correct movements. As one performs a behavior, one receives internal (sensory) and external (knowledge of results) feedback and compares the feedback to the trace. The discrepancy serves to correct the trace. Learning is enhanced when feedback is accurate, and eventually the behavior can be performed without feedback. Adams distinguished two memory mechanisms, one that produces the response and one that evaluates its correctness.

A different view is based on *schema theory* (Schmidt, 1975). (This theory as it relates to information processing is covered in Chapter 5.) Schmidt postulated that people store in memory much information regarding motor skill movements, including the initial conditions, the characteristics of the generalized motor sequence, the results of the movement, knowledge of results, and sensory feedback. Learners store this information in two general schemas, or organized memory networks comprising related information. The recall schema deals with response production; the recognition schema is used to evaluate responses.

Social cognitive theory contends that by observing others, people form a cognitive representation that initiates subsequent responses and serves as a standard for evaluating the correctness of responses (Bandura, 1986). Motor learning theories differ from social cognitive theory in that the former place greater emphasis on error correction after acting and postulate two memory mechanisms to store information and evaluate accuracy (McCullagh, 1993). Social cognitive theory also highlights the role of personal cognitions (goals and expectations) in the development of motor skills (Application 4.2).

A problem in motor skill learning is that learners cannot observe aspects of their performances that lie outside their field of vision. People who are swinging a golf club, hitting a tennis serve, kicking a football, throwing a baseball, or hurling a discus, cannot observe many aspects of these sequences. Not being able to see what one is doing requires one to rely on kinesthetic feedback and compare it with one's conceptual representation. The absence of visual feedback makes learning difficult.

Carroll and Bandura (1982) exposed learners to models performing a motor skill, and then asked them to reproduce the motor pattern. The experimenters gave some learners concurrent visual feedback of their performances by running a video camera and allowing them to observe their real-time performances on a monitor. Other learners

---

APPLICATION 4.2
Motor Skill Learning

Observational learning is useful for learning motor skills. To teach students to dribble a basketball, physical education teachers begin with skill exercises, such as standing stationary and bouncing the ball and moving and bouncing the ball with each step. After introducing each skill leading to the final sequence, teachers can demonstrate slowly and precisely what the students are to model. The students then should practice that skill. If students have

difficulty on a particular step, teachers can repeat the modeled demonstration before the students continue practicing.

For high school students to successfully learn a dance to perform in the spring musical, the teacher needs to demonstrate and slowly progress toward putting the dance to music. The teacher may break up the dance, working on each step separately, gradually combining steps and eventually putting all the various steps together with the music.

did not receive visual feedback. When visual feedback was given before learners formed a mental model of the motor behavior, it had no effect on performance. Once learners had an adequate model in mind, visual feedback enhanced their accurate reproduction of the modeled behaviors. Visual feedback eliminated discrepancies between their conceptual models and their actions once the former were in place.

Researchers also have examined the efficacy of using models to teach motor skills. Weiss (1983) compared the effects of a silent model (visual demonstration) with those of a verbal model (visual demonstration plus verbal explanation) on the learning of a six-part motor skill obstacle course. Older children (ages 7 through 9 years) learned equally well with either model; younger children (ages 4 through 6 years) learned better with the verbal model. Perhaps the addition of the verbalizations created a cognitive model that helped to maintain children's attention and assisted with coding of information in memory. Weiss and Klint (1987) found that children in visual-model and no-model conditions who verbally rehearsed the sequence of actions learned the motor skills better than children who did not verbally rehearse. Collectively these results suggest that some form of verbalization may be critically important in acquisition of motor skills.

INFLUENCES ON LEARNING AND PERFORMANCE

Observing models does not guarantee that learning will occur or that learned behaviors will be performed later. Several factors influence vicarious learning and performance of learned behaviors (Table 4.4). Developmental status, model prestige and competence, and vicarious consequences are discussed here; outcome expectations, goal setting, and self-efficacy are discussed in sections that follow.

Developmental Status of Learners

Learning depends heavily on developmental factors (Wigfield & Eccles, 2002), and these include students' abilities to learn from models (Bandura, 1986). Research shows that children as young as 6–12 months can perform behaviors displayed by models (Nielsen, 2006); however, young children have difficulty attending to modeled events for long periods and distinguishing relevant from irrelevant cues. Information processing functions such as rehearsing, organizing, and elaborating (Chapters 5 and 10) improve with development. Older children acquire a more extensive knowledge base to help them comprehend new information, and they become more capable of using memory strategies. Young children may encode modeled events in terms of physical properties (e.g., a ball is round, it bounces, you throw it), whereas older children often represent information visually or symbolically.

With respect to the production process, information acquired through observation cannot be performed if children lack the requisite physical capabilities. Production also requires translating into action information stored in memory, comparing performance with memorial representation, and correcting performance as necessary. The ability to self-regulate one's actions for longer periods increases with development. Motivational inducements for action also vary depending on development. Young children are motivated

Table 4.4
Factors affecting observational learning and performance.

Characteristic	Effects on Modeling
Developmental status	Improvements with development include longer attention and increased capacity to process information, use strategies, compare performances with memorial representations, and adopt intrinsic motivators.
Model prestige and competence	Observers pay greater attention to competent, high-status models. Consequences of modeled behaviors convey information about functional value. Observers attempt to learn actions that they believe they will need to perform.
Vicarious consequences	Consequences to models convey information about behavioral appropriateness and probable outcomes of actions. Valued consequences motivate observers. Similarity in attributes or competence signals appropriateness and heightens motivation.
Outcome expectations	Observers are more likely to perform modeled actions which they believe are appropriate and will result in rewarding outcomes.
Goal setting	Observers are more likely to attend to models who demonstrate behaviors that help observers attain goals.
Values	Observers are more likely to attend to models who display behaviors that the observers believe are important and find self-satisfying.
Self-efficacy	Observers attend to models when they believe they are capable of learning or performing the modeled behavior. Observation of similar models affects self-efficacy ("If they can do it, I can too").

by the immediate consequences of their actions. As children mature, they are more likely to perform modeled actions consistent with their goals and values (Bandura, 1986).

Model Prestige and Competence

Modeled behaviors vary in usefulness. Behaviors that successfully deal with the environment command greater attention than those that do so less effectively. People attend to a model in part because they believe they might face the same situation themselves and they want to learn the necessary actions to succeed. Students attend to a teacher because the teacher prompts them but also because they believe they will have to demonstrate the same skills and behaviors. Donnetta attends to her coach because the coach is an expert tennis player and because Donnetta knows she needs to improve her game. When models compete for attention, people are more likely to attend to competent models.

Model competence is inferred from the outcomes of modeled actions (success, failure) and from symbols that denote competence. An important attribute is prestige. Models who have gained distinction are more apt to command attention than those of lower prestige. Attendance usually is higher at a talk given by a well-known person than by one who is less known. In most instances, high-status models have ascended to their positions because they are competent and perform well. Their actions have greater functional value for observers, who are apt to believe that rewards will be forthcoming if they act accordingly.

APPLICATION 4.3
Model Attributes

People attend to models partly because they believe they will have to face the same situations themselves. Effective use of model prestige and competence can help motivate secondary students to attend to and learn from lessons.

If the use of alcohol is a problem in a high school, school personnel might deliver a program on alcohol education and abuse (prevention, treatment) to include speakers from outside the school. Influential speakers would be recent high school and college graduates, persons who have successfully overcome problems with alcohol, and those who work with alcohol abusers. The relative similarity in age of the models to the students, coupled with the models' personal experiences, should make the models appear highly competent. Such individuals might have more impact on the students than literature or lessons taught by teachers and counselors.

At the elementary school level, using peers to help teach academic skills can promote learning and self-efficacy among the learners. Children may identify with other children who have had the same difficulties. Kathy Stone has four students in her class who are having trouble learning to divide. She pairs these four students with students who have demonstrated that they understand how to perform long division. A child explaining to a classmate how to solve a long-division problem will do so in a way that the classmate can understand.

Parents and teachers are high-status models for most children. The scope of adult influence on children's modeling can generalize to many domains. Although teachers are important models in the development of children's intellect, their influence typically spreads to such other areas as social behaviors, educational attainments, dress, and mannerisms. The effects of model prestige often generalize to areas in which models have no particular competence, such as when adolescents adopt the dress and products touted by prominent entertainers in commercials (Schunk & Miller, 2002). Modeling becomes more prevalent with development, but young children are highly susceptible to adult influence (Application 4.3).

Vicarious Consequences to Models

Vicarious consequences to models can affect observers' learning and performance of modeled actions. Observers who watch as models are rewarded for their actions are more likely to attend to the models and rehearse and code their actions for retention. Vicarious rewards motivate observers to perform the same actions themselves. Thus, vicarious consequences serve to *inform* and *motivate* (Bandura, 1986).

Information. The consequences experienced by models convey information to observers about the types of actions most likely to be effective. Observing competent models perform actions that result in success conveys information to observers about the sequence of actions one should use to succeed. By observing modeled behaviors and their consequences, people form beliefs concerning which behaviors will be rewarded and which will be punished.

In a classic demonstration, Bandura, Ross, and Ross (1963) exposed children to live aggressive models, filmed aggression, or aggression portrayed by cartoon characters. The models, who pummeled a Bobo doll by hitting, throwing, kicking, and sitting on it, were neither rewarded nor punished, which most likely conveyed to the observers that the modeled behaviors were acceptable. Children subsequently were allowed to play with a Bobo doll. Compared with youngsters not exposed to aggression, children who viewed aggressive models displayed significantly higher levels of aggression. The type of aggressive model (live, filmed, cartoon) made no difference in children's level of aggression.

Similarity to models is important (Schunk, 1987, 1995). The more alike observers are to models, the greater is the probability that observers will consider similar actions socially appropriate for them to perform. Model attributes often are predictive of the functional value of behaviors. Most social situations are structured so that behavioral appropriateness depends on factors such as age, gender, or status. Similarity ought to be especially influential when observers have little information about functional value. Thus, modeled tasks with which observers are unfamiliar or those that are not immediately followed by consequences may be highly influenced by model similarity (Akamatsu & Thelen, 1974).

Although some research shows that children are more likely to attend to and learn from same-sex models (Maccoby & Jacklin, 1974), other research suggests that model gender has a greater effect on performance than on learning (Bandura & Bussey, 2004; Perry & Bussey, 1979; Spence, 1984). Children learn from models of both sexes and categorize behaviors as appropriate for both sexes or as more appropriate for members of one sex. Children who perform behaviors appropriate for members of either sex or for members of their sex may do so because they believe those behaviors are more likely to be rewarded (Schunk, 1987). Model gender, therefore, seems important as a conveyor of information about task appropriateness (Zimmerman & Koussa, 1975). When children are uncertain about the gender appropriateness of a modeled behavior, they may model same-sex peers because they are more likely to think that those actions are socially acceptable.

Model–observer similarity in age is important when children perceive the actions of same-age peers to be more appropriate for themselves than the actions of younger or older models (Schunk, 1987). Brody and Stoneman (1985) found that in the absence of competence information, children were more likely to model the actions of same-age peers. When children were provided with competence information, modeling was enhanced by similar competence regardless of model age.

Researchers have found no evidence that children consistently learn any better or worse from peers or adults (Schunk, 1987); however, children and adults use different teaching strategies. Children often use nonverbal demonstrations and link instruction to specific items (e.g., how to do it); adults typically employ more verbal instruction stressing general principles and relate information to be learned to other material (Ellis &

Rogoff, 1982). Peer instruction may be quite beneficial with students with learning problems and with those who do not process verbal material well.

The highest degree of model–observer similarity occurs when one is one's own model. *Self-modeling* has been used to develop social, vocational, motor, cognitive, and instructional skills (Bellini & Akullian, 2007; Dowrick, 1983, 1999; Hartley, Bray, & Kehle, 1998; Hitchcock, Dowrick, & Prater, 2003) In a typical procedure, one's performance is recorded, and he or she subsequently views the recording. Observing a self-modeled performance is a form of review and is especially informative for skills one cannot watch while performing (e.g., gymnastics).

Performances that contain errors are problematic (Hosford, 1981). Commentary from a knowledgeable individual while the performer is viewing the recording helps to prevent the performer from becoming discouraged; the expert can explain how to execute the skills better. Viewing a skillful performance conveys that one is capable of learning and can continue to make progress with further work, which raises self-efficacy.

Schunk and Hanson (1989b) found benefits of self-modeling during acquisition of arithmetic (fraction) skills. Children received instruction and problem-solving practice. Self-modeling students were videotaped while successfully solving problems and were shown their tapes, others were videotaped but not shown their tapes until after the study was completed (to control for effects of taping), and students in a third condition were not taped (to control for effects of participation). Self-modeling children scored higher on self-efficacy for learning, motivation, and posttest self-efficacy and achievement. Researchers found no differences between mastery self-model students who viewed tapes of their successful problem solving and self-model children whose tapes portrayed their gradual improvement as they acquired skills, which supports the point that the perception of progress or mastery can build efficacy (Schunk, 1995).

Motivation. Observers who see models rewarded become motivated to act accordingly. Perceived similarity enhances these motivational effects, which depend in part on self-efficacy (Bandura, 1982b, 1997). Observing similar others succeed raises observers' motivation and self-efficacy; they are apt to believe that if others can succeed, they can as well. Such motivational effects are common in classrooms. Students who observe other students performing a task well may be motivated to try their best.

Reinforcing models influences observers' behaviors (Rosenthal & Zimmerman, 1978). Of particular educational importance is the observation of effort that leads to success (Schunk, 1995). Seeing others succeed with effort and receiving praise from teachers may motivate observing peers to work harder. Students may become more motivated by watching similar others succeed than by those who they believe are superior in competence.

But vicarious success will not sustain behavior over long periods. Actual performance successes eventually become necessary. Motivation is boosted when students observe teachers giving praise and high grades to others for hard work and good performances; motivation is sustained over time when students believe their own efforts are leading to better performances.

MOTIVATIONAL PROCESSES

Among the important influences on enactive and vicarious learning and on performance of learned behaviors are observers' goals, outcome expectations, values, and self-efficacy. This section covers the first three; self-efficacy is addressed in the next section.

Goals

Much human behavior is sustained over long periods in the absence of immediate external incentives. Such persistence depends on goal setting and self-evaluations of progress. A *goal* reflects one's purpose and refers to quantity, quality, or rate of performance (Locke & Latham, 1990, 2002; Locke, Shaw, Saari, & Latham, 1981; Schunk, 1990). *Goal setting* involves establishing a standard or objective to serve as the aim of one's actions. People can set their own goals or goals can be established by others (parents, teachers, supervisors).

Goals were a central feature of Tolman's (1932, 1942, 1951, 1959) theory of *purposive behaviorism.* Like most psychologists of his time, Tolman was trained in behaviorism. His experiments resembled those of Thorndike and Skinner (Chapter 3) because they dealt with responses to stimuli under varying environmental conditions. But he disagreed with conditioning theorists over their view of behavior as a series of stimulus–response connections. He contended that learning is more than the strengthening of responses to stimuli, and he recommended a focus on *molar behavior*—a large sequence of goal-directed behavior.

The "purposive" aspect of Tolman's (1932) theory refers to his belief that behavior is goal directed: "Behavior . . . always seems to have the character of getting-to or getting-from a specific goal-object, or goal situation" (p. 10). Stimuli in the environment (e.g., objects, paths) are means to goal attainment. They cannot be studied in isolation; rather, entire behavioral sequences must be studied to understand why people engage in particular actions. High school students whose goal is to attend a leading university study hard in their classes. By focusing only on the studying, researchers miss the purpose of the behavior. The students do not study because they have been reinforced for studying in the past (i.e., by getting good grades). Rather, studying is a means to intermediate goals (learning, high grades), which, in turn, enhance the likelihood of acceptance to the university. "Because behavior is purposive it also is cognitive: And such purposes and such cognitions are just as evident . . . if this behavior be that of a rat as if it be that of a human being" (Tolman, 1932, p. 12).

Tolman's suggestion that rats and other lower animals pursue goals and act as if they have cognitions was rejected by conditioning theorists. Tolman qualified his use of "purpose" and "cognition" by noting that they are defined objectively. The behavior of people and animals is goal oriented. They act "as if" they are pursuing a goal and have chosen a means for attainment. Thus, Tolman went well beyond simple stimulus–response associations to discuss underlying cognitive mechanisms.

Social cognitive theory contends that goals enhance learning and performance through their effects on perceptions of progress, self-efficacy, and self-evaluations (Bandura, 1988, 1997; Locke & Latham, 1990, 2002; Schunk, 1990). Initially, people must make a *commitment* to attempt to attain their goals because goals do not affect performance without commitment. As they work on the task, they compare their current performances with goals. Positive self-evaluations of progress raise self-efficacy and sustain motivation. A perceived discrepancy between present performance and the goal may create dissatisfaction, which can enhance effort. Goals also can be acquired through modeling. People are more likely to attend to models when they believe the modeled behaviors will help them attain their goals.

Goals motivate people to exert effort necessary to meet task demands and to persist at the task over time (Locke & Latham, 1990, 2002). Goals also direct individuals' attention to relevant task features, behaviors to be performed, and potential outcomes and can affect how they process information. Goals give people "tunnel vision" to focus on the task, select task-appropriate strategies, and decide on the effectiveness of their approach, all of which are likely to raise performance.

But goals, by themselves, do not automatically enhance learning and motivation. Rather, the properties of specificity, proximity, and difficulty enhance self-perceptions, motivation, and learning (Locke & Latham, 2002; Nussbaum & Kardash, 2005; Application 4.4 and Table 4.5).

APPLICATION 4.4
Goal Properties

Goal properties are easily incorporated into lessons. In her third-grade class, Kathy Stone introduced a new spelling unit to her class by stating the following goal:

> Of our 20 words this week, I know that all of you will be able to learn to spell the first 15. We are going to work very diligently in class on these words, and I expect you to do the same at home. With our work at school and at home, I know that all of you will be able to spell these words correctly by Friday. The last 5 words are more difficult. These will be our bonus words.

This goal is specific, but for some children it is distant and might be viewed as too difficult. To ensure that all students achieve the overall goal, Kathy Stone sets short-term goals each day: "Today we are going to work on these 5 words. By the end of class time I know that you will be able to spell these 5 words." Children should view the daily goals as easier to attain than the weekly goal. To further

ensure goal attainment, she will make sure that the 15 words selected for mastery by Friday challenge the students but are not overly difficult.

A teacher working with students on keyboarding might establish a words-per-minute goal for students to reach by the end of the semester:

> Students, this semester I know that all of you will be able to learn to use the keyboard. Some of you, because of other experiences or certain dexterity talent, will be able to type faster, but I know that all of you will be able to enter at least 30 words per minute with no mistakes by the end of the semester.

To help students achieve this goal, the teacher might set weekly short-term goals. Thus, the first week the goal might be 10 words per minute with no mistakes, the second week 12 words per minute, and so forth, increasing the number each week.

Table 4.5
Goal properties and their effects.

Goal Property	Effects on Behavior
Specificity	Goals with specific standards of performance increase motivation and raise self-efficacy because goal progress is easy to gauge.
Proximity	Proximal goals increase motivation and self-efficacy and are especially important for young children who may not divide a long-term goal into a series of short-term goals.
Difficulty	Challenging but attainable goals raise motivation and self-efficacy better than easy or hard goals.

Specificity. Goals that incorporate specific standards of performance are more likely to enhance learning and activate self-evaluations than are general goals (e.g., "Do your best;" Locke & Latham, 1990). Specific goals boost task performance by better describing the amount of effort that success requires, and they promote self-efficacy because it is easy to evaluate progress toward an explicit goal.

Much research attests to the effectiveness of specific goals in raising performance (Bandura, 1988; Locke & Latham, 1990, 2002; Schunk, 1990). Schunk (1983b) provided children with instruction and practice solving long-division problems. During the sessions, some children received a specific goal denoting the number of problems to complete; others had a general goal to work productively. Within each condition, half of the children received social comparative information on the number of problems that peers completed (which matched the session goal) to convey that goals were attainable. Goals raised self-efficacy; goals plus comparative information led to the highest self-efficacy and achievement.

Schunk (1984a) compared the effects of goals with those of rewards. Children received long-division instruction and practice over sessions. Some were offered rewards based on the number of problems completed, others pursued goals (number of problems to complete), and children in a third condition received rewards and goals. The three conditions promoted motivation during the sessions; rewards plus goals resulted in the highest division self-efficacy and achievement. Combining rewards with goals provided children with two sources of information to use in gauging learning progress.

Proximity. Goals are distinguished by how far they project into the future. Proximal, short-term goals are closer at hand, are achieved quicker, and result in greater motivation directed toward attainment than more temporally distant, long-term goals. Although benefits of proximal goals are found regardless of developmental status, short-term goals are needed with children because they have short time frames of reference and are not fully capable of representing distant outcomes in thought (Bandura & Schunk, 1981). Proximal goals fit well with normal lesson planning as elementary teachers plan activities around blocks of time. Goals often are proximal and specific, such as when teachers ask children to read three pages (specific) in 5 minutes (proximal).

Bandura and Schunk (1981) gave children subtraction instruction with practice opportunities over seven sessions. Children received seven packets of material. Some pursued a proximal goal of completing one packet each session; a second group received a distant goal of completing all packets by the end of the last session; a third group was given a general goal of working productively. Proximal goals led to the highest motivation during the sessions, as well as the highest subtraction self-efficacy, achievement, and intrinsic interest (based on the number of problems solved during a free-choice period). The distant goal resulted in no benefits compared with the general goal. Manderlink and Harackiewicz (1984) found that proximal and distant goals did not differentially affect adults' performances on word puzzles, but proximal goal participants judged expectation of goal attainment and perceived competence higher.

Difficulty. Goal difficulty refers to the level of task proficiency required as assessed against a standard. The amount of effort people expend to attain a goal depends on the proficiency level required. Individuals expend greater effort to attain a difficult goal than an easy one (Locke & Latham, 2002); however, difficulty level and performance do not bear an unlimited positive relationship to each other. Positive effects due to goal difficulty depend on students having sufficient ability to reach the goal. Difficult goals do not enhance performance in the absence of needed skills. Self-efficacy also is important. Learners who think they cannot reach a goal hold low self-efficacy, do not commit to attempting the goal, and work halfheartedly. Teachers can encourage such students to work on the task and provide feedback on progress.

Schunk (1983c) gave children a difficult (but attainable) or an easier goal of completing a given number of long-division problems during each instructional session. To prevent students from believing goals were too difficult, the teacher gave half of each group attainment information ("You can work 25 problems"); the other half received social comparative information indicating that similar peers completed that many. Difficult goals enhanced motivation; children who received difficult goals and attainment information displayed the highest self-efficacy and achievement. Locke, Frederick, Lee, and Bobko (1984) found that assigning college students difficult goals led to better performance and to their subsequently setting higher goals for themselves compared with students who initially were allowed to set their own goals. When participants set their own goals, self-efficacy related positively to goal level and commitment.

Self-Set Goals. Researchers have found that allowing students to set their goals enhances self-efficacy and learning, perhaps because self-set goals produce high goal commitment. Schunk (1985) provided subtraction instruction to sixth graders with learning disabilities. Some set daily performance goals, others had comparable goals assigned, and a third group worked without goals. Self-set goals led to the highest judgments of confidence for attaining goals, self-efficacy for solving problems, and subtraction achievement. Children in the two goal groups demonstrated greater motivation during the instructional sessions than did those without goals.

Hom and Murphy (1985) assigned to self-set or assigned-goal conditions college students who were high or low in achievement motivation. Self-set participants decided how many anagrams they could solve; assigned-goal participants were given comparable goals.

Students high in achievement motivation performed equally well under the two goal conditions; self-set goals enhanced the performances of students low in achievement motivation.

Goal Progress Feedback. *Goal progress feedback* provides information about progress toward goals (Hattie & Timperley, 2007). Such feedback, which is especially valuable when people cannot derive reliable information on their own, should raise self-efficacy, motivation, and achievement when it informs people that they are competent and can continue to improve by working diligently. Higher self-efficacy sustains motivation when people believe that continued effort will allow them to attain their goals. Once individuals attain goals, they are more likely to set new goals (Schunk, 1990).

Schunk and Rice (1991) taught students with reading problems a strategy to answer comprehension questions. Children were given a product goal of answering questions, a process goal of learning to use the strategy, or a process goal plus progress feedback that linked performance with strategy use and conveyed that they were making progress toward their goal of learning to use the strategy to answer questions. Following the instruction, goal-plus-feedback children demonstrated higher reading self-efficacy and achievement than did learners assigned to the process and product goal conditions. Schunk and Swartz (1993a, 1993b) obtained comparable results in writing achievement with average-achieving and academically gifted elementary school children. Self-efficacy and achievement generalized across types of writing tasks and maintained themselves over time.

Contracts and Conferences. Contracts and conferences that incorporate goal-setting principles help promote students' learning. Tollefson, Tracy, Johnsen, Farmer, and Buenning (1984) worked with junior high students with learning disabilities. Students selected weekly spelling words or mathematical problems from a list of moderately difficult words or problems. Following the study, students predicted how many they would answer correctly on a test. The goal and a study plan were stated in a written contract, which was intended to help students take personal responsibility for their actions and show that effort enhances achievement (see the discussion of attribution theory in Chapter 8). After each test, students charted their scores and made an attribution for the outcome. Compared with students assigned to a no-treatment control condition, goal-setting students placed greater emphasis on effort as a cause of outcomes and set more attainable goals.

Gaa (1973, 1979) found that goal-setting conferences enhance children's learning and self-evaluations. Children were assigned to one of three conditions: conferences with goal setting, conferences without goal setting, or no conferences (Gaa, 1973). During in-class reading instruction, goal-conference children received a list of reading skills and selected those they would attempt the following week, along with feedback on their previous week's goal accomplishments. Children who participated in conferences without goals received general information about material covered previously and what would be covered the following week. Children who participated in goal-setting conferences developed the highest level of reading achievement and the most accurate perceptions of their reading capabilities.

Outcome Expectations

Outcome expectations are personal beliefs about the anticipated outcomes of actions (Schunk & Zimmerman, 2006). Outcome expectations were among the first cognitive variables to be included in explanations of learning. Tolman (1932, 1949) discussed *field expectancies,* which involved relations between stimuli (S_1–S_2) or among a stimulus, response, and stimulus (S_1–R–S_2). Relations between stimuli concern what stimulus is apt to follow what other stimulus; for example, thunder follows lightning. In three-term relations, people develop the belief that a certain response to a given stimulus produces a certain result. If one's goal is to get to a roof (S_2), the sight of the ladder (S_1) could lead one to think, "If I place this ladder against the house (R), I can get to the roof." This is similar to Skinner's (1953; Chapter 3) three-term contingency except that Tolman conceived of this type of relation as reflecting a cognitive expectancy.

Field expectancies were important because they helped people form *cognitive maps,* or internal plans comprising expectancies of which actions are needed to attain goals. People follow signs to a goal; they learn meanings rather than discrete responses. People use their cognitive maps to determine the best course of action to attain a goal.

Tolman tested his ideas in an ingenious series of experiments (Tolman, Ritchie, & Kalish, 1946a, 1946b). In one study, rats were trained to run an apparatus, shown in Figure 4.2 (Maze 1). Subsequently, the apparatus was replaced with one in which the original path was blocked. Conditioning theories predict that animals will choose a path close to the original one, as shown in Figure 4.2 (Maze 2a). In fact, rats most frequently chose a path following the direction in which they originally found food (Maze 2b). These results supported the idea that the animals formed a cognitive map of the location of the food and responded based on that map rather than on prior responses to stimuli.

Social cognitive theory contends that people form outcome expectations about the likely consequences of given actions based on personal experiences and observations of models. (Bandura, 1986, 1997). Individuals act in ways they believe will be successful and attend to models who teach them valued skills. Outcome expectations sustain behaviors over long periods when people believe their actions will eventually produce desired outcomes. They also figure prominently in transfer; people are apt to engage in actions in new situations that were successful in previous situations because they believe that similar consequences will follow.

Outcome expectations can refer to external outcomes ("If I try my best on this exam, I will make a good grade on it") or to internal ones ("If I try my best on this exam, I will feel good about myself"). An important type of outcome expectation relates to progress in skill learning ("If I try my best, I will become a better reader"). Students who believe they are making little or no progress in learning may become demoralized and lackadaisical. In many instances, progress occurs slowly and students notice little day-to-day change. For example, learners may improve their skills in reading longer and more difficult passages, in finding main ideas, in drawing inferences, and in reading for details; but progress is slow. Teachers may need to inform students of their reading comprehension progress when it is not immediately apparent.

Figure 4.2

Experimental arrangement to study expectancy learning.

Source: Adapted from content of article, "Studies in Spatial Learning," by E. C. Tolman, B. F. Ritchie, and D. Kalish, 1946, *Journal of Experimental Psychology,* 36, pp. 13–24.

Maze 1: Training

FOOD

Maze 2a: Expected test results (stimulus-response behavior)

FOOD

Maze 2b: Actual test results ("place" learning)

FOOD

The influential role of outcome expectations was demonstrated by Shell, Murphy, & Bruning (1989). College students completed measures of reading and writing self-efficacy, outcome expectancies, and achievement. The self-efficacy assessment asked students to rate their competencies in performing various reading and writing tasks (e.g., letter from a friend, employment application, short fiction story). For the outcome expectancy measure, students judged the importance of reading and writing for achieving such life goals as getting a job, being financially secure, and being happy.

Self-efficacy and outcome expectancies related positively to achievement in reading and writing. In both domains, self-efficacy was more strongly related to achievement than outcome expectancies. This study also showed that the expectancy beliefs for each domain related significantly to achievement in the other domain, which suggests that teachers' attempts to improve students' self-efficacy and outcome expectations in one literacy area may generalize to others.

Values

Value refers to the perceived importance or usefulness of learning. An important premise of social cognitive theory is that individuals' actions reflect their value preferences (Bandura, 1986). Learners do things that bring about what they desire and work to avoid outcomes that are inconsistent with their values. Learners are motivated to learn and perform when they deem that learning or performance important.

Values can be assessed against external and internal standards. There are many reasons why students might value high grades. Making As and making the honor roll may bring them external recognition (i.e., from parents and teachers), their names appearing in local newspapers, and acceptances at universities. But high grades also can produce internal self-satisfaction, as when students feel proud of their work and a sense of accomplishment. Such internal satisfaction also occurs when learners act in accordance with their personal ethical beliefs.

Values can be developed enactively or vicariously. When people learn by doing, they also experience the consequences of those actions. But many value beliefs are learned through observations of others. Children may observe some of their peers in class being rewarded by the teacher for turning in neat papers. Completing written assignments neatly then can become valued as a means of gaining teacher approval.

Values are covered in more depth in Chapter 8 because they figure prominently in theories of motivation. Values are intimately linked with the other motivational processes discussed here: goals, outcome expectations, and self-efficacy. For example, assume that Larissa's family has moved and that Larissa (a fifth grader) is starting at a new school. One of her goals is to make new friends. She values friendships; she enjoys spending time with other children and sharing on a personal level with them (she has no brothers or sisters). She believes that if she is nice to other children that they will be nice to her and may become her friends (positive outcome expectations). Although she is somewhat shy initially in her new school, she has made new friends before and feels reasonably self-efficacious about doing so again. Larissa observes the actions of her new peers to learn what types of things they like to do. She interacts with her peers in ways that she believes will lead to friendships, and as she begins to develop new friends, her social self-efficacy becomes strengthened.

An important part of a teacher's job is to determine students' value preferences and especially if any of these reflect stereotypes or cultural differences. Research by Wigfield and Eccles (1992) showed some stereotypes among adolescents: Boys valued mathematics more, whereas girls placed greater emphasis on English. Mickelson (1990) contended that perceived racial inequalities can result in some minority students devaluing school achievement. Teachers have the responsibility of promoting achievement values in all students, which they can do by teaching students how to set goals and assess their goal progress; showing students how their achievement results in positive outcomes; and building learners' self-efficacy for school success.

SELF-EFFICACY

Conceptual Overview

Self-efficacy (efficacy expectations) refers to personal beliefs about one's capabilities to learn or perform actions at designated levels (Bandura, 1977a, 1977b, 1986, 1993, 1997). Self-efficacy is a belief about what one is capable of doing; it is not the same as knowing what to do. In gauging self-efficacy, individuals assess their skills and their capabilities to translate those skills into actions. Self-efficacy is a key to promoting a sense of *agency* in people that they can influence their lives (Bandura, 1997, 2001).

Self-efficacy and outcome expectations do not have the same meaning (Schunk & Zimmerman, 2006). Self-efficacy refers to perceptions of one's capabilities to produce actions; outcome expectations involve beliefs about the anticipated outcomes of those actions. Students may believe that a positive outcome will result from certain actions but also believe that they lack the competence to produce those actions. For example, Jeremy may believe that if he correctly answers the teacher's questions, the teacher will praise him (positive outcome expectation). He also may value praise from the teacher. But he may not attempt to answer the teacher's questions if he doubts his capabilities to answer them correctly (low self-efficacy).

Despite self-efficacy and outcome expectations being conceptually distinct, they often are related. Students who typically perform well have confidence in their learning capabilities and expect (and usually receive) positive outcomes for their efforts. At the same time, there is no necessary relation between self-efficacy and outcome expectations. Even students with high self-efficacy for learning may expect a low grade as an outcome if they think that the teacher does not like them.

Although some evidence indicates that perceptions of self-efficacy generalize to different tasks (Smith, 1989), theory and research suggest that self-efficacy is primarily domain specific (Pajares, 1996, 1997). Thus, it is meaningful to speak of self-efficacy for drawing inferences from text, balancing chemical equations, solving fractions, running certain times at track events, and so on. Smith and Fouad (1999) found that self-efficacy, goals, and outcome expectations are specific to subject areas and show little generalization across areas. Self-efficacy might transfer to new situations, however, when learners believe that the same skills will produce success. Thus, learners who feel self-efficacious about outlining in English class also may feel confident about outlining in science class, and their self-efficacy may motivate them to construct an outline in science.

Self-efficacy is distinguished from *self-concept* (Pajares & Schunk, 2002; Schunk & Pajares, 2005), which refers to one's collective self-perceptions formed through experiences with and interpretations of the environment and which depends heavily on reinforcements and evaluations by significant others (Shavelson & Bolus, 1982; Wylie,1979). Self-efficacy refers to perceptions of specific capabilities; self-concept is one's general self-perception that includes self-efficacy in different areas (Schunk & Zimmerman, 2006; Chapter 8).

Self-efficacy depends in part on student abilities. In general, high-ability students feel more efficacious about learning compared with low-ability students; however, self-efficacy is not another name for ability. Collins (1982) identified high-, average-, and low-ability students in mathematics. Within each level, she found students of high and low self-efficacy. She gave students problems to solve, and told them they could rework those they missed.

Ability was positively related to achievement; but, regardless of ability level, students with high self-efficacy solved more problems correctly and chose to rework more problems they missed than those with low self-efficacy.

Self-efficacy can have diverse effects in achievement settings (Bandura, 1993; Pajares, 1996, 1997; Schunk, 1990, 1991). Self-efficacy can influence choice of activities. Students with low self-efficacy for learning may avoid attempting tasks; those who judge themselves efficacious should participate more eagerly. Self-efficacy also can affect effort expenditure, persistence, and learning. Students who feel efficacious about learning generally expend greater effort and persist longer than students who doubt their capabilities, especially when they encounter difficulties. In turn, these behaviors promote learning.

People acquire information about their self-efficacy in a given domain from their performances, observations of models (vicarious experiences), forms of social persuasion, and physiological indexes (e.g., heart rate, sweating). Actual performances offer the most valid information for assessing efficacy. Successes generally raise efficacy and failures lower it, although an occasional failure (success) after many successes (failures) should not have much effect.

Students acquire much information about their capabilities through knowledge of how others perform. *Similarity* to others is an important cue for gauging one's self-efficacy (Brown & Inouye, 1978; Rosenthal & Bandura, 1978; Schunk, 1987, 1998). Observing similar others succeed raises observers' self-efficacy and motivates them to try the task because they believe that if others can succeed, they can as well. At the same time, a vicarious increase in self-efficacy can be negated by subsequent personal failures. Students who observe peers fail may believe they lack the competence to succeed, which can dissuade them from attempting the task. Donnetta experienced some increase in self-efficacy from watching her coach demonstrate the backhand, but her doing it without hitting into the net is a more potent influence.

Students often receive persuasive information from teachers that they possess the capability to perform well (e.g., "You can do it"). Although positive feedback enhances self-efficacy, this increase will not endure for long if students subsequently perform poorly. Learners also acquire some self-efficacy information from physiological symptoms they experience. Emotional symptoms (sweating, trembling) might be interpreted to mean they are not capable of learning. When learners notice they are experiencing less stress in response to academic demands, they may feel more efficacious for mastering the task.

Information acquired from these sources does not influence self-efficacy automatically but is cognitively appraised (Bandura, 1982b, 1993, 1997). Appraising self-efficacy is an inferential process in which persons weigh and combine the contributions of personal, behavioral, and environmental factors. In forming efficacy assessments, students consider factors such as ability, effort expended, task difficulty, teacher assistance, and number and pattern of successes and failures (Bandura, 1981, 1997).

Self-Efficacy in Achievement Situations

Self-efficacy is especially germane to school learning and other achievement situations. Researchers have obtained the hypothesized effects of self-efficacy on choice, effort, persistence, and achievement (Pajares, 1996, 1997; Schunk & Pajares, 2005). Self-efficacy is related as well to career choices. Betz and Hackett (1981, 1983; Hackett & Betz,

1981) found that although there are structural and social influences on career choices, self-efficacy is an important mediator of these external influences and has a direct bearing on career choices. In addition, gender differences that emerge in vocational choices are due to differences in self-efficacy. Women are more self-efficacious for careers traditionally held by women than for careers traditionally held by men, whereas men's self-efficacy is less dependent on career gender typing.

Self-efficacy is strongly related to effort and task persistence (Bandura & Cervone, 1983, 1986; Schunk, 1995). Individuals with high self-efficacy beliefs are likely to exert effort in the face of difficulty and persist at a task when they have the requisite skills. There is, however, some evidence that self-doubts may foster learning when students have not previously acquired the skills. As Bandura (1986) noted, "Self-doubt creates the impetus for learning but hinders adept use of previously established skills" (p. 394). Salomon (1984) found that students high in self-efficacy were more likely to be cognitively engaged in learning when the task was perceived as difficult but less likely to be effortful and less cognitively engaged when the task was deemed easy.

Besides the quantity of effort, the quality of effort (deeper cognitive processing and general cognitive engagement) has been strongly linked to self-efficacy (Graham & Golan, 1991; Pintrich & Schrauben, 1992). Pintrich and De Groot (1990) found that junior high students high in self-efficacy were more likely to report using cognitive and self-regulatory learning strategies. In a series of experimental studies, Schunk (1982a, 1982b, 1983a, 1983b, 1983c, 1983d, 1984a, 1984b, 1996) found that self-efficacious students mastered various academic tasks better than students with weaker self-efficacy. Students' computer self-efficacy relates positively to their success in computer-based learning environments (Moos & Azevedo, 2009). Self-efficacy is a significant predictor of learning and achievement even after prior achievement and cognitive skills are taken into account (Schunk, 1981, 1982a).

In summary, self-efficacy is an important influence on motivation and achievement (Multon, Brown, & Lent, 1991; Pajares, 1996, 1997; Schunk & Pajares, 2005; Valentine, DuBois, & Cooper, 2004). Self-efficacy is assumed to be more situationally specific, dynamic, fluctuating, and changeable than the more static and stable measures of self-concept and general self-competence (Schunk & Pajares, 2002). One's self-efficacy for a specific task on a given day might fluctuate due to the individual's preparation, physical condition (sickness, fatigue), and affective mood, as well as external conditions such as the nature of the task (length, difficulty) and social milieu (general classroom conditions). In contrast, other views of self-competence view it more globally (e.g., mathematical competence) and are less concerned with instability of beliefs.

The reciprocal interaction between personal and environmental factors can be seen clearly with social and self variables. Social (environmental) factors can affect many self (personal) variables, such as learners' goals, self-efficacy, outcome expectations, attributions, self-evaluations of learning progress, and self-regulatory processes. In turn, self influences can affect social environments, as when learners decide they need more instruction on a skill and seek out a qualified teacher (Schunk, 1999).

Achievement outcomes such as goal progress, motivational indexes (choice of activities, effort, persistence), and learning are affected by social and self influences. In turn, learner actions affect these factors. As students work on tasks, they evaluate their learning progress. Perceptions of progress, which can be facilitated by feedback about progress, substantiate their self-efficacy for learning, which sustains motivation and learning (Hattie & Timperley, 2007; Schunk, 1995).

A key process is the *internalization* of social variables to self influences. Learners transform information acquired from the social environment into mechanisms of self-regulation (Chapter 9). With increased skill acquisition, this social-to-self transformation process becomes a bidirectional interactive process as learners alter and adjust their social environments to further enhance their achievement (Schunk, 1999).

Models and Self-Efficacy

The models in one's environment provide an important source of information for gauging self-efficacy. Parents and other influential adults (e.g., teachers, coaches) are key models in children's social environments. Bandura, Barbaranelli, Caprara, and Pastorelli (1996) found that parents' academic aspirations for their children affected both children's academic achievements and their self-efficacy.

Adult Models. Research shows that exposing students to adult models influences their self-efficacy for learning and performing well. Zimmerman and Ringle (1981) had children observe a model unsuccessfully attempt to solve a puzzle for a long or short time and verbalize statements of confidence or pessimism, after which children attempted to solve the puzzle. Observing a confident but nonpersistent model raised self-efficacy; children who observed a pessimistic but persistent model lowered their self-efficacy. Relich, Debus, and Walker (1986) found that exposing low-achieving children to models explaining mathematical division and providing them with feedback stressing the importance of ability and effort had a positive effect on self-efficacy.

Schunk (1981) showed that both cognitive modeling and didactic instruction raised self-efficacy; however, cognitive modeling led to greater gains in division skill and to more accurate perceptions of capabilities as these children's self-efficacy judgments corresponded more closely to their actual performances. Students who received only didactic instruction overestimated what they could do. Regardless of treatment condition, self-efficacy related positively to persistence and achievement.

Peer Models. Observing similar peer models performing a task well can raise observers' self-efficacy, which is validated when they work at the task successfully. Brown and Inouye (1978) investigated the effects of perceived similarity in competence to models. College students judged self-efficacy for solving anagrams and then attempted to solve them, after which they were told they performed better than or the same as a model. They then observed a model fail, judged self-efficacy, and attempted the anagrams again. Telling students they were more competent than the model led to higher self-efficacy and persistence than telling them they were equal in competence.

One way to raise self-efficacy is to use *coping models*, who initially demonstrate fears and skill deficiencies but gradually improve their performance and self-efficacy. Coping models illustrate how determined effort and positive self-thoughts overcome difficulties. In contrast, *mastery models* demonstrate faultless performance and high confidence from the outset (Thelen, Fry, Fehrenbach, & Frautschi, 1979). Coping models may enhance perceived similarity and self-efficacy for learning better than mastery models among students who are more likely to view the initial difficulties and gradual progress of coping models as more similar to their typical performances than the rapid learning of mastery models.

Children who had experienced difficulties learning subtraction with regrouping watched videos portraying a peer mastery model, a peer coping model, a teacher model, or no model (Schunk & Hanson, 1985). In the peer-model conditions, an adult teacher provided instruction, after which the peer solved problems. The peer mastery model easily grasped operations and verbalized positive achievement beliefs reflecting high self-efficacy and ability, low task difficulty, and positive attitudes. The peer coping model initially made errors and verbalized negative achievement beliefs but gradually performed better and verbalized coping statements (e.g., "I need to pay attention to what I'm doing"). Eventually, the coping model's problem-solving behaviors and verbalizations matched those of the mastery model. Teacher-model children observed videos portraying only the teacher providing instruction; no-model children did not view videos. All children judged self-efficacy for learning to subtract and received instruction and practice over sessions.

Observing a peer model raised self-efficacy and achievement more than observing a teacher model or no model; the teacher-model condition promoted these outcomes better than no model. The mastery and coping conditions led to similar outcomes. Possibly children focused more on what the models had in common (task success) than on their differences. Children may have drawn on their prior successes in subtraction without regrouping and concluded that if the model could learn, they could as well.

Another important variable is *number of models*. Compared with a single model, multiple models increase the probability that observers will perceive themselves as similar to at least one of the models (Thelen et al., 1979). Students who might easily discount the successes of a single model may be swayed by observing several successful peers and think that if all these models can learn, they can as well. Notice in the opening scenario that Donnetta's coach served as a model, and she gave Donnetta materials portraying backhands demonstrated by other models.

Schunk, Hanson, and Cox (1987) investigated the effects of single and multiple coping and mastery models with a task (fractions) on which children had experienced few prior successes. Viewing a single coping model or multiple coping or mastery models enhanced children's self-efficacy and achievement better than viewing a single mastery model. For these low achievers, the single mastery model was the least effective.

Schunk and Hanson (1989a) further explored variations in perceived similarity by having average-achieving children view one of three types of peer models. Mastery models easily grasped arithmetic operations and verbalized positive beliefs (e.g., "I know I can do this one"). Coping-emotive models initially experienced difficulties and verbalized negative statements (e.g., "I'm not very good at this"), after which they verbalized coping statements (e.g., "I'll have to work hard on this one") and displayed coping behaviors; eventually they performed as well as mastery models. Coping-alone models performed in identical fashion to coping-emotive models but never verbalized negative beliefs.

Coping-emotive models led to the highest self-efficacy for learning. Mastery and coping-alone children perceived themselves as equal in competence to the model; coping-emotive children viewed themselves as more competent than the model. The belief that one is more talented than an unsuccessful model can raise self-efficacy and motivation. The three conditions promoted self-efficacy and achievement equally well, which shows that actual task experience outweighed initial effects due to watching models.

Peer models have been used to increase prosocial behaviors. Strain et al. (1981) showed how peers can be taught to initiate social play with withdrawn children by using verbal signals (e.g., "Let's play blocks") and motor responses (handing child a toy). Such peer initiations typically increase target children's subsequent social initiations. Training peer initiators is time consuming but effective because methods of remedying social withdrawal (prompting, reinforcement) require nearly continuous teacher involvement. Application 4.5 discusses some additional uses of peer models.

APPLICATION 4.5
Building Self-Efficacy with Peer Models

Observing similar peers performing a task increases students' self-efficacy for learning. This idea is applied when a teacher selects certain students to complete mathematics problems at the board. By demonstrating success, the peer models help raise observers' self-efficacy for performing well. If ability levels in a class vary considerably, the teacher might pick peer models at different levels of ability. Students in the class are more likely to perceive themselves as similar in competence to at least one of the models.

Peers who readily master skills may help teach skills to observing students but may not have much impact on the self-efficacy of those students who experience learning difficulties. For the latter, students with learning difficulties who have mastered the skills may be excellent models. Jim Marshall's American history class has been learning the Civil War battles. Because so many battles occurred, learning all of them has been difficult for some of the students. Mr. Marshall places his students into three groups: Group 1 consists of students who mastered the material immediately; Group 2, students who have been working hard and are gradually developing mastery; and Group 3, students who still are having difficulty. Mr. Marshall pairs Groups 2 and 3 for peer tutoring. Using maps and charts, the

students work together, color coding and learning the groups of battles together.

Teachers also can refer to peer models who other students observe. Teachers can point out the concentration and hard work of the models. For instance, as Kathy Stone moves about the room monitoring seat work, she provides learners with social comparative information (e.g., "See how well Kevin is working? I'm sure that you can work just as well"). Teachers need to ensure that learners view the comparative performance level as one they can attain; judicious selection of referent students is necessary.

Peers also can enhance students' self-efficacy during small-group work. Successful groups are those in which each member has some responsibility and members share rewards based on their collective performance. The use of such groups helps to reduce negative ability-related social comparisons by students experiencing learning difficulties. Teachers need to select tasks carefully because unsuccessful groups do not raise self-efficacy.

In selecting students for working on group projects, Gina Brown might assess students' abilities for skills needed (e.g., writing, analyzing, interpreting, researching, organizing) and then form groups by assigning students with different strengths to each group.

Motor Skills

Self-efficacy has been shown to predict the acquisition and performance of motor skills (Bandura, 1997; Poag-DuCharme & Brawley, 1993; Wurtele, 1986). Gould and Weiss (1981) found benefits due to model similarity. College women viewed a similar model (female student with no athletic background) or dissimilar model (male physical education professor) perform a muscular endurance task. Students who viewed the similar model performed the task better and judged self-efficacy higher than those who observed the dissimilar model. Regardless of treatment condition, self-efficacy related positively to performance.

George, Feltz, and Chase (1992) replicated these results using female college students and models performing a leg-extension endurance task. Students who observed nonathletic male or female models extended their legs longer and judged self-efficacy higher than those who observed an athletic model. Among these unskilled observers, model ability was a more important similarity cue than model gender.

Lirgg and Feltz (1991) exposed sixth-grade girls to a skilled or unskilled teacher or peer video model demonstrating a ladder-climbing task; girls in a control group observed no model. Girls then judged self-efficacy for climbing successively higher levels on the ladder and performed the task over trials. Control students demonstrated poorer performance than those exposed to models; among the latter, children who viewed a skilled model (adult or peer) performed better than those who observed an unskilled model. Skilled-model girls judged self-efficacy higher.

Bandura and Cervone (1983) showed how feedback was important during motor skill acquisition. College students operated an ergometer by alternatively pushing and pulling arm levers that resisted their efforts. Some participants pursued a goal of increasing performance by 40% over the baseline, others were told they had increased their performance by 24%, those in a third condition received goals and feedback, and control-group participants received neither goals nor feedback. Goals combined with feedback improved performance most and instilled self-efficacy for goal attainment, which predicted subsequent effort.

In follow-up research (Bandura & Cervone, 1986), participants received a goal of 50% improvement over baseline. Following their performance, they received false feedback indicating they achieved an increase of 24%, 36%, 46%, or 54%. Self-efficacy was lowest for the 24% group and highest for the 54% condition. After students set goals for the next session and performed the task again, effort expenditure related positively to goals and self-efficacy across all conditions.

Poag-DuCharme and Brawley (1993) found that self-efficacy predicted involvement by individuals in community-based exercise programs. Self-efficacy was assessed for performing in-class activities and for overcoming barriers to exercising and scheduling problems. Self-efficacy related positively to the initiation and maintenance of regular exercise. In similar fashion, Motl, Dishman, Saunders, Dowda, and Pate (2007) found that self-efficacy for overcoming barriers to exercise predicted physical exercise by adolescent girls. These results suggest that promoting exercise requires attention to developing individuals' self-efficacy for coping with problems in scheduling and actual engagement.

Instructional Self-Efficacy

Self-efficacy is relevant to teachers as well as students (Pajares, 1996; Tschannen-Moran, Woolfolk Hoy, & Hoy, 1998). *Instructional self-efficacy* refers to personal beliefs about one's capabilities to help students learn. Instructional self-efficacy should influence teachers' activities, effort, and persistence with students (Ashton, 1985; Ashton & Webb, 1986). Teachers with low self-efficacy may avoid planning activities they believe exceed their capabilities, not persist with students having difficulties, expend little effort to find materials, and not reteach content in ways students might understand better. Teachers with higher self-efficacy are more apt to develop challenging activities, help students succeed, and persevere with students who have problems learning. These motivational effects on teachers enhance student achievement. Teachers with higher self-efficacy also show stronger commitment to their work (Chan, Lau, Nie, Lim, & Hogan, 2008). Ashton and Webb (1986) found that teachers with higher self-efficacy were likely to have a positive classroom environment, support students' ideas, and address students' needs. Teacher self-efficacy was a significant predictor of student achievement. Woolfolk and Hoy (1990) obtained comparable results with preservice teachers. Feltz, Chase, Moritz, and Sullivan (1999) showed that the same predictions for teacher self-efficacy also applied to coaches.

Much research has investigated the dimensions of instructional efficacy that relate best to student learning (Gibson & Dembo, 1984; Woolfolk & Hoy, 1990). Ashton and Webb (1986) distinguished *teaching efficacy*, or outcome expectations about the consequences of teaching in general, from *personal efficacy*, defined as self-efficacy to perform particular behaviors to bring about given outcomes. As noted earlier, self-efficacy and outcome expectations often are related but need not be. A teacher might have a high sense of personal efficacy but lower teaching efficacy if he or she believes that most student learning is due to home and environmental factors outside of the teacher's control. Other research suggests that instructional self-efficacy reflects an internal–external distinction: internal factors represent perceptions of personal influence and power and external factors relate to perceptions of influence and power of elements that lie outside the classroom (Guskey & Passaro, 1994).

Goddard, Hoy, and Woolfolk Hoy (2000) discussed *collective teacher efficacy*, or perceptions of teachers in a school that their efforts as a whole will positively affect students. Although research on collective teacher efficacy is scant (Bandura, 1993, 1997; Pajares, 1997), the notion is receiving increased attention because it often is reflected in 21st century skills curricula and standards and seems critical to effective school reform.

Collective teacher efficacy depends on having solid support from administrators who encourage and facilitate improvement by creating an environment free of roadblocks. Collective efficacy also depends on reliable sources of self-efficacy information (Bandura, 1997). Teachers who work collaboratively to achieve common goals (performance mastery) and who benefit from mentors as role models (vicarious information) are apt to feel collectively self-efficacious.

The role of collective teacher efficacy also may depend on the level of organizational coupling (Henson, 2002). Collective teacher efficacy may not predict outcomes in loosely knit schools; individual self-efficacy may be a better predictor. This situation may occur in some secondary schools where coupling, if present, resides at the departmental level rather than at the whole-school level. Conversely, elementary schools typically are more closely coupled, and the collective efficacy of the school's teachers may predict student outcomes.

Goddard et al. (2000) discussed the process whereby collective teacher efficacy can affect student learning. The same four sources of self-efficacy affect collective efficacy: performance attainments, vicarious experiences, social persuasion, and physiological indicators. Collective efficacy is apt to be strengthened when teachers successfully work together to implement changes, learn from one another and from other successful schools, receive encouragement for change from administrators and professional development sources, and work together to cope with difficulties and alleviate stress (Goddard, Hoy, & Woolfolk Hoy, 2004). As collective teacher efficacy is strengthened, teachers continue to improve educational opportunities for students.

Collective teacher efficacy also seems important for teachers' job satisfaction and retention in teaching. Caprara, Barbaranelli, Borgogni, and Steca (2003) found that teachers' collective efficacy beliefs bore a significant positive relation to their job satisfaction. Further, collective efficacy depends on teachers believing that other constituencies (e.g., principals, staff, parents, students) are working diligently to fulfill their obligations. Consistent with Bandura's (1997) position, even high self-efficacy will not lead to beneficial changes unless the environment is responsive to change. Retaining teachers in the profession—a critical priority given the teacher shortage in many areas—will be aided by creating an environment in which teachers' sense of agency is fostered and their efforts lead to positive changes.

An important challenge for pre- and in-service teacher education programs is to develop methods for increasing teachers' instructional self-efficacy by incorporating efficacy-building sources (actual performances, vicarious experiences, persuasion, physiological indexes). Internships where students work with teacher mentors provide actual performance success plus expert modeling. Teacher models not only teach observers skills but also build their self-efficacy for succeeding in the classroom (Application 4.6).

Health and Therapeutic Activities

Researchers have shown that self-efficacy predicts health and therapeutic behaviors (Bandura, 1997; Maddux, 1993; Maddux, Brawley, & Boykin, 1995). The Health Belief Model has been commonly applied to explain health behavior change (Rosenstock, 1974). This model assigns a prominent role to individuals' perceptions of four factors that affect health behaviors: susceptibility (personal assessment of risk for a given health threat), severity of the health threat, benefits of the behavior recommended to reduce the threat, and barriers to action (personal belief of possible undesirable consequences that could result from performing the recommended preventive behavior). The barriers factor has the strongest empirical support; it relates closely to self-efficacy (i.e., self-efficacy for overcoming barriers; Maddux, 1993). A newer health behavior goal model (Maes & Gebhardt, 2000) includes perceived competence (analogous to self-efficacy) as a key process.

The important function of self-efficacy as a predictor of health behaviors is evident in many studies (DiClemente, 1986; Strecher, DeVellis, Becker, & Rosenstock, 1986).

APPLICATION 4.6
Instructional Self-Efficacy

Self-efficacy among teachers is developed in the same ways as among students. An effective means of building self-efficacy is to observe someone else model specific teaching behaviors. A new elementary teacher might observe his or her mentor teacher implement the use of learning centers before the new teacher introduces the same activity. By observing the mentor, the new teacher acquires skill and self-efficacy for being able to implement the centers.

Self-efficacy in beginning teachers also may be aided by observing teachers with a few years of teaching experience successfully perform actions; new teachers may perceive greater similarity between themselves and other relatively new teachers than between themselves and those teachers with more experience.

Practicing behaviors helps to develop skills and also builds self-efficacy. Music teachers will increase their self-efficacy for teaching pieces to the class by practicing

those same pieces themselves on the piano after school until they know them well and feel confident about working with students. When teachers learn to use a new computer application before introducing it to their classes, they will feel more self-efficacious about teaching their students to use it.

Becoming more knowledgeable about a particular subject increases self-efficacy for discussing the subject more accurately and completely. Jim Marshall reads several books and articles about the Great Depression prior to developing the unit for class. The added knowledge should raise his self-efficacy for helping students learn about this significant period in American history. Gina Brown reviews the work of significant researchers for each major topic area included in the course discussions. This provides students with information beyond what is in the text and builds her self-efficacy for effectively teaching the content.

Self-efficacy correlates positively with controlled smoking (Godding & Glasgow, 1985), positively with longest period of smoking cessation (DiClemente, Prochaska, & Gilbertini, 1985), negatively with temptation to smoke (DiClemente et al., 1985), and positively with weight loss (Bernier & Avard, 1986). Love (1983) found that self-efficacy to resist bulimic behaviors correlated negatively with binging and purging. Bandura (1994) discussed the role of self-efficacy in the control of HIV infection.

In DiClemente's (1981) study, individuals who had recently quit smoking judged their self-efficacy to avoid smoking in situations of varying stress levels; they were surveyed months later to determine maintenance. Maintainers judged self-efficacy higher than those who relapsed. Self-efficacy was a better predictor of future smoking than was smoking history or demographic variables. Self-efficacy for avoiding smoking in various situations correlated positively with weeks of successful abstinence. People tended to relapse in situations where they had judged their self-efficacy low for avoiding smoking.

Bandura and others have investigated how well self-efficacy predicts therapeutic behavioral changes (Bandura, 1991). In one study (Bandura, Adams, & Beyer, 1977), adult snake phobics received a participant modeling treatment in which a therapist initially modeled a series of progressively more threatening encounters with a snake. After phobics jointly performed the various activities with the therapist, they were allowed to perform on their own to help enhance their self-efficacy. Compared with phobics who only observed the therapist model the activities and with those who received no training, participant-modeling clients demonstrated the greatest increases in self-efficacy and approach behaviors toward the snake. Regardless of treatment, self-efficacy for performing tasks was highly related to clients' actual behaviors. In a related study, Bandura and Adams (1977) found participant modeling superior to systematic desensitization (Chapter 3). These results support Bandura's (1982b, 1997) contention that performance-based treatments combining modeling with practice offer the best basis for gauging self-efficacy and produce greater behavioral change.

Bandura (2005) emphasized the importance of self-regulation in health and wellness. The development and maintenance of healthy lifestyles often have been explained in terms of prescriptive medical management, but increasingly researchers and practitioners are emphasizing collaborative self-management. The latter includes many of the social cognitive processes described in this chapter: self-monitoring of health-related behaviors, goals and self-efficacy for attaining them, self-evaluation of progress, and self-motivating incentives and social supports for healthy lifestyles (Maes & Karoly, 2005).

This view of health and wellness reflects Bandura's (2005) agentic perspective on human functioning described at the start of this chapter. Successful lifestyle change that is maintained over time requires that people feel self-efficacious for managing their own activities and controlling events that affect their lives. Self-efficacy affects actions through cognitive, motivational, affective, and decisional processes. Thus, self-efficacy affects whether people think in positive or negative ways, how they motivate themselves and persist during difficulties, how they handle their emotions and especially during periods of stress, how resilient they are to setbacks, and what choices they make at critical times (Benight & Bandura, 2004).

In summary, self-efficacy has generated much research. Evidence shows that self-efficacy predicts diverse outcomes such as smoking cessation, pain tolerance, athletic performance, assertiveness, coping with feared events, recovery from heart attack, and sales performance (Bandura, 1986, 1997). Self-efficacy is a key variable influencing career choices (Lent, Brown, & Hackett, 2000), and children's self-efficacy affects the types of occupations in which they believe they can succeed (Bandura, Barbaranelli, Caprara, & Pastorelli, 2001). Self-efficacy researchers have employed diverse settings, participants, measures, treatments, tasks, and time spans. The generality of self-efficacy undoubtedly will be extended in future research.

INSTRUCTIONAL APPLICATIONS

Many ideas in social cognitive theory lend themselves well to instruction and student learning. Instructional applications involving models, self-efficacy, worked examples, and tutoring and mentoring reflect social cognitive principles.

Models

Teacher models facilitate learning and provide self-efficacy information. Students who observe teachers explain and demonstrate concepts and skills are apt to learn and believe that they are capable of further learning. Teachers also provide persuasive self-efficacy information to students. Teachers who introduce lessons by stating that all students can learn and that by working diligently they will master the new skills instill in students self-efficacy for learning, which is substantiated when students successfully work on the task. In studies in which models act one way and tell observers to act differently, children are more influenced by actions than verbalizations (Bryan & Walbek, 1970). Teachers need to ensure that their instructions to students (e.g., "keep your desk tidy") are consistent with their own actions (teacher's desk is tidy).

In similar fashion, peer models can promote student motivation and learning. Relative to teachers, peers may be more focused on "how to do it," which improves learning in observers. Further, observing a similar peer succeed instills a vicarious sense of self-efficacy for learning in observers, which is validated when they perform well (Schunk, 1987). When using peers, it helps to choose models such that all students can relate to at least one. This may mean using multiple peer models, where the peers represent varying levels of skill.

Self-Efficacy

The role of self-efficacy in learning is well substantiated. In determining which instructional methods to use, it is important that teachers gauge their effects on students' self-efficacy as well as on their learning. It may be that a method that produces learning does not enhance self-efficacy. For example, providing students with extensive assistance is apt to aid their learning, but it will not do much for students' self-efficacy for being able to learn or perform well on their own. As Bandura (1986, 1997) recommended, periods of self-directed mastery, where students practice skills independently, are needed.

Competent models teach skills, but similar models are best for self-efficacy. Having the best mathematics student in the class demonstrate operations may teach skills to the observers, but many of the latter students may not feel efficacious because they may believe that they never will be as good as the model. Often top students serve as tutors for less-capable students, which may improve learning but should be accompanied by periods of independent practice to build self-efficacy (see section, Tutoring and Mentoring, below).

Pre-service teachers' self-efficacy can be developed through teacher preparation that includes internships with master teachers where the pre-service teachers can observe and practice teaching skills. For in-service teachers, continuing professional development can help them learn new strategies to use in challenging situations, such as how to foster learning in students with varying abilities, how to work with students with limited English proficiency, and how to involve parents in their children's learning. By removing impairments to teaching (e.g., excess paperwork), administrators allow teachers to focus on curricular improvement and student learning (see Application 4.6).

Worked Examples

Worked examples are graphic portrayals of problem solutions (Atkinson, Derry, Renkl, & Wortham, 2000). Worked examples present step-by-step problem solutions, often with accompanying diagrams or sound (narration). A worked example provides a model—with accompanying explanation—that illustrates how a proficient problem solver would proceed. Learners study worked examples before they attempt to solve problems themselves. Worked examples are often used in instruction in mathematics and science, although their use need not be confined to these disciplines.

The theoretical underpinnings for worked examples derive from information processing theory, and they are discussed in depth in Chapter 7. But worked examples also reflect many principles of social cognitive theory. Worked examples incorporate cognitive models and demonstration plus explanation. As with other complex forms of observational learning, students do not learn how to solve a particular problem but rather general skills and strategies that they can use to solve a wider class of problems. Worked examples also have motivational benefits. They may help to raise self-efficacy in learners when, after reviewing worked examples, they believe that they understand the model and can apply the skills and strategies themselves (Schunk, 1995).

Certain principles should be kept in mind when using worked examples. It is better to use more than one mode of presentation than a single mode. Thus, a worked example might include textual (words, numbers), graphical (arrows, charts), and aural (sounds) information. But too much complexity can overload learners' attention and memory capabilities. Research also shows that two examples are better than a single one, two varied examples are better than two examples of the same type, and intermixing practice with worked examples produces better learning than if all examples are presented first followed by practice (Atkinson et al., 2000). Thus, an algebra teacher teaching a lesson on solving equations in one unknown might present two worked examples of the form $4x + 2 = 10$, after which students solve problems. Then the teacher might present two worked examples of the form $x \div 2 + 1 = 5$, after which students solve problems of this type. The worked examples could be accompanied by graphics and sound, as in interactive computer-based learning environments.

Tutoring and Mentoring

Tutoring and mentoring reflect many of the social cognitive principles discussed in this chapter. *Tutoring* refers to a situation in which one or more persons serve as the instructional agents for another, usually in a specific subject or for a particular purpose (Stenhoff & Lignugaris/Kraft, 2007). When peers are the instructional agents, tutoring is a form of peer-assisted learning (Rohrbeck, Ginsburg-Block, Fantuzzo, & Miller, 2003; Chapter 6).

Tutors serve as instructional models for tutees by explaining and demonstrating skills, operations, and strategies that tutees are to learn. Both adults and children can be effective tutors for children. As noted earlier, however, there may be some motivational benefits that result from peer tutors. Effective peer tutors are those whom tutees perceive as similar to themselves except that tutors are farther along in their skill acquisition. The perception of similarity may lead tutees to believe that if the tutors could learn, they can as well, which can raise tutees' self-efficacy and motivation.

Researchers also have examined the effects of tutoring on tutors. Similar to the results of instructional self-efficacy, tutors with higher self-efficacy for tutoring are more apt to exert effort, tackle difficult material, and persist longer with tutees than are tutors with lower self-efficacy (Roscoe & Chi, 2007). There also is some evidence that tutoring can enhance tutors' motivation and self-efficacy (Roscoe & Chi, 2007).

Mentoring involves the teaching of skills and strategies to students or other professionals within advising and training contexts (Mullen, 2005). Mentoring can be formal/institutionalized or informal/casual. In a formal mentoring arrangement, the mentor may be assigned to the protégé based on organizational structure and procedures, whereas informal arrangements occur spontaneously and tend not to be officially structured or managed (Mullen, 2005). Ideally mentoring incorporates mutual learning and engagement between the mentor and protégé. Thus, mentoring is a fuller and deeper educational experience than tutoring, which is more apprenticeship oriented. While tutoring emphasizes content instruction within a short time period, mentoring typically involves modeled counsel and guidance over a longer time.

Mentoring is common at various levels of education, such as in learning communities, inquiry and writing groups, university–school partnerships, staff development, higher education, and peer coaching (Mullen, 2005). In higher education, mentoring often occurs between more- and less-experienced professors or between professors and students. In this context, mentoring ideally becomes a developmental relationship where more-experienced professors share their expertise with and invest time in less-experienced professors or students to nurture their achievement and self-efficacy (Johnson, 2006; Mullen, in press).

Mentoring reflects many social cognitive principles and can have instructional and motivational benefits. Protégés learn skills and strategies that can help them be successful in their environments from mentors who model, explain, and demonstrate these skills and strategies. Protégés who perceive themselves as similar in important ways to mentors may develop higher self-efficacy for being successful through their interactions with mentors. Similar to motivation, mentoring is a key self-regulated learning process that emphasizes goal-directed activity over time (Mullen, in press). Mentoring of doctoral students has been shown to improve their self-regulation, self-efficacy, motivation, and achievement (Mullen, in press). Mentors also can learn and refine their skills through their interactions with their protégés, which could raise their self-efficacy for continuing to succeed. Consistent with social cognitive theory, the mentoring relationship can result in reciprocal benefits for both parties.

SUMMARY

Social cognitive learning theory contends that people learn from their social environments. In Bandura's theory, human functioning is viewed as a series of reciprocal interactions among personal factors, behaviors, and environmental events. Learning is an information processing activity in which knowledge is cognitively represented as symbolic representations serving as guides for action. Learning occurs enactively through actual performances and vicariously by observing models, by listening to instructions, and by engaging with print or electronic materials. The consequences of behavior are especially important. Behaviors that result in successful consequences are retained; those that lead to failures are discarded.

Social cognitive theory presents an agentic perspective of human behavior in that persons can learn to set goals and self-regulate their cognitions, emotions, behaviors, and environments in ways to facilitate attainment of those goals. Key self-regulation processes are self-observation, self-judgment, and self-reaction. These processes occur prior to, during, and following task engagement.

Much historical work exists on imitation, but these perspectives do not fully capture the range and influence of modeling processes. Bandura and colleagues have shown how modeling greatly expands the range and rate of learning. Various modeling effects are distinguished: inhibition and disinhibition, response facilitation, and observational learning. Observational learning through modeling expands the learning rate, as well as the amount of knowledge acquired. Subprocesses of observational learning are attention, retention, production, and motivation.

According to social cognitive theory, observing a model does not guarantee learning or later ability to perform the behaviors. Rather, models provide information about probable consequences of actions and motivate observers to act accordingly. Factors influencing learning and performance are developmental status of learners, prestige and competence of models, and vicarious consequences to models.

Among the important motivational influences on learning are goals, outcome expectations, values, and self-efficacy. Goals, or what one is trying to accomplish, enhance learning through their effects on perceived progress, self-efficacy, and self-evaluations. As people work on a task, they compare their progress with their goal. The perception of progress raises self-efficacy and sustains motivation. Goal properties of specificity, proximity, and difficulty enhance self-perceptions and motivation, as do self-set goals and goals for which people make a commitment to attain.

Outcome expectations (perceived consequences of behavior) affect learning and motivation because people strive to attain desired outcomes and shun undesirable ones. People also act in concert with their values, working towards outcomes that they find self-satisfying.

Self-efficacy refers to perceived capabilities of learning or performing behaviors at designated levels. It is not the same as knowing what to do. People gauge their self-efficacy based on their performance attainments, vicarious consequences to models, forms of persuasion, and physiological indicators. Actual performances provide the most reliable information to use in assessing self-efficacy. Self-efficacy can affect choice of activities, effort, persistence, and achievement. Instructional self-efficacy and collective self-efficacy, which have been studied with teachers, bear a positive relation to student learning and achievement.

Researchers have found support for Bandura's theory in a variety of contexts involving cognitive, social, motor, health, instructional, and self-regulatory skills. Self-efficacy has been shown to predict behavioral change with different types of participants (e.g., adults, children) in various settings. This research also has shown that learning of complex skills occurs through a combination of enactive and vicarious learning. Observers acquire an approximation of the skill by observing models. Subsequent practice of the skill allows teachers to provide corrective feedback to learners. With additional practice, learners refine and internalize self-regulatory skills and strategies. Important instructional applications of social cognitive theory involve models (mastery, coping, teacher, peer, multiple), self-efficacy, worked examples, and tutoring and mentoring.

A summary of learning issues appears in Table 4.6.

Table 4.6
Summary of learning issues.

How Does Learning Occur?

Learning occurs enactively (by doing) and vicariously (by observing, reading, and listening). Much school learning requires a combination of vicarious and enactive experiences. Observational learning greatly expands the scope of human learning possible. Observational learning consists of four processes: attention, retention, production, and motivation. A major contribution of social cognitive theory is its emphasis on learning from the social environment.

What Is the Role of Memory?

Social cognitive researchers have not investigated in depth the role of human memory. Social cognitive theory predicts that memory includes information stored as images or symbols.

What Is the Role of Motivation?

Key motivational processes are goals, values, and expectations. People set goals for learning and assess progress against goals. Values reflect what persons find self-satisfying and believe are important. Expectations are of two types. Outcome expectations refer to the expected outcomes of actions. Efficacy expectations, or self-efficacy, refer to one's perceived capabilities for learning or performing tasks at designated levels. The belief that one is making goal progress substantiates self-efficacy and motivates one to continue learning.

How Does Transfer Occur?

Transfer is a cognitive phenomenon. It depends on people believing that certain actions in new or different situations are socially acceptable and will be met with favorable outcomes. Learners' self-efficacy also can facilitate transfer.

Which Processes Are Involved in Self-Regulation?

In the classical view, self-regulation consists of three processes: self-observation, self-judgment, and self-reaction. This view has been broadened to include activities before and after task engagement. Social cognitive theory stresses goals, self-efficacy, attributions, learning strategies, and self-evaluations. These processes reciprocally interact with one another such that goal attainment can lead to the adoption of new goals.

What Are the Implications for Instruction?

The use of modeling is highly recommended in instruction. The key is to begin with social influences, such as models, and gradually shift to self-influences as learners internalize skills and strategies. It also is important to determine how instruction affects not only learning but also learners' self-efficacy. Learners should be encouraged to set goals and assess goal progress. Teachers' self-efficacy affects instruction because efficacious teachers help promote student learning better. Social cognitive principles also are reflected in worked examples, tutoring, and mentoring.

FURTHER READING

Bandura, A. (1986). *Social foundations of thought and action: A social cognitive theory.* Englewood Cliffs, NJ: Prentice Hall.

Bandura, A. (1997). *Self-efficacy: The exercise of control.* New York: Freeman.

Goddard, R. D., Hoy, W. K., & Woolfolk Hoy, A. (2004). Collective efficacy beliefs: Theoretical developments, empirical evidence, and future directions. *Educational Researcher, 33*(3), 3–13.

Locke, E. A., & Latham, G. P. (2002). Building a practically useful theory of goal setting and task motivation: A 35-year odyssey. *American Psychologist, 57,* 705–717.

Pajares, F. (1996). Self-efficacy beliefs in achievement settings. *Review of Educational Research, 66,* 543–578.

Schunk, D. H. (1995). Self-efficacy and education and instruction. In J. E. Maddux (Ed.), *Self-efficacy, adaptation, and adjustment: Theory, research, and application.* (pp. 281–303). New York: Plenum Press.

Zimmerman, B. J., & Schunk, D. H. (2003). Albert Bandura: The scholar and his contributions to educational psychology. In B. J. Zimmerman & D. H. Schunk (Eds.), *Educational psychology: A century of contributions* (pp. 431–457). Mahwah, NJ: Erlbaum.

5

Information Processing Theory

Cass Paquin, a middle school mathematics teacher, seemed sad when she met with her team members Don Jacks and Fran Killian.

Don: What's the matter, Cass? Things got you down?

Cass: They just don't get it. I can't get them to understand what a variable is. "X" is a mystery to them.

Fran: Yes, "x" is too abstract for kids.

Don: It's abstract to adults too. "X" is a letter of the alphabet, a symbol. I've had the same problem. Some seem to pick it up, but many don't.

Fran: In my master's program they teach that you have to make learning meaningful. People learn better when they can relate the new learning to something they know. "X" has no meaning in math. We need to change it to something the kids know.

Cass: Such as what—cookies?

Fran: Well, yes. Take your problem $4x + 7 = 15$. How about saying: 4 times how many cookies plus 7 cookies equals 15 cookies? Or use apples. Or both. That way the kids can relate "x" to something tangible—real. Then "x" won't just be something they memorize how to work with. They'll associate "x" with things that can take on different values, such as cookies and apples.

Don: That's a problem with a lot of math—it's too abstract. When kids are little, we use real objects to make it meaningful. We cut pies into pieces to illustrate fractions. Then when they get older we stop doing that and use abstract symbols most of the time. Sure, they have to know how to use those symbols, but we should try to make the concepts meaningful.

Cass: Yes. I've fallen into that trap—teach the material like it's in the book. I need to try to relate the concepts better to what the kids know and what makes sense to them.

Information processing theories focus on how people attend to environmental events, encode information to be learned and relate it to knowledge in memory, store new knowledge in memory, and retrieve it as needed (Shuell, 1986). The tenets of these theories are as follows: "Humans are processors of information. The mind is an information-processing system. Cognition is a series of mental processes. Learning is the acquisition of mental representations." (Mayer, 1996, p. 154)

Information processing is not the name of a single theory; it is a generic name applied to theoretical perspectives dealing with the sequence and execution of cognitive events. Although certain theories are discussed in this chapter, there is no one dominant theory, and some researchers do not support any of the current theories (Matlin, 2009). Given this situation, one might conclude that information processing lacks a clear identity. In part this may be due to its influence by advances in various domains including communications, technology, and neuroscience.

Much early information processing research was conducted in laboratories and dealt with phenomena such as eye movements, recognition and recall times, attention to stimuli, and interference in perception and memory. Subsequent research has explored learning, memory, problem solving, visual and auditory perception, cognitive development, and artificial intelligence. Despite a healthy research literature, information processing principles have not always lent themselves readily to school learning, curricular structure, and instructional design. This situation does not imply that information processing has little educational relevance, only that many potential applications are yet to be developed. Researchers increasingly are applying principles to educational settings involving such subjects as reading, mathematics, and science, and applications remain research priorities. The participants in the opening scenario are discussing meaningfulness, a key aspect of information processing.

This chapter initially discusses the assumptions of information processing and gives an overview of a prototypical two-store memory model. The bulk of the chapter is devoted to explicating the component processes of attention, perception, short-term (working) memory, and long-term memory (storage, retrieval, forgetting). Relevant historical material on verbal learning and Gestalt psychology is mentioned, along with alternative views involving levels of processing and of memory activation. Language comprehension is discussed, and the chapter concludes by addressing mental imagery and instructional applications.

When you finish studying this chapter, you should be able to do the following:

■ Describe the major components of information processing: attention, perception, short-term (working) memory, long-term memory.

■ Distinguish different views of attention, and explain how attention affects learning.

■ Compare and contrast Gestalt and information processing theories of perception.

■ Discuss the major forms of verbal learning research.

■ Differentiate short- and long-term memory on the basis of capacity, duration, and component processes.

■ Define propositions, and explain their role in encoding and retrieval of long-term memory information.

■ Explain the major factors that influence encoding, retrieval, and forgetting.

■ Discuss the major components of language comprehension.

■ Explain the dual-code theory and apply it to mental imagery.

■ Identify information processing principles inherent in instructional applications involving advance organizers, the conditions of learning, and cognitive load.

INFORMATION PROCESSING SYSTEM

Assumptions

Information processing theorists challenged the idea inherent in behaviorism (Chapter 3) that learning involves forming associations between stimuli and responses. Information processing theorists do not reject associations, because they postulate that forming associations between bits of knowledge helps to facilitate their acquisition and storage in memory. Rather, these theorists are less concerned with external conditions and focus more on internal (mental) processes that intervene between stimuli and responses. Learners are active seekers and processors of information. Unlike behaviorists who said that people respond when stimuli impinge on them, information processing theorists contend that people select and attend to features of the environment, transform and rehearse information, relate new information to previously acquired knowledge, and organize knowledge to make it meaningful (Mayer, 1996).

Information processing theories differ in their views on which cognitive processes are important and how they operate, but they share some common assumptions. One is that information processing occurs in stages that intervene between receiving a stimulus and producing a response. A corollary is that the form of information, or how it is represented mentally, differs depending on the stage. The stages are qualitatively different from one another.

Another assumption is that information processing is analogous to computer processing, at least metaphorically. The human system functions similar to a computer: It receives information, stores it in memory, and retrieves it as necessary. Cognitive processing is remarkably efficient; there is little waste or overlap. Researchers differ in how far they extend this analogy. For some, the computer analogy is nothing more than a metaphor. Others employ computers to simulate activities of humans. The field of *artificial intelligence* is concerned with programming computers to engage in human activities such as thinking, using language, and solving problems (Chapter 7).

Researchers also assume that information processing is involved in all cognitive activities: perceiving, rehearsing, thinking, problem solving, remembering, forgetting, and imaging (Farnham-Diggory, 1992; Matlin, 2009; Mayer, 1996; Shuell, 1986; Terry, 2009). Information processing extends beyond human learning as traditionally delineated. This chapter is concerned primarily with those information functions most germane to learning.

Two-Store (Dual) Memory Model

Figure 5.1 shows an information processing model that incorporates processing stages. Although this model is generic, it closely corresponds to the classic model proposed by Atkinson and Shiffrin (1968, 1971).

Information processing begins when a stimulus input (e.g., visual, auditory) impinges on one or more senses (e.g., hearing, sight, touch). The appropriate *sensory register* receives the input and holds it briefly in sensory form. It is here that *perception (pattern recognition)* occurs, which is the process of assigning meaning to a stimulus input. This typically does not involve naming because naming takes time and information stays in the sensory register for only a fraction of a second. Rather, perception involves matching an input to known information.

Figure 5.1
Information processing model of
learning and memory.

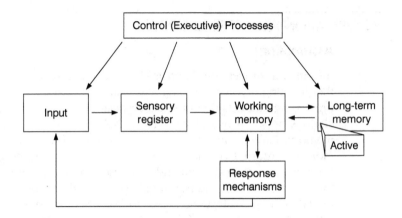

The sensory register transfers information to *short-term memory (STM)*. STM is a *working memory (WM)* and corresponds roughly to awareness, or what one is conscious of at a given moment. WM is limited in capacity. Miller (1956) proposed that it holds seven plus or minus two units of information. A unit is a meaningful item: a letter, word, number, or common expression (e.g., "bread and butter"). WM also is limited in duration; for units to be retained in WM they must be rehearsed (repeated). Without rehearsal, information is lost after a few seconds.

While information is in WM, related knowledge in *long-term memory (LTM)*, or permanent memory, is activated and placed in WM to be integrated with the new information. To name all the state capitals beginning with the letter A, students recall the names of states—perhaps by region of the country—and scan the names of their capital cities. When students who do not know the capital of Maryland learn "Annapolis," they can store it with "Maryland" in LTM.

It is debatable whether information is lost from LTM (i.e., forgotten). Some researchers contend that it can be, whereas others say that failure to recall reflects a lack of good retrieval cues rather than forgetting. If Sarah cannot recall her third-grade teacher's name (Mapleton), she might be able to if given the hint, "Think of trees." Regardless of theoretical perspective, researchers agree that information remains in LTM for a long time.

Control (executive) processes regulate the flow of information throughout the information processing system. Rehearsal is an important control process that occurs in WM. For verbal material, rehearsal takes the form of repeating information aloud or subvocally. Other control processes include coding (putting information into a meaningful context—an issue being discussed in the opening scenario), imaging (visually representing information), implementing decision rules, organizing information, monitoring level of understanding, and using retrieval, self-regulation, and motivational strategies. Control processes are discussed in this chapter and in Chapter 7.

The two-store model can account for many research results. One of the most consistent research findings is that when people have a list of items to learn, they tend to recall best the initial items (*primacy effect*) and the last items (*recency effect*), as portrayed in Figure 5.2. According to the two-store model, initial items receive the most rehearsal and

Figure 5.2
Serial position curve showing errors in recall as a function of item position.

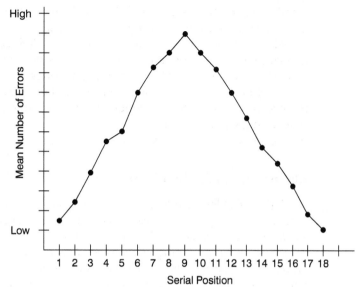

are transferred to LTM, whereas the last items are still in WM at the time of recall. Middle items are recalled the poorest because they are no longer in WM at the time of recall (having been pushed out by subsequent items), they receive fewer rehearsals than initial items, and they are not properly stored in LTM.

Research suggests, however, that learning may be more complex than the basic two-store model stipulates (Baddeley, 1998). One problem is that this model does not fully specify how information moves from one store to the other. The control processes notion is plausible but vague. We might ask: Why do some inputs proceed from the sensory registers into WM and others do not? Which mechanisms decide that information has been rehearsed long enough and transfer it into LTM? How is information in LTM selected to be activated? Another concern is that this model seems best suited to handle verbal material. How nonverbal representation occurs with material that may not be readily verbalized, such as modern art and well-established skills, is not clear.

The model also is vague about what really is learned. Consider people learning word lists. With nonsense syllables, they have to learn the words themselves and the positions in which they appear. When they already know the words, they must only learn the positions; for example, "cat" appears in the fourth position, followed by "tree." People must take into account their purpose in learning and modify learning strategies accordingly. What mechanism controls these processes?

Whether all components of the system are used at all times is also an issue. WM is useful when people are acquiring knowledge and need to relate incoming information to knowledge in LTM. But we do many things automatically: get dressed, walk, ride a bicycle, respond to simple requests (e.g., "Do you have the time?"). For many adults, reading (decoding) and simple arithmetic computations are automatic processes that place little demand on cognitive processes. Such automatic processing may not require the operation of WM. How does automatic processing develop and what mechanisms govern it?

These and other issues not addressed well by the two-store model (e.g., the role of motivation in learning and the development of self-regulation) do not disprove the model; rather, they are issues to be addressed. Although the two-store model is the best-known example of information processing theory, many researchers do not fully accept it (Matlin, 2009; Nairne, 2002). Alternative theories covered in this chapter are levels (or depth) of processing and activation level, and the newer connectionism and parallel distributed processing (PDP) theories. Before components of the two-store model are described in greater detail, levels of processing and activation level theories are discussed (connectionism and PDP are covered later in this chapter).

Alternatives to the Two-Store Model

Levels (Depth) of Processing. *Levels (depth) of processing* theory conceptualizes memory according to the type of processing that information receives rather than its location (Craik, 1979; Craik & Lockhart, 1972; Craik & Tulving, 1975; Lockhart, Craik, & Jacoby, 1976). This view does not incorporate stages or structural components such as WM or LTM (Terry, 2009). Rather, different ways to process information (such as levels or depth at which it is processed) exist: physical (surface), acoustic (phonological, sound), semantic (meaning). These three levels are dimensional, with physical processing being the most superficial (such as "*x*" as a symbol devoid of meaning as discussed by the teachers in the introductory scenario) and semantic processing being the deepest. For example, suppose you are reading and the next word is *wren.* This word can be processed on a surface level (e.g., it is not capitalized), a phonological level (rhymes with *den*), or a semantic level (small bird). Each level represents a more elaborate (deeper) type of processing than the preceding level; processing the meaning of *wren* expands the information content of the item more than acoustic processing, which expands content more than surface-level processing.

These three levels seem conceptually similar to the sensory register, WM, and LTM of the two-store model. Both views contend that processing becomes more elaborate with succeeding stages or levels. The levels of processing model, however, does not assume that the three types of processing constitute stages. In levels of processing, one does not have to move to the next process to engage in more elaborate processing; depth of processing can vary within a level. *Wren* can receive low-level semantic processing (small bird) or more extensive semantic processing (its similarity to and difference from other birds).

Another difference between the two information processing models concerns the order of processing. The two-store model assumes information is processed first by the sensory register, then by WM, and finally by LTM. The levels of processing model does not make a sequential assumption. To be processed at the meaning level, information does not have to be first processed at the surface and sound levels (beyond what processing is required for information to be received) (Lockhart et al., 1976).

The two models also have different views of how type of processing affects memory. In levels of processing, the deeper the level at which an item is processed, the better the memory because the memory trace is more ingrained. The teachers in the opening scenario are concerned about how they can help students process algebraic information at a deeper level. Once an item is processed at a particular point within a level, additional processing at that point should not improve memory. In contrast, the two-store model contends that memory can be improved with additional processing of the same type. This model predicts that the more a list of items is rehearsed, the better it will be recalled.

Some research evidence supports levels of processing. Craik and Tulving (1975) presented individuals with words. As each word was presented, they were given a question to answer. The questions were designed to facilitate processing at a particular level. For surface processing, people were asked, "Is the word in capital letters?" For phonological processing they were asked, "Does the word rhyme with *train?*" For semantic processing, "Would the word fit in the sentence, 'He met a _____ in the street'?" The time people spent processing at the various levels was controlled. Their recall was best when items were processed at a semantic level, next best at a phonological level, and worst at a surface level. These results suggest that forgetting is more likely with shallow processing and is not due to loss of information from WM or LTM.

Levels of processing implies that student understanding is better when material is processed at deeper levels. Glover, Plake, Roberts, Zimmer, and Palmere (1981) found that asking students to paraphrase ideas while they read essays significantly enhanced recall compared with activities that did not draw on previous knowledge (e.g., identifying key words in the essays). Instructions to read slowly and carefully did not assist students during recall.

Despite these positive findings, levels of processing theory has problems. One concern is whether semantic processing always is deeper than the other levels. The sounds of some words (*kaput*) are at least as distinctive as their meanings ("ruined"). In fact, recall depends not only on level of processing but also on type of recall task. Morris, Bransford, and Franks (1977) found that, given a standard recall task, semantic coding produced better results than rhyming coding; however, given a recall task emphasizing rhyming, asking rhyming questions during coding produced better recall than semantic questions. Moscovitch and Craik (1976) proposed that deeper processing during learning results in a higher potential memory performance, but that potential will be realized only when conditions at retrieval match those during learning.

Another concern with levels of processing theory is whether additional processing at the same level produces better recall. Nelson (1977) gave participants one or two repetitions of each stimulus (word) processed at the same level. Two repetitions produced better recall, contrary to the levels of processing hypothesis. Other research shows that additional rehearsal of material facilitates retention and recall as well as automaticity of processing (Anderson, 1990; Jacoby, Bartz, & Evans, 1978).

A final issue concerns the nature of a level. Investigators have argued that the notion of depth is fuzzy, both in its definition and measurement (Terry, 2009). As a result, we do not know how processing at different levels affects learning and memory (Baddeley, 1978; Nelson, 1977). Time is a poor criterion of level because some surface processing (e.g., "Does the word have the following letter pattern: consonant-vowel-consonant-consonant-vowel-consonant?") can take longer than semantic processing ("Is it a type of bird?"). Neither is processing time within a given level indicative of deeper processing (Baddeley, 1978, 1998). A lack of clear understanding of levels (depth) limits the usefulness of this perspective.

Resolving these issues may require combining levels of processing with the two-store idea to produce a refined memory model. For example, information in WM might be related to knowledge in LTM superficially or more elaborately. Also, the two memory stores might include levels of processing within each store. Semantic coding in LTM may lead to a more extensive network of information and a more meaningful way to remember information than surface or phonological coding.

Activation Level. An alternative concept of memory, but one similar to the two-store and levels of processing models, contends that memory structures vary in their *activation level* (Anderson, 1990). In this view, we do not have separate memory structures but rather one memory with different activation states. Information may be in an active or inactive state. When active, the information can be accessed quickly. The active state is maintained as long as information is attended to. Without attention, the activation level will decay, in which case the information can be activated when the memory structure is reactivated (Collins & Loftus, 1975).

Active information can include information entering the information processing system and information that has been stored in memory (Baddeley, 1998). Regardless of the source, active information either is currently being processed or can be processed rapidly. Active material is roughly synonymous with WM, but the former category is broader than the latter. WM includes information in immediate consciousness, whereas active memory includes that information plus material that can be accessed easily. For example, if I am visiting Aunt Frieda and we are admiring her flower garden, that information is in WM, but other information associated with Aunt Frieda's yard (trees, shrubs, dog) may be in an active state.

Rehearsal allows information to be maintained in an active state (Anderson, 1990). As with working memory, only a limited number of memory structures can be active at a given time. As one's attention shifts, activation level changes.

We encounter the activation level idea again later in this chapter (i.e., Anderson's ACT theory) because the concept is critical for storage of information and its retrieval from memory. The basic notion involves *spreading activation*, which means that one memory structure may activate another structure adjacent (related) to it (Anderson, 1990). Activation spreads from active to inactive portions of memory. The level of activation depends on the strength of the path along which the activation spreads and on the number of competing (interfering) paths. Activation spread becomes more likely with increased practice, which strengthens structures, and less likely with length of retention interval as strength weakens.

One advantage of activation level theory is that it can explain retrieval of information from memory. By dispensing with the notion of separate memory stores, the model eliminates the potential problem of transferring information from one store to the other. STM (WM) is that part of memory that is currently active. Activation decays with the passage of time, unless rehearsal keeps the information activated (Nairne, 2002).

At the same time, the activation level model has not escaped the dual-store's problems because it too dichotomizes the information system (active-inactive). We also have the problem of the strength level needed for information to pass from one state to another. Thus, we intuitively know that information may be partially activated (e.g., a crossword item on the "tip of your tongue"—you know it but cannot recall it), so we might ask how much activation is needed for material to be considered active. These concerns notwithstanding, the activation level model offers important insights into the processing of information.

We now examine in greater depth the components of the two-store model: attention, perception, encoding, storage, and retrieval (Shuell, 1986). The next section discusses attention; perception, encoding, storage, and retrieval are addressed in subsequent sections.

ATTENTION

The word *attention* is heard often in educational settings. Teachers and parents complain that students do not pay attention to instructions or directions. (This does not seem to be the problem in the opening scenario; rather, the issue involves meaningfulness of processing.) Even high-achieving students do not always attend to instructionally relevant events. Sights, sounds, smells, tastes, and sensations bombard us; we cannot and should not attend to them all. Our attentional capabilities are limited; we can attend to a few things at once. Thus, attention can be construed as the process of selecting some of many potential inputs.

Alternatively, attention can refer to a limited human resource expended to accomplish one's goals and to mobilize and maintain cognitive processes (Grabe, 1986). Attention is not a bottleneck in the information processing system through which only so much information can pass. Rather, it describes a general limitation on the entire human information processing system.

Theories of Attention

Research has explored how people select inputs for attending. In *dichotic listening* tasks, people wear headphones and receive different messages in each ear. They are asked to "shadow" one message (report what they hear); most can do this quite well. Cherry (1953) wondered what happened to the unattended message. He found that listeners knew when it was present, whether it was a human voice or a noise, and when it changed from a male to a female voice. They typically did not know what the message was, what words were spoken, which language was being spoken, or whether words were repeated.

Broadbent (1958) proposed a model of attention known as *filter (bottleneck) theory*. In this view, incoming information from the environment is held briefly in a sensory system. Based on their physical characteristics, pieces of information are selected for further processing by the perceptual system. Information not acted on by the perceptual system is filtered out—not processed beyond the sensory system. Attention is selective because of the bottleneck—only some messages receive further processing. In dichotic listening studies, filter theory proposes that listeners select a channel based on their instructions. They know some details about the other message because the physical examination of information occurs prior to filtering.

Subsequent work by Treisman (1960, 1964) identified problems with filter theory. Treisman found that during dichotic listening experiments, listeners routinely shifted their attention between ears depending on the location of the message they were shadowing. If they were shadowing the message coming into their left ear, and if the message suddenly shifted to the right ear, they continued to shadow the original message and not the new message coming into the left ear. Selective attention depends not only on the physical location of the stimulus but also on its meaning.

Treisman (1992; Treisman & Gelade, 1980) proposed a *feature-integration* theory. Sometimes we distribute attention across many inputs, each of which receives low-level processing. At other times we focus on a particular input, which is more cognitively demanding. Rather than blocking out messages, attention simply makes them less salient than those being attended to. Information inputs initially are subjected to different tests for physical characteristics and content. Following this preliminary analysis, one input may be selected for attention.

Treisman's model is problematic in the sense that much analysis must precede attending to an input, which is puzzling because presumably the original analysis involves some attention. Norman (1976) proposed that all inputs are attended to in sufficient fashion to activate a portion of LTM. At that point, one input is selected for further attention based on the degree of activation, which depends on the context. An input is more likely to be attended to if it fits into the context established by prior inputs. While people read, for example, many outside stimuli impinge on their sensory system, yet they attend to the printed symbols.

In Norman's view, stimuli activate portions of LTM, but attention involves more complete activation. Neisser (1967) suggested that preattentive processes are involved in head and eye movements (e.g., refocusing attention) and in guided movements (e.g., walking, driving). Preattentive processes are automatic—people implement them without conscious mediation. In contrast, attentional processes are deliberate and require conscious activity. In support of this point, Logan (2002) postulated that attention and categorization occur together. As an object is attended to, it is categorized based on information in memory. Attention, categorization, and memory are three aspects of deliberate, conscious cognition. Researchers currently are exploring the neurophysiological processes (Chapter 2) involved in attention (Matlin, 2009).

Attention and Learning

Attention is a necessary prerequisite of learning. In learning to distinguish letters, a child learns the distinctive features: To distinguish *b* from *d*, students must attend to the position of the vertical line on the left or right side of the circle, not to the mere presence of a circle attached to a vertical line. To learn from the teacher, students must attend to the teacher's voice and ignore other sounds. To develop reading comprehension skills, students must attend to the printed words and ignore such irrelevancies as page size and color.

Attention is a limited resource; learners do not have unlimited amounts of it. Learners allocate attention to activities as a function of motivation and self-regulation (Kanfer & Ackerman, 1989; Kanfer & Kanfer, 1991). As skills become routine, information processing requires less conscious attention. In learning to work multiplication problems, students must attend to each step in the process and check their computations. Once students learn multiplication tables and the algorithm, working problems becomes automatic and is triggered by the input. Research shows that much cognitive skill processing becomes automatic (Phye, 1989).

Differences in the ability to control attention are associated with student age, hyperactivity, intelligence, and learning disabilities (Grabe, 1986). Attention deficits are associated with learning problems. Hyperactive students are characterized by excessive motor activity, distractibility, and low academic achievement. They have difficulty focusing and sustaining attention on academic material. They may be unable to block out irrelevant stimuli, which overloads their processing systems. Sustaining attention over time requires that students work in a strategic manner and monitor their level of understanding. Normal achievers and older children sustain attention better than do low achievers and younger learners on tasks requiring strategic processing (Short, Friebert, & Andrist, 1990).

Teachers can spot attentive students by noting their eye focus, their ability to begin working on cue (after directions are completed), and physical signs (e.g., handwriting) indicating they are engaged in work (Good & Brophy, 1984). But physical signs alone may not be sufficient; strict teachers can keep students sitting quietly even though students may not be engaged in class work.

Teachers can promote student attention to relevant material through the design of classroom activities (Application 5.1). Eye-catching displays or actions at the start of lessons engage student attention. Teachers who move around the classroom—especially

APPLICATION 5.1
Student Attention in the Classroom

Various practices help keep classrooms from becoming predictable and repetitive, which decreases attention. Teachers can vary their presentations, materials used, student activities, and personal qualities such as dress and mannerisms. Lesson formats for young children should be kept short. Teachers can sustain a high level of activity through student involvement and by moving about to check on student progress.

Kathy Stone might include the following activities in a language arts lesson in her third-grade class. As students begin each section of a teacher-directed exercise, they can point to the location on their papers or in their book. The way sections are introduced can be varied: Students can read together in small groups, individual students can read and be called on to explain, or she can introduce the section. The way students' answers are checked also can be varied: Students can use hand signals or respond in

unison, or individual students can answer and explain their answers. As students independently complete the exercise, she moves about the room, checks students' progress, and assists those having difficulty learning or maintaining task focus.

A music teacher might increase student attention by using vocal exercises, singing certain selections, using instruments to complement the music, and adding movement to instruments. The teacher might combine activities or vary their sequence. Small tasks also can be varied to increase attention, such as the way a new music selection is introduced. The teacher might play the entire selection, then model by singing the selection, and then involve the students in the singing. Alternatively, for the last activity the teacher could divide the selection into parts, work on each of the small sections, and then combine these sections to complete the full selection.

Table 5.1
Suggestions for focusing and maintaining student attention.

Device	Implementation
Signals	Signal to students at the start of lessons or when they are to change activities.
Movement	Move while presenting material to the whole class. Move around the room while students are engaged in seat work.
Variety	Use different materials and teaching aids. Use gestures. Do not speak in a monotone.
Interest	Introduce lessons with stimulating material. Appeal to students' interests at other times during the lesson.
Questions	Ask students to explain a point in their own words. Stress that they are responsible for their own learning.

when students are engaged in seat work—help sustain student attention on the task. Other suggestions for focusing and maintaining student attention are given in Table 5.1.

Attention and Reading

A common research finding is that students are more likely to recall important text elements than less important ones (R. Anderson, 1982; Grabe, 1986). Good and poor readers locate important material and attend to it for longer periods (Ramsel & Grabe, 1983; Reynolds & Anderson, 1982). What distinguishes these readers is subsequent processing and comprehension. Perhaps poor readers, being more preoccupied with basic reading tasks (e.g., decoding), become distracted from important material and do not process it adequately for retention and retrieval. While attending to important material, good readers may be more apt to relate the information to what they know, make it meaningful, and rehearse it, all of which improve comprehension (Resnick, 1981).

The importance of text material can affect subsequent recall through differential attention (R. Anderson, 1982). Text elements apparently are processed at some minimal level so importance can be assessed. Based on this evaluation, the text element either is dismissed in favor of the next element (unimportant information) or receives additional attention (important information). Comprehension suffers when students do not pay adequate attention. Assuming attention is sufficient, the actual types of processing students engage in must differ to account for subsequent comprehension differences. Better readers may engage in much automatic processing initially and attend to information deemed important, whereas poorer readers might engage in automatic processing less often.

Hidi (1995) noted that attention is required during many phases of reading: processing orthographic features, extracting meanings, judging information for importance, and focusing on important information. This suggests that attentional demands vary considerably depending on the purpose of reading—for example, extracting details, comprehending, or new learning. Future research—especially neurophysiological—should help to clarify these issues (Chapter 2).

PERCEPTION

Perception (pattern recognition) refers to attaching meaning to environmental inputs received through the senses. For an input to be perceived, it must be held in one or more of the sensory registers and compared to knowledge in LTM. These registers and the comparison process are discussed in the next section.

Gestalt theory was an early cognitive view that challenged many assumptions of behaviorism. Although Gestalt theory no longer is viable, it offered important principles that are found in current conceptions of perception and learning. This theory is explained next, followed by a discussion of perception from an information processing perspective.

Gestalt Theory

The Gestalt movement began with a small group of psychologists in early twentieth-century Germany. In 1912, Max Wertheimer wrote an article on apparent motion. The article was significant among German psychologists but had no influence in the United States, where the Gestalt movement had not yet begun. The subsequent publication in English of Kurt Koffka's *The Growth of the Mind* (1924) and Wolfgang Köhler's *The Mentality of Apes* (1925) helped the Gestalt movement spread to the United States. Many Gestalt psychologists, including Wertheimer, Koffka, and Köhler, eventually emigrated to the United States, where they applied their ideas to psychological phenomena.

In a typical demonstration of the apparent motion perceptual phenomenon, two lines close together are exposed successively for a fraction of a second with a short time interval between each exposure. An observer sees not two lines but rather a single line moving from the line exposed first toward the line exposed second. The timing of the demonstration is critical. If the time interval between exposure of the two lines is too long, the observer sees the first line and then the second but no motion. If the interval is too short, the observer sees two lines side by side but no motion.

This apparent motion is known as the *phi phenomenon* and demonstrates that subjective experiences cannot be explained by referring to the objective elements involved. Observers perceive movement even though none occurs. Phenomenological experience (apparent motion) differs from sensory experience (exposure of lines). The attempt to explain this and related phenomena led Wertheimer to challenge psychological explanations of perception as the sum of one's sensory experiences because these explanations did not take into account the unique wholeness of perception.

Meaningfulness of Perception. Imagine a woman named Betty who is 5 feet tall. When we view Betty at a distance, our retinal image is much smaller than when we view Betty close up. Yet Betty is 5 feet tall and we know that regardless of how far away she is. Although the perception (retinal image) varies, the meaning of the image remains constant.

The German word *Gestalt* translates as "form," "figure," "shape," or "configuration." The essence of the *Gestalt psychology* is that objects or events are viewed as organized wholes (Köhler, 1947/1959). The basic organization involves a figure (what one focuses on) against a ground (the background). What is meaningful is the configuration, not the individual parts (Koffka, 1922). A tree is not a random collection of leaves, branches, roots, and trunk; it is a meaningful configuration of these elements. When viewing a tree, people typically do not focus on individual elements but rather on the whole. The human brain transforms objective reality into mental events organized as meaningful wholes. This capacity to view things as wholes is an inborn quality, although perception is modified by experience and training (Köhler, 1947/1959; Leeper, 1935).

Gestalt theory originally applied to perception, but when its European proponents came to the United States they found an emphasis on learning. Applying Gestalt ideas to learning was not difficult. In the Gestalt view, learning is a cognitive phenomenon involving reorganizing experiences into different perceptions of things, people, or events (Koffka, 1922, 1926). Much human learning is *insightful,* which means that the transformation from ignorance to knowledge occurs rapidly. When confronted with a problem, individuals figure out what is known and what needs to be determined. They then think about possible solutions. Insight occurs when people suddenly "see" how to solve the problem.

Gestalt theorists disagreed with Watson and other behaviorists about the role of consciousness (Chapter 3). In Gestalt theory, meaningful perception and insight occur only through conscious awareness. Gestalt psychologists also disputed the idea that complex phenomena can be broken into elementary parts. Behaviorists stressed associations—the whole is equal to the sum of the parts. Gestalt psychologists felt that the whole is meaningful and loses meaning when it is reduced to individual components. (In the opening scenario, "x" loses meaning unless it can be related to broader categories.) Instead, the whole is greater than the sum of its parts. Interestingly, Gestalt psychologists agreed with behaviorists in objecting to introspection, but for a different reason. Behaviorists viewed it as an attempt to study consciousness; Gestalt theorists felt it was inappropriate to modify perceptions to correspond to objective reality. People who used introspection tried to separate meaning from perception, whereas Gestalt psychologists believed that perception was meaningful.

Principles of Organization. Gestalt theory postulates that people use principles to organize their perceptions. Some of the most important principles are figure-ground relation, proximity, similarity, common direction, simplicity, and closure (Figure 5.3; Koffka, 1922; Köhler, 1926, 1947/1959).

The principle of *figure–ground relation* postulates that any perceptual field may be subdivided into a figure against a background. Such salient features as size, shape, color, and pitch distinguish a figure from its background. When figure and ground are ambiguous, perceivers may alternatively organize the sensory experience one way and then another (Figure 5.3a).

The principle of *proximity* states that elements in a perceptual field are viewed as belonging together according to their closeness to one another in space or time. Most people will view the lines in Figure 5.3b as three groups of three lines each, although other ways of perceiving this configuration are possible. This principle of proximity also is involved in the perception of speech. People hear (organize) speech as a series of words or phrases separated with pauses. When people hear unfamiliar speech sounds (e.g., foreign languages), they have difficulty discerning pauses.

Figure 5.3
Examples of Gestalt principles.

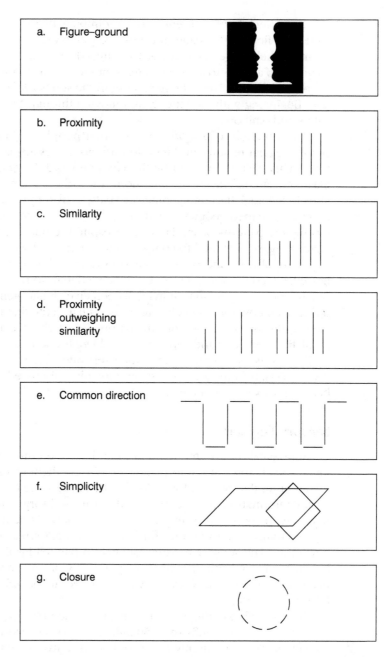

The principle of *similarity* means that elements similar in aspects such as size or color are perceived as belonging together. Viewing Figure 5.3c, people tend to see a group of three short lines, followed by a group of three long lines, and so on. Proximity can outweigh similarity; when dissimilar stimuli are closer together than similar ones (Figure 5.3d), the perceptual field tends to be organized into four groups of two lines each.

The principle of *common direction* implies that elements appearing to constitute a pattern or flow in the same direction are perceived as a figure. The lines in Figure 5.3e are most likely to be perceived as forming a distinct pattern. The principle of common direction also applies to an alphabetic or numeric series in which one or more rules define the order of items. Thus, the next letter in the series *abdeghjk* is *m,* as determined by the rule: Beginning with the letter *a* and moving through the alphabet sequentially, list two letters and omit one.

The principle of *simplicity* states that people organize their perceptual fields in simple, regular features and tend to form good Gestalts comprising symmetry and regularity. This idea is captured by the German word *Pragnanz,* which roughly translated means "meaningfulness" or "precision." Individuals are most likely to see the visual patterns in Figure 5.3f as one geometrical pattern overlapping another rather than as several irregularly shaped geometric patterns. The principle of *closure* means that people fill in incomplete patterns or experiences. Despite the missing lines in the pattern shown in Figure 5.3g, people tend to complete the pattern and see a meaningful picture.

Many of the concepts embodied in Gestalt theory are relevant to our perceptions; however, Gestalt principles are quite general and do not address the actual mechanisms of perception. To say that individuals perceive similar items as belonging together does not explain how they perceive items as similar in the first place. Gestalt principles are illuminating but vague and not explanatory. Research does not support some of the Gestalt predictions. Kubovy and van den Berg (2008) found that the joint effect of proximity and similarity was equal to the sum of their separate effects, not greater than it as Gestalt theory predicts. Information processing principles, discussed next, are clearer and provide a better explanation of perception.

Sensory Registers

Environmental inputs are attended to and received through the senses: vision, hearing, touch, smell, and taste. Information processing theories contend that each sense has its own register that holds information briefly in the same form in which it is received (e.g., visual information is held in visual form, auditory information in auditory form). Information stays in the sensory register for only a fraction of a second. Some sensory input is transferred to WM for further processing. Other input is erased and replaced by new input. The sensory registers operate in parallel fashion because several senses can be engaged simultaneously and independently of one another. The two sensory memories that have been most extensively explored are *iconic* (vision) and *echoic* (hearing) (Neisser, 1967).

In a typical experiment to investigate iconic memory, a researcher presents learners with rows of letters briefly (e.g., 50 milliseconds) and asks them to report as many as they remember. They commonly report only four to five letters from an array. Early work by Sperling (1960) provided insight into iconic storage. Sperling presented learners with rows of letters, then cued them to report letters from a particular row. Sperling estimated that, after exposure to the array, they could recall about nine letters. Sensory memory could hold more information than was previously believed, but while participants were recalling letters, the traces of other letters quickly faded. Sperling also found that the more time between the end of a presentation of the array and the beginning of recall, the poorer was the recall. This finding supports the idea that forgetting involves *trace decay,* or the loss of a stimulus from a sensory register over time.

Researchers debate whether the icon is actually a memory store or a persisting image. Sakitt argued that the icon is located in the rods of the eye's retina (Sakitt, 1976; Sakitt & Long, 1979). The active role of the icon in perception is diminished (but not eliminated) if the icon is a physical structure, although not all researchers agree with Sakitt's position.

There is evidence for an echoic memory similar in function to iconic memory. Studies by Darwin, Turvey, and Crowder (1972) and by Moray, Bates, and Barnett (1965) yielded results comparable to Sperling's (1960). Research participants heard three or four sets of recordings simultaneously and then were asked to report one. Findings showed that echoic memory is capable of holding more information than can be recalled. Similar to iconic information, traces of echoic information rapidly decay following removal of stimuli. The echoic decay is not quite as rapid as the iconic, but periods beyond 2 seconds between cessation of stimulus presentation and onset of recall produce poorer recall.

LTM Comparisons

Perception occurs through bottom-up and top-down processing (Matlin, 2009). In *bottom-up processing,* physical properties of stimuli are received by sensory registers and that information is passed to WM for comparisons with information in LTM to assign meanings. Environmental inputs have tangible physical properties. Assuming normal color vision, everyone who looks at a yellow tennis ball will recognize it as a yellow object, but only those familiar with tennis will recognize it as a tennis ball. The types of information people have acquired account for the different meanings they assign to objects.

But perception is affected not only by objective characteristics but also by prior experiences and expectations. *Top-down processing* refers to the influence of our knowledge and beliefs on perception (Matlin, 2009). Motivational states also are important. Perception is affected by what we wish and hope to perceive. We often perceive what we expect and fail to perceive what we do not expect. Have you ever thought you heard your name spoken, only to realize that another name was being called? While waiting to meet a friend at a public place or to pick up an order in a restaurant, you may hear your name because you expect to hear it. Also, people may not perceive things whose appearance has changed or that occur out of context. You may not recognize co-workers you meet at the beach because you do not expect to see them dressed in beach attire. Top-down processing often occurs with ambiguous stimuli or those registered only briefly (e.g., a stimulus spotted in the "corner of the eye").

An information processing theory of perception is *template matching*, which holds that people store *templates*, or miniature copies of stimuli, in LTM. When they encounter a stimulus, they compare it with existing templates and identify the stimulus if a match is found. This view is appealing but problematic. People would have to carry around millions of templates in their heads to be able to recognize everyone and everything in their environment. Such a large stock would exceed the brain's capability. Template theory also does a poor job of accounting for stimulus variations. Chairs, for example, come in all sizes, shapes, colors, and designs; hundreds of templates would be needed just to perceive a chair.

The problems with templates can be solved by assuming that they can have some variation. Prototype theory addresses this. *Prototypes* are abstract forms that include the basic ingredients of stimuli (Matlin, 2009; Rosch, 1973). Prototypes are stored in LTM and are compared with encountered stimuli that are subsequently identified based on the prototype they match or resemble in form, smell, sound, and so on. Some research supports the existence of prototypes (Franks & Bransford, 1971; Posner & Keele, 1968; Rosch, 1973).

A major advantage of prototypes over templates is that each stimulus has only one prototype instead of countless variations; thus, identification of a stimulus should be easier because comparing it with several templates is not necessary. One concern with prototypes deals with the amount of acceptable variability of the stimuli, or how closely a stimulus must match a prototype to be identified as an instance of that prototype.

A variation of the prototype model involves *feature analysis* (Matlin, 2009). In this view, one learns the critical features of stimuli and stores these in LTM as images or verbal codes (Markman, 1999). When a stimulus enters the sensory register, its features are compared with memorial representations. If enough of the features match, the stimulus is identified. For a chair, the critical features may be legs, seat, and a back. Many other features (e.g., color, size) are irrelevant. Any exceptions to the basic features need to be learned (e.g., bleacher and beanbag chairs that have no legs). Unlike the prototype analysis, information stored in memory is not an abstract representation of a chair but rather includes its critical features. One advantage of feature analysis is that each stimulus does not have just one prototype, which partially addresses the concern about the amount of acceptable variability. There is empirical research support for feature analysis (Matlin, 2009).

Treisman (1992) proposed that perceiving an object establishes a temporary representation in an object file that collects, integrates, and revises information about its current characteristics. The contents of the file may be stored as an object token. For newly perceived objects, we try to match the token to a memorial representation (dictionary) of object types, which may or may not succeed. The next time the object appears, we retrieve the object token, which specifies its features and structure. The token will facilitate perception if all of the features match but may impair it if many do not match.

Regardless of how LTM comparisons are made, research supports the idea that perception depends on bottom-up and top-down processing (Anderson, 1980; Matlin, 2009; Resnick, 1985). In reading, for example, bottom-up processing analyzes features and builds a meaningful representation to identify stimuli. Beginning readers typically use bottom-up processing when they encounter letters and new words and attempt to sound them out. People also use bottom-up processing when experiencing unfamiliar stimuli (e.g., handwriting).

Reading would proceed slowly if all perception required analyzing features in detail. In top-down processing, individuals develop expectations regarding perception based on the context. Skilled readers build a mental representation of the context while reading and expect certain words and phrases in the text (Resnick, 1985). Effective top-down processing depends on extensive prior knowledge.

TWO-STORE MEMORY MODEL

The two-store (dual) memory model serves as our basic information processing perspective on learning and memory, although as noted earlier not all researchers accept this model (Matlin, 2009). Research on verbal learning is covered next to provide a historical backdrop.

Verbal Learning

Stimulus-Response Associations. The impetus for research on verbal learning derived from the work of Ebbinghaus (Chapter 1), who construed learning as gradual strengthening of associations between verbal stimuli (words, nonsense syllables). With repeated pairings, the response *dij* became more strongly connected with the stimulus *wek*. Other responses also could become connected with *wek* during learning of a list of paired nonsense syllables, but these associations became weaker over trials.

Ebbinghaus showed that three important factors affecting the ease or speed with which one learns a list of items are *meaningfulness* of items, *degree of similarity* between them, and *length of time* separating study trials (Terry, 2009). Words (meaningful items) are learned more readily than nonsense syllables. With respect to similarity, the more alike items are to one another, the harder they are to learn. Similarity in meaning or sound can cause confusion. An individual asked to learn several synonyms such as *gigantic, huge, mammoth*, and *enormous* may fail to recall some of these but instead may recall words similar in meaning but not on the list (*large, behemoth*). With nonsense syllables, confusion occurs when the same letters are used in different positions (*xqv, khq, vxh, qvk*). The length of time separating study trials can vary from short (*massed practice*) to longer (*distributed practice*). When interference is probable (discussed later in this chapter), distributed practice yields better learning (Underwood, 1961).

Learning Tasks. Verbal learning researchers commonly employed three types of learning tasks: serial, paired-associate, and free-recall. In *serial learning*, people recall verbal stimuli in the order in which they were presented. Serial learning is involved in such school tasks as memorizing a poem or the steps in a problem-solving strategy. Results of many serial learning studies typically yield a *serial position curve* (Figure 5.2). Words at the beginning and end of the list are readily learned, whereas middle items require more trials for learning. The serial position effect may arise due to differences in distinctiveness of the various positions. People must remember not only the items themselves but also their positions in the list. The ends of a list appear to be more distinctive and are therefore "better" stimuli than the middle positions of a list.

In *paired-associate learning*, one stimulus is provided for one response item (e.g., *cat-tree, boat-roof, bench-dog*). Participants respond with the correct response upon presentation of the stimulus. Paired-associate learning has three aspects: discriminating among the stimuli, learning the responses, and learning which responses accompany which stimuli. Debate has centered on the process by which paired-associate learning occurs and the role of cognitive mediation. Researchers originally assumed that learning was incremental and that each stimulus–response association was gradually strengthened. This view was supported by the typical learning curve (Figure 5.4). The number of errors people make is high at the beginning, but errors decrease with repeated presentations of the list.

Research by Estes (1970) and others suggested a different perspective. Although list learning improves with repetition, learning of any given item has an *all-or-none* character: The learner either knows the correct association or does not know it. Over trials, the number of learned associations increases. A second issue involves cognitive mediation.

Figure 5.4
Learning curve showing errors as a
function of study trials.

Rather than simply memorizing responses, learners often impose their organization to make material meaningful. They may use cognitive mediators to link stimulus words with their responses. For the pair *cat-tree*, one might picture a cat running up a tree or think of the sentence, "The cat ran up the tree." When presented with *cat*, one recalls the image or sentence and responds with *tree*. Research shows that verbal learning processes are more complex than originally believed (Terry, 2009).

In *free-recall learning*, learners are presented with a list of items and recall them in any order. Free recall lends itself well to organization imposed to facilitate memory. Often during recall, learners group words presented far apart on the original list. Groupings often are based on similar meaning or membership in the same category (e.g., rocks, fruits, vegetables).

In a classic demonstration of the phenomenon of *categorical clustering*, learners were presented with a list of 60 nouns, 15 each drawn from the following categories: animals, names, professions, and vegetables (Bousfield, 1953). Words were presented in scrambled order; however, learners tended to recall members of the same category together. The tendency to cluster increases with the number of repetitions of the list (Bousfield & Cohen, 1953) and with longer presentation times for items (Cofer, Bruce, & Reicher, 1966). Clustering has been interpreted in associationist terms (Wood & Underwood, 1967); that is, words recalled together tend to be associated under normal conditions, either to one another directly (e.g., *pear-apple*) or to a third word (*fruit*). A cognitive explanation is that individuals learn both the words presented and the categories of which they are members (Cooper & Monk, 1976). The category names serve as mediational cues: When asked to recall, learners retrieve category names and then their members. Clustering provides insight into the structure of human memory and supports the Gestalt notion that individuals organize their experiences.

Verbal learning research identified the course of acquisition and forgetting of verbal material. At the same time, the idea that associations could explain learning of verbal material was simplistic. This became apparent when researchers moved beyond simple list learning to more meaningful learning from text. One might question the relevance of learning lists of nonsense syllables or words paired in arbitrary fashion. In school, verbal learning occurs within meaningful contexts, for example, word pairs (e.g., states and their capitals, English translations of foreign words), ordered phrases and sentences (e.g., poems, songs), and meanings for vocabulary words. With the advent of information processing views of learning and memory, many of the ideas propounded by verbal learning theorists were discarded or substantially modified. Researchers increasingly address learning and memory of context-dependent verbal material (Bruning, Schraw, Norby, & Ronning, 2004). We now turn to a key information processing topic—working memory.

Short-Term (Working) Memory

In the two-store model, once a stimulus is attended to and perceived, it is transferred to *short-term (working) memory* (*STM* or *WM;* Baddeley, 1992, 1998, 2001; Terry, 2009). WM is our memory of immediate consciousness. WM performs two critical functions: maintenance and retrieval (Unsworth & Engle, 2007). Incoming information is maintained in an active state for a short time and is worked on by being rehearsed or related to information retrieved from *long-term memory (LTM)*. As students read a text, WM holds for a few seconds the last words or sentences they read. Students might try to remember a particular point by repeating it several times (rehearsal) or by asking how it relates to a topic discussed earlier in the book (relate to information in LTM). As another example, assume that a student is multiplying 45 by 7. WM holds these numbers (45 and 7), along with the product of 5 and 7 (35), the number carried (3), and the answer (315). The information in WM ($5 \times 7 = ?$) is compared with activated knowledge in LTM ($5 \times 7 = 35$). Also activated in LTM is the multiplication algorithm, and these procedures direct the student's actions.

Research has provided a reasonably detailed picture of the operation of WM. WM is *limited in duration:* If not acted upon quickly, information in WM decays. In a classic study (Peterson & Peterson, 1959), participants were presented with a nonsense syllable (e.g., *khv*), after which they performed an arithmetic task before attempting to recall the syllable. The purpose of the arithmetic task was to prevent learners from rehearsing the syllable, but because the numbers did not have to be stored, they did not interfere with storage of the syllable in WM. The longer participants spent on the distracting activity, the poorer was their recall of the nonsense syllable. These findings imply that WM is fragile; information is quickly lost if not learned well. If, for example, you are given a phone number to call but then are distracted before being able to call or write it down, you may not be able to recall it.

WM also is *limited in capacity:* It can hold only a small amount of information. Miller (1956) suggested that the capacity of WM is seven plus or minus two items, where items are such meaningful units as words, letters, numbers, and common expressions. One can increase the amount of information by *chunking*, or combining information in a meaningful fashion. The phone number 555-1960 consists of seven items, but it can easily be chunked to two as follows: "Triple 5 plus the year Kennedy was elected president."

Sternberg's (1969) research on *memory scanning* provides insight into how information is retrieved from WM. Participants were presented rapidly with a small number of digits that did not exceed the capacity of WM. They then were given a test digit and were asked whether it was in the original set. Because the learning was easy, participants rarely made errors; however, as the original set increased from two to six items, the time to respond increased about 40 milliseconds per additional item. Sternberg concluded that people retrieve information from active memory by successively scanning items.

Control (executive) processes direct the processing of information in WM, as well as the movement of knowledge into and out of WM (Baddeley, 2001). Control processes include rehearsal, predicting, checking, monitoring, and metacognitive activities (Chapter 7). Control processes are goal directed; they select information relevant to people's plans and intentions from the various sensory receptors. Information deemed important is rehearsed. *Rehearsal* (repeating information to oneself aloud or subvocally) can maintain information in WM and improve recall (Baddeley, 2001; Rundus, 1971; Rundus & Atkinson, 1970).

Environmental or self-generated cues activate a portion of LTM, which then is more accessible to WM. This activated memory holds a representation of events occurring recently, such as a description of the context and the content. It is debatable whether active memory constitutes a separate memory store or merely an activated portion of LTM. Under the activation view, rehearsal keeps information in WM. In the absence of rehearsal, information decays with the passage of time (Nairne, 2002). High research interest on the operation of WM continues (Davelaar, Goshen-Gottstein, Ashkenazi, Haarmann, & Usher, 2005).

WM plays a critical role in learning. Compared with normally achieving students, those with mathematical and reading disabilities show poorer WM operation (Andersson & Lyxell, 2007; Swanson, Howard, & Sáez, 2006). A key instructional implication is not to overload students' WM by presenting too much material at once or too rapidly (see the section, Cognitive Load, later in this chapter). Where appropriate, teachers can present information visually and verbally to ensure that students retain it in WM sufficiently long enough to further cognitively process (e.g., relate to information in LTM).

Long-Term Memory

Knowledge representation in LTM depends on frequency and *contiguity* (Baddeley, 1998). The more often that a fact, event, or idea is encountered, the stronger is its representation in memory. Furthermore, two experiences that occur closely in time are apt to be linked in memory, so that when one is remembered, the other is activated. Thus, information in LTM is represented in *associative structures*. These associations are cognitive, unlike those in conditioning theories that are behavioral (stimuli and responses).

Information processing models often use computers for analogies, but some important differences exist, which are highlighted by associative structures. *Human memory is content addressable*. Information on the same topic is stored together, so that knowing what is being looked for will most likely lead to recalling the information (Baddeley, 1998). In contrast, *computers are location addressable*. Computers have to be told where information is to be stored. The nearness of the files or data sets on a hard drive to other files or data sets is purely arbitrary. Another difference is that information is stored precisely in computers. Human memory is less precise but often more colorful and informative. The name *Daryl Crancake* is stored in a computer's memory as "Daryl Crancake." In human memory it may be stored as "Daryl Crancake" or become distorted to "Darrell," "Darel," or "Derol," and "Cupcake," "Cranberry," or "Crabapple."

A useful analogy for the human mind is a library. Information in a library is content addressable because books on similar content are stored under similar call numbers. Information in the mind (as in the library) is also cross-referenced (Calfee, 1981). Knowledge that cuts across different content areas can be accessed through either area. For example, Amy may have a memory slot devoted to her 21st birthday. The memory includes what she did, whom she was with, and what gifts she received. These topics can be cross-referenced as follows: The jazz CDs she received as gifts are cross-referenced in the memory slot dealing with music. The fact that her next-door neighbor attended is filed in the memory slot devoted to the neighbor and neighborhood.

Knowledge stored in LTM varies in its richness. Each person has vivid memories of pleasant and unpleasant experiences. These memories can be exact in their details. Other types of knowledge stored in memories are mundane and impersonal: word meanings, arithmetic operations, and excerpts from famous documents.

To account for differences in memory, Tulving (1972, 1983) proposed a distinction between episodic and semantic memory. *Episodic memory* includes information associated with particular times and places that is personal and autobiographical. The fact that the word *cat* occurs in position three on a learned word list is an example of episodic information, as is information about what Amy did on her 21st birthday. *Semantic memory* involves general information and concepts available in the environment and not tied to a particular context. Examples include the words to the "Star Spangled Banner" and the chemical formula for water (H_2O). The knowledge, skills, and concepts learned in school are semantic memories. The two types of memories often are combined, as when a child tells a parent, "Today in school I learned [episodic memory] that World War II ended in 1945 [semantic memory]."

Researchers have explored differences between declarative and procedural memories (Gupta & Cohen, 2002). *Declarative memory* involves remembering new events and experiences. Information typically is stored in declarative memory quickly, and it is the memory most impaired in patients with amnesia. *Procedural memory* is memory for skills, procedures, and languages. Information in procedural memory is stored gradually—often with extensive practice—and may be difficult to describe (e.g., riding a bicycle). We return to this distinction shortly.

Another important issue concerns the *form* or *structure* in which LTM stores knowledge. Paivio (1971) proposed that knowledge is stored in *verbal* and *visual* forms, each of which is functionally independent but interconnected. Concrete objects (e.g., dog, tree, book) tend to be stored as images, whereas abstract concepts (e.g., love, truth, honesty) and linguistic structures (e.g., grammars) are stored in verbal codes. Knowledge can be stored both visually and verbally: You may have a pictorial representation of your home and also be able to describe it verbally. Paivio postulated that for any piece of knowledge, an individual has a preferred storage mode activated more readily than the other. Dual-coded knowledge may be remembered

Table 5.2

Characteristics and distinctions of memory systems.

Type of Memory	Characteristics
Short-term (working)	Limited capacity (about seven items), short duration (in the absence of rehearsal), immediate consciousness
Long-term	Theoretically unlimited capacity, permanent storage, information activated when cued
Episodic	Information in LTM associated with particular events, times, places
Semantic	Information in LTM involving general knowledge and concepts not tied to specific contexts
Verbal	Propositions (units of information) and procedures coded as meanings
Visual (iconic)	Information coded as pictures, images, scenes

better, which has important educational implications and confirms the general teaching principle of explaining (verbal) and demonstrating (visual) new material (Clark & Paivio, 1991).

Paivio's work is discussed further under mental imagery later in this chapter. His views have been criticized on the grounds that a visual memory exceeds the brain's capacity and requires some brain mechanism to read and translate the pictures (Pylyshyn, 1973). Some theorists contend that knowledge is stored only verbally (Anderson, 1980; Collins & Quillian, 1969; Newell & Simon, 1972; Norman & Rumelhart, 1975). Verbal models do not deny that knowledge can be represented pictorially but postulate that the ultimate code is verbal and that pictures in memory are reconstructed from verbal codes. Table 5.2 shows some characteristics and distinctions of memory systems.

The associative structures of LTM are *propositional networks*, or interconnected sets comprising nodes or bits of information (Anderson, 1990; Calfee, 1981; see next section). A *proposition* is the smallest unit of information that can be judged true or false. The statement, "My 80-year-old uncle lit his awful cigar," consists of the following propositions:

- I have an uncle.
- He is 80 years old.
- He lit a cigar.
- The cigar is awful.

Various types of propositional knowledge are represented in LTM. *Declarative knowledge* refers to facts, subjective beliefs, scripts (e.g., events of a story), and organized passages (e.g., Declaration of Independence). *Procedural knowledge* consists of concepts, rules, and algorithms. The declarative-procedural distinction also is referred to as explicit and implicit knowledge (Sun, Slusarz, & Terry, 2005). Declarative and procedural knowledge are discussed in this chapter. *Conditional knowledge* is knowing when to employ forms of declarative and procedural knowledge and why it is beneficial to do so (Gagné, 1985; Paris, Lipson, & Wixson, 1983; Chapter 7).

Information processing theories contend that learning can occur in the absence of overt behavior because learning involves the formation or modification of propositional networks; however, overt performance typically is required to ensure that students have acquired skills. Research on skilled actions (e.g., solving mathematical problems) shows that people typically execute behaviors according to a sequence of planned segments (Ericsson et al., 1993; Fitts & Posner, 1967; VanLehn, 1996). Individuals select a performance routine they expect will produce the desired outcome, periodically monitor their performances, make necessary corrections, and alter their performances following corrective feedback. Because performances often need to vary to fit contextual demands, people find that practicing adapting skills in different situations is helpful.

Transfer (Chapter 7) refers to the links between propositions in memory and depends on information being cross-referenced or the uses of information being stored along with it. Students understand that skills and concepts are applicable in different domains if that knowledge is stored in the respective networks. Teaching students how information is applicable in different contexts ensures that appropriate transfer occurs.

Influences on Encoding

Encoding is the process of putting new (incoming) information into the information processing system and preparing it for storage in LTM. Encoding usually is accomplished by making new information meaningful and integrating it with known information in LTM. Although information need not be meaningful to be learned—one unfamiliar with geometry could memorize the Pythagorean theorem without understanding what it means— meaningfulness improves learning and retention.

Attending to and perceiving stimuli do not ensure that information processing will continue. Many things teachers say in class go unlearned (even though students attend to the teacher and the words are meaningful) because students do not continue to process the information. Important factors that influence encoding are organization, elaboration, and schema structures.

Organization. Gestalt theory and research showed that well-organized material is easier to learn and recall (Katona, 1940). Miller (1956) argued that learning is enhanced by classifying and grouping bits of information into organized chunks. Memory research demonstrates that even when items to be learned are not organized, people often impose organization on the material, which facilitates recall (Matlin, 2009). Organized material improves memory because items are linked to one another systematically. Recall of one item prompts recall of items linked to it. Research supports the effectiveness of organization for encoding among children and adults (Basden, Basden, Devecchio, & Anders, 1991).

One way to organize material is to use a hierarchy into which pieces of information are integrated. Figure 5.5 shows a sample hierarchy for animals. The animal kingdom as a whole is on top, and underneath are the major categories (e.g., mammals, birds, reptiles). Individual species are found on the next level, followed by breeds.

Other ways of organizing information include the use of mnemonic techniques (Chapter 7) and mental imagery (discussed later in this chapter). Mnemonics enable

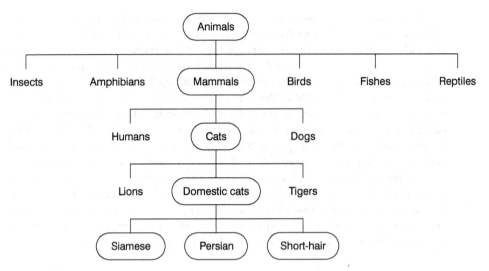

Figure 5.5
Memory network with hierarchical organization.

learners to enrich or elaborate material, such as by forming the first letters of words to be learned into an acronym, familiar phrase, or sentence (Matlin, 2009). Some mnemonic techniques employ imagery; in remembering two words (e.g., *honey* and *bread*), one might imagine them interacting with each other (honey on bread). Using audiovisuals in instruction can improve students' imagery.

Elaboration. *Elaboration* is the process of expanding upon new information by adding to it or linking it to what one knows. Elaborations assist encoding and retrieval because they link the to-be-remembered information with other knowledge. Recently learned information is easier to access in this expanded memory network. Even when the new information is forgotten, people often can recall the elaborations (Anderson, 1990). A problem that many students (not just the ones being discussed in the introductory scenario) have in learning algebra is that they cannot elaborate the material because it is abstract and does not easily link with other knowledge.

Rehearsing information keeps it in WM but does not necessarily elaborate it. A distinction can be drawn between *maintenance rehearsal* (repeating information over and over) and *elaborative rehearsal* (relating the information to something already known). Students learning U.S. history can simply repeat "D-Day was June 6, 1944," or they can elaborate it by relating it to something they know (e.g., In 1944 Roosevelt was elected president for the fourth time).

Mnemonic devices elaborate information in different ways. Once such device is to form the first letters into a meaningful sentence. For example, to remember the order of the planets from the sun you might learn the sentence, "*My very educated mother just served us nine pizzas,*" in which the first letters correspond to those of the planets

(*M*ercury, *V*enus, *E*arth, *M*ars, *J*upiter, *S*aturn, *U*ranus, *N*eptune, *P*luto). You first recall the sentence and then reconstruct planetary order based on the first letters.

Students may be able to devise elaborations, but if they cannot, they do not need to labor needlessly when teachers can provide effective elaborations. To assist storage in memory and retrieval, elaborations must make sense. Elaborations that are too unusual may not be remembered. Precise, sensible elaborations facilitate memory and recall (Bransford et al., 1982; Stein, Littlefield, Bransford, & Persampieri, 1984).

Schemas. A *schema* (plural *schemas* or *schemata*) is a structure that organizes large amounts of information into a meaningful system. Schemas include our generalized knowledge about situations (Matlin, 2009). Schemas are plans we learn and use during our environmental interactions. Larger units are needed to organize propositions representing bits of information into a coherent whole (Anderson, 1990). Schemas assist us in generating and controlling routine sequential actions (Cooper & Shallice, 2006).

In an early study, Bartlett (1932) found that schemas aid in comprehending information. In this experiment, a participant read a story about an unfamiliar culture, after which this person reproduced it for a second participant, who reproduced it for a third participant, and so on. By the time the story reached the 10th person, its unfamiliar context had been changed to one that participants were familiar with (e.g., a fishing trip). Bartlett found that as stories were repeated, they changed in predictable ways. Unfamiliar information was dropped, a few details were retained, and the stories became more like participants' experiences. They altered incoming information to fit their preexisting schemas.

Any well-ordered sequence can be represented as a schema. One type of schema is "going to a restaurant." The steps consist of activities such as being seated at a table, looking over a menu, ordering food, being served, having dishes picked up, receiving a bill, leaving a tip, and paying the bill. Schemas are important because they indicate what to expect in a situation. People recognize a problem when reality and schema do not match. Have you ever been in a restaurant where one of the expected steps did not occur (e.g., you received a menu but no one returned to your table to take your order)?

Common educational schemas involve laboratory procedures, studying, and comprehending stories. When given material to read, students activate the type of schema they believe is required. If students are to read a passage and answer questions about main ideas, they may periodically stop and quiz themselves on what they believe are the main points (Resnick, 1985). Schemas have been used extensively in research on reading and writing (McVee, Dunsmore, & Gavelek, 2005).

Schemas assist encoding because they elaborate new material into a meaningful structure. When learning material, students attempt to fit information into the schema's spaces. Less important or optional schema elements may or may not be learned. In reading works of literature, students who have formed the schema for a tragedy can easily fit the characters and actions of the story into the schema. They expect to find elements such as good versus evil, human frailties, and a dramatic denouement. When these events occur, they are fit into the schema students have activated for the story (Application 5.2).

APPLICATION 5.2
Schemas

Teachers can increase learning by helping students develop schemas. A schema is especially helpful when learning can occur by applying an ordered sequence of steps. Kathy Stone might teach the following schema to her children to assist their reading of unfamiliar words:

- Read the word in the sentence to see what might make sense.
- Look at the beginning and ending of the word—reading the beginning and the ending is easier than the whole word.
- Think of words that would make sense in the sentence and that would have the same beginning and ending.
- Sound out all the letters in the word.
- If these steps do not help identify the word, look it up in a dictionary.

With some modifications, this schema for figuring out new words can be used by students of any age.

In his American history class, Jim Marshall might teach his students to use a schema to locate factual answers to questions listed at the end of the chapter:

- Read through all of the questions.
- Read the chapter completely once.
- Reread the questions.
- Reread the chapter slowly and use paper markers if you find a section that seems to fit with one of the questions.
- Go back and match each question with an answer.
- When you find the answer, write it and the question on your paper.
- If you cannot find an answer, use your index to locate key words in the question.
- If you still cannot locate the answer, ask Mr. Marshall for help.

Schemas may facilitate recall independently of their benefits on encoding. Anderson and Pichert (1978) presented college students with a story about two boys skipping school. Students were advised to read it from the perspective of either a burglar or a home buyer; the story had elements relevant to both. Students recalled the story and later recalled it a second time. For the second recall, half of the students were advised to use their original perspective and the other half the other perspective. On the second recall, students recalled more information relevant to the second perspective but not to the first perspective and less information unimportant to the second perspective that was important to the first perspective. Kardash, Royer, and Greene (1988) also found that schemas exerted their primary benefits at the time of recall rather than at encoding. Collectively, these results suggest that at retrieval, people recall a schema and attempt to fit elements into it. This reconstruction may not be accurate but will include most schema elements. *Production systems*, which are discussed later, bear some similarity to schemas.

LONG-TERM MEMORY: STORAGE

This section discusses information storage in LTM. Although our knowledge about LTM is limited because we do not have a window into the brain, research has painted a reasonably consistent picture of the storage process.

The characterization of LTM in this chapter involves a structure with knowledge being represented as locations or nodes in networks, with networks connected (associated) with one another. Note the similarity between these cognitive networks and the neural networks discussed in Chapter 2. When discussing networks, we deal primarily with declarative knowledge and procedural knowledge. Conditional knowledge is covered in Chapter 7, along with metacognitive activities that monitor and direct cognitive processing. It is assumed that most knowledge is stored in LTM in verbal codes, but the role of imagery also is addressed at the end of this chapter.

Propositions

The Nature of Propositions. A *proposition* is the smallest unit of information that can be judged true or false. Propositions are the basic units of knowledge and meaning in LTM (Anderson, 1990; Kosslyn, 1984; Norman & Rumelhart, 1975). Each of the following is a proposition:

- The Declaration of Independence was signed in 1776.
- 2 + 2 = 4.
- Aunt Frieda hates turnips.
- I'm good in math.
- The main characters are introduced early in a story.

These sample propositions can be judged true or false. Note, however, that people may disagree on their judgments. Carlos may believe that he is bad in math, but his teacher may believe that he is very good.

The exact nature of propositions is not well understood. Although they can be thought of as sentences, it is more likely that they are meanings of sentences (Anderson, 1990). Research supports the point that we store information in memory as propositions rather than as complete sentences. Kintsch (1974) gave participants sentences to read that were of the same length but varied in the number of propositions they contained. The more propositions contained in a sentence, the longer it took participants to comprehend it. This implies that, although students can generate the sentence, "The Declaration of Independence was signed in 1776," what they most likely have stored in memory is a proposition containing only the essential information (Declaration of Independence—signed—1776). With certain exceptions (e.g., memorizing a poem), it seems that people usually store meanings rather than precise wordings.

Propositions form networks that are composed of individual nodes or locations. Nodes can be thought of as individual words, although their exact nature is unknown but probably abstract. For example, students taking a history class likely have a "history class" network comprising such nodes as "book," "teacher," "location," "name of student who sits on their left," and so forth.

Propositional Networks. Propositions are formed according to a set of rules. Researchers disagree on which rules constitute the set, but they generally believe that rules combine nodes into propositions and, in turn, propositions into higher-order structures or *networks*, which are sets of interrelated propositions.

Anderson's *ACT theory* (Anderson, 1990, 1993, 1996, 2000; Anderson et al., 2004; Anderson, Reder, & Lebiere, 1996) proposes an *ACT-R* (*Adaptive Control of Thought-Rational*) network model of LTM with a propositional structure. ACT-R is a model of cognitive architecture that attempts to explain how all components of the mind work together to produce coherent cognition (Anderson et al., 2004). A proposition is formed by combining two nodes with a *subject–predicate link*, or association; one node constitutes the subject and another node the predicate. Examples are (implied information in parentheses): "Fred (is) rich" and "Shopping (takes) time." A second type of association is the *relation–argument link*, where the relation is verb (in meaning) and the argument is the recipient of the relation or what is affected by the relation. Examples are "eat cake" and "solve puzzles." Relation arguments can serve as subjects or predicates to form complex propositions. Examples are "Fred eat(s) cake," and "solv(ing) puzzles (takes) time."

Propositions are interrelated when they share a common element. Common elements allow people to solve problems, cope with environmental demands, draw analogies, and so on. Without common elements, transfer would not occur; all knowledge would be stored separately and information processing would be slow. One would not recognize that knowledge relevant to one domain is also relevant to other domains.

Figure 5.6 shows an example of a propositional network. The common element is "cat" because it is part of the propositions, "The cat walked across the front lawn," and "The cat caught a mouse." One can imagine that the former proposition is linked with other propositions relating to one's house, whereas the latter is linked with propositions about mice.

Evidence suggests that propositions are organized in hierarchical structures. Collins and Quillian (1969) showed that people store information at the highest level of generality. For example, the LTM network for "animal" would have stored at the highest level such facts as "moves" and "eats." Under this category would come such species as "birds" and "fish." Stored under "birds" are "has wings," "can fly," and "has feathers" (although there are exceptions—chickens are birds but they do not fly). The fact that birds eat and move is not stored at the level of "bird" because that information is stored at the higher level of animal. Collins and Quillian found that retrieval times increased the farther apart concepts were stored in memory.

Propositions:
"The cat walked across the front lawn."
"The cat caught a mouse."

Figure 5.6
Sample propositional network.

The hierarchical organization idea has been modified by research showing that information is not always hierarchical. Thus, "collie" is closer to "mammal" than to "animal" in an animal hierarchy, but people are quicker to agree that a collie is an animal than to agree that it is a mammal (Rips, Shoben, & Smith, 1973).

Furthermore, familiar information may be stored both with its concept and at the highest level of generality (Anderson, 1990). If you have a bird feeder and you often watch birds eating, you might have "eat" stored with both "birds" and "animals." This finding does not detract from the central idea that propositions are organized and interconnected. Although some knowledge may be hierarchically organized, much information is probably organized in a less systematic fashion in propositional networks.

Storage of Knowledge

Declarative Knowledge. Declarative knowledge (knowing that something is the case) includes facts, beliefs, opinions, generalizations, theories, hypotheses, and attitudes about oneself, others, and world events (Gupta & Cohen, 2002; Paris et al., 1983). It is acquired when a new proposition is stored in LTM, usually in a related propositional network (Anderson, 1990). ACT theory postulates that declarative knowledge is represented in chunks comprising the basic information plus related categories (Anderson, 1996; Anderson, Reder, & Lebiere, 1996).

The storage process operates as follows. First, the learner receives new information, such as when the teacher makes a statement or the learner reads a sentence. Next, the new information is translated into one or more propositions in the learner's WM. At the same time, related propositions in LTM are cued. The new propositions are associated with the related propositions in WM through the process of spreading activation (discussed in the following section). As this point, learners might generate additional propositions. Finally, all the new propositions—those received and those generated by the learner—are stored together in LTM (Hayes-Roth & Thorndyke, 1979).

Figure 5.7 illustrates this process. Assume that a teacher is presenting a unit on the U.S. Constitution and says to the class, "The vice president of the United States serves as president of the Senate but does not vote unless there is a tie." This statement may cue other

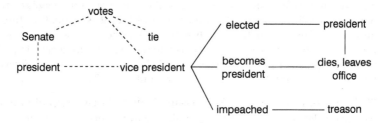

Figure 5.7
Storage of declarative knowledge.
Note: Dotted lines represent new knowledge; solid lines indicate knowledge in long-term memory.

propositional knowledge stored in students' memories relating to the vice president (e.g., elected with the president, becomes president when the president dies or resigns, can be impeached for crimes of treason) and the Senate (e.g., 100 members, two elected from each state, 6-year terms). Putting these propositions together, the students should infer that the vice president would vote if 50 senators voted for a bill and 50 voted against it.

Storage problems can occur when students have no preexisting propositions with which to link new information. Students who have not heard of the U.S. Constitution and do not know what a constitution is will draw a blank when they hear the word for the first time. Conceptually meaningless information can be stored in LTM, but students learn better when new information is related to something they know. Showing students a facsimile of the U.S. Constitution or relating it to something they have studied (e.g., Declaration of Independence) gives them a referent to link with the new information.

Even when students have studied related material, they may not automatically link it with new information. Often the links need to be made explicit. When discussing the function of the vice president in the Senate, teachers could remind students of the composition of the U.S. Senate and the other roles of the vice president. Propositions sharing a common element are linked in LTM only if they are active in WM simultaneously. This point helps to explain why students might fail to see how new material relates to old material, even though the link is clear to the teacher. Instruction that best establishes propositional networks in learners' minds incorporates review, organization of material, and reminders of things they know but are not thinking of now.

As with many memory processes, meaningfulness, organization, and elaboration facilitate storing information in memory. Meaningfulness is important because meaningful information can be easily associated with preexisting information in memory. Consequently, less rehearsal is necessary, which saves space and time of information in WM. The students being discussed in the opening scenario are having a problem making algebra meaningful, and the teachers express their frustration at not teaching the content in a meaningful fashion.

A study by Bransford and Johnson (1972) provides a dramatic illustration of the role of meaningfulness in storage and comprehension. Consider the following passage:

> The procedure is actually quite simple. First you arrange things into different groups. Of course, one pile may be sufficient depending on how much there is to do. If you have to go somewhere else due to lack of facilities that is the next step, otherwise you are pretty well set. It is important not to overdo things. That is, it is better to do too few things at once than too many. In the short run this may not seem important, but complications can easily arise. A mistake can be expensive as well. At first the whole procedure will seem complicated. Soon, however, it will become just another facet of life. It is difficult to foresee any end to the necessity for this task in the immediate future, but then one never can tell. After the procedure is completed one arranges the materials into different groups again. Then they can be put into their appropriate places. Eventually they will be used once more and the whole cycle will then have to be repeated. However, that is part of life. (p. 722)

Without prior knowledge this passage is difficult to comprehend and store in memory because relating it to existing knowledge in memory is hard to do. However, knowing that it is about "washing clothes" makes remembering and comprehension easier. Bransford and Johnson found that students who knew the topic recalled about twice as much as those who were unaware of it. The importance of meaningfulness in learning has been demonstrated in numerous other studies (Anderson, 1990; Chiesi, Spilich, & Voss, 1979; Spilich, Vesonder, Chiesi, & Voss, 1979).

Organization facilitates storage because well-organized material is easier to relate to preexisting memory networks than is poorly organized material (Anderson, 1990). To the extent that material can be organized into a hierarchical arrangement, it provides a ready structure to be accepted into LTM. Without an existing LTM network, creating a new LTM network is easier with well-organized information than with poorly organized information.

Elaboration, or the process of adding information to material to be learned, improves storage because by elaborating information learners may be able to relate it to something they know. Through spreading activation, the elaborated material may be quickly linked with information in memory. For example, a teacher might be discussing the Mt. Etna volcano. Students who can elaborate that knowledge by relating it to their personal knowledge of volcanoes (e.g., Mt. St. Helens) will be able to associate the new and old information in memory and better retain the new material.

Spreading Activation. *Spreading activation* helps to explain how new information is linked to knowledge in LTM (Anderson, 1983, 1984, 1990, 2000; Collins & Loftus, 1975). The basic underlying principles are as follows (Anderson, 1984):

- Human knowledge can be represented as a network of nodes, where nodes correspond to concepts and links to associations among these concepts.
- The nodes in this network can be in various states that correspond to their levels of activation. More active nodes are processed "better."
- Activation can spread along these network paths by a mechanism whereby nodes can cause their neighboring nodes to become active. (p. 61)

Anderson (1990) cites the example of an individual presented with the word *dog*. This word is associatively linked with such other concepts in the individual's LTM as *bone, cat*, and *meat*. In turn, each of these concepts is linked to other concepts. The activation of *dog* in LTM will spread beyond *dog* to linked concepts, with the spread lessening with concepts farther away from *dog*.

Experimental support for the existence of spreading activation was obtained by Meyer and Schvaneveldt (1971). These investigators used a reaction time task that presented participants with two strings of letters and asked them to decide whether both were words. Words associatively linked (*bread, butter*) were recognized faster than words not linked (*nurse, butter*).

Spreading activation results in a larger portion of LTM being activated than knowledge immediately associated with the content of WM. Activated information stays in LTM unless it is deliberately accessed, but this information is more readily accessible to WM. Spreading activation also facilitates transfer of knowledge to different domains. Transfer depends on propositional networks in LTM being activated by the same cue, so students recognize that knowledge is applicable in the domains.

Schemas. Propositional networks represent small pieces of knowledge. *Schemas (or schemata)* are large networks that represent the structure of objects, persons, and events

(Anderson, 1990). Structure is represented with a series of "slots," each of which corresponds to an attribute. In the schema or slot for *houses*, some attributes (and their values) might be as follows: material (wood, brick), contents (rooms), and function (human dwelling). Schemas are hierarchical; they are joined to superordinate ideas (building) and subordinate ones (roof).

Brewer and Treyens (1981) found research support for the underlying nature of schemas. Individuals were asked to wait in an office for a brief period, after which they were brought into a room where they wrote down everything they could recall about the office. Recall reflected the strong influence of a schema for *office*. They correctly recalled the office having a desk and a chair (typical attributes) but not that the office contained a skull (nontypical attribute). Books are a typical attribute of offices; although the office had no books, many persons incorrectly recalled books.

Schemas are important during teaching and for transfer (Matlin, 2009). Once students learn a schema, teachers can activate this knowledge when they teach any content to which the schema is applicable. Suppose an instructor teaches a general schema for describing geographical formations (e.g., mountain, volcano, glacier, river). The schema might contain the following attributes: height, material, and activity. Once students learn the schema, they can employ it to categorize new formations they study. In so doing, they would create new schemata for the various formations.

Procedural Knowledge. Procedural knowledge, or knowledge of how to perform cognitive activities (Anderson, 1990; Gupta & Cohen, 2002; Hunt, 1989; Paris et al., 1983), is central to much school learning. We use procedural knowledge to solve mathematical problems, summarize information, skim passages, and perform laboratory techniques.

Procedural knowledge may be stored as verbal codes and images, much the same way as declarative knowledge is stored. ACT theory posits that procedural knowledge is stored as a production system (Anderson, 1996; Anderson, Reder, & Lebiere, 1996). A *production system* (or *production*) is a network of condition–action sequences (rules), in which the condition is the set of circumstances that activates the system and the action is the set of activities that occurs (Anderson, 1990; Andre, 1986; see next section). Production systems seem conceptually similar to neural networks (discussed in Chapter 2).

Production Systems and Connectionist Models

Production systems and connectionist models provide paradigms for examining the operation of cognitive learning processes (Anderson, 1996, 2000; Smith, 1996). Connectionist models represent a relatively new perspective on cognitive learning. To date, there is little research on connectionist models that is relevant to education. Additional sources provide further information about connectionist models (Bourne, 1992; Farnham-Diggory, 1992; Matlin, 2009; Siegler, 1989).

Production Systems. ACT—an activation theory—specifies that a *production system* (or *production*) is a network of condition–action sequences (rules), in which the condition is a set of circumstances that activates the system and the action is the set of activities that occurs (Anderson, 1990, 1996, 2000; Anderson, Reder, & Lebiere, 1996; Andre, 1986). A production consists of *if–then statements: If* statements (the condition) include the goal and test statements and *then* statements are the actions. As an example:

- IF I see two numbers and they must be added,
- THEN decide which is larger and start with that number and count up to the next one. (Farnham-Diggory, 1992, p. 113)

Although productions are forms of procedural knowledge that can have conditions (conditional knowledge) attached to them, they also include declarative knowledge.

Learning procedures for performing skills often occurs slowly (J. Anderson, 1982). First, learners represent a sequence of actions in terms of declarative knowledge. Each step in the sequence is represented as a proposition. Learners gradually drop out individual cues and integrate the separate steps into a continuous sequence of actions. For example, children learning to add a column of numbers are apt initially to perform each step slowly, possibly even verbalizing it aloud. As they become more skillful, adding becomes part of an automatic, smooth sequence that occurs rapidly and without deliberate, conscious attention. Automaticity is a central feature of many cognitive processes (e.g., attention, retrieval) (Moors & De Houwer, 2006). When processes become automatic, this allows the processing system to devote itself to complex parts of tasks (Chapter 7).

A major constraint on skill learning is the size limitation of WM (Baddeley, 2001). Procedures would be learned quicker if WM could simultaneously hold all the declarative knowledge propositions. Because it cannot, students must combine propositions slowly and periodically stop and think (e.g., "What do I do next?"). WM contains insufficient space to create large procedures in the early stages of learning. As propositions are combined into small procedures, the latter are stored in WM simultaneously with other propositions. In this fashion, larger productions are gradually constructed.

These ideas explain why skill learning proceeds faster when students can perform the prerequisite skills (i.e., when they become automatic). When the latter exist as well-established productions, they are activated in WM at the same time as new propositions to be integrated. In learning to solve long-division problems, students who know how to multiply simply recall the procedure when necessary; it does not have to be learned along with the other steps in long division. Although this does not seem to be the problem in the opening scenario, learning algebra is difficult for students with basic skill deficiencies (e.g., addition, multiplication), because even simple algebra problems become difficult to answer correctly. Children with reading disabilities seem to lack the capability to effectively process and store information at the same time (de Jong, 1998).

In some cases, specifying the steps in detail is difficult. For example, thinking creatively may not follow the same sequence for each student. Teachers can model creative thinking to include such self-questions as, "Are there any other possibilities?" Whenever steps can be specified, teacher demonstrations of the steps in a procedure, followed by student practice, are effective (Rosenthal & Zimmerman, 1978).

One problem with the learning of procedures is that students might view them as lockstep sequences to be followed regardless of whether they are appropriate. Gestalt psychologists showed how *functional fixedness*, or an inflexible approach to a problem, hinders problem solving (Duncker, 1945; Chapter 7). Adamantly following a sequence while learning may assist its acquisition, but learners also need to understand the circumstances under which other methods are more efficient.

Sometimes students overlearn skill procedures to the point that they avoid using alternative, easier procedures. At the same time, there are few, if any, alternatives for many of the procedures students learn (e.g., decoding words, adding numbers, determining subject–verb agreement). Overlearning these skills to the point of automatic production becomes an asset to students and makes it easier to learn new skills (e.g., drawing inferences, writing term papers) that require mastery of these basic skills.

One might argue that teaching problem-solving or inference skills to students who are deficient in basic mathematical facts and decoding skills, respectively, makes little sense. Research shows that poor grasp of basic number facts is related to low performance on complex arithmetic tasks (Romberg & Carpenter, 1986), and slow decoding relates to poor comprehension (Calfee & Drum, 1986; Perfetti & Lesgold, 1979). Not only is skill learning affected, but self-efficacy (Chapter 4) suffers as well.

Practice is essential to instate basic procedural knowledge (Lesgold, 1984). In the early stages of learning, students require corrective feedback highlighting the portions of the procedure they implemented correctly and those requiring modification. Often students learn some parts of a procedure but not others. As students gain skill, teachers can point out their progress in solving problems quicker or more accurately.

Transfer of procedural knowledge occurs when the knowledge is linked in LTM with different content. Transfer is aided by having students apply the procedures to the different content and altering the procedures as necessary. General problem-solving strategies (Chapter 7) are applicable to varied academic content. Students learn about their generality by applying them to different subjects (e.g., reading, mathematics).

Productions are relevant to cognitive learning, but several issues need to be addressed. ACT theory posits a single set of cognitive processes to account for diverse phenomena (Matlin, 2009). This view conflicts with other cognitive perspectives that delineate different processes depending on the type of learning (Shuell, 1986). Rumelhart and Norman (1978) identified three types of learning. *Accretion* involves encoding new information in terms of existing schemata; *restructuring* (schema creation) is the process of forming new schemata; and *tuning* (schema evolution) refers to the slow modification and refinement of schemata that occurs when using them in various contexts. These involve different amounts of practice: much for tuning and less for accretion and restructuring.

ACT is essentially a computer program designed to simulate learning in a coherent manner. As such, it may not address the range of factors involved in human learning. One issue concerns how people know which production to use in a given situation, especially if situations lend themselves to different productions being employed. Productions may be ordered in terms of likelihood, but a means for deciding what production is best given the circumstance must be available. Also of concern is the issue of how productions are altered. For example, if a production does not work effectively, do learners discard it, modify it, or retain it but seek more evidence? What is the mechanism for deciding when and how productions are changed?

Another concern relates to Anderson's (1983, 1990) claim that productions begin as declarative knowledge. This assumption seems too strong given evidence that this sequence is not always followed (Hunt, 1989). Because representing skill procedures as pieces of declarative knowledge is essentially a way station along the road to mastery, one might question whether students should learn the individual steps. The individual steps will eventually not be used, so time may be better spent allowing students to practice them. Providing students with a list of steps they can refer to as they gradually develop a procedure facilitates learning and enhances self-efficacy (Schunk, 1995).

Finally, one might question whether production systems, as generally described, are nothing more than elaborate stimulus-response (S-R) associations (Mayer, 1992). Propositions (bits of procedural knowledge) become linked in memory so that when one piece is cued, others also are activated. Anderson (1983) acknowledged the associationist nature of productions but believes they are more advanced than simple S-R associations because they incorporate goals. In support of this point, ACT associations are analogous to neural network connections (Chapter 2). Perhaps, as is the case with behaviorist theories, ACT can explain performance better than it can explain learning. These and other questions (e.g., the role of motivation) need to be addressed by research and related to learning of academic skills to establish the usefulness of productions in education better.

Connectionist Models. A line of recent theorizing about complex cognitive processes involves *connectionist models* (or *connectionism*, but not to be confused with Thorndike's connectionism discussed in Chapter 3; Baddeley, 1998; Farnham-Diggory, 1992; Smith, 1996). Like productions, connectionist models represent computer simulations of learning processes. These models link learning to neural system processing where impulses fire across synapses to form connections (Chapter 2). The assumption is that higher-order cognitive processes are formed by connecting a large number of basic elements such as neurons (Anderson, 1990, 2000; Anderson, Reder, & Lebiere, 1996; Bourne, 1992). Connectionist models include distributed representations of knowledge (i.e., spread out over a wide network), parallel processing (many operations occur at once), and interactions among large numbers of simple processing units (Siegler, 1989). Connections may be at different stages of activation (Smith, 1996) and linked to input into the system, output, or one or more in-between layers.

Rumelhart and McClelland (1986) described a system of *parallel distributed processing (PDP)*. This model is useful for making categorical judgments about information in memory. These authors provided an example involving two gangs and information about gang members, including age, education, marital status, and occupation. In memory, the similar characteristics of each individual are linked. For example, Members 2 and 5 would be linked if they both were about the same age, married, and engaged in similar gang activities. To retrieve information about Member 2, we could activate the memory unit with the person's name, which in turn would activate other memory units. The pattern created through this spread of activation corresponds to the memory representation for the individual. Borowsky and Besner (2006) described a PDP model for making lexical decisions (e.g., deciding whether a stimulus is a word).

Connectionist units bear some similarity to productions in that both involve memory activation and linked ideas. At the same time, differences exist. In connectionist models all units are alike, whereas productions contain conditions and actions. Units are differentiated in terms of pattern and degree of activation. Another difference concerns rules. Productions are governed by rules. Connectionism has no set rules. Neurons "know" how to activate patterns; after the fact we may provide a rule as a label for the sequence (e.g., rules for naming patterns activated; Farnham-Diggory, 1992).

One problem with the connectionist approach is explaining how the system knows which of the many units in memory to activate and how these multiple activations become linked in integrated sequences. This process seems straightforward in the case of well-established patterns; for example, neurons know how to react to a ringing telephone, a cold wind, and a teacher announcing, "Everyone pay attention!" With less-established patterns the activations may be problematic. We also might ask how neurons become self-activating in the first place. This question is important because it helps to explain the role of connections in learning and memory. Although the notion of connections seems plausible and grounded in what we know about neurological functioning (Chapter 2), to date this model has been more useful in explaining perception rather than learning and problem solving (Mayer, 1992). The latter applications require considerable research.

LONG-TERM MEMORY: RETRIEVAL AND FORGETTING

Retrieval

Retrieval Strategies. What happens when a student is asked a question such as, "What does the vice president of the United States do in the Senate?" The question enters the student's WM and is broken into propositions. The process by which this occurs has a neurological basis and is not well understood, but available evidence indicates that information activates associated information in memory networks through *spreading activation* to determine if they answer the question. If they do, that information is translated into a sentence and verbalized to the questioner or into motor patterns to be written. If the activated propositions do not answer the query, activation spreads until the answer is located. When insufficient time is available for spreading activation to locate the answer, students may make an educated guess (Anderson, 1990).

Much cognitive processing occurs automatically. We routinely remember our home address and phone number, Social Security number, and close friends' names. People are often unaware of all the steps taken to answer a question. However, when people must judge several activated propositions to determine whether the propositions properly answer the question, they are more aware of the process.

Because knowledge is encoded as propositions, retrieval proceeds even though the information to be retrieved does not exist in exact form in memory. If a teacher asks whether the vice president would vote on a bill when the initial vote was 51 for and 49 against, students could retrieve the proposition that the vice president votes only in the event of a tie. By implication, the vice president would not vote. Processing like this, which involves construction, takes longer than when a question requires information coded in memory in the same form, but students should respond correctly assuming they activate the relevant propositions in LTM. The same process is involved in rule learning and transfer (Chapter 7): students learn a rule (e.g., the Pythagorean theorem in mathematics) and recall and apply it to arrive at solutions of problems they have never seen before.

Encoding Specificity. Retrieval depends on the manner of encoding. According to the *encoding specificity hypothesis* (Brown & Craik, 2000; Thomson & Tulving, 1970), the manner in which knowledge is encoded determines which retrieval cues will effectively activate that knowledge. In this view, the best retrieval occurs when retrieval cues match those present during learning (Baddeley, 1998).

Some experimental evidence supports encoding specificity. When people are given category names while they are encoding specific instances of the categories, they recall the instances better if they are given the category names at recall than if not given the names (Matlin, 2009). A similar benefit is obtained if they learn words with associates and then are given the associate names at recall than if not given the associates. Brown (1968) gave students a partial list of U.S. states to read; others read no list. Subsequently all students recalled as many states as they could. Students who received the list recalled more of the states on the list and fewer states not on it.

Encoding specificity also includes context. In one study (Godden & Baddeley, 1975), scuba divers learned a word list either on shore or underwater. On a subsequent free recall task, learners recalled more words when they were in the same environment as the one in which they learned the words than when they were in the other environment.

Encoding specificity can be explained in terms of spreading activation among propositional networks. Cues associated with material to be learned are linked in LTM with the material at the time of encoding. During recall, presentation of these cues activates the relevant portions in LTM. In the absence of the same cues, recall depends on recalling individual propositions. Because the cues lead to spreading activation (not the individual propositions or concepts), recall is facilitated by presenting the same cues at encoding and recall. Other evidence suggests that retrieval is guided in part by expectancies about what information is needed and that people may distort inconsistent information to make it coincide with their expectations (Hirt, Erickson, & McDonald, 1993).

Retrieval of Declarative Knowledge. Although declarative knowledge often is processed automatically, there is no guarantee that it will be integrated with relevant information in LTM. We can see this in the scenario at the start of this chapter. Information about algebraic variables and operations has little meaning for students, and they cannot integrate it well with existing information in memory. Meaningfulness, elaboration, and organization enhance the potential for declarative information to be effectively processed and retrieved. Application 5.3 provides some classroom examples.

Meaningfulness improves retrieval. Nonmeaningful information will not activate information in LTM and will be lost unless students rehearse it repeatedly until it becomes established in LTM, perhaps by forming a new propositional network. One also can connect the sounds of new information, which are devoid of meaning, to other similar sounds. The word *constitution*, for example, may be linked phonetically with other uses of the word stored in learners' memories (e.g., *Constitution Avenue*).

Meaningful information is more likely to be retained because it easily connects to propositional networks. In the opening scenario, one suggestion offered is to relate algebraic variables to tangible objects—things that students understand—to give the algebraic notation some meaning. Meaningfulness not only promotes learning, but it also saves time. Propositions in WM take time to process; Simon (1974) estimated that each new

APPLICATION 5.3
Organizing Information by Networks

Teachers enhance learning when they develop lessons to assist students to link new information with knowledge in memory. Information that is meaningful, elaborated, and organized is more readily integrated into LTM networks.

A teacher planning a botany unit on the reproduction of different species of plants might start by reviewing common plant knowledge that students have stored in their memories (e.g., basic structure, conditions necessary for growth). As the teacher introduces new information, students examine familiar live plants that reproduce differently to make the experience more meaningful. Factual information to be learned can be elaborated by providing visual drawings and written

details regarding the reproductive processes. For each live plant examined, students can organize the new information by creating outlines or charts to show the means of reproduction.

An art teacher planning a design unit might start by reviewing the various elements of color, shape, and texture. As the teacher introduces new techniques related to placement, combination of the various elements, and balance as it relates to the whole composition, manipulatives of various shapes, colors, and textures are provided for each student to use in creating different styles. The students can use the manipulatives to organize the elements and media they want to include in each of their design compositions.

piece of information takes 10 seconds to encode, which means that only six new pieces of information can be processed in a minute. Even when information is meaningful, much knowledge is lost before it can be encoded. Although every piece of incoming information is not important and some loss usually does not impair learning, students typically retain little information even under the best circumstances.

When we elaborate we add to information being learned with examples, details, inferences, or anything that serves to link new and old information. A learner might elaborate the role of the vice president in the Senate by thinking through the roll call and, when there is a tie, having the vice president vote.

Elaboration facilitates learning because it is a form of rehearsal: By keeping information active in WM, elaboration increases the likelihood that information will be permanently stored in LTM. This facilitates retrieval, as does the fact that elaboration establishes links between old and new information. Students who elaborate the role of the vice president in the Senate link this new information with what they know about the Senate and the vice president. Well-linked information in LTM is easier to recall than poorly linked information (Stein et al., 1984).

Although elaboration promotes storage and retrieval, it also takes time. Comprehending sentences requiring elaboration takes longer than sentences not requiring elaboration (Haviland & Clark, 1974). For example, the following sentences require drawing an inference that Marge took her credit card to the grocery store: "Marge went to the grocery store," and "Marge charged her groceries." The link is clarified in the following sentences: "Marge took her credit card to the grocery store," and "Marge used her credit card to pay for her groceries." Making explicit links between adjoining propositions assists their encoding and retention.

An important aspect of learning is deciding on the importance of information. Not all learned information needs to be elaborated. Comprehension is aided when students elaborate only the most important aspects of text (Reder, 1979). Elaboration aids retrieval by providing alternate paths along which activation can spread, so that if one path is blocked, others are available (Anderson, 1990, 2000). Elaboration also provides additional information from which answers can be constructed (Reder, 1982), such as when students must answer questions with information in a different form from that of the learned material.

In general, almost any type of elaboration assists encoding and retrieval; however, some elaborations are more effective than others. Activities such as taking notes and asking how new information relates to what one knows build propositional networks. Effective elaborations link propositions and stimulate accurate recall. Elaborations not linked well to the content do not aid recall (Mayer, 1984).

Organization takes place by breaking information into parts and specifying relationships between parts. In studying U.S. government, organization might involve breaking government into three branches (executive, legislative, judicial), breaking each of these into subparts (e.g., functions, agencies), and so on. Older students employ organization more often, but elementary children are capable of using organizational principles (Meece, 2002). Children studying leaves may organize them by size, shape, and edge pattern.

Organization improves retrieval by linking relevant information; when retrieval is cued, spreading activation accesses the relevant propositions in LTM. Teachers routinely organize material, but student-generated organization is also effective for retrieval. Instruction on organizational principles assists learning. Consider a schema for understanding stories with four major attributes: setting, theme, plot, and resolution (Rumelhart, 1977). The setting ("Once upon a time . . .") places the action in a context. The theme is then introduced, which consists of characters who have certain experiences and goals. The plot traces the actions of the characters to attain their goals. The resolution describes how the goal is reached or how the characters adjust to not attaining the goal. By describing and exemplifying these phases of a story, teachers help students learn to identify them on their own.

Retrieval of Procedural Knowledge. Retrieval of procedural knowledge is similar to that of declarative knowledge. Retrieval cues trigger associations in memory, and the process of spreading activation activates and recalls relevant knowledge. Thus, if students are told to perform a given procedure in chemistry laboratory, they will cue that production in memory, recall it, and implement it.

When declarative and procedural knowledge interact, retrieval of both is necessary. While adding fractions, students use procedures (i.e., convert fractions to their lowest common denominator, add numerators) and declarative knowledge (addition facts). During reading comprehension, some processes operate as procedures (e.g., decoding, monitoring comprehension), whereas others involve only declarative knowledge (e.g., word meanings, functions of punctuation marks). People typically employ procedures to acquire declarative knowledge, such as mnemonic techniques to remember declarative knowledge (see Chapter 7). Having declarative information is typically a prerequisite for successfully implementing procedures. To solve for roots using the quadratic formula, students must know multiplication facts.

Declarative and procedural knowledge vary tremendously in scope. Individuals possess declarative knowledge about the world, themselves, and others; they understand procedures for accomplishing diverse tasks. Declarative and procedural knowledge are different in that *procedures transform information.* Such declarative statements as "$2 \times 2 = 4$" and "Uncle Fred smokes smelly cigars" change nothing, but applying the long-division algorithm to a problem changes an unsolved problem into a solved one.

Another difference is in speed of processing. Retrieval of declarative knowledge often is slow and conscious. Even assuming people know the answer to a question, they may have to think for some time to answer it. For example, consider the time needed to answer "Who was the U.S. president in 1867?" (Andrew Johnson). In contrast, once procedural knowledge is established in memory, it is retrieved quickly and often automatically. Skilled readers decode printed text automatically; they do not have to consciously reflect on what they are doing. Processing speed distinguishes skilled from poor readers (de Jong, 1998). Once we learn how to multiply, we do not have to think about what steps to follow to solve problems.

The differences in declarative and procedural knowledge have implications for teaching and learning. Students may have difficulty with a particular content area because they lack domain-specific declarative knowledge or because they do not understand the prerequisite procedures. Discovering which is deficient is a necessary first step for planning remedial instruction. Not only do deficiencies hinder learning, they also produce low self-efficacy (Chapter 4). Students who understand how to divide but do not know multiplication facts become demoralized when they consistently arrive at wrong answers.

Language Comprehension

An application illustrating storage and retrieval of information in LTM is language comprehension (Carpenter, Miyake, & Just, 1995; Corballis, 2006; Clark, 1994; Matlin, 2009). Language comprehension is highly relevant to school learning and especially in light of the increasing number of students whose native language is not English (Fillmore & Valadez, 1986; Hancock, 2001; Padilla, 2006).

Comprehending spoken and written language represents a problem-solving process involving domain-specific declarative and procedural knowledge (Anderson, 1990). Language comprehension has three major components: perception, parsing, and utilization. *Perception* involves attending to and recognizing an input; sound patterns are translated into words in working memory (WM). *Parsing* means mentally dividing the sound patterns into units of meaning. *Utilization* refers to the disposition of the parsed mental representation: storing it in LTM if it is a learning task, giving an answer if it is a question, asking a question if it is not comprehended, and so forth. This section covers parsing and utilization; perception was discussed earlier in this chapter (Application 5.4).

APPLICATION 5.4
Language Comprehension

Students presented with confusing or vague information may misconstrue it or relate it to the wrong context. Teachers need to present clear and concise information and ensure that students have adequate background information to build networks and schemata.

Assume that Kathy Stone plans to present a social studies unit comparing city life with life in the country, but that most of her students have never seen a farm; thus, they will have difficulty comprehending the unit. They may never have heard words such as *silo, milking, sow,* and *livestock.* Mrs. Stone can produce better student understanding by providing farm-related experiences: take a field trip to a farm; show films about farm life; or bring in small farm equipment, seeds, plants, small animals, and photographs. As students become familiar with farms, they will be better able to comprehend spoken and written communication about farms.

Young children may have difficulty following directions in preschool and kindergarten. Their limited use and understanding of language may cause them to interpret certain words or phrases differently than intended. For instance, if a teacher said to a small group of children playing in a "dress-up" center, "Let's get things tied up so we can work on our next activity," the teacher might return to find children tying clothes together instead of cleaning up! Or a teacher might say, "Make sure you color this whole page," to children working with crayons. Later the teacher may discover that some children took a single crayon and colored the entire page from top to bottom instead of using various colors to color the items on the page. Teachers must explain, demonstrate, and model what they want children to do. Then they can ask the children to repeat in their own words what they think they are supposed to do.

Parsing. Linguistic research shows that people understand the grammatical rules of their language, even though they usually cannot verbalize them (Clark & Clark, 1977). Beginning with the work of Chomsky (1957), researchers have investigated the role of deep structures containing prototypical representations of language structure. The English language contains a deep structure for the pattern "noun 1–verb–noun 2," which allows us to recognize these patterns in speech and interpret them as "noun 1 did verb to noun 2." Deep structures may be represented in LTM as productions. Chomsky postulated that the capacity for acquiring deep structures is innately human, although which structures are acquired depends on the language of one's culture.

Parsing includes more than just fitting language into productions. When people are exposed to language, they construct a mental representation of the situation. They recall from LTM propositional knowledge about the context into which they integrate new knowledge. A central point is that *all communication is incomplete.* Speakers do not provide all information relevant to the topic being discussed. Rather, they omit the information listeners are most likely to know (Clark & Clark, 1977). For example, suppose

Sam meets Kira and Kira remarks, "You won't believe what happened to me at the concert!" Sam is most likely to activate propositional knowledge in LTM about concerts. Then Kira says, "As I was locating my seat . . ." To comprehend this statement, Sam must know that one purchases a ticket with an assigned seat. Kira did not tell Sam these things because she assumed he knew them.

Effective parsing requires knowledge and inferences (Resnick, 1985). When exposed to verbal communication, individuals access information from LTM about the situation. This information exists in LTM as propositional networks hierarchically organized as schemas. Networks allow people to understand incomplete communications. Consider the following sentence: "I went to the grocery store and saved five dollars with coupons." Knowledge that people buy merchandise in grocery stores and that they can redeem coupons to reduce cost enables listeners to comprehend this sentence. The missing information is filled in with knowledge in memory.

People often misconstrue communications because they fill in missing information with the wrong context. When given a vague passage about four friends getting together for an evening, music students interpreted it as a description of playing music, whereas physical education students described it as an evening of playing cards (Anderson, Reynolds, Schallert, & Goetz, 1977). The interpretative schemas salient in people's minds are used to comprehend problematic passages. As with many other linguistic skills, interpretations of communications become more reliable with development as children realize both the literal meaning of a message and its intent (Beal & Belgrad, 1990).

That spoken language is incomplete can be shown by decomposing communications into propositions and identifying how propositions are linked. Consider this example (Kintsch, 1979):

> The Swazi tribe was at war with a neighboring tribe because of a dispute over some cattle. Among the warriors were two unmarried men named Kakra and his younger brother Gum. Kakra was killed in battle.

Although this passage seems straightforward, analysis reveals the following 11 distinct propositions:

1. The Swazi tribe was at war.
2. The war was with a neighboring tribe.
3. The war had a cause.
4. The cause was a dispute over some cattle.
5. Warriors were involved.
6. The warriors were two men.
7. The men were unmarried.
8. The men were named Kakra and Gum.
9. Gum was the younger brother of Kakra.
10. Kakra was killed.
11. The killing occurred during battle.

Even this propositional analysis is incomplete. Propositions 1 through 4 link together, as do Propositions 5 through 11, but a gap occurs between 4 and 5. To supply the missing link, one might have to change Proposition 5 to "The dispute involved warriors."

Kintsch and van Dijk (1978) showed that features of communication influence comprehension. Comprehension becomes more difficult when more links are missing and when propositions are further apart (in the sense of requiring inferences to fill in the gaps). When much material has to be inferred, WM becomes overloaded and comprehension suffers.

Just and Carpenter (1992) formulated a *capacity theory of language comprehension,* which postulates that comprehension depends on WM capacity and individuals differ in this capacity. Elements of language (e.g., words, phrases) become activated in WM and are operated on by other processes. If the total amount of activation available to the system is less than the amount required to perform a comprehension task, then some of the activation maintaining older elements will be lost (Carpenter et al., 1995). Elements comprehended at the start of a lengthy sentence may be lost by the end. Production-system rules presumably govern activation and the linking of elements in WM.

We see the application of this model in parsing of ambiguous sentences or phrases (e.g., "The soldiers warned about the dangers . . ."; MacDonald, Just, & Carpenter, 1992). Although alternative interpretations of such constructions initially may be activated, the duration of maintaining them depends on WM capacity. Persons with large WM capacities maintain the interpretations for quite a while, whereas those with smaller capacities typically maintain only the most likely (although not necessarily correct) interpretation. With increased exposure to the context, comprehenders can decide which interpretation is correct, and such identification is more reliable for persons with large WM capacities who still have the alternative interpretations in WM (Carpenter et al., 1995; King & Just, 1991).

In building representations, people include important information and omit details (Resnick, 1985). These *gist representations* include propositions most germane to comprehension. Listeners' ability to make sense of a text depends on what they know about the topic (Chiesi et al., 1979; Spilich et al., 1979). When the appropriate network or schema exists in listeners' memories, they employ a production that extracts the most central information to fill the slots in the schema. Comprehension proceeds slowly when a network must be constructed because it does not exist in LTM.

Stories exemplify how schemas are employed. Stories have a prototypical schema that includes setting, initiating events, internal responses of characters, goals, attempts to attain goals, outcomes, and reactions (Black, 1984; Rumelhart, 1975, 1977; Stein & Trabasso, 1982). When hearing a story, people construct a mental model of the situation by recalling the story schema and gradually fitting information into it (Bower & Morrow, 1990). Some categories (e.g., initiating events, goal attempts, consequences) are nearly always included, but others (internal responses of characters) may be omitted (Mandler, 1978; Stein & Glenn, 1979). Comprehension proceeds quicker when schemas are easily activated. People recall stories better when events are presented in the expected order (i.e., chronological) rather than in a nonstandard order (i.e., flashback). When a schema is well established, people rapidly integrate information into it. Research shows that early home literacy experiences that include exposure to books relate positively to the development of listening comprehension (Sénéchal & LeFevre, 2002).

Utilization. *Utilization* refers to what people do with the communications they receive. For example, if the communicator asks a question, listeners retrieve information from LTM to answer it. In a classroom, students link the communication with related information in LTM.

To use sentences properly, as speakers intend them, listeners must encode three pieces of information: speech act, propositional content, and thematic content. A *speech act* is the speaker's purpose in uttering the communication, or what the speaker is trying to accomplish with the utterance (Austin, 1962; Searle, 1969). Speakers may be conveying information to listeners, commanding them to do something, requesting information from them, promising them something, and so on. *Propositional content* is information that can be judged true or false. *Thematic content* refers to the context in which the utterance is made. Speakers make assumptions about what listeners know. On hearing an utterance, listeners infer information not explicitly stated but germane to how it is used. The speech act and propositional and thematic contents are most likely encoded with productions.

As an example of this process, assume that Jim Marshall is giving a history lesson and is questioning students about text material. Mr. Marshall asks, "What was Churchill's position during World War II?" The speech act is a request and is signaled by the sentence beginning with a WH word (e.g., who, which, where, when, and why). The propositional content refers to Churchill's position during World War II; it might be represented in memory as follows: Churchill–Prime Minister–Great Britain–World War II. The thematic content refers to what the teacher left unsaid; the teacher assumes students have heard of Churchill and World War II. Thematic content also includes the classroom question-and-answer format. The students understand that Mr. Marshall will be asking questions for them to answer.

Of special importance for school learning is how students encode assertions. When teachers utter an assertion, they are conveying to students they believe the stated proposition is true. If Mr. Marshall says, "Churchill was the Prime Minister of Great Britain during World War II," he is conveying his belief that this assertion is true. Students record the assertion with related information in LTM.

Speakers facilitate the process whereby people relate new assertions with information in LTM by employing the *given-new contract* (Clark & Haviland, 1977). Given information should be readily identifiable and new information should be unknown to the listener. We might think of the given-new contract as a production. In integrating information into memory, listeners identify given information, access it in LTM, and relate new information to it (i.e., store it in the appropriate "slot" in the network). For the given-new contract to enhance utilization, given information must be readily identified by listeners. When given information is not readily available because it is not in listeners' memories or has not been accessed in a long time, using the given-new production is difficult.

Although language comprehension is often overlooked in school in favor of reading and writing, it is a central component of literacy. Educators lament the poor listening and speaking skills of students, and these are valued attributes of leaders. Habit 5 of Covey's (1989) *Seven Habits of Highly Effective People* is "Seek first to understand, then to be understood," which emphasizes listening first and then speaking. Listening is intimately linked with high achievement. A student who is a good listener is rarely a poor reader. Among college students, measures of listening comprehension may be indistinguishable from those of reading comprehension (Miller, 1988).

Forgetting

We forget a lot despite our best intentions. *Forgetting* refers to the loss of information from memory or to the inability to access information. Researchers disagree about whether information is lost from memory or whether it still is present but cannot be retrieved because it has been distorted, the retrieval cues are inadequate, or other information is interfering with its recall. Forgetting has been studied experimentally since the time of Ebbinghaus (Chapter 1). Before presenting information processing perspectives on forgetting, which involve interference and decay, some historical work on interference is discussed.

Interference Theory. One of the contributions of the verbal learning tradition was the *interference theory of forgetting.* According to this theory, learned associations are never completely forgotten. Forgetting results from competing associations that lower the probability of the correct association being recalled; that is, other material becomes associated with the original stimulus (Postman, 1961). The problem lies in retrieving information from memory rather than in memory itself (Crouse, 1971).

Two types of interference were experimentally identified (Table 5.3). *Retroactive interference* occurs when new verbal associations make remembering prior associations difficult. *Proactive interference* refers to older associations that make newer learning more difficult.

To demonstrate retroactive interference, an experimenter might ask two groups of individuals to learn Word List A. Group 1 then learns Word List B, while group 2 engages in a competing activity to prevent rehearsal of List A. Both groups then attempt to recall List

Table 5.3
Interference and forgetting.

Task	Retroactive Interference		Proactive Interference	
	Group 1	Group 2	Group 1	Group 2
Learn	A	A	A	—
Learn	B	—	B	B
Test	A	A	B	B

Note: Each group learns the task to some criterion of mastery. The "—" indicates a period of time in which the group is engaged in another task that prevents rehearsal but does not interfere with the original learning. Interference is demonstrated if Group 2 outperforms Group 1 on the test.

APPLICATION 5.5
Interference in Teaching and Learning

Proactive and retroactive interference occur often in teaching and learning. Teachers cannot completely eliminate interference, but they can minimize its effects by recognizing areas in the curriculum that easily lend themselves to interference. For example, students learn to subtract without regrouping and then to subtract with regrouping. In Kathy Stone's third-grade class she often finds that when she gives students review problems requiring regrouping, some students do not regroup. To minimize interference, she teaches students the underlying rules and principles and has them practice applying the skills in different contexts. She points out similarities and differences between the two types of problems and teaches students how to

decide whether regrouping is necessary. Frequent reviews help to minimize interference.

When spelling words are introduced at the primary level, words often are grouped by phonetic similarities (e.g., *crate, slate, date, state, mate, late*); however, when children learn certain spelling patterns, it may confuse them as they encounter other words (e.g., *weight* or *wait* rather than *wate; freight* rather than *frate*). Kathy Stone provides additional instruction regarding other spellings for the same sounds and exceptions to phonetic rules along with periodic reviews over time. This reinforcement should help alleviate confusion and interference among students.

A. Retroactive interference occurs if the recall of Group 2 is better than that of Group 1. For proactive interference, Group 1 learns List A while Group 2 does nothing. Both groups then learn List B and attempt to recall List B. Proactive interference occurs if the recall of Group 2 surpasses that of Group 1.

Retroactive and proactive interference occur often in school. Retroactive interference is seen among students who learn words with regular spellings and then learn words that are exceptions to spelling rules. If, after some time, they are tested on the original words, they might alter the spellings to those of the exceptions. Proactive interference is evident among students taught first to multiply and then to divide fractions. When subsequently tested on division, they may simply multiply without first inverting the second fraction. Developmental research shows that proactive interference decreases between the ages of 4 and 13 (Kail, 2002). Application 5.5 offers suggestions for dealing with interference.

Interference theory represented an important step in specifying memory processes. Early theories of learning postulated that learned connections leave a memory "trace" that weakens and decays with nonuse. Skinner (1953; Chapter 3) did not postulate an internal memory trace but suggested that forgetting results from lack of opportunity to respond due to the stimulus being absent for some time. Each of these views has shortcomings. Although some decay may occur (discussed later), the memory trace notion is vague and difficult to verify experimentally. The nonuse position holds at times, but exceptions do exist; for example, being able to recall information after many years of nonuse (e.g., names of some elementary school teachers) is not unusual. Interference theory surmounts these problems by postulating how information in memory becomes confused with other information. It also specifies a research model for investigating these processes.

Postman and Stark (1969) suggested that *suppression*, rather than interference, causes forgetting. Participants in learning experiments hold in active memory material they believe they will need to recall later. Those who learn List A and then are given List B are apt to suppress their responses to the words on List A. Such suppressions would last while they are learning List B and for a while thereafter. In support of this point, the typical retroactive interference paradigm produces little forgetting when learners are given a recognition test on the original Word List A rather than asked to recall the words.

Tulving (1974) postulated that forgetting represents *inaccessibility of information* due to improper retrieval cues. Information in memory does not decay, become confused, or get lost. Rather, the memory trace is intact but cannot be accessed. Memory of information depends on the trace being intact and on having adequate retrieval cues. Perhaps you cannot remember your home phone number from many years ago. You may not have forgotten it; the memory is submerged because your current environment is different from that of years ago and the cues associated with your old home phone number—your house, street, neighborhood—are absent. This principle of *cue-dependent forgetting* also is compatible with the common finding that people perform better on recognition than on recall tests. In the cue-dependent view, they should perform better in recognition tests because more retrieval cues are provided; in recall tests, they must supply their own cues.

Later research on interference suggests that interference occurs (e.g., people confuse elements) when the same cognitive schema or plan is used on multiple occasions (Thorndyke & Hayes-Roth, 1979; Underwood, 1983). Interference theory continues to provide a viable framework for investigating forgetting (Brown, Neath, & Chater, 2007; Oberauer & Lewandowsky, 2008).

Information Processing. From an information processing perspective, *interference* refers to a blockage of the spread of activation across memory networks (Anderson, 1990). For various reasons, when people attempt to access information in memory, the activation process is thwarted. Although the mechanism blocking activation is not completely understood, theory and research suggest various causes of interference.

One factor that can affect whether structures are activated is the *strength of original encoding*. Information that originally is strongly encoded through frequent rehearsal or extensive elaboration is more likely to be accessed than information that originally is weakly encoded.

A second factor is the number of *alternative network paths* down which activation can spread (Anderson, 1990). Information that can be accessed via many routes is more likely to be remembered than information that is only accessible via fewer paths. For example, if I want to remember the name of Aunt Frieda's parakeet (Mr. T), I should associate that with many cues, such as my friend Mr. Thomas, the fact that when Mr. T spreads his wings it makes the letter T, and the idea that his constant chirping taxes my tolerance. Then, when I attempt to recall the name of the parakeet I can access it via my memory networks for Aunt Frieda and for parakeets. If these fail, then I still have available the networks for my friends, the letter T, and things that tax my tolerance. In contrast, if I associate only the name "Mr. T" with the bird, then the number of alternative paths available for access is fewer and the likelihood of interference is greater.

A third factor is the *amount of distortion or merging of information.* Throughout this chapter we have discussed the memory benefits of organizing, elaborating, and making information meaningful by relating it to what we know. Whenever we engage in these practices, we change the nature of information, and in some cases we merge it with other information or subsume it under more general categories. Such merging and subsumption facilitate *meaningful reception learning* (Ausubel, 1963, 1968; discussed later in this chapter). Sometimes, however, such distortion and merging may cause interference and make recall more difficult than if information is remembered on its own.

Interference is an important cause of forgetting, but it is unlikely that it is the only one (Anderson, 1990). It appears that some information in LTM decays systematically with the passage of time and independently of any interference. Wickelgren (1979) traced systematic decay of information in time intervals ranging from 1 minute to 2 weeks. The data decay rapidly at first with decay gradually tapering off. Researchers find little forgetting after 2 weeks.

The position that forgetting occurs because of decay is difficult to affirm or refute. Failure to recall even with extensive cuing does not unequivocally support a decay position because it still is possible that the appropriate memory networks were not activated. Similarly, the fact that the decay position posits no psychological processes responsible for forgetting (rather only the passage of time) does not refute the position. Memory traces include both perceptual features and reactions to the experiences (Estes, 1997). Decay or changes in one or both cause forgetting and memory distortions. Furthermore, the decay process may be neurological (Anderson, 1990). Synapses can deteriorate with lack of use in the same way muscles do with nonuse (Chapter 2).

Decay is commonly cited as a reason for forgetting (Nairne, 2002). You may have learned French in high school but now some years later cannot recall many vocabulary words. You might explain that as, "I haven't used it for so long that I've forgotten it." Furthermore, forgetting is not always bad. Were we to remember everything we have ever learned, our memories would be so overcrowded that new learning would be very difficult. Forgetting is facilitative when it rids us of information that we have not used and thus may not be important, analogous to your discarding things that you no longer need. Forgetting leads people to act, think, judge, and feel differently than they would in the absence of forgetting (Riccio, Rabinowitz, & Axelrod, 1994). Forgetting has profound effects on teaching and learning (Application 5.6).

APPLICATION 5.6
Minimizing Forgetting of Academic Learning

Forgetting is a problem when learned knowledge is needed for new learning. To help children retain important information and skills, teachers might do the following:

- Periodically review important information and skills during classroom activities.
- Assign class work and homework that reinforce previously learned material and skills.
- Send home fun learning packets during long vacation breaks that will reinforce various information and skills acquired.
- When introducing a new lesson or unit, review previously learned material that is needed for mastering the new material.

When Kathy Stone introduces long division, some third graders have forgotten how to regroup in subtraction, which can slow the new learning. She spends a couple of days reviewing subtraction—especially problems requiring regrouping—as well as drilling the students on multiplication and simple division facts. She also gives homework that reinforces the same skills.

Assume that a physical education teacher is teaching a basketball unit over several days. At the start of each class, the teacher might review the skills taught in the previous class before he or she introduces the new skill. Periodically the teacher could spend an entire class period reviewing all the skills (e.g., dribbling, passing, shooting, playing defense) that the students have been working on up to that point. Some remedial instruction may be necessary if students have forgotten some of these skills so that they will be able to play well once the teacher begins to organize games.

In Gina Brown's educational psychology class the students have been assigned an application paper that focuses on motivation techniques. During the semester, she introduced various motivational theories. Many of the students have forgotten some of these. To help the students prepare for writing their papers, she spends one class period reviewing the major motivation theories. Then she divides students into small groups and has each group write a brief summary of one of the theories with some classroom applications. After working in small groups, each group shares its findings with the entire class.

MENTAL IMAGERY

Mental imagery is central to the study of LTM (Matlin, 2009). This section discusses how information is represented in images and individual differences in the ability to use imagery.

Representation of Spatial Information

Mental imagery refers to mental representations of visual/spatial knowledge including physical properties of the objects or events represented. Visual stimuli that are attended to are held briefly in veridical (true) form in the sensory register and then are transferred to WM. The WM representation appears to preserve some of the physical attributes of the stimulus it represents (Gagné, Yekovich, & Yekovich, 1993). Images are analog representations that are similar but not identical to their referents (Shepard, 1978).

Imagery has been valued as far back as the time of the ancient Greeks. Plato felt that thoughts and perceptions are impressed on the mind as a block of wax and are remembered as long as the images last (Paivio, 1970). Simonides, a Greek poet, believed that images are associative mediators. He devised the *method of loci* as a memory aid (Chapter 7). In this method, information to be remembered is paired with locations in a familiar setting.

Mental imagery also has been influential in discoveries. Shepard (1978) described Einstein's *Gedanken experiment* that marked the beginning of the relativistic reformulation of electromagnetic theory. Einstein imagined himself traveling with a beam of light (186,000 miles per second), and what he saw corresponded neither to light nor to anything described by Maxwell's equations in classical electromagnetic theory. Einstein reported that he typically thought in terms of images and only reproduced his thoughts in words and mathematical equations once he conceptualized the situation visually. The German chemist Kekulé supposedly had a dream in which he visualized the structure of benzene, and Watson and Crick apparently used mental rotation to break the genetic code.

In contrast to images, propositions are discrete representations of meaning not resembling their referents in structure. The expression "New York City" no more resembles the actual city than virtually any three words picked at random from a dictionary. An image of New York City containing skyscrapers, stores, people, and traffic is more similar in structure to its referent. The same contrast is evident for events. Compare the sentence, "The black dog ran across the lawn," with an image of this scene.

Mental imagery is a controversial topic (Matlin, 2009). A central issue is how closely mental images resemble actual pictures: Do they contain the same details as pictures or are they fuzzy pictures portraying only highlights? The visual pattern of a stimulus is perceived when its features are linked to a LTM representation. This implies that images can only be as clear as the LTM representations (Pylyshyn, 1973). To the extent that mental images are the products of people's perceptions, images are likely to be incomplete representations of stimuli.

Support for the idea that people use imagery to represent spatial knowledge comes from studies where participants were shown pairs of two-dimensional pictures, each of which portrayed a three-dimensional object (Cooper & Shepard, 1973; Shepard & Cooper, 1983). The task was to determine if the two pictures in each pair portrayed the same object. The solution strategy involved mentally rotating one object in each pair until it matched the other object or until the individual decided that no amount of rotation would yield an identical object. Reaction times were a direct function of the number of mental rotations needed. Although these and other data suggest that people employ images to represent knowledge, they do not directly address the issue of how closely images correspond to actual objects.

To the extent that students use imagery to represent spatial and visual knowledge, imagery is germane to educational content involving concrete objects. When teaching a unit about different types of rock formations (mountains, plateaus, ridges), an instructor could show pictures of the various formations and ask students to imagine them. In geometry, imagery could be employed when dealing with mental rotations. Pictorial illustrations improve students' learning from texts (Carney & Levin, 2002; see Application 5.7 for more examples).

APPLICATION 5.7
Using Imagery in the Classroom

Imagery can be used to increase student learning. One application involves instructing students on three-dimensional figures (e.g., cubes, spheres, cones) to include calculating their volumes. Verbal descriptors and two-dimensional diagrams are also used, but actual models of the figures greatly enhance teaching effectiveness. Allowing students to hold the shapes fosters their understanding of the concept of volume.

Imagery can be applied in physical education. When students are learning an exercise routine accompanied by music, the teacher can model in turn each portion of the routine initially without music, after which students close their eyes and think about what they saw. The students then perform each part of the routine. Later the teacher can add music to the individual portions.

Imagery can be used in language arts. For a unit involving writing a paragraph that gives directions for performing a task or making something, Kathy Stone asks her third-grade students to think about the individual steps (e.g., of making a peanut butter and jelly sandwich). Once students finish imagining the task, they can visualize each step while writing it down.

Art teachers can use imagery to teach students to follow directions. The teacher might give the following directions orally and write them on the board: "Visualize on a piece of art paper a design including four circles, three triangles, and two squares, with some of the shapes overlapping one another." The teacher might ask the following questions to ensure that students are using imagery: How many circles do you see? How many triangles? How many squares? Are any of the shapes touching? Which ones?

Dance teachers might have their students close their eyes while listening to the music to which they will be performing. Then they might ask the students to imagine themselves dancing, visualizing every step and movement. The teacher also might ask students to visualize where they and their classmates are on the stage as they dance.

Jim Marshall took his American history classes to a Civil War battlefield and had them imagine what it must have been like to fight a battle at that site. Later in class he had students produce a map on the computer that duplicated the site and then create various scenarios for what could have happened as the Union and Confederate forces fought.

Evidence shows that people also use imagery to think about abstract dimensions. Kerst and Howard (1977) asked students to compare pairs of cars, countries, and animals on the concrete dimension of size and on an appropriate abstract dimension (e.g., cost, military power, ferocity). The abstract and concrete dimensions yielded similar results: As items became more similar, reaction times increased. For instance, in comparing size, comparing a bobcat and an elephant is easier than comparing a rhinoceros and a hippopotamus. How participants imagined abstract dimensions or whether they even used imagery is not clear. Perhaps they represented abstract dimensions in terms of propositions, such as by comparing the United States and Jamaica on military power using the proposition, "(The) United States (has) more military power (than) Jamaica." Knowledge maps, which are pictorial representations of linked ideas, aid student learning (O'Donnell, Dansereau, & Hall, 2002).

Imagery in LTM

Many researchers agree that images are used in WM but disagree whether they are retained in LTM (Kosslyn & Pomerantz, 1977; Pylyshyn, 1973). *Dual-code theory* directly addresses this issue (Clark & Paivio, 1991; Paivio, 1971, 1978, 1986). LTM has two means of representing knowledge: A *verbal system* incorporating knowledge expressed in language and an *imaginal system* storing visual and spatial information. These systems are interrelated—a verbal code can be converted into an imaginal code and vice versa—but important differences exist. The verbal system is suited for abstract information, whereas the imaginal system is used to represent concrete objects or events.

Shepard's experiments support the utility of imagery and offer indirect support for the dual-code theory. Other supporting evidence comes from research showing that when recalling lists of concrete and abstract words, people recall concrete words better than abstract ones (Terry, 2009). The dual-code theory explanation of this finding is that concrete words can be coded verbally and visually, whereas abstract words usually are coded only verbally. At recall, people draw on both memory systems for the concrete words, but only the verbal system for the abstract words. Other research on imaginal mnemonic mediators supports the dual-code theory (Chapter 7).

In contrast, *unitary theory* postulates that all information is represented in LTM in verbal codes (propositions). Images in WM are reconstructed from verbal LTM codes. Indirect support for this notion comes from Mandler and Johnson (1976) and Mandler and Ritchey (1977). As with verbal material, people employ schemas while acquiring visual information. They remember scenes better when elements are in a typical pattern; memory is poorer when elements are disorganized. Meaningful organization and elaboration of information into schemas improve memory for scenes much as they do for verbal material. This finding suggests the operation of a common process regardless of the form of information presented.

This debate notwithstanding, using concrete materials and pictures enhances memory (Terry, 2009). Such instructional tools as manipulatives, audiovisual aids, and computer graphics facilitate learning. Although concrete devices are undoubtedly more important for young children because they lack the cognitive capability to think in abstract terms, students of all ages benefit from information presented in multiple modes.

Individual Differences

The extent to which people actually use imagery to remember information varies as a function of cognitive development. Kosslyn (1980) proposed that children are more likely to use imagery to remember and recall information than adults, who rely more on propositional representation. Kosslyn gave children and adults statements such as, "A cat has claws," and "A rat has fur." The task was to determine accuracy of the statements. Kosslyn reasoned that adults could respond quicker because they could access the propositional information from LTM, whereas children would have to recall the image of the animal and scan it. To control for adults' better information processing in general, some adults were asked to scan an image of the animal, whereas others were free to use any strategy.

Adults were slower to respond when given the imagery instructions than when free to choose a strategy, but no difference was found for children. These results suggest that children use imagery even when they are free to do otherwise, but they do not address whether children cannot use propositional information (because of cognitive limitations) or whether they can but choose not to because they find imagery to be more effective.

Use of imagery also depends on effectiveness of performing the component processes. Apparently two types are involved. One set of processes helps to activate stored memories of parts of images. Another set serves to arrange parts into the proper configuration. These processes may be localized in different parts of the brain. Individual differences in imagery can result because people differ in how effectively this dual processing occurs (Kosslyn, 1988).

The use of imagery by people of any age depends on what is to be imagined. Concrete objects are more easily imagined than abstractions. Another factor that influences use of imagery is one's ability to employ it. *Eidetic imagery*, or photographic memory (Leask, Haber, & Haber, 1969), actually is unlike a photograph; the latter is seen as a whole, whereas eidetic imagery occurs in pieces. People report that an image appears and disappears in segments rather than all at once.

Eidetic imagery is found more often in children than in adults (Gray & Gummerman, 1975), yet even among children it is uncommon (about 5%). Eidetic imagery may be lost with development, perhaps because propositional representation replaces imaginal thinking. It also is possible that adults retain the capacity to form clear images but do not routinely do so because their propositional systems can represent more information. Just as memory can be improved, the capacity to form images can be developed, but most adults do not explicitly work to sharpen their imagery.

INSTRUCTIONAL APPLICATIONS

Information processing principles increasingly have been applied to school learning settings. The theory's relevance to education will continue to expand with future research. Three instructional applications that reflect information processing principles are advance organizers, the conditions of learning, and cognitive load.

Advance Organizers

Advance organizers are broad statements presented at the outset of lessons that help to connect new material with prior learning (Mayer, 1984). Organizers direct learners' attention to important concepts to be learned, highlight relationships among ideas, and link new material to what students know (Faw & Waller, 1976). Organizers also can be maps that are shown with accompanying text (Verdi & Kulhavy, 2002). It is assumed that learners' cognitive structures are hierarchically organized so that inclusive concepts subsume subordinate ones. Organizers provide information at high levels in hierarchies.

The conceptual basis of organizers derives from Ausubel's (1963, 1968, 1977, 1978; Ausubel & Robinson, 1969) theory of *meaningful reception learning*. Learning is meaningful when new material bears a systematic relation to relevant concepts in LTM; that is, new material expands, modifies, or elaborates information in memory. Meaningfulness also depends on personal variables such as age, background experiences, socioeconomic status, and educational background. Prior experiences determine whether students find learning meaningful.

Ausubel advocated deductive teaching: General ideas are taught first, followed by specific points. This requires teachers to help students break ideas into smaller, related points and to link new ideas to similar content in memory. In information processing terms, the aims of the model are to expand propositional networks in LTM by adding knowledge and to establish links between networks. Deductive teaching works better with older students (Luiten, Ames, & Ackerson, 1980).

Advance organizers set the stage for meaningful reception learning. Organizers can be expository or comparative. *Expository organizers* provide students with new knowledge needed to comprehend the lesson. Expository organizers include concept definitions and generalizations. *Concept definitions* state the concept, a superordinate concept, and characteristics of the concept. In presenting the concept "warm-blooded animal," a teacher might define it (i.e., animal whose internal body temperature remains relatively constant), relate it to superordinate concepts (animal kingdom), and give its characteristics (birds, mammals). *Generalizations* are broad statements of general principles from which hypotheses or specific ideas are drawn. A generalization appropriate for the study of terrain would be: "Less vegetation grows at higher elevations." Teachers can present examples of generalizations and ask students to think of others.

Comparative organizers introduce new material by drawing analogies with familiar material. Comparative organizers activate and link networks in LTM. If a teacher were giving a unit on the body's circulatory system to students who have studied communication systems, the teacher might relate the circulatory and communication systems with relevant concepts such as the source, medium, and target. For comparative organizers to be effective, students must have a good understanding of the material used as the basis for the analogy. Learners also must perceive the analogy easily. Difficulty perceiving analogous relationships impedes learning.

Evidence suggests that organizers promote learning and transfer (Ausubel, 1978; Faw & Waller, 1976; Mautone & Mayer, 2007). Maps are effective organizers and lend themselves well to infusion in lessons via technology (Verdi & Kulhavy, 2002). Mayer (1979) reported research with college students who had no computer programming experience. Students were given programming materials to study; one group was given a conceptual model as

APPLICATION 5.8
Advance Organizers

Advance organizers help students connect new material with prior learning. Kathy Stone is teaching her students to develop comprehensive paragraphs. The students have been learning to write descriptive and interesting sentences. Mrs. Stone writes the students' sentences on the board and uses them as an organizer to show how to put sentences together to create a complete paragraph.

A middle school teacher might employ an organizer during geography. The teacher might begin a lesson on landforms (surfaces with characteristic shapes and compositions) by reviewing the definition and components of geography concepts previously discussed. The teacher wants to show that geography includes elements of the physical environment, human beings and the physical environment, and different world regions and their ability to support human beings. To do this, the teacher

initially could focus on elements of the physical environment and then move to landforms. The teacher then might discuss types of landforms (e.g., plateaus, mountains, hills) by showing mock-ups and asking students to identify key features of each landform. This approach gives students an overall framework or outline into which they can integrate new knowledge about the components.

In medical school an instructor teaching the effects of blood disorders might begin by reviewing the basic parts of blood (e.g., plasma, white and red cells, platelets). Then the teacher could list various categories of blood disease (e.g., anemia, bleeding and bruising, leukemia, bone marrow disease). The students can build on this outline by exploring the diseases in the different categories and by studying the symptoms and treatments for each condition.

an organizer, whereas the other group received the same materials without the model. The advance organizer group performed better on posttest items requiring transfer to items different from those discussed in the instructional material. Organizers may help students relate new material to a broader set of experiences, which facilitates transfer (Application 5.8).

Conditions of Learning

One of the best known instructional theories based on cognitive principles was formulated by Robert Gagné (1985). This theory involves the *conditions of learning*, or the circumstances that prevail when learning occurs (Ertmer, Driscoll, & Wager, 2003). Two steps are critical. The first is to *specify the type of learning outcome*; Gagné identified five major types (discussed later). The second is to *determine the events of learning*, or factors that make a difference in instruction.

Learning Outcomes. Gagné (1984) identified five types of learning outcomes: intellectual skills, verbal information, cognitive strategies, motor skills, and attitudes (Table 5.4).

Table 5.4
Learning outcomes in Gagné's theory.

Learning Outcomes	
Type	**Examples**
Intellectual skills	Rules, procedures, concepts
Verbal information	Facts, dates
Cognitive strategies	Rehearsal, problem-solving
Motor skills	Hitting a ball, juggling
Attitudes	Generosity, honesty, fairness

Intellectual skills include rules, procedures, and concepts. They are forms of procedural knowledge or productions. This type of knowledge is employed in speaking, writing, reading, solving mathematical problems, and applying scientific principles to problems.

Verbal information, or declarative knowledge, is knowledge that something is the case. Verbal information involves facts or meaningfully connected prose recalled verbatim (e.g., words to a poem or the "Star Spangled Banner"). Schemas are forms of verbal information.

Cognitive strategies are executive control processes. They include information processing skills such as attending to new information, deciding to rehearse information, elaborating, using LTM retrieval strategies, and applying problem-solving strategies (Chapter 7).

Motor skills are developed through gradual improvements in the quality (smoothness, timing) of movements attained through practice. Whereas intellectual skills can be acquired abruptly, motor skills develop gradually with continued, deliberate practice (Ericsson et al., 1993). Practice conditions differ: Intellectual skills are practiced with different examples; motor-skill practice involves repetition of the same muscular movements.

Attitudes are internal beliefs that influence actions and reflect characteristics such as generosity, honesty, and commitment to healthy living. Teachers can arrange conditions for learning intellectual skills, verbal information, cognitive strategies, and motor skills, but attitudes are learned indirectly through experiences and exposures to live and symbolic (televised, videotaped) models.

Learning Events. The five types of learning outcomes differ in their conditions. *Internal conditions* are prerequisite skills and cognitive processing requirements; *external conditions* are environmental stimuli that support the learner's cognitive processes. One must specify as completely as possible both types of conditions when designing instruction.

Internal conditions are learners' current capabilities stored in LTM as knowledge. Instructional cues from teachers and materials activate relevant LTM knowledge (Gagné & Glaser, 1987). External conditions differ as a function of the learning outcome and the internal conditions. To teach students a classroom rule, a teacher might inform them of the rule and visually display it. To teach students a strategy for checking their comprehension, a teacher might demonstrate the strategy and give students practice and feedback on its effectiveness. Proficient readers are instructed differently from those with decoding problems. Each phase of instruction is subject to alteration as a function of learning outcomes and internal conditions.

Learning Hierarchies. *Learning hierarchies* are organized sets of intellectual skills. The highest element in a hierarchy is the *target skill.* To devise a hierarchy, one begins at the top and asks what skills the learner must perform prior to learning the target skill or what skills are immediate prerequisites for the target skill. Then one asks the same question for each prerequisite skill, continuing down the hierarchy until one arrives at the skills the learner can perform now (Dick & Carey, 1985; Merrill, 1987; Figure 5.8).

Figure 5.8
Sample learning hierarchy.

Table 5.5
Gagné's phases of learning.

Category	Phase
Preparation for learning	Attending
	Expectancy
	Retrieval
Acquisition and performance	Selective perception
	Semantic encoding
	Retrieval and responding
	Reinforcement
Transfer of learning	Cueing retrieval
	Generalizability

Hierarchies are not linear orderings of skills. One often must apply two or more prerequisite skills to learn a higher-order skill with neither of the prerequisites dependent on the other. Nor are higher-order skills necessarily more difficult to learn than lower-order ones. Some prerequisites may be difficult to acquire; once learners have mastered the lower-order skills, learning a higher-order one may seem easier.

Phases of Learning. *Instruction* is a set of external events designed to facilitate internal learning processes. Table 5.5 shows the nine phases of learning grouped into the three categories (Gagné, 1985).

Preparation for learning includes introductory learning activities. During *attending*, learners focus on stimuli relevant to material to be learned (audiovisuals, written materials, teacher-modeled behaviors). The learner's *expectancy* orients the learner to the goal (learn a motor skill, learn to reduce fractions). During retrieval of relevant information from LTM, learners activate the portions relevant to the topic studied (Gagné & Dick, 1983).

The main phases of learning are *acquisition* and *performance*. *Selective perception* means that the sensory registers recognize relevant stimulus features and transfer them to WM. *Semantic encoding* is the process whereby new knowledge is transferred to LTM. During *retrieval and responding*, learners retrieve new information from memory and make a response demonstrating learning. *Reinforcement* refers to feedback that confirms the accuracy of a student's response and provides corrective information as necessary.

Transfer of learning phases include cueing retrieval and generalizability. In *cueing retrieval*, learners receive cues signaling that previous knowledge is applicable in that situation. When solving word problems, for instance, a mathematics teacher might inform learners that their knowledge of right triangles is applicable. *Generalizability* is enhanced by providing learners the opportunity to practice skills with different content and under different circumstances (e.g., homework, spaced review sessions).

Table 5.6

Instructional events accompanying learning phases (Gagné).

Phase	Instructional Event
Attending	Inform class that it is time to begin.
Expectancy	Inform class of lesson objective and type and quantity of performance to be expected.
Retrieval	Ask class to recall subordinate concepts and rules.
Selective perception	Present examples of new concept or rule.
Semantic encoding	Provide cues for how to remember information.
Retrieval and responding	Ask students to apply concept or rule to new examples.
Reinforcement	Confirm accuracy of students' learning.
Cueing retrieval	Give short quiz on new material.
Generalizability	Provide special reviews.

These nine phases are equally applicable for the five types of learning outcomes. Gagné and Briggs (1979) specified types of instructional events that might accompany each phase (Table 5.6). Instructional events enhancing each phase depend on the type of outcome. Instruction proceeds differently for intellectual skills than for verbal information.

One issue is that developing learning hierarchies can be difficult and time consuming. The process requires expertise in the content domain to determine the successive prerequisite skills—the scope and sequence of instruction. Even a seemingly simple skill may have a complex hierarchy if learners must master several prerequisites. For those skills with less well-defined structures (e.g., creative writing), developing a hierarchy may be difficult. Another issue is that the system allows for little learner control because it prescribes how learners should proceed. These issues notwithstanding, the theory offers solid suggestions for ways to apply information processing principles to the design of instruction (Ertmer et al., 2003).

Cognitive Load

The information processing system can handle only so much processing at once. If too many stimuli impinge simultaneously, observers will miss many of them because of their limited attentional capacity. The capacity of WM is limited. Because information processing takes time and involves multiple cognitive processes, at any given time only a limited amount of information can be held in WM, transferred to LTM, rehearsed, and so forth.

Cognitive load theory takes these processing limitations into account in the design of instruction (DeLeeuw & Mayer, 2008; Schnotz & Kürschner, 2007; Sweller, van Merriënboer, & Pass, 1998). *Cognitive load*, or the demands on the information processing system, can be of two types. *Intrinsic cognitive load* depends on the unalterable properties of the information to be learned and is eased only when learners acquire an effective cognitive schema to deal with the information. *Extrinsic cognitive load* is caused by the manner in which the material is presented or the activities required of the learner (Bruning et al., 2004). For example, in learning key trigonometric relationships (e.g., sine, tangent), a certain cognitive load (intrinsic) is inherent in the material to be learned, namely, developing knowledge about the ratios of sides of a right triangle. How the material is taught influences the extrinsic cognitive load. Teachers who give clear presentations help to minimize extrinsic cognitive load, whereas those who explain these concepts poorly increase extrinsic load.

In similar fashion, Mayer and Moreno (2003) distinguished three types of cognitive demands. *Essential processing* refers to cognitive processes necessary to understand the material (similar to intrinsic load). *Incidental processing* refers to processing not necessary for learning but which may help to increase understanding. *Representational holding* denotes temporarily holding information in memory while other information is being processed. Mayer and Moreno suggested that learning proceeds best when learners can focus their resources on essential processing and little or no resources on the other types.

A key idea is that instructional methods should decrease extraneous cognitive load so that existing resources can be devoted to learning (van Merriënboer & Sweller, 2005). The use of scaffolding should be beneficial (van Merriënboer, Kirschner, & Kester, 2003). Initially the scaffold helps learners acquire skills that they would be unlikely to acquire without the assistance. The scaffolding helps to minimize the extrinsic load so learners can focus their resources on the intrinsic demands of the learning. As learners develop a schema to work with the information, the scaffold assistance can be phased out.

Another suggestion is to use simple-to-complex sequencing of material (van Merriënboer et al., 2003), in line with Gagné's theory. Complex learning is broken into simple parts that are acquired and combined into a larger sequence. This procedure minimizes cognitive load, so learners can focus their cognitive resources on the learning at hand.

A third suggestion is to use authentic tasks in instruction. Reigeluth's (1999) *elaboration theory*, for example, requires identifying conditions that simplify performance of the task and then beginning instruction with a simple but authentic case (e.g., one that might be encountered in the real world). Tasks that have real-world significance help to minimize extrinsic load because they do not require learners to engage in extraneous processing to understand the context. It is more meaningful, for example, for students to determine the sine of the angle formed by joining a point 40 feet from the school's flagpole to the top of the pole than it is to solve comparable trigonometric problems in a textbook.

These considerations also suggest the use of collaborative learning. As cognitive load increases, learning by individuals becomes less effective and efficient (Kirschner, Paas, & Kirschner, 2009). With greater task complexity, dividing the cognitive processing demands across individuals reduces cognitive load on individual students. These ideas fit well with the constructivist emphasis on peer collaboration (Chapter 6).

SUMMARY

Information processing theories focus on attention, perception, encoding, storage, and retrieval of knowledge. Information processing has been influenced by advances in communications, computer technology, and neuroscience.

Important historical influences on contemporary information processing views are Gestalt psychology and verbal learning. Gestalt theorists stressed the role of organization in perception and learning. Verbal learning researchers used serial learning, free recall, and paired-associate tasks. A number of important findings were obtained from verbal learning research. Free-recall studies showed that organization improves recall and that people impose their own organization when none is present. One of the major contributions was work in interference and forgetting.

A two-store (dual) memory model has been widely applied. Information enters through the sensory registers. Although there is a register for each sense, most research has been conducted on the visual and auditory registers. At any one time, only a limited amount of information can be attended to. Attention may act as a filter or a general limitation on capacity of the human system. Inputs attended to are perceived by being compared with information in LTM.

Information enters STM (WM), where it is retained through rehearsal and linked with related information in LTM. Information may be encoded for storage in LTM. Encoding is facilitated through organization, elaboration, meaningfulness, and links with schemas. LTM is organized by content, and information is cross-referenced with related content. Control processes monitor and direct the flow of information through the system.

Alternative views of memory conceive of it in terms of levels of processing, activation level, connectionism, and parallel distributed processing. Each of these views has advantages and disadvantages, and some integration of views may best characterize memory.

Attention and perception processes involve critical features, templates, and prototypes. Whereas WM is limited in capacity and duration, LTM appears to be very large. The basic unit of knowledge is the proposition, and propositions are organized in networks. Types of knowledge include declarative, procedural, and conditional. Large bits of procedural knowledge may be organized in production systems. Networks further are linked in connectionist fashion through spreading activation to enhance cross-referencing and transfer. Retrieval of knowledge depends on its being accessed in LTM. Failure to retrieve may result from decay of information or interference. Information may be best retrieved with cues present during encoding (encoding specificity).

An area that illustrates the storage and retrieval of information in LTM is language comprehension, which involves perception, parsing, and utilization. Communications are incomplete; speakers omit information they expect that listeners will know. Effective language comprehension requires that listeners possess adequate propositional knowledge and schemas and understand the context. To integrate information into memory, listeners identify given information, access it in LTM, and relate new information to it. Language comprehension is a central aspect of literacy and relates strongly to academic success—especially in subjects that require extensive reading.

Although much evidence exists for information being stored in memory in verbal form (meanings), evidence also exists for storage of images. Images are analog representations: They are similar but not identical to their referents. Dual-code theory postulates that the imaginal system primarily stores concrete objects and events and the verbal system stores more abstract information expressed in language. Conversely, images may be reconstructed in WM from verbal codes stored in LTM. Developmental evidence shows that children are more likely than adults to represent knowledge as images, but imaginal representation can be developed in persons of any age.

Although much early research on information processing was basic in nature and conducted in experimental laboratories, researchers increasingly are conducting research in applied settings and especially on learning of academic content. Three instructional applications that reflect information processing principles involve advance organizers, the conditions of learning, and cognitive load.

A summary of learning issues appears in Table 5.7.

Table 5.7
Summary of learning issues.

How Does Learning Occur?

Learning, or encoding, occurs when information is stored in LTM. Information initially enters the information processing system through a sensory register after it is attended to. It then is perceived by being compared with information in LTM and enters STM (WM). This information can stay activated, be transferred to LTM, or be lost. Factors that help encoding are meaningfulness, elaboration, organization, and links with schema structures.

What Is the Role of Memory?

Memory is a key component of the information processing system. There is debate about how many memories there are. The classical model postulated two memory stores: short- and long-term. Other perspectives contend that there is one memory with different levels of activation or processing. Memory receives information and through associative networks links it with other information in memory.

What Is the Role of Motivation?

Relative to other learning theories, motivation has received less attention by information processing theories. In the classical view, control processes—which direct the flow of information through the system—can be thought of as having motivational properties. Learners presumably engage their cognitive processes to support attainment of their goals. Motivational processes such as goals and self-efficacy likely are represented in memory as propositions embedded in networks.

How Does Transfer Occur?

Transfer occurs through the process of spreading activation in memory, where information is linked to other information such that recall of information can produce recall of related information. It is important when learning that cues be attached to information so that the learning may be linked with different contexts, skills, or events.

Which Processes Are Involved in Self-Regulation?

Key self-regulation processes are goals, learning strategies, production systems, and schemas (Chapter 9). Information processing theories contend that learners control the processing of information in their own systems.

What Are the Implications for Instruction?

Information processing theories emphasize the transformation and flow of information through the cognitive system. It is important that information be presented in such a way that students can relate the new information to known information (meaningfulness) and that they understand the uses for the knowledge. These points suggest that learning be structured so that it builds on existing knowledge and can be clearly comprehended by learners. Teachers also should provide advance organizers and cues that learners can use to recall information when needed and that minimize cognitive load.

FURTHER READING

Anderson, J. R. (1996). ACT: A simple theory of complex cognition. *American Psychologist, 51,* 355–365.

Baddeley, A. D. (2001). Is working memory still working? *American Psychologist, 56,* 851–864.

Gagné, R. M. (1985). *The conditions of learning* (4th ed.). New York: Holt, Rinehart & Winston.

Mayer, R. E. (1996). Learners as information processors: Legacies and limitations of educational psychology's second metaphor. *Educational Psychologist, 31,* 151–161.

Riccio, D. C., Rabinowitz, V. C., & Alexrod, S. (1994). Memory: When less is more. *American Psychologist, 49,* 917–926.

Triesman, A. M. (1992). Perceiving and re-perceiving objects. *American Psychologist, 47,* 862–875.

Van Merriënboer, J. J. G., & Sweller, J. (2005). Cognitive load theory and complex learning: Recent developments and future directions. *Educational Psychology Review, 14,* 331–351.

6

Constructivism

During a first-grade math lesson on measurement and equivalency, children were asked to use a balance to determine how many plastic links equaled one metal washer in weight. The teacher recognized and seized an opportunity to help one particularly eager child, Anna, begin to construct a rudimentary notion of ratio and proportion.

Teacher: How many links does it take to balance one washer?

Anna: (After a few seconds of experimenting) Four.

Teacher: If I placed one more washer on this side, how many more links do you think we would need to balance it?

Anna: One.

Teacher: Try it.

Anna placed one more link in the balance tray and noticed that balance was not achieved. She looked confused and placed another link in the tray and then a third. Still no balance. She placed one more link in the tray. Balance was achieved. She smiled and looked at the teacher.

Teacher: How many cubes did it take to balance one washer?

Anna: Four.

Teacher: And how many to balance two washers?

Anna: (Counting) Eight.

Teacher: If I put one more washer on this side, how many more links will you need to balance it?

Anna: (Pondered and looked quizzically at the teacher) Four.

Teacher: Try it.

Anna: (After successfully balancing with four links) Each washer is the same as four links.

Teacher: Now, let me give you a really hard question. If I took four links off of the balance, how many washers would I need to take off in order to balance it?

Anna: One!

(Brooks & Brooks, 1999, p. 73)

Constructivism is a psychological and philosophical perspective contending that individuals form or construct much of what they learn and understand (Bruning et al., 2004). A major influence on the rise of constructivism has been theory and research in human development, especially the theories of Piaget and Vygotsky. Human development is the subject of Chapter 10; however, the present chapter covers Piaget's and Vygotsky's theories because they form a cornerstone of the constructivist movement. The emphasis that these theories place on the role of knowledge construction is central to constructivism.

In recent years, constructivism increasingly has been applied to learning and teaching. The history of learning theory reveals a shift away from environmental influences and toward human factors as explanations for learning. This shift began with the advent of cognitive psychology (Chapter 5), which disputed the claim of behaviorism (Chapter 3) that stimuli, responses, and consequences were adequate to explain learning. Cognitive theories place great emphasis on learners' information processing as a central cause of learning. Despite the elegance of cognitive learning theories, some researchers believe that these theories fail to capture the complexity of human learning. This point is underscored by the fact that some cognitive perspectives use behavioral terminology such as the "automaticity" of performance and "forming connections" between items in memory.

Today a number of learning researchers have shifted even more toward a focus on learners. Rather than talk about how knowledge is acquired, they speak of how it is constructed. Although these researchers differ in their emphasis on factors that affect learning and learners' cognitive processes, the theoretical perspectives they espouse may be loosely grouped and referred to as *constructivism*. Anna's construction of understanding is evident in the opening scenario.

This chapter begins by providing an overview of constructivism to include a description of its key assumptions and the different types of constructivist theories. The theories of Piaget and Vygotsky are described next, with emphasis on those aspects relevant to learning. The critical roles of social processes and private speech are discussed, followed by coverage of motivation from a constructivist perspective. The chapter concludes with a discussion of constructivist learning environments and instructional applications that reflect principles of constructivism.

When you finish studying this chapter, you should be able to do the following:

- Discuss the major assumptions and various types of constructivism.

- Summarize the major processes in Piaget's theory that are involved in learning and some implications for instruction.

- Explain the key principles of Vygotsky's sociocultural theory and implications for teaching in the zone of proximal development.

- Explain the function of private speech for learning and self-regulation.

- Discuss how classroom structure and TARGET variables affect student motivation.

- Describe how teacher expectations are formed and how they can affect teachers' interactions with students.

- List the key features of constructivist learning environments and the major components of the APA learner-centered principles.

- Describe how discovery learning, inquiry teaching, peer-assisted learning, discussions, and debates can be structured to reflect constructivist principles.

- Explain how teachers can become more reflective and thereby enhance student achievement.

CONSTRUCTIVISM: ASSUMPTIONS AND PERSPECTIVES

Many researchers and practitioners question some of cognitive psychology's assumptions about learning and instruction because they believe that these assumptions do not completely explain students' learning and understanding. These questionable assumptions are as follows (Greeno, 1989):

- Thinking resides in the mind rather than in interaction with persons and situations.
- Processes of learning and thinking are relatively uniform across persons, and some situations foster higher-order thinking better than others.
- Thinking derives from knowledge and skills developed in formal instructional settings more than on general conceptual competencies that result from one's experiences and innate abilities.

Constructivists do not accept these assumptions because of evidence that thinking takes place in situations and that cognitions are largely constructed by individuals as a function of their experiences in these situations (Bredo, 1997). Constructivist accounts of learning and development highlight the contributions of individuals to what is learned. Social constructivist models further emphasize the importance of social interactions in acquisition of skills and knowledge. Let us examine further what constructivism is, its assumptions, and its forms.

Overview

What Is Constructivism? Unlike other theories discussed in this text, there is a lack of consistency about the meaning of constructivism (Harlow, Cummings, & Aberasturi, 2006). Strictly speaking, constructivism is not a theory but rather an *epistemology,* or philosophical explanation about the nature of learning (Hyslop-Margison & Strobel, 2008; Simpson, 2002). As discussed in Chapter 1, a theory is a scientifically valid explanation for learning. Theories allow for hypotheses to be generated and tested. Constructivism does not propound that learning principles exist and are to be discovered and tested, but rather that learners create their own learning. Readers who are interested in exploring the historical and philosophical roots of constructivism are referred to Bredo (1997) and Packer and Goicoechea (2000).

Nonetheless, constructivism makes general predictions that can be tested. Although these predictions are general and thus open to different interpretations (i.e., what does it mean that learners construct their own learning?), they could be the focus of research.

Constructivist theorists reject the notion that scientific truths exist and await discovery and verification. They argue that no statement can be assumed as true but rather should be viewed with reasonable doubt. The world can be mentally constructed in many different ways, so no theory has a lock on the truth. This is true even for constructivism: There are many varieties and no one version should be assumed to more correct than any other (Derry, 1996; Simpson, 2002).

Rather than viewing knowledge as truth, constructivists construe it as a working hypothesis. Knowledge is not imposed from outside people but rather formed inside them. A person's constructions are true to that person but not necessarily to anyone else. This is because people produce knowledge based on their beliefs and experiences in situations (Cobb & Bowers, 1999), which differ from person to person. All knowledge, then, is subjective and personal and a product of our cognitions (Simpson, 2002). Learning is situated in contexts (Bredo, 2006).

Assumptions. Constructivism highlights the interaction of persons and situations in the acquisition and refinement of skills and knowledge (Cobb & Bowers, 1999). Constructivism contrasts with conditioning theories that stress the influence of the environment on the person as well as with information processing theories that place the locus of learning within the mind with little attention to the context in which it occurs. It shares with social cognitive theory the assumption that persons, behaviors, and environments interact in reciprocal fashion (Bandura, 1986, 1997).

A key assumption of constructivism is that people are active learners and develop knowledge for themselves (Geary, 1995). To understand material well, learners must discover the basic principles, as Anna did in the opening lesson. Constructivists differ in the extent to which they ascribe this function entirely to learners. Some believe that mental structures come to reflect reality, whereas others (radical constructivists) believe that the individual's mental world is the only reality. Constructivists also differ in how much they ascribe the construction of knowledge to social interactions with teachers, peers, parents, and others (Bredo, 1997).

Many of the principles, concepts, and ideas discussed in this text reflect the idea of constructivism, including cognitive processing, expectations, values, and perceptions of self and others (Derry, 1996). Thus, although constructivism seems to be a recent arrival on the learning scene, its basic premise that learners construct understandings underlies many learning principles. This is the epistemological aspect of constructivism. Some constructivist ideas are not as well developed as those of other theories discussed in this text, but constructivism has affected theory and research in learning and development.

Constructivism also has influenced educational thinking about curriculum and instruction. It underlies the emphasis on the integrated curriculum in which students study a topic from multiple perspectives. For example, in studying hot-air balloons, students might read about them, write about them, learn new vocabulary words, visit one (hands-on experience), study the scientific principles involved, draw pictures of them, and learn songs about them. Constructivist ideas also are found in many professional standards and affect design of curriculum and instruction, such as the learner-centered principles developed by the American Psychological Association (discussed later).

Another constructivist assumption is that teachers should not teach in the traditional sense of delivering instruction to a group of students. Rather, they should structure situations such that learners become actively involved with content through manipulation of materials and social interaction. How the teacher structured the lesson allowed Anna to construct her understanding. Activities include observing phenomena, collecting data, generating and testing hypotheses, and working collaboratively with others. Classes visit sites outside of the classroom. Teachers from different disciplines plan the curriculum together. Students are taught to be self-regulated and take an active role in their learning by setting goals, monitoring and evaluating progress, and going beyond basic requirements by exploring interests (Bruning et al., 2004; Geary, 1995).

Table 6.1
Perspectives on constructivism.

Perspective	Premises
Exogenous	The acquisition of knowledge represents a reconstruction of the external world. The world influences beliefs through experiences, exposure to models, and teaching. Knowledge is accurate to the extent it reflects external reality.
Endogenous	Knowledge derives from previously acquired knowledge and not directly from environmental interactions. Knowledge is not a mirror of the external world; rather, it develops through cognitive abstraction.
Dialectical	Knowledge derives from interactions between persons and their environments. Constructions are not invariably tied to the external world nor wholly the workings of the mind. Rather, knowledge reflects the outcomes of mental contradictions that result from one's interactions with the environment.

Perspectives

Constructivism is not a single viewpoint but rather has different perspectives (Table 6.1; Bruning et al., 2004; Moshman, 1982; Phillips, 1995). *Exogenous constructivism* refers to the idea that the acquisition of knowledge represents a reconstruction of structures that exist in the external world. This view posits a strong influence of the external world on knowledge construction, such as by experiences, teaching, and exposure to models. Knowledge is accurate to the extent it reflects that reality. Contemporary information processing theories reflect this notion (e.g., schemas, productions, memory networks; Chapter 5).

In contrast, *endogenous constructivism* emphasizes the coordination of cognitive actions (Bruning et al., 2004). Mental structures are created from earlier structures, not directly from environmental information; therefore, knowledge is not a mirror of the external world acquired through experiences, teaching, or social interactions. Knowledge develops through the cognitive activity of abstraction and follows a generally predictable sequence. Piaget's (1970) theory of cognitive development (discussed later) fits this framework.

Between these extremes lies *dialectical constructivism*, which holds that knowledge derives from interactions between persons and their environments. Constructions are not invariably bound to the external world nor are they wholly the result of the workings of the mind; rather, they reflect the outcomes of mental contradictions that result from interactions with the environment. This perspective has become closely aligned with many contemporary theories. For example, it is compatible with Bandura's (1986) social cognitive theory (Chapter 4) and with many motivation theories (Chapter 8). It also is referred to as *cognitive constructivism* (Derry, 1996). The developmental theories of Bruner (Chapter 10) and Vygotsky (discussed later) also emphasize the influence of the social environment.

Each of these perspectives has merit and is potentially useful for research and teaching. Exogenous views are appropriate when we are interested in determining how accurately learners perceive the structure of knowledge within a domain. The endogenous perspective is relevant to explore how learners develop from novices through greater levels of competence (Chapter 7). The dialectical view is useful for designing interventions to challenge children's thinking and for research aimed at exploring the effectiveness of social influences such as exposure to models and peer collaboration.

Situated Cognition

A core premise of constructivism is that cognitive processes (including thinking and learning) are situated (located) in physical and social contexts (Anderson, Reder, & Simon, 1996; Cobb & Bowers, 1999; Greeno et al., 1998). *Situated cognition* (or *situated learning*) involves relations between a person and a situation; cognitive processes do not reside solely in one's mind (Greeno, 1989).

The idea of person–situation interaction is not new. Most contemporary theories of learning and development assume that beliefs and knowledge are formed as people interact in situations. This emphasis contrasts with the classical information processing model that highlights the processing and movement of information through mental structures (e.g., sensory registers, WM, LTM; Chapter 5). Information processing downplays the importance of situations once environmental inputs are received. Research in a variety of disciplines—including cognitive psychology, social cognitive learning, and content domains (e.g., reading, mathematics)—shows this to be a limited view and that thinking involves an extended reciprocal relation with the context (Bandura, 1986; Cobb & Bowers, 1999; Derry, 1996; Greeno, 1989).

Research highlights the importance of exploring situated cognition as a means of understanding the development of competence in domains such as literacy, mathematics (as we see in the opening scenario), and science (Cobb, 1994; Cobb & Bowers, 1999; Driver, Asoko, Leach, Mortimer, & Scott, 1994; Lampert, 1990; Chapter 7). Situated cognition also is relevant to motivation (this chapter and Chapter 8). As with learning, motivation is not an entirely internal state as posited by classical views or wholly dependent on the environment as predicted by reinforcement theories (Chapter 3). Rather, motivation depends on cognitive activity in interaction with sociocultural and instructional factors, which include language and forms of assistance such as scaffolding (Sivan, 1986).

Situated cognition addresses the intuitive notion that many processes interact to produce learning. We know that motivation and instruction are linked: Good instruction can raise motivation for learning and motivated learners seek effective instructional environments (Schunk, 1995). A further benefit of the situated cognition perspective is that it leads researchers to explore cognition in authentic learning contexts such as schools, workplaces, and homes, many of which involve mentoring or apprenticeships.

Research on the effectiveness of situated learning is recent, but results are promising. Griffin (1995) compared traditional (in-class) instruction on map skills with a situated learning approach in which college students received practice in the actual environments depicted on the maps. The situated learning group performed better on a map-skill assessment. Although Griffin found no benefit of situated learning on transfer, the results of situated learning studies should be highly generalizable to similar contexts.

The situated idea also is pertinent to how learning occurs (Greeno et al., 1998). Students exposed to a certain procedure for learning a subject experience situated cognition for that method; in other words, that is how this content is learned. For example, if students repeatedly receive mathematics instruction taught in didactic fashion by a teacher explaining and demonstrating, followed by their engaging in independent problem solving at their desks, then mathematics learning is apt to become situated in this context. The same students might have difficulty adjusting to a new teacher who favors using guided discovery (as done by the teacher in the opening lesson) by collaborative peer groups.

The instructional implication is that teaching methods should reflect the outcomes we desire in our learners. If we are trying to teach them inquiry skills, the instruction must incorporate inquiry activities. The method and the content must be properly situated.

Situated cognition fits well with the constructivist idea that context is an inherent part of learning. Especially in subject domains (Chapter 7), this idea increasingly has been shown to be valid. Nonetheless, extending the idea of situated learning too far may be erroneous. As Anderson, Reder, and Simon (1996) showed, there is plenty of empirical evidence for contextual independence of learning and transfer of learning between contexts. We need more information on which types of learning proceed best when they are firmly linked to contexts and when it is better to teach broader skills and show how they can be applied in different contexts.

Contributions and Applications

Given the recency of constructivism, research exploring constructivist assumptions about learning is in its infancy. Another factor that makes determining the contributions of constructivism difficult is that the approach is not a unified one that offers specific hypotheses to be tested. Bereiter (1994) noted that the claim that "students construct their own knowledge" is not falsifiable but rather is true of all cognitive learning theories. Cognitive theories view the mind as a repository of beliefs, values, expectations, schemata, and so forth, so any feasible explanation of how those thoughts and feelings come to reside in the mind must assume that they are formed there. For example, social cognitive theory emphasizes the roles of expectations (e.g., self-efficacy, outcome) and goals; these beliefs and cognitions do not arise from nowhere but, rather, are constructed by learners.

Constructivism eventually must be evaluated not on whether its premises are true or false. Rather, it seems imperative to determine the process whereby students construct knowledge and how social, developmental, and instructional factors may influence that process. Research also is needed on when situational influences have greater effects on mental processes. A drawback of many forms of constructivism is the emphasis on *relativism* (Phillips, 1995), or the idea that all forms of knowledge are justifiable because they are constructed by learners, especially if they reflect societal consensus. Educators cannot accept this premise in good conscience because education demands that we inculcate values such as honesty, fairness, and responsibility in our students regardless of whether societal constituencies deem them important.

Furthermore, nature may constrain our thinking more than we wish to admit. Research suggests that some mathematical competencies—such as one-to-one correspondence and being able to count—are not constructed but rather largely genetically driven (Geary, 1995; Gelman & Gallistel, 1978; Chapter 7). Far from being relative, some forms of knowledge may be universally endogenous. Acquisition of other competencies (e.g., multiplying, word processing) requires environmental input. Constructivism—with its emphasis on minimal instructional guidance—may downplay the importance of human cognitive structures. Instructional methods that are mapped better onto this cognitive structure may actually produce better learning (Kirschner, Sweller, & Clark, 2006). Research will help to establish the scope of constructivist processes in the sequence of competency acquisition and how these processes change as a function of development (Muller, Sokol, & Overton, 1998).

Constructivism has important implications for instruction and curriculum design (Phillips, 1995). The most straightforward recommendations are to involve students actively in their learning and to provide experiences that challenge their thinking and force them to rearrange their beliefs. Constructivism also underlies the current emphasis on *reflective teaching* (discussed later in this chapter). Social constructivist views (e.g., Vygotsky's) stress that social group learning and peer collaboration are useful (Ratner, Foley, & Gimpert, 2002). As students model for and observe each other, they not only teach skills but also experience higher self-efficacy for learning (Schunk, 1995). Application 6.1 gives constructivist applications. We now turn to a more in-depth examination of constructivism and its applications to human learning.

APPLICATION 6.1
Constructivism and Teaching

Constructivism emphasizes integrated curricula and having teachers use materials in such a way that learners become actively involved. Kathy Stone implements various constructivist ideas in her third-grade classroom using integrated units. In the fall she presents a unit on pumpkins. In social studies children learn where pumpkins are grown and about the products made from pumpkins. They also study the uses of pumpkins in history and the benefits of pumpkins to early settlers.

Kathy takes her class on a field trip to a pumpkin farm, where they learn how pumpkins are grown. Each student selects a pumpkin and brings it back to class. The pumpkin becomes a valuable learning tool. In mathematics the students estimate the size and weight of their pumpkins and then measure and weigh them. They establish class graphs by comparing all the pumpkins by size, weight, shape, and color. The children also estimate the number of seeds they think Kathy Stone's pumpkin has, and then they count the seeds when she cuts open her pumpkin. As another class activity, the students make pumpkin bread with her pumpkin. For art they design a shape for the carving of their pumpkins, and then with Kathy's assistance they carve them. In language arts they write a story about pumpkins. They also write a thank-you letter to the pumpkin farm. For spelling, Kathy uses words that they have used in the study of pumpkins. These examples illustrate how she integrates the study of pumpkins across the curriculum.

PIAGET'S THEORY OF COGNITIVE DEVELOPMENT

Piaget's theory was little noticed when it first appeared, but gradually it ascended to a major position in the field of human development. Piaget's theory covers many types of development and is complex; a complete summary is beyond the scope of this text. Interested readers should consult other sources (Brainerd, 2003; Furth, 1970; Ginsburg & Opper, 1988; Meece, 2002; Phillips, 1969; Piaget, 1952, 1970; Piaget & Inhelder, 1969; Wadsworth, 1996). What follows is a concise overview of the major points relevant to constructivism and learning. Although Piaget's theory no longer is a leading theory of cognitive development, it remains important and has several useful implications for instruction and learning.

Developmental Processes

Equilibration. According to Piaget, cognitive development depends on four factors: biological maturation, experience with the physical environment, experience with the social environment, and equilibration. The first three are self-explanatory, but their effects depend on the fourth. *Equilibration* refers to a biological drive to produce an optimal state of equilibrium (or *adaptation*) between cognitive structures and the environment (Duncan, 1995). Equilibration is the central factor and the motivating force behind cognitive development. It coordinates the actions of the other three factors and makes internal mental structures and external environmental reality consistent with each other.

To illustrate the role of equilibration, consider 6-year-old Allison riding in a car with her father. They are going 65 mph, and about 100 yards in front of them is a car. They have been following this car for some time, and the distance between them stays the same. Her dad points to the car and asks Allison, "Which car is going faster, our car or that car, or are we going the same speed?" Allison replies that the other car is going faster. When her dad asks why, she replies, "Because it's in front of us." If her dad then said, "We're actually going the same speed," this would create a conflict for Allison. She believes the other car is going faster, but she has received conflicting environmental input.

To resolve this conflict, Allison can use one of the two component processes of equilibration: assimilation and accommodation. *Assimilation* refers to fitting external reality to the existing cognitive structure. When we interpret, construe, and frame, we alter the nature of reality to make it fit our cognitive structure. To assimilate the information, Allison might alter reality by believing that her dad is teasing her or perhaps at that moment the two cars were going the same speed but that the other car had been going faster beforehand.

Accommodation refers to changing internal structures to provide consistency with external reality. We accommodate when we adjust our ideas to make sense of reality. To accommodate her belief system (structures) to the new information, she might believe her dad without understanding why or she might change her belief system to include the idea that all cars in front of them are going the same speed as they are.

Assimilation and accommodation are complementary processes. As reality is assimilated, structures are accommodated.

Table 6.2
Piaget's stages of cognitive development.

Stage	Approximate Age Range (Years)
Sensorimotor	Birth to 2
Preoperational	2 to 7
Concrete operational	7 to 11
Formal operational	11 to adult

Stages. Piaget concluded from his research that children's cognitive development passed through a fixed sequence. The pattern of operations that children can perform may be thought of as a level or *stage*. Each level or stage is defined by how children view the world. Piaget's and other stage theories make certain assumptions (see Chapter 10):

- Stages are discrete, qualitatively different, and separate. Progression from one stage to another is not a matter of gradual blending or continuous merging.
- The development of cognitive structures is dependent on preceding development.
- Although the order of structure development is invariant, the age at which one may be in a particular stage will vary from person to person. Stages should not be equated with ages.

Table 6.2 shows how Piaget characterized his stage progression. Much has been written on these stages and an extensive research literature exists on each. The stages are only briefly described here; interested readers should consult other sources (Brainerd, 2003; Byrnes, 1996; Meece, 2002; Wadsworth, 1996).

In the *sensorimotor* stage, children's actions are spontaneous and represent an attempt to understand the world. Understanding is rooted in present action; for example, a ball is for throwing and a bottle for sucking. The period is characterized by rapid change; a two-year-old is cognitively far different from an infant. Children actively equilibrate, albeit at a primitive level. Cognitive structures are constructed and altered, and the motivation to do this is internal. The notion of *effectance motivation (mastery motivation;* Chapter 8) is relevant to sensorimotor children. By the end of the sensorimotor period, children have attained sufficient cognitive development to progress to new conceptual-symbolic thinking characteristic of the preoperational stage (Wadsworth, 1996).

Preoperational children are able to imagine the future and reflect on the past, although they remain heavily perceptually oriented in the present. They are apt to believe that 10 coins spread out in a row are more than 10 coins in a pile. They also are unable to think in more than one dimension at a time; thus, if they focus on length, they are apt to think a longer object (a yardstick) is bigger than a shorter one (a brick) even though the shorter one is wider and deeper. Preoperational children demonstrate *irreversibility;* that is, once things are done, they cannot be changed (e.g., the box flattened cannot be remade into a box). They have difficulty distinguishing fantasy from reality. Cartoon characters appear as real as people. The period is one of rapid language development. Another characteristic is that children become less *egocentric:* They realize that others may think and feel differently than they do.

The *concrete operational* stage is characterized by remarkable cognitive growth and is a formative one in schooling, because it is when children's language and basic skills acquisition accelerate dramatically. Children begin to show some abstract thinking, although it typically is defined by properties or actions (e.g., honesty is returning money to the person who lost it). Concrete operational children display less egocentric thought, and language increasingly becomes social. *Reversibility* in thinking is acquired along with classification and seriation—concepts essential for the acquisition of mathematical skills. Concrete operational thinking no longer is dominated by perception; children draw on their experiences and are not always swayed by what they perceive.

The *formal operational* stage extends concrete operational thought. No longer is thought focused exclusively on tangibles; children are able to think about hypothetical situations. Reasoning capabilities improve, and children can think about multiple dimensions and abstract properties. Egocentrism emerges in adolescents' comparing reality to the ideal; thus, they often show idealistic thinking.

Piaget's stages have been criticized on many grounds (Byrnes, 1996). One problem is that children often grasp ideas and are able to perform operations earlier than Piaget found. Another problem is that cognitive development across domains typically is uneven; rarely does a child think in stage-typical ways across all topics (e.g., mathematics, science, history). This also is true for adults; the same topic may be understood quite differently. For example, some adults may think of baseball in preoperational terms ("Hit the ball and run"), others might think of it as concrete operationally ("What do I do in different situations?"), and some can reason using formal operational thought (e.g., "Explain why a curve ball curves"). As a general framework, however, the stages describe the thought patterns that tend to co-occur, which is useful knowledge for educators, parents, and others who work with children.

Mechanisms of Learning. Equilibration is an internal process (Duncan, 1995). As such, cognitive development can occur only when *disequilibrium* or *cognitive conflict* exists. Thus, an event must occur that produces a disturbance in the child's cognitive structures so that the child's beliefs do not match the observed reality. Equilibration seeks to resolve the conflict through assimilation and accommodation.

Piaget felt that development would proceed naturally through regular interactions with the physical and social environments. The impetus for developmental change is internal. Environmental factors are extrinsic; they can influence development but not direct it. This point has profound implications for education because it suggests that teaching may have little impact on development. Teachers can arrange the environment to cause conflict, but how any particular child resolves the conflict is not predictable.

Learning occurs, then, when children experience cognitive conflict and engage in assimilation or accommodation to construct or alter internal structures. Importantly, however, the conflict should not be too great because this will not trigger equilibration. Learning will be optimal when the conflict is small and especially when children are in transition between stages. Information must be partially understood (assimilated) before it can promote structural change (accommodation). Environmental stimulation to facilitate change should have negligible effect unless the critical stage transitions have begun so that the conflict can be successfully resolved via equilibration. Thus, learning is limited by developmental constraints (Brainerd, 2003).

The research evidence on cognitive conflict is not overwhelmingly supportive of Piaget's position (Zimmerman & Blom, 1983a, 1983b; Zimmerman & Whitehurst, 1979). Rosenthal and Zimmerman (1978) summarized data from several research studies showing that preoperational children can master concrete operational tasks through teaching involving verbal explanations and modeled demonstrations. According to the theory, this should not happen unless the children are in stage transition, at which time cognitive conflict would be at a reasonable level.

The stagelike changes in children's thinking seem to be linked to more gradual changes in attention and cognitive processing (Meece, 2002). Thus, children may not demonstrate Piagetian stage understanding for various reasons, including not attending to the relevant stimuli, improperly encoding information, not relating information to prior knowledge, or using ineffective means to retrieve information (Siegler, 1991). When children are taught to use cognitive processes more effectively, they often can perform tasks at higher cognitive levels.

Piaget's theory is constructivist because it assumes that children impose their concepts on the world to make sense of it (Byrnes, 1996). These concepts are not inborn; rather, children acquire them through their normal experiences. Information from the environment (including people) is not automatically received but rather is processed according to the child's prevailing mental structures. Children make sense of their environments and construct reality based on their capabilities at the present time. In turn, these basic concepts develop into more sophisticated views with experience.

Implications for Instruction

Piaget contended that cognitive development could not be taught, although research evidence shows that it can be accelerated (Zimmerman & Whitehurst, 1979). The theory and research have implications for instruction (Table 6.3).

Understand Cognitive Development. Teachers will benefit when they understand at what levels their students are functioning. All students in a class should not be expected to operate at the same level. Many Piagetian tasks are easy to administer (Wadsworth, 1996). Teachers can try to ascertain levels and gear their teaching accordingly. Students who seem to be in stage transition may benefit from teaching at the next higher level, because the conflict will not be too great for them.

Keep Students Active. Piaget decried passive learning. Children need rich environments that allow for active exploration and hands-on activities. This arrangement facilitates active construction of knowledge.

Table 6.3
Implications of Piaget's theory for education.

- Understand cognitive development.
- Keep students active.
- Create incongruity.
- Provide social interaction.

APPLICATION 6.2
Piaget and Education

At all grades teachers should evaluate the developmental levels of their students prior to planning lessons. Teachers need to know how their students are thinking so they can introduce cognitive conflict at a reasonable level, where students can resolve it through assimilation and accommodation. Kathy Stone, for example, is apt to have students who operate at both the preoperational and concrete operational levels, which means that one lesson will not suffice for any particular unit. Furthermore, because some children will grasp operations more quickly than others, she needs to build enrichment activities into her lessons.

In developing units for his history classes, Jim Marshall includes components that require basic understanding and also those that necessitate abstract reasoning. Thus, he incorporates activities that require factual answers, as well as activities that have no right or wrong answers but that require students to think abstractly and construct their ideas through reasoned judgments based on data. For students who are not fully operating at the formal operational level, the components requiring abstract reasoning may produce desired cognitive conflict and enhance a higher level of thinking. For students who already are operating at a formal operational level, the reasoning activities will continue to challenge them.

Create Incongruity. Development occurs only when environmental inputs do not match students' cognitive structures. Material should not be readily assimilated but not too difficult to preclude accommodation. Incongruity also can be created by allowing students to solve problems and arrive at wrong answers. Nothing in Piaget's theory says that children always have to succeed; teacher feedback indicating incorrect answers can promote disequilibrium.

Provide Social Interaction. Although Piaget's theory contends that development can proceed without social interaction, the social environment is nonetheless a key source for cognitive development. Activities that provide social interactions are useful. Learning that others have different points of view can help children become less egocentric. Application 6.2 discusses ways that teachers can help to foster cognitive development.

VYGOTSKY'S SOCIOCULTURAL THEORY

Like Piaget's theory, Vygotsky's also is a constructivist theory; however, Vygotsky's places more emphasis on the social environment as a facilitator of development and learning (Tudge & Scrimsher, 2003). The background of the theory is discussed, along with its key assumptions and principles.

Background

Lev Semenovich Vygotsky, who was born in Russia in 1896, studied various subjects in school, including psychology, philosophy, and literature, and received a law degree from Moscow Imperial University in 1917. Following graduation, he returned to his hometown of Gomel, which was beset with problems stemming from German occupation, famine, and civil war. Two of his brothers died, and he contracted tuberculosis—the disease that eventually killed him. He taught courses in psychology and literature, wrote literary criticism, and edited a journal. He also worked at a teacher training institution, where he founded a psychology laboratory and wrote an educational psychology book (Tudge & Scrimsher, 2003).

A critical event in Vygotsky's life occurred in 1924 at the Second All-Russian Congress of Psychoneurology in Leningrad. Prevailing psychological theory at that time neglected subjective experiences in favor of Pavlov's conditioned reflexes and behaviorism's emphasis on environmental influences. Vygotsky presented a paper ("The Methods of Reflexological and Psychological Investigation") in which he criticized the dominant views and spoke on the relation of conditioned reflexes to human consciousness and behavior. Pavlov's experiments with dogs (Chapter 3) and Köhler's studies with apes (Chapter 7) erased many distinctions between animals and humans.

Vygotsky contended that, unlike animals that react only to the environment, humans have the capacity to alter the environment for their own purposes. This adaptive capacity distinguishes humans from lower forms of life. His speech made such an impression on one listener—Alexander Luria (discussed later in this chapter)—that he was invited to join the prestigious Institute of Experimental Psychology in Moscow. He helped to establish the Institute of Defektology, the purpose of which was to study ways to help handicapped individuals. Until his death in 1934, he wrote extensively on the social mediation of learning and the role of consciousness, often in collaboration with colleagues Luria and Leontiev (Rohrkemper, 1989).

Understanding Vygotsky's position requires keeping in mind that he was a Marxist and that his views represented an attempt to apply Marxist ideas of social change to language and development (Rohrkemper, 1989). After the 1917 Russian Revolution, an urgency among the new leaders produced rapid change in the populace. Vygotsky's strong sociocultural theoretical orientation fit well with the revolution's goals of changing the culture to a socialist system.

Vygotsky had some access to Western society (e.g., writers such as Piaget; Bredo, 1997; Tudge & Winterhoff, 1993), but little of what he wrote was published during his lifetime or for some years following his death (Gredler, 2009). A negative political climate prevailed in the former Soviet Union; among other things, the Communist Party curtailed psychological testing and publications. Vygotsky espoused revisionist thinking (Bruner, 1984). He moved from a Pavlovian view of psychology focusing on reflexes to a cultural–historical perspective that stressed language and social interaction (Tudge & Scrimsher, 2003). Some of his writings were at odds with Stalin's views and because of that were not published. References to his work were banned in the Soviet Union until the 1980s (Tudge & Scrimsher, 2003). In recent years, Vygotsky's writings have been increasingly translated and circulated, which has expanded their impact on such disciplines as education, psychology, and linguistics.

Basic Principles

One of Vygotsky's central contributions to psychological thought was his emphasis on socially meaningful activity as an important influence on human consciousness (Bredo, 1997; Kozulin, 1986; Tudge & Winterhoff, 1993). Vygotsky attempted to explain human thought in new ways. He rejected introspection (Chapter 1) and raised many of the same objections as the behaviorists. He wanted to abandon explaining states of consciousness by referring to the concept of consciousness; similarly, he rejected behavioral explanations of action in terms of prior actions. Rather than discarding consciousness (which the behaviorists did) or the role of the environment (which the introspectionists did), he sought a middle ground of taking environmental influence into account through its effect on consciousness.

Vygotsky's theory stresses the interaction of interpersonal (social), cultural–historical, and individual factors as the key to human development (Tudge & Scrimsher, 2003). Interactions with persons in the environment (e.g., apprenticeships, collaborations) stimulate developmental processes and foster cognitive growth. But interactions are not useful in a traditional sense of providing children with information. Rather, children transform their experiences based on their knowledge and characteristics and reorganize their mental structures.

The cultural–historical aspects of Vygotsky's theory illuminate the point that learning and development cannot be dissociated from their context. The way that learners interact with their worlds—with the persons, objects, and institutions in it—transforms their thinking. The meanings of concepts change as they are linked with the world (Gredler, 2009). Thus, "school" is not simply a word or a physical structure but also an institution that seeks to promote learning and citizenship.

There also are individual, or inherited, factors that affect development. Vygotsky was interested in children with mental and physical disabilities. He believed that their inherited characteristics produced learning trajectories different from those of children without such challenges.

Of these three influences, the one that has received the most attention—at least among Western researchers and practitioners—is the interpersonal. Vygotsky considered the social environment critical for learning and thought that social interactions transformed learning experiences. Social activity is a phenomenon that helps explain changes in consciousness and establishes a psychological theory that unifies behavior and mind (Kozulin, 1986; Wertsch, 1985).

The social environment influences cognition through its "tools"—that is, its cultural objects (e.g., cars, machines) and its language and social institutions (e.g., schools, churches). Social interactions help to coordinate the three influences on development. Cognitive change results from using cultural tools in social interactions and from internalizing and mentally transforming these interactions (Bruning et al., 2004). Vygotsky's position is a form of dialectical (cognitive) constructivism because it emphasizes the interaction between persons and their environments. *Mediation* is the key mechanism in development and learning:

> All human psychological processes (higher mental processes) are mediated by such psychological tools as language, signs, and symbols. Adults teach these tools to children in the course of their joint (collaborative) activity. After children internalize these tools they function as mediators of the children's more advanced psychological processes. (Karpov & Haywood, 1998, p. 27)

Table 6.4
Key points in Vygotsky's theory.

- Social interactions are critical; knowledge is coconstructed between two or more people.
- Self-regulation is developed through internalization (developing an internal representation) of actions and mental operations that occur in social interactions.
- Human development occurs through the cultural transmission of tools (language, symbols).
- Language is the most critical tool. Language develops from social speech, to private speech, to covert (inner) speech.
- The zone of proximal development (ZPD) is the difference between what children can do on their own and what they can do with assistance from others. Interactions with adults and peers in the ZPD promote cognitive development.

(Meece, 2002)

Vygotsky's most controversial contention was that all higher mental functions originated in the social environment (Vygotsky, 1962). This is a powerful claim, but it has a good degree of truth to it. The most influential process involved is language. Vygotsky thought that a critical component of psychological development was mastering the external process of transmitting cultural development and thinking through symbols such as language, counting, and writing. Once this process was mastered, the next step involved using these symbols to influence and self-regulate thoughts and actions. Self-regulation uses the important function of private speech (discussed later in this chapter).

In spite of this impressive theorizing, Vygotsky's claim appears to be too strong. Research evidence shows that young children mentally figure out much knowledge about the way the world operates long before they have an opportunity to learn from the culture in which they live (Bereiter, 1994). Children also seem biologically predisposed to acquire certain concepts (e.g., understanding that adding increases quantity), which does not depend on the environment (Geary, 1995). Although social learning affects knowledge construction, the claim that all learning derives from the social environment seems overstated. Nonetheless, we know that learners' cultures are critical and need to be considered in explaining learning and development. A summary of major points in Vygotsky's (1978) theory appears in Table 6.4 (Meece, 2002).

Zone of Proximal Development

A key concept is the *zone of proximal development (ZPD)*, defined as "the distance between the actual developmental level as determined by independent problem solving and the level of potential development as determined through problem solving under adult guidance or in collaboration with more capable peers" (Vygotsky, 1978, p. 86). The ZPD represents the amount of learning possible by a student given the proper instructional conditions (Puntambekar & Hübscher, 2005). It is largely a test of a student's developmental readiness or intellectual level in a specific domain, and it shows how learning and development are related (Bredo, 1997; Campione, Brown, Ferrara, & Bryant, 1984) and can be viewed as an alternative to the conception of intelligence

(Belmont, 1989). In the ZPD, a teacher and learner (adult/child, tutor/tutee, model/observer, master/apprentice, expert/novice) work together on a task that the learner could not perform independently because of the difficulty level. The ZPD reflects the marxist idea of collective activity, in which those who know more or are more skilled share that knowledge and skill to accomplish a task with those who know less (Bruner, 1984).

Cognitive change occurs in the ZPD as teacher and learner share cultural tools, and this culturally mediated interaction produces cognitive change when it is internalized in the learner (Bruning et al., 2004; Cobb, 1994). Working in the ZPD requires a good deal of guided participation (Rogoff, 1986); however, children do not acquire cultural knowledge passively from these interactions, nor is what they learn necessarily an automatic or accurate reflection of events. Rather, learners bring their own understandings to social interactions and construct meanings by integrating those understandings with their experiences in the context. The learning often is sudden, in the gestalt sense of insight (Chapter 7), rather than reflecting a gradual accretion of knowledge (Wertsch, 1984).

For example, assume that a teacher (Trudy) and a child (Laura) will work on a task (making a picture of mom, dad, and Laura doing something together at home). Laura brings to the task her understandings of what the people and the home look like and of the types of things they might work on, combined with knowledge of how to draw and make pictures. Trudy brings the same understandings plus knowledge of conditions necessary to work on various tasks. Suppose they decide to make a picture of the three working in the yard. Laura might draw a picture of dad cutting grass, mom trimming shrubs, and Laura raking the lawn. If Laura were to draw herself in front of dad, Trudy would explain that Laura must be behind dad to rake up the grass left behind by dad's cutting. During the interaction, Laura modifies her beliefs about working in the yard based on her current understanding and on the new knowledge she constructs.

Despite the importance of the ZPD, the overarching emphasis it has received in Western cultures has served to distort its meaning and downplay the complexity of Vygotsky's theory. As Tudge and Scrimsher (2003) explain:

> Moreover, the concept itself has too often been viewed in a rather limited way that emphasized the interpersonal at the expense of the individual and cultural-historical levels and treats the concept in a unidirectional fashion. As if the concept were synonymous with "scaffolding," too many authors have focused on the role of the more competent other, particularly the teacher, whose role is to provide assistance just in advance of the child's current thinking. . . . The concept thus has become equated with what sensitive teachers might do with their children and has lost much of the complexity with which it was imbued by Vygotsky, missing both what the child brings to the interaction and the broader setting (cultural and historical) in which the interaction takes place. (p. 211)

The influence of the cultural-historical setting is seen clearly in Vygotsky's belief that schooling was important not because it was where children were scaffolded but, rather, because it allowed them to develop greater awareness of themselves, their language, and their role in the world order. Participating in the cultural world transforms mental functioning rather than simply accelerate processes that would have developed anyway. Broadly speaking, therefore, the ZPD refers to new forms of awareness that occur as people interact with their societies' social institutions. The culture affects the course of one's mental development. It is unfortunate that in most discussions of the ZPD, it is conceived so narrowly as an expert teacher providing learning opportunities for a student (although that is part of it).

Applications

Vygotsky's ideas lend themselves to many educational applications (Karpov & Haywood, 1998; Moll, 2001). The field of self-regulation (Chapter 9) has been strongly influenced by the theory. Self-regulation requires metacognitive processes such as planning, checking, and evaluating. This section and Application 6.3 discuss other examples.

Helping students acquire cognitive mediators (e.g., signs, symbols) through the social environment can be accomplished in many ways. A common application involves the concept of *instructional scaffolding*, which refers to the process of controlling task elements that are beyond the learners' capabilities so that they can focus on and master those features of the task that they can grasp quickly (Bruning et al., 2004; Puntambekar & Hübscher, 2005). To use an analogy of scaffolding employed in construction projects, instructional scaffolding

---

APPLICATION 6.3
Vygotsky's Theory

Vygotsky postulated that one's interactions with the environment assist learning. The experiences one brings to a learning situation can greatly influence the outcome.

Ice skating coaches may work with advanced students who have learned a great deal about ice skating and how their bodies perform on the ice. Students bring with them their concepts of balance, speed, movement, and body control based on their experiences skating. Coaches take the strengths and weaknesses of these students and help them learn to alter various movements to improve their performances. For example, a skater who has trouble completing a triple axel toe loop has the height and speed needed to complete the jump, but the coach notices

that she turns her toe at an angle during the spin that alters the smooth completion of the loop. After the coach points this out to the skater and helps her learn to alter that movement, she is able to successfully complete the jump.

Veterinary students who have grown up on farms and have experienced births, illnesses, and care of various types of animals bring valuable knowledge to their training. Veterinary instructors can use these prior experiences to enhance students' learning. In teaching students how to treat an injured hoof of a cow or horse, the instructor might call on some of these students to discuss what they have observed and then build on that knowledge by explaining the latest and most effective methods of treatment.

has five major functions: provide support, function as a tool, extend the range of the learner, permit the attainment of tasks not otherwise possible, and use selectively only as needed.

In a learning situation, a teacher initially might do most of the work, after which the teacher and the learners share responsibility. As learners become more competent, the teacher gradually withdraws the scaffolding so learners can perform independently (Campione et al., 1984). The key is to ensure that the scaffolding keeps learners in the ZPD, which is raised as they develop capabilities. Students are challenged to learn within the bounds of the ZPD. We see in the opening lesson how Anna was able to learn given the proper instructional support.

It is critical to understand that scaffolding is not a formal part of Vygotsky's theory (Puntambekar & Hübscher, 2005). The term was coined by Wood, Bruner, and Ross (1976). It does, however, fit nicely within the ZPD. Scaffolding is part of Bandura's (1986) participant modeling technique (Chapter 4), in which a teacher initially models a skill, provides support, and gradually reduces aid as learners develop the skill. The notion also bears some relation to shaping (Chapter 3), as instructional supports are used to guide learners through various stages of skill acquisition.

Scaffolding is appropriate when a teacher wants to provide students with some information or to complete parts of tasks for them so that they can concentrate on the part of the task they are attempting to master. Thus, if Kathy Stone were working with her third-grade children on organizing sentences in a paragraph to express ideas in a logical order, she might assist the students by initially giving them the sentences with word meanings and spellings so that these needs would not interfere with their primary task. As they became more competent in sequencing ideas, she might have students compose their own paragraphs while still assisting with word meanings and spellings. Eventually students will assume responsibility for these functions. In short, the teacher creates a ZPD and provides the scaffolding for students to be successful (Moll, 2001).

Another application that reflects Vygotsky's ideas is *reciprocal teaching*. This technique is discussed and exemplified in Chapter 7 in conjunction with reading. Reciprocal teaching involves an interactive dialogue between a teacher and small group of students. Initially the teacher models the activities, after which teacher and students take turns being the teacher. If students are learning to ask questions during reading comprehension, the instructional sequence might include the teacher modeling a question-asking strategy for determining level of understanding. From a Vygotskian perspective, reciprocal teaching comprises social interaction and scaffolding as students gradually develop skills.

An important application area is *peer collaboration*, which reflects the notion of collective activity (Bruner, 1984; Ratner et al., 2002; see section on peer-assisted learning later in this chapter). When peers work on tasks cooperatively, the shared social interactions can serve an instructional function. Research shows that cooperative groups are most effective when each student has assigned responsibilities and all must attain competence before any are allowed to progress (Slavin, 1995). Peer groups are commonly used for learning in fields such as mathematics, science, and language arts (Cobb, 1994; Cohen, 1994; DiPardo & Freedman, 1988; Geary, 1995; O'Donnell, 2006), which attests to the recognized impact of the social environment during learning.

An application relevant to Vygotsky's theory and to situated cognition is social guidance through *apprenticeships* (Radziszewska & Rogoff, 1991; Rogoff, 1990). In apprenticeships, novices work closely with experts in joint work-related activities. Apprenticeships fit well with the ZPD because they occur in cultural institutions (e.g., schools, agencies) and thus help to transform learners' cognitive development. On the job, apprentices operate within a ZPD because they often work on tasks beyond their capabilities. By working with experts, novices develop a shared understanding of important processes and integrate this with their current understandings. Apprenticeships represent a type of dialectical constructivism that depends heavily on social interactions.

An example of apprenticeships set within a particular cultural context was described by Childs and Greenfield (1981) regarding the teaching of weaving in the Zincantecan culture of Mexico. Young girls observed their mothers and other older women weave from the time they were born, so when instruction began, they already had been exposed to many models. In the early phases of instruction, the adult spent more than 90% of the time weaving with the child, but this dropped to 50% after weaving one garment. The adult then worked on the more difficult aspects of the task. The adult's participation dropped to less than 40% after completion of four garments. This instructional procedure exemplifies close social interaction and scaffolding operating within the ZPD.

Apprenticeships are used in many areas of education. Student teachers work with co-operating teachers in schools and, once on the job, often are paired with experienced teachers for mentoring. Students conduct research with and are mentored by professors (Mullen, 2005). Counselor trainees serve internships under the direct guidance of a supervisor. On-the-job training programs use the apprentice model as students acquire skills while in the actual work setting and interacting with others. There is much emphasis on expanding youth apprenticeships, especially for non–college-bound adolescents (Bailey, 1993). Future research should evaluate the factors that influence the success of apprenticeships as a means of fostering skill acquisition in students of various ages.

Critique

It is difficult to evaluate the contributions of Vygotsky's theory to human development and learning (Tudge & Scrimsher, 2003). His works were not circulated for many years, translations have only recently become available, and only a small number of sources exist (Vygotsky, 1978, 1987). Researchers and practitioners have tended to focus on the ZPD without placing it in a larger theoretical context that is centered around cultural influence.

Another issue is that when applications of Vygotsky's theory are discussed, they often are not part of the theory, but rather seem to fit with it. When Wood et al. (1976) introduced the term *scaffolding*, for example, they presented it as a way for teachers to structure learning environments. As such, it has little relation to the dynamic ZPD that Vygotsky wrote about. Although *reciprocal teaching* also is not a Vygotskian concept, the term captures much better this sense of dynamic, multidirectional interaction.

Given these issues, there has been little debate on the adequacy of the theory. Debate that has ensued often has focused on "Piaget versus Vygotsky," contrasting their presumably discrepant positions on the course of human development, although on many points they do not differ (Duncan, 1995). While such debates may illuminate differences and provide testable research hypotheses, they are not helpful to educational practitioners seeking ways to help children learn.

Possibly the most significant implication of Vygotsky's theory for education is that the cultural–historical context is relevant to all forms of learning because learning does not occur in isolation. Student–teacher interactions are part of that context. Research has identified, for example, different interaction styles between Hawaiian, Anglo, and Navajo children (Tharp, 1989; Tharp & Gallimore, 1988). Whereas the Hawaiian culture encourages collaborative activity and more than one student talking at once, Navajo children are less acculturated to working in groups and more likely to wait to talk until the speaker is finished. Thus, the same instructional style would not be equally beneficial for all cultures. This point is especially noteworthy given the large influx of nonnative English speaking children in U.S. schools. Being able to differentiate instruction to fit children's learning preferences is a key 21st century skill.

PRIVATE SPEECH AND SOCIALLY MEDIATED LEARNING

A central premise of constructivism is that learning involves transforming and internalizing the social environment. Language plays a key role. This section discusses how private speech helps to perform these critical transforming and internalizing processes.

Private Speech

Private speech refers to the set of speech phenomena that has a self-regulatory function but is not socially communicative (Fuson, 1979). Various theories—including constructivism, cognitive-developmental, and social cognitive—establish a strong link between private speech and the development of self-regulation (Berk, 1986; Frauenglass & Diaz, 1985; Harris, 1982).

The historical impetus derives in part from work by Pavlov (1927). Recall from Chapter 3 that Pavlov distinguished the first (perceptual) from the second (linguistic) signal systems. Pavlov realized that animal conditioning results do not completely generalize to humans; human conditioning often occurs quickly with one or a few pairings of conditioned stimulus and unconditioned stimulus, in contrast to the multiple pairings required with animals. Pavlov believed that conditioning differences between humans and animals are largely due to the human capacity for language and thought. Stimuli may not produce conditioning automatically; people interpret stimuli in light of their prior experiences. Although Pavlov did not conduct research on the second signal system, subsequent investigations have validated his beliefs that human conditioning is complex and language plays a mediating role.

The Soviet psychologist Luria (1961) focused on the child's transition from the first to the second signal system. Luria postulated three stages in the development of verbal control of motor behavior. Initially, the speech of others is primarily responsible for directing the child's behavior (ages $1\frac{1}{2}$ to $2\frac{1}{2}$). During the second stage (ages 3 to 4), the child's overt verbalizations initiate motor behaviors but do not necessarily inhibit them. In the third stage, the child's private speech becomes capable of initiating, directing, and inhibiting motor behaviors (ages $4\frac{1}{2}$ to $5\frac{1}{2}$). Luria believed this private, self-regulatory speech directs behavior through neurophysiological mechanisms.

The mediating and self-directing role of the second signal system is embodied in Vygotsky's theory. Vygotsky (1962) believed private speech helps develop thought by organizing behavior. Children employ private speech to understand situations and surmount difficulties. Private speech occurs in conjunction with children's interactions in the social environment. As children's language facility develops, words spoken by others acquire meaning independent of their phonological and syntactical qualities. Children internalize word meanings and use them to direct their behaviors.

Vygotsky hypothesized that private speech follows a curvilinear developmental pattern: Overt verbalization (thinking aloud) increases until ages 6 to 7, after which it declines and becomes primarily covert (internal) by ages 8 to 10. However, overt verbalization can occur at any age when people encounter problems or difficulties. Research shows that although the amount of private speech decreases from approximately ages 4 or 5 to 8, the proportion of private speech that is self-regulating increases with age (Fuson, 1979). In many research investigations, the actual amount of private speech is small, and many children do not verbalize at all. Thus, the developmental pattern of private speech seems more complex than originally hypothesized by Vygotsky.

Verbalization and Achievement

Verbalization of rules, procedures, and strategies can improve student learning. Although Meichenbaum's (1977, 1986) *self-instructional training* procedure (Chapter 4) is not rooted in constructivism, it re-creates the overt-to-covert developmental progression of private speech. Types of statements modeled are *problem definition* ("What is it I have to do?"), *focusing of attention* ("I need to pay attention to what I'm doing"), *planning and response guidance* ("I need to work carefully"), *self-reinforcement* ("I'm doing fine"), *self-evaluation* ("Am I doing things in the right order?"), and *coping* ("I need to try again when I don't get it right"). Teachers can use self-instructional training to teach learners cognitive and motor skills, and it can result in creating a positive task outlook and fostering perseverance in the face of difficulties (Meichenbaum & Asarnow, 1979). The procedure need not be scripted; learners can construct their own verbalizations.

Verbalization is beneficial for students who often experience difficulties and perform in a deficient manner (Denney, 1975; Denney & Turner, 1979). Teachers have obtained benefits with children who do not spontaneously rehearse material to be learned, impulsive learners, students with learning disabilities and mental retardation, and learners who require remedial experiences (Schunk, 1986). Verbalization helps students with learning problems work at tasks systematically (Hallahan et al., 1983). It forces students to attend to tasks and to rehearse material, both of which enhance learning. Verbalization does not seem to facilitate learning when students can handle task demands adequately without verbalizing. Because verbalization constitutes an additional task, it might interfere with learning by distracting children from the task at hand.

Research has identified the conditions under which verbalization promotes performance. Denney (1975) modeled a performance strategy for 6-, 8-, and 10-year-old normal learners on a 20-question task. The 8- and 10-year-olds who verbalized the model's strategy as they performed the task scored no higher than children who did not verbalize. Verbalization interfered with the performance of 6-year-olds. Children verbalized specific statements (e.g., "Find the right picture in the fewest questions"); apparently performing this additional task proved too distracting for the youngest children. Denney and Turner (1979) found that among normal learners ranging in age from 3 to 10 years, adding verbalization to a strategy modeling treatment resulted in no benefits on cognitive tasks compared with modeling alone. Participants constructed their own verbalizations, which might have been less distracting than Denney's (1975) specific statements. Coates and Hartup (1969) found that 7-year-olds who verbalized a model's actions during exposure did not subsequently produce them better than children who passively observed the behaviors. The children regulated their attention and cognitively processed the model's actions without verbalizing.

Berk (1986) studied first and third graders' spontaneous private speech. Task-relevant overt speech was negatively related and faded verbalization (whispers, lip movements, muttering) was positively related to mathematical performance. These results were obtained for first graders of high intelligence and third graders of average intelligence; among third graders of high intelligence, overt and faded speech showed no relationship to achievement. For the latter students, internalized self-guiding speech apparently is the most effective. Daugherty and White (2008) found that private speech related positively to indexes of creativity among Head Start and low socioeconomic status preschoolers.

Keeney, Cannizzo, and Flavell (1967) pretested 6- and 7-year-olds on a serial recall task and identified those who failed to rehearse prior to recall. After these children learned how to rehearse, their recall matched that of spontaneous rehearsers. Asarnow and Meichenbaum (1979) identified kindergartners who did not spontaneously rehearse on a serial recall test. Some were trained to use a rehearsal strategy similar to that of Keeney et al., whereas others received self-instructional training. Both treatments facilitated recall relative to a control condition, but the self-instructional treatment was more effective. Taylor and his colleagues (Taylor, Josberger, & Whitely, 1973; Whitely & Taylor, 1973) found that educable mentally retarded children who were trained to generate elaborations between word associate pairs recalled more associates if they verbalized their elaborations than if they did not. In the Coates and Hartup (1969) study, 4-year-olds who verbalized a model's actions as they were being performed later reproduced them better than children who merely observed the model.

Schunk (1982b) instructed students who lacked division skills. Some students verbalized explicit statements (e.g., "check," "multiply," "copy"), others constructed their own verbalizations, a third group verbalized the statements and their own verbalizations, and students in a fourth condition did not verbalize. Self-constructed verbalizations—alone or combined with the statements—led to the highest division skill.

In summary, verbalization is more likely to promote student achievement if it is relevant to the task and does not interfere with performance. Higher proportions of task-relevant statements produce better learning (Schunk & Gunn, 1986). Private speech follows an overt-to-covert developmental cycle, and speech becomes internalized earlier in students with higher intelligence (Berk, 1986; Frauenglass & Diaz, 1985). Private speech relates positively to creativity. Allowing students to construct their verbalizations—possibly in conjunction with verbalizing steps in a strategy—is more beneficial than limiting verbalizing to specific statements. To facilitate transfer

APPLICATION 6.4
Self-Verbalization

A teacher might use self-verbalization (self-talk) in a special education resource room or in a regular classroom to assist students having difficulty attending to material and mastering skills. When Kathy Stone introduces long division to her third-grade students, she uses verbalization to help those children who cannot remember the steps to complete the procedure. She works individually with the students by verbalizing and applying the following steps:

- Will (number) go into (number)?
- Divide.
- Multiply: (number) × (number) = (number).
- Write down the answer.
- Subtract: (number) − (number) = (number).
- Bring down the next number.
- Repeat steps.

Use of self-talk helps students stay on task and builds their self-efficacy to work systematically through the long process. Once they begin to grasp the content, it is to their advantage to fade verbalizations to a covert (silent) level so they can work more rapidly.

Self-verbalization also can help students who are learning sport skills and strategies. They might verbalize what is happening and what moves they should make. A tennis coach, for example, might encourage students to use self-talk during practice matches: "high ball—overhand return," "low ball—underhand return," "cross ball—backhand return."

Aerobic and dance instructors often use self-talk during practice. A ballet teacher might have young students repeat "paint a rainbow" for a flowing arm movement, and "walk on eggs" to get them to move lightly on their toes. Participants in aerobic exercise classes also might verbalize movements (e.g., "bend and stretch," "slide right and around") as they perform them.

and maintenance, overt verbalization should eventually be faded to whispering or lip movements and then to a covert level. Internalization is a key feature of self-regulation (Schunk, 1999; Chapter 9).

These benefits of verbalization do not mean that all students ought to verbalize while learning. That practice would result in a loud classroom and would distract many students! Rather, verbalization could be incorporated into instruction for students having difficulties learning. A teacher or classroom aide could work with such students individually or in groups to avoid disrupting the work of other class members. Application 6.4 discusses ways to integrate verbalization into learning.

Socially Mediated Learning

Many forms of constructivism, and Vygotsky's theory in particular, stress the idea that learning is a socially mediated process. This focus is not unique to constructivism; many other learning theories emphasize social processes as having a significant impact on learning. Bandura's (1986, 1997) social cognitive theory (Chapter 4), for example, highlights the reciprocal relations among learners and social environmental influences, and much research has shown that social modeling is a powerful influence on learning (Rosenthal & Zimmerman, 1978; Schunk, 1987). In Vygotsky's theory, however, social mediation of learning is the central construct (Karpov & Haywood, 1998; Moll, 2001; Tudge & Scrimsher, 2003). All learning is mediated by tools such as language, symbols, and signs. Children acquire these tools during their social interactions with others. They internalize these tools and then use them as mediators of more advanced learning (i.e., higher cognitive processes such as concept learning and problem solving).

The centrality of social mediation is apparent in self-regulation and constructivist learning environments (discussed later). For now, let us examine how social mediation influences concept acquisition. Young children acquire concepts spontaneously by observing their worlds and formulating hypotheses. For example, they hear the noise that cars make and the noise that trucks make, and they may believe that bigger objects make more noise. They have difficulty accommodating discrepant observations (e.g., a motorcycle is smaller than a car or truck but may make more noise than either).

Through social interactions, children are taught concepts by others (e.g., teachers, parents, older siblings). This is often a direct process, such as when teachers teach children the difference between squares, rectangles, triangles, and circles. As cognitive psychologists might say, such concepts are internalized as declarative knowledge. Thus, children use the tools of language and symbols to internalize these concepts.

It is, of course, possible to learn concepts on one's own without social interactions. But even such independent learning is, in a constructivist sense, socially mediated, because it involves the tools (i.e., language, signs, symbols) that have been acquired through previous social interactions. Further, a certain amount of labeling is needed. Children may learn a concept but not have a name for it ("What do you call a thing that looks like ————?"). The label involves language and likely will be supplied by another person.

Tools are useful not only for learning but also for teaching. Children teach one another things they have learned. Vygotsky (1962, 1978) believed that by being used for social purposes, tools exert powerful influences on others.

These points suggest that preparation is needed for children to effectively construct knowledge. The teaching of the basic tools to learn can be direct. There is no need for students to construct the obvious or what they can be easily taught. Constructed discoveries are the result of basic learning, not their cause (Karpov & Haywood, 1998). Teachers should prepare students to learn by teaching them the tools and then providing opportunities for learning. Applications of socially mediated learning are discussed in Application 6.5.

Self-Regulation

Vygotsky's theory in general, and the ideas covered in this section on private speech and on socially mediated learning in particular, has high relevance to self-regulation. In Vygotsky's theory, self-regulation involves the coordination of mental (cognitive) processes such as planning, synthesizing, and forming concepts (Henderson &

APPLICATION 6.5
Socially Mediated Learning

Socially mediated learning is appropriate for students of all ages. Gina Brown knows that success in teaching depends in part on understanding the culture of the communities served by the school. She obtains consent from the schools where her students are placed and from the parents, and she assigns each student to be a "buddy" of a schoolchild. As part of their placements, her students spend extra time with their buddies—for example, working one-to-one, eating lunch with them, riding home on the school bus with them, and visiting them in their homes. She pairs her students, and the members of each dyad meet regularly to discuss the culture of their assigned buddies, such as what their buddies like about school, what their parents or guardians do, and characteristics of the neighborhoods where their buddies live. She meets regularly with each dyad to discuss the implications of the cultural variables for school learning. Through social interactions with buddies, with Gina, and with other class members, Gina's students develop a better understanding of the role of culture in schooling.

Historical events typically are open to multiple interpretations, and Jim Marshall uses social mediation to develop his students' thinking about events. As part of a unit on post–World War II changes in American life, he organizes students into five teams. Each team is assigned a topic: medicine, transportation, education, technology, suburbs. Teams prepare a presentation on why their topic represents a significant advance in American life. Students on each team work together to prepare the presentation, and each member presents part of it. After the presentations are finished, Jim leads a discussion with the class. He tries to get them to see how advances are interrelated: for example, technology influences medicine, transportation, and education; more automobiles and roads lead to growth in suburbs; and better education results in preventative medicine. Social mediation through discussions and presentations helps students gain a deeper understanding of changes in American life.

Cunningham, 1994). But such coordination does not proceed independently of the individual's social environment and culture.

The process of self-regulation involves the gradual internalization of language and concepts. Young children primarily respond to the directions from others (e.g., older persons in their environments). Through the use of private speech and other cognitive tools, children internalize directions to self-regulate their behaviors in different situations. Thought processes become self-directed. Internalization is critical for the development of self-regulation (Schunk, 1999).

Children's earliest self-regulation may be crude and reflect largely the verbalizations of others. But as they develop a greater capability for self-directed thought, they construct effective and idiosyncratic cognitive self-regulators. The constructivist perspective on self-regulation is discussed in more depth in Chapter 9.

MOTIVATION

Constructivism is primarily a theory of human development that in recent years has been applied to learning. Less has been written about the role of motivation in constructivism. Nonetheless, constructivism is applicable to motivation, and some motivational principles explored by researchers in other theoretical traditions fit well with constructivism (Sivan, 1986). Aspects of motivation especially relevant include contextual factors, implicit theories, and teachers' expectations (Chapter 8).

Contextual Factors

Organization and Structure. Constructivism stresses situated cognition and the importance of taking the context of environments into account to explain behavior. A topic relevant to constructivism is the *organization and structure of learning environments,* that is, how students are grouped for instruction, how work is evaluated and rewarded, how authority is established, and how time is scheduled. Many researchers and practitioners believe that environments are complex and that to understand learning we must take into account many factors (Marshall & Weinstein, 1984; Roeser, Urdan, & Stephens, 2009).

An important aspect of organization is *dimensionality* (Rosenholtz & Simpson, 1984). *Unidimensional classrooms* include a few activities that address a limited range of student abilities. *Multidimensional classrooms* have more activities and allow for diversity in student abilities and performances. Multidimensional classes are compatible with constructivist tenets about learning.

Classroom characteristics that indicate dimensionality include differentiation of task structure, student autonomy, grouping patterns, and salience of formal performance evaluations (Table 6.5). Unidimensional classrooms have *undifferentiated task structures.* All students work on the same or similar tasks, and instruction employs a small number of materials and methods (Rosenholtz & Simpson, 1984). The more undifferentiated the structure, the more likely the daily activities will produce consistent performances from each student and the greater the probability that students will socially compare their work with

Table 6.5
Characteristics of dimensionality.

Characteristic	Unidimensional	Multidimensional
Differentiation of task structure	Undifferentiated; students work on same tasks	Differentiated; students work on different tasks
Student autonomy	Low; students have few choices	High; students have choices
Grouping patterns	Whole class; students are grouped by ability	Individual work; students are not grouped by ability
Performance evaluations	Students are graded on same assignments; grades are public; much social comparison	Students are graded on different assignments; less public grading and social comparison

that of others to determine relative standing. Structures become *differentiated* (and classrooms become multidimensional) when students work on different tasks at the same time.

Autonomy refers to the extent to which students have choices about what to do and when and how to do it. Classrooms are unidimensional when autonomy is low, which can hinder self-regulation and stifle motivation. Multidimensional classrooms offer students more choices, which can enhance intrinsic motivation.

With respect to *grouping patterns*, social comparisons become more prominent when students work on whole-class activities or are grouped by ability. Comparisons are not as prevalent when students work individually or in mixed-ability groups. Grouping affects motivation and learning and has added influence over the long-term if groups remain intact and students understand they are bound to the groups regardless of how well they perform.

Salience of formal *performance evaluations* refers to the public nature of grading. In unidimensional classrooms, students are graded on the same assignments and grades are public, so everyone knows the grade distribution. Those receiving low grades may not be motivated to improve. As grading becomes less public or as grades are assigned for different projects (as in multidimensional classes), grading can motivate a higher proportion of students, especially those who believe they are progressing and capable of further learning (Schunk, Pintrich, & Meece, 2008).

Unidimensional classrooms have high visibility of performance (Rosenholtz & Rosenholtz, 1981), which can motivate high achievers to learn but often has a negative effect on everyone else. Multidimensional classrooms are more likely to motivate more students because they feature greater differentiation and autonomy, less ability grouping, and more flexibility in grading with less public evaluation.

TARGET. Classrooms include other factors that can affect learners' perceptions, motivation, and learning. Some of these, as shown in Table 6.6, can be summarized by the acronym *TARGET*: *task* design, distribution of *authority*, *recognition* of students, *grouping* arrangements, *evaluation* practices, and *time* allocation (Epstein, 1989).

Table 6.6
TARGET factors affecting motivation and learning.

Factor	Characteristics
Task	Design of learning activities and assignments
Authority	Extent that students can assume leadership and develop independence and control over learning activities
Recognition	Formal and informal use of rewards, incentives, praise
Grouping	Individual, small group, large group
Evaluation	Methods for monitoring and assessing learning
Time	Appropriateness of workload, pace of instruction, time allotted for completing work

The task dimension involves the design of learning activities and assignments. Chapter 8 discusses ways to structure tasks to promote a mastery (learning) goal orientation in students—for example, by making learning interesting, using variety and challenge, assisting students to set realistic goals, and helping students develop organizational, management, and other strategic skills (Ames, 1992a, 1992b). Task structure is a distinguishing feature of dimensionality. In unidimensional classes, students have the same materials and assignments, so variations in ability can translate into motivational differences. In multidimensional classes, students may not all work on the same task simultaneously and thereby have fewer opportunities for social comparisons.

Authority refers to whether students can assume leadership and develop independence and control over learning activities. Teachers foster authority by allowing students to participate in decisions, giving them choices and leadership roles, and teaching them skills that allow them to take responsibility for learning. Self-efficacy tends to be higher in classes that allow students some measure of authority (Ames, 1992a, 1992b).

Recognition, which involves the formal and informal use of rewards, incentives, and praise, has important consequences for motivated learning (Schunk, 1995). Ames (1992a, 1992b) recommended that teachers help students develop mastery goal orientations by recognizing progress, accomplishments, effort, and self-directed strategy use; providing opportunities for all learners to earn rewards; and using private forms of recognition that avoid comparing students or emphasizing the difficulties of others.

The grouping dimension focuses on students' ability to work with others. Teachers should use heterogeneous cooperative groups and peer interaction where possible to ensure that differences in ability do not translate into differences in motivation and learning. Low achievers especially benefit from small-group work because contributing to the group's success engenders feelings of self-efficacy. Group work also allows more students to share in the responsibility for learning so that a few students do not do all of the work. At the same time, individual work is important because it provides for clear indicators of learning progress.

Evaluation involves methods for monitoring and assessing student learning, for example, evaluating students for individual progress and mastery, giving students opportunities to improve their work (e.g., revise work for a better grade), using different forms of evaluation, and conducting evaluations privately. Although normative grading systems are common in schools (i.e., students compared to one another), such normative comparisons can lower self-efficacy among students who do not perform as well as their peers.

Time involves the appropriateness of workload, pace of instruction, and time allotted for completing work (Epstein, 1989). Effective strategies for enhancing motivation and learning are to adjust time or task requirements for those having difficulty and allowing students to plan their schedules and timelines for making progress. Giving students control over their time management helps allay anxiety about completing work and can promote use of self-regulatory strategies and self-efficacy for learning (Schunk & Zimmerman, 1994). Application 6.6 lists classroom applications of TARGET.

Implicit Theories

Constructivist theories call attention to many facets of motivation, including the cognitive and the affective. A central premise of many contemporary theories of learning and motivation,

APPLICATION 6.6
Applying TARGET in the Classroom

Incorporating TARGET components into a unit can positively affect motivation and learning. As Kathy Stone develops a unit on deserts, she plans part of the unit but also involves her students in planning activities. She sets up learning centers, plans reading and research assignments, organizes large- and small-group discussions, and designs unit pre- and posttests as well as tasks for checking mastery throughout the unit. The class helps her plan a field trip to a museum with an area devoted to life in the desert, develop small-group project topics, and decide how to create a desert in the classroom. Kathy and the students then develop a calendar and timeline for working on and completing the unit. Notice in this example how Kathy incorporates motivational components into the TARGET classroom features: task, authority, recognition, grouping, evaluation, and time.

and one that fits nicely with constructivist assumptions, is that people hold *implicit theories* about issues, such as how they learn, what contributes to school achievement, and how motivation affects performance. Learning and thinking occur in the context of learners' beliefs about cognition, which differ as a function of personal, social, and cultural factors (Greeno, 1989; Moll, 2001).

Research shows that implicit theories about such processes as learning, thinking, and ability influence how students engage in learning and their views about what leads to success in and outside of the classroom (Duda & Nicholls, 1992; Dweck, 1999, 2006; Dweck & Leggett, 1988; Dweck & Molden, 2005; Nicholls, Cobb, Wood, Yackel, & Patashnick, 1990). Motivation researchers have identified two distinct implicit theories (or mindsets) about the role of ability in achievement: *entity theory (fixed mindset)* and *incremental theory (growth mindset)*. Students who hold an entity theory, or fixed mindset, view their abilities as representing fixed traits over which they have little control; whereas those who hold an incremental theory, or growth mindset, believe that abilities are skills that they can improve through learning (Dweck, 1999; Dweck & Leggett, 1988; Dweck & Molden, 2005). These perspectives influence motivation and ultimately learning and achievement. Wood and Bandura (1989) found that adults who view managerial skills as capable of being developed use better strategies, hold higher self-efficacy for success, and set more challenging goals than those who believe such skills are relatively fixed and not capable of being altered.

Students with a fixed mindset are apt to be discouraged if they encounter difficulty because they think they can do little to alter their status. Such discouragement results in low self-efficacy (Chapter 4), which can affect learning adversely (Schunk, 1995; Schunk & Zimmerman, 2006). Conversely, students with a growth mindset are less apt to give up when they encounter difficulty and instead are likely to alter their strategy, seek assistance, consult additional sources of information, or engage in other self-regulatory strategies (Dweck, 2006; Zimmerman, 1994, 1998; Zimmerman & Martinez-Pons, 1992).

Evidence also shows that implicit theories can affect the way that learners process information (Graham & Golan, 1991). Students who believe that learning outcomes are under their control may expend greater mental effort, rehearse more, use organizational strategies, and employ other tactics to improve learning. In contrast, students who hold a fixed view may not expend the same type of effort.

Students differ in how they view kinds of classroom learning. Nicholls and Thorkildsen (1989) found that elementary school students perceived learning substantive matters (e.g., mathematical logic, facts about nature) as more important than learning intellectual conventions (e.g., spelling, methods of representing addition). Students also saw didactic teaching as more appropriate for teaching of conventions than for matters of logic and fact. Nicholls, Patashnick, and Nolen (1985) found that high school students held definite beliefs about what types of activities should lead to success. *Task orientation*, or a focus during learning on mastery of the task, was positively associated with student perceptions that success depends on being interested in learning, working hard, trying to understand (as opposed to memorizing), and working collaboratively. (Goal orientations are discussed in Chapter 8.)

Implicit theories likely are formed as children encounter socialization influences. Dweck (1999) found evidence for implicit theories in children as young as $3^{1}/_{2}$ years. Early on, children are socialized by significant others about right and wrong, good and bad. Through what they are told and what they observe, they form implicit theories about rightness, badness, and the like. At achievement tasks, praise and criticism from others influence what they believe produce good and poor outcomes (e.g., "You worked hard and got it right," "You don't have what it takes to do this right"). As with other beliefs, these may be situated within contexts, and teachers and parents may stress different causes of achievement (effort and ability). By the time children enter school, they hold a wide range of implicit theories that they have constructed and that cover most situations.

Research on implicit theories suggests that the premise that learning requires providing students with information to build propositional networks is incomplete. Also important is how children refine, modify, combine, and elaborate their conceptual undestandings as a function of experience. Those understandings are situated in a personal belief system and include beliefs about the usefulness and importance of knowledge, how it relates to what else one knows, and in what situations it may be appropriate.

Teachers' Expectations

A motivation topic that has attracted much attention and integrates nicely with constructivism is *teachers' expectations*. Theory and research suggest teachers' expectations for students relate to teacher actions and student achievement outcomes (Cooper & Good, 1983; Cooper & Tom, 1984; Dusek, 1985; Jussim, Robustelli, & Cain, 2009; Rosenthal, 2002).

The impetus for exploring expectations came from a study by Rosenthal and Jacobson (1968), who gave elementary school students a test of nonverbal intelligence at the start of the academic year. Teachers were told that this test predicted which students would bloom intellectually during the year. The researchers actually randomly identified 20% of the school population as bloomers and gave these names to the teachers. Teachers were not aware of the deception: The test did not predict intellectual blooming and names bore no relation to test scores. Teachers taught in their usual fashion and students were retested one semester, 1 year, and 2 years later. For the first two tests, students were in the classes of teachers given bloomers' names; for the last test, students were in new classes with teachers who did not have these names.

After the first year, significant differences in intelligence were seen between bloomers and control students (those not identified as bloomers); differences were greater among children in the first and second grades. During the subsequent year, these younger children lost their advantage, but bloomers in upper grades showed an increasing advantage over control students. Differences were greater among average achievers than among high or low achievers. Similar findings were obtained for grades in reading. Overall the differences between bloomers and control students were small, both in reading and on the intelligence test.

Rosenthal and Jacobson concluded that teacher expectations can act as *self-fulfilling prophecies* because student achievement comes to reflect the expectations. They suggested that results are stronger with young children because they have close contact with teachers. Older students may function better after they move to a new teacher.

This study is controversial: It has been criticized on conceptual and methodological grounds, and many attempts at replication have not been successful (Cooper & Good, 1983; Jussim et al., 2009). Nonetheless, teacher expectations exist and have been found to relate to various student outcomes. A model to explain self-fulfilling prophecies is as follows:

- Teachers develop erroneous expectations.
- These expectations lead teachers to treat high expectancy students differently than they treat low expectancy students.
- Students react to this differential treatment in such a manner as to confirm the originally erroneous expectation. (Jussim et al., 2009, p. 361)

Brophy and Good (1974) contended that early in the school year teachers form expectations based on initial interactions with students and information in records. Teachers then may begin to treat students differently consistent with these expectations. Teacher behaviors are reciprocated; for example, teachers who treat students warmly are apt to receive warmth in return. Student behaviors begin to complement and reinforce teacher behaviors and expectations. Effects will be most pronounced for rigid and inappropriate expectations. When they are appropriate or inappropriate but flexible, student behavior may substantiate or redefine expectations. When expectations are inappropriate or not easily changed, student performance might decline and become consistent with expectations.

Once teachers form expectations, they can convey them to students through socioemotional climate, verbal input, verbal output, and feedback (Rosenthal, 1974). *Socioemotional climate* includes smiles, head nods, eye contact, and supportive and friendly actions. Teachers may create a warmer climate for students for whom they hold high expectations than for those for whom expectations are lower (Cooper & Tom, 1984). *Verbal input*, or opportunities to learn new material and difficulty of material, varies when high-expectation students have more opportunities to interact with and learn new material and be exposed to more difficult material. *Verbal output* refers to number and length of academic interactions. Teachers engage in more academic interchanges with high- than with low-expectation students (Brophy & Good, 1974). They also are more persistent with highs and get them to give answers by prompting or rephrasing questions.

Feedback refers to use of praise and criticism. Teachers praise high-expectation students and criticize low-expectation students more (Cooper & Tom, 1984).

Although these factors are genuine, wide differences exist between teachers (Schunk et al., 2008). Some teachers consistently encourage lower achievers and treat them much like the patterns described above for high achievers (e.g., give more praise, get them to answer more questions). Appropriate teacher expectations for students can improve learning. Tailoring difficulty of material and level of questioning to students based on their prior performances is instructionally sound. Expecting all students to learn with requisite effort also is reasonable. Greatly distorted expectations are not credible and typically have little effect on learning. Most elementary teachers (when expectation effects may be strongest) hold positive expectations for students, provide for a lot of successes, and use praise often (Brophy & Good, 1974).

It seems likely that students construct implicit theories about what their teachers think and expect of them. How these theories might influence their achievement actions is less predictable. Our beliefs about what others expect of us may motivate ("She thinks I can do it, so I'll try"), demotivate ("She thinks I can't do it, so I won't try"), or lead us to act contrary to our theories ("She thinks I can't do it, so I'll show her I can"). The best advice is to expect that all students can learn, and provide support for them, which should help them construct appropriate expectations for themselves. Application 6.7 gives suggestions for conveying positive expectations to students.

APPLICATION 6.7
Teacher Expectations

Expectations that teachers hold for students can positively and negatively affect their interactions with students. The following practices help preclude negative effects:

- Enforce rules fairly and consistently.
- Assume that all students can learn and convey that expectation to them.
- Do not form differential student expectations based on qualities unrelated to performance (e.g., gender, ethnicity, parents' background).
- Do not accept excuses for poor performance.
- Realize that upper limits of student ability are unknown and not relevant to school learning.

A college English professor told her class that they would be expected to do a lot of writing throughout the semester. Some of the students looked apprehensive, and the professor assured them that it was a task they could do. "We can all work together to improve our writing. I know some of you have had different experiences in high school with writing, but I will work with each of you, and I know by the end of the semester you will be writing well."

One student waited after class and told the professor that he had been in a special-education class in school and said, "I can hardly write a good sentence; I don't think you can make a writer out of me." To which the professor replied, "Well, sentences are a good place to begin. I'll see you Wednesday morning in class."

CONSTRUCTIVIST LEARNING ENVIRONMENTS

Learning environments created to reflect constructivist principles look quite different from traditional classrooms (Brooks & Brooks, 1999). This section describes key features of constructivist learning environments.

Key Features

Learning in a constructivist setting is not allowing students to do whatever they want. Rather, constructivist environments should create rich experiences that encourage learning.

Constructivist classrooms differ from traditional classrooms in several ways (Brooks & Brooks, 1999). In traditional classes, basic skills are emphasized. The curriculum is presented in small parts using textbooks and workbooks. Teachers disseminate information to students didactically and seek correct answers to questions. Assessment of student learning is distinct from teaching and usually done through testing. Students often work alone.

In constructivist classrooms, the curriculum focuses on big concepts. Activities typically involve primary sources of data and manipulative materials. Teachers interact with students by seeking their questions and points of view. Assessment is authentic; it is interwoven with teaching and includes teacher observations and student portfolios. Students often work in groups. The key is to structure the learning environment such that students can effectively construct new knowledge and skills (Schuh, 2003).

Some guiding principles of constructivist learning environments are shown in Table 6.7 (Brooks & Brooks, 1999). One principle is that teachers should *pose problems of emerging relevance* to students, where relevance is preexisting or emerges through teacher mediation. Thus, a teacher might structure a lesson around questions that challenge students' preconceptions. This takes time, which means that other critical content may not be covered. Relevance is not established by threatening to test students, but rather by stimulating their interest and helping them discover how the problem affects their lives.

A second principle is that *learning should be structured around primary concepts.* This means that teachers design activities around conceptual clusters of questions and problems so that ideas are presented holistically rather than in isolation (Brooks & Brooks, 1999). Being able to see the whole helps to understand the parts.

Holistic teaching does not require sacrificing content, but it does involve structuring content differently. A piecemeal approach to teaching history is to present information chronologically as a series of events. In contrast, a holistic method involves presenting

Table 6.7
Guiding principles of constructivist learning environments.

- Pose problems of emerging relevance to students.
- Structure learning around primary concepts.
- Seek and value students' points of view.
- Adapt curriculum to address students' suppositions.
- Assess student learning in the context of teaching.

(Brooks & Brooks, 1999)

themes that recur in history (e.g., economic hardships, disputes over territory) and structuring content so that students can discover these themes in different eras. Students then can see that although environmental features change over time (e.g., armies → air forces; farming → technology), the themes remain the same.

Holistic teaching also can be done across subjects. In the middle school curriculum, for example, the theme of "courage" can be explored in social studies (e.g., courage of people to stand up and act based on their beliefs when these conflict with governments), language arts (e.g., characters in literature who display courage), and science (e.g., courage of scientists who dispute prevailing theories). An integrated curriculum in which teachers plan units together reflects this holism.

Third, it is important to *seek and value students' points of view*. Understanding students' perspectives is essential for planning activities that are challenging and interesting. This requires that teachers ask questions, stimulate discussions, and listen to what students say. Teachers who make little effort to understand what students think fail to capitalize on the role of their experiences in learning. This is not to suggest that teachers should analyze every student utterance; that is not necessary, nor is there time to do it. Rather, teachers should try to learn students' conceptions of a topic.

With the current emphasis on achievement test scores, it is easy to focus only on students' correct answers. Constructivist education, however, requires that—where feasible—we go beyond the answer and learn how the students arrived at that answer. Teachers do this by asking students to elaborate on their answers; for example, "How did you arrive at that answer?" or "Why do you think that?" It is possible for a student to arrive at a correct answer through faulty reasoning and, conversely, to answer incorrectly but engage in sound thinking. Students' perspectives on a situation or theories about a phenomenon help teachers in curriculum planning.

Fourth, we should *adapt curriculum to address students' suppositions*. This means that curricular demands on students should align with the beliefs they bring to the classroom. When there is a gross mismatch, lessons will lack meaning for students. But alignment need not be perfect. Demands that are slightly above students' present capabilities (i.e., within the zone of proximal development) produce challenge and learning.

When students' suppositions are incorrect, the typical response is to inform them of such. Instead, constructivist teaching challenges students to discover the information. Recall the opening scenario describing a first-grade lesson on measurement and equivalence. Children were using a balance to determine how many plastic links equaled one metal washer in weight (Brooks & Brooks, 1999). This example shows how the teacher modified the lesson based on Anna's suppositions and how she challenged Anna to discover the correct principle. Even after Anna answered "four" correctly, the teacher did not respond by saying "correct" but rather continued to question her.

Finally, constructivist education requires that we *assess student learning in the context of teaching*. This point runs counter to the typical classroom situation where most learning assessments are disconnected from teaching—for example, end-of-grade tests, end-of-unit exams, pop quizzes. Although the content of these assessments may align well with learning objectives addressed during instruction, the assessment occasions are separate from teaching.

In a constructivist environment, assessment occurs continuously during teaching and is an assessment of both students and teacher. Anna's learning was being assessed throughout the sequence, as was the success of the teacher in designing an activity and guiding Anna to understand the concept.

Of course, assessment methods must reflect the type of learning (Chapter 1). Constructivist environments are best designed for meaningful, deep-structure learning, not for superficial understanding. True-false and multiple-choice tests may be inappropriate to assess learning outcomes. Authentic forms of assessment may require students to write reflective pieces, discussing what they learned and why this knowledge is useful in the world, or to demonstrate and apply skills they have acquired.

Constructivist assessment is less concerned about right and wrong answers than about next steps after students answer. This type of authentic assessment guides instructional decisions, but it is difficult because it forces teachers to design activities that elicit student feedback and then alter instruction as needed. It is much easier to design and score a multiple-choice test, but encouraging teachers to teach constructively and then assess separately in a traditional manner sends a mixed message. Given the present emphasis on accountability, we may never completely move to authentic assessment; but encouraging it facilitates curricular planning and provides for more-interesting lessons than drilling students to pass test.

APA Learner-Centered Principles

The American Psychological Association formulated a set of learner-centered psychological principles (American Psychological Association Work Group of the Board of Educational Affairs, 1997; Table 6.8) that reflect a constructivist learning approach. They were developed as guidelines for school design and reform.

The principles are grouped into four major categories: cognitive and metacognitive factors, motivational and affective factors, developmental and social factors, and individual differences. Cognitive and metacognitive factors involve the nature of the learning process, learning goals, construction of knowledge, strategic thinking, thinking about thinking, and the content of learning. Motivational and affective factors reflect motivational and emotional influences on learning, the intrinsic motivation to learn, and the effects of motivation on effort. Developmental and social factors include developmental and social influences on learning. Individual differences comprise individual difference variables, learning and diversity, and standards and assessment. These principles are reflected in current work on standards reform to address 21st century skills.

Application 6.8 illustrates ways to apply these principles in learning environments. In considering their application, teachers should keep in mind the purpose of the instruction and the uses to which it will be put. Teacher-centered instruction often is the appropriate means of instruction and the most efficient. But when deeper student understanding is desired—along with greater student activity—the principles offer sound guidelines.

Table 6.8
APA learner-centered principles.

Cognitive and Metacognitive Factors

1. *Nature of the learning process.* The learning of complex subject matter is most effective when it is an intentional process of constructing meaning from information and experience.

2. *Goals of the learning process.* The successful learner, over time and with support and instructional guidance, can create meaningful, coherent representations of knowledge.

3. *Construction of knowledge.* The successful learner can link new information with existing knowledge in meaningful ways.

4. *Strategic thinking.* The successful learner can create and use a repertoire of thinking and reasoning strategies to achieve complex learning goals.

5. *Thinking about thinking.* Higher-order strategies for selecting and monitoring mental operations facilitate creative and critical thinking.

6. *Context of learning.* Learning is influenced by environmental factors, including culture, technology, and instructional practices.

Motivational and Affective Factors

7. *Motivational and emotional influences on learning.* What and how much is learned is influenced by the learner's motivation. Motivation to learn, in turn, is influenced by the individual's emotional states, beliefs, interests and goals, and habits of thinking.

8. *Intrinsic motivation to learn.* The learner's creativity, higher-order thinking, and natural curiosity all contribute to motivation to learn. Intrinsic motivation is stimulated by tasks of optimal novelty and difficulty, tasks that are relevant to personal interests, and tasks that provide for personal choice and control.

9. *Effects of motivation on effort.* Acquisition of complex knowledge and skills requires extended learner effort and guided practice. Without learners' motivation to learn, the willingness to exert this effort is unlikely without coercion.

Development and Social Factors

10. *Developmental influences on learning.* As individuals develop, there are different opportunities and constraints for learning. Learning is most effective when differential development within and across physical, intellectual, emotional, and social domains is taken into account.

11. *Social influences on learning.* Learning is influenced by social interactions, interpersonal relations, and communication with others.

Individual Differences Factors

12. *Individual differences in learning.* Learners have different strategies, approaches, and capabilities for learning that are a function of prior experience and heredity.

13. *Learning and diversity.* Learning is most effective when differences in learners' linguistic, cultural, and social backgrounds are taken into account.

14. *Standards and assessment.* Setting appropriately high and challenging standards and assessing the learner as well as learning progress—including diagnostic, process, and outcome assessment—are integral parts of the learning process.

Source: From "Learner-Centered Psychological Principles: A Framework for School Reform and Redesign." Copyright ©1997 by the American Psychological Association. Reproduced with permission. No further reproduction or distribution is permitted without written permission from the American Psychological Association. The full document may be viewed at http://www.apa.org/ed/governance/ea/learner-centered.pdf. The "Learner-Centered Psychological Principles" is a historical document which was derived from a 1990 APA presidential task force and was revised in 1997.

APPLICATION 6.8
Learner-Centered Principles

Jim Marshall applies the APA learner-centered principles in his history classes. He knows that many students are not intrinsically motivated to learn history and take it only because it is required, so he builds into the curriculum strategies to enhance interest. He makes use of films, field trips, and class reenactments of historical events to link history better with real-world experiences. Jim also does not want students to simply memorize content but rather learn to think critically. He teaches them a strategy to analyze historical events that includes key questions such as, What preceded the event? How might it have turned out differently? and How did this event influence future developments? Because he likes to focus on historical themes (e.g., economic development, territorial conflict), he has students apply these themes throughout the school year to different historical periods.

Being a psychologist, Gina Brown is familiar with the APA principles and incorporates them into her teaching. She knows that her students must have a good understanding of developmental, social, and individual difference variables if they are to be successful teachers. For their field placements, Gina ensures that students work in a variety of settings. Thus, students are assigned at different times to classes with younger and older students. She also ensures that students have the opportunity to work in classes where there is diversity in ethnic and socioeconomic backgrounds of students and with teachers whose methods use social interactions (e.g., cooperative learning, tutoring). Gina understands the importance of students' reflections on their experiences. They write journals on the field placement experiences and share these in class. She helps students understand how to link these experiences to topics they study in the course (e.g., development, motivation, learning).

INSTRUCTIONAL APPLICATIONS

The educational literature is replete with examples of instructional applications that reflect constructivist principles. Some are summarized in this section.

The task facing teachers who attempt to implement constructivist principles can be challenging. Many are unprepared to teach in a constructivist fashion (Elkind, 2004), especially if their preparation programs have not stressed it. There also are factors associated with schools and school systems that work against constructivism (Windschitl, 2002). For example, school administrators and teachers are held accountable for students' scores on standardized tests. These tests typically emphasize lower-level, basic skills and downgrade the importance of deeper conceptual understanding. School cultures also may work against constructivism, especially if teachers have been teaching in the same fashion for many years and have standard curricula and lessons. Parents, too, may not be fully supportive of teachers using less direction in the classroom in favor of time for students to construct their understandings. Despite these potential problems, there are many ways that teachers can incorporate constructivist teaching into their instruction and especially for topics that lend themselves well to it (e.g., discussion issues where there is no clearly correct answer).

Discovery Learning

The Process of Discovery. *Discovery learning* refers to obtaining knowledge for oneself (Bruner, 1961). Discovery involves constructing and testing hypotheses rather than simply reading or listening to teacher presentations. Discovery is a type of *inductive reasoning,* because students move from studying specific examples to formulating general rules, concepts, and principles. Discovery learning also is referred to as problem-based, inquiry, experiential, and constructivist learning (Kirschner et al., 2006).

Discovery is a form of problem solving (Klahr & Simon, 1999; Chapter 7); it is not simply letting students do what they want. Although discovery is a minimally guided instructional approach, it involves direction; teachers arrange activities in which students search, manipulate, explore, and investigate. The opening scenario represents a discovery situation. Students learn new knowledge relevant to the domain and such general problem-solving skills as formulating rules, testing hypotheses, and gathering information (Bruner, 1961).

Although some discoveries may be accidents that happen to lucky people, in fact most are to some degree planned and predictable. Consider how Pasteur developed the cholera vaccine (Root-Bernstein, 1988). Pasteur went on vacation during the summer of 1879. He had been conducting research on chicken cholera and left out germ cultures when he departed for 2 months.

> Upon his return, he found that the cultures, though still active, had become avirulent; they no longer could sicken a chicken. So he developed a new set of cultures from a natural outbreak of the disease and resumed his work. Yet he found . . . that the hens he had exposed to the weakened germ culture still failed to develop cholera. Only then did it dawn on Pasteur that he had inadvertently immunized them. (p. 26)

This exemplifies most discoveries, which are not flukes but rather a natural (albeit possibly unforeseen) consequence of systematic inquiry by the discoverer. Discoverers cultivate their discoveries by expecting the unexpected. Pasteur did not leave the germ cultures unattended but rather in the care of his collaborator, Roux. When Pasteur returned from vacation, he inoculated chickens with the germs, and they did not become sick.

> But when the same chickens were later injected with a more virulent strain, they died. No discovery here . . . Pasteur did not even initiate his first successful enfeeblement experiment until a few months later... . He and Roux had tried to enfeeble the germs by passing them from one animal to another, by growing them in different media . . . and only after many such attempts did one of the experiments succeed. . . . For some time, the strains that failed to kill chickens were also too weak to immunize them. But by March of 1880, Pasteur had developed two cultures with the properties of vaccines. The trick . . . was to use a mildly acidic medium, not a strong one, and to leave the germ culture sitting in it for a long time.

Thus, he produced an attenuated organism capable of inducing an immune response in chickens. The discovery . . . was not an accident at all; Pasteur had posed a question—Is it possible to immunize an animal with a weakened infectious agent?—and then systematically searched for the answer. (Root-Bernstein, 1988, p. 29)

To discover knowledge, students require background preparation (the well-prepared mind requires declarative, procedural, and conditional knowledge; Chapter 5). Once students possess prerequisite knowledge, careful structuring of material allows them to discover important principles.

Teaching for Discovery. Teaching for discovery requires presenting questions, problems, or puzzling situations to resolve and encouraging learners to make intuitive guesses when they are uncertain. In leading a class discussion, teachers could ask questions that have no readily available answers and tell students that their answers will not be graded, which forces students to construct their understandings. Discoveries are not limited to activities within school. During a unit on ecology, students could discover why animals of a given species live in certain areas and not in others. Students might seek answers in classroom workstations, in the school media center, and on or off the school grounds. Teachers provide structure by posing questions and giving suggestions on how to search for answers. Greater teacher structure is beneficial when students are not familiar with the discovery procedure or require extensive background knowledge. Other examples are given in Application 6.9.

APPLICATION 6.9
Discovery Learning

Learning becomes more meaningful when students explore their learning environments rather than listen passively to teachers. Kathy Stone uses guided discovery to help her third-grade children learn animal groups (e.g., mammals, birds, reptiles). Rather than providing students with the basic animal groups and examples for each, she asks students to provide the names of types of animals. Then she helps students classify the animals by examining their similarities and differences. Category labels are assigned once classifications are made. This approach is guided to ensure that classifications are proper, but students are active contributors as they discover the similarities and differences among animals.

A high school chemistry teacher might use "mystery" liquids and have students discover the elements in each. The students could proceed through a series of tests designed to determine if certain substances are present in a sample. By using the experimental process, students learn about the reactions of substances to certain chemicals and also how to determine the contents of their substances.

Gina Brown uses other problem-based learning activities in her class. She creates different classroom scenarios that describe situations involving student learning and behaviors as well as teacher actions. She divides her educational psychology students into small groups and asks them to work through each scenario and discover which learning principles best describe the situations presented.

Discovery is not appropriate for all types of learning. Discovery can impede learning when students have no prior experience with the material or background information (Tuovinen & Sweller, 1999). Teaching for discovery learning may not be appropriate with well-structured content that is easily presented. Students could discover which historical events occurred in which years, but this is trivial learning. If they arrived at the wrong answers, time would be wasted in reteaching the content. Discovery seems more appropriate when the learning process is important, such as with problem-solving activities that motivate students to learn and acquire the requisite skills. However, establishing discovery situations (e.g., growing plants) often takes time, and experiments might not work.

As a type of minimally guided instruction, discovery learning has drawn criticism. Mayer (2004) reviewed research from the 1950s to the 1980s that compared pure discovery learning (i.e., unguided, problem-based learning) with guided instruction. The research showed that guided instruction produced superior learning. Kirschner et al. (2006) contended that such instruction does not take into account the organization, or architecture, of cognitive structures (e.g., working memory, long-term memory). Although minimally guided instruction can enhance students' problem solving and self-directed learning (Hmelo-Silver, 2004), most promising research has been conducted in medical or gifted education.

Notice that these criticisms pertain to minimally guided instruction. Guided discovery, in which teachers arrange the situation such that learners are not left to their own devices but rather receive support, can lead to effective learning. Guided discovery also makes good use of the social environment—a key feature of constructivism. Supports (scaffolding) for learning can be minimized when learners have developed some skills and therefore can guide themselves. In deciding whether to use discovery, teachers should take into account the learning objectives (e.g., acquire knowledge or learn problem-solving skills), time available, and cognitive capacities of the students.

Inquiry Teaching

Inquiry teaching is a form of discovery learning, although it can be structured to have greater teacher direction. Collins (1977; Collins & Stevens, 1983) formulated an inquiry model based on the Socratic teaching method. The goals are to have students reason, derive general principles, and apply them to new situations. Appropriate learning outcomes include formulating and testing hypotheses, differentiating necessary from sufficient conditions, making predictions, and determining when making predictions requires more information.

In implementing the model, the teacher repeatedly questions the student. Questions are guided by rules such as "Ask about a known case," "Pick a counterexample for an insufficient factor," "Pose a misleading question," and "Question a prediction made without enough information" (Collins, 1977). Rule-generated questions help students formulate general principles and apply them to specific problems.

The following is a sample dialogue between teacher (T) and student (S) on the topic of population density (Collins, 1977):

T: In Northern Africa, is there a large population density?

S: In Northern Africa? I think there is.

T: Well, there is in the Nile valley, but elsewhere there is not. Do you have any idea why not?

S: Because it's not good for cultivating purposes?

T: It's not good for agriculture?

S: Yeah.

T: And do you know why?

S: Why?

T: Why is the farming at a disadvantage?

S: Because it's dry.

T: Right. (p. 353)

Although this instructional approach was designed for one-to-one tutoring, with some modifications it seems appropriate with small groups of students. One issue is that persons who serve as tutors require extensive training to pose appropriate questions in response to a student's level of thinking. Also, good content-area knowledge is a prerequisite for problem-solving skills. Students who lack a decent understanding of basic knowledge are not likely to function well under an inquiry system designed to teach reasoning and application of principles. Other student characteristics (e.g., age, abilities) also may predict success under this model. As with other constructivist methods, teachers must consider the student outcomes and the likelihood that students can successfully engage in the inquiry process.

Peer-Assisted Learning

Peer-assisted learning methods fit well with constructivism. *Peer-assisted learning* refers to instructional approaches in which peers serve as active agents in the learning process (Rohrbeck et al., 2003). Methods emphasizing peer-assisted learning include peer tutoring (Chapter 4 and this section), reciprocal teaching (Chapter 7), and cooperative learning (covered in this section) (Palincsar & Brown, 1984; Slavin, 1995; Strain et al., 1981).

Peer-assisted learning has been shown to promote achievement. In their review of the literature, Rohrbeck et al. (2003) found that peer-assisted learning was most effective with younger (first through third graders), urban, low-income, and minority children. These are promising results, given the risk to academic achievement associated with urban, low-income, and minority students. Rohrbeck et al. did not find significant differences due to content area (e.g., reading, mathematics). In addition to the learning benefits, peer-assisted learning also can foster academic and social motivation for learning (Ginsburg-Block, Rohrbeck, & Fantuzzo, 2006; Rohrbeck et al., 2003). Peers who stress academic learning convey its importance, which then can motivate others in the social environment.

As with other instructional models, teachers need to consider the desired learning outcomes in determining whether peer-assisted learning should be used. Some types of lessons (e.g., those emphasizing inquiry skills) would seem to be ideally suited for this approach, and especially if the development of social outcomes also is an objective.

Peer Tutoring. *Peer tutoring* captures many of the principles of constructive teaching (Chapter 4). Students are active in the learning process; tutor and tutee freely participate. The one-to-one context may encourage tutees to ask questions that they might be reluctant to ask in a large class. There is evidence that peer tutoring can lead to greater achievement gains than traditional instruction (Fuchs, Fuchs, Mathes, & Simmons, 1997).

Peer tutoring also encourages cooperation among students and helps to diversify the class structure. A teacher might split the class into small groups and tutoring groups while continuing to work with a different group. The content of the tutoring is tailored to the specific needs of the tutee.

Teachers likely will need to instruct peer tutors to ensure that they possess the requisite academic and tutoring skills. It also should be clear what the tutoring session is expected to accomplish. A specific goal is preferable to a general one—thus, "Work with Mike to help him understand how to regroup from the 10s column," rather than "Work with Mike to help him get better in subtraction."

Cooperative Learning. *Cooperative learning* is frequently used in classrooms (Slavin, 1994, 1995), but when not properly structured can lead to poorer learning compared with whole-class instruction. In cooperative learning the objective is to develop in students the ability to work collaboratively with others. The task should be one that is too extensive for a single student to complete in a timely fashion. The task also should lend itself well to a group, such as by having components that can be completed by individual students who then merge their individual work into a final product.

There are certain principles that help cooperative groups be successful. One is to form groups with students who are likely to work together well and who can develop and practice cooperative skills. This does not necessarily mean allowing students to choose groups, since they may select their friends and some students may be left without a group. It also does not necessarily mean heterogeneous groupings, where different ability levels are represented. Although that strategy often is recommended, research shows that high-achieving peers do not always benefit from being grouped with lower achievers (Hogan & Tudge, 1999), and the self-efficacy of lower achievers will not necessarily improve by watching higher achievers succeed (Schunk, 1995). Whatever the means of grouping, teachers should ensure that each group can succeed with reasonable effort.

Groups also need guidance on what they are to accomplish—what is the expected product—as well as the expected mode of behavior. The task should be one that requires interdependence; no group member should be able to accomplish most of the entire task single-handedly. Ideally, the task also will allow for different approaches. For example, to address the topic of "Pirates in America," a group of middle school students might give a presentation, use posters, conduct a skit, and involve class members in a treasure hunt.

Finally, it is important to ensure that each group member is accountable. If grades are given, it is necessary for group members to document what their overall contributions were to the group. A group in which only two of six members do most of the work but everyone receives an "A" is likely to breed resentment.

Two variations of cooperative learning are the jigsaw method and STAD (student-teams-achievement divisions). In the *jigsaw method*, teams work on material that is subdivided into parts. After each team studies the material, each team member takes responsibility for one part. The team members from each group meet together to discuss their part, after which they return to their teams to help other team members learn more about their part (Slavin, 1994). This jigsaw method combines many desirable features of cooperative learning, including group work, individual responsibility, and clear goals.

STAD groups study material after it has been presented by the teacher (Slavin, 1994). Group members practice and study together but are tested individually. Each member's score contributes to the overall group score; but, because scores are based on improvement, each group member is motivated to improve—that is, individual improvements raise the overall group score. Although STAD is a form of cooperative learning, it seems best suited for material with well-defined objectives or problems with clear answers—for example, mathematical computations and social studies facts. Given its emphasis on improvement, STAD will not work as well where conceptual understanding is involved because student gains may not occur quickly.

Discussions and Debates

Class discussions are useful when the objective is to acquire greater conceptual understanding or multiple sides of a topic. The topic being discussed is one for which there is no clear right answer but rather involves a complex or controversial issue. Students enter the discussion with some knowledge of the topic and are expected to gain understanding as a result of the discussion.

Discussions lend themselves to various disciplines, such as history, literature, science, and economics. Regardless of the topic, it is critical that a class atmosphere be created that is conducive to free discussion. Students likely will have to be given rules for the discussion (e.g., do not interrupt someone who is speaking, keep arguments to the topic being discussed, do not personally attack other students). If the teacher is the facilitator of the discussion, then he or she must support multiple viewpoints, encourage students to share, and remind students of the rules when they are violated. Teachers also can ask students to elaborate on their opinions (e.g., "Tell us why you think that.").

When class size is large, small-group discussions may be preferable to whole-class ones. Students reluctant to speak in a large group may feel less inhibited in a smaller one. Teachers can train students to be facilitators of small-group discussions.

A variation of the *discussion* is the *debate*, in which students selectively argue sides of an issue. This requires preparation by the groups and, likely, some practice if they will be giving short presentations on their sides. Teachers enforce rules of the debate and ensure that all team members participate. A larger discussion with the class can follow, which allows for points to be reinforced or new points brought up.

Reflective Teaching

Reflective teaching is based on thoughtful decision making that takes into account knowledge about students, the context, psychological processes, learning and motivation, and

Table 6.9
Components of reflective teaching decisions.

- Sensitive to the context

- Guided by fluid planning

- Informed by professional and personal knowledge that is critically examined

- Enhanced by formal and informal professional growth opportunities

(Henderson, 1996)

knowledge about oneself. Although reflective teaching is not part of a constructivist perspective on learning, its premises are based on the assumptions of constructivism (Armstrong & Savage, 2002).

Components. Reflective teaching stands in stark contrast to traditional teaching in which a teacher prepares a lesson, presents it to a class, gives students assignments and feedback, and evaluates their learning. Reflective teaching assumes that teaching cannot be reduced to one method to use with all students. Each teacher brings a unique set of experiences to teaching. How teachers interpret situations will differ depending on their experiences and perceptions. Professional development requires that teachers reflect on their beliefs and theories about students, content, context, and learning and check the validity of these beliefs and theories against reality.

Henderson (1996) listed four components of reflective teaching that involve decision making (Table 6.9). Teaching decisions must be sensitive to the context, which includes the school, content, students' backgrounds, time of the year, educational expectations, and the like. Fluid planning means that instructional plans must be flexible and change as conditions warrant. When students do not understand a lesson, it makes little sense to reteach it in the same way. Rather, the plan must be modified to aid student understanding.

Henderson's model puts emphasis on teachers' personal knowledge. They should be aware of why they do what they do and be keen observers of situations. They must reflect on and process a wide variety of information about situations. Their decisions are strengthened by professional development. Teachers must have a strong knowledge base from which to draw in order to engage in flexible planning and tailor lessons to student and contextual differences.

Reflective teachers are active persons who seek solutions to problems rather than wait for others to tell them what to do. They persist until they find the best solution rather than settle for one that is less than satisfactory. They are ethical and put students' needs above their own; they ask what is best for students rather than what is best for them. Reflective teachers also thoughtfully consider evidence by mentally reviewing classroom events and revising their practices to better serve students' needs. In summary, reflective teachers (Armstrong & Savage, 2002):

- Use context considerations
- Use personal knowledge

- Use professional knowledge
- Make fluid plans
- Commit to formal and informal professional growth opportunities

We can see assumptions of constructivism that underlie these points. Constructivism places heavy emphasis on the context of learning because learning is situated. People construct knowledge about themselves (e.g., their capabilities, interests, attitudes) and about their profession from their experiences. Teaching is not a lockstep function that proceeds immutably once a lesson is designed. And finally, there is no "graduation" from teaching. Conditions always are changing, and teachers must stay at the forefront in terms of content, psychological knowledge of learning and motivation, and student individual differences.

Becoming a Reflective Teacher. Being a reflective teacher is a skill, and like other skills it requires instruction and practice. The following suggestions are useful in developing this skill.

Being a reflective teacher requires good *personal knowledge*. Teachers have beliefs about their teaching competencies to include subject knowledge, pedagogical knowledge, and student capabilities. To develop personal knowledge, teachers reflect on and assess these beliefs. Self-questioning is helpful. For example, teachers might ask themselves: "What do I know about the subjects I teach?" "How confident am I that I can teach these subjects so that students can acquire skills?" "How confident am I that I can establish an effective classroom climate that facilitates learning?" "What do I believe about how students can learn?" "Do I hold biases (e.g., that students from some ethnic or socioeconomic backgrounds cannot learn as well as other students)?"

Personal knowledge is important because it forms the basis from which to seek improvement. For example, teachers who feel they are not well skilled in using technology to teach social studies can seek out professional development to aid them. If they find that they have biases, they can employ strategies so that their beliefs do not cause negative effects. Thus, if they believe that some students cannot learn as well as others, they can seek ways to help the former students learn better.

Being a reflective teacher also requires *professional knowledge*. Effective teachers are well skilled in their disciplines, understand classroom management techniques, and have knowledge about human development. Teachers who reflect on their professional knowledge and recognize deficiencies can correct them, such as by taking university courses or participating in staff development sessions on those topics.

Like other professionals, teachers must keep abreast of current developments in their fields. They can do this by belonging to professional organizations, attending conferences, subscribing to journals and periodicals, and discussing issues with colleagues.

Third, reflective teaching means *planning and assessing*. When reflective teachers plan, they do so with the goal of reaching all students. Many good ideas for lesson plans can be garnered from colleagues and practitioner journals. When students have difficulty grasping content presented in a certain way, reflective teachers consider other methods for attaining the same objective.

Assessment works together with planning. Reflective teachers ask how they will assess students' learning outcomes. To gain knowledge of assessment methods, teachers may need to take courses or participate in staff development. The authentic methods that have come into vogue in recent years offer many possibilities for assessing outcomes, but teachers may need to consult with assessment experts and receive training on their use.

SUMMARY

Constructivism is an epistemology, or philosophical explanation about the nature of learning. Constructivist theorists reject the idea that scientific truths exist and await discovery and verification. Knowledge is not imposed from outside people but rather formed inside them. Constructivist theories vary from those that postulate complete self-construction, through those that hypothesize socially mediated constructions, to those that argue that constructions match reality. Constructivism requires that we structure teaching and learning experiences to challenge students' thinking so that they will be able to construct new knowledge. A core premise is that cognitive processes are situated (located) within physical and social contexts. The concept of situated cognition highlights these relations between persons and situations.

Piaget's theory is constructivist and postulates that children pass through a series of qualitatively different stages: sensorimotor, preoperational, concrete operational, and formal operational. The chief developmental mechanism is equilibration, which helps to resolve cognitive conflicts by changing the nature of reality to fit existing structures (assimilation) or changing structures to incorporate reality (accommodation).

Vygotsky's sociocultural theory emphasizes the social environment as a facilitator of development and learning. The social environment influences cognition through its tools—cultural objects, language, symbols, and social institutions. Cognitive change results from using these tools in social interactions and from internalizing and transforming these interactions. A key concept is the zone of proximal development (ZPD), which represents the amount of learning possible by a student given proper instructional conditions. It is difficult to evaluate the contributions of Vygotsky's theory to learning because most research is recent and many educational applications that fit with the theory are not part of it. Applications that reflect Vygotsky's ideas are instructional scaffolding, reciprocal teaching, peer collaboration, and apprenticeships.

Private speech has a self-regulatory function, but is not socially communicative. Vygotsky believed that private speech develops thought by organizing behavior. Children employ private speech to understand situations and surmount difficulties. Private speech becomes covert with development, although overt verbalization can occur at any age. Verbalization can promote student achievement if it is relevant to the task and does not interfere with performance. Self-instructional training is useful for helping individuals verbally self-regulate their performances.

Vygotsky's theory contends that learning is a socially mediated process. Children learn many concepts during social interactions with others. Structuring learning environments to promote these interactions facilitates learning. Self-regulation includes the coordination of mental processes, such as memory, planning, synthesis, and evaluation. Vygotsky believed that language and the zone of proximal development are critical for the development of self-regulation. A key is the internalization of self-regulatory processes.

Aspects of motivation relevant to constructivism include contextual factors, implicit theories, and teachers' expectations. Multidimensional classrooms, which have many activities and allow for greater diversity in student performances, are more compatible with constructivism than are unidimensional classes. Characteristics that indicate dimensionality are differentiation of task structure, student autonomy, grouping patterns, and salience of performance evaluations. The TARGET variables (task, authority, recognition, grouping, evaluation, and time) affect learners' motivation and learning.

Students hold implicit theories about such issues as how they learn and what contributes to achievement. Implicit theories are formed during socialization practices and self-reflection and influence students' motivation and learning. Incremental theorists believe that skills can be increased through effort. Entity theorists view their abilities as fixed traits over which they have little control. Research shows that students who believe learning is under their control expend greater effort, rehearse more, and use better learning strategies. Teachers convey their expectations to students in many ways. Teachers' expectations influence teacher–student interactions, and some research shows that, under certain conditions, expectations may affect student achievement. Teachers should expect all students to succeed and provide support (scaffolding) for them to do so.

The goal of constructivist learning environments is to provide rich experiences that encourage students to learn. Constructivist classrooms teach big concepts using much student activity, social interaction, and authentic assessments. Students' ideas are avidly sought, and, compared with traditional classes, there is less emphasis on superficial learning and more emphasis on deeper understanding. The APA learner-centered principles, which address various factors (cognitive, metacognitive, motivational, affective, developmental, social, and individual differences), reflect a constructivist learning approach.

Some instructional methods that fit well with constructivism are discovery learning, inquiry teaching, peer-assisted learning, discussions and debates, and reflective teaching. Discovery learning allows students to obtain knowledge for themselves through problem solving. Discovery requires that teachers arrange activities such that students can form and test hypotheses. It is not simply letting students do what they want. Inquiry teaching is a form of discovery learning that may follow Socratic principles with much teacher questioning of students. Peer-assisted learning refers to instructional approaches in which peers serve as active agents in the learning process. Peer tutoring and cooperative learning are forms of peer-assisted learning. Discussions and debates are useful when the objective is to acquire greater conceptual understanding or multiple viewpoints of a topic. Reflective teaching is thoughtful decision making that considers such factors as students, contexts, psychological processes, learning, motivation, and self-knowledge. Becoming a reflective teacher requires developing personal and professional knowledge, planning strategies, and assessment skills.

A summary of learning issues relevant to constructivism appears in Table 6.10.

Table 6.10
Summary of learning issues.

How Does Learning Occur?

Constructivism contends that learners form or construct their own understandings of knowledge and skills. Perspectives on constructivism differ as to how much influence environmental and social factors have on learners' constructions. Piaget's theory stresses equilibration, or the process of making internal cognitive structures and external reality consistent. Vygotsky's theory places a heavy emphasis on the role of social factors in learning.

What Is the Role of Memory?

Constructivism has not dealt explicitly with memory. Its basic principles suggest that learners are more apt to remember information if their constructions are personally meaningful to them.

What Is the Role of Motivation?

The focus of constructivism has been on learning rather than motivation, although some educators have written about motivation. Constructivists hold that learners construct motivational beliefs in the same fashion as they construct beliefs about learning. Learners also construct implicit theories that concern their strengths and weaknesses, what is necessary for learning to occur, and what others think of their capabilities (e.g., parents, teachers).

How Does Transfer Occur?

As with memory, transfer has not been a central issue in constructivist research. The same idea applies, however: To the extent that learners' constructions are personally meaningful to them and linked with other ideas, transfer should be facilitated.

Which Processes Are Involved in Self-Regulation?

Self-regulation involves the coordination of mental functions—memory, planning, synthesis, evaluation, and so forth. Learners use the tools of their culture (e.g., language, symbols) to construct meanings. The key is for self-regulatory processes to be internalized. Learners' initial self-regulatory activities may be patterned after those of others, but as learners construct their own they become idiosyncratic.

What Are the Implications for Instruction?

The teacher's central task is to structure the learning environment so that learners can construct understandings. To this end, teachers need to provide the instructional support (scaffolding) that will assist learners to maximize their learning in their zone of proximal development. The teacher's role is to provide a supportive environment, not to lecture and give students answers.

FURTHER READING

Brainerd, C. J. (2003). Jean Piaget, learning research, and American education. In B. J. Zimmerman & D. H. Schunk (Eds.), *Educational psychology: A century of contributions* (pp. 251–287). Mahwah, NJ: Erlbaum.

Brooks, J. G., & Brooks, M. G. (1999). *In search of understanding: The case for constructivist classrooms.* Alexandria, VA: Association for Supervision and Curriculum Development.

Epstein, J. L. (1989). Family structures and student motivation: A developmental perspective. In C. Ames & R. Ames (Eds.), *Research on motivation in education* (Vol. 3, pp. 259–295). San Diego: Academic Press.

Karpov, Y. V., & Haywood, H. C. (1998). Two ways to elaborate Vygotsky's concept of mediation: Implications for instruction. *American Psychologist, 53,* 27–36.

Rosenthal, R., & Jacobson, L. (1968). *Pygmalion in the classroom.* New York: Holt, Rinehart & Winston.

Tudge, J. R. H., & Scrimsher, S. (2003). Lev S. Vygotsky on education: A cultural-historical, interpersonal, and individual approach to development. In B. J. Zimmerman & D. H. Schunk (Eds.), *Educational psychology: A century of contributions* (pp. 207–228). Mahwah, NJ: Erlbaum.

Vygotsky, L. (1978). *Mind in society: The development of higher psychological processes.* Cambridge, MA: Harvard University Press.

Cognitive Learning Processes

Meg LaMann, the principal of Franklin U. Nikowsky Middle School, was holding a faculty meeting. The previous day the school's teachers had participated in a professional development session on helping students learn problem solving and critical-thinking skills. Meg asked the teachers for feedback on the session.

"Tiny" Lawrance, one of the more outspoken teachers in the school, spoke first. "Well Meg, I thought the presenters had lots of good things to say and suggestions for developing skills in the students. But, you know what the problem is. We don't have time to do any of this. We're too crunched with covering what we need to so that the kids are ready for the state's end-of-grade tests. And besides, those tests, as you know, cover mostly low-level factual information, not what you need problem solving for. So realistically I don't see how I'll use any of what I learned yesterday."

Piper Rowland spoke up next. "That's right, Meg. I thought it was wonderful information. And surely our kids would benefit from learning some of these strategies. But if we neglect the basic skills to teach this stuff and our test results fall, we'll hear about it from Central Office. So I don't know what to do."

Meg replied, "I hear you and have the same concern. But I don't think we need to work on problem solving and critical thinking in everything we teach. There are facts and basic skills to be learned, and those can be taught effectively through direct teaching. But sometimes we don't think enough about how we might incorporate problem solving into our instruction. I think we all can do that.

Tiny said, "I agree, Meg. What about some time set aside periodically to work on problem-solving skills?"

"Well, you heard what the presenters said," replied Meg. "Problem solving and critical thinking are best taught in the context of regular learning. That way the kids see how they can apply these skills as they're learning math, English, science, social studies, and so on. The stand-alone thinking skills programs are less effective and the kids usually don't apply any of those skills outside of the training setting."

"Well, I'm willing to work on this more in social studies," said Tiny. "And I will in math," replied Piper. "I just hope the test scores don't fall."

"Don't worry about the test scores," said Meg. "Let me address that issue with Central Office."

The teachers made a concerted effort to incorporate suggestions they learned from the session into their teaching for the rest of the school year. The end-of-grade test scores for the school actually rose by a small amount.

At the start of the next academic year the school held a parent "walk the schedule" night. Several parents told Meg how much they appreciated the teachers working more on problem solving. One parent remarked, "Those strategies are great, not just for school but for other things. I'm working with my son now, having him set goals for what he needs to do, check his progress, and so on." Another parent told Meg, "My daughter loves the new emphasis on problem solving. She says that school now isn't so boring and is more like its initials—FUN!"

Previous chapters covered cognitive theories of learning: social cognitive (Chapter 4), information processing (Chapter 5), and constructivism (Chapter 6). This chapter extends this perspective to the operation of key cognitive processes during learning. Following a discussion of skill acquisition, the topics of conditional knowledge and metacognition are covered, which are central to learning. Subsequent sections address concept learning, problem solving, transfer, technology and instruction, and instructional applications.

There is debate among professionals on the extent that the cognitive processes discussed in this chapter are involved in most, if not all, learning. Problem solving, for example, is thought by some to be the central process in learning (Anderson, 1993), whereas others limit its application to settings where specific conditions prevail (Chi & Glaser, 1985). Teachers generally agree on the importance of concept learning, problem solving, transfer, and metacognition, and educators recommend that these topics be incorporated into instruction (Pressley & McCormick, 1995). The opening scenario describes a schoolwide effort to integrate problem solving in the curriculum. The processes discussed in this chapter are integral components of complex types of learning that occur in school subjects such as reading, writing, mathematics, and science.

When you finish studying this chapter you should be able to do the following:

- Distinguish between general and specific skills, and discuss how they work together in the acquisition of competence.

- Describe the novice-to-expert research methodology.

- Understand why conditional knowledge is important for learning, and discuss variables affecting metacognition.

- Distinguish properties of concepts, and explain models of concept learning.

- Discuss historical views of problem solving and the role of general strategies (heuristics).

- Describe problem solving from an information processing perspective.

- Differentiate historical views of transfer, and provide a cognitive explanation for transfer of knowledge, skills, and strategies.

- Discuss key learning features of computer-based learning environments and distance learning.

- Explain learning from worked examples and the development of writing and mathematical skills.

SKILL ACQUISITION

Developing competence in any domain represents a process of skill acquisition. We begin by examining issues relevant to the acquisition of general and specific skills.

General and Specific Skills

Skills may be differentiated according to degree of specificity. *General skills* apply to a wide variety of disciplines; *specific skills* are useful only in certain domains. As discussed in the opening scenario, problem solving and critical thinking are general skills because they are useful in acquiring a range of cognitive, motor, and social skills, whereas factoring polynomials and solving square-root problems involve specific skills because they have limited mathematical applications.

Acquisition of general skills facilitates learning in many ways. Bruner (1985) noted that tasks such as "learning how to play chess, learning how to play the flute, learning mathematics, and learning to read the sprung rhymes in the verse of Gerard Manley Hopkins" (pp. 5–6) are similar in that they involve attention, memory, and persistence.

At the same time, each type of skill learning has unique features. Bruner (1985) contended that views of learning are not unambiguously right or wrong; rather, they can be evaluated only in light of such conditions as the nature of the task to be learned, the type of learning to be accomplished, and the characteristics that learners bring to the situation. The many differences between tasks, such as learning to balance equations in chemistry and learning to balance on a beam in gymnastics, require different processes to explain learning.

Domain specificity is defined in various ways. Ceci (1989) used the term to refer to discrete declarative knowledge structures (Chapter 5). Other researchers include procedural knowledge and view specificity as pertaining to the usefulness of knowledge (Perkins & Salomon, 1989). The issue really is not one of proving or disproving one position because we know that both general and specific skills are involved in learning (Voss, Wiley, & Carretero, 1995). Rather, the issue is one of specifying the extent to which any type of learning involves general and specific skills, what those skills are, and what course their acquisition follows.

Thinking of skill specificity ranging along a continuum is preferable, as Perkins & Salomon (1989) explained:

> General knowledge includes widely applicable strategies for problem solving, inventive thinking, decision making, learning, and good mental management, sometimes called autocontrol, autoregulation, or metacognition. In chess, for example, very specific knowledge (often called local knowledge) includes the rules of the game as well as lore about how to handle innumerable specific situations, such as different openings and ways of achieving checkmate. Of intermediate generality are strategic concepts, like control of the center, that are somewhat specific to chess but that also invite far-reaching application by analogy. (p. 17)

We then can ask: What counts most for ensuring success in learning? Some local knowledge is needed—one cannot become skilled at fractions without learning the rules governing fraction operations (e.g., adding, subtracting). As Perkins and Salomon (1989) noted, however, the more important questions are: Where are the bottlenecks in developing mastery? Can one become an expert with only domain-specific knowledge? If not, at what point do general competencies become important?

Ohlsson (1993) advanced a model of skill acquisition through practice that comprises three subfunctions: generate task-relevant behaviors, identify errors, and correct errors. This model includes both general and task-specific processes. As learners practice, they monitor their progress by comparing their current state to their prior knowledge. This is a general strategy, but as learning occurs, it becomes increasingly adapted to specific task conditions. Errors often are caused by applying general procedures inappropriately (Ohlsson, 1996), but prior domain-specific knowledge helps learners detect errors and identify the conditions that caused them. With practice and learning, therefore, general methods become more specialized.

Problem solving is useful for learning skills in many content areas, but task conditions often require specific skills for the development of expertise. In many cases a merging of the two types of skills is needed. Research shows that expert problem solvers often use general strategies when they encounter unfamiliar problems and that asking general metacognitive questions (e.g., "What am I doing now?" "Is it getting me anywhere?") facilitates problem solving (Perkins & Salomon, 1989). Despite these positive results, general principles often do not transfer (Pressley et al., 1990; Schunk & Rice, 1993). Transfer requires combining general strategies with factors such as instruction on self-monitoring and practice in specific contexts. The goal in the opening scenario is that once students learn general strategies, they will be able to adapt them to specific settings.

In short, expertise is largely domain specific (Lajoie, 2003). It requires a rich knowledge base that includes the facts, concepts, and principles of the domain, coupled with learning strategies that can be applied to different domains and that may have to be tailored to each domain. One would not expect strategies such as seeking help and monitoring goal progress to operate in the same fashion in disparate domains (e.g., calculus and pole vaulting). At the same time, Perkins and Salomon (1989) pointed out that general strategies are useful for coping with atypical problems in different domains regardless of one's overall level of competence in the domain. These findings imply that students need to be well grounded in basic content-area knowledge (Ohlsson, 1993), as well as in general problem-solving and self-regulatory strategies (Chapter 9). Application 7.1 provides suggestions for integrating the teaching of general and specific skills.

Novice-to-Expert Research Methodology

With the growth of cognitive and constructivist views of learning, researchers have moved away from viewing learning as changes in responses due to differential reinforcement (Chapter 3) and have become interested in students' beliefs and thought processes during learning. The focus of learning research has shifted accordingly.

To investigate academic learning, many researchers have used a *novice-to-expert methodology* with the following steps:

- Identify the skill to be learned.
- Find an expert (i.e., one who performs the skill well) and a novice (one who knows something about the task but performs it poorly).
- Determine how the novice can be moved to the expert level as efficiently as possible.

APPLICATION 7.1
Integrating the Teaching of General and Specific Skills

As teachers work with students, they can effectively teach general skills to increase success in various domains, but they also must be aware of the specific skills that are needed for learning within a specific domain.

Kathy Stone might work with her third-grade students on using goal setting to complete assignments. In reading, she might help students determine how to finish reading two chapters in a book by the end of the week. The students might establish a goal to read a certain number of pages or a subsection each day of the week. Because the goal comprises more than just reading the words on the pages, she also must teach specific comprehension skills, such as locating main ideas and reading for details. Goal setting can be applied in mathematics by having students decide how many problems or activities to do each day to complete a particular unit by the end of the week. Specific skills that come into play in this context are determining what the problem is asking for, representing the problem, and knowing how to perform the computations.

In physical education, students may use goal setting to master skills, such as working toward running a mile in 6 minutes. The students might begin by running the mile in 10 minutes and then work to decrease the running time every week. Motor and endurance skills must be developed to successfully meet the goal. Such skills are most likely to be specific to the context of running a short distance in a good time.

This methodology is intuitively plausible. The basic idea is that if you want to understand how to become more skillful in an area, closely study someone who performs that skill well. In so doing you can learn what knowledge he or she possesses, what procedures and strategies are useful, how to handle difficult situations, and how to correct mistakes. The model has many real-world counterparts and is reflected in apprenticeships, on-the-job training, and mentoring.

Much of the knowledge on how more- and less-competent persons differ in a domain comes from research based in part on assumptions of this methodology (VanLehn, 1996). Compared with novices, experts have more-extensive domain knowledge, have better understanding of what they do not know, spend more time initially analyzing problems, and solve them quicker and more accurately (Lajoie, 2003). Research also has identified differences in the stages of skill acquisition. Conducting such research is labor intensive and time consuming because it requires studying learners over time, but it yields rich results.

At the same time, this model is descriptive rather than explanatory: It describes what learners do rather than explaining why they do it. The model also tacitly assumes that a fixed constellation of skills exists that constitutes expertise in a given domain, but this is not always the case. With respect to teaching, Sternberg and Horvath (1995) argued that no one standard exists; rather, expert teachers resemble one another in prototypical fashion. This makes sense given our experiences with master teachers who typically differ in several ways.

Finally, the model does not automatically suggest teaching methods. As such, it may have limited usefulness for classroom teaching and learning. Explanations for learning and corresponding teaching suggestions should be firmly grounded in theories and identify important personal and environmental factors. These factors are emphasized in this and other chapters in this book.

Expert–Novice Differences in Science

A good place to explore expert–novice differences is in science because much research in scientific domains has compared novices with experts to identify the components of expertise. Researchers also have investigated students' construction of scientific knowledge and the implicit theories and reasoning processes that they use during problem solving and learning (Linn & Eylon, 2006; Voss et al., 1995; White, 2001; C. Zimmerman, 2000; Chapter 6).

Experts in scientific domains differ from novices in quantity and organization of knowledge. Experts possess more domain-specific knowledge and are more likely to organize it in hierarchies, whereas novices often demonstrate little overlap between scientific concepts.

Chi, Feltovich, and Glaser (1981) had expert and novice problem solvers sort physics textbook problems on any basis they wanted. Novices classified problems based on superficial features (e.g., apparatus); experts classified the problems based on the principle needed to solve the problem. Experts and novices also differed in declarative knowledge memory networks. "Inclined plane," for example, was related in novices' memories with descriptive terms such as "mass," "friction," and "length." Experts had these descriptors in their memories, but in addition had stored principles of mechanics (e.g., conservation of energy, Newton's force laws). The experts' greater knowledge of principles was organized with descriptors subordinate to principles.

Novices often use principles erroneously to solve problems. McCloskey and Kaiser (1984) posed the following question to college students:

> A train is speeding over a bridge that spans a valley. As the train rolls along, a passenger leans out of a window and drops a rock. Where will it land?

About one-third of the students said the rock would fall straight down (Figure 7.1). They believed that an object pushed or thrown acquires a force but that an object being carried by a moving vehicle does not acquire a force, so it drops straight down. The analogy the students made was with a person standing still who drops an object, which falls straight down. The path of descent of the rock from the moving train is, however, parabolic. The idea that objects acquire force is erroneous because objects move in the same direction and at the same speed as their moving carriers. When the rock is dropped, it continues to move forward with the train until the force of gravity pulls it down. Novices generalized their basic knowledge and arrived at an erroneous solution.

As discussed later in this chapter, another difference between novices and experts concerns the use of *problem-solving strategies* (Larkin, McDermott, Simon, & Simon, 1980; White & Tisher, 1986). When confronted with scientific problems, novices often use a

Figure 7.1
Possible answers to falling rock problem.

means–ends analysis, determining the goal of the problem and deciding which formulas might be useful to reach that goal. They work backward and recall formulas containing quantities in the target formula. If they become uncertain how to proceed, they may abandon the problem or attempt to solve it based on their current knowledge.

Experts quickly recognize the problem format, work forward toward intermediate sub-goals, and use that information to reach the ultimate goal. Experience in working scientific problems builds knowledge of problem types. Experts often automatically recognize familiar problem features and carry out necessary productions. Even when they are less certain how to solve a problem, experts begin with some information given in the problem and work forward to the solution. Notice that the last step experts take is often novices' first step. Klahr and Simon (1999) contended that the process of scientific discovery is a form of problem solving and that the general heuristic approach is much the same across domains.

CONDITIONAL KNOWLEDGE AND METACOGNITION

An issue with information processing theories is that they primarily describe learning rather than explain it. Thus, we know that inputs are received into working memory (WM), rehearsed, coded, linked with relevant information, and stored in long-term memory (LTM), but we might ask why any of these activities happen. Especially during learning—when processing is not automatic—we need an explanation for why the system processes information. For example, what determines how much rehearsal takes place? How is relevant information selected in LTM? How do people know what knowledge is required in different situations?

The topic of metacognition addresses these questions. *Metacognition* refers to higher-order cognition. Conditional knowledge is discussed next, followed by an explanation of how metacognitive processes help to integrate information processing.

Conditional Knowledge

Declarative and procedural knowledge refer to knowledge of facts and procedures, respectively (Chapter 5). *Conditional knowledge* is understanding when and why to employ forms of declarative and procedural knowledge (Paris et al., 1983). Possessing requisite declarative and procedural knowledge to perform a task does not guarantee students will perform it well. Students reading a social studies text may know what to do (read a chapter), understand the meanings of vocabulary words (declarative knowledge), and know how to decode, skim, find main ideas, and draw inferences (procedural knowledge). When they start reading, they might skim the chapter. As a consequence, they perform poorly on a comprehension test.

This type of situation is common. In this example, conditional knowledge includes knowing when skimming is appropriate. One might skim a newspaper or a web page for the gist of the news, but skimming should not be used to comprehend textual content.

Conditional knowledge helps students select and employ declarative and procedural knowledge to fit task goals. To decide to read a chapter carefully and then do it, students should believe that careful reading is appropriate for the task at hand; that is, this strategy has functional value because it will allow them to comprehend the material.

Learners who do not possess conditional knowledge about when and why skimming is valuable will employ it at inappropriate times. If they believe it is valuable for all reading tasks, they may indiscriminately employ it unless otherwise directed. If they believe it has no value, they may never use it unless directed.

Conditional knowledge likely is represented in LTM as propositions in networks and linked with the declarative and procedural knowledge to which it applies. Conditional knowledge actually is a form of declarative knowledge because it is "knowledge that"—for example, knowledge that skimming is valuable to get the gist of a passage and knowledge that summarizing text is valuable to derive greater understanding. Conditional knowledge also is included in procedures: Skimming is valuable as long as I can get the gist; but if I find that I am not getting the gist, I should abandon skimming and read more carefully. The three types of knowledge are summarized in Table 7.1.

Conditional knowledge is an integral part of self-regulated learning (Schunk & Zimmerman, 1994, 1998; Chapter 9). Self-regulated learning requires that students decide which learning strategy to use prior to engaging in a task (Zimmerman, 1994, 2000). While students are engaged in a task, they assess task progress (e.g., their level of comprehension) using metacognitive processes. When comprehension problems are detected, students alter their strategy based on conditional knowledge of what might prove

Table 7.1

Comparison of types of knowledge.

Type	Knowing	Examples
Declarative	That	Historical dates, number facts, episodes (what happened when), task features (stories have a plot and setting), beliefs ("I am good in math")
Procedural	How	Math algorithms, reading strategies (skimming, scanning, summarizing), goals (breaking long-term goals into subgoals)
Conditional	When, Why	Skim the newspaper because it gives the gist but does not take much time; read texts carefully to gain understanding

more effective. It also has been suggested that computer-based learning environments can serve as metacognitive tools to foster students' self-regulated learning (Azevedo, 2005a, 2005b), a point we return to later.

Metacognition and Learning

Metacognition refers to the deliberate conscious control of cognitive activity (Brown, 1980; Matlin, 2009):

> What is metacognition? It has usually been broadly and rather loosely defined as any knowledge or cognitive activity that takes as its object, or regulates, any aspect of any cognitive enterprise. . . . It is called metacognition because its core meaning is "cognition about cognition." Metacognitive skills are believed to play an important role in many types of cognitive activity, including oral communication of information, oral persuasion, oral comprehension, reading comprehension, writing, language acquisition, perception, attention, memory, problem solving, social cognition, and various forms of self-instruction and self-control. (Flavell, 1985, p. 104)

Metacognition comprises two related sets of skills. First, one must understand what skills, strategies, and resources a task requires. Included in this cluster are finding main ideas, rehearsing information, forming associations or images, using memory techniques, organizing material, taking notes or underlining, and using test-taking techniques. Second, one must know how and when to use these skills and strategies to ensure the task is completed successfully. These monitoring activities include checking level of understanding, predicting outcomes, evaluating the effectiveness of efforts, planning activities, deciding how to budget time, and revising or switching to other activities to overcome difficulties (Baker & Brown, 1984). Collectively, metacognitive activities reflect the strategic application of declarative, procedural, and conditional knowledge to tasks (Schraw & Moshman, 1995). Kuhn (1999) argued that metacognitive skills were the key to the development of critical thinking.

Metacognitive skills develop slowly. Young children are not fully aware of which cognitive processes various tasks involve. For example, they typically are poor at recognizing that they have been thinking and then recalling what they were thinking about (Flavell, Green, & Flavell, 1995). They may not understand that disorganized passages are harder to comprehend than organized ones or that passages containing unfamiliar material are more

APPLICATION 7.2
Metacognition

Teachers can help students develop their metacognitive skills. A teacher working with students on listening comprehension might include situations such as listening to an enjoyable story, a set of explicit directions, and a social studies lecture. For each situation, the teacher could ask students why they would listen in that setting; for example, enjoyment and general theme (stories), specific elements (directions), facts and concepts (social studies). Then the teacher could work with students to develop listening skills such as retelling in their own words, visualizing, and taking notes. To foster conditional knowledge, the teacher can discuss with students the various listening techniques that seem most appropriate for each situation.

A teacher helping students with memory skills might give them a list of items to memorize. The teacher could teach them to reconstruct the list of items given partial cues. The students might be encouraged to explore various memorization techniques: putting the items into categories; visualizing a picture that contains the items; associating the items with a familiar setting or task; using acronyms that include the first letter of each item; creating a jingle, poem, or song that incorporates the items; or repeating the list several times. Then the teacher could help the students determine which technique works best for each individual and with which type of memorization task.

difficult than those composed of familiar material (Baker & Brown, 1984). Dermitzaki (2005) found that second graders used metacognitive strategies, but that their use bore little relation to children's actual self-regulatory activities. Monitoring activities are employed more often by older children and adults than by young children; however, older children and adults do not always monitor their comprehension and often are poor judges of how well they have comprehended text (Baker, 1989).

At the same time, young children are cognitively capable of monitoring their activities on simple tasks (Kuhn, 1999). Learners are more likely to monitor their activities on tasks of intermediate difficulty as opposed to easy tasks (where monitoring may not be necessary) or on very difficult tasks (where one may not know what to do or may quit working).

Metacognitive abilities begin to develop around ages 5 to 7 and continue throughout the time children are in school, although within any age group there is much variability (Flavell, 1985; Flavell et al., 1995). Preschool children are capable of learning some strategic behaviors (Kail & Hagen, 1982), but as a result of schooling, children develop the awareness they can control what they learn by the strategies they use (Duell, 1986). Flavell and Wellman (1977) hypothesized that children form generalizations concerning how their actions influence the environment; for example, they learn "what works" for them to promote school achievement. This is especially true with memory strategies, perhaps because much school success depends on memorizing information (Application 7.2).

Variables Influencing Metacognition

Metacognitive awareness is influenced by variables associated with learners, tasks, and strategies (Duell, 1986; Flavell & Wellman, 1977).

Learner Variables. Learners' levels of development influence their metacognition (Alexander, Carr, & Schwanenflugel, 1995). Older children understand their own memory abilities and limitations better than younger children do (Flavell, Friedrichs, & Hoyt, 1970; Flavell et al., 1995). Flavell et al. (1970) presented children with material and told them to study it until they thought they could accurately recall the information. Children aged 7 to 10 were more accurate in judging their readiness to recall than were the children aged 4 to 6. Older children were also more aware that their memory abilities differ from one context to another. Children of the same age showed variations in memory abilities.

Learners' abilities to monitor how well they have done on a memory task also vary. Older children are more accurate in judging whether they have recalled all items they were to recall and whether they can recall information. Wellman (1977) presented children with pictures of objects and asked them to name the objects. If children could not name them, they were asked whether they would recognize the name. Compared with kindergartners, third graders were more accurate at predicting which object names they would be able to recognize.

Task Variables. Knowing the relative difficulty of different forms of learning and retrieving from memory various types of information are parts of metacognitive awareness. Although kindergartners and first graders believe that familiar or easily named items are easier to remember, older children are better at predicting that categorized items are easier to recall than conceptually unrelated items (Duell, 1986). Older children are more likely to believe that organized stories are easier to remember than disorganized pieces of information. With respect to the goal of learning, sixth graders know better than second graders that students should use different reading strategies depending on whether the goal is to recall a story word for word or in their own words (Myers & Paris, 1978).

Some school tasks do not require metacognition because they can be handled routinely. Part of the issue in the opening scenario is to use more tasks that require metacognition, with a corresponding decrease in low-level learning that can be accomplished easily.

Strategy Variables. Metacognition depends on the strategies learners employ. Children as young as ages 3 and 4 can use memory strategies to remember information, but their ability to use strategies improves with development. Older children are able to state more ways that help them remember things. Regardless of age, children are more likely to think of external things (e.g., write a note) than internal ones (e.g., think about doing something). Students' use of memory strategies such as rehearsal and elaboration also improves with development (Duell, 1986).

Although many students are capable of using metacognitive strategies, they may not know which strategies aid learning and LTM retrieval, and they may not employ those that are helpful (Flavell, 1985; Zimmerman & Martinez-Pons, 1990). Salatas and Flavell (1976) asked kindergartners, third graders, and college students to recall all list items that exhibited a given property (e.g., were breakable). Even though the young children often reported that conducting a thorough search for information is important (Duell, 1986), only the college students spontaneously recalled each item and decided whether it exhibited the given property.

Simply generating a strategy does not guarantee its use. This *utilization deficiency* is more common in younger children (Justice, Baker-Ward, Gupta, & Jannings, 1997) and appears to stem from children's understanding of how a strategy works. Older learners understand that the intention to use a strategy leads to strategy use, which produces an outcome. Younger children typically have only partial understanding of the links between intentions, actions, and outcomes. Such understanding develops between the ages of 3 and 6 (Wellman, 1990).

Task, strategy, and learner variables typically interact when students engage in metacognitive activities. Learners consider the type and length of material to be learned (task), the potential strategies to be used (strategy), and their skill at using the various strategies (learner). If learners think that note taking and underlining are good strategies for identifying main points of a technical article and if they believe they are good at underlining but poor at taking notes, they likely will decide to underline. As Schraw and Moshman (1995) noted, learners construct metacognitive theories that include knowledge and strategies that they believe will be effective in a given situation. Such metacognitive knowledge is critical for effective self-regulated learning (Dinsmore, Alexander, & Loughlin, 2008; Chapter 9).

Metacognition and Behavior

Understanding which skills and strategies help us learn and remember information is necessary but not sufficient to enhance our achievement. Even students who are aware of what helps them learn do not consistently engage in metacognitive activities for various reasons. In some cases, metacognition may be unnecessary because the material is easily learned. Learners also might be unwilling to invest the effort to employ metacognitive activities. The latter are tasks in their own right; they take time and effort. Learners may not understand fully that metacognitive strategies improve their performances, or they may believe they do but that other factors, such as time spent or effort expended, are more important for learning (Borkowski & Cavanaugh, 1979; Flavell & Wellman, 1977; Schunk & Rice, 1993).

Metacognitive activities improve achievement, but the fact that students often do not use them presents a quandary for educators. Students need to be taught a menu of activities ranging from those applying to learning in general (e.g., determining the purpose in learning) to those applying to specific situations (e.g., underlining important points in text), and they need to be encouraged to use them in various contexts (Belmont, 1989). Although the *what* component of learning is important, so are the *when, where,* and *why* of strategy use. Teaching the *what* without the latter will only confuse students and could prove demoralizing; students who know what to do but not when, where, or why to do it might hold low self-efficacy for performing well (Chapter 4).

Learners often need to be taught basic declarative or procedural knowledge along with metacognitive skills (Duell, 1986). Students need to monitor their understanding of main ideas, but the monitoring is pointless if they do not understand what a main idea is or how to find one. Students must be encouraged to employ metacognitive strategies—this is one of the implications of the discussion at the Nikowsky Middle School—and given opportunities to apply what they have learned outside of the instructional context. Students also need feedback on how well they are applying a strategy and how strategy use improves their performance (Schunk & Rice, 1993; Schunk & Swartz, 1993a). A danger of teaching a metacognitive strategy in conjunction with only a single task is that students will see the strategy as applying only to that task or to highly similar tasks, which does not foster transfer. It is desirable to use multiple tasks to teach strategies (Borkowski, 1985; Borkowski & Cavanaugh, 1979).

Metacognition and Reading

Metacognition is relevant to reading because it is involved in understanding and monitoring reading purposes and strategies (Paris, Wixson, & Palincsar, 1986). Beginning readers often do not understand the conventions of printed material: In the English language, one reads words from left to right and top to bottom. Beginning and poorer readers typically do not monitor their comprehension or adjust their strategies accordingly (Baker & Brown, 1984). Older and skilled readers are better at comprehension monitoring than are younger and less-skilled readers, respectively (Alexander et al., 1995; Paris et al., 1986).

Metacognition is involved when learners set goals, evaluate goal progress, and make necessary corrections (McNeil, 1987). Skilled readers do not approach all reading tasks identically. They determine their goal: find main ideas, read for details, skim, get the gist, and so on. They then use a strategy they believe will accomplish the goal. When reading skills are highly developed, these processes may occur automatically.

While reading, skilled readers check their progress. If their goal is to locate important ideas, and if after reading a few pages they have not located any important ideas, they are apt to reread those pages. If they encounter a word they do not understand, they try to determine its meaning from context or consult a dictionary rather than continue reading.

Developmental evidence indicates a trend toward greater recognition and correction of comprehension deficiencies (Alexander et al., 1995; Byrnes, 1996). Younger children recognize comprehension failures less often than do older children. Younger children who are good comprehenders may recognize a problem but may not employ a strategy to solve it (e.g., rereading). Older children who are good comprehenders recognize problems and employ correction strategies.

Children develop metacognitive abilities through interactions with parents and teachers (Langer & Applebee, 1986). Adults help children solve problems by guiding them through solution steps, reminding them of their goal, and helping them plan how to reach their goal. An effective teaching procedure includes informing children of the goal, making them aware of information relevant to the task, arranging a situation conducive to problem solving, and reminding them of their goal progress.

Strategy instruction programs generally have been successful in helping students learn strategies and maintain their use over time (Pressley & Harris, 2006). Brown and her colleagues advocated strategy training incorporating practice in use of skills, instruction in how to monitor outcomes of one's efforts, and feedback on when and where a strategy may be useful (Brown, 1980; Brown, Palincsar, & Armbruster, 1984).

Palincsar and Brown (1984) identified seventh graders with poor comprehension skills. They trained students in self-directed summarizing (review), questioning, clarifying, and predicting. Summarizing included stating what had happened in the text and also served as a self-test on the content. Questioning was directed at determining what main idea question a teacher or test might ask about that material. Clarifying was used when portions of the text were unclear and students could not adequately summarize. Predicting was used when text cues signaled forthcoming information.

Researchers taught these activities as part of an interactive dialogue between teacher and student known as *reciprocal teaching*. During the lessons, an adult teacher met with two students. Initially the teacher modeled the activities. The teacher and students silently read a passage, after which the teacher asked a question that a teacher or test might ask, summarized the content, clarified troublesome points, and predicted future content. Following the teacher's modeled demonstration, the teacher and students took turns being the teacher. At first, students had difficulty assuming the role of teacher; the teacher often had to construct paraphrases and questions for students. Eventually students became more capable of following the procedure and implementing the four activities.

Compared with a condition in which students received instruction on locating information in text, reciprocal teaching led to greater comprehension gains, better maintenance over time, and better generalization to classroom comprehension tests. Students exposed to reciprocal teaching also showed greater improvements in quality of summaries and questions asked. The maintenance and generalization results are important because changes brought about by strategy training programs may not maintain themselves or generalize to other tasks (Phye, 2001).

The dialogue about the following text occurred between teacher (T) and student (S) early in the training program (Palincsar & Brown, 1984).

The snake's skeleton and parts of its body are very flexible—something like a rubber hose with bones. A snake's backbone can have as many as 300 vertebrae, almost 10 times as many as a human's. These vertebrae are connected by loose and rubbery tissues that allow easy movement. Because of this bendable, twistable spinal construction, a snake can turn its body in almost any direction at almost any point.

S: Like, if a snake is turning around, he wouldn't break any bones because he is flexible.

T: And the reason he is so flexible is . . .

S: If someone stepped on his tail, he wouldn't be able to move unless he was flexible.

T: Okay. That explains why it would be helpful to be so flexible, but what makes the snake so flexible? I think that is an important part of the summary.

S: So he can move faster?

T: That is another reason for being flexible. Let me do a summary for you. Sara [the student] is right. The most important thing we have learned is that snake[s are] very flexible. The reason they can bend so easily is that they have so many little bones in their backbones and each of them can move separately, making the snake very flexible. Does that make sense? (p. 142)

The last statement by the teacher is a modeled demonstration of summarization.

There are other reading programs that incorporate strategy instruction and teach students to self-regulate. For example, the *Self-Regulated Strategy Development* program combines strategy instruction with instruction in self-regulation (e.g., self-monitoring, self-instructions, goal setting, self-reinforcement; Graham & Harris, 2003; Mason, 2004). This program has proven to be effective with children with learning disabilities and reading problems.

Concept-Oriented Reading Instruction (CORI) incorporates cognitive strategy instruction on the strategies of activating background knowledge, questioning, searching for information, summarizing, organizing graphically, and identifying story structure (Guthrie et al., 2004; Guthrie, Wigfield, & Perencevich, 2004). CORI has shown to be effective in raising students' reading comprehension.

Motivation plays a critical role in reading comprehension (Schunk, 1995). Guthrie, Wigfield, and VonSecker (2000) integrated reading strategy instruction with science content and found significant benefits on students' motivation compared with traditional instruction emphasizing coverage of material. Student interest presumably was heightened with the real-world use of effective reading strategies. The CORI program also incorporates motivational practices such as goal setting and giving students choices. Compared with strategy instruction alone, Guthrie et al. (2004) found that CORI led to greater benefits in comprehension, motivation, and use of strategies.

Other research shows that motivational factors affect reading outcomes. Meece and Miller (2001) found that task-mastery goals predicted students' use of learning strategies in reading instruction. After reviewing a large number of studies, Blok, Oostdam, Otter, and Overmaat (2002) concluded that computer-assisted instruction was effective in beginning reading instruction. It is possible that the motivational benefits of computers may aid in the development of early reading skill. Morgan and Fuchs (2007) examined 15 studies and found a positive correlation between children's reading skills and motivation and also obtained evidence suggesting that skills and motivation can affect one another.

The rapid influx of nonnative English speaking students in U.S. schools has necessitated expansion of programs for English language learners. For English instruction students often are placed in immersion or second language programs. In immersion programs students learn English in an all-English speaking classroom with formal or informal support when they have difficulties. In second language programs students receive instruction in reading and possibly other subjects in their native languages. Students often transition to English instruction around grade 2 or 3. Slavin and Cheung (2005) compared immersion with second language programs and found an advantage of second language programs on students' reading competencies; however, the number of studies in their review was small, and longitudinal studies are needed to determine long-term effects.

CONCEPT LEARNING

The Nature of Concepts

In many different contexts, students learn concepts. *Concepts* are labeled sets of objects, symbols, or events that share common characteristics, or critical attributes. A concept is a mental construct or representation of a category that allows one to identify examples and nonexamples of the category (Howard, 1987). Concepts may involve concrete objects (e.g., "table," "chair," "cat") or abstract ideas (e.g., "love," "democracy," "wholeness"). In fact, there are many types of concepts (for a detailed review, see Medin, Lynch, & Solomon, 2000). *Concept learning* refers to forming representations to identify attributes, generalize them to new examples, and discriminate examples from nonexamples.

Early studies by Bruner, Goodnow, and Austin (1956) explored the nature of concepts. Learners were presented with boxes portraying geometrical patterns. Each pattern could be classified using four different attributes: number of stimuli (one, two, three); shape (circle, square, cross); color (red, green, black); and number of borders on the box (one, two, three). The task was to identify the concept represented in different subsets of the boxes.

The configuration of features in a concept-learning task can be varied to yield different concepts. A *conjunctive concept* is represented by two or more features (e.g., two red circles). Other features (number of borders) are not relevant. A *disjunctive concept* is represented by one of two or more features; for example, two circles of any color or one red circle. A *relational concept* specifies a relationship between features that must be present, such as the number of objects in the figure must outnumber the number of borders (type of object and color are unimportant).

Bruner et al. (1956) found that learners formulated a hypothesis about the rule underlying the concept. Rules can be expressed in if-then form. A rule classifying a cat might be: "If it is domesticated, has four legs, fur, whiskers, a tail, is relatively small, purrs, and vocalizes 'meow,' then it is a cat." Although exceptions exist, this rule will accurately classify cats most of the time. Generalization occurs when the rule is applied to a variety of cats.

People tend to form rules quickly (Bruner et al., 1956). For any given concept, they retain the rule as long as it correctly identifies instances and noninstances of the concept and they modify it when it fails to do so. Learners acquire concepts better when they are presented with *positive instances*, or examples of the concept. Learning is much slower with *negative (non-) instances*. When trying to confirm the rule underlying the concept, people prefer to receive positive rather than negative instances.

Since this early work, other views have emerged concerning the nature of concepts. The *features analysis theory* derives from the work of Bruner and others and postulates that concepts involve rules that define the critical features, or the intrinsic (necessary) attributes, of the concept (Gagné, 1985; Smith & Medin, 1981). Through experiences with the concept, one formulates a rule that satisfies the conditions and retains the rule as long as it functions effectively.

This view predicts that different instances of a concept should be recognized equally quickly because each instance is judged against critical features; but this is not always the case. Most people find some instances of a category (e.g., a dolphin is a mammal) more difficult to verify than others (e.g., a dog is a mammal). This highlights the problem that many concepts cannot be defined precisely in terms of a set of critical attributes.

A second perspective is *prototype theory* (Rosch, 1973, 1975, 1978). A *prototype* is a generalized image of the concept, which may include only some of the concept's defining attributes. When confronted with an instance, one recalls the most likely prototype from LTM and compares it to the instance to see if they match. Prototypes may include some nondefining (optional) attributes. In cognitive psychology, prototypes often are thought of as *schemas* (Andre, 1986), or organized forms for the knowledge we have about a particular concept (Chapter 5).

Research supports the prototype theory prediction that instances closer to the prototype (e.g., prototype = "bird"; instances = "robin," "sparrow") are recognized quicker than those less typical (e.g., "owl," "ostrich"; Rosch, 1973). One concern is that prototype theory implies that people would store thousands of prototypes in LTM, which would consume much more space than rules. A second concern is that learners easily could form incorrect prototypes if they are allowed to include some nondefining characteristics and not all necessary ones.

Combining the features-analysis and prototype positions is possible. Given that prototypes include critical features, we might employ prototypes to classify instances of concepts that are fairly typical (Andre, 1986). For instances that are ambiguous, we may employ critical feature analysis, which might modify the list of critical features to incorporate the new features.

Children's understandings of concepts change with development and experience. Children in transition about the meaning of a concept may simultaneously keep a prior hypothesis in mind as they are developing a revised one (Goldin-Meadow, Alibali, & Church, 1993). This interpretation is consistent with Klausmeier's position, which is discussed next.

Concept Attainment

Research indicates that there are multiple ways to learn and modify concepts (Chinn & Samarapungavan, 2009). One way to develop prototypes is to be exposed to a typical instance of the concept that reflects the classic attributes (Klausmeier, 1992). A second way is by abstracting features from two or more examples; for birds, features might be "feathers," "two legs," "beak," and "flies," although not every feature applies to every member of the class. Prototypes are refined and expanded when one is exposed to new examples of the concept; thus, "lives in the jungle" (parrot) and "lives by the ocean" (seagull).

Gagné's (1985) theory (Chapter 5) includes concepts as a central form of learning. Learners initially must have basic prerequisite capabilities to discriminate among stimulus features (i.e., distinguish relevant from irrelevant features).

In Gagné's (1985) view, concept learning involves a *multistage sequence*. First, the stimulus feature is presented as an instance of the concept along with a noninstance. The learner confirms the ability to make the discrimination. In the next (generalization) stage, the learner identifies instances and noninstances. Third, the stimulus feature—which is to become the concept—is varied and presented along with noninstances. Concept attainment is verified by asking for identification of several instances of the class using stimuli not previously employed in learning. Throughout the process, correct responses are reinforced and contiguity learning occurs (Chapter 3) by presenting several instances of the concept in close association.

Klausmeier (1990, 1992) developed and tested a model of concept attainment. This model postulates a four-stage sequence: concrete, identity, classificatory, and formal. Competence at each level is necessary for attainment at the next level. The process of concept attainment represents an interaction of development, informal experience, and formal education.

At the *concrete level*, learners can recognize an item as the same one previously encountered when the context or spatial orientation in which it was originally encountered remains the same. This level requires learners to attend to the item, discriminate it as different from its surroundings on the basis of one or more defining attributes, represent it in LTM as a visual image, and retrieve it from LTM to compare it with a new image and determine that it is the same item. Thus, a learner might learn to recognize an equilateral triangle and discriminate it from a right or isosceles triangle.

The *identity level* is characterized by recognizing an item as the same one previously encountered when the item is observed from a different perspective or in a different modality. This stage involves the same processes as at the concrete level as well as the process of generalization. Thus, the learner will be able to recognize equilateral triangles in different orientations or positions on a page.

The *classificatory level* requires that learners recognize at least two items as being equivalent. Additional generalization is involved; in the case of equilateral triangles, this involves recognizing a smaller and larger equilateral triangle as equivalent. The process continues until the learner can recognize examples and nonexamples; at this stage, however, the learner may not understand the basis for classification (e.g., equality of side length and angles). Being able to name the concept is not necessary at this level, but, as in the preceding stages, it can facilitate concept acquisition.

Finally, the *formal level* requires the learner to identify examples and nonexamples of the concept, name the concept and its defining attributes, give a definition of the concept, and specify the attributes that distinguish the concept from other closely related ones (i.e., three equal sides and angles). Mastery of this stage requires the learner to implement classificatory-level cognitive processes and a set of higher-order thinking processes involving hypothesizing, evaluating, and inferring.

This stage model has instructional implications for learners at various points in development. Instruction can be spread over several grades in which concepts are periodically revisited at higher levels of attainment. Young children initially are provided with concrete referents and, with development, become able to operate at more abstract cognitive levels. For example, young children may learn the concept of "honesty" by seeing specific examples (e.g., not stealing, giving back something that is not yours); as they grow older, they can understand the concept in more abstract and complex terms (e.g., recognize honest feedback by a supervisor of a worker's performance; discuss benefits of honesty).

Teaching of Concepts

Tennyson (1980, 1981; Tennyson, Steve, & Boutwell, 1975) also developed a model of concept teaching based on empirical research. This model includes the following steps (Tennyson & Park, 1980):

- Determine the structure of the concept to include superordinate, coordinate, and subordinate concepts, and identify the critical and variable attributes (e.g., features that can legitimately vary and not affect the concept).
- Define the concept in terms of the critical attributes, and prepare several examples with the critical and variable attributes.
- Arrange the examples in sets based on the attributes, and ensure that the examples have similar variable attributes within any set containing examples from each coordinate concept.
- Order and present the sets in terms of the divergence and difficulty of the examples, and order the examples within any set according to the learner's current knowledge.

Most concepts can be represented in a hierarchy with *superordinate* (higher) and *subordinate* (lower) concepts. For any given concept, similar concepts may be at roughly the same level in the hierarchy; these are known as *coordinate* concepts. For example, the concept "domestic cat" has "cat family" and "mammal" as superordinate concepts, the various breeds (short hair, Siamese) as subordinate concepts, and other members of the cat family (lion, jaguar) as coordinate concepts. The concept has critical attributes (e.g., paws, teeth) and variable attributes (e.g., hair length, eye color). A *set* comprises examples and nonexamples (e.g., dog, squirrel) of the concept.

Although the concept should be defined with its critical attributes before examples and nonexamples are given, presenting a definition does not ensure that students will learn the concept. Examples should differ widely in variable attributes, and nonexamples should differ from examples in a small number of critical attributes at once. This mode of presentation prevents students from overgeneralizing (classifying nonexamples as examples) and undergeneralizing (classifying examples as nonexamples).

Pointing out relationships among examples is an effective way to foster generalization. One means is by using *concept (knowledge) maps,* or diagrams that represent ideas as node-link assemblies (Nesbit & Adescope, 2006). O'Donnell et al. (2002) showed that learning is facilitated with knowledge maps where ideas are interlinked. Nesbit and Adescope found that concept maps improved students' knowledge retention. Application 7.3 contains suggestions for teaching concepts.

The optimal number of examples to present depends on such concept characteristics as number of attributes and degree of abstractness of the concept. Abstract concepts usually have fewer tangible examples than concrete concepts, and examples of the former may be difficult for learners to grasp. Concept learning also depends on learner attributes such as age and prior knowledge (Tennyson & Park, 1980). Older students learn better than younger ones, and students with more relevant knowledge outperform those lacking such knowledge.

In teaching concepts, it is helpful to present examples that differ in optional attributes but have relevant attributes in common so that the latter can be clearly pointed out, along with the irrelevant dimensions. In teaching the concept "right triangle," for example, the size is irrelevant, as is the direction it faces. One might present right triangles of various sizes pointing in different directions. Using worked examples is an effective cognitive instructional strategy (Atkinson et al., 2000).

Not only must students learn to generalize right triangles, they also must learn to distinguish them from other triangles. To foster concept discrimination, teachers should present negative instances that clearly differ from positive instances. As students' skills develop, they can be taught to make finer discriminations. The suggestions shown in Table 7.2 are helpful in teaching students to generalize and discriminate among concepts.

This model requires a careful analysis of the taxonomic structure of a concept. Structure is well specified for many concepts (e.g., the animal kingdom), but for many others—especially abstract concepts—the links with higher- and lower-order concepts, as well as with coordinate concepts, are problematic.

APPLICATION 7.3
Teaching of Concepts

Concept learning involves identifying attributes, generalizing them to new examples, and discriminating examples from nonexamples. Using superordinate, coordinate, and subordinate concepts and critical and variable attributes to present the concept to be learned should help students clearly define its structure.

A kindergarten teacher presenting a unit to teach students to identify and distinguish shapes (circle, square, rectangle, oval, triangle, diamond) might initially have children group objects alike in shape and identify critical attributes (e.g., a square has four straight sides, the sides are the same length) and variable attributes (squares, rectangles, triangles, and diamonds have straight sides but a different number of sides of different lengths and arranged in different ways). The teacher might then focus on a particular shape by presenting different examples representing each shape so children can compare attributes with those of other shapes. As for content progression, the teacher might introduce

shapes familiar to students (e.g., circle and square) before moving to less common ones (e.g., parallelogram).

Kathy Stone introduced a unit on mammals by having her third-grade students sort a list of various animals into the major animal groups. Then the students discussed the major differences between the animal groups. After reviewing these facts, she focused on the amphibian group by expanding the knowledge about the physical characteristics and by reviewing other attributes such as eating habits and the ideal environment and climate.

In American history, Jim Marshall listed on the board the various immigrant groups that settled in America. After reviewing the time periods when each group came to America, he and the students discussed the reasons why each group came, where they predominantly settled in the country, and what types of trades they practiced. Then they described the impact of each group separately and collectively on the growth and progress of America.

Table 7.2
Steps for generalizing and discriminating concepts.

Step	Examples
Name concept	Chair
Define concept	Seat with a back for one person
Give relevant attributes	Seat, back
Give irrelevant attributes	Legs, size, color, material
Give examples	Easy chair, high chair, beanbag chair
Give nonexamples	Bench, table, stool

Motivational Processes

In a seminal article, Pintrich, Marx, and Boyle (1993) contended that conceptual change also involves *motivational processes* (e.g., goals, expectations, needs), which information processing models have tended to neglect. These authors argued that four conditions are necessary for conceptual change to occur. First, dissatisfaction with one's current conceptions is needed; change is unlikely if people feel their conceptions are accurate or useful. Second, the new conception must be intelligible—people must understand a conception in order to adopt it. Third, the new conception must be plausible—learners must understand how it fits with other understandings of how it might be applied. Finally, they must perceive the new conception as fruitful—being able to explain phenomena and suggesting new areas of investigation or application.

Motivational processes enter at several places in this model. For example, research shows that students' goals direct their attention and effort, and their self-efficacy relates positively to motivation, use of effective task strategies, and skill acquisition (Schunk, 1995). Furthermore, students who believe that learning is useful and that task strategies are effective display higher motivation and learning (Borkowski, 1985; Pressley et al., 1990; Schunk & Rice, 1993). Goals, self-efficacy, and self-evaluations of competence have been shown to promote learning and self-regulation in such domains as reading comprehension, writing, mathematics, and decision making (Pajares, 1996; Schunk & Pajares, 2009; Schunk & Swartz, 1993a; Wood & Bandura, 1989; Zimmerman & Bandura, 1994). We see in the opening scenario that the shift toward more problem solving actually has improved some students' motivation for learning.

In short, the literature suggests that conceptual change involves an interaction of students' cognitions and motivational beliefs (Pintrich et al., 1993), which has implications for teaching. Rather than simply provide knowledge, teachers must take students' pre-existing ideas into account when planning instruction and ensure that instruction includes motivation for learning.

These ideas are highly applicable to science. Many science educators believe that knowledge is built by learners rather than simply transmitted (Driver et al., 1994; Linn & Eylon, 2006). An interesting issue is how students develop scientific misconceptions and simplistic scientific models (Windschitl & Thompson, 2006). An important task is to help students challenge and correct misconceptions (Sandoval, 1995). Experiences that produce cognitive conflict can be helpful (Mayer, 1999; Sandoval, 1995; Williams & Tolmie, 2000). This might entail having students engage in hands-on activities and work with others (e.g., in discussions) to interpret their experiences through selective questioning (e.g., "Why do you think that?" "How did you figure that?"). This approach fits well with the Vygotskian emphasis on social influences on knowledge construction (Chapter 6).

Nussbaum and Novick (1982) proposed a three-stage model for changing student beliefs:

- Reveal and understand student preconceptions.
- Create conceptual conflict with those conceptions.
- Facilitate the development of new or revised schemas about the phenomena under consideration.

The role of motivation is critical. Although science has many themes that ought to be interesting, studying science holds little interest for many students. Learning benefits from hands-on instruction and links to aspects of students' lives. For example, motion can be linked to the path of soccer balls, electricity to DVD players, and ecology to community recycling programs. Enhancing interest in topics also can improve the quality of student learning (Sandoval, 1995). Thus, using illustrations and diagrams helps students to understand scientific concepts (Carlson, Chandler, & Sweller, 2003; Hannus & Hyönä, 1999), although some students may need to be taught how to study illustrations as part of text learning.

PROBLEM SOLVING

One of the most important types of cognitive processing that occurs often during learning is problem solving. Problem solving has been a topic of study for a long time—historical material is reviewed in this section—but interest in the topic has burgeoned with the growth of cognitive theories of learning. Some theorists consider problem solving to be the key process in learning, especially in domains such as science and mathematics (Anderson, 1993). Although "problem solving" and "learning" are not synonymous, the former often is involved in the latter and particularly when learners can exert some degree of self-regulation over learning (Chapter 9) and when the learning involves challenges and nonobvious solutions. In the opening scenario, Meg recommends more emphasis on problem solving.

A *problem* exists when there is a "situation in which you are trying to reach some goal, and must find a means for getting there" (Chi & Glaser, 1985, p. 229). The problem may be to answer a question, compute a solution, locate an object, secure a job, teach a student, and so on. *Problem solving* refers to people's efforts to achieve a goal for which they do not have an automatic solution.

Regardless of content area and complexity, all problems have certain commonalities. Problems have an initial state—the problem solver's current status or level of knowledge. Problems have a goal—what the problem solver is attempting to attain. Most problems also require the solver to break the goal into subgoals that, when mastered (usually sequentially), result in goal attainment. Finally, problems require performing operations (cognitive and behavioral activities) on the initial state and the subgoals, which alter the nature of those states (Anderson, 1990; Chi & Glaser, 1985).

Given this definition, not all learning activities include problem solving. Problem solving likely is not involved when students' skills become so well established that they automatically execute actions to attain goals, which happens with many skills in different domains. Problem solving also may not occur in low-level (possibly trivial) learning, where students know what to do to learn. This seems to be an issue at Nikowsky Middle School, as teachers are focusing on basic skills needed for the tests. At the same time, students learn new skills and new uses for previously learned skills, so many school activities might involve problem solving at some point during learning.

Historical Influences

Some historical perspectives on problem solving are examined as a backdrop to current cognitive views: trial and error, insight, and heuristics.

Trial and Error. Thorndike's (1913b) research with cats (Chapter 3) required problem solving; the problem was how to escape from the cage. Thorndike conceived of problem solving as *trial and error.* The animal was capable of performing certain behaviors in the cage. From this behavioral repertoire, the animal performed one behavior and experienced the consequences. After a series of random behaviors, the cat made the response that opened the hatch leading to escape. With repeated trials, the cat made fewer errors before performing the escape behavior, and the time required to solve the problem diminished. The escape behavior (response) became connected to cues (stimuli) in the cage.

We occasionally use trial and error to solve problems; we simply perform actions until one works. But trial and error is not reliable and often not effective. It can waste time, may never result in a solution, may lead to a less-than-ideal solution, and can have negative effects. In desperation, a teacher might use a trial-and-error approach by trying different reading materials with Kayla until she begins to read better. This approach might be effective but also might expose her to materials that prove frustrating and thereby retard her reading progress.

Insight. Problem solving often is thought to involve *insight*, or the sudden awareness of a likely solution. Wallas (1921) studied great problem solvers and formulated a four-step model as follows:

- *Preparation:* A time to learn about the problem and gather information that might be relevant to its solution.
- *Incubation:* A period of thinking about the problem, which may also include putting the problem aside for a time.
- *Illumination:* A period of insight when a potential solution suddenly comes into awareness.
- *Verification:* A time to test the proposed solution to ascertain whether it is correct.

Wallas's stages were descriptive and not subjected to empirical verification. Gestalt psychologists (Chapter 5) also postulated that much human learning was insightful and involved a change in perception. Learners initially thought about the ingredients necessary to solve a problem. They integrated these in various ways until the problem was solved. When learners arrived at a solution, they did so suddenly and with insight.

Many problem solvers report having moments of insight; Watson and Crick had insightful moments in discovering the structure of DNA (Lemonick, 2003). An important educational application of Gestalt theory was in the area of problem solving, or *productive thinking* (Duncker, 1945; Luchins, 1942; Wertheimer, 1945). The Gestalt view stressed the role of *understanding*—comprehending the meaning of some event or grasping the principle or rule underlying performance. In contrast, rote memorization—although used often by students—was inefficient and rarely used in life outside of school (Application 7.4).

Research by Katona (1940) demonstrated the utility of rule learning compared with memorization. In one study, participants were asked to learn number sequences (e.g., 816449362516941). Some learned the sequences by rote, whereas others were given clues to aid learning (e.g., "Think of squared numbers"). Learners who determined the rule for generating the sequences retained them better than those who memorized.

APPLICATION 7.4
Role of Understanding in Learning

Teachers want students to understand concepts rather than simply memorize how to complete tasks. Gestalt psychologists believed that an emphasis on drill and practice, memorization, and reinforcement resulted in trivial learning and that understanding was achieved by grasping rules and principles underlying concepts and skills.

Teachers often use hands-on experiences to help students understand the structure and principles involved in learning. In biology, students might memorize what a cross section of a bean stem looks like under a microscope, but they may have difficulty conceptualizing the structures in the living organism. Mock-ups assist student learning. A large, hands-on model of a bean stem that can be taken apart to illustrate the internal structures should enhance student understanding of the stem's composition and how the parts function.

Talking about child care in a high school family studies class is not nearly as beneficial as the hour each week students spend helping children at a local day care center and applying what they have been studying.

In discussing the applications of learning theories, it is preferable that students see firsthand the utilization of techniques that enhance student learning. Gina Brown has her educational psychology students observe in school classrooms. As they observe, she has them list examples of situations where various learning principles are evident.

Rules lead to better learning and retention than memorization because rules give a simpler description of the phenomenon so less information must be learned. In addition, rules help organize material. To recall information, one recalls the rule and then fills in the details. In contrast, memorization entails recalling more information. Memorization generally is inefficient because most situations have some organization (Wertheimer, 1945). Problems are solved by discovering the organization of the situation and the relationship of the elements to the problem solution. By arranging and rearranging elements, learners eventually gain insight into the solution.

Köhler (1926) did well-known work on problem solving with apes on the island of Tenerife during World War I. In one experiment, Köhler put a banana just out of reach of an ape in a cage; the ape could fetch the banana by using a long stick or by putting two sticks together. Köhler concluded that problem solving was insightful: Animals surveyed the situation, suddenly "saw" the means for attaining the goal, and tested the solution. The apes' first problem-solving attempts failed as they tried different ineffective strategies (e.g., throwing a stick at the banana). Eventually they saw the stick as an extension of their arms and used it accordingly.

In another situation (Köhler, 1925), the animal could see the goal but not attain it without turning away and taking an indirect route. For example, the animal might be in a room with a window and see food outside. To reach the goal, the animal must exit the room via a door and proceed down a corridor that led outside. In going from the presolution to the solution phase, the animal might try a number of alternatives before settling on one and employing it. Insight occurred when the animal tested a likely solution.

A barrier to problem solving is *functional fixedness*, or the inability to perceive different uses for objects or new configurations of elements in a situation (Duncker, 1945). In a classic study, Luchins (1942) gave individuals problems that required them to obtain a given amount of water using three jars of different sizes. Persons from ages 9 to adult easily learned the formula that always produced the correct amount. Intermixed in the problem set were some problems that could be solved using a simpler formula. Persons generally continued to apply the original formula. Cuing them that there might be an easier solution led some to discover the simpler methods, although many persisted with the original formula. This research shows that when students do not understand a phenomenon, they may blindly apply a known algorithm and fail to understand that easier methods exist. This procedure-bound nature of problem solving can be overcome when different procedures are emphasized during instruction (Chen, 1999).

Gestalt theory had little to say about how problem-solving strategies are learned or how learners could be taught to be more insightful. Wertheimer (1945) believed that teachers could aid problem solving by arranging elements of a situation so that students would be more likely to perceive how the parts relate to the whole. Such general advice may not be helpful for teachers.

Heuristics

Another way to solve problems is to use *heuristics*, which are general methods for solving problems that employ principles (rules of thumb) that usually lead to a solution (Anderson, 1990). Polya's (1945/1957) list of mental operations involved in problem solving is as follows:

- Understand the problem.
- Devise a plan.
- Carry out the plan.
- Look back.

Understanding the problem involves asking such questions as "What is the unknown?" and "What are the data?" It often helps to draw a diagram representing the problem and the given information. In devising a plan, one tries to find a connection between the data and the unknown. Breaking the problem into subgoals is useful, as is thinking of a similar problem and how that was solved (i.e., use analogies). The problem may need to be restated. While carrying out the plan, checking each step to ensure it is being properly implemented is important. Looking back means examining the solution: Is it correct? Is there another means of attaining it?

Bransford and Stein (1984) formulated a similar heuristic known as IDEAL:

- *I*dentify the problem.
- *D*efine and represent the problem.

- *E*xplore possible strategies.
- *A*ct on the strategies.
- *L*ook back and evaluate the effects of your activities.

The Creative Problem Solving (CPS) model offers another example of a generic problem-solving framework (Treffinger, 1985; Treffinger & Isaksen, 2005). This model comprises three major components: understanding the challenge, generating ideas, and preparing for action (Treffinger, 1995; Treffinger & Isaksen, 2005). Metacognitive components (e.g., planning, monitoring, modifying behavior) are present throughout the process.

Understanding the challenge begins with a general goal or direction for problem solving. After important data (e.g., facts, opinions, concerns) are obtained, a specific goal or question is formulated. The hallmark of generating ideas is divergent thinking to produce options for attaining the goal. Preparing for action includes examining promising options and searching for sources of assistance and ways to overcome resistance.

General heuristics are most useful when one is working with unfamiliar content (Andre, 1986). They are less effective in a familiar domain, because as domain-specific skills develop, students increasingly use established procedural knowledge. General heuristics have an instructional advantage: They can help students become systematic problem solvers. Although the heuristic approach may appear to be inflexible, there actually is flexibility in how steps are carried out. For many students, a heuristic will be more systematic than their current problem-solving approaches and will lead to better solutions.

Newell and Simon (1972) proposed an information processing model of problem solving that included a problem space with a beginning state, a goal state, and possible solution paths leading through subgoals and requiring application of operations. The problem solver forms a mental representation of the problem and performs operations to reduce the discrepancy between the beginning and goal states. The process of operating on the representation to find a solution is known as the *search* (Andre, 1986).

The first step in problem solving is to form a mental representation. Similar to Polya's first step (understand the problem), representation requires translating known information into a model in memory. The internal representation consists of propositions, and possibly images, in WM. The problem also can be represented externally (e.g., on paper, computer screen). Information in WM activates related knowledge in LTM, and the solver eventually selects a problem-solving strategy. As people solve problems, they often alter their initial representation and activate new knowledge, especially if their problem solving does not succeed. Thus, problem solving includes evaluating goal progress.

The problem representation determines what knowledge is activated in memory and, consequently, how easy the problem is to solve (Holyoak, 1984). If solvers incorrectly represent the problem by not considering all aspects or by adding too many constraints, the search process is unlikely to identify a correct solution path (Chi & Glaser, 1985). No matter how clearly solvers subsequently reason, they will not reach a correct solution unless they form a new representation. Not surprisingly, problem-solving training programs typically devote a lot of time to the representation phase (Andre, 1986).

Problem-Solving Strategies

Like skills (discussed earlier), problem-solving strategies can be general or specific. *General strategies* can be applied to problems in several domains regardless of content; *specific strategies* are useful only in a particular domain. For example, breaking a complex problem into subproblems (subgoal analysis) is a general strategy applicable to problems such as writing a term paper, choosing an academic major, and deciding where to live. Conversely, tests that one might perform to classify laboratory specimens are task specific. The professional development given to Nikowsky's teachers probably included general and specific strategies.

General strategies are useful when one is working on problems where solutions are not immediately obvious. Useful general strategies are generate-and-test strategies, means–ends analysis, analogical reasoning, and brainstorming. General strategies are less useful than domain-specific strategies when working with highly familiar content. Some examples of problem solving in learning contexts are given in Application 7.5.

Generate-and-Test Strategy. The generate-and-test strategy is useful when a limited number of problem solutions can be tested to see if they attain the goal (Resnick, 1985). This strategy works best when multiple solutions can be ordered in terms of likelihood and at least one solution is apt to solve the problem.

As an example, assume that you walk into a room, flip the light switch, but the light does not come on. Possible causes include: the bulb is burned out; the electricity is turned off; the switch is broken; the lamp socket is faulty; the circuit breaker is tripped; the fuse is blown; or the wiring has a short. You will probably generate and test the most likely solution (replace the bulb); if this does not solve the problem, you may generate and test other likely solutions. Although content does not need to be highly familiar, some knowledge is needed to use this method effectively. Prior knowledge establishes the hierarchy of possible solutions; current knowledge influences solution selection. Thus, if you notice an electric utility truck in your neighborhood, you would determine if the power is shut off.

Means–Ends Analysis. To use *means–ends analysis*, one compares the current situation with the goal and identifies the differences between them (Resnick, 1985). Subgoals are set to reduce the differences. One performs operations to accomplish the subgoal, at which point the process is repeated until the goal is attained.

Newell and Simon (1972) studied means–ends analysis and formulated the General Problem Solver (GPS)—a computer simulation program. GPS breaks a problem into subgoals, each representing a difference from the current state. GPS starts with the most important difference and uses operations to eliminate that difference. In some cases, the operations must first eliminate another difference that is prerequisite to the more important one.

Means-ends analysis is a powerful problem-solving heuristic. When subgoals are properly identified, means–ends analysis is most likely to solve the problem. One drawback is that with complex problems means–ends analysis taxes WM because one may have to keep track of several subgoals. Forgetting a subgoal thwarts problem solution.

Means–ends analysis can proceed from the goal to the initial state (*working backward*) or from the initial state to the goal (*working forward*). In working backward, one

APPLICATION 7.5
Problem Solving

Various ways exist to help students improve their problem-solving skills. When students solve mathematical word problems, Kathy Stone encourages them to state each problem in their own words, draw a sketch, decide what information is relevant, and state the ways they might solve the problem. These and other similar questions help focus students' attention on important task aspects and guide their thinking:

- What information is important?
- What information is missing?
- Which formulas are necessary?
- What is the first thing to do?

Another way to assist students is to encourage them to view a problem from varying perspectives. During an exercise in which Jim Marshall's high school students categorized wartime figures who had a predominant impact on the United States (e.g., Churchill, Hitler), they discussed ways these figures could be categorized, such as by personality type, political makeup of countries they ruled, goals of the war, and the effect their leadership and goals had on the United States. This exercise illustrates different ways to organize information, which aids problem solving.

Teachers also can teach strategies. In a geography lesson, students might be given the following problem: "Pick a state (not your own) that you believe could attract new residents, and create a poster depicting the most important attributes of that state."

A working backward strategy could be taught as follows:

Goal: Create a poster depicting the state's important attributes.

Subgoal: Decide how to portray the attributes in a poster.

Subgoal: Decide which attributes to portray.

Subgoal: Decide which state to pick.

Initial Subgoal: Decide which attributes attract new residents.

To attain the initial subgoal, students could brainstorm in small groups to determine which factors attract people to a state. They then could conduct library research to check on which states possess these attributes. Students could reconvene to discuss the attributes of different states and decide on one. They then would decide which attributes to portray in the poster and how to portray them, after which they would create their poster and present it to the class.

When students are developing problem-solving skills, teachers might want to give clues rather than answers. A teacher working with younger children on categorizing might give the children a word list of names of animals, colors, and places to live. Children are most likely to experience some difficulty categorizing the names. Rather than telling them the answers, the teacher could provide clues such as, "Think of how the words go together. How are *horse* and *lion* alike? How are *pink* and *house* different?

Figure 7.2
Means–ends analysis applied to a geometry problem.

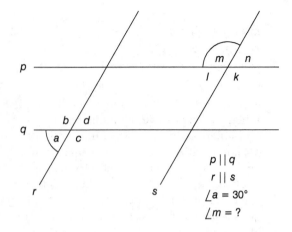

$p \parallel q$
$r \parallel s$
$\angle a = 30°$
$\angle m = ?$

starts with the goal and asks what subgoals are necessary to accomplish it. One then asks what is necessary to attain these subgoals and so forth, until the initial state is reached. To work backward, therefore, one plans a series of moves, each designed to attain a subgoal. Successfully working backward requires a fair amount of knowledge in the problem domain to determine goal and subgoal prerequisites.

Working backward is frequently used to prove geometric theorems. One starts by assuming that the theorem is true and then works backward until the postulates are reached. A geometric example is shown in Figure 7.2. The problem is to solve for angle m. Working backward, students realize that they need to determine angle n, because angle $m = 180° -$ angle n (straight line $= 180°$). Continuing to work backward, students understand that because the parallel lines intersect, the corresponding angle d on line q equals angle n. Drawing on their geometric knowledge, students determine that angle $d =$ angle a, which is 30°. Thus, angle $n = 30°$, and angle $m = 180° - 30° = 150°$.

As another example of working backward, suppose one has a term paper due in 3 weeks. The last step before turning it in is to proofread it (to do the day before the paper is due). The step before that is to type and print the final copy (allow 1 day). Before that, one makes final revisions (1 day), revises the paper (3 days), and types and prints the draft copy (1 day). Continuing to work backward, we might allow 5 days to write the draft, 1 day to outline, 3 days for library research, and 1 day to decide on a topic. We allow a total of 17 days to spend in part working on the paper. So we need to begin 4 days from today.

A second type of means–ends analysis is working forward, sometimes referred to as *hill climbing* (Matlin, 2009; Mayer, 1992). The problem solver starts with the current situation and alters it in the hope of moving closer to the goal. Several alterations usually are necessary to attain the goal. One danger is that working forward sometimes proceeds based on superficial problem analysis. Although each step represents an attempt to attain a necessary subgoal, one can easily veer off on a tangent or arrive at a dead end because typically one cannot see many alternatives ahead but rather only the next step (Matlin, 2009).

As an example of a working forward strategy, consider students in a laboratory who have various substances in jars. Their goal is to label the substances in their jars. To do so, they perform a series of tests on the substances which, if correctly done, will result in a solution. This represents a working forward strategy because each test moves students closer to their goal of classifying their substances. The tests are ordered, and the results show what the substances are not, as well as what they might be. To prevent students from going off on the wrong track, the teacher sets up the procedure carefully and ensures that students understand how to perform the tests.

Analogical Reasoning. Another general problem-solving strategy is to use *analogical reasoning*, which involves drawing an analogy between the problem situation (the target) and a situation with which one is familiar (the base or source; Anderson, 1990; Chen, 1999; Hunt, 1989). One works the problem through the familiar domain and then relates the solution to the problem situation (Holyoak & Thagard, 1997). Analogical reasoning involves accessing the familiar domain's network in LTM and mapping it onto (relating it to) the problem situation in WM (Halpern, Hansen, & Riefer, 1990). Successful application requires that the familiar situation be structurally similar to the problem situation, although the situations may differ in surface features (e.g., one might involve the solar system and the other molecular structures). The subgoals in this approach are relating the steps in the original (familiar) domain to those in the transfer (problem) area. Students often use the analogy method to solve problems in textbooks. Examples are worked in the text (familiar domain), then students relate these steps to the problems they must solve.

Gick and Holyoak (1980, 1983) demonstrated the power of analogical problem solving. They presented learners with a difficult medical problem and, as an analogy, a solved military problem. Simply giving them the analogical problem did not automatically prompt them to use it. However, giving them a hint to use the military problem to solve the medical problem improved problem solving. Gick and Holyoak also found that giving students two analog stories led to better problem solving than giving one story. However, having them summarize the analog story, giving them the principle underlying the story while they read it, or providing them with a diagram illustrating the problem-solution principle did not enhance problem solving. These results suggest that in an unfamiliar domain, students need guidance for using analogies and that multiple examples increase the likelihood of students' linking at least one example to the problem to be solved.

To be most effective, analogical problem solving requires good knowledge of the familiar and problem domains. Students often have enough difficulty using analogies to solve problems even when the solution strategy is highlighted. With inadequate knowledge, students are unlikely to see the relation between the problem and the analogue. Even assuming good knowledge, the analogy is most likely to fail when the familiar and problem domains are conceptually dissimilar. Learners may understand how fighting a battle (the military problem) is similar to fighting a disease (the medical problem), but they may not grasp other analogies (e.g., fighting a corporate takeover attempt).

Developmental evidence indicates that, despite its difficulties, children can employ analogical reasoning (Siegler, 1989). Teaching analogies to children—including those with learning disabilities—can improve their subsequent problem solving (Grossen, 1991). The use of case studies and case-based reasoning can help develop analogical thinking (Kolodner, 1997). Effective techniques for using analogies include having the adult teacher and child verbalize the solution principle that underlies the original and transfer problems, prompting children to recall elements of the original problem's causal structure, and presenting the two problems such that the causal structures proceed from most to least obvious (Crisafi & Brown, 1986). Other suggestions include using similar original and transfer problems, presenting several similar problems, and using pictures to portray causal relations.

This is not to suggest that all children can become experts at using analogies. The task is difficult, and children often draw inappropriate analogies. Compared with older students, younger ones require more hints, are more apt to be distracted by irrelevant perceptual features, and process information less efficiently (Crisafi & Brown, 1986). Children's success depends heavily on their knowledge about the original problem and their skill at encoding and making mental comparisons, which show wide individual differences (Richland, Morrison, & Holyoak, 2006; Siegler, 1989). Children learn problem-solving strategies better when they observe and explain them than when they merely observe (Crowley & Siegler, 1999).

Analogical problem solving is useful in teaching. Teachers often have students in their classes whose native language is not English. Teaching students in their native language is impossible. Teachers might relate this problem to teaching students who have difficulty learning. With the latter students, teachers would proceed slowly, use concrete experiences whenever possible, and provide much individual instruction. They might try the same tactics with limited-English-proficiency students, while simultaneously teaching them English words and phrases so they can follow along with the other students in class.

This analogy is appropriate because students with learning problems and students who speak little English have difficulties in the classroom. Other analogies might be inappropriate. Unmotivated students also have learning difficulties. Using them for the analogy, the teacher might offer the limited-English-proficiency students rewards for learning. This solution is not apt to be effective because the issue with limited-English-proficiency students is instructional rather than motivational.

Brainstorming. Brainstorming is a general problem-solving strategy that is useful for formulating possible problem solutions (Isaksen & Gaulin, 2005; Mayer, 1992; Osborn, 1963). The steps in brainstorming are as follows:

- Define the problem.
- Generate as many solutions as possible without evaluating them.
- Decide on criteria for judging potential solutions.
- Use these criteria to select the best solution.

Successful brainstorming requires that participants withhold criticism of ideas until after all ideas are generated. In addition, participants may generate ideas that build onto one another. Thus, "wild" and unusual ideas should be encouraged (Mayer, 1992).

As with analogical problem solving, the amount of knowledge one has about the problem domain affects the success of brainstorming because better domain knowledge allows one to generate more potential solutions and criteria for judging their feasibility. Brainstorming can be used individually, although the group interaction usually leads to more solutions.

Brainstorming lends itself well to many instructional and administrative decisions made in schools. It is most useful for generating many varied—and possibly some unique—ideas (Isaksen & Gaulin, 2005). Assume that a new school principal finds low staff morale. Staff members agree that better communication is needed. The grade-level leaders meet with the principal, and the group arrives at the following potential solutions: Hold a weekly meeting with staff, send out a weekly (electronic) bulletin, post notices on a bulletin board, hold weekly meetings with grade-level leaders (after which they meet with teachers), send e-mail informational messages frequently, make announcements over the public address system. The group formulates two criteria: (a) minimally time-consuming for teachers and (b) minimally disrupting to classes. With the criteria in mind, they decide that the principal should send out a weekly bulletin and frequent e-mail messages and meet with grade-level leaders as a group. Although they will take time, meetings between the principal and grade-level leaders will be more focused than those between the principal and the entire staff.

Problem Solving and Learning

Problem solving often is involved in learning, but the concepts are not synonymous in meaning. According to a contemporary information processing view (Anderson, 1990, 1993, 2000), problem solving involves the acquisition, retention, and use of production systems, which are networks of condition–action sequences (rules) in which the conditions are the sets of circumstances that activate the system and the actions are the sets of activities that occur (Anderson, 1990; Andre, 1986; Chapter 5). A production system consists of if-then statements. If statements (the condition) include the goal and test statements, then statements are the actions.

Productions are forms of procedural knowledge that include declarative knowledge and the conditions under which these forms are applicable. Productions are represented in LTM as propositional networks and are acquired in the same fashion as other procedural knowledge. Productions also are organized hierarchically with subordinate and superordinate productions. To solve two equations with two unknowns, one first represents one unknown in terms of the second unknown (subordinate production), after which one solves for the second unknown (production) and uses that value to solve for the first unknown (superordinate production).

Productions can be general or specific. Specific productions apply to content in well-defined areas. In contrast, heuristics are general productions because they apply to diverse content. A means–ends analysis might be represented as follows (Anderson, 1990):

> IF the goal is to transform the current state into the goal state and D is the largest
>   difference between the states
> THEN set as subgoals
> 1. To eliminate the difference D
> 2. To convert the resulting state into the goal state. (p. 243)

A second production will then need to be employed with the if-then statement, "If the goal is to eliminate the difference D." This sequence continues until the subgoals have been identified at a specific level; then domain-specific rules are applied. In short, general productions are broken down until the level at which domain-specific knowledge is applied. Production systems offer a means of linking general with specific problem-solving procedures. Other problem-solving strategies (e.g., analogical reasoning) also can be represented as productions.

School learning that is highly regulated may not require problem solving. Problem solving is not applicable when students have a goal and a clear means for attaining it. Problem solving becomes more important when teachers move away from lockstep, highly regimented instruction and encourage more original and critical thinking by students. This is what the teachers at Nikowsky worked on after their meeting with Meg. There is a movement in education to encourage problem solving by students, and many educators believe that this trend will continue. In the meantime, students need to learn both general and specific problem-solving strategies so they can handle these added demands associated with learning.

Experts and Novices

As with skill acquisition, researchers have identified differences between novice and expert problem solvers (Anderson, 1990, 1993; Bruning et al., 2004; Resnick, 1985). One difference involves the demands made on WM. Expert problem solvers do not activate large amounts of potentially relevant information; they identify key features of the problem, relate them to background knowledge, and generate one or a small number of potential solutions (Mayer, 1992). Experts reduce complex problems to manageable size by separating the problem space from the larger task environment, which includes the domain of facts and knowledge within which the problem is embedded (Newell & Simon, 1972). Coupled with the fact that experts can hold more information in WM (Chi, Glaser, & Farr, 1988), this reduction process retains relevant information, discards irrelevant information, fits within the limits of WM, and is accurate enough to allow a solution.

Experts often employ a working forward strategy by identifying the problem format and generating an approach to fit it (Mayer, 1992). This typically entails breaking the problem into parts and solving the parts sequentially (Bruning et al., 2004). Novice problem solvers, however, often attempt problem solving in piecemeal fashion, in part because of the poorer organization in their memories. They may use trial and error or try to work backward from what they are trying to find to the problem givens—an ineffective strategy if they are unaware of the substeps needed (Mayer, 1992). Their means–ends analyses often are based on surface features of problems. In mathematics, novices generate formulas from memory when confronted with word problems. Trying to store excess information in WM clutters their thinking (Resnick, 1985).

Experts and novices also differ in background domain-specific knowledge, although they appear to be comparably versed in knowledge of general problem-solving strategies (Elstein, Shulman, & Sprafka, 1978; Simon, 1979). Experts have more extensive and better organized LTM structures in their area of expertise (Chi et al., 1981). The greater amount of knowledge experts can use in solving problems, the more likely they are to solve them and the better their memory organization facilitates efficiency.

Qualitative differences are evident in how knowledge is structured in memory (Chi, Glaser, & Rees, 1982). Experts' knowledge is more hierarchically organized. Experts tend to classify problems according to "deep structure," whereas novices rely more on surface features (Hardiman, Dufresne, & Mestre, 1989). Interestingly, training of novices to recognize deep features improves their performances relative to those of untrained novices.

Novices typically respond to problems in terms of how they are presented; experts reinterpret problems to reveal an underlying structure, one that most likely matches their own LTM network (Resnick, 1985). Novices attempt to translate the given information directly into formulas and solve for the missing quantities. Rather than generate formulas, experts may initially draw diagrams to clarify the relations among problem aspects. They often construct a new version of the problem. By the time they are ready to perform calculations, they usually have simplified the problem and perform fewer calculations than novices. While working, experts monitor their performances better to assess goal progress and the value of the strategy they are using (Gagné et al., 1993).

Finally, experts spend more time planning and analyzing. They are more thoughtful and do not proceed until they have some strategy in mind. Moore (1990) found that experienced teachers spend more time planning than do less-experienced teachers, as well as more time exploring new classrooms. Such planning makes strategy implementation easier.

In summary, the differences between novice and expert problem solvers are many. Compared with novices, experts:

- Possess more declarative knowledge
- Have better hierarchical organization of knowledge
- Spend more time planning and analyzing
- Recognize problem formats more easily
- Represent problems at a deeper level
- Monitor their performances more carefully
- Understand better the value of strategy use

Reasoning

Reasoning refers to the mental processes involved in generating and evaluating logical arguments (Anderson, 1990). Reasoning yields a conclusion from thoughts, percepts, and assertions (Johnson-Laird, 1999) and involves working through problems to explain why something happened or what will happen (Hunt, 1989). Reasoning skills include clarification, basis, inference, and evaluation (Ennis, 1987; Quellmalz, 1987; Table 7.3 and Application 7.6).

Table 7.3
Reasoning skills.

Skill	Definition	Sample Questions
Clarification	Identifying and formulating questions, analyzing elements, defining terms	"What do I know?" "What do I need to figure out?"
Basis	Determining source(s) of support for conclusions about a problem	"Is this a fact or opinion?" "What is the source of this information?"
Inference	Reasoning inductively from specific cases to general principles or deductively from general principles to specific cases	"What do these diverse examples have in common?" (induction) "How can I apply these general rules to this example?" (deduction)
Evaluation	Using criteria to judge adequacy of a problem solution	"Do I need more information?" "Is my conclusion reasonable?"

APPLICATION 7.6
Reasoning

Teachers can teach students how to ask questions to produce an accurate mental representation of a problem. A teacher might give primary students objects to classify according to shape. To help students identify and clarify the problem, the teacher could ask questions such as:

- What have you been asked to do?
- What items do you have?
- What are some of the shapes you know?
- Does it matter if the items are different colors?
- Does it matter if some of the items are little and some are big?
- Does it matter if some of the items are soft and some are hard?
- What do you think you will do with the items you have?

Students verbalize what information they need to use and what they are supposed to do with that information. Each time the teacher works with students in solving a problem, the teacher can help them generate questions to determine what information is important for solving the problem.

A medical researcher working with a group of interns gives them information about a virus, and their task is to identify the virus. To assist the students in the identification process, the instructor might generate a list of questions similar to the following:

- What effect does the virus have on blood cells?
- What effect does the virus have on human tissue?
- How quickly does the virus appear to grow, and under what conditions does it grow?
- What does the virus do when exposed to warmth?
- What does the virus do when exposed to cold?
- What does the virus do when exposed to moisture?
- What does the virus do in an airtight environment?
- What reaction does the virus have when exposed to various drugs?

Clarification. *Clarification* requires identifying and formulating questions, analyzing elements, and defining terms. These skills involve determining which elements in a situation are important, what they mean, and how they are related. At times, scientific questions are posed, but at other times students must develop questions such as "What is the problem, hypothesis, or thesis?" Clarification corresponds to the representation phase of problem solving; students define the problem to obtain a clear mental representation. Little productive reasoning occurs without a clear problem statement.

Basis. People's conclusions about a problem are supported by information from personal observations, statements by others, and previous inferences. Judging the credibility of a source is important. In so doing, one must distinguish between fact, opinion, and reasoned judgment. Assume that a suspect armed with a gun is apprehended near the scene of a murder. That the suspect had a gun when arrested is a fact. Laboratory tests on the gun, the bullets, and the victim lead to the reasoned judgment that the gun was used in the crime. Someone investigating the case might be of the opinion that the suspect is the murderer.

Inference. Scientific reasoning proceeds inductively or deductively. *Inductive reasoning* refers to developing general rules, principles, and concepts from observation and knowledge of specific examples (Pellegrino, 1985). It requires determination of a model and its associated rules of inference (Hunt, 1989). People reason inductively when they extract similarities and differences among specific objects and events and arrive at generalizations, which are tested by applying them to new experiences. Individuals retain their generalizations as long as they are effective, and they modify them when they experience conflicting evidence.

Some of the more common types of tasks used to assess inductive reasoning are *classification, concept,* and *analogy problems.* Consider the following analogy (Pellegrino, 1985):

sugar : sweet :: lemon : _____
yellow sour fruit squeeze tea

The appropriate mental operations represent a type of production system. Initially, the learner mentally represents critical attributes of each term in the analogy. She activates networks in LTM involving each term, which contain critical attributes of the terms to include subordinate and superordinate concepts. Next, she compares the features of the first pair to determine the link. "Sweet" is a property of sugar that involves taste. She then searches the "lemon" network to determine which of the five features listed corresponds in meaning to "lemon" as "sweet" does to "sugar." Although all five terms are most likely stored in her "lemon" network, only "sour" directly involves taste.

Children begin to display basic inductive reasoning around age 8. With development, children can reason faster and with more complex material. This occurs because their LTM networks become more complex and better linked, which in turn reduces the burden on the WM. To help foster inductive thinking, teachers might use a guided discovery approach (Chapter 6) in which children learn different examples and try to formulate a general rule. For example, children may collect leaves and formulate some general principles involving stems, veins, sizes, and shapes of leaves from different trees. Teachers might pose a problem for students, such as "Why does metal sink in water but metal ships float?" Rather than tell students how to solve the problem, the teacher might provide materials and encourage them to formulate and test hypotheses as they work on the task. Phye (1997; Klauer & Phye, 2008) discussed effective teaching methods and programs that have been used to teach inductive reasoning to students.

Deductive reasoning refers to applying inference rules to a formal model of a problem to decide whether specific instances logically follow. When individuals reason deductively, they proceed from general concepts (premises) to specific instances (conclusions) to determine whether the latter follow from the former. A deduction is valid if the premises are true and if the conclusion follows logically from the premises (Johnson-Laird, 1985, 1999).

Linguistic and deductive reasoning processes are intimately linked (Falmagne & Gonsalves, 1995; Polk & Newell, 1995). One type of deduction problem is the *three-term series* (Johnson-Laird, 1972). For example,

> If Karen is taller than Tina, and
> If Mary Beth is not as tall as Tina, then
> Who is the tallest?

The problem-solving processes employed with this problem are similar to those discussed previously. Initially one forms a mental representation of the problem, such as K > T, MB < T. One then works forward by combining the propositions (K > T > MB) to solve the problem. Developmental factors limit children's proficiency in solving such problems. Children may have difficulty keeping relevant problem information in WM and may not understand the language used to express the relationships.

Another type of deductive reasoning problem is the *syllogism*. Syllogisms are characterized by premises and a conclusion containing the words *all, no,* and *some.* The following are sample premises:

> All university professors are lazy.
> Some graduate students are not lazy.
> No undergraduate student is lazy.

A sample syllogism is as follows:

> All the students in Ken's class are good in math.
> All students who are good in math will attend college.
> (Therefore) All the students in Ken's class will attend college.

Researchers debate what mental processes people use to solve syllogisms, including whether people represent the information as Venn (circle) diagrams or as strings of propositions (Johnson-Laird, 1985). A production system analysis of syllogisms gives a basic rule: A syllogism is true only if there is no way to interpret the premises to imply the opposite of the conclusion; that is, a syllogism is true unless an exception to the conclusion can be found. Research needs to examine the types of rules people apply to test whether the premises of a syllogism allow an exception.

Different views have been proposed to explain the mechanisms of deductive reasoning (Johnson-Laird, Byrne, & Tabossi, 1989). One view holds that reasoning proceeds on the basis of formal rules of inference. People learn the rules (e.g., the *modus ponens* rule governs "if p then q" statements) and then match instances to the rules.

A second, related view postulates content-specific rules. They may be expressed as productions such that specific instances trigger the production rules. Thus, a production may involve all cars and may be triggered when a specific car ("my brand X") is encountered.

A third view holds that reasoning depends on semantic procedures that search for interpretations of the premises that are counterexamples to conclusions. According to this view, people construct one or more mental models for the assertions they encounter (interpretations of the premises); the models differ in structure and are used to test the logic of the situation. Students may repeatedly re-encode the problem based on information; thus, deduction largely is a form of verbal reasoning (Polk & Newell, 1995). Johnson-Laird and colleagues (Johnson-Laird, 1999; Johnson-Laird, Byrne, & Schaeken, 1992; Johnson-Laird et al., 1989) have extended this semantic analysis to various classes of inferences (e.g., those involving *if, or, and, not*, and multiple quantifiers). Further research also will help determine instructional implications of these theoretical analyses.

Evaluation. *Evaluation* involves using criteria to judge the adequacy of a problem solution. In evaluating, students address questions such as, "Are the data sufficient to solve the problem?" "Do I need more information?" and "Are my conclusions based on facts, opinions, or reasoned judgments?" Evaluation also involves deciding what ought to happen next—that is, formulating hypotheses about future events assuming that one's problem solving is correct so far.

Deductive reasoning also can be affected by content apart from the logic. Wason (1966) put four cards (showing *A B 2 3*) in front of participants. They were told that each card contained a letter on one side and a number on the other, and they were given a conditional rule: "If a card has *A* on one side, then it has *2* on the other." Their task was to select the cards that needed to be turned over to determine whether the rule was true. Although most participants picked the *A* card and many also chose the *2*, few picked the *3*; however, it must be turned over because if there is an *A* on the other side, then the rule is false. When the content was changed to an everyday generalization (e.g., letter = hair color, number = eye color, *A* = blond hair, *2* = blue eyes), most people made the correct selections (Wason & Johnson-Laird, 1972). These results speak to the importance of not assuming generalization in reasoning but rather giving students experience working on different types of content.

Metacognitive processes enter into all aspects of scientific reasoning. Learners monitor their efforts to ensure that questions are properly posed, that data from adequate sources are available and used to draw inferences, and that relevant criteria are employed in evaluation. Teaching reasoning requires instruction in skills and in metacognitive strategies. Cognitive load also seems important (Chapter 5). Scientific reasoning is difficult if multiple sources of information must be processed simultaneously, which taxes WM. Carlson et al. (2003) found that students' science performance benefited from two procedures designed to reduce cognitive load: diagrams and instructions that minimized the amount of information to be processed at the same time.

Implications for Instruction

The links between learning and problem solving suggest that students can learn heuristics and strategies and become better problem solvers (Bruning et al., 2004). In addition, for information to be linked in memory, it is best to integrate problem solving with academic content (as Meg recommended in the opening scenario) rather than to teach problem solving with stand-alone programs. Nokes, Dole, and Hacker (2007) found that heuristics instruction can be infused into classroom teaching without sacrificing students' content learning.

Andre (1986) listed several suggestions that are derived from theory and research and that are useful for training students in problem-solving skills, especially as they represent productions in memory.

- *Provide students with metaphorical representations.* A concrete analogical passage given to students prior to an instructional passage facilitates learning from the target passage.
- *Have students verbalize during problem solving.* Verbalization of thoughts during problem solving can facilitate problem solutions and learning.
- *Use questions.* Ask students questions that require them to practice concepts they have learned; many such questions may be necessary.
- *Provide examples.* Give students many worked-out examples showing application of problem-solving strategies. Students may have difficulty seeing on their own how strategies apply to situations.
- *Coordinate ideas.* Show how productions and knowledge relate to one another and in what sequence they might need to be applied.
- *Use discovery learning.* Discovery learning often facilitates transfer and problem solving better than expository teaching. Discovery may force students to generate rules from examples. The same can be accomplished through expository teaching, but discovery may lend itself better to certain content (e.g., science experiments).
- *Give a verbal description.* Providing students with a verbal description of the strategy and its rules for application can be helpful.
- *Teach learning strategies.* Learners may need assistance in using effective learning strategies. As discussed in Chapter 9, strategies help learning and problem solving.
- *Use small groups.* A number of studies have found that small-group learning helps develop students' problem-solving skills. Group members must be held accountable for their learning, and all students must share in the work.
- *Maintain a positive psychological climate.* Psychological factors are important to effective problem solving. Minimize excessive anxiety among students and help to create a sense of self-efficacy among students for improving their skills (Chapter 4).

Another instructional suggestion is to phase in problem solving, which may be especially helpful with students who have little experience with it. This can be done by using worked examples (Atkinson, Renkl, & Merrill, 2003; Renkl & Atkinson, 2003; discussed later in this chapter). Mathematics texts, for example, often state a rule or theorem, followed by one or more worked examples. Students then solve comparable problems by applying the steps from the worked examples (a type of analogical reasoning). Renkl and Atkinson recommended reliance on examples in the early stages of learning, followed by a transition to problem solving as students develop skills. This process also helps to minimize demands on WM, or the cognitive load that learners experience (Chapter 5). Thus, the transition might proceed as follows. Initially a complete example is given, then an example where one step is omitted. With each succeeding example an additional step is omitted until the learners reach independent problem solving.

Problem-based learning (*PBL;* Hmelo-Silver, 2004) offers another instructional application. In this approach, students work in groups on a problem that does not have one correct answer. Students identify what they need to know to solve the problem. Teachers act as facilitators by providing assistance but not answers. PBL has been shown to be effective in teaching problem-solving and self-regulation skills, but most research has been conducted in medical and gifted education (Evenson, Salisbury-Glennon, & Glenn, 2001; Hmelo-Silver, 2004). PBL is useful for the exploration of meaningful problems. Because it is time consuming, teachers need to consider its appropriateness given the instructional goals.

TRANSFER

Transfer is a critical topic for learning and relies upon cognitive processes. *Transfer* refers to knowledge being applied in new ways, in new situations, or in familiar situations with different content. Transfer also explains how prior learning affects subsequent learning. Transfer is involved in new learning because students transfer to this situation their prior relevant knowledge and experience (National Research Council, 2000). The cognitive capability for transfer is important, because without it all learning would be situationally specific and much instructional time would be spent reteaching skills in new situations.

There are different types of transfer. *Positive transfer* occurs when prior learning facilitates subsequent learning. Learning how to drive a car with standard transmission should facilitate learning to drive other cars with standard transmission. *Negative transfer* means that prior learning interferes with subsequent learning or makes it more difficult. Learning to drive a standard transmission car might have a negative effect on subsequently learning to drive a car with automatic transmission because one would be apt to hit the phantom clutch and possibly shift gears while the car is moving, which could ruin the transmission. *Zero transfer* means that one type of learning has no noticeable influence on subsequent learning. Learning to drive a standard transmission car should have no effect on learning to operate a computer.

Current cognitive conceptions of learning highlight the complexity of transfer (Phye, 2001). Although some forms of simple skill transfer seem to occur automatically, much transfer requires higher-order thinking skills and beliefs about the usefulness of knowledge. This section begins with a brief overview of historical perspectives on transfer, followed by a discussion of cognitive views and the relevance of transfer to school learning.

Historical Views

Identical Elements. Conditioning theories (Chapter 3) stress that transfer depends on identical elements or similar features (stimuli) among situations. Thorndike (1913b) contended that transfer occurs when situations have identical elements (stimuli) and call for similar responses. A clear and known relation must exist between the original and transfer tasks, as is often the case between drill/practice and homework.

This view is intuitively appealing. Students who learn to solve the problem $602 - 376 = ?$ are apt to transfer that knowledge and also solve the problem $503 - 287 = ?$ We might ask, however, what elements are, and how similar they must be to be considered identical. In subtraction, do the same types of numbers need to be in the same column? Students who can solve the problem $42 - 37 = ?$ will not necessarily be able to solve the problem $7428 - 2371 = ?$, even though the former problem is contained within the latter one. Findings such as this call into question the validity of identical elements. Furthermore, even when identical elements exist, students must recognize them. If students believe no commonality exists between situations, no transfer will occur. The identical elements position, therefore, is inadequate to explain all transfer.

Mental Discipline. Also relevant to transfer is the *mental discipline* doctrine (Chapter 3), which holds that learning certain subjects (e.g., mathematics, the classics) enhances general mental functioning and facilitates learning of new content better than does learning other subjects. This view was popular in Thorndike's day and periodically reemerges in the form of recommendations for basic or core skills and knowledge (e.g., Hirsch, 1987).

Research by Thorndike (1924) provided no support for the mental discipline idea (Chapter 3). Instead, Thorndike concluded that what facilitates new learning is students' beginning level of mental ability. Students who were more intelligent when they began a course gained the most from the course. The intellectual value of studies reflects not how much they improve students' ability to think but rather how they affect students' interests and goals.

Generalization. Skinner (1953) propounded another view of transfer. According to operant conditioning theory, transfer involves *generalization* of responses from one discriminative stimulus to another. Thus, students might be taught to put their books in their desks when the bell rings. When students go to another class, putting books away when the bell rings might generalize to the new setting.

The notion of generalization, like identical elements, has intuitive appeal. Surely some transfer occurs through generalization, and it may even occur automatically. Students who are punished for misbehavior in one class may not misbehave in other classes. Once drivers learn to stop their cars at a red light, then that response will generalize to other red lights regardless of location, weather, time of day, and so forth.

Nonetheless, the generalization position has problems. As with identical elements, we can ask what features of the situation are used to generalize responses. Situations share many common features, yet we respond only to some of them and disregard others. We respond to the red light regardless of many other features in the situation. At the same time, we might be more likely to run a red light when no other cars are around or when we are in a hurry. Our response is not fixed but rather depends on our cognitive assessment of the situation. The same can be said of countless other situations where generalization does not occur automatically. Cognitive processes are involved in most generalization as people determine whether responding in similar fashion is appropriate in that setting. The generalization position, therefore, is incomplete because it neglects the role of cognitive processes.

Activation of Knowledge in Memory

In information processing theory (Chapter 5), transfer involves activating knowledge in memory networks. It requires that information be cross-referenced with propositions linked in memory (Anderson, 1990; Gagné et al., 1993). The more links between bits of information in memory, the likelier that activating one piece of information will cue other information in memory. Such links can be made within and between networks.

The same process is involved in transfer of procedural knowledge and productions (Bruning et al., 2004). Transfer occurs when knowledge and productions are linked in LTM with different content. Students must also believe that productions are useful in various situations. Transfer is aided by the uses of knowledge being stored with the knowledge itself. For example, learners may possess a production for skimming text. This may be linked in memory with other reading procedures (e.g., finding main ideas, sequencing) and may have various uses stored with it (e.g., skimming web page text to get the gist, skimming memos to determine meeting place and time). The more links in LTM and the more uses stored with skimming, the better the transfer. Such links are formed by having students practice skills in various settings and by helping them understand the uses of knowledge.

This cognitive description of transfer fits much of what we know about cued knowledge. Where more LTM links are available, accessing information in different ways is possible. We may not be able to recall the name of Aunt Martha's dog by thinking about her (cuing the "Aunt Martha" network), but we might be able to recall the name by thinking about (cuing) breeds of dogs ("collie"). Such cuing is reminiscent of the experiences we periodically have of not being able to recall someone's name until we think about that person from a different perspective or in a different context.

At the same time, we still do not know many things about how such links form. Links are not automatically made simply by pointing out uses of knowledge to students or having them practice skills in different contexts (National Research Council, 2000). Different forms of transfer, governed by different conditions, exist.

Types of Transfer

Research indicates that transfer is not a unitary phenomenon but rather is complex (Barnett & Ceci, 2002; Table 7.4). One distinction is between near and far transfer (Royer,

Table 7.4

Types of transfer.

Type	Characteristics
Near	Much overlap between situations; original and transfer contexts are highly similar
Far	Little overlap between situations; original and transfer contexts are dissimilar
Literal	Intact skill or knowledge transfers to a new task
Figural	Use of some aspects of general knowledge to think or learn about a problem, such as with analogies or metaphors
Low road	Transfer of well-established skills in spontaneous and possibly automatic fashion
High road	Transfer involving abstraction through an explicit conscious formulation of connections between situations
Forward reaching	Abstracting behavior and cognitions from the learning context to one or more potential transfer contexts
Backward reaching	Abstracting in the transfer context features of the situation that allow for integration with previously learned skills and knowledge

1986). *Near transfer* occurs when situations overlap a great deal, such as between the stimulus elements during instruction and those present in the transfer situation. An example is when fraction skills are taught and then students are tested on the content in the same format in which it was taught. In contrast, *far transfer* involves a transfer context much different from that in which original learning occurred. An example would be applying fraction skills in an entirely different setting without explicitly being told to do so. Thus, students might have to add parts of a recipe (1/2 cup milk and 1/4 cup water) to determine the amount of liquid without being told the task involves fractions.

Another distinction is between literal and figural transfer. *Literal transfer* involves transfer of an intact skill or knowledge to a new task (Royer, 1986). Literal transfer occurs when students use fraction skills in and out of school. *Figural transfer* refers to using some aspect of our general knowledge to think or learn about a particular problem. Figural transfer often involves using analogies, metaphors, or comparable situations. Figural transfer occurs when students encounter new learning and employ the same study strategies that they used to master prior learning in a related area. Figural transfer requires drawing an analogy between the old and new situations and transferring that general knowledge to the new situation.

Although some overlap exists, the forms of transfer involve different types of knowledge. Near transfer and literal transfer involve primarily declarative knowledge and mastery of basic skills. Far transfer and figurative transfer involve declarative and procedural knowledge, as well as conditional knowledge concerning the types of situations in which the knowledge may prove useful (Royer, 1986).

Salomon and Perkins (1989) distinguished low-road from high-road transfer. *Low-road transfer* refers to transfer of well-established skills in a spontaneous and perhaps automatic fashion. In contrast, *high-road transfer* is abstract and mindful; it "involves the explicit conscious formulation of abstraction in one situation that allows making a connection to another" (Salomon & Perkins, 1989, p. 118).

Low-road transfer occurs with skills and actions that have been practiced extensively in varied contexts. The behaviors tend to become performed automatically in response to characteristics of a situation that are similar to those of the situation in which they were acquired. Examples are learning to drive a car and then driving a different but similar car, brushing one's teeth with a regular toothbrush and with an electric toothbrush, or solving algebra problems at school and at home. At times the transfer may occur with little conscious awareness of what one is doing. The level of cognitive activity increases when some aspect of the situation differs and requires attention. Thus, most people have little trouble accommodating to features in rental cars. When features differ (e.g., the headlight control works differently or is in a different position from what one is used to), people have to learn them.

High-road transfer occurs when students learn a rule, principle, prototype, schema, and so forth, and then use it in a more general sense than how they learned it. Transfer is mindful because students do not apply the rule automatically. Rather, they examine the new situation and decide what strategies will be useful to apply. Abstraction is involved during learning and later when students perceive basic elements in the new problem or situation and decide to apply the skill, behavior, or strategy. Low-road transfer primarily involves declarative knowledge, and high-road transfer uses productions and conditional knowledge to a greater extent.

Salomon and Perkins (1989) distinguished two types of high-road transfer—forward reaching and backward reaching—according to where the transfer originates. *Forward-reaching transfer* occurs when one abstracts behavior and cognitions from the learning context to one or more potential transfer contexts. For example, while students are studying precalculus, they might think about how some of the material (e.g., limits) might be pertinent in calculus. Another example is while being taught in a class how a parachute works, students might think about how they will use the parachute in actually jumping from an airplane.

Forward-reaching transfer is proactive and requires self-monitoring of potential contexts and uses of skills and knowledge. To determine potential uses of precalculus, for example, learners must be familiar with other content knowledge of potential contexts in which knowledge might be useful. Forward-reaching transfer is unlikely when students have little knowledge about potential transfer contexts.

In *backward-reaching transfer*, students abstract in the transfer context features of the situation that allow for integration with previously learned ideas (Salomon & Perkins, 1989). While students are working on a calculus problem, they might try to think of any situations in precalculus that could be useful for solving the calculus problem. Students who have difficulty learning new material employ backward-reaching transfer when they think back to other times when they experienced difficulty and ask what they did in those situations (e.g., seek help from friends, go to the library, reread the text, talk with the teacher). They then might be apt to implement one of those solutions in hopes of remedying their current difficulty. Analogical reasoning might involve backward-reaching transfer, as students apply steps from the original problem to the current one. Consistent with the effects of analogical reasoning on learning, Gentner, Loewenstein, and Thompson (2003) found that analogical reasoning enhanced transfer, especially when two original cases were presented together.

Earlier we noted that transfer involves linked information in LTM such that the activation of one item can cue other items. Presumably low-road transfer is characterized by relatively automatic cuing. A central distinction between the two forms is degree of mindful abstraction, or the volitional, metacognitively guided employment of nonautomatic processes (Salomon & Perkins, 1989). Mindful abstraction requires that learners not simply act based on the first possible response, but rather that they examine situational cues, define alternative strategies, gather information, and seek new connections between information. LTM cuing is not automatic with high-road transfer but rather deliberate, and can result in links being formed in LTM as individuals think of new ways to relate knowledge and contexts.

Anderson, Reder, and Simon (1996) contended that transfer is more likely when learners attend to the cues that signal the appropriateness of using a particular skill. They then will be more apt to notice those cues on transfer tasks and employ the skill. In this sense, the learning and transfer tasks share symbolic elements. These shared elements are important in strategy transfer.

Strategy Transfer

Transfer applies to strategies as well as to skills and knowledge (Phye, 2001). An unfortunate finding of much research is that students learn strategies and apply them effectively but fail to maintain their use over time or generalize them beyond the instructional setting. This is a common issue encountered in problem solving (Jonassen & Hung, 2006). Many factors impede strategy transfer, including not understanding that the strategy is appropriate for different settings, not understanding how to modify its use with different content, believing that the strategy is not as useful for performance as other factors (e.g., time available), thinking that the strategy takes too much effort, or not having the opportunity to apply the strategy with new material (Borkowski & Cavanaugh, 1979; Dempster & Corkill, 1999; Paris et al., 1983; Pressley et al., 1990; Schunk, 1991; Schunk & Rice, 1993).

Phye (1989, 1990, 1992, 2001; Phye & Sanders, 1992, 1994) developed a model useful for enhancing strategy transfer and conducted research testing its effectiveness. During the initial acquisition phase, learners receive instruction and practice to include assessment of their metacognitive awareness of the uses of the strategy. A later retention phase includes further practice on training materials and recall measures. The third transfer phase occurs when participants attempt to solve new problems that have different surface characteristics but that require the same solution strategy practiced during training. Phye also stressed the role of learner motivation for transfer and ways to enhance motivation by showing learners uses of knowledge. Motivation is a critical influence on transfer (National Research Council, 2000; Pugh & Bergin, 2006).

In one study in which adults worked on verbal analogy problems, some received corrective feedback during trials that consisted of identifying the correct solutions, whereas others were given advice concerning how to solve analogies. All students judged confidence in the correctness of solutions they generated. During training, corrective feedback was superior to advice in promoting transfer of problem-solving skills; however, on a delayed transfer task, no difference occurred between conditions. Regardless of condition, confidence in problem-solving capabilities bore a positive relation to actual performance.

Transfer of problem-solving strategies requires knowledge of the strategy plus conditional knowledge of the uses of the strategy, which is facilitated when learners explain the strategy as they acquire it (Crowley & Siegler, 1999). In addition, feedback about how the strategy helps improve performance facilitates strategy retention and transfer (Phye & Sanders, 1994; Schunk & Swartz, 1993a, 1993b). Phye's research highlights the link of strategy transfer with information processing and the key roles played by practice, corrective feedback, and motivation. It also underscores the point that teaching students self-regulated learning strategies can facilitate transfer (Fuchs et al., 2003a; Fuchs, Fuchs, Finelli, Courey, & Hamlett, 2004; Chapter 9).

Teaching for Transfer

Although different forms of transfer may be distinct, they often work in concert. While working on a task, some behaviors may transfer automatically whereas others may require mindful application. For example, assume that Jeff is writing a short paper. In thinking through the organization, Jeff might employ high-road, backward-reaching transfer by thinking about how he organized papers in previous, similar situations. Many aspects of the task, including word choice and spellings, will occur automatically (low-road transfer).

As Jeff writes, he also might think about how this information could prove useful in other settings. Thus, if the paper is on some aspect of the Civil War, Jeff might think of how to use this knowledge in history class. Salomon and Perkins cited another example involving chess masters, who accumulate a repertoire of configurations from years of play. Although some of these may be executed automatically, expert play depends on mindfully analyzing play and potential moves. It is strategic and involves high-road transfer.

In some situations, low-road transfer could involve a good degree of mindfulness. With regard to strategy transfer, even minor variations in formats, contexts, or requirements can make transfer problematic among students, especially among those who experience learning problems (Borkowski & Cavanaugh, 1979). Conversely, some uses of analogical reasoning can occur with little conscious effort if the analogy is relatively clear. A good rule is never to take transfer for granted; it must be directly addressed.

This raises the issue of how teachers might encourage transfer in students. A major goal of teaching is to promote long-term retention and transfer (Halpern & Hakel, 2003). We know that having students practice skills in varied contexts and ensuring that they understand different uses for knowledge builds links in LTM (Anderson, Reder, & Simon, 1996). Homework is a mechanism for transfer because students practice and refine, at home, skills learned in school. Research shows a positive relation between homework and student achievement with the relation being stronger in grades 7–12 than in grades K–6 (Cooper, Robinson, & Patall, 2006).

But students do not automatically transfer strategies for the reasons noted earlier. Practice addresses some of these concerns, but not others. Cox (1997) recommended that as students learn in many contexts, they should determine what they have in common. More complex skills, such as comprehension and problem solving, will probably benefit most from this situated cognition approach (Griffin, 1995). Motivation should be addressed (Pugh & Bergin, 2006). Teachers may need to provide students with explicit motivational feedback that links strategy use with improved performance and provides information about how the strategy will prove useful in that setting. Studies show that such motivational feedback enhances strategy use, academic performance, and self-efficacy for performing well (Schunk & Rice, 1993). At the Nikowsky Middle School, teachers combined cognitive strategy instruction with motivational factors to enhance students' problem solving.

Establishing academic goals (another motivational variable), the attainment of which requires careful deliberation and use of available resources, also should help students. By cuing students at appropriate times, teachers may help them use relevant knowledge in new ways. Teachers might ask a question such as, "What do you know that might help you in this situation?" Such cuing tends to be associated with greater generation of ideas. Teachers can serve as models for transfer. Modeling strategies that bring related knowledge to bear on a new situation encourages students to seek ways to enhance transfer in both forward- and backward-reaching fashion and feel more efficacious about doing so. Working with children in grades 3–5 during mathematical problem solving, Rittle-Johnson (2006) found that having children explain how answers were arrived at and whether they were correct promoted transfer of problem-solving strategies. Application 7.7 discusses teaching for transfer.

APPLICATION 7.7
Teaching for Transfer

Kathy Stone helps students build on the knowledge they already have learned. She has her students recall the major points of each page of a story in their reading book before they write a summary paragraph about the story. She also reviews with them how to develop a complete paragraph. Building on former learning helps her children transfer knowledge and skills to a new activity.

In preparing for a class discussion about influential presidents of the United States,

Jim Marshall sends a study sheet home with his students asking them to list presidents that they feel had a major impact on American history. He instructs them not only to rely on what has been discussed in class, but also to rely on knowledge they have from previous courses or other readings and research they have done. He encourages students to pull the information together from the class discussion and incorporate the former learning into the learning that occurs from new material presented.

TECHNOLOGY AND INSTRUCTION

The last few years have witnessed a rapid explosion of technology in instruction through electronic and distance learning (Bernard et al., 2009; Brown, 2006; Campbell, 2006; Clark, 2008; Jonassen, 1996; Jonassen et al., 1999; Larreamendy-Joerns & Leinhardt, 2006; Roblyer, 2006; Winn, 2002). Technology often is equated with equipment (e.g., computers), but its meaning is much broader. *Technology* refers to the designs and environments that engage learners (Jonassen et al., 1999). Research on the effects of technology on learning is increasing, as are efforts to remove barriers to infusing technology into instruction (Ertmer, 1999).

Technology has the potential to facilitate instruction in ways that formerly were unimaginable. Not long ago technological classroom applications were limited to movies, televisions, slide projectors, radios, and the like. Today, students can experience simulations of environments and events that they never could in regular classes, receive instruction from and communicate with others at long distances, and interact with large knowledge bases and expert tutoring systems.

A challenge for researchers is to determine how technology affects learners' cognitive processes during encoding, retention, transfer, problem solving, and so forth. The material in this section on computer-based learning environments and distance education is not a practical guide on how to use technology in education. Rather, this section focuses on the role that technology plays in learning. Readers interested in in-depth applications of technology should consult other sources (Brown, 2006; Kovalchick & Dawson, 2004a, 2004b; Roblyer, 2006; Winn, 2002).

Computer-Based Learning Environments

Students increasingly are learning in computer-based environments. Researchers are highly interested in the roles that computers play in teaching and learning. Although learning in computer-based environments is not a theory of learning, it is important to know whether computers improve school achievement and help develop critical thinking and problem-solving skills.

It is tempting to evaluate computer-based learning by comparing it to learning not involving computers, but such comparisons can be misleading because other factors (e.g., authenticity of the content, teacher-student/student-student interactions) also may differ. Rather than focusing on this issue, it seems more productive to examine the types of cognitive processes that can occur in computer-based environments and from other technological applications.

Jonassen et al. (1999) presented a dynamic perspective on the role of technology in learning. The maximum benefits of technology derive when it energizes and facilitates thinking and knowledge construction. In this conceptualization, technology can serve the functions shown in Table 7.5. The technological applications relevant to learning described in this section are differentially effective in accomplishing these functions.

Computer-Based Instruction. Until a few years ago, when it was supplanted by the Internet, *computer-based instruction (CBI)* (or *CAI—computer-assisted instruction*) was the most common application of computer learning in schools (Jonassen, 1996). CBI is often used for drills and tutorials (Chapter 3), which present information and feedback to students and respond based on students' answers.

Although CBI is limited in what it can do, several CBI features are firmly grounded in learning theory and research (Lepper, 1985). The material can command students' attention and provide immediate response feedback. Feedback can be of a type not often given in the classroom, such as how students' present performances compare with their prior performances (to show progress in learning). Computers individualize content and rate of presentation.

Another advantage of CBI is that many programs allow personalization; students enter information about themselves, parents, and friends, which is then included in the instructional presentation. Personalization can produce higher achievement than other formats (Anand & Ross, 1987). Personalizing instruction may improve meaningfulness

Table 7.5
Functions of technology.

- *Tool* to support knowledge construction
- *Information vehicle* for exploring knowledge to support learning by constructing
- *Context* to support learning by doing
- *Social medium* to support learning by conversing
- *Intellectual partner* to support learning by reflecting

(Jonassen et al., 1999)

and facilitate integration of content into LTM networks. Knowledge construction should be aided with familiar referents.

Simulations and Games. *Simulations* represent real or imaginary situations that cannot be brought into the learning setting. Examples are programs simulating the flights of aircraft, underwater expeditions, and life in a fictional city. Learners can build memory networks better when they have tangible referents during learning. *Games* are designed to create an enjoyable learning context by linking material with sport, adventure, or fantasy. Games can emphasize thinking skills and problem solving but also can be used to teach content (e.g., basketball game to teach fractions).

Lepper (1985; Lepper & Hodell, 1989) suggested that games also influence learning by increasing motivation. Motivation is greater when an *endogenous* (natural) relationship exists between the content and the means ("special effects") by which the game or simulation presents the content. Fractions are endogenously related to a basketball game, for example, when students are asked to determine how much of the court is covered by players dribbling down the floor. Such an endogenous relationship enhances meaningfulness and LTM coding and storage. In many games and simulations, however, the relation between content and means is arbitrary, such as when a student's correct response to a question produces fantasy elements (e.g., cartoon characters). When the relation is arbitrary, the game does not produce better learning than traditional instruction, although the former may be more interesting.

As a type of computer-based environment, simulations seem well suited for discovery and inquiry learning (Chapter 6). In their review of studies using computer simulations in discovery learning, de Jong and van Joolingen (1998) concluded that simulations were more effective than traditional instruction in inculcating students' "deep" (intuitive) cognitive processing. Simulations also may be beneficial for developing problem-solving skills. Similar to the results for CBI, Moreno and Mayer (2004) found that personalized messages from an on-screen agent during simulations improved retention and problem solving better than did nonpersonalized messages. Woodward, Carnine, and Gersten (1988) found that the addition of computer simulations to structured teaching produced problem-solving gains for special-education high school students compared with traditional instruction alone. The authors noted, however, that the mechanism producing these results was unclear, and the results may not generalize to stand-alone computer simulations.

Multimedia/Hypermedia. *Multimedia* refers to technology that combines the capabilities of various media such as computers, film, video, sound, music, and text (Galbreath, 1992); *hypermedia* refers to linked or interactive media (Roblyer, 2006). Multimedia and hypermedia learning occurs when students interact with information presented in more than one mode (e.g., words and pictures; Mayer, 1997). The capabilities of computers to interface with other media have advanced rapidly. Video streaming, CDs, and DVDs are commonly used with computers for instructional purposes (Hannafin & Peck, 1988; Roblyer, 2006).

Multimedia and hypermedia have important implications for teaching because they offer many possibilities for infusing technology into instruction (Roblyer, 2006). Research evidence provides some support for the benefits of multimedia for learning. In his review of research studies, Mayer (1997) found that multimedia enhanced students' problem solving and transfer; however, effects were strongest for students with little prior knowledge and high spatial ability. Dillon and Gabbard (1998) also concluded from their review that effects depended in part on ability: Students with lower general ability had the greatest difficulty with multimedia. Learning style was important: Students willing to explore obtained the greatest benefits. Multimedia seems especially advantageous on specific tasks requiring rapid searching through information.

Researchers have investigated the conditions favoring learning from multimedia. When verbal and visual (e.g., narration and animation) information are combined during instruction, students benefit from dual coding (Paivio, 1986; Chapter 5). The simultaneous presentation helps learners form connections between words and pictures because they are in WM at the same time (Mayer, Moreno, Boire, & Vagge, 1999). Multimedia may facilitate learning better than tailoring media to individual student differences (Reed, 2006). By using different media, teachers increase the likelihood that at least one type will be effective for every student. Some instructional devices that assist multimedia learning are: text signals that emphasize the structure of the content and its relationship to other material (Mautone & Mayer, 2001); personalized messages that address students and make them feel like participants in the lesson (Mayer, Fennell, Farmer, & Campbell, 2004; Moreno & Mayer, 2000); allowing learners to exercise control over the pace of instruction (Mayer & Chandler, 2001); animations that include movement and simulations (Mayer & Moreno, 2002); being able to interact with an on-screen speaker (Mayer, Dow, & Mayer, 2003); taking a practice test on the material (Johnson & Mayer, 2009); and being exposed to a human rather than a machine-generated speaker (Mayer, Sobko, & Mantone, 2003).

Maximal benefits of multimedia require that some logistical and administrative issues be addressed. Interactive capabilities are expensive to develop and produce, although they are very effective (Moreno & Mayer, 2007). Costs may prohibit many school systems from purchasing components. Interactive video may require additional instruction time because it presents more material and requires greater student time. But interactive multimodal learning environments provide great potential for increasing students' motivation (Scheiter & Gerjets, 2007). The greater amount of learner control that is possible yields better benefits on learning and can foster self-regulation (Azevedo, 2005b; Chapter 9).

Despite potential issues involving costs and technological skills needed, multimedia and hypermedia seem to benefit student learning, and research increasingly is showing that this technology can help to develop students' self-regulated learning (Azevedo, 2005a, 2005b; Azevedo & Cromley, 2004; Azevedo, Guthrie, & Siebert, 2004). Applications will continue to be developed as the technology advances (Roblyer, 2006). Further research is needed on multimedia's effects on motivation and how to link it with a sequence of acquiring self-regulatory skills (e.g., social influence to self-influence; Zimmerman & Tsikalas, 2005; Chapter 9).

E-learning. *E-learning* refers to learning through electronically delivered means. The term often is used to refer to any type of electronic communication (e.g., videoconferencing, e-mail); however, here it is used in the narrower sense of Internet (Web-based) instruction.

The *Internet* (an international collection of computer networks) is a system of shared resources that no one owns. The Internet provides access to other people (users) through e-mail and conferences (chat rooms), files, and the World Wide Web (WWW)—a multi-computer interactive multimedia resource. It also stores information that can be copied for personal use.

The Internet is a wonderful resource for information, but the relevant issue here is its role in learning. On the surface, the Internet has advantages. Web-based instruction provides students with access to more resources in less time than is possible in traditional ways; however, more resources do not automatically mean better learning. The latter is accomplished only if students acquire new skills, such as methods for conducting research on a topic or critical thinking about the accuracy of material on the Web. Web resources also can promote learning when students take information from the Web and incorporate it into classroom activities (e.g., discovery learning; Chapter 6).

Teachers can assist the development of students' Internet skills with scaffolding (Chapter 6). Students must be taught search strategies (e.g., ways to use browsers), but teachers also might conduct the initial Web search and provide students with names of helpful websites. Grabe and Grabe (1998) offer other suggestions. Applications involving technology in classroom instruction are given in Application 7.8.

A danger in students using the Internet is that the large array of information available could inculcate the belief that everything is important and reliable. Students then may engage in "associative writing" by trying to include too much information in reports and papers. To the extent that e-learning helps teach students the higher-level skills of analysis and synthesis, they will acquire strategies for determining what is important and merging information into a coherent product.

Distance Learning

Distance learning (distance education) occurs when instruction that originates in one location is transmitted to students at one or more remote sites. Interactive capabilities allow two-way feedback and discussions to become part of the learning experience. Distance learning saves time, effort, and money because instructors and students do not have to make long journeys to classes. Universities, for example, can recruit students from a wide geographical area. There is less concern about the students traveling great distances to attend classes. School districts can conduct in-service programs by transmitting from a central site to all of the schools. Distance learning sacrifices face-to-face contact with instructors, although if two-way interactive video is used the interactions are real-time (synchronous). In their review of distance education programs, Bernard et al. (2004) found their effects on student learning and retention comparable to those of traditional instruction. Effects for synchronous instruction favored classroom instruction, whereas distance education was more effective for asynchronous applications (involving lag time).

Another networking application is the *electronic bulletin board (conference)*. People networked with computers can post messages, but more important for learning can be part of a discussion (chat) group. Participants ask questions and raise issues, as well as respond to the comments of others. A fair amount of research has examined whether such exchanges facilitate writing skill acquisition (Fabos & Young, 1999).

APPLICATION 7.8
Technology and Learning

Technological applications can be applied effectively to help improve student learning. Jim Marshall works with an American history teacher in a neighboring high school in developing a Civil War computer simulation. The classes draw straws to determine which class will be the Union and which the Confederacy. The students in each class then study the battles of the Civil War and look for information about the terrain, the weather at the time of each battle, the number of soldiers involved, and the leadership abilities of the individuals in charge. The students in both classes then simulate the battles on the computer, interacting with each other, using the data, trying to see if they might change the outcome of the original battle. When students make a strategic move, they have to defend and support their move with historical data.

Gina Brown uses streaming video and the Web to have her students study and reflect on educational psychology principles applied in classrooms. As students observe the video of an elementary class lesson, they stop the video and enter responses to relate educational practices to psychological principles they have been discussing in class. Then students are able to interact with other students and with her to share thoughts on the lesson observed. She also has a fictional classroom set up on a website. She poses questions to her students (e.g., "How might the teacher use authentic assessment in science?"), after which they go to the website, read and reflect, and construct a response that is distributed to her and all other students. Thus, everyone can respond and interact with others.

Kathy Stone uses her computers for various activities in her third-grade class, but one of the fun activities that incorporates creative writing abilities and word-processing skills becomes a class project each month. At the beginning of each month, Mrs. Stone starts a story on the computer entitled, "The Adventures of Mrs. Stone's Class." Children have the opportunity to add to the story as often as they wish. At the end of the month, they print the story and read it aloud in class. The computer provides a unique means for constructing a story collaboratively.

Whether this asynchronous means of telecommunication exchange promotes learning any better than face-to-face interaction is problematic because much of the research is conflicting or inconclusive (Fabos & Young, 1999); however, the review by Bernard et al. (2004) suggests that distance education may be more effective with asynchronous learning. Telecommunication has the benefit of convenience in that people can respond at any time, not just when they are gathered together. The receptive learning environment may indirectly promote learning.

Being forms of *computer-mediated communication (CMC)*, distance learning and computer conferencing greatly expand the possibilities for learning through social interaction. Further research is needed to determine whether personal characteristics of learners and types of instructional content can affect students' learning and motivation.

Web-based (online) learning is commonly incorporated into traditional instruction as a *blended* model of instruction (i.e., some face-to-face instruction and the rest via online). Web-based learning also is useful in conjunction with multimedia projects. In many teacher preparation programs, preservice teachers use the Web to obtain resources and then selectively incorporate these into multimedia projects as part of lesson designs.

In their review of online courses, Tallent-Runnels et al. (2006) found that students liked moving at their own pace, students with more computer experience expressed greater satisfaction, and asynchronous communication facilitated in-depth discussions. Distance education that incorporates interactions (student–student, student–teacher, student–content) helps to increase student achievement (Bernard et al., 2009). Other types of interactions (e.g., wikis, blogs) also may be useful. Infusing multimedia presentations into distance education increases its personalization and thus makes it more akin to face-to-face instruction (Larreamendy-Joerns & Leinhardt, 2006), which may increase student motivation.

Attempting to compare online with traditional courses is difficult because there are so many differences, one of which is that, to date, most online courses have enrolled largely nontraditional and White American students. This demographic will change as online courses become more prevalent, which will permit better assessment of online learning outcomes and environmental characteristics that facilitate learning.

Future Directions

From the preceding evidence, we can conclude that technology can enhance learning. How technologically enhanced instruction compares with conventional instruction is difficult to assess, and comparisons can present misleading results (Oppenheimer, 1997). No one instructional medium is consistently superior to others, regardless of content, learners, or setting (Clark & Salomon, 1986). Technology is not a cause of learning; rather, it is a means for applying principles of effective instruction and learning.

Clark and Salomon (1986) recommended that researchers determine the conditions under which computers facilitate instruction and learning. This is still true today and may be said for technology in general. Use of technology should depend on the learning goals. Although technology has the potential to foster different learning goals, it may not be the best way to promote student interaction through peer teaching, group discussions, or cooperative learning.

More research evaluating the effectiveness of computer-based learning environments and distance education clearly is needed. Some research shows that computer-based problem solving is differentially effective for male and female students (Littleton, Light, Joiner, Messer, & Barnes, 1998). Exploring gender and ethnic differences should be a research priority.

Another area that needs to be addressed is the motivational effects of technology on teachers and students (Ertmer, 1999; Lepper & Gurtner, 1989). Lepper and Malone (1987) noted that computers can focus attention on the task through motivational enhancements, maintain level of arousal at an optimal level, and direct students to engage in task-directed information processing rather than attend to focusing on irrelevant task aspects. The idea is that effective motivational principles can enhance deep (rather than shallow) processing (Hooper & Hannafin, 1991).

Predicting the future of technology in education is difficult. A few years ago, few would have predicted that laptops would supplant desktops or that handheld devices may eventually supplant laptops. As technology becomes more elaborate, it will offer a far greater range of instructional possibilities (Brown, 2006). We will be able to access and create knowledge in new, sophisticated ways. Research will explore the effects of these developments on student learning, as well as effective ways to infuse technology into instruction.

Exciting developments are likely on several fronts (Roblyer, 2006). Wireless connectivity now is common, which greatly expands the convenience of using laptops in instruction. Wireless and the portability of devices (e.g., laptops, handheld devices) help instructors infuse technology into instruction. The merging of technologies will continue (e.g., cell phones that can perform multiple functions), which may ultimately lead to students requiring minimal hardware to perform different applications. Technological advances will continue to improve accessibility for persons with disabilities, and assistive technology should become more common in schools. Distance education and online learning opportunities will increase. Today we have virtual universities and high schools, which may be expanded to earlier levels (e.g., middle, elementary grades). Finally, as the convenience of technology continues to improve, we may see a gradual moving away from traditional instruction and toward a model containing fewer class meetings and more electronic communications.

At a basic research level, investigations on artificial intelligence (AI) may provide important insights into human learning, thinking, and problem solving. *Artificial intelligence* refers to computer programs that simulate human abilities to infer, evaluate, reason, solve problems, understand speech, and learn (Trappl, 1985). John McCarthy coined the term in 1956 as a conference theme.

Expert systems are an application of AI. *Expert systems* are large computer programs that supply the knowledge and problem-solving processes of one or more experts (Anderson, 1990; Fischler & Firschein, 1987). Analogous to human consultants, expert systems have been applied to diverse fields such as medicine, chemistry, electronics, and law. Expert systems have a vast knowledge base consisting of declarative knowledge (facts) and procedural knowledge (system of rules used to draw inferences). An interface poses questions to users and gives recommendations or solutions. A common application of expert systems is to teach by providing expertise to students. Instruction often employs guided discovery; students formulate and test hypotheses and experience consequences.

Future expert systems will be applied to a wider array of domains. One challenge is to improve systems' capabilities to understand natural languages, especially speech. Although expert systems can perform pattern-recognition tasks, most of these tasks involve only visual stimuli. But voice recognition systems continue to improve. The use of assistive technology in education is expanding, as students with disabilities are integrated as much as possible in regular classroom instruction. Expert systems should enhance the capabilities of computers such that they will be accessible to all learners (e.g., auditory, visual, multiple handicaps).

AI holds exciting possibilities for helping us understand human thought processes. This application involves programming computers with some knowledge and rules that allow them to alter and acquire new knowledge and rules based on experiences. In concept learning, for example, a computer might be programmed with an elementary rule and then be exposed to instances and noninstances of the concept. The program modifies itself by storing the new information in memory and altering its rule. Learning also can occur from exposure to case histories. A computer can be programmed with facts and case histories of a disease. As the computer analyzes these histories, it alters its memory to incorporate the etiology, symptoms, and course of the disease. When the computer acquires an extensive knowledge base for a particular disease, it can diagnose future cases with precision.

INSTRUCTIONAL APPLICATIONS

Several instructional applications have been given in this chapter for the principles covered. This section describes three additional applications that reflect many of the principles discussed in this chapter: worked examples, writing, and mathematics.

Worked Examples

Worked examples, which were discussed briefly in Chapter 4, present step-by-step problem solutions and often include accompanying diagrams. They portray an expert's problem-solving model for learners to study before they begin to emulate it. A worked example is shown in Figure 7.3 (Glover, Ronning, & Bruning, 1990).

Worked examples reflect Anderson's ACT-R theory (Lee & Anderson, 2001) and are especially appropriate for complex forms of learning, such as algebra, physics,

Problem Statement: Find the Square Root of 7,225

Steps		Algorithm	
1.		$\sqrt{7225}$	
2.		$\sqrt{72.25}$	Mark off in units of two from the decimal point.
3.	8 x 8	$\begin{array}{r} 8 \\ \sqrt{72.25} \\ \underline{64} \\ 825 \end{array}$	Find the largest perfect square in the two numbers to the left of the decimal. Subtract from 72 and "bring down" the next two numbers.
4.	160	$\begin{array}{r} 8 \\ \sqrt{72.25} \\ \underline{64} \\ 825 \end{array}$	Double the 8 and add a zero. Use the number (160) as a trial divisor: 825 divided by 160 = 5, plus a remainder.
5.	165 x 5	$\begin{array}{r} 8\,5 \\ \sqrt{72.25} \\ \underline{64} \\ 825 \\ \underline{825} \end{array}$	Substitute the 5 for the zero and multiply (165 x 5). Product equals 825. Solution achieved.

Figure 7.3
Sample worked example.

and geometry (Atkinson et al., 2000, 2003). Applying the novice–expert model, researchers have found that experts typically focus on deeper (structural) aspects of problems and that novices more often deal with surface features. Practice alone is less effective in promoting skills than is practice coupled with worked examples (Atkinson et al., 2000).

Worked examples seem most beneficial with students in the early stages of skill acquisition, as opposed to proficient learners who are refining skills. Its applicability is seen clearly in the four-stage model of skill acquisition within the ACT-R framework (Anderson, Fincham, & Douglass, 1997; Chapter 5). In stage 1 learners use analogies to relate examples to problems to be solved. In stage 2 they develop abstract declarative rules through practice. During stage 3, performance becomes quicker and smoother as aspects of problem solution become automatized. By stage 4 learners have in memory many types of problems and can retrieve the appropriate solution strategy quickly when confronted with a problem. Use of worked examples is best suited for stage 1 and early stage 2 learners. During later stages, people benefit from practice to hone their strategies, although even at advanced stages, studying solutions of experts can be helpful.

A key instructional issue is how to integrate the components of an example, such as diagram, text, and aural information. It is imperative that a worked example not overload the learner's WM, which multiple sources of information presented simultaneously can do. Stull and Mayer (2007) found that providing graphic organizers (similar to worked examples) produced better problem-solving transfer than did allowing learners to construct their own. The latter task may have produced excessive cognitive load (Chapter 5). Other evidence shows that worked examples can reduce cognitive load (Renkl, Hilbert, & Schworm, 2009).

Research supports the prediction that dual presentation facilitates learning better than single-mode presentation (Atkinson et al., 2000; Mayer, 1997). This result is consistent with dual-coding theory (Paivio, 1986; Chapter 5), with the caveat that too much complexity is not desirable. Similarly, examples intermixed with subgoals help create deep structures and facilitate learning.

A key point is that examples that include multiple presentation modes should be unified so that learners' attention is not split across nonintegrated sources. Aural and verbal explanations should indicate to which aspect of the example they refer, so learners do not have to search on their own. Subgoals should be clearly labeled and visually isolated in the overall display.

A second instructional issue concerns how examples should be sequenced. Research supports the conclusions that two examples are superior to a single one, that varied examples are better than two of the same type, and that intermixing examples and practice is more effective than a lesson that presents examples followed by practice problems (Atkinson et al., 2000). Gradually fading out worked examples in an instructional sequence is associated with better student transfer of learning (Atkinson et al., 2003).

Chi, Bassok, Lewis, Reimann, and Glaser (1989) found that students who provided *self-explanations* while studying examples subsequently achieved at higher levels compared with students who did not self-explain. Presumably the self-explanations helped students understand the deep structure of the problems and thereby encode it more

Table 7.6
Suggestions for using worked examples in instruction.

- Present examples in close proximity to problems students will solve.
- Present multiple examples showing different types of problems.
- Present information in different modalities (aural, visual).
- Indicate subgoals in examples.
- Ensure that examples present all information needed to solve problems.
- Teach students to self-explain examples, and encourage self-explanations.
- Allow sufficient practice on problem types so students refine skills.

meaningfully. Self-explanation also is a type of rehearsal, and the benefit of rehearsal on learning is well established. Thus, students should be encouraged to self-explain while studying worked examples, such as by verbalizing subgoals.

Another issue is that worked examples can produce passive learning since learners may process them superficially. Including interactive elements, such as by providing prompts or leaving gaps that learners must complete, leads to more active cognitive processing and learning (Atkinson & Renkl, 2007). Animations also are helpful (Wouters, Paas, & van Merriënboer, 2008).

In summary, there are several features that when incorporated with worked examples help learners create cognitive schemas to facilitate subsequent achievement (Table 7.6). These instructional strategies are best employed during the early stages of skill learning. Through practice, the initial cognitive representations should evolve into the refined schemas that experts employ.

Writing

Writing reflects many of the cognitive processes discussed in this chapter. Good writers are not born but developed; effective instruction is critical for the development of writing skills (Graham, 2006; Harris, Graham, & Mason, 2006; Scardamalia & Bereiter, 1986; Sperling & Freedman, 2001).

Contemporary models examine writers' mental processes as they engage in different aspects of writing (Byrnes, 1996; de Beaugrande, 1984; Graham, 2006; Mayer, 1999; McCutchen, 2000). A research goal is to define expertise. By comparing expert writers with novices, researchers identify how their mental processes diverge (Bereiter & Scardamalia, 1986).

Flower and Hayes (1980, 1981a; Hayes, 1996; Hayes & Flower, 1980) formulated a model that reflects the general problem-solving framework developed by Newell and Simon (1972). Writers define a problem space and perform operations on their mental representation of the problem to attain their goals. Key components of this model are the rhetorical problem, planning, organizing, goal setting, translating, and reviewing.

The *rhetorical problem* includes the writer's topic, intended audience, and goals. The rhetorical problem for students often is well defined. Teachers assign a term paper topic, the audience is the teacher, and the goal (e.g., to inform, to persuade) is provided;

however, the rhetorical problem is never defined completely by someone other than the writer. Writers interpret problems in their own ways.

The writer's LTM plays a crucial role. Writers differ in their knowledge of the topic, audience, and mechanics (e.g., grammar, spelling, punctuation). Writers knowledgeable about their topics include fewer irrelevant statements but more auxiliary statements (designed to elaborate upon main points) compared with less knowledgeable writers (Voss, Vesonder, & Spilich, 1980). Differences in declarative knowledge affect the quality of writing.

Planning involves forming an internal representation of knowledge to be used in composing. The internal representation generally is more abstract than the actual writing. Planning includes several processes such as generating ideas by retrieving relevant information from memory or other sources. These ideas may be well formed or fragmentary.

There are wide individual differences in planning. Children's writing typically resembles "knowledge telling" (McCutchen, 1995; Scardamalia & Bereiter, 1982). They often follow a "retrieve and write" strategy by accessing LTM with a cue and writing what they know. Children do little planning and reviewing and much translating. Whereas older writers also retrieve content from LTM, they do it as part of planning, after which they evaluate its appropriateness prior to translating. Children's retrieval and translating are integrated in seamless fashion (Scardamalia & Bereiter, 1986).

Young children produce fewer ideas than older ones (Scardamalia & Bereiter, 1986). They benefit from prompting (e.g., "Can you write some more?"). Englert, Raphael, Anderson, Anthony, and Stevens (1991) showed that fourth and fifth graders' writing improved when they were exposed to teachers who modeled metacognitive components (e.g., which strategies were useful, when and why they were useful) and when they were taught to generate questions during planning. Older and better writers make greater use of internal prompts. They search relevant topics in LTM and assess knowledge before they begin composing. Teachers can foster idea generation by cueing students to think of ideas (Bruning et al., 2004).

Organizing is conveyed through cohesion among sentence parts and coherence across sentences. Cohesive devices tie ideas together with pronouns, definite articles, conjunctions, and word meanings. Young children have more difficulty with cohesion, but unskilled writers of any age use cohesion less well. Developmental differences also are found in coherence. Young and poor writers have difficulty linking sentences with one another and with the topic sentence (McCutchen & Perfetti, 1982).

A major subprocess is *goal setting*. Goals are substantive (what the writer wants to communicate) and procedural (how to communicate or how points should be expressed). Good writers often alter their goals based on what they produce. Writers have goals in mind prior to writing, but as they proceed, they may realize that a certain goal is not relevant to the composition. New goals are suggested by actual writing.

The primary goal of skilled writers is to communicate meaning, whereas poor writers often practice *associative writing* (Bereiter, 1980). They may believe the goal of writing is to regurgitate everything they know about the topic; order is less important than inclusiveness. Another goal of less-skilled writers is to avoid making errors. When asked to critique their own writing, good writers focus on how well they communicated their intentions, whereas poor writers cite surface considerations (e.g., spelling, punctuation) more often.

Translation refers to putting one's ideas into print. For children and inexperienced writers, translating often overburdens WM. They must keep in mind their goal, the ideas they wish to express, and the necessary organization and mechanics. Good writers concern themselves less with surface features during translation; they focus more on meaning and correct surface problems later. Poor writers concentrate more on surface features and write more slowly than good writers. Better writers take stylistic and surface considerations into account when they pause during writing. Poorer writers benefit when they read what they have written as they prepare to compose.

Reviewing consists of evaluating and revising. Reviewing occurs when writers read what they have written as a precursor to further translation or systematic evaluation and revision (Flower & Hayes, 1981a; Hayes & Flower, 1980). During reviewing, writers evaluate and modify plans and alter subsequent writing.

These processes are important because writers may spend as much as 70% of their writing time pausing (Flower & Hayes, 1981b), much of which is spent on sentence-level planning. Writers reread what they have written and decide what to say next. These bottom-up processes construct a composition a section at a time. When such building up is accomplished with the overall plan in mind, the composition continues to reflect the writers' goals.

Poor writers typically depend on bottom-up writing. While pausing, good writers engage in rhetorical planning not directly linked to what they have produced. This type of planning reflects a top-down view of writing as a problem-solving process; writers keep an overall goal in mind and plan how to attain it or decide that they need to alter it. Planning includes content (deciding what topic to discuss) and style (deciding to alter the style by inserting an anecdote). This planning subsumes sentence-level planning and is characteristic of mature writers (Bereiter & Scardamalia, 1986).

Children may do little revising without teacher or peer support (Fitzgerald, 1987). Students benefit from instruction designed to improve the quality of their writing. Fitzgerald and Markham (1987) gave average sixth-grade writers instruction on types of revisions: additions, deletions, substitutions, and rearrangements. The teacher explained and modeled each revision strategy, after which students worked in pairs (peer conferences). Instruction improved students' knowledge of revision processes and their actual revisions. Beal, Garrod, and Bonitatibus (1990) found that teaching third- and sixth-grade children a self-questioning strategy (e.g., "What is happening in the story?") led to significantly greater text revising.

Evaluation skills develop earlier than revision skills. Even when fourth graders recognize writing problems, they may not successfully correct them as often as 70% of the time (Scardamalia & Bereiter, 1983). When children correct problems, poor writers revise errors in spelling and punctuation, whereas better writers revise for stylistic reasons (Birnbaum, 1982).

Given the complexity of writing, the course of skill acquisition is better characterized as the development of fluency rather than automaticity (McCutchen, 1995). Automatic processes become routinized and require few attentional or WM resources, whereas fluent processes—although rapid and resource efficient—are thoughtful and can be altered "online." Good writers follow plans but revise them as they write. Were this process automatic, writers' plans—once adopted—would be followed without interruption.

APPLICATION 7.9
Writing

Teachers can incorporate planning, transcribing, and revising activities into lessons. If Kathy Stone wanted her third-grade students to write a paragraph describing their summer vacations, she might have students share what they did during the summer. Following this large-group activity, she and the children might jointly develop and edit a paragraph about the teacher's summer vacation. This exercise would emphasize the important elements of a good paragraph and components of the writing process.

Students then could be paired and share orally with each other some things done during the summer. Sharing helps students generate ideas to use in transcribing. Following this activity, children can write their summer activities. For the transcribing, students will use their lists to formulate sentences of a paragraph and share their written products with their partners. Partners will provide feedback about clarity and grammar, after which students revise their paragraphs.

The faculty sponsor of the high school yearbook can incorporate planning, transcribing, and revising activities into producing the yearbook. When the sponsor meets with the students, the sponsor and the students generate sections and topics to be covered (e.g., school news highlights, sports, clubs), as well as who will be responsible for each section. Then the students work in teams to transcribe and revise their articles with input from the sponsor.

Gina Brown works with members of her class as they write their first research paper. She has each student select a topic, develop a basic outline, and compile a list of possible sources, after which she meets with students individually. Then she has students begin the first draft of the paper, giving more attention to the introduction and conclusion. She meets again with students individually to discuss their first drafts and progress and guides them toward what should be done to complete the finished product.

Although component skills of writing (i.e., spelling, vocabulary) often become automatic, the overall process does not. Some classroom applications are given in Application 7.9.

Mathematics

Mathematics has been a fertile area of cognitive and constructivist research (Ball, Lubienski, & Mewborn, 2001; National Research Council, 2000; Newcombe et al., 2009; Schoenfeld, 2006; Voss et al., 1995). Researchers have explored how learners construct knowledge, how experts and novices differ, and which methods of instruction are most effective (Byrnes, 1996; Mayer, 1999; Schoenfeld, 2006). The improvement of instruction is important given that so many students have difficulty learning mathematics.

A distinction typically is made between mathematical *computation* (use of rules, procedures, and algorithms) and *concepts* (problem solving and use of strategies). Computational and conceptual problems require students to implement productions involving rules and algorithms. The difference between these two categories lies in how explicitly the problem tells students which operations to perform. The following are computational problems.

- $26 + 42 = ?$
- $5x + 3y = 19$
  $7x - y = 11$

Solve for x and y.

- What is the length of the hypotenuse of a right triangle with sides equal to 3 and 4 inches?

Although students are not explicitly told what to do in problems 2 and 3, recognition of the problem format and knowledge of procedures lead them to perform the correct operations.

Now contrast those problems with the following:

- Alex has 20 coins composed of dimes and quarters. If the quarters were dimes and the dimes were quarters, he would have 90 cents more than he has now. How much money does Alex have?
- If a passenger train takes twice as long to pass a freight train, after it first overtakes the freight train, as it takes the two trains to pass when going in opposite directions, how many times faster than the freight train is the passenger train?
- When she hikes, Shana can average 2 mph going uphill and 6 mph going downhill. If she goes uphill and downhill and spends no time at the summit, what will be her average speed for an entire trip?

These word problems do not explicitly tell students what to do, but they require computations no more difficult than those needed in the first set. Solving word problems involves recognizing their problem formats, generating appropriate productions, and performing the computations.

This is not to suggest that conceptual expertise is better than computational proficiency, although Rittle-Johnson and Alibali (1999) found that conceptual understanding had a greater influence on procedural knowledge than did the reverse. Deficiencies in either area cause problems. Understanding how to solve a problem but not being able to perform the computations results in incorrect answers, as does being computationally proficient but not being able to conceptualize problems.

Computation. The earliest computational skill children use is *counting* (Byrnes, 1996; Resnick, 1985). Children count objects on their fingers and in their heads using a strategy (Groen & Parkman, 1972). The *sum model* involves setting a hypothetical counter at zero, counting in the first addend in increments of one, and then counting in the second addend to arrive at the answer. For the problem "2 + 4 = ?" children might count from 0 to 2 and then count out 4 more. A more efficient strategy is to set the counter at the first addend (2) and then count in the second addend (4) in increments of one. Still more efficient is the *min model:* Set the counter at the larger of the two addends (4) and then count in the smaller addend (2) in increments of one (Romberg & Carpenter, 1986).

These types of invented procedures are successful. Children and adults often construct procedures to solve mathematical problems. Errors generally are not random but rather reflect *buggy algorithms*, or systematic mistakes in thinking and reasoning (Brown & Burton, 1978). Buggy algorithms reflect the constructivist assumption that students form procedures based on their interpretation of experiences (Chapter 6). A common mistake in subtraction is to subtract the smaller number from the larger number in each column, regardless of direction, as follows:

$$\begin{array}{r} 53 \\ -27 \\ \hline 34 \end{array} \qquad \begin{array}{r} 602 \\ -274 \\ \hline 472 \end{array}$$

Mathematical bugs probably develop when students encounter new problems and incorrectly generalize productions. In subtraction without regrouping, for example, students subtract the smaller number from the larger one column by column. It is easy to see how they could generalize this procedure to problems requiring regrouping. Buggy algorithms are durable and can instill in students a false sense of self-efficacy (Chapter 4), perhaps because their computations produce answers.

Another source of computational difficulties is poor declarative knowledge of number facts. Many children do not know basic facts and show deficiencies in numerical processing (Geary, Hoard, Byrd-Craven, Nugent, & Numtee, 2007). Until facts become established in LTM through practice, children count or compute answers. Speed of fact retrieval from memory relates directly to overall mathematical achievement in students from elementary school through college (Royer, Tronsky, Chan, Jackson, & Marchant, 1999). Computational skill improves with development, along with WM and LTM capabilities (Mabbott & Bisanz, 2003).

Many difficulties in computation result from using overly complex but technically correct productions to solve problems. Such procedures produce correct answers, but because they are complex, the risk of computational errors is high. The problem 256 divided by 5 can be solved by the division algorithm or by successively subtracting 5 from 256 and counting the number of subtractions. The latter procedure is technically correct but inefficient and has a high probability of error.

Learners initially represent computational skill as declarative knowledge in a propositional network. Facts concerning the different steps (e.g., in the algorithm) are committed to memory through mental rehearsal and overt practice. The production that guides performance at this stage is general; for example: "If the goal is to solve this division problem, then apply the method the teacher taught us." With added practice, the declarative representation changes into a domain-specific procedural representation and eventually becomes automated. Early counting strategies are replaced with more-efficient rule-based strategies (Hopkins & Lawson, 2002). At the automatic stage, learners quickly recognize the problem pattern (e.g., division problem, square root problem) and implement the procedure without much conscious deliberation.

Problem Solving. Problem solving requires that students first accurately represent the problem to include the given information and the goal and then select and apply a problem-solving strategy (Mayer, 1985, 1999). Translating a problem from its linguistic representation to a mental representation is often difficult (Bruning et al., 2004). The more abstract the language, the more difficult the text comprehension and the lower the likelihood of solution (Cummins, Kintsch, Reusser, & Weimer, 1988). Students who have difficulty comprehending show poorer recall of information and lower performance. This is especially true for younger children, who have difficulty translating abstract linguistic representations.

Translation also requires good declarative and procedural knowledge. Solving the earlier problem about Alex with 20 coins requires knowledge that dimes and quarters are coins, that a dime is one-tenth ($0.10) of $1, and that a quarter is one-fourth ($0.25) of $1. This declarative knowledge needs to be coupled with procedural understanding that dimes and quarters are variables such that the number of dimes plus the number of quarters equals 20.

One reason experts translate problems better is that their knowledge is better organized in LTM; the organization reflects the underlying structure of the subject matter (Romberg & Carpenter, 1986). Experts overlook surface features of a problem and analyze it in terms of the operations required for solution. Novices are swayed more by surface features. Silver (1981) found that good problem solvers organized problems according to the process required for solution, whereas poor problem solvers were more likely to group problems with similar content (e.g., money, trains).

In addition to problem translation and classification, experts and novices differ in productions (Greeno, 1980). Novices often adopt a working backward strategy, beginning with the goal and working their way back to the givens. This is a good heuristic useful in the early stages of learning when learners have acquired some domain knowledge but are not competent enough to recognize problem formats quickly.

In contrast, experts often work forward. They identify the problem type and select the appropriate production to solve the problem. Hegarty, Mayer, and Monk (1995) found that successful problem solvers used a problem model approach, translating the problem into a mental model in which the numbers in the problem statement were tied to their variable names. In contrast, less successful solvers were more likely to employ a direct translation approach, combining the numbers in the problem with the arithmetic operations primed by the key words (e.g., addition is the operation linked with the key word "more"). The latter strategy is superficial and based on surface features, whereas the former strategy is linked better with meanings.

Experts develop sophisticated procedural knowledge for classifying mathematical problems according to type. High school algebra problems fall into roughly 20 general categories, such as motion, current, coins, and interest/investment (Mayer, 1992). These categories can be aggregated into six major groups. For example, the amount-per-time group includes motion, current, and work problems. These problems are solvable with the general formula: amount = rate × time. The development of mathematical problem-solving expertise depends on classifying a problem into the correct group and then applying the strategy. Verbalizing steps in problem solving aids the development of proficiency (Gersten et al., 2009). Application 7.10 discusses teaching problem solving.

APPLICATION 7.10
Mathematical Problem Solving

Teachers use various ways to help students improve problem-solving skills. As students solve mathematical word problems, they can state each problem in their own words, draw a sketch, decide what information is relevant, and state the ways they might solve the problem. Kathy Stone could use these and other similar questions to help focus her third-grade students' attention on important task aspects and guide their thinking:

- What information is important?
- What information is missing?
- Which formulas are necessary?
- What is the first thing to do?

Constructivism. Many theorists contend that constructivism (Chapter 6) represents a viable model for explaining how mathematics is learned (Ball et al., 2001; Cobb, 1994; Lampert, 1990; Resnick, 1989). Mathematical knowledge is not passively absorbed from the environment, but rather is constructed by individuals as a consequence of their interactions. This construction process also includes children's inventing of procedures that incorporate implicit rules.

The following unusual example illustrates rule-based procedural invention. Some time ago I was working with a teacher to identify children in her class who might benefit from additional instruction in long division. She named several students and said that Tim also might qualify, but she was not sure. Some days he worked his problems correctly, whereas other days his work was incorrect and made no sense. I gave him problems to solve and asked him to verbalize while working because I was interested in what children thought about while they solved problems. This is what Tim said: "The problem is 17 divided into 436. I start on the side of the problem closest to the door . . ." I then knew why on some days his work was accurate and on other days it was not. It depended on which side of his body was closest to the door!

The process of constructing knowledge begins in the preschool years (Resnick, 1989). Geary (1995) distinguished *biologically primary* (biologically based) from *biologically secondary* (culturally taught) *abilities*. Biologically primary abilities are grounded in neurobiological systems that have evolved in particular ecological and social niches and that serve functions related to survival or reproduction. They should be seen cross-culturally, whereas biologically secondary abilities should show greater cultural specificity (e.g., as a function of schooling). Furthermore, many of the former should be seen in very young children. Indeed, counting is a natural activity that preschoolers do without direct teaching (Gelman & Gallistel, 1978; Resnick, 1985). Even infants may be sensitive to different properties of numbers (Geary, 1995). Preschoolers show increasing numerical competence involving the concepts of part–whole additivity and changes as increases/decreases in quantities. Conceptual change proceeds quickly during the elementary years (Resnick, 1989). Teaching children to use schematic diagrams to represent word problems facilitates problem solving (Fuson & Willis, 1989).

Mathematical competence also depends on sociocultural influence (Cobb, 1994; Chapter 6). Vygotsky (1978) stressed the role of competent other persons in the *zone of proximal development (ZPD)*. In contrast to the constructivist emphasis on cognitive reorganizations among individual students, sociocultural theorists advocate cultural practices—especially social interactions (Cobb, 1994). The sociocultural influence is incorporated through such activities as peer teaching, instructional scaffolding, and apprenticeships.

Research supports the idea that social interactions are beneficial. Rittle-Johnson and Star (2007) found that seventh graders' mathematical proficiency was enhanced when they were allowed to compare solution methods with partners. Results of a literature review by Springer, Stanne, and Donovan (1999) showed that small-group learning significantly raised college students' achievement in mathematics and science. Kramarski and Mevarech (2003) found that combining cooperative learning with metacognitive instruction (e.g., reflect on relevant concepts, decide on appropriate strategies to use) raised eighth graders' mathematical reasoning more than either procedure alone. In addition to these benefits of cooperative learning (Stein & Carmine, 1999), the literature on peer and cross-age tutoring in mathematics reveals that it is effective in raising children's achievement (Robinson, Schofield, & Steers-Wentzell, 2005). Coordination of the constructivist and sociocultural perspectives is possible; students can develop knowledge through social interactions but then idiosyncratically construct uses of that knowledge.

SUMMARY

Cognitive and constructivist learning processes apply to basic forms of learning, but they assume greater significance in complex learning. Developing competence in an academic domain requires knowledge of the facts, principles, and concepts of that domain, coupled with general strategies that can be applied across domains and specific strategies that pertain to each domain. Research has identified many differences between experts and novices in a given domain.

Conditional knowledge is knowing when and why to employ declarative and procedural knowledge. Simply knowing what to do and how to do it does not produce success. Students also must understand when knowledge and procedures are useful. Conditional knowledge most likely is stored in LTM as propositions linked with other declarative and procedural knowledge. Metacognition refers to deliberate, conscious control of mental activities. Metacognition includes knowledge and monitoring activities designed to ensure that tasks are completed successfully. Metacognition begins to develop around ages 5 to 7 and continues throughout schooling. One's metacognitive awareness depends on task, strategy, and learner variables. Learners benefit from instruction on metacognitive activities.

Concept learning involves higher-order processes of forming mental representations of critical attributes of categories. Current theories emphasize analyzing features and forming hypotheses about concepts (feature analysis), as well as forming generalized images of concepts that include only some defining features (prototypes). Prototypes may be used to classify typical instances of concepts, and feature analysis may be used for less typical ones. Models of concept acquisition and teaching have been proposed, and motivational processes also are involved in conceptual change.

Problem solving consists of an initial state, a goal, subgoals, and operations performed to attain the goal and subgoals. Researchers have examined the mental processes of learners engaged in problem solving and the differences between experts and novices. Problem solving has been viewed as reflecting trial and error, insight, and heuristics. These general approaches can be applied to academic content. As people gain experience in a domain, they acquire knowledge and production systems, or sets of rules to apply strategically to accomplish goals. Problem solving requires forming a mental representation of the problem and applying a production to solve it. With well-defined problems where potential solutions can be ordered in likelihood, a generate-and-test strategy is useful. For more difficult or less well-defined problems, means–ends analysis is used, which requires working backward or forward. Other problem-solving strategies involve analogical reasoning and brainstorming.

Transfer is a complex phenomenon. Historical views include identical elements, mental discipline, and generalization. From a cognitive perspective, transfer involves activation of memory structures and occurs when information is linked. Distinctions are drawn between near and far, literal and figural, and low-road and high-road transfer. Some forms of transfer may occur automatically, but much is conscious and involves abstraction. Providing students with feedback on the usefulness of skills and strategies makes transfer more likely to occur.

Technology continues to increase in importance in learning and instruction. Two areas that have seen rapid growth are computer-based learning environments and distance learning. Applications involving computer-based environments include computer-based instruction, games and simulations, hypermedia/multimedia, and e-learning. Distance learning occurs when instruction originates in one location and is transmitted to students at one or more remote sites. Interactive capabilities allow two-way feedback and synchronous discussions. Distance learning often involves online (Web-based) asynchronous instruction, and courses can be organized using a blended model (some face-to-face and some online instruction). Research shows benefits of technology on metacognition, deep processing, and problem solving. Future innovations will result in greater accessibility and interactive capabilities.

Applications involving the principles summarized in this chapter include worked examples, writing, and mathematics. Worked examples present problem solutions in step-by-step fashion and often include accompanying diagrams. Worked examples incorporate many features that facilitate learners' problem solving. Writing requires composing and reviewing. Experts plan text around a goal of communicating meaning and keep the goal in mind during reviewing. Novices tend to write what they can recall about a topic rather than focusing on their goal. Children display early mathematical competence with counting. Computational skills require algorithms and declarative knowledge. Students often overgeneralize procedures (buggy algorithms). Students acquire knowledge of problem types through experience. Experts recognize types and apply the correct productions to solve them (working forward). Novices work backward by applying formulas that include quantities given in the problem.

FURTHER READING

Brown, J. S. (2006). New learning environments for the 21st century: Exploring the edge. *Change, 38*(5), 18–24.

Halpern, D. F., & Hakel, M. D. (2003). Applying the science of learning to the university and beyond: Teaching for long-term retention and transfer. *Change, 35*(4), 36–41.

Isaksen, S. G., & Gaulin, J. P. (2005). A reexamination of brainstorming research: Implications for research and practice. *Gifted Child Quarterly, 49,* 315–329.

Kuhn, D. (1999). A developmental model of critical thinking. *Educational Researcher, 28*(2), 16–25, 46.

Lajoie, S. P. (2003). Transitions and trajectories for studies of expertise. *Educational Researcher, 32*(8), 21–25.

Medin, D. L., Lynch, E. B., & Solomon, K. O. (2000). Are there kinds of concepts? *Annual Review of Psychology, 51,* 121–147.

Pintrich, P. R., Marx, R. W., & Boyle, R. A. (1993). Beyond cold conceptual change: The role of motivational beliefs and classroom contextual factors in the process of conceptual change. *Review of Educational Research, 63,* 167–199.

8

Motivation

Kerri Townsend, an elementary teacher, has been working with her students on subtraction with regrouping. In teaching the concept, she used everyday examples, cutouts, and manipulatives, to help spark students' interest. Now the students are solving problems at their desks, and Kerri is walking around, talking with students individually and checking their work.

The first student she checks on is Margaret, who feels she is not very good in math. Kerri says to Margaret, "Margaret, you got them all correct. You're really getting good at this. That should make you feel good. I know that you'll keep doing well in math this year."

Next is Derrick, who's having a hard time concentrating and hasn't done much work. Kerri says to him, "Derrick, I know you can do much better. See how well Jason is working. (Jason and Derrick are friends.) I know that you can work just as well and do great on these problems. Let's try."

Jared likes to do better than others. As Kerri approaches, Jared says to her, "Ms. Townsend, see how good I'm doing, better than most others." Kerri says, "Yes, you are doing very well. But instead of thinking about how others are doing, think about how you're doing. See, you can do these problems now, and just a few weeks ago you couldn't. So you really have learned a lot."

As Kerri approaches Amy, she sees that Amy is wasting time. "Amy, why aren't you working better?" Amy replies, "I don't like these problems. I'd rather be working on the computer." Kerri replies, "You'll get your chance for that. I know that you can work better on these, so let's try to finish them before the end of the period. I think you'll like subtraction more when you see how well you can solve the problems."

Matt enjoys learning and is a very hard worker. As Kerri comes up to his desk, Matt is working hard on the problems. Unfortunately he's also making some mistakes. Kerri gives him feedback, showing him what he's doing correctly and what he needs to correct. Then she says, "Matt, you're a hard worker. I know that if you keep working on these, you will learn how to do them. I'm sure that soon you'll find that you can do them easier."

Kerri has been working with Rosetta on setting goals for completing her work accurately. Rosetta's goal is to complete her work with at least 80% accuracy. Earlier in the year Rosetta averaged only about 30% accuracy. Kerri checks her work and says, "Rosetta, I'm so proud of you. You did 10 problems and got 8 of them completely correct, so you made your goal. See how much better you're doing now than before? You're getting much better in math!"

We have seen throughout this text that much human learning—regardless of content—has common features. Learning begins with the knowledge and skills that learners bring to the situation, which they expand and refine as a function of learning. Learning involves the use of cognitive strategies and processes such as attention, perception, rehearsal, organization, elaboration, storage, and retrieval.

This chapter discusses motivation—a topic intimately linked with learning. *Motivation* is the process of instigating and sustaining goal-directed behavior (Schunk et al., 2008). This is a cognitive definition because it postulates that learners set goals and employ cognitive processes (e.g., planning, monitoring) and behaviors (e.g., persistence, effort) to attain their goals. Although behavioral views of motivation are reviewed, the bulk of this chapter is devoted to cognitive perspectives.

As with learning, motivation is not observed directly, but rather inferred from behavioral indexes such as verbalizations, task choices, and goal-directed activities. Motivation is an explanatory concept that helps us understand why people behave as they do.

Although some simple types of learning can occur with little or no motivation, most learning is motivated. Students motivated to learn attend to instruction and engage in such activities as rehearsing information, relating it to previously acquired knowledge, and asking questions. Rather than quit when they encounter difficult material, motivated students expend greater effort. They choose to work on tasks when they are not required to do so; in their spare time they read books on topics of interest, solve problems and puzzles, and work on computer projects. In short, motivation engages students in activities that facilitate learning. Teachers understand the importance of motivation for learning, and—as the opening scenario shows—do many things to raise student motivation.

This chapter begins by discussing some historical views of motivation; the remainder of the chapter covers cognitive perspectives. Key motivational processes are explained and linked to learning. Topics covered are achievement motivation theory, attribution theory, social cognitive theory, goal theory, perceptions of control, self-concept, and intrinsic motivation. The chapter concludes with some educational applications.

When you finish studying this chapter, you should be able to do the following:

■ Briefly discuss some important historical theories of motivation: drive, conditioning, cognitive consistency, humanistic.

■ Sketch a model of motivated learning, and describe its major components.

■ Explain the major features in a current model of achievement motivation.

■ Discuss the causal dimensions in Weiner's attribution theory and the effects they have in achievement situations.

■ Explain how the social cognitive processes of goals and expectations can be formed and interact to affect motivation.

■ Distinguish between learning (process) and performance (product) goals, and explain how they can influence motivation and learning.

- Explain the potential effects of perceived control on learning, behavior, and emotions.

- Define self-concept, and explain the major factors that affect its development.

- Distinguish intrinsic from extrinsic motivation and the conditions under which

rewards may increase or decrease intrinsic motivation.

- Discuss educational applications involving achievement motivation, attributions, and goal orientations.

HISTORICAL PERSPECTIVES

We begin by discussing historical perspectives on motivation. Whereas some variables included in historical theories are not relevant to current theories, historical views helped set the stage for current cognitive theories, and several historical ideas have contemporary relevance.

Some early views reflected the idea that motivation results primarily from *instincts*. Ethologists, for example, based their ideas on Darwin's theory, which postulates that instincts have survival value for organisms. Energy builds within organisms and releases itself in behaviors designed to help species survive. Others have emphasized the individual's need for *homeostasis*, or optimal levels of physiological states. A third perspective involves *hedonism*, or the idea that humans seek pleasure and avoid pain. Although each of these views may explain some instances of human motivation, they are inadequate to account for a wide range of motivated activities, especially those that occur during learning. Readers interested in these views should consult other sources (Petri, 1986; Schunk et al., 2008; Weiner, 1992).

Four historical perspectives on motivation with relevance to learning are drive theory, conditioning theory, cognitive consistency theory, and humanistic theory.

Drive Theory

Drive theory originated as a physiological theory; eventually, it was broadened to include psychological needs. Woodworth (1918) defined *drives* as internal forces that sought to maintain homeostatic body balance. When a person or animal is deprived of an essential element (e.g., food, air, water), this activates a drive that causes the person or animal to respond. The drive subsides when the element is obtained.

Much of the research that tested predictions of drive theory was conducted with laboratory animals (Richter, 1927; Woodworth & Schlosberg, 1954). In these experiments, animals often were deprived of food or water for some time, and their behaviors to get food or water were assessed. For example, rats might be deprived of food for varying amounts of time and placed in a maze. The time that it took them to run to the end to receive food was measured. Not surprisingly, response strength (running speed) normally varied directly with the number of prior reinforcements and with longer deprivation up to 2 to 3 days, after which it dropped off because the animals became progressively weaker.

Hull (1943) broadened the drive concept by postulating that physiological deficits were primary needs that instigated drives to reduce the needs. *Drive (D)* was the motivational force that energized and prompted people and animals into action. Behavior that obtained reinforcement to satisfy a need resulted in *drive reduction*. This process is as follows:

$$\text{Need} \rightarrow \text{Drive} \rightarrow \text{Behavior}$$

Hull (1943) defined *motivation* as the "initiation of learned, or habitual, patterns of movement or behavior" (p. 226). He believed that innate behaviors usually satisfied primary needs and that learning occurred only when innate behaviors proved ineffective. *Learning* represented one's adaptation to the environment to ensure survival.

Hull also postulated the existence of *secondary reinforcers* because much behavior was not oriented toward satisfying primary needs. Stimulus situations (e.g., work to earn money) acquired secondary reinforcing power by being paired with primary reinforcement (e.g., money buys food).

Drive theory generated much research as a consequence of Hull's writings (Weiner, 1992). As an explanation for motivated behavior, drive theory seems best applied to immediate physiological needs; for example, one lost in a desert is primarily concerned with finding food, water, and shelter. Drive theory is not an ideal explanation for much human motivation. Needs do not always trigger drives oriented toward need reduction. Students hastily finishing an overdue term paper may experience strong symptoms of hunger, yet they may not stop to eat because the desire to complete an important task outweighs a physiological need. Conversely, drives can exist in the absence of biological needs. A sex drive can lead to promiscuous behavior even though sex is not immediately needed for survival.

Although drive theory may explain some behaviors directed toward immediate goals, many human behaviors reflect long-term goals, such as finding a job, obtaining a college degree, and sailing around the world. People are not in a continuously high drive state while pursuing these goals. They typically experience periods of high, average, and low motivation. High drive is not conducive to performance over lengthy periods and especially on complex tasks (Broadhurst, 1957; Yerkes & Dodson, 1908). In short, drive theory does not offer an adequate explanation for academic motivation.

Conditioning Theory

Conditioning theory (Chapter 3) explains motivation in terms of responses elicited by stimuli (classical conditioning) or emitted in the presence of stimuli (operant conditioning). In the *classical conditioning model*, the motivational properties of an unconditioned stimulus (UCS) are transmitted to the conditioned stimulus (CS) through repeated pairings. Conditioning occurs when the CS elicits a conditioned response (CR) in the absence of the UCS. This is a passive view of motivation, because it postulates that once conditioning occurs, the CR is elicited when the CS is presented. As discussed in Chapter 3, conditioning is not an automatic process, but rather depends on information conveyed to the individual about the likelihood of the UCS occurring when the CS is presented.

In *operant conditioning*, motivated behavior is an increased rate of responding or a greater likelihood that a response will occur in the presence of a stimulus. Skinner (1953) contended that internal processes accompanying responding are not necessary to explain behavior. Individuals' immediate environment and their history must be examined for the causes of behavior. Labeling a student "motivated" does not explain why the student works productively. The student is productive because of prior reinforcement for productive work and because the current environment offers effective reinforcers.

Ample evidence shows that reinforcers can influence what people do; however, what affects behavior is not reinforcement but rather are beliefs about reinforcement. People engage in activities because they believe they will be reinforced and value that reinforcement (Bandura, 1986). When reinforcement history conflicts with current beliefs, people act based on their beliefs (Brewer, 1974). By omitting cognitive elements, conditioning theories offer an incomplete account of human motivation.

Cognitive Consistency Theory

Cognitive consistency theory assumes that motivation results from interactions of cognitions and behaviors. This theory is *homeostatic* because it predicts that when tension occurs among elements, the problem needs to be resolved by making cognitions and behaviors consistent with one another. Two prominent perspectives are balance theory and dissonance theory.

Balance Theory. Heider (1946) postulated that individuals have a tendency to cognitively balance relations among persons, situations, and events. The basic situation involves three elements, and relations can be positive or negative.

For example, assume the three elements are Janice (teacher), Ashley (student), and chemistry (subject). Balance exists when relations among all elements are positive; Ashley likes Janice, Ashley likes chemistry, Ashley believes Janice likes chemistry. Balance also exists with one positive and two negative relations: Ashley does not like Janice, Ashley does not like chemistry, Ashley believes Janice likes chemistry (Figure 8.1).

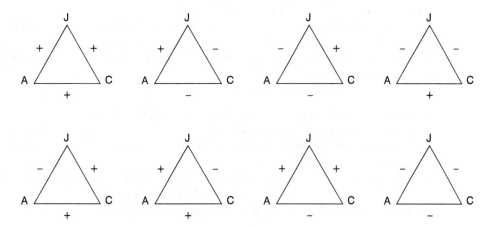

Figure 8.1
Predictions of balance theory.

Note: J, Janice (chemistry teacher); A, Ashley (student); C, chemistry (subject). The symbols "+" and "−" stand for "likes" and "does not like," respectively, so that the top left balance can be read as follows: Ashley likes Janice, Ashley likes chemistry, and Ashley believes Janice likes chemistry.

Cognitive imbalance exists with one negative and two positive relations (Ashley likes Janice, Ashley does not like chemistry, Ashley believes Janice likes chemistry) and with three negative relations. Balance theory predicts no tendency to change relationships exists when the triad is balanced, but people will try (cognitively and behaviorally) to resolve conflicts when imbalance exists. For example, Ashley might decide that because she likes Janice and Janice likes chemistry, maybe chemistry is not so bad after all (i.e., Ashley changes her attitude about chemistry).

That people seek to restore cognitive imbalance is intuitively plausible, but balance theory contains problems. It predicts when people will attempt to restore balance but not how they will do it. Ashley might change her attitude toward chemistry, but she also could establish balance by disliking chemistry and Janice. The theory also does not adequately take into account the importance of imbalanced relationships. People care very much when imbalance exists among people and situations they value, but they may make no effort to restore balance when they care little about the elements.

Cognitive Dissonance. Festinger (1957) formulated a theory of *cognitive dissonance*, which postulates that individuals attempt to maintain consistent relations among their beliefs, attitudes, opinions, and behaviors. Relations can be consonant, irrelevant, or dissonant. Two cognitions are *consonant* if one follows from or fits with the other; for example, "I have to give a speech in Los Angeles tomorrow morning at 9" and "I'm flying there today". Many beliefs are *irrelevant* to one another; for example, "I like chocolate" and "There is a hickory tree in my yard". *Dissonant* cognitions exist when one follows from the opposite of the other; for example, "I don't like Deborah" and "I bought Deborah a gift." Dissonance is tension with drivelike properties leading to reduction. Dissonance should increase as the discrepancy between cognitions increases. Assuming I bought Deborah a gift, the cognition "I don't like Deborah" ought to produce more dissonance than "Deborah and I are acquaintances."

Cognitive dissonance theory also takes the importance of the cognitions into account. Large discrepancies between trivial cognitions do not cause much dissonance. "Yellow is not my favorite color" and "I drive a yellow car" will not produce much dissonance if car color is not important to me.

Dissonance can be reduced in various ways:

- Change a discrepant cognition ("Maybe I actually like Deborah").
- Qualify cognitions ("The reason I do not like Deborah is because 10 years ago she borrowed $100 and never repaid it. But she's changed a lot since then and probably would never do that again").
- Downgrade the importance of the cognitions ("It's no big deal that I gave Deborah a gift; I give gifts to lots of people for different reasons").
- Alter behavior ("I'm never giving Deborah another gift").

Dissonance theory calls attention to how cognitive conflicts can be resolved (Aronson, 1966). The idea that dissonance propels us into action is appealing. By dealing with discrepant cognitions, the theory is not confined to three relations as is balance theory. But dissonance and balance theories share many of the same problems. The dissonance notion is vague and difficult to verify experimentally. To predict whether cognitions will conflict in a given situation is problematic because they must be clear and important. The theory does not predict how dissonance will be reduced—by changing behavior or by altering thoughts. These problems suggest that additional processes are needed to explain human motivation. Shultz and Lepper (1996) presented a model that reconciled discrepant findings from dissonance research and integrated dissonance better with other motivational variables.

Humanistic Theory

Humanistic theory as applied to learning is largely constructivist (Chapter 6) and emphasizes cognitive and affective processes. It addresses people's capabilities and potentialities as they make choices and seek control over their lives.

Humanistic theorists make certain assumptions (Schunk et al., 2008). One is that the study of persons is *holistic*: To understand people, we must study their behaviors, thoughts, and feelings (Weiner, 1992). Humanists disagree with behaviorists who study individual responses to discrete stimuli. Humanists emphasize individuals' self-awareness.

A second assumption is that human choices, creativity, and self-actualization are important areas to study (Weiner, 1992). To understand people, researchers should not study animals but rather people who are psychologically functioning and attempting to be creative and to maximize their capabilities and potential. Motivation is important for attaining basic needs, but greater choices are available when striving to maximize one's potential.

Well-known humanistic theories include those of Abraham Maslow and Carl Rogers. Maslow's theory, which emphasizes motivation to develop one's full potential, is discussed next, followed by Rogers's theory, which addresses both learning and instruction.

Hierarchy of Needs. Maslow (1968, 1970) believed that human actions are unified by being directed toward goal attainment. Behaviors can serve several functions simultaneously; for example, attending a party could satisfy needs for self-esteem and social interaction. Maslow felt that conditioning theories did not capture the complexity of human behavior. To say that one socializes at a party because one has previously been reinforced for doing so fails to take into account the current role that socialization plays for the person.

Most human action represents a striving to satisfy needs. Needs are *hierarchical* (Figure 8.2). Lower-order needs have to be satisfied adequately before higher-order needs can influence behavior. *Physiological needs*, the lowest on the hierarchy, concern necessities such as food, air, and water. These needs are satisfied for most people most of the time, but they become potent when they are not satisfied. *Safety needs*, which involve environmental security, dominate during emergencies: People fleeing from rising waters will abandon valuable property to save their lives. Safety needs are also manifested in activities such as saving money, securing a job, and taking out an insurance policy.

Once physiological and safety needs are adequately met, *belongingness (love) needs* become important. These needs involve having intimate relationships with others, belonging to groups, and having close friends and acquaintances. A sense of belonging is attained through marriage, interpersonal commitments, volunteer groups, clubs,

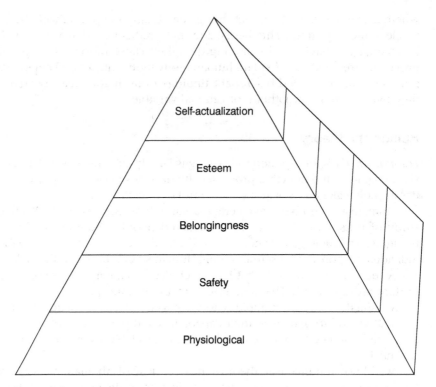

Figure 8.2
Maslow's hierarchy of needs.
Source: Motivation and Personality by A. Maslow, © 1970. Reprinted by permission of Pearson Education, Inc., Upper Saddle River, NJ.

churches, and the like. *Esteem needs* comprise self-esteem and esteem from others. These needs manifest themselves in high achievement, independence, competent work, and recognition from others.

The first four needs are *deprivation needs*: Their lack of satisfaction produces deficiencies that motivate people to satisfy them. Severe or prolonged deficiencies can lead to mental problems: "Most neuroses involved, along with other complex determinants, ungratified wishes for safety, for belongingness and identification, for close love relationships and for respect and prestige" (Maslow, 1968, p. 21).

At the highest level is the *need for self-actualization*, or the desire for self-fulfillment. Self-actualization manifests itself in the need to become everything that one is capable of becoming. Behavior is not motivated by a deficiency but rather by a desire for personal growth.

> Healthy people have sufficiently gratified their basic needs for safety, belongingness, love, respect, and self-esteem so that they are motivated primarily by trends to self-actualization [defined as ongoing actualization of potentials, capacities and talents, as fulfillment of mission (or call, fate, destiny, or vocation), as a fuller knowledge of, and acceptance of, the person's own intrinsic nature, as an unceasing trend toward unity, integration or synergy within the person]. (Maslow, 1968, p. 25)

APPLICATION 8.1
Maslow's Hierarchy

Maslow's hierarchy can help teachers understand students and create an environment to enhance learning. It is unrealistic to expect students to show interest in classroom activities if they have physiological or safety deficiencies. Children who come to school without having had breakfast and who have no lunch money cannot focus properly on classroom tasks. Teachers can work with counselors, principals, and social workers to assist children's families or to have children approved for free or reduced-cost meal programs.

Some students will have difficulty working on tasks with nearby distractions (e.g., movement, noise). Teachers can meet with parents to assess whether home conditions are disruptive. Disruption at home can result in an unfilled safety need—a desire to feel more secure about learning. Parents can be urged to provide a favorable home environment for studying, ensure few classroom distractions, and teach students skills for coping with them (e.g., how to concentrate and pay close attention to academic activities).

Some high schools have problems with violence and pressures associated with gang behaviors. If students are afraid that they may be physically harmed or often must deal with pressures to join a gang, concentrating on academic tasks may be impossible. Teachers and administrators might consider working with students, parents, community agencies, and law enforcement officials to develop effective strategies for eliminating the safety concerns. These issues must be addressed in order to create an atmosphere conducive for learning. Once the appropriate atmosphere is created, teachers should provide activities that students can complete successfully.

Although most people go beyond the deficiency needs and strive toward self-actualization, few people ever fully reach this level—perhaps 1% of the population (Goble, 1970). Self-actualization can be manifested in various ways.

> The specific form that these needs will take will of course vary greatly from person to person. In one individual it may take the form of the desire to be an ideal mother, in another it may be expressed athletically, and in still another it may be expressed in painting pictures or in inventions. At this level, individual differences are greatest. (Maslow, 1970, p. 46)

A strong motive to achieve is another manifestation of self-actualization (Application 8.1).

Maslow informally studied personal acquaintances and historical figures. Characteristics of self-actualized individuals included an increased perception of reality, acceptance (of self, others, nature), spontaneity, problem-centering, detachment and desire for privacy, autonomy and resistance to enculturation, freshness of appreciation and richness of emotional reaction, frequency of peak experiences (loss of self-awareness), and identification with the human species (Maslow, 1968).

When self-actualized persons attempt to solve important problems, they look outside of themselves for a cause and dedicate their efforts to solving it. They also display great interest in the means for attaining their goals. The outcome (righting a wrong or solving a problem) is as important as the means to the end (the actual work involved).

Maslow's hierarchy is a useful general guide for understanding behavior. It demonstrates that it is unrealistic to expect students to learn well in school if they are suffering from physiological or safety deficiencies. The hierarchy provides educators with clues concerning why students act as they do. Educators stress intellectual achievement, but many adolescents are preoccupied with belongingness and esteem.

At the same time, the theory has problems. One is conceptual vagueness; what constitutes a deficiency is not clear. What one person considers a deficiency in some area, someone else may not. Another problem is that lower-order needs are not always stronger than higher-order ones. Many people risk their safety to rescue others from danger. Third, research on the qualities of self-actualized individuals has yielded mixed results (Petri, 1986). Apparently, self-actualization can take many forms and be manifested at work, school, home, and so forth. How it may appear and how it can be influenced are unclear. Despite these problems, the idea that people strive to feel competent and lead self-fulfilling lives is a central notion in many theories of motivation (Schunk et al., 2008).

Actualizing Tendency. Carl Rogers was a renowned psychotherapist whose approach to counseling is known as *client-centered therapy*. According to Rogers (1963), life represents an ongoing process of personal growth or achieving wholeness. This process, or *actualizing tendency*, is motivational and presumably innate (Rogers, 1963). Rogers considered this motive the only fundamental one from which all others (e.g., hunger, thirst) derive. The actualizing tendency is oriented toward personal growth, autonomy, and freedom from control by external forces.

> We are, in short, dealing with an organism which is always motivated, is always "up to something," always seeking. So I would reaffirm . . . my belief that there is one central source of energy in the human organism; that it is a function of the whole organism rather than some portion of it; and that it is perhaps best conceptualized as a tendency toward fulfillment, toward actualization, toward the maintenance and enhancement of the organism. (Rogers, 1963, p. 6)

The environment can affect the actualizing tendency. Our experiences and interpretations of them foster or hinder attempts at growth. With development, individuals become more aware of their own being and functioning (*self-experience*). This awareness becomes elaborated into a self-concept through interactions with the environment and significant others (Rogers, 1959). The development of self-awareness produces a need for *positive regard*, or feelings such as respect, liking, warmth, sympathy, and acceptance. We experience positive regard for others when we have these feelings about them. We perceive ourselves as receiving positive regard when we believe that others feel that way about us. This relation is reciprocal: When people perceive themselves as satisfying another's need for positive regard, they experience satisfaction of their need for positive regard.

People also have a need for *positive self-regard*, or positive regard that derives from self-experiences (Rogers, 1959). Positive self-regard develops when people experience positive regard from others, which creates a positive attitude toward oneself. A critical element is receiving *unconditional positive regard*, or attitudes of worthiness and acceptance with no strings attached. Unconditional positive regard is what most parents feel for their children. Parents value or accept ("prize") their children all the time, even though they do not value or accept all of their children's behaviors. People who experience unconditional positive regard believe they are valued, even when their actions disappoint others. The actualizing tendency grows because people accept their own experiences, and their perceptions of themselves are consistent with the feedback they receive.

Problems occur when people experience *conditional regard*, or regard contingent on certain actions. People act in accordance with these conditions of worth when they seek or avoid experiences that they believe are more or less worthy of regard. Conditional regard creates tension because people feel accepted and valued only when they behave appropriately. To protect themselves, people may selectively perceive or distort experiences or block out awareness.

Rogers and Education. Rogers (1969; Rogers & Frieberg, 1994) discussed education in his book *Freedom to Learn*. Meaningful, experiential learning has relevance to the whole person, has personal involvement (involves learners' cognitions and feelings), is self-initiated (impetus for learning comes from within), is pervasive (affects learners' behavior, attitudes, and personality), and is evaluated by the learner (according to whether it is meeting needs or leading to goals). Meaningful learning contrasts with meaningless learning, which does not lead to learners being invested in their learning, is initiated by others, does not affect diverse aspects of learners, and is not evaluated by learners according to whether it is satisfying their needs.

Rogers (1969) believed people have a natural potentiality for learning and are eager to learn.

> I become very irritated with the notion that students must be "motivated." The young human being is intrinsically motivated to a high degree. Many elements of his environment constitute challenges for him. He is curious, eager to discover, eager to know, eager to solve problems. A sad part of most education is that by the time the child has spent a number of years in school this intrinsic motivation is pretty well dampened. (p. 131)

Students perceive meaningful learning as relevant because they believe it will enhance them personally. Learning requires active participation combined with self-criticism and self-evaluation by learners and the belief that learning is important. Rogers felt that learning that can be taught to others was of little value. Rather than imparting learning, the primary job of teachers is to act as *facilitators* who establish a classroom climate oriented toward significant learning and help students clarify their goals. Facilitators arrange resources so that learning can occur and, because they are resources, share their feelings and thoughts with students.

Instead of spending a lot of time writing lesson plans, facilitators should provide resources for students to use to meet their needs. Individual contracts are preferable to lockstep sequences in which all students work on the same material at the same time. Contracts allow students considerable freedom (i.e., self-regulation) in deciding on goals and timelines. Freedom itself should not be imposed; students who want more teacher

APPLICATION 8.2
Humanistic Teaching

Humanistic principles are highly relevant to classrooms. Some important principles that can be built into instructional goals and practices are:

- Show positive regard for students.
- Separate students from their actions.
- Encourage personal growth by providing students with choices and opportunities.
- Facilitate learning by providing resources and encouragement.

Jim Marshall employed all four of these principles with Tony, a student in his American history class who was known to be a neighborhood troublemaker. Other teachers in the building told Mr. Marshall negative things about Tony. Mr. Marshall noticed, however, that Tony seemed to have an outstanding knowledge of American history. Undaunted by Tony's reputation among others, Mr. Marshall often called on him to share in the classroom, provided him with a variety of project opportunities and resources, and praised him to further develop his interest in history. At the end of the semester, Mr. Marshall worked with Tony to prepare a project for the state history fair, after which Tony submitted it and won second place.

direction should receive it. Rogers advocated greater use of inquiry, simulations, and self-evaluation as ways to provide freedom. Application 8.2 offers suggestions for applying humanistic principles.

Rogers's theory has seen wide psychotherapeutic application. The focus on helping people strive for challenges and maximize their potential is important for motivation and learning. The theory is developed only in general terms and the meanings of several constructs are unclear. Additionally, how one might assist students to develop self-regard is not clear. Still, the theory offers teachers many good principles to use to enhance learner motivation. Many of the ideas that Rogers discussed are found in other theories discussed in this and other chapters of this text.

MODEL OF MOTIVATED LEARNING

The central thesis of this chapter is that motivation is intimately linked with learning. Motivation and learning can affect one another. Students' motivation can influence what and how they learn. In turn, as students learn and perceive that they are becoming more skillful, they are motivated to continue to learn.

This close connection of motivation and learning is portrayed in Table 8.1 (Schunk et al., 2008; Schunk, 1995). The model is generic and is not intended to reflect any one theoretical perspective. It is a cognitive model because it views motivation arising largely from thoughts and beliefs. The model portrays three phases: pretask, during task, posttask. This is a convenient way to think about the changing role of motivation during learning.

Table 8.1
Model of motivated learning

Pretask	During Task	Posttask
Goals	Instructional variables Teacher	Attributions

Expectations
  Self-efficacy
  Outcome
	Feedback
	  Materials
	  Equipment
		Goals
		
		Expectations

Values	Contextual variables	Affects
Affects	Peers Environment	Values
Needs	Personal variables	Needs

Social support	Knowledge construction
	  Skill acquisition
	  Self-regulation
	  Choice of activities
	  Effort
	  Persistence
		Social support

Pretask

Several variables influence students' incoming motivation for learning. Students enter tasks with various goals, such as to learn the material, perform well, finish first, and so on. Not all goals are academic. As Wentzel (1992, 1996) has shown, students have social goals that can integrate with their academic ones. During a group activity, Matt may want to learn the material but also become friends with Amy.

Students enter with various *expectations*. As discussed in Chapter 4, expectations may involve capabilities for learning (self-efficacy) and perceptions of the consequences of learning (outcome expectations). Students have differing perceptions of the *value*, or perceived importance, of learning. Wigfield and Eccles (1992) distinguished different values, which are explained later.

Students differ in their *affects* associated with learning. They may be excited, anxious, or feel no particular emotion. These affects may relate closely to students' *needs*, which some theories postulate to be important.

Finally, we expect that the social support in students' lives will vary. *Social support* includes the types of assistance available at school from teachers and peers, as well as help and encouragement from parents and significant others in students' lives. Learning often requires that others provide time, money, effort, transportation, and so forth.

During Task

Instructional, contextual (social/environmental), and personal variables come into play during learning. *Instructional variables* include teachers, forms of feedback, materials, and equipment. Although these variables typically are viewed as influencing learning, they also affect motivation. For instance, teacher feedback can encourage or discourage; instruction can clarify or confuse; materials can provide for many or few successes.

Contextual variables include social and environmental resources. Factors such as location, time of day, distractions, temperature, ongoing events, and the like can enhance or retard motivation for learning. Many investigators have written about how highly competitive conditions can affect motivation (Ames, 1992a; Meece, 1991, 2002). Students' social comparisons of ability with peers directly link to motivation.

Personal variables include those associated with learning, such as knowledge construction and skill acquisition, self-regulation variables, and motivational indexes (e.g., choice of activities, effort, persistence). Students' perceptions of how well they are learning and of the effects of instructional, contextual, and personal variables influence motivation for continued learning.

Posttask

Posttask denotes the time when the task is completed, as well as periods of self-reflection when students pause during the task and think about their work. The same variables important prior to task engagement are critical during self-reflection with the addition of *attributions*, or perceived causes of outcomes. All of these variables, in cyclical fashion, affect future motivation and learning. Students who believe that they are progressing toward their learning goals and who make positive attributions for success are apt to sustain their self-efficacy for learning, outcome expectations, perceived value, and positive emotional climate. Factors associated with instruction, such as teacher feedback, provide information about goal progress and outcome expectations. Thus, students who expect to do well and receive positive outcomes from learning are apt to be motivated to continue to learn, assuming they believe they are making progress and can continue to do so by using effective learning strategies.

ACHIEVEMENT MOTIVATION

The study of achievement motivation is central to education and learning. *Achievement motivation* refers to striving to be competent in effortful activities (Elliot & Church, 1997). Murray (1938) identified the achievement motive, along with other physiological and psychological needs contributing to personality development. Motivation to act presumably results because of a desire to satisfy needs. Over the years achievement motivation has been heavily researched, with results that bear on learning.

Murray (1936) devised the *Thematic Apperception Test* (*TAT*) to study personality processes. The TAT is a projective technique in which an individual views a series of ambiguous pictures and for each makes up a story or answers a series of questions. McClelland and his colleagues adapted the TAT to assess the achievement motive (McClelland, Atkinson, Clark, & Lowell, 1953). Researchers showed respondents pictures of individuals in unclear situations and asked questions such as "What is happening?" "What led up to this situation?" "What is wanted?" and "What will happen?" They scored responses according to various criteria and categorized participants on strength of achievement motive. Although many experimental studies have employed the TAT, it suffers from problems, including low reliability and low correlation with other achievement measures. To address these problems, researchers have devised other measures of achievement motivation (Weiner, 1992).

The next section discusses the historical foundations of achievement motivation theory, followed by contemporary perspectives.

Expectancy-Value Theory

John Atkinson (1957; Atkinson & Birch, 1978; Atkinson & Feather, 1966; Atkinson & Raynor, 1974, 1978) developed an *expectancy-value theory of achievement motivation.* The basic idea of this and other expectancy-value theories is that behavior depends on one's *expectancy* of attaining a particular outcome (e.g., goal, reinforcer) as a result of performing given behaviors and on how much one *values* that outcome. People judge the likelihood of attaining various outcomes. They are not motivated to attempt the impossible, so they do not pursue outcomes perceived as unattainable. Even a positive outcome expectation does not produce action if the outcome is not valued. An attractive outcome, coupled with the belief that it is attainable, motivates people to act.

Atkinson postulated that achievement behaviors represent a conflict between approach (*hope for success*) and avoidance (*fear of failure*) tendencies. Achievement actions carry with them the possibilities of success and failure. Key concepts are as follows: the *tendency to approach an achievement-related goal* (T_s), the *tendency to avoid failure* (T_{af}), and the *resultant achievement motivation* (T_a). T_s is a function of the *motive to succeed* (M_s), the *subjective probability of success* (P_s), and the *incentive value of success* (I_s):

$$T_s = M_s \times P_s \times I_s$$

Atkinson believed that M_s (*achievement motivation*) is a stable disposition, or characteristic trait of the individual, to strive for success. P_s (the individual's estimate of how likely goal attainment is) is inversely related to I_s: Individuals have a greater incentive to work hard at difficult tasks than at easy tasks. Greater pride is experienced in accomplishing difficult tasks.

In similar fashion, the *tendency to avoid failure* (T_{af}) is a multiplicative function of the *motive to avoid failure* (M_{af}), the *probability of failure* (P_f), and the *inverse of the incentive value of failure* ($-I_f$):

$$T_{af} = M_{af} \times P_f \times (-I_f)$$

The *resultant achievement motivation* (T_a) is represented as follows:

$$T_a = T_s - T_{af}$$

Notice that simply having a high hope for success does not guarantee achievement behavior because the strength of the motive to avoid failure must be considered. The best way to promote achievement behavior is to combine a strong hope for success with a low fear of failure (Application 8.3).

This model predicts that students high in resultant achievement motivation will choose tasks of intermediate difficulty; that is, those they believe are attainable and will produce a sense of accomplishment. These students should avoid difficult tasks for which

APPLICATION 8.3
Achievement Motivation

Achievement motivation theory has implications for teaching and learning. If an academic assignment is perceived as too hard, students may not attempt it or may quit readily because of high fear of failure and low hope for success. Lowering fear of failure and raising hope for success enhance motivation, which can be done by conveying positive expectations for learning to students and by structuring tasks so students can successfully complete them with reasonable effort. Viewing an assignment as too easy is not beneficial: Students who feel that the material is not challenging may become bored. (Notice in the opening scenario that Amy seems to be bored with the assignment.) If lessons are not planned to meet the varying needs of students, the desired achievement behaviors will not be displayed.

In working on division, some of Kathy Stone's third-grade students are still having difficulty with multiplication. They may need to spend the majority of their time learning facts and using manipulatives to reinforce learning of new concepts. Success on these activities in a nonthreatening classroom environment builds hope for success and lowers fear of failure. Students who are proficient in multiplication, have mastered the steps for solving division

problems, and understand the relationship between multiplication and division do not need to spend lots of class time on review. Instead, they can be given a brief review and then guided into more difficult skills, which maintains challenge and produces optimal achievement motivation.

College professors such as Gina Brown benefit by becoming familiar with the research knowledge and writing skills of their students prior to assigning a lengthy paper or research project. Student background factors (e.g., type of high school attended, expectations and guidance of former teachers) can influence student confidence for completing such challenging tasks. She should seek students' input regarding their past research and writing experiences and should highlight model research and writing projects in the classroom. When making assignments, she might begin with short writing tasks and by having students critique various research projects. Then she can provide students with detailed input and feedback regarding the effectiveness of their writing. As the semester progresses, assignments can become more challenging. This approach helps to build hope for success and diminish fear of failure, which collectively raise achievement motivation and lead students to set more difficult goals.

successful accomplishment is unlikely, as well as easy tasks for which success, although guaranteed, produces little satisfaction. Students low in resultant achievement motivation are more apt to select either easy or difficult tasks. To accomplish the former, students have to expend little effort to succeed. Although accomplishing the latter seems unlikely, students have an excuse for failure—the task is so difficult that no one can succeed at it. This excuse gives these students a reason for not expending effort, because even great effort is unlikely to produce success.

Research on task difficulty preference as a function of level of achievement motivation has yielded conflicting results (Cooper, 1983; Ray, 1982). In studies of task difficulty by Kuhl and Blankenship (1979a, 1979b), individuals repeatedly chose tasks. These researchers assumed that fear of failure would be reduced following task success, so they predicted the tendency to choose easy tasks would diminish over time. They expected this change to be most apparent among subjects for whom $M_{af} > M_s$. Kuhl and Blankenship found a shift toward more difficult tasks for participants in whom $M_{af} > M_s$, as well as for those in whom $M_s > M_{af}$. Researchers found no support for the notion that this tendency would be greater in the former participants.

These findings make sense when interpreted differently. Repeated success builds perceptions of competence (self-efficacy). People then are more likely to choose difficult tasks because they feel capable of accomplishing them. In short, people choose to work on easy or difficult tasks for many reasons, and Atkinson's theory may have overestimated the strength of the achievement motive.

Classical achievement motivation theory has generated much research. One problem with a global achievement motive is that it rarely manifests itself uniformly across different achievement domains. Students typically show greater motivation to perform well in some content areas than in others. Because the achievement motive varies with the domain, how well such a global trait predicts achievement behavior in specific situations is questionable. Some theorists (Elliot & Church, 1997; Elliot & Harackiewicz, 1996) have proposed an integration of classical theory with goal theory; the latter is discussed later in this chapter.

Familial Influences

It is plausible that achievement motivation depends strongly on factors in children's homes. An early investigation studied parents' interactions with their sons (Rosen & D'Andrade, 1959). Children were given tasks, and parents could interact in any fashion. Parents of boys with high achievement motivation interacted more, gave more rewards and punishments, and held higher expectations for their children than parents of boys with low achievement motivation. The authors concluded that parental pressure to perform well is a more important influence on achievement motivation than parental desire for child independence.

Other research, however, shows that family influences are not automatic. For example, Stipek and Ryan (1997) found that whereas economically disadvantaged preschoolers scored lower than advantaged children on cognitive measures, researchers found virtually no differences between these groups on motivation measures. Children's achievement motivation suffers when parents show little involvement in children's academics (Ratelle, Guay, Larose, & Senécal, 2004). Children who form insecure attachments with their parents are at greater risk for developing perfectionism (Neumeister & Finch, 2006).

Although families can influence children's motivation, attempts to identify parental behaviors that encourage achievement strivings are complicated because parents display many behaviors with their children. Determining which behaviors are most influential is difficult. Thus, parents may encourage their children to perform well, convey high expectations, give rewards and punishments, respond with positive affect (warmth, permissiveness), and encourage independence. These behaviors also are displayed by teachers and other significant persons in a child's life, which complicates determining the precise nature of familial influence. Another point is that although parents influence children, children also influence parents (Meece, 2002). Parents help children develop achievement behaviors when they encourage preexisting tendencies in their children; for example, children develop independence through interactions with peers and then are praised by parents.

Contemporary Model of Achievement Motivation

The classical view of achievement motivation contrasts sharply with theories that stress needs, drives, and reinforcers. Atkinson and others moved the field of motivation away from a simple stimulus–response ($S \rightarrow R$) perspective to a more complex cognitive model. By stressing the person's perceptions and beliefs as influences on behavior, these researchers also shifted the focus of motivation from inner needs and environmental factors to the subjective world of the individual.

An important contribution was emphasizing both expectancies for success and perceived value of engaging in the task as factors affecting achievement. Contemporary models of achievement motivation reflect this subjective emphasis and, in addition, have incorporated other cognitive variables such as goals and perceptions of capabilities. Current models also place greater emphasis on contextual influences on achievement motivation, realizing that people alter their motivation depending on perceptions of their current situations.

This section considers a contemporary theoretical perspective on achievement motivation as espoused by Eccles and Wigfield. In the following section, another current view of achievement motivation—self-worth theory—is presented. Collectively, these two approaches represent valuable attempts to refine achievement motivation theory to incorporate additional elements.

Figure 8.3 shows the contemporary model (Eccles, 1983, 2005; Wigfield, 1994; Wigfield, Byrnes, & Eccles, 2006; Wigfield & Eccles, 1992, 2000, 2002; Wigfield, Tonks, & Eccles, 2004; Wigfield, Tonks, & Klauda, 2009). This model is complex. Only its features most germane to the present discussion will be described here. Interested readers are referred to Wigfield and Eccles (2000, 2002) for in-depth coverage of the model.

We see on the left that factors in the social world affect the types of cognitive processes and motivational beliefs that students possess. These social influences include factors associated with the culture and the beliefs and behaviors of important socialization influences in the individual's environment. Students' aptitudes and their past experiences also influence their motivation.

The middle part of the model focuses on students' achievement beliefs in the current situation. Their cognitive processes involve their perceptions of social factors and their interpretations of past events (attributions, or perceived causes of outcomes, are discussed later in this chapter). Students' initial motivational beliefs center on goals, self-concepts of abilities, and perceptions of task demands. More is said about goals later in this chapter, but the point is that students' goals may not coincide with those of teachers, parents, and significant others.

Self-concepts of abilities are students' perceptions of their ability or competence in different domains. These perceptions are task specific and vary greatly by domain; thus,

Figure 8.3 Contemporary model of achievement motivation.

Source: The development of competence beliefs, expectancies for success, and achievement values from childhood through adolescence, by A. Wigfield & J. S. Eccles, 2002, p. 93. In A. Wigfield & J. S. Eccles (Eds.), *Development of achievement motivation* (pp. 91–120). Published in 2002 by Academic Press. Copyright Taylor & Francis Group LLC-Books. Used with permission.

students may feel highly competent in mathematics and English composition but less able in English grammar and science. Task-specific self-concept bears a close relation to Bandura's (1986) notion of self-efficacy (see Chapter 4 and later in this chapter); however, task-specific self-concept is more reflective of one's perceived ability whereas self-efficacy incorporates perceptions of various factors such as ability, effort, task difficulty, help from others, and similarity to models.

Perceptions of task demands refer to judgments of how difficult the task is to accomplish. Task difficulty is always considered relative to perceived capabilities; the actual difficulty level is less important than people's beliefs about whether they are capable enough to overcome the challenges and master the task.

The task value and expectancy components are shown on the right. *Value* refers to the perceived importance of the task, or the belief about why one should engage in the task. The overall value of any task depends on four components. *Attainment value* is the importance of doing well on the task, for example, because the task conveys important information about the self, provides a challenge, or offers the opportunity to fulfill achievement or social needs. *Intrinsic* or *interest value* refers to the inherent, immediate enjoyment one derives from the task. This construct is roughly synonymous with *intrinsic motivation* discussed later in this chapter. *Utility value* relates to task importance relative to a future goal (e.g., taking a course because it is necessary to attain a career goal). Finally, there is a *cost belief* component, defined as the perceived negative aspects of engaging in the task (Wigfield & Eccles, 1992). When people work on one task, then they cannot work on others, and there may be associated costs (e.g., academic, social).

The *expectancy* construct refers to individuals' perceptions concerning the likelihood of success on tasks; that is, their perceptions about how well they will do. This construct is not synonymous with perceived competence; rather, it bears some resemblance to Bandura's (1986) outcome expectation in the sense that it is forward looking and reflects the person's perception of doing well. In the opening scenario, Jared seems to have high expectancies for success, although he is overly concerned with doing better than others. It also contrasts with task-specific self-concept, which involves current beliefs about perceived ability. Research shows that higher expectancies for success are positively related to achievement behaviors, including choice of tasks, effort, persistence, and actual achievement (Bandura, 1986, 1997; Eccles, 1983; Eccles & Wigfield, 1985; Wigfield, 1994; Wigfield & Eccles, 2000, 2002; Wigfield et al., 2009). Collectively, expectancies for success and task values are predicted to affect achievement-related outcomes.

Research by Eccles, Wigfield, and others demonstrates support for many of the relations depicted in the model. Studies have used both cross-sectional and longitudinal designs that assess the beliefs and achievement of upper elementary and junior high students over time. A general finding across several studies is that expectancies and task-specific self-concepts are mediators between environmental contexts and achievement, as proposed by the model. Another finding is that expectancies are closely linked to cognitive engagement and achievement and that values are strong predictors of students' choices (Schunk et al., 2008). These findings have good generalizability because the studies use students in actual classrooms and follow them over lengthy periods (Eccles, 1983, 2005; Wigfield et al., 2006). A challenge for the future is to explore in greater depth the links between variables and determine how these vary depending on the classroom context and variables associated with students (e.g., developmental status, ability level, gender).

Self-Worth Theory

Atkinson's theory predicts that achievement behavior results from an emotional conflict between hope for success and fear of failure. This notion is intuitively appealing. Thinking about beginning a new job or taking a difficult course produces anticipated satisfaction from being successful as well as anxiety over the possibility of failing.

Self-worth theory refines this idea by combining the emotions with cognitions (Covington, 1983, 1984, 1992, 2004, 2009; Covington & Beery, 1976; Covington & Dray, 2002). This theory assumes that success is valued and that failure, or the belief that one has failed, should be avoided because it implies low ability. People want to be viewed as able, but failure creates feelings of unworthiness. To preserve a basic sense of self-worth, individuals must feel able and demonstrate that ability often to others. The key is to be perceived as able by oneself and by others.

One means of avoiding failure is to pursue easy goals that guarantee success. Another means is to cheat, although cheating is problematic. Shannon might copy answers from Yvonne, but if Yvonne does poorly, then Shannon will too. Shannon also might get caught copying answers by her teacher. Another way to avoid failure is to escape from a negative situation. Students who believe they will fail a course are apt to drop it; those who are failing several courses may quit school.

Strangely, students can avoid the perception of low ability through deliberate failure. One can pursue a difficult goal, which increases the likelihood of failure (Covington, 1984). Setting high aspirations is valued, and failing to attain them does not automatically imply low ability. A related tactic is to blame failure on low effort: One could have succeeded if circumstances had allowed one to expend greater effort. Kay cannot be faulted for failing an exam for which she did not properly study, especially if she had a job and had inadequate study time.

Expending effort carries risk. High effort that produces success maintains the perception of ability, but high effort that results in failure implies that one has low ability. Low effort also carries risk because teachers routinely stress effort and criticize students for not expending effort (Weiner & Kukla, 1970). Effort is a "double-edged sword" (Covington & Omelich, 1979). Excuses can help students maintain the perception of ability; for example, "I would have done better had I been able to study more," "I didn't work hard enough" [when in fact the student worked very hard], or "I was unlucky—I studied the wrong material."

Self-worth theory stresses perceptions of ability as the primary influences on motivation. Research shows that perceived ability bears a strong positive relationship to students' expectations for success, motivation, and achievement (Eccles & Wigfield, 1985; Wigfield et al., 2009). That effect, however, seems most pronounced in Western societies. Cross-cultural research shows that effort is more highly valued as a contributor to success among students from China and Japan than it is among students from the United States (Schunk et al., 2008).

Another problem with self-worth theory is that perceived ability is only one of many influences on motivation. Self-worth predictions depend somewhat on students' developmental levels. Older students perceive ability to be a more important influence on achievement than younger students (Harari & Covington, 1981; Schunk et al., 2008). Young children do not clearly differentiate between effort and ability (Nicholls, 1978, 1979). At approximately age 8, they begin to distinguish the concepts and realize that their performances do not necessarily reflect their abilities. With development, students increasingly value ability while somewhat devaluing effort (Harari & Covington, 1981). In the opening scenario, Matt is a hard worker, and effort does not yet seem to imply lower ability to him. Teachers and adolescents will work at cross-purposes if teachers stress working harder while adolescents (believing that hard work implies low ability) attempt to shy away from expending effort. A mature conception eventually emerges in which successes are attributed to a combination of ability and effort. Despite these limitations, self-worth theory captures the all-too-common preoccupation with ability and its negative consequences.

Task and Ego Involvement

Achievement motivation theories have shifted their focus away from general achievement motives to task-specific beliefs. Later in this chapter, goal theory is discussed, which stresses the roles of goals, conceptions of ability, and motivational patterns in achievement contexts. In this section we discuss task and ego involvement, which are types of motivational patterns that derive largely from work in achievement motivation (Schunk et al., 2008).

Task involvement stresses learning as a goal. Task-involved students focus on task demands such as solving the problem, balancing the equation, and writing the book report. Learning is valued as an important goal. In contrast, *ego involvement* is a type of self-preoccupation. Ego-involved students want to avoid looking incompetent. Learning is valued not for itself but only as a means to avoid appearing incapable (Nicholls, 1983, 1984).

Task and ego involvement reflect different beliefs about ability and effort (Jagacinski & Nicholls, 1984, 1987). Ego-involved students perceive ability as synonymous with *capacity.* Ability is a relatively fixed quantity assessed by comparisons with others (norms). The role of effort is limited; effort can improve performance only to the limit set by ability. Success achieved with great effort implies high ability only if others require more effort to attain the same performance or if others perform less well with the same effort. Task-involved students perceive ability as close in meaning to *learning,* such that more effort can raise ability. Students feel more competent if they expend greater effort to succeed, because learning is their goal and implies greater ability. Feelings of competence arise when students' current performance is seen as an improvement over prior performance.

Ego and task involvement are not fixed characteristics and can be affected by conditions in school (Nicholls, 1979, 1983). Ego involvement is promoted by competition, which fosters self-evaluation of abilities relative to those of others. Students typically compete for teacher attention, privileges, and grades. Elementary and middle-grades students often are grouped for reading and mathematics instruction based on ability differences; secondary students are tracked. Teacher feedback may unwittingly foster ego involvement (e.g., "Tommy, finish your work; everyone else is done"), as can teacher introductions to a lesson (e.g., "This is hard material; some of you may have trouble learning it").

Task involvement can be raised by individual learning conditions. Students evaluate their own progress relative to how they, rather than others, performed previously. Task involvement also is enhanced by cooperative learning conditions (students in a group collectively work on tasks). In support of these predictions, Ames (1984) found that students placed greater emphasis on ability as a determinant of outcomes in competitive contexts but stressed effort in noncompetitive (i.e., cooperative or individual) situations. Much research has examined how instructional and social factors affect students' motivational involvement (Ames, 1987, 1992a; Brophy, 1985; Meece, 1991, 2002; Schunk et al., 2008).

ATTRIBUTION THEORY

Attribution theory has been widely applied to the study of motivation (Graham & Williams, 2009; Schunk et al., 2008). *Attributions* are perceived causes of outcomes. *Attribution theory* explains how people view the causes of their behaviors and those of others (Weiner, 1985, 1992, 2000, 2004). The theory assumes that people are inclined to seek information to form attributions. The process of assigning causes is presumably governed by rules, and much attributional research has addressed how rules are used. From a motivational perspective, attributions are important because they influence beliefs, emotions, and behaviors.

Before discussing attributions in achievement settings, some relevant background material will be described. Rotter's *locus of control* and Heider's *naïve analysis of action* incorporate important attributional concepts.

Locus of Control

A central tenet of most cognitive motivation theories is that people seek to control important aspects of their lives (Schunk & Zimmerman, 2006). This tenet reflects the idea of *locus of control,* or a generalized expectancy concerning whether responses influence the attainment of outcomes such as successes and rewards (Rotter, 1966). People believe that outcomes occur independently of how they behave (*external locus of control*) or that outcomes are highly contingent on their behavior (*internal locus of control*).

Other investigators, however, have noted that locus of control may vary depending on the situation (Phares, 1976). It is not unusual to find students who generally believe they have little control over academic successes and failures but also believe they can exert much control in a particular class because the teacher and peers are helpful and because they like the content.

Locus of control is important in achievement contexts because expectancy beliefs are hypothesized to affect behavior. Students who believe they have control over their successes and failures should be more inclined to engage in academic tasks, expend effort, and persist than students who believe their behaviors have little impact on outcomes. In turn, effort and persistence promote achievement (Lefcourt, 1976; Phares, 1976).

Regardless of whether locus of control is a general disposition or is situationally specific, it reflects *outcome expectations* (beliefs about the anticipated outcomes of one's actions; Chapter 4). Outcome expectations are important determinants of achievement behaviors, but they alone are insufficient (Bandura, 1982b, 1997). Students may not work on tasks because they do not expect competent performances to produce favorable results (negative outcome expectation), as might happen if they believe the teacher dislikes them and will not reward them no matter how well they do. Positive outcome expectations do not guarantee high motivation; students may believe that hard work will produce a high grade, but they will not work hard if they doubt their capability to put forth the effort (low self-efficacy).

These points notwithstanding, self-efficacy and outcome expectations usually are related (Bandura, 1986, 1997). Students who believe they are capable of performing well (high self-efficacy) expect positive reactions from their teachers following successful performances (positive outcome expectation). Outcomes, in turn, validate self-efficacy because they convey that one is capable of succeeding (Schunk & Pajares, 2005, 2009).

Naïve Analysis of Action

The origin of attribution theory generally is ascribed to Heider (1958), who referred to his theory as a *naïve analysis of action. Naïve* means that the average individual is unaware of the objective determinants of behavior. Heider's theory examines what ordinary people believe are the causes of important events in their lives.

Heider postulated that people attribute causes to internal or external factors. He referred to these factors, respectively, as the *effective personal force* and the *effective environmental force*, as follows:

Outcome = personal force + environmental force

Internal causes are within the individual: needs, wishes, emotions, abilities, intentions, and effort. The *personal force* is allocated to two factors: *power* and *motivation*. Power refers to abilities and motivation (trying) to intention and exertion:

Outcome = trying + power + environment

Collectively, power and environment constitute the *can factor*, which, combined with the *try factor*, is used to explain outcomes. One's power (or ability) reflects the environment. Whether Beth can swim across a lake depends on Beth's swimming ability relative to the forces of the lake (current, width, and temperature). Similarly, Jason's success or failure on a test depends on his ability relative to the difficulty of the test, along with his intentions and efforts in studying. Assuming that ability is sufficient to conquer environmental forces, then trying (effort) affects outcomes.

Although Heider sketched a framework for how people view significant events in their lives, this framework provided researchers with few empirically testable hypotheses. Investigators subsequently clarified his ideas and conducted attributional research testing refined hypotheses.

Attribution Theory of Achievement

In achievement settings, the search for causes elicits the following types of questions: "Why did I do well (poorly) on my social studies test?" and "Why did I get an A (D) in biology?" A series of studies by Weiner and his colleagues provided the empirical base for developing an attribution theory of achievement (Weiner, 1979, 1985, 1992, 2000, 2004, 2005; Weiner et al., 1971; Weiner, Graham, Taylor, & Meyer, 1983; Weiner & Kukla, 1970). This section discusses those aspects of Weiner's theory relevant to motivated learning.

Causal Factors. Guided by Heider's work, Weiner et al. (1971) postulated that students attribute their academic successes and failures largely to ability, effort, task difficulty, and luck. These authors assumed that these factors were given general weights, and that for any given outcome one or two factors would be judged as primarily responsible. For example, if Kara received an A on a social studies test, she might attribute it mostly to ability ("I'm good in social studies") and effort ("I studied hard for the test"), somewhat to task difficulty ("The test wasn't too hard"), and very little to luck ("I guessed right on a couple of questions"; Table 8.2).

Weiner et al. (1971) did not imply that ability, effort, task difficulty, and luck are the only attributions students use to explain their successes and failures, but rather that they are commonly given by students as causes of achievement outcomes. Subsequent research identified other attributions, such as other people (teachers, students), mood, fatigue, illness, personality, and physical appearance (Frieze, 1980; Frieze, Francis, & Hanusa, 1983). Of the four attributions identified by Weiner et al. (1971), luck gets relatively less emphasis,

Table 8.2
Sample attributions for grade on mathematics exam.

Grade	Attribution	Example
High	Ability	I'm good in math.
	Effort	I studied hard for the exam.
	Ability + Effort	I'm good in math, and I studied hard for the exam.
	Task ease	It was an easy test.
	Luck	I was lucky; I studied the right material for the exam.
Low	Ability	I'm no good in math.
	Effort	I didn't study hard enough.
	Ability + Effort	I'm no good in math, and I didn't study hard enough.
	Task difficulty	The test was impossible; nobody could have done well.
	Luck	I was unlucky; I studied the wrong material for the exam.

although it is important in some situations (e.g., games of chance). Frieze et al. (1983) showed that task conditions are associated with particular attributional patterns. Exams tend to generate effort attributions, whereas art projects are ascribed to ability and effort. In the opening vignette, we might speculate that Margaret attributes her difficulties to low ability and Matt attributes his successes to high effort.

Causal Dimensions. Drawing on the work of Heider (1958) and Rotter (1966), Weiner et al. (1971) originally represented causes along two dimensions: (a) internal or external to the individual, and (b) relatively stable or unstable over time (Table 8.3). Ability is internal and relatively stable. Effort is internal but unstable; one can alternatively work diligently and lackadaisically. Task difficulty is external and relatively stable because task conditions do not vary much from moment to moment; luck is external and unstable—one can be lucky one moment and unlucky the next.

Weiner (1979) added a third causal dimension: controllable or uncontrollable by the individual (Table 8.3). Although effort is generally viewed as internal and unstable (immediate effort), a general effort factor (typical effort) also seems to exist: People may be typically lazy or hardworking. Effort is considered to be controllable; mood factors (to include fatigue and illness) are not. The classification in Table 8.3 has some problems (e.g.,

Table 8.3
Weiner's model of causal attribution.

	Internal		External	
	Stable	**Unstable**	**Stable**	**Unstable**
Controllable	Typical effort	Immediate effort	Teacher bias	Help from others
Uncontrollable	Ability	Mood	Task difficulty	Luck

the usefulness of including both immediate and typical effort; the issue of whether an external factor can be controllable), but it has served as a framework to guide research and attributional intervention programs.

In forming attributions, people use situational cues, the meanings of which they have learned via prior experiences (Schunk, 1994; Weiner et al., 1971). Salient cues for ability attributions are success attained easily or early in the course of learning, as well as many successes. With motor skills, an important effort cue is physical exertion. On cognitive tasks, effort attributions are credible when we expend mental effort or persist for a long time to succeed. Task difficulty cues include task features; for example, reading passages with fewer or easier words indicate easier tasks than those with more words or more difficult words. Task difficulty also is judged from social norms. If everyone in class fails a test, failure is more likely to be attributed to high task difficulty; if everyone makes an A, then success may be attributed to task ease. A prominent cue for luck is random outcomes; how good students are (ability) or how hard they work (effort) has no obvious connection to how well they do.

Attributional Consequences. Attributions affect expectations for subsequent successes, achievement behaviors, and emotional reactions (Graham & Williams, 2009; Weiner, 1979, 1985, 1992, 2000). The *stability* dimension is thought to influence *expectancy of success*. Assuming that task conditions remain much the same, attributions of success to stable causes (high ability, low task difficulty) should result in higher expectations of future success than attributions to unstable causes (immediate effort, luck). Students may be uncertain whether they can sustain the effort needed to succeed or whether they will be lucky in the future. Failure ascribed to low ability or high task difficulty is apt to result in lower expectations for future success than failure attributed to insufficient effort or bad luck. Students may believe that increased effort will produce more favorable outcomes or that their luck may change in the future.

The *locus* dimension is hypothesized to influence *affective reactions*. One experiences greater pride (shame) after succeeding (failing) when outcomes are attributed to internal causes rather than to external ones. Students experience greater pride in their accomplishments when they believe they succeeded on their own (ability, effort) than when they believe external factors were responsible (teacher assistance, easy task).

The *controllability* dimension has diverse effects (Weiner, 1979). Feelings of control seem to promote choosing to engage in academic tasks, effort and persistence at difficult tasks, and achievement (Bandura, 1986; Dweck & Bempechat, 1983; Monty & Perlmuter, 1987; Schunk & Zimmerman, 2006). Students who believe they have little control over academic outcomes hold low expectations for success and display low motivation to succeed (Licht & Kistner, 1986). Research shows that students who attribute failures to low ability—which is not controllable—demonstrate lower classroom engagement up to a year later (Glasgow, Dornbusch, Troyer, Steinberg, & Ritter, 1997).

Individual Differences. Some research indicates that attributions may vary as a function of gender and ethnic background (Graham & Williams, 2009). With respect to gender, a common finding (although there are exceptions) is that in subjects such as mathematics and science, girls tend to hold lower expectancies for success than do boys (Bong &

Clark, 1999; Meece, 2002; Meece & Courtney, 1992; Meece, Parsons, Kaczala, Goff, & Futterman, 1982). Margaret exemplifies this in the opening classroom scenario. What is not clear is whether this difference is mediated by different attributions, as might be predicted by attributional theories. Some studies have found that women are more likely to attribute success to external causes (e.g., good luck, low task difficulty) or unstable causes (effort) and attribute failure to internal causes (low ability; Eccles, 1983; Wolleat, Pedro, Becker, & Fennema, 1980); however, other research has not yielded differences (Diener & Dweck, 1978; Dweck & Repucci, 1973). Eccles (1983) noted the difficulties of attempting to make sense of this research because of differences in participants, instruments, and methodologies.

With respect to ethnic differences, some early research suggested that African American students used information about effort less often and less systematically than did Anglo American students and were more likely to use external attributions and hold an external locus of control (Friend & Neale, 1972; Weiner & Peter, 1973). Graham (1991, 1994) reexamined these and other findings and concluded that although many studies show greater externality among African American students because researchers often did not control for social class, African American students were overrepresented in lower socioeconomic backgrounds. When the effect of social class is controlled, researchers find few, if any, ethnic differences (Graham, 1994; Pajares & Schunk, 2001), and some research has shown that African American students place greater emphasis on low effort as a cause of failure—a more adaptive attributional pattern (Graham & Long, 1986; Hall, Howe, Merkel, & Lederman, 1986).

Van Laar (2000) found a tendency toward external attributions in African American college students; however, these students also held high expectancies for success and felt that their efforts might not be properly rewarded (i.e., negative outcome expectations). This seeming paradox of high success expectancies amidst lower achievement outcomes has been reported by others (Graham & Hudley, 2005). In summary, research investigating ethnic differences in achievement beliefs has not yielded reliable differences (Graham & Taylor, 2002), and these inconsistent results warrant further research before conclusions are drawn.

Attribution theory has had a tremendous impact on motivation theory, research, and practice. To ensure an optimal level of motivation, students need to make facilitative attributions concerning the outcomes of achievement behaviors. Dysfunctional judgments about abilities, the importance of effort and strategies, and the role of significant others can lead to low levels of motivation and learning.

Social cognitive theory provides another important cognitive perspective on motivation, and much of Chapter 4 is relevant to motivation as well as to learning. The next section provides a brief recap.

SOCIAL COGNITIVE THEORY

Although different perspectives on motivation are relevant to learning, social cognitive theorists have directed considerable attention to the relation between motivation and learning (Bandura, 1986, 1997; Pajares, 1996; Pajares & Miller, 1994, 1995; Pajares &

Schunk, 2001, 2002; Pintrich, 2000a, 2000b, 2003; Schunk, 1995; Schunk & Pajares, 2005, 2009; Schunk & Zimmerman, 2006). In social cognitive theory, *goals* and *expectations* are important learning mechanisms. Motivation is goal-directed behavior instigated and sustained by people's expectations concerning the anticipated outcomes of their actions and their self-efficacy for performing those actions (Bandura, 1986, 1991, 1997). Attributions and other cognitions (e.g., values, perceived similarity) influence motivation through their effects on goals and expectations.

Goals and Expectations

Goal setting and *self-evaluation of goal progress* constitute important motivational mechanisms (Bandura, 1977b, 1986, 1991; Schunk & Ertmer, 2000; Schunk & Pajares, 2009; Zimmerman, 2000). The perceived negative discrepancy between a goal and current performance creates an inducement for change. As people work toward goals, they note their progress and sustain their motivation. In the opening classroom scene, Rosetta's goal progress should build her self-efficacy and sustain her motivation.

Goal setting works in conjunction with outcome expectations and self-efficacy. People act in ways they believe will help attain their goals. A sense of self-efficacy for performing actions to accomplish goals is necessary for goals to affect behavior (Chapter 4). One of Kerri's goals is to help build Margaret's self-efficacy. Margaret may want teacher praise (goal) and believe she will earn it if she volunteers correct answers (positive outcome expectation). But she may not volunteer answers if she doubts her capabilities to give correct ones (low self-efficacy).

Unlike conditioning theorists who believe that reinforcement is a response strengthener (Chapter 3), Bandura (1986) contended that reinforcement informs people about the likely outcomes of behaviors and motivates them to behave in ways they believe will result in positive consequences. People form expectations based on their experiences, but another important source of motivation is social comparison.

Social Comparison

Social comparison is the process of comparing ourselves with others (Wheeler & Suls, 2005). Festinger (1954) hypothesized that when objective standards of behavior are unclear or unavailable, people evaluate their abilities and opinions through comparisons with others. He also noted that the most accurate self-evaluations derive from comparisons with those similar in the ability or characteristic being evaluated. The more alike observers are to models, the greater the probability that similar actions by observers are socially appropriate and will produce comparable results (Schunk, 1987). In the opening classroom scene, Jared uses social comparison as he compares his progress with that of his classmates.

Model–observer similarity in competence can improve learning (Braaksma, Rijlaarsdam, & van den Bergh, 2002). This effect on learning may result largely from the motivational effects of vicarious consequences, which depend on self-efficacy. Observing similar others succeed raises observers' self-efficacy and motivates them to try the task because they are apt to believe that if others can succeed, they will too. By comparing

Derrick to Jason, Kerri hopes that Derrick's behavior will improve. Observing similar others fail can lead people to believe they also lack the competencies to succeed, which dissuades them from attempting the behavior. Similarity may be especially influential in situations in which individuals have experienced difficulties and possess self-doubts about performing well (Application 8.4).

Developmental status is important in social comparison. The ability to use comparative information depends on higher levels of cognitive development and on experience in making comparative evaluations (Veroff, 1969). Festinger's hypothesis may not apply to children younger than 5 or 6, because they tend not to relate two or more elements in thought and are egocentric in that the "self" dominates their cognitive focus (Higgins, 1981; Chapter 6). This does not mean that young children cannot evaluate themselves relative to others, only that they may not automatically do so. Children show increasing

APPLICATION 8.4
Social Comparison

Teachers can use social comparison as a motivation tool for improving behavior and effort in completing assigned tasks. As Kathy Stone works with a small reading group, she compliments students for appropriate displays of behavior, which emphasizes expected behaviors and instills self-efficacy in students for performing accordingly. She might say:

- "I really like the way Adrian is sitting quietly and waiting for all of us to finish reading."
- "I like the way Carrie read that sentence clearly so we could hear her."

Observing student successes leads other students to believe they are capable of succeeding. A teacher might ask a student to go to the board and match contractions with the original words. Because the students in the group have similar abilities, the successes of the student at the board should raise self-efficacy in the others.

A swimming coach might group swimmers with similar talents and skills when planning practices and simulated competitions. With students of like skills in the same group, a coach can use social comparison while working on improving certain movements and speed. The coach might say:

- "Dan is really working to keep his legs together with little bending and splashing as he moves through the water. Look at the extra momentum he is gaining from this movement. Good job, Dan!"
- "Joel is doing an excellent job of cupping his hands in a way that acts like a paddle and that pulls him more readily through the water. Good work!"

Teachers and coaches should be judicious in their use of social comparison. Students who serve as models must succeed and be perceived by others as similar in important attributes. If models are perceived as dissimilar (especially in underlying abilities) or if they fail, social comparisons will not positively motivate observers.

interest in comparative information in elementary school, and by fourth grade they regularly use this information to form self-evaluations of competence (Ruble, Boggiano, Feldman, & Loebl, 1980; Ruble, Feldman, & Boggiano, 1976).

The meaning and function of comparative information change with development, especially after children enter school. Preschoolers actively compare at an overt level (e.g., amount of reward). Other social comparisons involve how one is similar to and different from others and competition based on a desire to be better than others (e.g., Jared) without involving self-evaluation (e.g., "I'm the general; that's higher than the captain"; Mosatche & Bragioner, 1981). As children become older, social comparisons shift to a concern for how to perform a task (Ruble, 1983). First graders engage in peer comparisons—often to obtain correct answers from peers. Providing comparative information to young children increases motivation for practical reasons. Direct adult evaluation of children's capabilities (e.g., "You can do better") influences children's self-evaluations more than comparative information.

Comparing one's current and prior performances (temporal comparison) and noting progress enhances self-efficacy and motivation. Developmentally this capability is present in young children; however, they may not employ it. R. Butler (1998) found among children ages 4 to 8 that temporal comparisons increased with age, but that children most often attended only to their last outcome. In contrast, children frequently employed social comparisons and evaluated their performances higher if they exceeded those of peers. Butler's results suggest that teachers need to assist children in making temporal comparisons, such as by showing children their prior work and pointing out areas of improvement. Kerri does this with Jared, Matt, and Rosetta.

In summary, with its emphasis on goals, expectations, and related cognitive processes, social cognitive theory offers a useful perspective on motivation. Application 8.5 gives some classroom applications of social cognitive principles. We now turn to goal theory, a relatively recent perspective on motivation that uses social cognitive principles as well as ideas from other theories.

GOAL THEORY

Goal theory represents a relatively new conception of human motivation, although it incorporates many variables hypothesized to be important by other theories (Schunk et al., 2008). Goal theory postulates that important relations exist among goals, expectations, attributions, conceptions of ability, motivational orientations, social and self comparisons, and achievement behaviors (Anderman & Wolters, 2006; Blumenfeld, 1992; Elliot, 2005; Maehr & Zusho, 2009; Pintrich, 2000a, 2000b; Pintrich & Zusho, 2002; Weiner, 1990).

Although goal theory bears some similarity to goal-setting theory (Bandura, 1988; Locke & Latham, 1990, 2002; Chapter 4), important differences exist. Educational and developmental psychologists developed goal theory to explain and predict students' achievement behaviors. Goal-setting theory, in contrast, has drawn from various disciplines, including social psychology, management, and clinical and health psychology. A central construct in goal theory is *goal orientation*, which refers to the purpose and focus of an individual's engagement in achievement activities. Goal-setting theory is

APPLICATION 8.5
Social Cognitive Theory

Students enter learning situations with a sense of self-efficacy for learning based on prior experiences, personal qualities, and social support mechanisms. Teachers who know their students well and incorporate various educational practices can positively affect motivation and learning.

Instruction presented such that students can comprehend it fosters self-efficacy for learning. Some students learn well in large group instruction, whereas others benefit from small group work. If a university English professor is introducing a unit on the major works of Shakespeare, the instructor initially might provide background on Shakespeare's life and literary reputation. Then the professor could divide the students into small groups to review and discuss what had been introduced. This process would help build the self-efficacy of both students who learn well in large groups and those who do better in small groups.

As the professor moves through the unit and introduces the major periods of Shakespeare's dramatic career, the student activities, exercises, and assignments should provide students with performance feedback. Progress made toward the acquisition of basic facts about Shakespeare and his works can be assessed through short tests or self-checked assignments. Individual student growth as it relates to

understanding specific Shakespearean works can be conveyed through written comments on essays and papers and through verbal comments during class discussions.

Students should be encouraged to share their insights and frustrations in working with interpretations of various Shakespearean plays. Guiding students to serve as models during the analysis and discussion of the plays will promote their self-efficacy better than will having a professor who has built his or her career studying Shakespeare provide the interpretation.

In working with students to develop goals toward learning the material and understanding Shakespeare and his works, the professor could help each student focus on short-term and specific goals. For example, the professor might have students read a portion of one major work and write a critique, after which they could discuss their analyses with one another. Breaking the material into short segments helps to instill self-efficacy for eventually mastering it. Commenting on the quality of the critiques by students is more beneficial than rewarding them for just reading a certain number of plays. Being able to interpret Shakespeare's work is more difficult than simply reading, and rewarding students for progress on difficult assignments strengthens self-efficacy.

more concerned with how goals are established and altered and with the role of their properties (e.g., specificity, difficulty, and proximity) in instigating and directing behavior. Goal theory also considers a wide array of variables in explaining goal-directed behavior, some of which may not directly involve goals (e.g., comparisons with others). Goal-setting theory typically considers a more restricted set of influences on behavior.

Goal Orientations

A central feature of goal theory is its emphasis on how different types of goals can influence behavior in achievement situations (Anderman & Wolters, 2006; Elliot, 2005; Maehr & Zusho, 2009; Pintrich, 2003). *Goal orientations* may be thought of as students' reasons for engaging in academic tasks (Anderman, Austin, & Johnson, 2002). Researchers have identified different orientations (Elliot & McGregor, 2001; Elliot & Thrash, 2001).

One distinction is between learning and performance goals (Dweck, 1991, 1999, 2002; Dweck & Leggett, 1988; Elliott & Dweck, 1988; Schunk, 1996; Schunk & Swartz, 1993a, 1993b). A *learning goal* refers to what knowledge, behavior, skill, or strategy students are to acquire; a *performance goal* denotes what task students are to complete. Other types of goals mentioned in the literature that are conceptually similar to learning goals include *mastery, task-involved,* and *task-focused goals* (Ames & Archer, 1987; Butler, 1992; Meece, 1991; Nicholls, 1984); synonyms for performance goals include *ego-involved* and *ability-focused goals*. In the opening scenario, Matt seems to hold a learning goal orientation, whereas Jared is more performance-goal oriented.

Although these goal orientations at times may be related (e.g., learning produces faster performance), the importance of these goals for achievement behavior and learning stems from the effects they can have on learners' beliefs and cognitive processes (Pintrich, 2000a). Learning goals focus students' attention on processes and strategies that help them acquire capabilities and improve their skills (Ames, 1992a). The task focus motivates behavior and directs and sustains attention on task aspects critical for learning. Students who pursue a learning goal are apt to feel efficacious for attaining it and be motivated to engage in task-appropriate activities (e.g., expend effort, persist, and use effective strategies; Bandura, 1986; Schunk, 1995). Self-efficacy is substantiated as they work on the task and assess their progress (Wentzel, 1992). Perceived progress in skill acquisition and self-efficacy for continued learning sustain motivation and enhance skillful performance (Schunk, 1996; Figure 8.4a). From a related perspective, students who pursue learning goals are apt to hold a *growth mindset,* which reflects the belief that one's qualities and abilities can be developed through effort (Dweck, 2006).

In contrast, performance goals focus attention on completing tasks (Figure 8.4b). Such goals may not highlight the importance of the processes and strategies underlying task completion or raise self-efficacy for acquiring skills (Schunk & Swartz, 1993a, 1993b).

Figure 8.4a
Effects of learning goals on motivation.

Figure 8.4b
Effects of performance goals on motivation.

As students work on tasks, they may not compare their present and past performances to determine progress. Performance goals can lead to social comparisons of one's work with that of others to determine progress. Social comparisons can result in low perceptions of ability among students who experience difficulties, which adversely affect task motivation (Schunk, 1996). Students who pursue performance goals may hold a *fixed mindset,* reflecting the idea that one's qualities and abilities are limited and cannot change very much (Dweck, 2006).

Research supports these ideas. During science lessons, Meece, Blumenfeld, and Hoyle (1988) found that students who emphasized task-mastery goals reported more active cognitive engagement characterized by self-regulatory activities (e.g., reviewing material not understood). Intrinsic motivation (discussed later in this chapter) related positively to goals stressing learning and understanding.

Elliott and Dweck (1988) gave children feedback indicating they had high or low ability, along with instructions highlighting a learning goal of developing competence or a performance goal of appearing competent. Learning-goal children sought to increase competence by choosing challenging tasks and using problem-solving strategies. Performance-goal children who received high-ability feedback persisted at the task but also avoided challenging tasks that might have entailed public errors. Performance-goal children given low-ability feedback selected easier tasks, did not persist to overcome mistakes, and displayed negative affect.

During reading comprehension instruction, Schunk and Rice (1989) found that with children deficient in reading skills, a process goal (e.g., learning to use a comprehension strategy) and a product (e.g., performance) goal (e.g., answering questions) led to higher self-efficacy than did a general goal of working productively; however, the process and product conditions did not differ. Schunk and Rice (1991) found that combining a process goal with feedback on progress toward the goal of learning to use a strategy promoted self-efficacy and skill better than process and product goal conditions. These two studies suggest that without progress feedback, learning goals may not be more effective than performance goals among students with reading problems.

Schunk and Swartz (1993a, 1993b) provided children in regular and gifted classes with a process goal of learning to use a paragraph-writing strategy or a product (performance) goal of writing paragraphs. Half of the process-goal students periodically received feedback on their progress in learning the strategy. Schunk and Swartz found that the process goal with feedback was the most effective and that the process goal with or without feedback led to higher achievement outcomes than did the product goal.

Schunk (1996) provided fourth graders with instruction and practice on fractions, along with either a learning goal (e.g., learning how to solve problems) or a performance goal (e.g., solving problems). In the first study, half of the students in each goal condition evaluated their problem-solving capabilities. The learning goal with or without self-evaluation and the performance goal with self-evaluation led to higher self-efficacy, skill, motivation, and task orientation, than did the performance goal without self-evaluation. In the second study, all students in each goal condition evaluated their progress in skill acquisition. The learning goal led to higher motivation and achievement outcomes than did the performance goal. These findings were replicated with college students by Schunk and Ertmer (1999), who found that self-efficacy for applying computer skills was enhanced when students received a process (learning) goal and an opportunity to evaluate their learning progress.

Investigators have examined additional distinctions in the mastery–performance dichotomy (Elliot, 2005; Elliot & McGregor, 2001; Elliot & Thrash, 2001; Maehr & Zusho, 2009). Drawing on the work of Carver and Scheier (1998), Linnenbrink and Pintrich (2002) proposed classifying mastery and performance goals according to whether they involve approach or avoidance and hypothesized that goals have different emotional consequences. Approach mastery goals are predicted to lead to positive affect, whereas both types of avoidance goals are expected to result in negative affect. Linnenbrink and Pintrich reported support for these predictions. The role of affect in goal choice and outcomes often is not addressed, yet the emotional consequences of motivation for schooling are important (Meyer & Turner, 2002).

Goal orientations play a key role in self-regulation (Chapter 9), because they provide a framework within which learners interpret and react to events (Dweck & Leggett, 1988; Meece, 1994). Students who develop and maintain high self-efficacy for learning have higher expectancies for success, greater perceived control over learning, and more intrinsic interest in learning (Covington, 1992; Eccles, 1983; Harter & Connell, 1984). Harackiewicz, Barron, Tauer, Carter, and Elliot (2000) found that mastery goals predicted immediate and long-term interest in the discipline among college students, whereas performance goals predicted grades better. Students are more likely to adopt a task/learning-goal orientation when they believe they can improve their ability through expending effort (Dweck & Leggett, 1988; Meece, 1994; Nicholls & Miller, 1984). Purdie, Hattie, and Douglas (1996) found among Australian and Japanese students that a conception of learning as understanding was related to greater use of learning strategies. In contrast to this incremental conception of ability, students with a fixed conception believe that effort will improve ability only to a set limit. Effort becomes less important when ability is fixed.

Achievement goal patterns also can motivate self-regulatory efforts (Zimmerman & Cleary, 2009). Providing students with feedback stressing a learning-goal orientation can enhance self-efficacy, motivation, self-regulatory activities, and achievement more than providing feedback emphasizing performance goals (Schunk & Swartz, 1993a, 1993b). Achievement goals affect students' task persistence and effort expenditure (Elliott & Dweck, 1988; Stipek & Kowalski, 1989). Under performance-oriented conditions, children with low perceived ability experience performance deterioration when they begin to fail (Meece, 1994); however, this pattern is not found among learning-oriented children regardless of perceived ability and among performance-oriented students with high perceived ability. Ames and Archer (1988) found that classroom mastery (learning) goal orientation relates positively to students' reported use of effective learning strategies and effort attributions.

Research shows that achievement goals can affect how students study and what they learn. Learning-oriented students tend to use deep processing strategies that enhance conceptual understandings and that require cognitive effort (e.g., integrating information, monitoring comprehension; Graham & Golan, 1991; Nolen, 1988, 1996; Pintrich & Garcia, 1991). In contrast, ego-oriented goal patterns are associated with such short-term and surface-level processing strategies as rehearsal and memorization (Graham & Golan, 1991; Meece, 1994).

Factors in the home and school can affect the role of learning-goal orientation in self-regulation. Learning situations that emphasize self-improvement, discovery of new information, and usefulness of learning material can promote a learning-goal orientation (Ames & Archer, 1988; Graham & Golan, 1991; Jagacinski & Nicholls, 1984). In contrast, interpersonal competition, tests of intellectual skills, and normative evaluations can enhance performance goals. Murdock and Anderman (2006) found that performance goals related to cheating, whereas students who pursued mastery goals were less likely to cheat.

In sum, evidence demonstrates that a learning-goal orientation facilitates achievement motivation, beliefs, and skill acquisition better than a performance-goal orientation, although performance goals bear a relation to grades. We now consider a mechanism that may explain such effects.

Conceptions of Ability

Several investigators have hypothesized that goal orientation is intimately related to one's theory about the nature of intelligence or ability (Dweck, 1986, 1991, 1999, 2006; Dweck & Leggett, 1988; Dweck & Molden, 2005; Nicholls, 1983, 1984). Dweck (1991, 2006) proposed two theories of intelligence: entity and incremental. People who hold an *entity theory* (or *fixed mindset*) believe that intelligence is relatively fixed, stable, and unchanging over time and task conditions. Effort helps to reach one's limit, not for progressing much beyond it. Difficulties are viewed as obstacles and can lower self-efficacy and lead students to display ineffective strategies and give up or work halfheartedly.

In contrast, people who hold an *incremental theory* (or *growth mindset*) roughly equate intelligence with learning. Students believe that intelligence can change and increase with experience, effort, and learning. An upper limit of intelligence—if it exists—is sufficiently high and does not preclude one from working harder to improve. Difficulties are viewed as challenges and can raise self-efficacy if students mobilize effort, persist at the task, and use effective strategies.

With some exceptions, students who hold a growth mindset, or an incremental view of intelligence, are more likely to believe that learning will raise their overall ability and thus should be more likely to adopt learning goals. Conversely, students holding a fixed mindset, or an entity view, may be less likely to adopt learning goals because they believe that learning will not raise their overall level of ability. These predictions have received research support (Dweck, 1991, 1999, 2006; Dweck & Molden, 2005).

Research also shows important relations among conceptions of ability, motivation, and achievement outcomes. Wood and Bandura (1989) had adults engage in a managerial decision-making task and told them that decision-making ability was fixed (reflecting their basic cognitive capabilities) or incremental (developed through practice). These ability conceptions often are associated with ego and task orientations, respectively (Dweck & Leggett, 1988; Jagacinski & Nicholls, 1984; Nicholls, 1983). Incremental decision makers maintained high self-efficacy, set challenging goals, applied rules efficiently, and performed better; entity participants showed a decline in self-efficacy. Jourden, Bandura, and Banfield (1991) obtained similar results among college students on a motor task. Participants who were led to believe that performance was an acquirable skill showed increased self-efficacy, positive self-reactions to their performance, and greater skill acquisition and task interest; those led to believe that performance reflected inherent aptitude showed no gain in self-efficacy, little increase in skill and interest, and negative self-reactions. Bempechat, London, & Dweck (1991) found important relations between theories of intelligence and achievement beliefs and behaviors in kindergarten through fifth-grade children.

PERCEIVED CONTROL

Although cognitive conceptions of motivation differ in many ways, they are unified in their espousing that *perceived control* over task engagement and outcomes is a critical influence on motivation (Schunk & Zimmerman, 2006). Perceived control also forms the core of the belief system of learned helplessness, which is a psychological perspective on behavior relevant to academic motivation. Later in this chapter we will see how perceptions of control are important determinants of intrinsic motivation.

Control Beliefs

People might believe that they have greater or lesser amounts of control over many types of situations and circumstances. Recall that Bandura (1986; Chapter 4) distinguished self-efficacy from outcome expectations; the former refers to perceived capabilities to learn or perform behaviors and the latter to beliefs about the consequences of actions. Perceived control is central to both of these expectations. People who believe they can control what they learn and perform, as well as the consequences of their actions, have a sense of agency. They are more apt to initiate and sustain behaviors directed toward those ends than are individuals who hold a low sense of control over their capabilities and outcomes of their actions.

Skinner, Wellborn, and Connell (1990) distinguished three types of beliefs that contribute to perceived control. *Strategy beliefs* are expectations about factors that influence success (e.g., ability, effort, other persons, luck, unknown factors). *Capacity beliefs* refer to personal capabilities with respect to ability, effort, others, and luck. For example, a strategy belief might be, "The best way for me to get good grades is to work hard"; a capacity belief could be, "I cannot seem to work very hard in school." *Control beliefs* are expectations about one's chances of doing well in school without reference to specific means (e.g., "I can do well in school if I want to").

Similar to Bandura's social cognitive theory in which self-efficacy and outcome expectations contribute to an individual's sense of agency, Skinner et al. described a three-part system of perceived control. Their research showed that these beliefs influence academic performance by promoting or decreasing active engagement in learning and that teachers contributed to students' perceptions of control by providing *contingency* (clear and consistent guidelines and feedback) and *involvement* (interest in and dedication of resources to students).

Evidence also indicates that when people think they have control over their environment, they tolerate aversive stimuli better and perform at a higher level. Glass and Singer

(1972) had adults work on tasks and periodically exposed them to a loud, irritating noise. No-control participants could not control the sound. Researchers told perceived direct-control participants they could terminate the noise by pushing a button, but advised them not to do so unless they needed to. Researchers told perceived indirect-control participants that pushing a button would send a signal to a confederate who could terminate the noise; the experimenter also advised these participants not to push unless they needed to. Perceived control (direct or indirect) led to significantly longer persistence and fewer errors compared with no perceived control. Perceived-control individuals judged the noise as less aversive than did no-control participants. These results suggest that students holding a sense of agency or control are better able to recover from setbacks and eventually achieve.

Learned Helplessness

Learned helplessness is a psychological phenomenon that highlights perceptions of control. *Learned helplessness* refers to a psychological state involving a disturbance in motivation, cognitive processes, and emotions due to previously experienced uncontrollability (Maier & Seligman, 1976; Peterson, 2000; Seligman, 1975, 1991). The key to producing learned helplessness is a perceived independence between responses and outcomes.

Helplessness was identified in laboratory studies in which dogs given inescapable shocks were moved to another location, where they could avoid shocks by jumping a hurdle. The prior inescapable shocks conditioned the dogs; they made little attempt to escape in the new setting but, rather, passively endured the shock. Dogs not previously exposed to inescapable shock easily learned to escape.

One manifestation of helplessness is passivity. People may do nothing when they believe they have no control over a situation. Helplessness also retards learning. People and animals exposed to uncontrollable situations may never learn adaptive responses or may learn them more slowly than those not exposed to uncontrollability. Helplessness has emotional manifestations. Prior uncontrollable situations may initially make one respond more aggressively, but eventually behavior becomes less assertive.

Learned helplessness has been applied in diverse clinical contexts (Fincham & Cain, 1986). Seligman (1975) proposed helplessness as an explanation for *reactive depression* brought about by sudden, dramatic changes in one's life (e.g., death of loved one, divorce, or loss of job). This explanation is intuitively plausible because people typically feel helpless in these situations. At the same time, many depressed people blame themselves for the negative events in their lives. Alex may believe, for example, that he was fired because he continually was late to work and could have avoided being fired had he arrived a few minutes earlier each day. Feeling personally responsible for negative events is incompatible with the notion that helplessness results from perceived lack of control.

Seligman's original model of learned helplessness was reformulated to incorporate attributions (Abramson, Seligman, & Teasdale, 1978). The reformulated model postulates that explanations (attributions) for outcomes influence future expectancies of outcomes and reactions to them. Explanations vary along three dimensions: *stable–unstable*, *global–specific*, and *internal–external*. One who attributes negative outcomes to stable causes (e.g., "I always arrive late for everything") is more likely to expect bad events in the future and may acquire helplessness than is one who makes attributions to unstable causes (e.g., "I arrived late when the weather was bad"). Causes can affect many areas of one's life (global) or only one area (specific). Students may believe they lack ability in all school subjects or only in one subject. Global attributions are more likely to produce helplessness. Causes for negative events may be internal to the person (low intelligence) or external (the teacher gives unfair tests). Internal attributions are apt to result in help-lessness. Collectively, people most prone to helplessness are those who typically explain negative events with internal, global, and stable attributions (e.g., "I do poorly in school because I'm not very smart").

Students with Learning Problems

Learned helplessness characterizes many students with learning problems who enter a vi-cious cycle in which negative beliefs reciprocally interact with academic failures (Licht & Kistner, 1986). For various reasons, students fail in school, and they begin to doubt their learning capabilities and view academic successes as uncontrollable. These beliefs pro-duce frustration and giving up readily on tasks. Lack of effort and persistence contribute to further failures, which reinforce negative beliefs. Eventually, students interpret their successes as externally caused; for example, the task was easy, they were lucky, or the teacher helped them. They attribute failures to low ability, which is internal, global, and stable, and which negatively affects self-efficacy, motivation, and achievement (Nolen-Hoeksema, Girgus, & Seligman, 1986). In the opening scene, Margaret may be a candidate for learned helplessness.

Compared with normal learners, students with learning problems hold lower expec-tations for success, judge themselves lower in ability, and emphasize lack of ability as a cause of failure (Boersma & Chapman, 1981; Butkowsky & Willows, 1980; Chapman, 1988; Harris et al., 2006; Palmer, Drummond, Tollison, & Zinkgraff, 1982). Such students often do not attribute failure to low effort (Andrews & Debus, 1978; Dweck, 1975; Pearl, Bryan, & Donohue, 1980). They give up readily when they encounter difficulties, cite un-controllable causes for successes and failures, and hold low perceptions of internal con-trol over outcomes (Johnson, 1981; Licht & Kistner, 1986). Students may even generalize these negative beliefs to situations in which they previously have not failed.

Dweck integrated learned helplessness into a model of achievement motivation (Dweck, 1986, 1999; Dweck & Leggett, 1988). Ego involvement characterizes helpless stu-dents. Their school goals are to complete tasks and avoid negative judgments of their competence. They may hold a fixed mindset and believe that intelligence is a stable quantity (Dweck, 2006). They avoid challenges, display low persistence in the face of dif-ficulty, hold low perceptions of their capabilities, and may experience anxiety while en-gaged in tasks (Diener & Dweck, 1978, 1980). In contrast, mastery-oriented students are more likely to hold a growth mindset and display a task-involved achievement pattern. They believe intelligence can improve, and their school goals are to learn and become more competent. They hold high perceptions of their learning capabilities, frequently seek challenges, and persist at difficult tasks.

Mastery-oriented and helpless students often do not differ in intellectual ability. Although helpless students may possess cognitive skill deficits, these alone do not cause failure. Not all students with learning problems enter this cycle; some continue to feel confident and display positive attributional patterns. One factor that may be important is frequency of failure: Students who fail in many school subjects are especially susceptible. Reading deficits are particularly influential; poor reading skills affect learning in many content areas. Reading deficits can promote negative beliefs even in areas that involve little or no reading (e.g., mathematics; Licht & Kistner, 1986).

Variables associated with the instructional environment can prevent students with learning problems from entering this cycle and can help them overcome it (Friedman & Medway, 1987). Attributional feedback can alter students' maladaptive achievement beliefs and behaviors. Teachers also need to give students tasks they can accomplish and feedback highlighting progress toward learning goals (Schunk, 1995; Stipek, 2002). Stipek and Kowalski (1989) found that teaching task strategies to children who de-emphasized the role of effort raised their academic performance.

We will now examine an important influence on motivation—self-concept, which has received much attention by researchers and practitioners as they attempt to understand student motivation and achievement.

SELF-CONCEPT

Psychologists and educators have studied self-concept for years, stimulated in large part by attempts to understand human personality and functioning. Although many believed that self-concept related positively to academic achievement, theoretical and research evidence to support this claim was missing.

This situation has been dramatically altered as theory and research on self-concept have undergone a resurgence (Hattie, 1992). Teachers are concerned with issues such as how self-concept relates to motivation and learning, how self-concept can be improved, and how social and instructional factors influence self-concept. This section provides an overview of the makeup of the self-concept and its role in academic motivation and learning.

Dimensions and Development

Self-concept refers to one's collective self-perceptions (a) formed through experiences with, and interpretations of, the environment and (b) heavily influenced by reinforcements and evaluations by significant other persons (Shavelson & Bolus, 1982). Self-concept is multidimensional and comprises elements such as self-confidence, self-esteem, self-concept stability, and self-crystallization (Pajares & Schunk, 2001, 2002; Rosenberg & Kaplan, 1982; Schunk & Pajares, 2009). *Self-esteem* is one's perceived sense of self-worth, or whether one accepts and respects oneself. Self-esteem is the evaluative component of self-concept. *Self-confidence* denotes the extent to which one believes one can produce results, accomplish goals, or perform tasks competently (analogous to self-efficacy). Self-esteem and self-confidence are related. The belief that one is capable of performing a task can raise self-esteem. High self-esteem might lead one to attempt difficult tasks, and subsequent success enhances self-confidence.

Self-concept stability refers to the ease or difficulty of changing the self-concept. Stability depends in part on how crystallized or structured beliefs are. Beliefs become crystallized with development and repeated similar experiences. By adolescence, individuals have relatively well-structured perceptions of themselves in areas such as intelligence, sociability, and sports. Brief experiences providing evidence that conflicts with personal beliefs may not have much effect. Conversely, self-concept is modified more easily when people have poorly formed ideas about themselves, usually because they have little or no experience.

The development of self-concept proceeds from a concrete view of oneself to a more abstract one (Montemayor & Eisen, 1977). Young children perceive themselves concretely; they define themselves in terms of their appearance, actions, name, possessions, and so forth. Children do not distinguish among behaviors and underlying abilities or personal characteristics. They also do not have a sense of enduring personality because their self-concepts are diffuse and loosely organized. They acquire a more abstract view with development and as a function of schooling. As they develop separate conceptions of underlying traits and abilities, their self-concepts become better organized and more complex.

Development also produces a differentiated self-concept. Although most investigators postulate the existence of a general self-concept, evidence indicates that it is hierarchically organized (Marsh & Shavelson, 1985; Pajares & Schunk, 2001, 2002; Schunk & Pajares, 2005, 2009; Shavelson & Bolus, 1982). A general self-concept tops the hierarchy and specific subarea self-concepts fall below. Self-perceptions of specific behaviors influence subarea self-concepts (e.g., mathematics, social studies), which in turn combine to form the academic self-concept. For example, Chapman and Tunmer (1995) found that children's reading self-concept comprised perceived competence in reading, perceived difficulty with reading, and attitudes toward reading. General self-concept comprises self-perceptions in the academic, social, emotional, and physical domains. Vispoel (1995) examined artistic domains and found evidence for the multifaceted nature of self-concept but less support for the hierarchical framework.

Experiences that help form the self-concept emanate from personal actions and vicarious (modeled) experiences (Schunk & Pajares, 2005, 2009). The role of social comparison is important, especially in school (see discussion earlier in this chapter). This idea is reflected in the *big-fish-little-pond effect* (Marsh & Hau, 2003): Students in selective schools (who have intelligent peers) may have lower self-concepts than those in less-selective schools. Marsh and Hau found evidence for this effect among students in 26 countries. Research also shows that being placed in a high-achieving group is associated with lower self-concept (Trautwein, Lüdtke, Marsh, & Nagy, 2009).

Evidence indicates that self-concept is not passively formed but rather is a dynamic structure that mediates significant intrapersonal and interpersonal processes (Cantor & Kihlstrom, 1987). Markus and colleagues (Markus & Nurius, 1986; Markus & Wurf, 1987) hypothesized that the self-concept is made up of self-schemas or generalizations formed through experiences. These schemas process personal and social information much as academic schemas process cognitive information. The multidimensional nature of self-concept is captured by the notion of *working self-concept*, or self-schemas that are mentally active at any time (presently accessible self-knowledge). Thus, a stable core (general) self-concept exists, surrounded by domain-specific self-concepts capable of being altered.

Self-Concept and Learning

The idea that self-concept is positively related to school learning is intuitively plausible. Students who are confident of their learning abilities and feel self-worthy display greater interest and motivation in school, which enhances achievement. Higher achievement, in turn, validates self-confidence for learning and maintains high self-esteem.

Unfortunately, these ideas have not been consistently supported by research. Wylie (1979) reviewed many research studies. The general correlation between academic achievement measures (grade point averages) and measures of self-concept was $r = +.30$, which is a moderate and positive relation suggesting a direct correspondence between the two. Correlation does not imply causality, so it cannot be determined whether self-concept influences achievement, achievement influences self-concept, each influences the other, or each is influenced by other variables (e.g., factors in the home). Wylie found somewhat higher correlations when standardized measures of self-concept were employed and lower correlations with researcher-developed measures. That higher correlations were obtained between achievement and academic self-concept than between achievement and overall self-concept supports the hierarchical organization notion. The highest correlations with achievement have been found with domain-specific self-concepts (e.g., in areas such as English or mathematics; Schunk & Pajares, 2009).

It is reasonable to assume that self-concept and learning affect one another. Given the general nature of self-concept, brief interventions designed to alter it may not have much effect. Rather, interventions tailored to specific domains may alter domain-specific self-concepts, which may extend up the hierarchy and influence higher-level self-concepts.

The research literature supports this proposition. The moderate relation between self-concept and achievement found in research studies may result because general self-concept measures were used. Conversely, when domain-specific self-concept measures are compared with achievement in that domain, the relation is strong and positive (Pajares & Schunk, 2001, 2002; Schunk & Pajares, 2005. 2009). As self-concept is defined more specifically, it increasingly resembles self-efficacy, and there is much evidence showing that self-efficacy predicts achievement (Bandura, 1997; Pajares, 1996; Schunk, 1995; Schunk & Pajares, 2009; Chapter 4).

Many of the suggestions made in this chapter have relevance for influencing self-concept. In their review of research on self-concept interventions, O'Mara, Marsh, Craven, and Debus (2006) found that domain-specific interventions had stronger effects on self-concept than did interventions designed to raise global self-concept. Teachers who show students they are capable of learning and have made academic progress in specific content areas, provide positive feedback, use models effectively, and minimize negative social comparisons, can help develop students' self-concepts (see Chapter 4 for ways to enhance self-efficacy).

INTRINSIC MOTIVATION

Intrinsic motivation refers to a desire to engage in an activity for no obvious reward except task engagement itself (Deci, 1975). The importance of intrinsic motivation for learning is underscored by research showing that interest in learning relates positively to cognitive processing and achievement (Alexander & Murphy, 1998; Schiefele, 1996, 2009). Some perspectives on intrinsic motivation are examined below.

Theoretical Perspectives

Effectance Motivation. In a seminal paper, White (1959) defined effectance motivation as:

> Fitness or ability, and the suggested synonyms capability, capacity, efficiency, proficiency, and skill. It is therefore a suitable word to describe such things as grasping and exploring, crawling and walking, attention and perception, language and thinking, manipulating and changing the surroundings, all of which promote an effective—a competent—interaction with the environment. The behavior . . . is directed, selective, and persistent, and it is continued not because it serves primary drives, which indeed it cannot serve until it is almost perfected, but because it satisfies an intrinsic need to deal with the environment. (pp. 317–318)

Effectance motivation is seen in young children when they interact with environmental features that catch their attention. A youngster may reach out and grab an object, turn it over, and push it away in an effort to control it. Effectance motivation is undifferentiated in young children; it is directed toward all aspects of the environment. With development, motivation becomes increasingly specialized. Once children enter school, they manifest effectance motivation in achievement behaviors in various school subjects.

Effectance motivation arises when biological motives are satisfied; it also facilitates future need satisfaction. Taking the top off of a jar initially satisfies the effectance motive, but in so doing the child learns that cookies are in the jar. This knowledge is used in the future to satisfy hunger.

Mastery Motivation. The notion of effectance motivation is intuitively appealing, but its generality limits the search for its causes and its effectiveness as an explanation for actions. The way to influence such a global construct, and thereby improve academic motivation, is unclear.

Harter (1978, 1981) attempted to specify the antecedents and consequences of effectance motivation in a developmental model of *mastery motivation*. Whereas White focused on success, Harter took success and failure into account. Harter also stressed the roles of socializing agents and rewards, the process whereby children internalize mastery goals and develop a self-reward system, and the important correlates of effectance motivation (e.g., perceived competence and control; Figure 8.5).

The left side of the model portrays success and is somewhat similar to White's formulation. Effectance motivation can trigger mastery attempts. White considered the motive generic, but Harter differentiated it according to domain (school, peers, athletics). Most behaviors involve optimally challenging tasks. Successes produce intrinsic pleasure and perceptions of competence and control, which in turn strengthen effectance motivation.

Figure 8.5
Model of mastery motivation.
Source: A Model of Mastery Motivation in Children: Individual Differences and Developmental Change, by S. Harter, 1981. In W. A. Collins (Ed.), *Aspects on the Development of Competence: The Minnesota Symposia on Child Psychology* (Vol. 14, pp. 215–255). Published in 1981 by Lawrence Erlbaum Associates. Copyright Taylor & Francis Group LLC-Books. Used by permission.

The bottom part highlights the role played by socializing agents. Some positive reinforcement for mastery attempts is necessary to develop and maintain motivation. Much of this reinforcement comes from primary caregivers, and eventually a self-reward system is internalized, which allows children to reinforce themselves for mastery attempts. Children acquire mastery goals through observation (social learning), and internalization becomes more complete with development. In support of these points, research shows that children from homes in which learning opportunities and activities are emphasized display higher intrinsic motivation for learning (Gottfried, Fleming, & Gottfried, 1998).

On the left side of the model are positive outcomes that result when social environments satisfy children's natural desires. The right side portrays negative outcomes, or the development of extrinsically oriented individuals. Unsuccessful mastery attempts, coupled with a nonresponsive environment, can lead to low perceptions of competence, an external locus of control, and anxiety. Effectance motivation ebbs if children increasingly depend on others to set goals and reward actions.

Research supports many of the propositions of the model. For example, intrinsic motivation relates positively to perceived competence and internal control (Harter, 1981; Harter & Connell, 1984). Social models are important sources of mastery behavior and learning (Bandura, 1986, 1997; Schunk, 1987). Perceived competence relates positively to intrinsic motivation (Gottfried, 1985, 1990). At the same time, the model relies heavily on socializing agents. They are important, but research has identified other ways to foster mastery behavior, including setting learning goals, providing attributional feedback, and teaching self-regulatory strategies (Ames, 1992a; Pintrich & Schrauben, 1992; Schunk, 1995; Zimmerman, 1989, 2000; Zimmerman & Cleary, 2009). Relatively little attention has been paid to educational implications of the theory—for example, how students can be taught to adopt an intrinsic orientation toward school. The theory must be broadened to address these points.

Incongruity and Arousal. Some investigators postulate that intrinsic motivation reflects an inherent need for a moderate amount of environmental stimulation. Hunt (1963) argued that exploratory behaviors and curiosity are intrinsically motivated and result from incongruity between prior experiences and new information. People extract information from the environment and compare it to internal representations. When incongruity exists between the input and internal knowledge or expectation, people become intrinsically motivated to reduce the incongruity. Hunt postulated that people require an optimal level of incongruity. When deprived of that level, they seek situations that provide it. Too much incongruity proves frustrating and triggers a drive to reduce frustration. Although Hunt's views have intuitive merit, they have been criticized because "optimal level of incongruity" is vague and how much incongruity is required to trigger motivation is not clear (Deci, 1975).

Berlyne (1960, 1963) similarly hypothesized that an optimal level of physiological incongruity (stimulation to the nervous system) is necessary and adaptive. If it becomes too low, people are intrinsically motivated to increase it; conversely, they are motivated to reduce it if it becomes too great. Berlyne's "arousal potential" may be interpreted as being approximately equivalent on a physiological level to Hunt's psychological incongruity. Properties of stimuli involving their novelty, ambiguity, incongruity, and surprise affect arousal and motivate people to explore the objects.

Although the notions of arousal and incongruity seem intuitively sensible, the idea of an optimal level of arousal or incongruity is vague, and it is unclear how much is needed to stimulate motivation. Practically speaking, we know novelty and surprise raise student interest, but how much of either is optimal? Too much may lead to frustration, attempts to escape from the situation, and lower interest in learning.

Self-Determination. Deci and colleagues (Deci, 1980; Deci & Moller, 2005; Deci & Ryan, 1991; Grolnick, Gurland, Jacob, & Decourcey, 2002; Reeve, Deci, & Ryan, 2004; Ryan, Connell, & Deci, 1985; Ryan & Deci, 2000, 2009) postulated that intrinsic motivation is an innate human need and originates in infants as an undifferentiated need for competence and *self-determination.* As children develop, the need differentiates into specific areas (e.g., athletics, academics), and environmental interactions influence the direction of differentiation.

This self-determination view emphasizes the internalization of social values and mores. Society contains many extrinsic rewards and controls that may not fit with children's quest for self-determination but may produce good behavior and social functioning. With development, these external motivators can become an internalized part of the self-regulatory system (Chapter 9).

Motivation is conceptualized as a continuum: Intrinsic and extrinsic motivation anchor the ends and in the middle are behaviors that originally were extrinsically motivated but have become internalized and now are self-determined. For instance, students may want to avoid some academic activities but they work on them to obtain rewards and avoid teacher punishment. As skills develop and students believe they are becoming more competent, they perceive a sense of control and self-determination over learning. The activities become more intrinsically motivating, and positive social reinforcers (e.g., praise, feedback) assist the process.

Deci's position is thought-provoking and has generated much research. It also has implications for educational practice because it stresses the role of self-determination in learning. Some points in the model are not clearly specified, but research continues to test its ideas (Reeve et al., 2004).

Overjustification and Reward

Lepper and Hodell (1989) hypothesized that there are four *sources of intrinsic motivation:* challenge, curiosity, control, and fantasy. The perspectives on intrinsic motivation discussed earlier in this chapter support the importance of the first three sources. Fantasy contexts (e.g., involving role-playing, simulations) seem well designed to heighten intrinsic motivation. Despite their differences, the various perspectives contend that intrinsic motivation is a strong, positive force in people's lives.

We typically think of intrinsic motivation increasing, but it also can diminish. Research shows that engaging in an intrinsically interesting activity to obtain an extrinsic reward can undermine intrinsic motivation (Deci, Koestner, & Ryan, 1999, 2001; Lepper, Corpus, & Iyengar, 2005; Lepper & Greene, 1978; Lepper, Henderlong, & Gingras, 1999). This finding has important educational implications given the prevalence of rewards.

When people are *intrinsically motivated*, they engage in an activity as an end in itself. Csikszentmihalyi (1975) studied persons who engaged in intrinsically motivating activities and found that their experiences reflected total involvement or flow with the activities. *Flow* is a personal process and reflects *emergent motivation* stemming from the discovery of new goals and rewards as a consequence of interacting with the environment (Csikszentmihalyi & Rathunde, 1993; Meyer & Turner, 2002).

In contrast, *extrinsic motivation* involves engaging in an activity for reasons external to the task. This activity is a means to some end: an object, a grade, feedback or praise, or being able to work on another activity. Students are extrinsically motivated if they try to perform well in school primarily to please their parents, earn high grades, or receive teacher approval.

Intrinsic reasons for working on a task are internal to it. The reward comes from working on the task; the task is both the means and the end. The rewards for intrinsic motivation may be feelings of competence and control, self-satisfaction, task success, or pride in one's work.

We engage in many activities for both intrinsic and extrinsic reasons. Many students like to feel competent in school and experience pride for a job done well, but they also desire teacher praise and good grades. Rewards are not inherently extrinsically motivating. Deci (1975) contended that rewards have an *informational* and a *controlling* aspect. Reward systems may be primarily structured to convey information about one's capabilities or to control one's behavior, and the relative salience of each (information or control) influences subsequent behavior. A salient informational aspect indicating successful performance should promote feelings of competence, whereas a salient controlling aspect can lead to perceptions of the reward as the cause of the behavior.

For example, suppose that in a classroom reward system the more work students accomplish, the more points they earn. Although students will want to work to earn points (because the points can be exchanged for privileges), the points convey information about their capabilities: The more points students earn, the more capable they are. In contrast, if points are given simply for time spent on a task regardless of learning or output, the task may be viewed primarily as a means to an end. The points convey nothing about capabilities; students are more likely to view the rewards as controlling their task engagement. Expected, tangible rewards offered to students for simply doing a task diminish intrinsic motivation (Cameron & Pierce, 1994, 2002).

Lepper (1983; Lepper & Greene, 1978; Lepper et al., 1999) postulated that the perception of reward influences students' intrinsic motivation. Motivation is largely a function of one's perceptions for engaging in the task. When external constraints are salient, unambiguous, and sufficient to explain the behavior, individuals attribute their behaviors to those constraints. If external constraints are viewed as weak, unclear, or psychologically insufficient to account for their behavior, people are more likely to attribute their actions to their desires or personal dispositions.

In a classic experiment (Lepper, Greene, & Nisbett, 1973), preschoolers were observed during free play. Those who spent a lot of time drawing were selected for the study and assigned to one of three conditions. In the expected-award group, children were offered a good player certificate if they drew a picture. Unexpected-award children were not offered the certificate, but unexpectedly received it after they drew a picture. No-award children were not offered the award and did not receive it. Two weeks later children were again observed during free play.

The expected-award children engaged in drawing for a significantly shorter time following the experiment than they had prior to the study, whereas the other two conditions showed no significant change. Expected-award children spent less time drawing following the study compared with the other conditions. It was not the reward itself that was important but rather the contingency. Lepper et al. (1973) postulated the *overjustification hypothesis*: Engaging in an intrinsically interesting activity under conditions that make it salient as a means to an end (reward) decreases subsequent interest in that activity. The overjustification hypothesis has been supported in experimental investigations with different tasks and participants of all ages (Lepper & Greene, 1978; Lepper et al., 1999; Lepper & Hodell, 1989).

Rewards need not have detrimental effects on performance. Rewards can help develop skills, self-efficacy, and interest when they are linked to one's actual performance and convey that one is making progress in learning. Offering children rewards based on the amount of work they accomplish during learning activities increases self-efficacy, motivation, and skill acquisition compared with offering rewards merely for task participation or not offering rewards (Schunk, 1983e). During a subtraction instruction program, Bandura and Schunk (1981) found that higher self-efficacy related positively to the amount of intrinsic interest children subsequently showed in solving arithmetic problems.

Thus, when rewards convey that one has learned, they can increase self-efficacy and intrinsic motivation. As a form of reward, grades can function in the same way. A grade that improves shows that one is performing better in the subject, which promotes self-efficacy and motivation for further learning. Unfortunately, research shows that children's intrinsic motivation in learning declines with development (Lepper, Sethi, Dialdin, & Drake, 1997), although other research shows that interest and self-efficacy are related positively in elementary and middle-grades students (Tracey, 2002). Application 8.6 demonstrates ways to enhance and sustain intrinsic motivation.

APPLICATION 8.6
Intrinsic Motivation

Intrinsic motivation involves perceptions of control and competence. Individuals develop perceived competence by mastering difficult situations. If elementary teachers are helping slower learners complete assigned tasks in an allotted time, they may begin by offering a reward (extrinsic motivator) and work toward building student pride in their accomplishments (intrinsic motivator). Initially teachers might reward students for increased output with time on the computer, verbal praise, or special notes home to parents. Gradually teachers could reward intermittently and then decrease it to allow students to focus more on their accomplishments. The ability to complete tasks in the appropriate time span provides students with information about their capabilities and their ability to control situations. When pride from successfully completing tasks becomes a reward, students are intrinsically motivated to continue to display the new behavior.

High school and college students often are motivated to achieve in school primarily to earn good grades (extrinsic motivators). Teachers and professors should attempt to show the connection between what is being taught in each course and the outside world and to link each student's accomplishments with his or her ability to be successful in that world. Instructors should help move students toward wanting to learn for the sake of learning and to be able to better address future challenges (intrinsic motivator). Thus, subjects such as chemistry, physics, and biology are not stale subjects studied in artificial laboratories but have direct relevance to what we eat, what we wear, what we do, and how we conduct our daily lives. The field experience component of Gina Brown's educational psychology class allows students to observe applications of teaching and learning principles during actual teaching. Enhanced perceived value of learning strengthens intrinsic motivation to learn.

INSTRUCTIONAL APPLICATIONS

The material in this chapter suggests many educational applications. Three applications that are linked closely with learning involve achievement motivation training, attribution change programs, and goal orientations.

Achievement Motivation Training

Achievement motivation training aims to help students develop thoughts and behaviors typical of learners high in achievement motivation (de Charms, 1968, 1984). De Charms (1976) initially prepared teachers, who then worked with students. The goal was to help students develop personal responsibility for their learning outcomes.

The teacher preparation included self-study of academic motivation, realistic goal setting, development of concrete plans to accomplish goals, and evaluation of goal progress. Student motivation was integrated with academic content. Classroom activities included self-study of academic motives, achievement motivation thinking, development of self-concept, realistic goal setting, and promotion of personal responsibility. During a spelling activity designed to teach goal setting, students could choose to learn easy, moderate, or difficult words. To teach personal responsibility, teachers had students write stories about achievement, which were then used in a classroom essay contest. The results showed that the program raised teachers' and students' motivation, halted the trend among low achievers to fall increasingly behind their peers in achievement, and reduced student absenteeism and tardiness.

Integrating instruction on achievement motivation with academic content, rather than including it as an add-on activity with special content, seems imperative. The danger of the latter approach is that students may not understand how to apply achievement motivation principles to other content.

Alderman (1985, 1999) recommended several useful components of achievement motivation instruction. One is having teachers assist students to set realistic goals and provide feedback concerning their goal progress. Another aspect is self-study to examine one's motives for learning and to develop personal responsibility. The distinction between task and ego involvement seems useful. A series of questions helps students examine how they feel about tasks and what they see as their goals (e.g., learning versus pleasing others). Attributional training (discussed next) also is relevant. One means of teaching personal responsibility is to help students place greater emphasis on effort as a cause of outcomes rather than blaming others when they fail or believing they were lucky when they succeed. As students experience successes, they should develop increased self-efficacy for continued learning and assume greater control of their learning.

Alderman (1985) applied these ideas to a senior high girls' physical education class. On the first day of class, students completed a self-evaluation of their health, physical fitness status, and competence and interest in various activities, and they set fitness goals. They took weekly self-tests in different activities (e.g., aerobics, flexibility, strength, and posture). At the end of the first grading period, students set goals for the final exam. They had various ways to accomplish the aerobic goal (running, walking, and jumping rope). The teacher met with individual students to assess goals and made suggestions if these did not seem realistic. Students established practice schedules of at least three times a week for 9 weeks and kept a record of practices. Following the final exam, students completed a self-evaluation of what they had learned. Alderman noted: "To the instructor, the most striking comment made by students on the final self-evaluation was, 'I learned to set a goal and accomplish it'" (p. 51).

Attribution Change Programs

Attribution change programs attempt to enhance motivation by altering students' attributions for successes and failures. Students commonly have some difficulties when learning new material. Some learners attribute these problems to low ability (e.g., Margaret in the opening scenario). Students who believe they lack the requisite ability to perform well may work at tasks in a lackadaisical fashion, which retards skill development. Researchers have identified students who fit this attributional pattern and have trained them to attribute failure to controllable factors (e.g., low effort, improper strategy use) rather than to low ability. Effort has received special attention; students who believe that they fail largely because of low ability may not expend much effort to succeed. Because effort is under one's control, teaching students to believe that prior difficulties resulted from low effort may lead them to work harder with the expectation that it will produce better outcomes (Application 8.7).

In an early study, Dweck (1975) identified children who had low expectations for success and whose achievement behaviors deteriorated after they experienced failure (e.g., low effort, lack of persistence). Dweck presented the children with arithmetic problems (some of which were insolvable) to assess the extent of performance decline following failure. Children largely attributed their failures to low ability. During training, children solved problems with a criterion number set for each trial. For some (*success-only*) children, the criterion was set at or below their capabilities as determined by the pretest. A similar criterion applied on most trials for *attribution retraining* children, but on some trials the criterion was set beyond their capabilities. When these children failed, they were told they did not try hard enough. On the posttest, success-only children continued to show deterioration in performance following failure, whereas attribution-retraining children showed less impairment. Success-only children continued to stress low ability; attribution-retraining students emphasized low effort.

Dweck did not assess self-efficacy or expectancies for success, so the effect of attributions on expectancies could not be determined. Other investigations have shown that teaching students to attribute failures to low effort enhances effort attributions, expectancies, and achievement behaviors (Andrews & Debus, 1978; Chapin & Dyck, 1976; Horner & Gaither, 2004; Robertson, 2000).

Providing effort-attributional feedback to students for their successes also promotes achievement expectancies and behaviors (Schunk, 1982a; Schunk & Cox, 1986; Schunk & Rice, 1986). In the context of subtraction instruction, Schunk (1982a) found that linking children's prior achievements with effort (e.g., "You've been working hard") enhanced task motivation, perceived competence, and skill acquisition better than linking their future achievement with effort (e.g., "You need to work hard") or not providing effort feedback. For effort feedback to be effective, students must believe that it is credible.

APPLICATION 8.7
Attributional Feedback

Providing effort attributional feedback to students for their successes promotes achievement expectancies and behaviors, but the feedback must be perceived as credible. When a student is having trouble mastering difficult multiplication problems, the teacher can use past student successes and attributional feedback to build confidence in learning. If the student has mastered addition and multiplication concepts and facts, the teacher might say, "I know these new problems look hard, but you can learn how to work them because you know all the things you need to know. You just need to work hard and you'll do fine."

As the student works, the teacher can interject comments similar to the following:

- "You're doing well; you completed the first step. I was sure you knew your multiplication facts. Keep working hard."
- "Wow! Look at that! You did those so quickly. I knew you could do that because you're working hard."

- "You did it! You got it right because you worked hard."

In a nursing program an instructor should give the future nurses positive and accurate feedback regarding their administration of various clinical procedures and their effectiveness in interacting with patients. For example, after a trainee has completed the drawing of blood for testing purposes, the instructor might say:

- "I'm glad to see you used all the correct safety procedures in handling the blood. You know what to do."
- "You did a great job of explaining the procedure to the patient before starting the process. You are really good at giving explanations!"
- "You completed the procedure very calmly and with a smile. You have real talent at this."

These types of remarks reflect positive attributional feedback concerning students' competencies, which can raise their self-efficacy and motivation for further learning.

Feedback is credible when students realistically have to work hard to succeed, as in the early stages of learning. Notice in the opening vignette how Kerri provides effort feedback to Derrick, Amy, and Matt.

Effort feedback may be especially useful for students with learning problems. Schunk and Cox (1986) provided subtraction instruction and practice opportunities to middle school students with learning disabilities. Some students received effort feedback ("You've been working hard") during the first half of a multisession instructional program, others received it during the second half, and learners in a third condition did not receive effort feedback. Each type of feedback promoted self-efficacy, motivation, and skill acquisition better than no feedback. Feedback during the first half of the program enhanced students' effort attributions for successes. Given students' learning disabilities, effort feedback for early or later successes may have seemed credible.

Young children attribute successes to effort, but by age 8 they begin to form a distinct conception of ability and continue to differentiate the concepts up to about age 12 (Nicholls, 1978, 1979; Nicholls & Miller, 1984). Ability attributions become increasingly important, whereas the influence of effort as a causal factor declines (Harari & Covington, 1981). During arithmetic instruction and practice, Schunk (1983a) found that providing children with ability feedback for prior successes (e.g., "You're good at this") enhanced perceived competence and skill better than providing effort feedback or ability-plus-effort (combined) feedback. Children in the latter condition judged effort expenditure greater than ability-only children and apparently discounted some of the ability information in favor of effort. In a follow-up study using a similar methodology (Schunk, 1984b), ability feedback given when children succeeded early in the course of learning enhanced achievement outcomes better than early effort feedback regardless of whether the ability feedback was continued or discontinued during the later stages of learning.

The *structure* of classroom activities conveys attributional information (Ames, 1992a, 1992b). Students who compete for grades and other rewards are more likely to compare their ability among one another. Students who succeed under *competitive* conditions are more likely to emphasize their abilities as contributing to their successes; those who fail believe they lack the requisite ability to succeed. These conditions create an ego-involved motivational state. Students begin to ask themselves, "Am I smart?" (Ames, 1985).

Cooperative, or *individualistic,* reward structures, on the other hand, minimize ability differences. Cooperative structures stress student effort when each student is responsible for completing some aspect of the task and for instructing other group members on that aspect, and when the group is rewarded for its collective performance. In individualistic structures, students compare their current work with their prior performances. Students in individualistic structures focus on their efforts ("Am I trying hard enough?") and on learning strategies for enhancing their achievement ("How can I do this?").

The current educational emphasis on *inclusion* means that students with high-incidence (e.g., learning) disabilities and low-incidence (e.g., severe) disabilities are grouped with other learners in the regular classroom as much as possible. In inclusive classrooms learners often work on tasks cooperatively. To date, there has not been much research on the effectiveness of inclusive classrooms (McGregor & Vogelsberg, 1998), but related research shows that grouping is a beneficial practice as long as the group succeeds (Ames, 1984). Group success enhances the self-evaluations of poor performers. Cooperative groups comprising students with and without learning disabilities function well if they are first taught how to work in small groups (Bryan, Cosden, & Pearl, 1982). When group members do not work well together, the performances and self-evaluations of students with and without learning disabilities suffer (Licht & Kistner, 1986). Furthermore, if the group fails, students may blame the slower learners (often unfairly), which negatively affects self-efficacy and motivation of group members.

Goal Orientations

Goal theory and research suggest several ways that teachers can foster a productive learning goal orientation. Teachers might help students alter their beliefs about limits to their abilities and the usefulness of effort as a means to improve their motivation. Giving students progress feedback showing how their skills have improved (i.e., how much they have learned), along with information showing that effort has helped to produce learning, can create a growth mindset, raise self-efficacy, and motivate students to improve skills further.

Another suggestion is to use more collaborative student activities. Duda and Nicholls (1992) found for both sport and schoolwork that task orientation (growth mindset) related to high school students' beliefs that success depends on effort and collaboration with peers, whereas ego orientation (fixed mindset) was associated with beliefs that success is due to high ability and attempting to perform better than others. Goal orientations and beliefs about success were not strongly related to perceived ability. Perceived ability related better to satisfaction in sport than in school; the opposite pattern was obtained for task orientation.

A third way to promote a learning-goal orientation is to help students adopt learning goals. Teachers can stress acquiring skills, learning new strategies, developing problem-solving methods, and so forth. They also can de-emphasize goals such as completing work, finishing earlier than other students, and rechecking work. Assignments should involve learning; when students practice skills, teachers can stress the reasons for the practice (e.g., to retard forgetting) and inform students that skillful practice shows skills have been retained (i.e., recast practice in terms of skill acquisition). Application 8.8 gives some other suggestions for instilling a task orientation, incremental ability conception, and focus on learning goals in students.

APPLICATION 8.8
Goal Orientations

Promoting learning goal orientations in the classroom can foster self-efficacy and enhance learning. In working with her third-grade students on multiplication, Kathy Stone might introduce the unit by saying, "Boys and girls, today we are going to learn some things about putting numbers together that will make you much better math students." Then she could emphasize acquisition of skills ("As we work today, you are going to learn how to multiply numbers together"), learning of new strategies ("We are going to use these manipulatives to help us figure out different ways to group numbers together and multiply"), and development of problem-solving methods ("I want all of you to put on your thinking caps as we work to figure out different numbers you can multiply together to make

20"). It is important to stress these goals and de-emphasize goals such as completing work and finishing before other students.

Working together in a large group, in small groups, or in pairs to solve problems helps to diminish competition and to allow students to focus more on learning rather than on completing a certain amount of work. With law students, an instructor could pair them to help one another locate prior cases on child abuse and encourage them with statements such as, "I want you to put your efforts toward learning how to research a case," and "I want you to work to prepare precise short and direct opening statements." These types of statements focus students on goals for the task at hand; students can then assess learning progress against these statements.

SUMMARY

Motivation refers to the process of instigating and sustaining goal-directed behavior. Some early views on motivation were drive theory, conditioning theory, cognitive consistency theory, and humanistic theory. Each of these contributed to the understanding of motivation, but none was adequate to explain human motivated behavior. Current theories view motivation as reflecting cognitive processes, although these theories differ in the importance ascribed to various cognitions. Models of motivated learning assume that motivation operates before, during, and after learning.

Atkinson's achievement motivation theory postulates that need for achievement is a general motive leading individuals to perform their best in achievement contexts. Achievement behavior represents an emotional conflict between hope for success and fear of failure. Eccles and Wigfield developed an expectancy-value theory of achievement motivation that surmounts many problems of older views. The self-worth theory of Covington and his colleagues hypothesizes that achievement behavior is a function of students' efforts to preserve the perception of high ability among themselves and others. Other researchers have focused on motivational states such as task and ego involvement.

Attribution theory incorporates Rotter's locus of control and many elements of Heider's naïve analysis of action. Weiner's attribution theory, which is relevant to achievement settings, categorizes attributions along three dimensions: internal–external, stable–unstable, and controllable–uncontrollable. Attributions are important because they affect achievement beliefs, emotions, and behaviors.

Social cognitive theory views motivation as resulting from goals and expectations. People set goals and act in ways they believe will help them attain their goals. By comparing present performance to the goal and noting progress, people experience a sense of self-efficacy for improvement. Motivation depends on believing that one will achieve desired outcomes from given behaviors (positive outcome expectations) and that one is capable of performing or learning to perform those behaviors (high self-efficacy). Social comparisons with others are important sources of information to form outcome and efficacy expectations.

Goal theory postulates important links between people's goals, expectations, attributions, conceptions of ability, motivational orientations, social and self comparisons, and achievement behaviors. In achievement contexts, learners may possess learning (mastery) or performance (ability-focused) goals. The theory predicts that learning goals focus attention better on skills and competencies needed for learning and that as students perceive progress, their self-efficacy and motivation are enhanced. In contrast, performance goals may not lead to the same focus on progress, but rather result in social comparisons, which may not raise motivation. Goal orientations are linked with conceptions of ability that reflect an entity (fixed mindset) or incremental (growth mindset) perspective.

Many theories stress people's desire to exert control over important aspects of their lives. Control beliefs have especially powerful effects in achievement settings. When people perceive independence between responses and outcomes, learned helplessness manifests itself in motivational, learning, and emotional deficits. Learned helplessness is applicable to many students with learning problems who display negative attributional patterns and low self-efficacy in their learning capabilities.

Theory and research on self-concept are relevant to motivation. Research suggests that self-concept is hierarchically organized and multifaceted. It develops from a concrete to a more abstract self-view. Self-concept and learning appear to influence one another in reciprocal fashion.

Intrinsically interesting activities are ends in themselves, in contrast to extrinsically motivated actions, which are means to some ends. White and Harter hypothesized that young children have intrinsic motivation to understand and control their environments, which becomes more specialized with development and progression in school. Harter's theory highlights the role of socializing agents and perceived competence. Other theorists hypothesize that intrinsic motivation depends on the needs for optimal levels of psychological or physiological incongruity, on attempts to engage in self-determination, and on a flow-type involvement with activities. Much research has addressed the effect of rewards on intrinsic motivation. Offering rewards for task engagement decreases intrinsic motivation when rewards are seen as controlling behavior. Rewards given contingent on one's level of performance are informative of capabilities and foster students' self-efficacy, interest, and skill acquisition.

Achievement motivation, attributions, and goal orientations have important educational applications. Achievement motivation programs are designed to foster students' desire to learn and perform well at achievement tasks. Attributional change programs attempt to alter students' dysfunctional attributions for failure, such as from low ability to insufficient effort. Attributional feedback for prior successes improves self-efficacy, motivation, and skill acquisition. Teachers can foster productive goal orientations in students by teaching them to set learning goals and providing feedback on their goal progress.

FURTHER READING

Dweck, C. S. (2006). *Mindset: The new psychology of success*. New York: Random House.

Elliot, A. J. (2005). A conceptual history of the achievement goal construct. In A. J. Elliot & C. S. Dweck (Eds.), *Handbook of competence and motivation* (pp. 52–72). New York: Guilford Press.

Pintrich, P. R. (2003). A motivational science perspective on the role of student motivation in learning and teaching contexts. *Journal of Educational Psychology, 95,* 667–686.

Reeve, J., Deci, E. L., & Ryan, R. M. (2004). Self-determination theory: A dialectical framework for understanding sociocultural influences on student motivation. In D. M. McInerney & S. Van Etten (Eds.), *Big theories revisited* (pp. 31–60). Greenwich, CT: Information Age Publishing.

Rogers, C. R., & Frieberg, A. J. (1994). *Freedom to learn* (3rd ed.). Columbus, OH: Merrill/Prentice Hall.

Weiner, B. (2005). Motivation from an attributional perspective and the social psychology of perceived competence. In A. J. Elliot & C. S. Dweck (Eds.), *Handbook of competence and motivation* (pp. 73–84). New York: Guilford Press.

Wigfield, A., & Eccles, J. S. (2002). The development of competence beliefs, expectancies for success, and achievement values from childhood through adolescence. In A. Wigfield & J. S. Eccles (Eds.), *Development of achievement motivation* (pp. 91–120). San Diego: Academic Press.

Chapter **9**

Self-Regulation

Kim Danola, a high school sophomore, is meeting with her counselor Connie Smith. Kim is struggling in school, making Cs and Ds in her courses. Connie knows that Kim can do better in school. Kim's home is full of distractions and she has a hard time studying there. The two are meeting to discuss a plan to help Kim academically.

Kim: I don't know; my classes are all so different. Algebra, chemistry, history: they don't have anything in common.

Connie: Well, I agree they are different subjects. But let's think about it. Do you have a textbook in each class?

Kim: Sure.

Connie: So then, in all of them you have to do what?

Kim: Read?

Connie: Sure, read. They all involve reading right?

Kim: Yeah, but the readings are so different. It's like you have to read and study one way in math, a different way in chemistry, and another different way in history.

Connie: Yes, I understand. Kim, there are lots of students in our school who have trouble in these classes. We have student tutors at the school. I'm going to set you up with a tutor for each subject. That student will teach you learning strategies for each subject. But let's go back to what they all have in common. I'm taking a class at the university, and I've learned some general study strategies that you can use in all subjects. So I'm going to help you with those.

Kim: Such as?

Connie: Such as checking yourself when you read something to make sure you understood what you read. It's called "comprehension monitoring," and you can do it whenever you read anything. Then there are some other general strategies, such as setting goals, taking notes, and summarizing information. These are general skills. You learn them and how to adapt them to the subject you're studying. I'll help you with those.

Kim: Do you think there's hope for me? My parents are really mad about my grades.

Connie: If I didn't think there was hope, I wouldn't be talking with you. Now let's get started!

The preceding chapters discuss learning processes that are applicable to diverse content in varied settings. For example, processes such as modeling, encoding, and metacognition apply to many types of learning; they are not unique to certain learners or a few content areas. This is what Connie says in the above scenario.

The focus of this chapter is self-regulation. *Self-regulation* (or *self-regulated learning*) refers to processes that learners use to systematically focus their thoughts, feelings, and actions, on the attainment of their goals (Zimmerman, 2000). Research on self-regulation during learning began as an outgrowth of psychological investigations into the development of self-control by adults and children (Zimmerman, 2001). Much early self-regulation research was conducted in clinical contexts, where researchers taught participants to alter such dysfunctional behaviors as aggression, addictions, sexual disorders, interpersonal conflicts, and behavioral problems at home and in school (Mace & West, 1986). Self-regulation has expanded to address academic learning and achievement (Zimmerman & Schunk, 2001).

The present chapter makes it clear that self-regulation can take many forms. Most notably, self-regulation involves behaviors, as individuals regulate their behaviors to keep themselves focused on goal attainment. But self-regulation also involves cognitive and affective variables. Thus, while involved in learning activities, it is helpful for learners to maintain a sense of self-efficacy for learning, value the learning, believe that positive outcomes will result, and maintain a positive emotional climate (e.g., enjoy what they are doing).

The self-regulatory processes and strategies that learners apply vary in whether they are general (apply to many types of learning) or specific (apply only to a particular type of learning). This distinction is highlighted in the opening scenario. Some self-regulatory processes, such as setting goals and evaluating goal progress, can be employed generally, whereas others pertain only to specific tasks (e.g., applying the quadratic formula to solve quadratic equations).

Self-regulation has been addressed by the various theories covered in earlier chapters in this text, and how these differing perspectives treat self-regulation is explained in this chapter. In recent years, researchers have increasingly been concerned with the self-regulation of motivation, and that topic also is addressed.

The first four sections of this chapter cover different theoretical perspectives on self-regulation: behavioral, social cognitive, information processing, and constructivist. The relation of self-regulation with motivation then is discussed, and the chapter concludes by discussing instructional applications involving self-regulation in the areas of academic studying, writing, and mathematics.

When you finish studying this chapter, you should be able to do the following:

■ Define and exemplify the key behavioral subprocesses of self-regulation: self-monitoring, self-instruction, and self-reinforcement.

■ Define and exemplify the social-cognitive self-regulation subprocesses of self-observation, self-judgment, and self-reaction.

■ Discuss the various processes that operate during the social cognitive phases of self-regulation: forethought, performance/volitional control, and self-reflection.

■ Explain self-regulation from an information processing perspective, and give examples of self-regulatory strategies used by proficient learners.

- Discuss self-regulation from a constructivist perspective to include the role of students' implicit theories.

- Discuss how different motivational variables (e.g., self-efficacy, goals, values) relate to self-regulation.

- Devise a plan that students might use to improve their academic studying.

- Explain how self-regulation principles can promote achievement in writing and mathematics.

BEHAVIORAL THEORY

A behavioral theory perspective on self-regulation derives largely from the work of Skinner (Mace et al., 2001; Chapter 3). Researchers working within the framework of his operant conditioning theory apply operant principles in diverse settings (e.g., clinical, academic) with adults and children. The aim of these studies is to reduce dysfunctional behaviors and replace them with more-adaptive behaviors (Zimmerman, 2001).

Much behavioral research has been characterized by certain design features. Studies typically use few participants and sometimes only one participant. Participants are followed over time to determine behavioral changes resulting from interventions. The outcome measures are frequency and duration of the dysfunctional behaviors and the behaviors to be conditioned.

From a behavioral theory perspective, self-regulation involves choosing among different behaviors and deferring immediate reinforcement in favor of delayed, and usually greater, reinforcement. People self-regulate their behaviors by initially deciding which behaviors to regulate. They then establish discriminative stimuli for their occurrence, provide self-instruction as needed, and monitor their performances to determine whether the desired behavior occurs. This phase often involves self-recording the frequency or duration of behavior. When desirable behavior occurs, people administer self-reinforcement. These three key subprocesses of self-monitoring, self-instruction, and self-reinforcement are discussed next.

Self-Monitoring

Self-monitoring refers to deliberate attention to some aspect of one's behavior and often is accompanied by recording its frequency or intensity (Mace et al., 2001; Mace & Kratochwill, 1988). People cannot regulate their actions if they are not aware of what they do. Behaviors can be assessed on such dimensions as quality, rate, quantity, and originality. While writing a term paper, students may periodically assess their work to determine whether it states important ideas, whether they will finish it by the due date, whether it will be too long or too short, and whether it integrates their ideas. One can engage in self-monitoring in such diverse areas as motor skills (e.g., how fast one runs the 100-meter dash), art (e.g., how original one's pen-and-ink drawings are), and social behavior (e.g., how much one talks at social functions).

Often students must be taught one or more self-monitoring methods (Belfiore & Hornyak, 1998; Lan, 1998; Ollendick & Hersen, 1984; Application 9.1). Methods include narrations, frequency counts, duration measures, time-sampling measures, behavior ratings, and behavioral traces and archival records (Mace et al., 1989). *Narrations* are written accounts of behavior and the context in which it occurs. Narrations can range from very detailed to open-ended. *Frequency counts* are used to self-record instances of specific behaviors during a given period (e.g., number of times a student turns around in his or her seat during a 30-minute seat work exercise). *Duration measures* record the amount

---

APPLICATION 9.1
Self-Monitoring

Self-monitoring makes students aware of existing behaviors and assists them in evaluating and improving those behaviors. In a special education self-contained or resource class, self-monitoring could help students improve on-task behavior, particularly if it is coupled with goal setting. The teacher might create individual charts divided into small blocks representing a short time period (e.g., 10 minutes). Once students are working independently at their seats or work stations, a signal could be given every 10 minutes. When the signal occurs, students could record on their charts what they are doing—writing, reading, daydreaming, talking with others, and so forth. The teacher could help each student set individual goals related to the number of on-task behaviors expected in a day, which would be increased as the student's behavior improves.

It is important that teachers be careful about how they indicate time periods to self-monitoring students. Using a bell might disrupt other students and draw embarrassing attention to the students having difficulty. Kathy Stone seats her third-grade self-monitoring students close to her so that she can gently tap the students' desks at the end of each time period or otherwise quietly indicate its end to these students.

Jim Marshall has a few students who have difficulty completing assignments and reading all the material required for his history class. He meets with these students after school each Monday and Friday to help them establish realistic goals for developing productive study habits and evaluate goal progress. He also works with the students to record how much reading (by pages), note studying, writing, and so forth, they accomplish in a set time period. Using the goals and a timer, students can monitor their progress toward achieving the goals.

Some students in Gina Brown's class had difficulty completing their first paper. She provided considerable guidance, but it was clear that these students were not working in sequential steps to complete the paper by the deadline. For the next paper, she initially met individually with each of these students and created a checklist of items and timetable necessary for completing the paper. She then met with them weekly, at which time they shared with her their progress on the checklist and completion of the assignment. This helped the students develop a tool that they could use to self-monitor progress toward completing assignments in any course.

of time a behavior occurs during a given period (e.g., number of minutes a student studies during 30 minutes). *Time-sampling measures* divide a period into shorter intervals and record how often a behavior occurs during each interval. A 30-minute study period might be divided into six 5-minute periods; for each 5-minute period, students record whether they studied the entire time. *Behavior ratings* require estimates of how often a behavior occurs during a given time (e.g., always, sometimes, never). *Behavioral traces* and *archival records* are permanent records that exist independently of other assessments (e.g., number of worksheets completed, number of problems solved correctly).

In the absence of self-recording, selective memory of successes and failures can occur. Our beliefs about outcomes often do not faithfully reflect our actual outcomes (e.g., we may think we performed better than we actually did). Self-recording can yield surprising results. Students having difficulties studying who keep a written record of their activities may learn they are wasting more than half of their study time on nonacademic tasks.

There are two important criteria for self-monitoring: regularity and proximity (Bandura, 1986). *Regularity* means monitoring behavior on a continual basis instead of intermittently; for example, keeping a daily record rather than recording behavior one day per week. Nonregular observation often yields misleading results. *Proximity* means that behavior is monitored close in time to its occurrence rather than long afterward. It is better to write down what we do at the time it occurs, rather than to wait until the end of the day to reconstruct events.

Self-monitoring methods place responsibility for behavioral assessment on the student (Belfiore & Hornyak, 1998). These methods often lead to significant behavioral improvements, known as reactive effects. Self-monitored responses are consequences of behaviors, and like other consequences, they affect future responding. Self-recordings are immediate responses that serve to mediate the relationship between preceding behavior and longer-term consequences (Mace & West, 1986; Nelson & Hayes, 1981). Students who monitor their completion of problems during seat work provide themselves with immediate reinforcers that mediate the link between seat work and such distant consequences as teacher praise and good grades.

Research supports the benefits of self-monitoring on achievement outcomes. Sagotsky, Patterson, and Lepper (1978) had children periodically monitor their performances during mathematics sessions and record whether they were working on the appropriate instructional material. Other students set daily performance goals, and students in a third condition received self-monitoring and goal setting. Self-monitoring increased time on task and mathematical achievement; goal setting had minimal effects. For goal setting to affect performance, students initially may need to learn how to set challenging but attainable goals.

Schunk (1983d) provided subtraction instruction and practice to children who failed to master subtraction operations in their classrooms. One group (self-monitoring) reviewed their work at the end of each instructional session and recorded the number of workbook pages they completed. A second group (external monitoring) had their work reviewed at the end of each session by an adult who recorded the number of pages completed. No-monitoring children received the instructional program, but were not monitored or told to monitor their work.

Self- and external-monitoring conditions led to higher self-efficacy, skill, and persistence, compared with no monitoring. The effects of the two monitoring conditions were comparable. The benefits of monitoring did not depend on children's performances during the instructional sessions, because the three treatment conditions did not result in different amounts of work completed. Monitoring progress, rather than who evaluated it, enhanced children's perceptions of their learning progress and self-efficacy.

Reid, Trout, and Schartz (2005) reviewed the literature on self-regulation interventions to promote on-task behavior and academic performance and reduce disruptive behaviors among children with attention deficits and hyperactivity. Self-monitoring, alone and in combination with self-reinforcement, often was a key component in effective interventions.

Self-Instruction

Self-instruction refers to establishing discriminative stimuli that set the occasion for self-regulatory responses leading to reinforcement (Mace et al., 1989). As used here, self-instruction is not the same as self-instructional training (Meichenbaum, 1977; Chapter 4). One type of self-instruction involves arranging the environment to produce discriminative stimuli. Students who realize they need to review class notes the next day might write themselves a reminder before going to bed. The written reminder serves as a cue to review, which makes reinforcement (i.e., a good grade on a quiz) more likely. Another type of self-instruction takes the form of statements (rules) that serve as discriminative stimuli to guide behavior. This type of self-instruction is included in the self-instructional training procedure.

Strategy instruction is an effective means of enhancing comprehension and self-efficacy among poor readers. Schunk and Rice (1986, 1987) taught remedial readers to use the following self-instruction strategy for working on reading comprehension passages:

> What do I have to do? (1) Read the questions. (2) Read the passage to find out what it is mostly about. (3) Think about what the details have in common. (4) Think about what would make a good title. (5) Reread the story if I don't know the answer to a question. (Schunk & Rice, 1987, pp. 290–291)

Children verbalized the individual steps prior to applying them to passages.

Self-instructional statements have been used to teach a variety of academic, social, and motor skills. These statements are especially helpful for students with learning disabilities or attention deficits. Verbalizing statements keeps learners focused on a task. A self-instruction procedure used to improve the handwriting of a student with learning disabilities is as follows (Kosiewicz, Hallahan, Lloyd, & Graves, 1982):

> (1) Say aloud the word to be written. (2) Say the first syllable. (3) Name each of the letters in that syllable three times. (4) Repeat each letter as it is written down. (5) Repeat steps 2 through 4 for each succeeding syllable.

This sequence appeared on a card on the student's desk. During training, the student was praised for completing the steps. Once the student learned the procedure, praise was discontinued and the sequence was maintained by the consequence of better handwriting.

Self-Reinforcement

Self-reinforcement refers to the process whereby individuals reinforce themselves contingent on their performing a desired response, which increases the likelihood of future responding (Mace et al., 1989). As discussed in Chapter 3, a reinforcer is defined on the basis of its effects. To illustrate, assume that Mitch is on a point system: He awards himself one point for each page he reads in his geography book. He keeps a record each week, and if his week's points exceed his previous week's points by 5%, he earns 30 minutes of free time on Friday. Whether this arrangement functions as self-reinforcement cannot be determined until it is known whether he regularly earns the free time. If he does (i.e., his average performance increases as the semester proceeds), then the reinforcement contingency is regulating his academic behaviors.

Much research shows that reinforcement contingencies improve academic performance (Bandura, 1986), but it is unclear whether self-reinforcement is more effective than externally administered reinforcement (such as given by the teacher). Studies investigating self-reinforcement often contain problems (Brigham, 1982; Martin, 1980). In academic settings, the reinforcement contingency typically occurs in a context that includes instruction and rules. Students usually do not work on materials when they choose but rather when told to do so by the teacher. Students may stay on task primarily because of the teacher's classroom control and fear of punishment rather than because of reinforcement.

Self-reinforcement is hypothesized to be an effective component of self-regulated behavior (O'Leary & Dubey, 1979), but the reinforcement may be more important than the agent of reinforcement (self or others). Although self-reinforcement may enhance maintenance of behavior over time, explicitly providing reinforcement may be more important while self-regulatory skills are being learned.

Behavioral theory has been widely applied to teach self-regulated behaviors. The subprocesses of self-monitoring, self-instruction, and self-reinforcement are types of self-regulatory processes that can be taught to students. At the same time, the behavioral position does not take cognitive and affective factors into consideration. This limits its applicability to self-regulation of complex academic learning, because learning requires self-regulating more than just behaviors; for example, goals, self-evaluations of goal progress, and judgments of self-efficacy. These factors are considered critical in a social cognitive theoretical perspective on self-regulation, as discussed next.

SOCIAL COGNITIVE THEORY

Conceptual Framework

The principles of social cognitive theory have been applied extensively to self-regulation (Bandura, 1997, 2001; Pintrich, 2004; Pintrich & Zusho, 2002; B. Zimmerman, 2000; Zimmerman & Schunk, 2004). From a social cognitive perspective, self-regulation requires learner *choice* (Zimmerman, 1994, 1998, 2000; Table 9.1). This does not mean that learners always take advantage of the available choices, especially when they are uncertain about what to do and ask the teacher. When all task aspects are controlled, however,

Table 9.1
Learner choices and self-regulatory processes.

Choice	Self-Regulatory Processes
Choose to participate	Goals, self-efficacy, values
Choose method	Strategy use, relaxation
Choose outcomes	Self-monitoring, self-judgment
Choose social and physical setting	Environmental structuring, help seeking

it is accurate to speak of achievement behavior being "externally controlled" or "controlled by others." This type of situation results when a teacher gives students no latitude in methods, outcomes, and other conditions. The potential for self-regulation varies depending on choices available to learners.

Table 9.1 shows choices potentially available to learners and some corresponding self-regulatory processes. One choice is whether to participate in the task. This depends on such processes as learners' goals, values, and self-efficacy. Learners also may choose the methods they use while performing the task; for example, which strategies they employ and which relaxation techniques they use if they become anxious. A third type of choice involves outcomes: Which outcomes do learners desire? As they work on the task they monitor their performances and judge whether their performances are moving them toward outcome attainment. Finally, learners may be able to choose the social and physical settings they use to work on the task. This may require that they structure their environments to make them conducive to learning and seek help when they need it.

In some classrooms, little self-regulation is possible. Suppose that a teacher tells students to write a 10-page typewritten, double-spaced paper on an assigned topic, containing at least 10 references, completed in 3 weeks, and written individually in the media center and at home. Assuming the teacher further specifies the paper format, the teacher is directing most of this assignment.

In contrast, assume Jim wants to learn to play the guitar. He chooses to engage in this task. The method he chooses is to take lessons from a teacher. He takes one 45-minute lesson per week and practices 1 hour per day. His goal is to be proficient enough to play at social gatherings so others can sing along. He practices the guitar at home at night. Besides his teacher, he enlists the aid of a friend who plays the guitar and asks him technical questions about finger positions and tuning. Jim has almost complete control over the situation, so it allows for maximum self-regulation.

Many situations lie somewhere between these extremes. Teachers may give a term paper assignment but allow students to choose from several topics. Students also may be able to decide on the resources they use, where they write, and how long the paper will be. High school senior graduation projects typically specify some elements (e.g., research paper, oral presentation), but give students choices with other elements (e.g., topic, props). It thus makes more sense to ask to what degree one engages in self-regulation rather than whether one is self-regulated.

Table 9.2
Processes of self-regulation.

Self-Observation	Self-Judgment	Self-Reaction
Regularity	Types of standards	Evaluative motivators
Proximity	Goal properties	Tangible motivators
Self-recording	Goal importance	
	Attributions	

Source: Social Foundations of Thought and Action, by A. Bandura, © 1986. Reprinted by permission of Pearson Education, Inc., Upper Saddle River, NJ.

Interventions designed to enhance self-regulation in students often focus on one or more self-regulatory processes and provide students with instruction and practice on those processes. A wealth of evidence shows that self-regulatory competencies can be enhanced through educational interventions (Schunk & Ertmer, 2000; Schunk & Zimmerman, 1994, 1998, 2008).

Social Cognitive Processes

Early applications of social cognitive theoretical principles of self-regulation involved investigating the operation of three subprocesses: self-observation (or self-monitoring), self-judgment, and self-reaction (Bandura, 1986; Kanfer & Gaelick, 1986; Schunk, 1994; Zimmerman, 1990; Table 9.2). Notice the similarity of these to the three subprocesses espoused by behavioral theory: self-monitoring, self-instruction, and self-reinforcement.

Students enter learning activities with such goals as acquiring knowledge and problem-solving strategies, finishing workbook pages, and completing experiments. With these goals in mind, students observe, judge, and react to their perceived progress. These processes are not mutually exclusive, but rather interact with one another.

Self-Observation. *Self-observation* involves judging observed aspects of one's behavior against standards and reacting positively or negatively. People's evaluations and reactions set the stage for additional observations of the same behavioral aspects or others. These processes also do not operate independently of the environment (Zimmerman, 1986, 1989, 1990, 2000). Students who judge their learning progress as inadequate may react by asking for teacher assistance, which alters their environment. In turn, teachers may instruct students in a more efficient strategy, which students then use to promote their learning. That environmental influences (e.g., teachers) can assist the development of self-regulation is important, because educators advocate that students be taught self-regulatory skills (Schunk & Zimmerman, 1994, 1998, 2008).

Self-observation is conceptually similar to self-monitoring and is commonly taught as part of self-regulatory instruction (Lan, 1998; Zimmerman, Bonner, & Kovach, 1996); however, by itself self-observation usually is insufficient to self-regulate behavior over time. Standards of goal attainment and criteria in assessing goal progress are necessary.

Self-Judgment. *Self-judgment* refers to comparing present performance level with one's goal. Self-judgments depend on the type of self-evaluative standards employed, properties of the goal, importance of goal attainment, and attributions.

Self-evaluative standards may be absolute or normative. Absolute standards are fixed; normative standards are based on performances of others. Students whose goal is to read six workbook pages in 30 minutes gauge their progress against this absolute standard. Grading systems often reflect absolute standards (e.g., A = 90–100, B = 80–89).

Normative standards frequently are acquired by observing models (Bandura, 1986). Socially comparing one's performances with those of others is an important way to determine the appropriateness of behaviors and self-evaluate performances. Social comparisons become more probable when absolute standards are nonexistent or ambiguous (Festinger, 1954). Students have numerous opportunities to compare their work with that of their peers. Absolute and normative standards often are employed in concert, as when students have 30 minutes to read six pages and compare their progress with peers to gauge who will be the first to finish.

Standards inform and motivate. Comparing performance with standards indicates goal progress. Students who read three pages in 10 minutes realize they have finished half of the work in less than half of the time. The belief that they are making progress enhances their self-efficacy, which sustains their motivation to complete the task. Similar others, rather than those much higher or lower in ability, offer the best basis for comparison, because students are apt to believe that if others can succeed, they will too (Schunk, 1987).

Schunk (1983b) compared the effects of social comparative information with those of goal setting during a division training program. Half of the children were given performance goals during each instructional session; the other half were advised to work productively. Within each goal condition, half of the students were told the number of problems other similar children had completed (which matched the session goal) to convey that goals were attainable; the other half were not given comparative information. Goals enhanced self-efficacy; comparative information promoted motivation. Children who received both goals and comparative information demonstrated the highest skill acquisition.

An important means of acquiring self-evaluative standards is through observation of models. Bandura and Kupers (1964) exposed children to a peer or adult demonstrating stringent or lenient standards while playing a bowling game. Children exposed to high-standard models were more likely to reward themselves for high scores and less likely to reward themselves for lower scores compared with those assigned to the low-standard condition. Adult models produced stronger effects than peers. Davidson and Smith (1982) had children observe a superior adult, equal peer, or inferior younger child set stringent or lenient task standards. Children who observed a lenient model rewarded themselves more often for lower scores than those who observed a stringent model. Children's self-reward standards were lower than those of the adult, equal to those of the peer, and higher than those of the younger child. Model–observer similarity in age might have led children to believe that what was appropriate for the peer was appropriate for them.

Observation of models affects self-efficacy and achievement behaviors (Chapter 4). Zimmerman and Ringle (1981) exposed children to an adult model who unsuccessfully

APPLICATION 9.2
Goal Setting and Self-Regulation

Goal setting is a useful self-regulatory skill for completing long-term tasks. Many students have doubts about finishing a history project that includes a display and a research paper. Jim Marshall assists his students by breaking the assignment into short-term goals. If students have a 6-week period to complete the project, their first task might be to choose a topic after researching various topics. He allows 1 week for research, after which students submit their topics with a brief explanation of their selections. The second week is spent in more specific research and in developing an outline for the paper. After the outlines are submitted and feedback from him is received, students have 2 weeks to work on the initial drafts of their papers and to draw a sketch of the items to be included in their displays. He then reviews their progress and provides

feedback. Students can revise papers and develop displays during the final 2 weeks.

A law student can become overwhelmed when trying to memorize and analyze numerous landmark cases in preparing for moot court. Law professors can help throughout the semester by having students set realistic goals and by helping students organize their studying. Students might begin by establishing goals to learn the cases for major categories (e.g., substantive, procedural, public, private, and international law) in a set time period. Within each major goal category subgoals can be created; for example, for the major goal category of private law, subgoals can be established for ownership and use of property, contracts between individuals, family relationships, and redress by way of compensation for harm inflicted on one person by another.

attempted to solve a wire puzzle for a long or short period and who verbalized statements of confidence or pessimism. Children who observed a pessimistic model persist for a long time lowered their efficacy judgments. Perceived similarity to models is especially influential when observers experience difficulties and possess self-doubts about performing well (Schunk & Hanson, 1985; Schunk et al., 1987).

Goal properties—specificity, proximity, difficulty—are especially influential with long-term tasks (Kanfer & Kanfer, 1991; Chapter 4). Teachers can assist students who have doubts about writing a good term paper by breaking the task into short-term goals (e.g., selecting a topic, conducting background research, writing an outline). Learners are apt to believe they can accomplish the subtasks, and completing each subtask develops their self-efficacy for producing a good term paper. Other examples are given in Application 9.2.

Allowing students to set goals for learning enhances goal commitment (Locke & Latham, 1990, 2002) and promotes self-efficacy (Schunk, 1990). Schunk (1985) found support for this in a study with children with learning disabilities. Some children set mathematical subtraction problem-solving goals for themselves each session, others were assigned comparable goals by a teacher, and others received instruction but no goals. Self-set goals led to higher expectancies of goal attainment compared with goals set by others. Relative to the other two conditions, self-set goals produced the highest self-efficacy and greatest skill acquisition.

Self-judgments reflect in part the importance of goal attainment. When individuals care little about how they perform, they may not assess their performance or expend effort to improve it (Bandura, 1986). People judge their progress in learning for goals they value. Sometimes goals that originally hold little value become more important when people receive feedback indicating they are becoming skillful. Thus, novice piano players initially may hold ill-defined goals for themselves (e.g., play better). As their skill develops, people begin to set specific goals (e.g., learn to play a particular piece) and judge progress relative to these goals.

Attributions (perceived causes of outcomes; Chapter 8), along with goal progress judgments, can affect self-efficacy, motivation, achievement, and affective reactions (Schunk, 2001, 2008). Students who believe they are not making good progress toward their goals may attribute their performances to low ability, which negatively impacts expectancies and behaviors. Students who attribute poor progress to lackadaisical effort or an inadequate learning strategy may believe they will perform better if they work harder or switch to a different strategy (Schunk, 2008). With respect to affective reactions, people take more pride in their accomplishments when they attribute them to ability and effort than to external causes (Weiner, 1985). People are more self-critical when they believe that they failed due to personal reasons rather than to circumstances beyond their control.

Attributional feedback can enhance self-regulated learning (Schunk, 2008). Being told that one can achieve better results through harder work can motivate one to do so, because the feedback conveys that one is capable (Andrews & Debus, 1978; Dweck, 1975; Schunk, 2008). Providing effort feedback for prior successes supports students' perceptions of their progress, sustains their motivation, and increases their efficacy for further learning (Schunk, 1982a; Schunk & Cox, 1986).

The timing of attributional feedback may be important. Early task successes constitute a prominent cue for forming ability attributions. Feedback linking early successes with ability (e.g., "That's correct; you're good at this") should enhance learning efficacy. Many times, however, effort feedback for early successes is more credible, because when students lack skills they have to expend effort to succeed. As students develop skills, ability feedback better enhances self-efficacy (Schunk, 1983a).

Self-Reaction. *Self-reactions* to goal progress motivate behavior (Bandura, 1986; Zimmerman & Schunk, 2004). The belief that one is making acceptable progress, along with the anticipated satisfaction of accomplishing the goal, enhances self-efficacy and sustains motivation. Negative evaluations do not decrease motivation if individuals believe they are capable of improving (Schunk, 1995). If students believe they have been lackadaisical but can progress with enhanced effort, they are apt to feel efficacious and redouble their efforts. Motivation does not improve if students believe they lack the ability and will not succeed no matter how hard they try (Schunk, 1982a, 2008).

Instructions to people to respond evaluatively to their performances promote motivation; people who think they can perform better persist longer and expend greater effort

(Kanfer & Gaelick, 1986). Perceived progress is relative to one's goals; the same level of performance can be evaluated differently. Some students are content with a B in a course, whereas others will be dissatisfied with a B because they want an A. Assuming that people feel capable of improving, higher goals lead to greater effort and persistence than lower goals (Bandura & Cervone, 1983).

People routinely reward themselves tangibly with work breaks, new clothes, and evenings out with friends, contingent on their making progress toward goal attainment. Social cognitive theory postulates that the anticipated consequences of behavior, rather than the actual consequences, enhance motivation (Bandura, 1986). Grades are given at the end of courses, yet students typically set subgoals for accomplishing their work and reward and punish themselves accordingly.

Tangible consequences also affect self-efficacy. External rewards that are given based on actual accomplishments enhance efficacy. Telling students that they will earn rewards based on what they accomplish instills a sense of self-efficacy for learning (Schunk, 1995). Self-efficacy is validated as students work on a task and note their progress. Receipt of the reward further validates efficacy, because it symbolizes progress. Rewards not tied to performances (e.g., given for spending time on the task regardless of what one accomplishes) may convey negative self-efficacy information; students might infer they are not expected to learn much because they are not capable (Schunk, 1983e).

Cyclical Nature of Self-Regulation

Social cognitive theory emphasizes the interaction of personal, behavioral, and environmental factors (Bandura, 1986, 1997; Pintrich & Zusho, 2002; Zimmerman, 2000, 2001; Zimmerman & Schunk, 2004; Chapter 4). Self-regulation is a cyclical process because these factors typically change during learning and must be monitored. Such monitoring leads to changes in an individual's strategies, cognitions, affects, and behaviors.

This cyclical nature is captured in Zimmerman's (1998, 2000) three-phase self-regulation model (Figure 9.1). This model also expands the classical view, which covers task engagement, because it includes self-regulatory processes performed before and after engagement. The forethought phase precedes actual performance and refers to processes that set the stage for action. The performance (volitional) control phase involves processes that occur during learning and affect attention and action. During the self-reflection phase, which occurs after performance, people respond to their efforts (Zimmerman & Schunk, 2004).

Figure 9.1
Self-regulation cycle phases.
Source: From "Developing Self-Fulfilling Cycles of Academic Regulation: An Analysis of Exemplary Instructional Models," by B. J. Zimmerman, 1998, in D. H. Schunk and B. J. Zimmerman, (Eds.)., *Self-Regulated Learning: From Teaching to Self Reflective Practice* (p. 3). New York: Guilford Press.

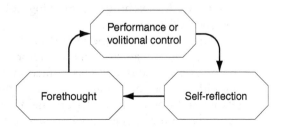

Various self-regulatory processes come into play during the different phases. In the forethought phase, learners set goals, engage in strategic planning, and hold a sense of self-efficacy for attaining their goals. Performance control involves implementing learning strategies that affect motivation and learning, as well as observing and recording one's performances. During periods of self-reflection, learners engage in self-evaluation (addressed next) and make attributions for their performances. There is evidence that teaching students to engage in self-regulation in all three phases has desirable effects on strategic thinking and attributions (Cleary, Zimmerman, & Keating, 2006).

Self-Evaluation. Effective self-regulation requires goals and motivation (Bandura, 1986; Kanfer & Kanfer, 1991; Zimmerman, 1989, 2000). Students must regulate their actions and underlying achievement cognitions, beliefs, intentions, and affects. Research substantiates the prediction that self-monitoring of achievement beliefs sustains learning and promotes achievement (Schunk & Zimmerman, 1994, 2008; B. Zimmerman, 2000; Zimmerman et al., 1996; Zimmerman & Martinez-Pons, 1992).

Effective self-regulators develop self-efficacy for self-regulating their learning (Caprara et al., 2008; Pajares, 2008; Zimmerman, Bandura, & Martinez-Pons, 1992) and for performing well (Bouffard-Bouchard, Parent, & Larivee, 1991). Research shows that self-efficacy for self-regulated learning bears a significant and positive relation to students' academic achievement and grades (Caprara et al., 2008).

Of critical importance is self-evaluation of capabilities and progress in skill acquisition. *Self-evaluation* comprises self-judgments of present performance by comparing one's goal and self-reactions to those judgments by deeming performance noteworthy, unacceptable, and so forth. Positive self-evaluations lead students to feel efficacious about learning and motivated to continue to work diligently because they believe they are capable of making further progress (Schunk, 1991). Low self-judgments of progress and negative self-reactions will not necessarily diminish self-efficacy and motivation if students believe they are capable of succeeding but that their present approach is ineffective (Bandura, 1986). Such students may alter their self-regulatory processes by working harder, persisting longer, adopting what they believe is a better strategy, or seeking help from teachers and peers (Schunk, 1990). These and other self-regulatory activities are likely to lead to success (Schunk, 2001; Zimmerman & Martinez-Pons, 1992).

Research substantiates the hypothesis that self-evaluations of capabilities and progress in skill acquisition affect achievement outcomes (Schunk & Ertmer, 2000). Investigations with children during learning of mathematical skills (Schunk & Hanson, 1985; Schunk et al., 1987) and writing skills (Schunk & Swartz, 1993a, 1993b) show that self-efficacy for learning or improving skills assessed prior to instruction predict motivation and skill acquisition.

Bandura and Cervone (1983) obtained benefits of goals and self-evaluative feedback among college students on motor-skill performance. A similar study showed that the greater the students' dissatisfaction with their performances and the higher their self-efficacy for performing well, the stronger was their subsequent effort expenditure (Bandura & Cervone, 1986). Cervone, Jiwani, and Wood (1991) found that providing individuals with a specific goal enhanced the effects of self-efficacy and self-evaluation on performance.

Students may not spontaneously self-evaluate their capabilities. One means of high-lighting progress is to have them periodically assess their progress. Explicit capability self-evaluations constitute a type of self-monitoring because students must attend to their present performance and compare it with their prior performance to note progress. By making performance improvements salient, such self-monitoring is apt to raise self-efficacy, sustain self-regulatory activities, and promote skills. White, Kjelgaard, and Harkins (1995) noted that self-evaluation augments the effects of goals on performance when goals are informative of one's capabilities.

Schunk (1996) conducted two studies that investigated how goals and self-evaluation affect achievement outcomes. Fourth graders received instruction and practice on fractions over several sessions. Students worked under conditions involving either a goal of learning how to solve problems (process goal) or a goal of merely solving them (product goal). In Study 1, half of the students in each goal condition evaluated their problem-solving capabilities. The process goal (with or without self-evaluation) and the product goal with self-evaluation led to higher self-efficacy, skill, self-directed performance, and task orientation than did the product goal without self-evaluation. In Study 2, all students in each goal condition evaluated their progress in skill acquisition. The process goal led to higher motivation and achievement outcomes than did the product goal.

Schunk and Ertmer (1999) examined how goals and self-evaluation affected self-efficacy, achievement, and self-reported competence and use of self-regulatory strategies. College undergraduates worked on computer projects over three sessions. Students received a process goal of learning computer applications or a product goal of performing them. In the first study, half of the students in each goal condition evaluated their progress in learning after the second session. The process goal led to higher self-efficacy, self-judged learning progress, and self-regulatory competence and strategy use; the opportunity for self-evaluation promoted self-efficacy. In the second study, self-evaluation students assessed their progress after each session. Frequent self-evaluation produced comparable results when coupled with a process or product goal. Collectively, these results suggest that infrequent self-evaluation complements learning process goals, but that multiple self-evaluations outweigh the benefits of process goals and raise achievement outcomes for all students.

Having students self-monitor their performance and evaluate their capabilities or progress in learning makes it clear that they have become more competent, and this perception strengthens self-efficacy and enhances self-regulated learning efforts. This research has implications for teaching. Students may not normally be in the habit of evaluating their skills or learning progress; thus, they may require instruction in self-evaluation and frequent opportunities to practice it. Suggestions for incorporating self-evaluation in learning settings are given in Application 9.3.

Learning Strategies. The opening scenario underscores the importance of *learning strategies*. Self-regulated learners believe acquisition of proficiency is a strategically controllable process and accept responsibility for their achievement outcomes (Zimmerman & Martinez-Pons, 1992). According to social cognitive theory, self-regulated strategy use is influenced by students' self-belief systems. Self-regulated learners are metacognitively aware of strategic relations between self-regulatory processes and learning outcomes, feel

APPLICATION 9.3
Incorporating Self-Evaluation into Learning

Teaching students to evaluate their progress and learning can begin as early as preschool and kindergarten. Teachers initially might use simple self-checking. Children might be asked to assemble various shaped blocks to form a larger shape (rectangle, square, triangle, hexagon). Samples of various ways to combine the smaller blocks to make the shape can be drawn on cards and placed in an envelope at an activity center. Older elementary students might be given an activity sheet that accompanies a hands-on task with the answers for the sheet listed on the back so they can check their work.

For older students, self-checking can be integrated into daily activities. They also can also be taught to evaluate their learning by utilizing pretests and practice tests; for example, with the learning of spelling words and mathematical facts. More complicated and thorough practice tests can be used with middle school and high school students, allowing them to determine how much studying to do and what activities they need to complete to master the unit goals.

self-efficacious about using strategies, have academic goals of learning, have control over debilitating thoughts and anxiety, and believe that strategy use will help them attain goals at higher levels (Zimmerman, 1989, 1990, 2000, 2001, 2008; Zimmerman & Cleary, 2009).

Social and Self Influences

The social cognitive perspective on self-regulation reflects Bandura's (1986) notion of triadic reciprocality. This system contrasts with noncognitive (behavioral) views (Chapter 3), which, although they employ some of the same methods (e.g., self-recording), are limited in that they do not include powerful cognitive learning strategies. This system also contrasts with closed negative feedback loops (Carver & Scheier, 1990, 2000). In this view, learners compare performance feedback continuously against learning goals. If feedback indicates substandard performance, they try to improve. Reductions in negative feedback are motivating, and once the goal is achieved, work on the task ceases. This closed feature is a significant impediment to students' continuing motivation (Anderman & Maehr, 1994).

Social cognitive theorists argue that self-regulatory systems are open: Goals and strategic activities change based on self-evaluations of feedback. Goal progress and attainment raises learners' self-efficacy and can lead to their adopting new, more-difficult goals (Schunk, 1990). Further, students who feel efficacious about learning select what they believe are useful learning strategies, monitor their performances, and alter their task approach when their present methods do not appear to function properly (Zimmerman, 1989, 1990). Research shows that self-efficacy relates positively to productive use of self-regulatory strategies (Pajares, 2008; Pintrich & Zusho, 2002; Zimmerman et al., 1992; Zimmerman & Cleary, 2009; Zimmerman & Martinez-Pons, 1990). Results from a series of

Table 9.3
Social and self influences on self-regulation.

Level of Development	Social Influences	Self Influences
Observational	Modeling, verbal description	
Imitative	Social guidance and feedback	
Self-controlled		Internal standards, self-reinforcement
Self-regulated		Self-regulatory processes, self-efficacy beliefs

studies support the notion that altering goals and strategies is adaptive during learning (Kitsantas & Zimmerman, 1998; Zimmerman & Kitsantas, 1996, 1997). In particular, self-regulation was enhanced by shifting from process to product goals as learning improved.

The dynamic nature of self-regulation is further highlighted in the interaction of social and self influences (Schunk, 1999; Schunk & Zimmerman, 1996, 1997; Table 9.3). Initial learning often proceeds best when learners observe social models, after which they become able to perform skills in rudimentary fashion with appropriate guidance and feedback. As learners develop competence, they enter a self-controlled phase where they can match their actions with internal representations of the skill. At the final level, learners develop self-regulatory processes that they employ to further refine skills and select new goals. Skills and self-efficacy beliefs are strengthened and internalized throughout this sequence. Although it is possible that learners could skip early phases if they enter with some skill, this sequence is useful in planning instruction to develop skills and self-regulatory competence (Zimmerman & Kitsantas, 2005).

INFORMATION PROCESSING THEORY

Information processing theories have evolved from their original formulations to incorporate cognitive and motivational self-regulatory processes. This section presents an information processing model of self-regulation that includes these components, and discusses research and applications on learning strategies—a key feature of self-regulation from an information processing perspective.

Model of Self-Regulation

Information processing theories view learning as the encoding of information in long-term memory (LTM; Chapter 5). Learners activate relevant portions of LTM and relate new knowledge to existing information in working memory (WM). Organized, meaningful information is easier to integrate with existing knowledge and more likely to be remembered.

Self-regulation is roughly equivalent to *metacognitive awareness* or *metacognition* (Gitomer & Glaser, 1987), where individuals monitor, direct, and regulate actions toward goals (Paris & Paris, 2001). This awareness includes knowledge of the task (what is to be learned, when and how it is to be learned), as well as self-knowledge of personal capabilities, interests, and attitudes. Self-regulation requires learners to have a sound knowledge base comprising task demands, personal qualities, and strategies for completing the task.

Metacognitive awareness also includes procedural knowledge or productions that regulate learning of the material by monitoring one's level of learning, deciding when to take a different task approach, and assessing readiness for a test. Self-regulatory (metacognitive) activities are types of *control processes* (Chapter 5) under the learner's direction. They facilitate processing and movement of information through the system.

The basic (superordinate) unit of self-regulation may be a *problem-solving production system*, in which the problem is to reach the goal and the monitoring serves to ascertain whether the learner is making progress. This system compares the present situation against a standard and attempts to reduce discrepancies.

An early formulation of this system was Miller, Galanter, and Pribham's (1960) *Test-Operate-Test-Exit (TOTE)* model. The initial test phase compares the present situation against a standard. If they are the same, no further action is required. If they do not match, control is switched to the operate function to change behavior to resolve the discrepancy. One perceives a new state of affairs that is compared to the standard during the second test phase. Assuming that these match, one exits the model. If they do not match, further behavioral changes and comparisons are necessary.

We can illustrate this with Lisa, who is reading her economics text and stops periodically to summarize what she has read. She recalls information from LTM pertaining to what she has read and compares the information to her internal standard of an adequate summary. This standard also may be a production characterized by rules (e.g., be precise, include information on all topics covered, be accurate) developed through experiences in summarizing. Assuming that her summary matches her standard, she continues reading. If they do not match, Lisa evaluates where the problem lies (in her understanding of the second paragraph) and executes a correction strategy (rereads the second paragraph).

Winne and Hadwin (1998, 2008; Winne, 2001) developed an information processing model of self-regulated learning that is highly relevant to education (Greene & Azevedo, 2007). This model comprises three necessary phases (definition of task, goals and plans, studying tactics) and one optional phase (adaptations).

In the first phase, learners process information about the conditions that characterize the task in order to clearly define it (Winne, 2001). There are two main sources of information. Task conditions include information about the task that learners interpret based on the external environment (e.g., teacher's directions for an assignment). Cognitive conditions are those that learners retrieve from long-term memory. These include information about how they did on prior work, as well as motivational variables (e.g., perceived competence, attributions). In the second phase, learners decide on a goal and a plan for attaining it. The plan will include relevant learning strategies. As they begin to apply these strategies, they move into the third phase (studying tactics). In phase four students make adaptations to their plans based on their evaluations of how successful they are. This phase is optional because if the original plan is successful there is no need to adapt it.

Within each phase, information processing occurs and constructs information products, or new information. Information processes work on existing information and are characterized by the acronym SMART: searching, monitoring, assembling, rehearsing, translating. Working on a task requires using a schema, or script, and each script has five possible slots to fill characterized by the acronym COPES: conditions, operations, products, evaluations, standards. Figuratively speaking, these are the elements a student "copes with" to learn (Winne, 2001). Information processing outcomes are judged against standards, and these evaluations (e.g., on target, too high) serve as the basis for bringing new conditions to bear on the student's learning activities.

The importance of this model for education derives heavily from its development and use with learning content and on its inclusion of motivational variables. These motivational variables are combined with cognitive variables to determine the usefulness of a particular self-regulatory schema, or script. This model represents a great advance over traditional and contemporary cognitive information processing models that emphasized cognitive components (Chapter 5). Much research supports the idea that motivational variables are important during self-regulated learning (Zimmerman & Schunk, 2001).

There are other information processing models of self-regulation (e.g., Carver & Scheier, 1998), but they are in agreement in their emphasis on learning strategies. These are discussed next.

Learning Strategies

Learning strategies are cognitive plans oriented toward successful task performance (Pressley et al., 1990; Weinstein & Mayer, 1986). Strategies include activities such as selecting and organizing information, rehearsing material to be learned, relating new material to information in memory, and enhancing meaningfulness of material. Strategies also include techniques that create and maintain a positive learning climate—for example, ways to overcome test anxiety, enhance self-efficacy, appreciate the value of learning, and develop positive outcome expectations and attitudes (Weinstein & Mayer, 1986). Use of strategies is an integral part of self-regulated learning because strategies give learners better control over information processing (Winne, 2001). In the opening vignette, Connie stresses the importance of Kim using learning strategies in her courses.

Learning strategies assist encoding in each of its phases. Thus, learners initially attend to relevant task information and transfer it from the sensory register to WM. Learners also activate related knowledge in LTM. In WM, learners build connections (links) between new information and prior knowledge and integrate these links into LTM networks.

Table 9.4 outlines the steps in formulating and implementing a learning strategy. Initially learners analyze an activity or situation in terms of the activity's goal, aspects of the situation relevant to that goal, personal characteristics that seem to be important, and potentially useful self-regulated learning methods. Learners then might develop a strategy or plan along the following lines: "Given this task to be accomplished at this time and place according to these criteria and given these personal characteristics, I should use these procedures to accomplish the goal" (paraphrased from Snowman, 1986). Learners next implement the methods, monitor their goal progress, and modify the strategy when the methods are not producing goal progress. Guiding the implementation of these methods is metacognitive knowledge, which involves knowing that one must carry out the methods, why they are important, and when and how to perform them.

Table 9.4
Steps in constructing and implementing a learning strategy.

Step	Learner Tasks
Analyze	Identify learning goal, important task aspects, relevant personal characteristics, and potentially useful learning techniques.
Plan	Construct plan: "Given this task _____ to be done _____ according to these criteria _____ and given these personal characteristics _____, I should use these techniques _____."
Implement	Employ tactics to enhance learning and memory.
Monitor	Assess goal progress to determine how well tactics are working.
Modify	Continue strategy use if assessment is positive; modify the plan if progress seems inadequate.
Metacognitive knowledge	Guide operation of steps.

Source: Adapted and reprinted from "Learning Tactics and Strategies," by J. Snowman, in G. D. Phye & T. Andre (Eds.), *Cognitive classroom learning: Understanding, thinking, and problem solving* (pp. 243–275). Orlando, FL: Academic Press. © 1986. Reprinted by permission of Elsevier and the author.

Self-regulated learning methods are specific procedures or techniques included in strategies to attain goals. The categories of learning methods shown in Table 9.4 are interdependent (Weinstein & Mayer, 1986). For example, procedures that elaborate information also often rehearse and organize it. Methods that organize information may relieve one's stress about learning and help one cope with anxiety. Methods are not equally appropriate with all types of tasks. Rehearsal may be the method of choice when one must memorize simple facts, but organization is more appropriate for comprehension. The sections that follow discuss different methods (Application 9.4).

Rehearsal. Repeating information verbatim, underlining, and summarizing are forms of *rehearsal.* Repeating information to oneself—aloud, subvocally (whispering), or covertly—is an effective procedure for tasks requiring rote memorization. For example, to learn the names of the 50 state capitals, Janna might say the name of each state followed by the name of its capital. Rehearsal also can help learners memorize lines to a song or poem and learn English translations of foreign-language words.

Rehearsal that rotely repeats information does not link information with what one already knows. Nor does rehearsal organize information in hierarchical or other fashion. As a consequence, LTM does not store rehearsed information in any meaningful sense, and retrieval after some time is often difficult.

Rehearsal can be useful for complex learning, but it must involve more than merely repeating information. One useful rehearsal procedure is *underlining (highlighting).* This method, which is popular among high school and college students, improves learning if employed judiciously (Snowman, 1986). When too much material is underlined, underlining loses its effectiveness because less important material is underlined along with more important ideas. Underlined material should represent points most relevant to learning goals.

APPLICATION 9.4
Learning Methods

Learning methods are useful at all educational levels. An elementary teacher might use rhyming schemes or catchy songs to teach the alphabet (the "ABC Song"). Kathy Stone uses familiar words to assist her third-grade students in learning the directions north, south, east, and west (e.g., learn to draw a line connecting north-east-west-south, this spells "news").

In his history classes, Jim Marshall shows students ways to organize material to be studied—the text, class notes, and supplementary readings. He also shows them how to create new notes that integrate material from the various sources, and he demonstrates how to create a time line that incorporates the related material to provide a sequenced list of events.

In medical school, acronyms and pictures can help students memorize the terminology for parts of the body. When students learn the appropriate drugs to prescribe for various conditions, having them place the names of drugs, their uses,

and their side effects into categories may assist with the learning.

Track coaches may help their broad jump and pole vault team members by asking them to close their eyes and slowly visualize every movement their bodies must make to accomplish the jumps. By visualizing their movements, team members can focus on specific positions they need to work on. Executing the actual jump happens so quickly that focusing on what one is doing is difficult, whereas the use of imagery helps to slow the action down.

Gina Brown uses a memory technique with her students to group psychologists who have similar views by developing a catchy phrase or acronym. For example, when she introduces the major behavioral theorists she teaches her students: "The (Thorndike) Sisters (Skinner) Won't (Watson) Play (Pavlov) Together (Tolman)." This helps the undergraduates remember these people: They recall the sentence, then add the names.

In *summarizing*—another popular rehearsal procedure—students put into their own words (orally or in writing) the main ideas expressed in the text. As with underlining, summarizing loses its effectiveness if it includes too much information (Snowman, 1986). Limiting the length of students' summaries forces them to identify main ideas.

The *reciprocal teaching* method of Palincsar and Brown (1984) includes summarization as a means for promoting reading comprehension (Chapter 7). Reciprocal teaching is based on Vygotsky's (1978) *zone of proximal development (ZPD)*, or the amount a student can learn given the proper instructional conditions (Chapter 6). Instruction begins with the teacher performing the activity, after which students and teacher perform together. Students gradually assume more responsibility and teach one another.

Palincsar and Brown taught children to summarize, question, clarify, and predict. Children periodically summarized what they read in the passage, asked teacher-type questions about main ideas, clarified unclear portions of text, and predicted what would happen next. Readers should note that these procedures are not unique to reading comprehension instruction; they are good problem-solving methods that can be used with effective results across domains (e.g., science, mathematics, social studies).

Elaboration. *Elaboration* procedures (imagery, mnemonics, questioning, and note taking) expand information by adding something to make learning more meaningful. Imagery (Chapter 5) adds a mental picture. Consider the definition of a turnip ("a biennial plant of the mustard family with edible hairy leaves and a roundish, light-colored fleshy root used as a vegetable"). One could memorize this definition through rote rehearsal or elaborate it by looking at a picture of a turnip and forming a mental image to link with the definition.

Mnemonics are popular elaboration methods (Weinstein, 1978). A mnemonic makes information meaningful by relating it to what one knows. Mnemonics take various forms (Table 9.5). *Acronyms* combine the first letters of the material to be remembered into a meaningful word. "HOMES" is an acronym for the five Great Lakes (Huron, Ontario,

Table 9.5
Learning methods.

Category	Types
Rehearsal	Repeating information verbatim
	Underlining
	Summarizing
Elaboration	Using imagery
	Using mnemonics: acronym, sentence, narrative story, pegword, method of loci, keyword
	Questioning
	Note taking
Organization	Using mnemonics
	Grouping
	Outlining
	Mapping
Comprehension	Self-questioning
Monitoring	Rereading
	Checking consistencies
	Paraphrasing
Affective	Coping with anxiety
	Holding positive beliefs: self-efficacy, outcome expectations, attitudes
	Creating a positive environment
	Managing time

Source: C. E. Weinstein & R. E. Mayer, 1986, The Teaching of Learning Strategies, in M. C. Wittrock (Ed.), *Handbook of research on teaching* (3rd ed., pp. 315–327). New York: Macmillan. Reprinted by permission.

Michigan, Erie, Superior); "ROY G. BIV" for the colors of the spectrum (Red, Orange, Yellow, Green, Blue, Indigo, Violet). *Sentence mnemonics* use the first letters of the material to be learned as the first letters of words in a sentence. For example, "Every Good Boy Does Fine" is a sentence mnemonic for the notes on the treble clef staff (E, G, B, D, F), and "My Very Educated Mother Just Served Us Nine Pizzas" for the order of the planets from the sun (Mercury, Venus, Earth, Mars, Jupiter, Saturn, Uranus, Neptune, Pluto).

Also possible is combining material to be remembered into a *paragraph* or *narrative story*. This type of mnemonic might be useful when long lists have to be remembered (e.g., 50 state capitals). Student-generated acronyms, sentences, and stories are as effective as those supplied by others (Snowman, 1986).

The *pegword method* requires that learners first memorize a set of objects rhyming with integer names; for example, one-bun, two-shoe, three-tree, four-door, five-hive, six-sticks, seven-heaven, eight-gate, nine-wine, ten-hen. Then the learner generates an image of each item to be learned and links it with the corresponding object image. Thus, if Joan needs to buy some items at the grocery store (butter, milk, apples), she might imagine a buttered bun, milk in a shoe, and apples growing on a tree. To recall the shopping list, she recalls the rhyming scheme and its paired associates. Successful use of this technique requires that learners first learn the rhyming scheme.

To use the *method of loci*, learners imagine a familiar scene, such as a room in their house, after which they take a mental walk around the room and stop at each prominent object. Each new item to be learned is paired mentally with one object in the room. Assuming that the room contains (in order) a table, a lamp, and a television, and using the previous grocery list example, Joan might first imagine butter on the table, a milky-colored lamp, and apples on top of the television. To recall the grocery list, she mentally retraces the path around the room and recalls the appropriate object at each stop.

Atkinson (1975; Atkinson & Raugh, 1975) developed the *keyword method* for learning foreign language vocabulary words. For example, *pato* (pronounced "pot-o") is a Spanish word meaning "duck." Learners initially think of an English word (*pot*) that sounds like the foreign word (*pato*). Then they link an image of a pot with the English translation of the foreign word ("duck"); for example, a duck with a pot on its head. When the learners encounter *pato*, they recall the image of a duck with a pot on its head. Although the keyword method has been employed effectively with various types of academic content (Pressley, Levin, & Delaney, 1982), its success with young children often requires supplying them with the keyword and the picture incorporating the keyword and its English translation.

Mnemonic techniques incorporate several valid learning principles including rehearsal and relating new information to prior knowledge. Informal evidence indicates that most students have favorite memorization techniques, many of which employ mnemonics. Experiments that compare recall of students instructed in a mnemonic with recall of students not given a memory technique generally indicate that learning benefits from mnemonics instruction (Weinstein, 1978). Students must understand how to use the technique, which generally entails instruction.

Elaboration methods also are useful with complex learning tasks. For example, *questioning* requires that learners stop periodically as they read text and ask themselves questions. To address higher-order learning outcomes, learners might ask, "How does this information relate to what the author discussed in the preceding section?" (synthesis) or, "How can this idea be applied in a school setting?" (application).

We might assume that questioning should improve comprehension, but research has not yielded strong support for this correlation (Snowman, 1986). To be effective, questions must reflect the types of desired learning outcomes. Questioning will not aid comprehension if questions address low-level, factual knowledge. Unfortunately, most research studies have used relatively brief passages of fewer than 1,500 words. With older students, questioning is most useful with longer passages. Among elementary children, rereading or reviewing (rehearsing) material is equally effective. This may be due to children's limited knowledge of how to construct good questions.

Note taking, another elaboration technique, requires learners to construct meaningful paraphrases of the most important ideas expressed in text. Note taking is similar to summarizing except that the former is not limited to immediately available information. While taking notes, students might integrate new textual material with other information in personally meaningful ways. To be effective, notes must not reflect verbatim textual information. Rote copying of material is a form of rehearsal and may improve recall, but it is not elaboration. The intent of note taking is to elaborate (integrate and apply) information. Students generally need instruction in how to take good notes for this method to be effective. Note taking works best when the notes include content highly relevant to the learning goals.

Organization. Organization techniques include mnemonics, grouping, outlining, and mapping. Mnemonics elaborate information and organize it in meaningful fashion. Acronyms, for example, organize information into a meaningful word. Information can be organized by grouping it before using rehearsal or mnemonics. If students are learning mammal names, they might first group the names into common families (apes, cats, etc.) and then rehearse or use a mnemonic. Organization imposed by learners is an effective aid to recall; learners first recall the organizational scheme and then the individual components (Weinstein & Mayer, 1986).

Organization techniques are useful with complex material. A popular one is *outlining,* which requires that learners establish headings. Outlining improves comprehension, but as with other learning methods, students usually require instruction in how to construct a good outline. One way to teach outlining is to use a text with headings that are set off from the text or that appear in the margins, along with embedded (**boldface** or *italic*) headings interspersed throughout the text. Another way is to have students identify topic sentences and points that relate to each sentence. Simply telling students to outline a passage does not facilitate learning if students do not understand the procedure.

Mapping is an organizational technique that improves learners' awareness of text structure. Mapping involves identifying important ideas and specifying their interrelationship. Concepts or ideas are identified, categorized, and related to one another. The exact nature of the map varies depending on the content and types of relationships to be specified. The following steps are useful in teaching mapping:

- Discuss how different sentences in a paragraph relate to one another by giving the categories into which sentences will fit: main idea, example, comparison/contrast, temporal relationship, and inference.
- Model the application of this categorization with sample paragraphs.

- Give students guided practice on categorizing sentences and on explaining the reasons for their choices.
- Have students practice independently on paragraphs. Once students acquire these basic skills, more complex textual material can be used (multiple paragraphs, short sections of stories or chapters) with new categories introduced as needed (e.g., transition; McNeil, 1987).

A *map* is conceptually akin to a *propositional network* because mapping involves creating a hierarchy, with main ideas, or superordinate concepts, listed at the top, followed by supporting points, examples, and subordinate concepts. Branching off from the main hierarchy are lines to related points, such as might be used if a concept is being contrasted with related concepts. Figure 9.2 shows a sample map.

Research indicates differential effectiveness for mapping as a means of improving comprehension (Snowman, 1986). The skill to discern some relationships is learned easily (main idea-example), but the skill to discern others is more difficult to acquire (cause-effect). Students often have difficulty linking ideas between sections or paragraphs. In teaching students to construct maps, having them first map each section or paragraph separately and then link the maps is helpful. Mapping is especially effective with students who experience difficulty integrating ideas (Holley, Dansereau, McDonald, Garland, & Collins, 1979).

Figure 9.2
Cognitive map for "city."

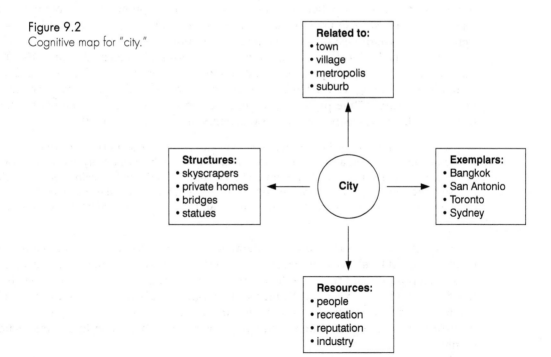

Comprehension Monitoring. *Comprehension monitoring* helps learners determine whether they are properly applying declarative and procedural knowledge to material to be learned, evaluate whether they understand the material, decide whether their strategy is effective or whether a better strategy is needed, and know why strategy use will improve learning. Teaching students comprehension monitoring is a central component of strategy-instruction programs (Baker & Brown, 1984; Borkowski & Cavanaugh, 1979; Paris et al., 1983). *Self-questioning, rereading, checking consistencies,* and *paraphrasing* are monitoring processes. Using a hypermedia learning environment with middle- and high-school students, Greene and Azevedo (2009) found that monitoring activities (e.g., self-questioning) significantly enhanced students' understanding of complex science topics.

Some textual material periodically provides students with questions about content. Students who answer these questions as they read the material are engaging in self-questioning. When questions are not provided, students need to generate their own. As a means of training students to ask questions, teachers can instruct students to stop periodically while reading and ask themselves a series of questions (i.e., who, what, when, where, why, how).

Rereading is often accomplished in conjunction with self-questioning; when students cannot answer questions about the text or otherwise doubt their understanding, these cues prompt them to reread. Checking for consistencies involves determining whether the text is internally consistent, that is, whether parts of the text contradict others and whether conclusions that are drawn follow from what has been discussed. A belief that textual material is inconsistent serves as a cue for rereading to determine whether the author is inconsistent or whether the reader has failed to comprehend the content. Students who periodically stop and paraphrase material are checking their level of understanding. Being able to paraphrase is a cue that rereading is unnecessary (Paris & Oka, 1986).

A useful method to teach comprehension monitoring is Meichenbaum's (1986) *self-instructional training* (Chapter 4). Cognitive modeling portrays a systematic approach to comprehension along with statements to self-check understanding and take corrective action as necessary. While presenting comprehension instruction to remedial readers, a teacher might verbalize the following (Meichenbaum & Asarnow, 1979):

> Well, I've learned three big things to keep in mind before I read a story and while I read it. One is to ask myself what the main idea of the story is. What is the story about? A second is to learn important details of the story as I go along. The order of the main events or their sequence is an especially important detail. A third is to know how the characters feel and why. So, get the main idea. Watch sequences. And learn how the characters feel and why. (p. 17)

Students learn to verbalize such statements and internalize them by gradually fading them to a covert level. To remind learners what to think about, teachers might display key ideas on a poster board (e.g., get the main idea, watch sequences, learn how the characters feel and why). Winsler and Naglieri (2003) found that between the ages of 5 and 17, children's verbal problem-solving strategies moved from overt (aloud) to partially covert (whispers) to fully covert (silent), which supports the progression in self-instructional training.

Affective Techniques. *Affective learning techniques* create a favorable psychological climate for learning (Weinstein & Mayer, 1986). These methods help one cope with anxiety, develop positive beliefs (self-efficacy, outcome expectations, attitudes), set goals, establish a regular time and place for studying, and minimize distractions (setting such rules as no talking on the phone and no watching television).

Affective techniques help learners focus and maintain attention on important task aspects, manage time effectively, and minimize anxiety. *Self-verbalization* helps keep students' attention on the academic task. At the outset of an academic activity, students might think to themselves, "This might be tough. I need to pay close attention to the teacher." If they notice their attention is waning, they might think, "Stop thinking about _____. I need to concentrate on what the teacher is saying."

Goal setting is an effective time-management strategy (Chapter 4). Learners who set overall learning goals, subdivide them into short-term goals, and periodically evaluate their goal progress are self-regulating their academic performances. The belief that they are making progress strengthens students' self-efficacy for continued learning (Schunk, 1995).

Anxiety about tests, grades, and failure interferes with learning. Students who ruminate about potential failure waste time and strengthen doubts about their capabilities. Anxiety-reduction programs employ systematic desensitization, modeling, and guided self-talk. Models verbalize positive achievement beliefs (e.g., "I know that if I work hard, I can do well on the test") rather than dysfunctional beliefs (e.g., "I can't pass the test"). Coping models, who initially are anxious but use effective self-regulated learning methods and persist until they perform better, are important therapeutic agents of change (Schunk, 1987).

For students who have difficulties taking tests, a specific program to teach test-taking skills may prove beneficial (Kirkland & Hollandsworth, 1980). These programs typically teach students to subdivide the test, establish time limits for each part, and not spend too long on any one question. To conquer negative thoughts while taking a test, students are taught relaxation techniques and ways to refocus attention on test items. Test performance and beliefs exert reciprocal effects. Experiencing some test success creates a sense of self-efficacy for performing well, which leads to more productive studying and better performance.

Effectiveness of Strategy Instruction. The research literature on strategy instruction has expanded dramatically in recent years (Corno, 2008). Hattie, Biggs, and Purdie (1996) conducted an extensive review of interventions aimed at improving student learning. They concluded that most interventions were effective, and they obtained evidence for near transfer. When transfer is a goal, it is imperative that students understand the conditions under which the strategy is effective. The best self-regulated strategy instruction programs are those that are integrated with academic content and implemented in classrooms that support students' self-regulated learning (Butler, 1998a, 1998b; Perry, 1998; Winne & Hadwin, 2008).

As with other aspects of learning, strategy instruction is most effective when the methods are meaningful to students and they perceive them as valuable to use. The research literature contains many examples of strategy-instruction programs with immediate effects that did not endure over time or transfer beyond the learning context (Borkowski & Cavanaugh, 1979; Borkowski, Johnston, & Reid, 1987). Strategy instruction programs with children often have participants who demonstrate production deficiencies (i.e., they fail to use a strategy that is available to them) and utilization deficiencies (i.e., they use the strategy but it does not enhance their performances; Schwenck, Bjorklund, & Schneider, 2007).

Pressley and his colleagues (Harris & Pressley, 1991; Pressley, Harris, & Marks, 1992; Pressley et al., 1990) contended that several factors should be taken into account when designing and implementing strategy-instruction programs. Strategies should not be foisted on students; teaching strategies in the hope that students will realize their benefits and use them is preferable.

> Good strategy instruction sends the message that students can control how they do academically, with much gained by creatively applying the cognitive strategies that are taught to them. Good strategy instruction encourages student reflection, permitting powerful tools for reflective "meaning-getting" from texts, creation of reflective stances via writing, and reflective decision making about whether and how to use strategies they know to tackle new situations. (Pressley & McCormick, 1995, p. 515)

Strategy instruction is likely to be most effective when the constructivist nature of the acquisition and use of strategies is stressed (Goldin-Meadow et al., 1993; Paris & Paris, 2001; Chapter 6). A key point is that students are motivated to construct understanding from inputs they receive. Good teaching complements this process because it provides rich inputs and the context for constructions to take place. In the opening vignette, Connie hopes that eventually Kim will adapt strategies to be most effective for her.

Pressley et al. (1992) recommended several steps to follow in strategy instruction (Table 9.6). *Introducing a few strategies at a time* does not overload students, and the strategies can be coalesced into a large package to show how they interrelate. The advantage of *providing distributed practice on diverse tasks* is to facilitate transfer and maintenance. The importance of *teachers as models* cannot be underestimated, and we must

Table 9.6
Steps to follow in strategy instruction.

Introduce a few strategies at a time
Provide distributed practice on diverse tasks
Have teachers serve as models
Stress to students the value of strategy use
Personalize feedback and teaching
Determine opportunities for transfer
Sustain student motivation
Encourage habitual reflection and planning

Source: M. Pressley, K. R. Harris & M. B. Marks, 1992, But good strategy instructors are constructivists! *Educational Psychology Review, 4*, pp. 10–11. Reprinted by permission.

remember that the modeling is rule governed; students learn strategies and how to modify them rather than rotely copying the model's actions (Rosenthal & Zimmerman, 1978). *Stressing the value of strategies* to students is necessary to encourage greater strategy use. Teachers can enhance perceived value with feedback showing how strategy use improves performance.

The importance of *feedback and personal teaching* is highlighted; teachers tailor feedback to individual student needs and teachers and students collaborate to work out understandings of strategies. Azevedo, Greene, and Moos (2007) obtained benefits on college students' self-regulated learning by having a human tutor facilitate their use of strategies (i.e., prompt students to activate prior knowledge, plan time, monitor goal progress, summarize, use mnemonics). Teachers and students also must *determine opportunities for transfer* through discussions, prompts to students, and opportunities to practice adapting strategies to new tasks. *Sustaining student motivation*, especially by highlighting empowerment that accompanies strategy learning, is necessary. Finally, teachers encourage *habitual reflection and planning*. They model reflection, provide opportunities for students to think through problems, and create an environment that values reflection more than simply completing assignments or arriving at correct answers.

CONSTRUCTIVIST THEORY

Constructivist researchers have addressed self-regulation, which seems natural given that a central constructivist assumption is that learners construct knowledge and ways for acquiring and applying it. There are various sources for constructivist accounts of self-regulation, including cognitive-developmental theories (Chapters 6 and 10), precursors of contemporary cognitive theories (e.g., Gestalt psychology, memory; Chapter 5), and Vygotsky's theory (Paris & Byrnes, 1989; Chapter 6). Regardless of the source, constructivist views of self-regulation rest on certain assumptions, as shown in Table 9.7 (Paris & Byrnes, 1989).

Two key points underlying these assumptions are that sociocultural influences are critical and that people form implicit theories about themselves, others, and how to best manage demands. These are discussed in turn.

Table 9.7
Constructivist assumptions of self-regulation.

- There is an intrinsic motivation to seek information.
- Understanding goes beyond the information given.
- Mental representations change with development.
- There are progressive refinements in levels of understanding.
- There are developmental constraints on learning.
- Reflection and reconstruction stimulate learning.

Sociocultural Influences

Vygotsky's (1978) constructivist theory of human development lends itself well to self-regulation (Chapter 6). Recall that Vygotsky believed that people and their cultural environments constituted an interacting social system. Through their communications and actions, people in children's environments taught children the tools (e.g., language, symbols, signs) they needed to acquire competence. Using these tools within the system, learners develop higher-level cognitive functions, such as concept acquisition and problem solving. As Vygotsky used the term *higher mental function*, he meant a consciously directed thought process. In this sense, self-regulation may be thought of as a higher mental function (Henderson & Cunningham, 1994).

In the Vygotskian view, self-regulation includes the coordination of such mental processes as memory, planning, synthesis, and evaluation (Henderson & Cunningham, 1994). These coordinated processes do not operate independently of the context in which they are formed. Indeed, the self-regulatory processes of an individual reflect those that are valued and taught within the person's culture.

Vygotsky believed that people came to control their own deliberate actions (i.e., learned to self-regulate). The primary mechanisms affecting self-regulation are language and the zone of proximal development (ZPD).

Kopp (1982) provided a useful framework for understanding the development of the self-regulatory function of speech. In her view, self-regulation involves a transition from responding to the commands of others to the use of speech and other cognitive tools to plan, monitor, and direct one's activities.

Self-regulation also depends on learners being aware of socially approved behaviors (Henderson & Cunningham, 1994). The meaning of actions depends on both the context and the tools (language, signs, and symbols) used to describe the actions. Through interactions with adults in the ZPD, children make the transition from behaviors regulated by others to behaviors regulated by themselves (self-regulation).

Wertsch (1979) described four stages of intersubjectivity that correspond to the degrees of responsibility held by parties in a social context. Initially the child does not understand the adult's words or gestures, so there is no intersubjectivity. With maturation of the child and greater sensitivity of the adult to the child's situation, a shared understanding of the situation develops, although responsibility for regulating behavior still lies with the adult. In the third phase, the child learns the relation between speech and activity and takes responsibility for the task. During the third phase, private speech is commonly used to self-regulate behavior. As this speech is internalized to self-directed thought, intersubjectivity becomes complete and self-regulation occurs independently. Internalization becomes the key to use of self-regulatory processes (Schunk, 1999). Some examples of internalization are given in Application 9.5.

It is noteworthy that even after an adult or teacher is no longer present, the child's self-regulatory activity may heavily reflect that person's influence. Although the action is self-directed, it is the internalized regulation of the other's influence. Often the child may repeat the same words used by the adult. In time, the child will construct his or her self-regulatory activity and it will become idiosyncratic.

APPLICATION 9.5
Promoting Internalization

Many influences on students' self-regulation originate in their social environments, such as when teachers explain and demonstrate specific strategies for students to use on academic content. But as the theories covered in this chapter make clear, these external inputs are not passively received by students but rather transformed by them into personal self-regulatory influences. As learners develop skills, the unidimensional social-to-self process becomes a bidirectional interactive process as learners modify their environments and enhance their learning. A key process is internalization of information. Self-regulatory processes that are internalized are under the learner's control, whereas noninternalized processes are under the control of others. Internalized processes are represented mentally as thoughts, beliefs, procedures, strategies, and so forth. Although it is possible to learn without internalization (e.g., when teachers direct students' actions), internalization is needed for skill improvement over time and beyond the present learning setting. The net result of internalization is a set of self-regulatory influences that learners employ to promote their motivation and learning.

Kathy Stone works with her children to help them internalize spelling rules. For example, she teaches them the rhyme, "I before E except after C or when sounded like A as in Neighbor or Weigh." When she gives them spelling words with ie or ei in them, she asks them to verbalize aloud the rhyme. Then once they regularly do this, she advises them to whisper the rhyme, and eventually to say it quietly to themselves (subvocally). She uses this same procedure with other spelling rules, teaching students to internalize rules so that they can generate them in response to various spelling words.

Jim Marshall does not want his students to think of history as the memorizing of facts. Instead, he wants them to develop skills of historical analysis. He teaches them questions to ask to analyze historical events, such as: What happened? Who were the influential people? What events led up to this event? How might this event have turned out differently if the events leading up to it had changed? Early in his course he has students write out the answers to these questions as they analyze events. As students develop skills of historical analysis, he asks them to formulate their own strategy that will capture the same type of information. They internalize this strategy as their own as they apply it to historical events, as well as to current events involving elections, the economy, and wars.

As part of her educational psychology course, Gina Brown teaches her students self-regulation strategies to use when studying the course content. For example, she teaches them how to effectively underline and highlight information in text, how to summarize chapter content, how to budget their study time, and how to create an effective study environment. Each student formulates a study plan to use for the chapters. She provides feedback on these and asks the students to revise their plans as the semester progresses based on their evaluations of the plan's effectiveness. By the end of the semester, the goal is for students to be using their study plans routinely and adapting them as needed based on study requirements (e.g., studying some chapters requires access to the Internet).

Implicit Theories

Implicit theories (Chapters 6 and 8) are inherent features of constructivist accounts of learning, cognition, and motivation. Students also construct theories about self-regulated learning. These theories exist along with theories about others and their worlds, so self-regulated learning theories are highly contextualized (Paris, Byrnes, & Paris, 2001).

A major type of implicit theory involves children's beliefs about their academic abilities. Children who experience learning problems and who believe that these problems reflect poor ability are apt to demonstrate low motivation to succeed. The beliefs that effort leads to success and that learning produces higher ability are positively related to effective self-regulation (Chapter 8).

Children also develop theories about their competence relative to their peers. Through social comparisons with similar others, they formulate perceptions of ability and of their relative standing within their class. They also begin to differentiate their perceptions by subject area and to ascertain how smart they are in subjects such as reading and mathematics.

In line with these beliefs, children formulate theories about what contributes to success in different domains. Self-regulatory strategies may be general in nature, such as taking notes and rehearsing information to be learned, or they may be idiosyncratic to a particular area. Whether these strategies truly are useful is not the point. Because they are constructed, they may be misleading.

Learners also develop theories about agency and control that they have in academic situations. This power to act to obtain desired outcomes is central to social cognitive theory (Bandura, 1997) and to constructivist theories (Martin, 2004). Bandura contended that self-efficacy is a key influence on agency, whereas constructivist theories place greater emphasis on learners' activities in their physical and sociocultural environments (Martin, 2004). With respect to learners' theories, they may feel self-efficacious (Chapter 4) and believe that they are capable of learning what is being taught in school. Conversely, they may entertain serious doubts about their learning capabilities. Again, these beliefs may or may not accurately capture reality. Research has shown, for example, that children often feel highly self-efficacious about successfully solving mathematical problems even after being given feedback showing that they had failed most or all of the problems they attempted to solve (Bandura & Schunk, 1981). The correspondence between self-efficacy judgments and actual performance can be affected by many factors (Bandura, 1997; Schunk & Pajares, 2009).

Another class of theories involves schooling and academic tasks (Paris et al., 2001). These theories contain information about the content and skills taught in school and what is required to learn the content and skills. The goals that students formulate for schooling may not be consistent with those of teachers and parents. For example, teachers and parents may want students to perform well, but students' goals might be to make friends and stay out of trouble. For a subject area (e.g., reading), students may have a goal of understanding the text or simply verbalizing the words on a page. A goal of writing may be to fill the lines on a page or create a short story.

Self-regulation, therefore, involves individuals constructing theories about themselves (e.g., abilities, capabilities, typical effort), others, and their environments. These theories are constructed partly through direct instruction from others (e.g., teachers, peers, and parents), but also largely through their personal reflections on their performances, environmental effects, and responses from others. Theories are constructed using the tools (language, signs, and symbols) and in social contexts, often through instruction in the ZPD.

The goal is for students to construct a self-identity as students. Their beliefs are influenced by parents, teachers, and peers and may include stereotypes associated with gender, culture, and ethnic background. Paris et al. (2001) contended that the separation of identity development and self-regulated learning is impossible because achievement behaviors are indicators of who students believe they are or who they want to become. Strategies cannot be taught independently of goals, roles, and identities of students. In other words, self-regulation is intimately linked with personal development.

Children are intrinsically motivated to construct explanatory frameworks and understand their educational experiences (Paris et al., 2001). When they are successful, they construct theories of competence, tasks, and themselves, which aid learning and usage of adaptive learning strategies. But when they are not successful, they may construct inappropriate goals and strategies. To use terminology from cognitive psychology, implicit theories include declarative and conditional knowledge that underlie procedural knowledge. In short, self-regulation is heavily dependent on how children perceive themselves and achievement tasks (Dweck & Master, 2008).

MOTIVATION AND SELF-REGULATION

Motivation is intimately linked with self-regulation (Pintrich, 2003; Wolters, 2003). People motivated to attain a goal engage in self-regulatory activities they believe will help them (e.g., organize and rehearse material, monitor learning progress and adjust strategies). In turn, self-regulation promotes learning, and the perception of greater competence sustains motivation and self-regulation to attain new goals (Schunk & Ertmer, 2000). Thus, motivation and self-regulation influence one another.

The link between motivation and self-regulation is seen clearly in theoretical models (Pintrich, 2000b; Vollmeyer & Rheinberg, 2006; Zimmerman, 2000; Zimmerman & Schunk, 2004). Pintrich's model is heavily motivation dependent, since motivation underlies learners' setting and pursuit of goals and also is a focus of their self-regulation as they engage in tasks. In Zimmerman's model, motivation enters at all phases: forethought (e.g., self-efficacy, outcome expectations, interest, value, goal orientations), performance control (e.g., attention focusing, self-monitoring), and self-reflection (e.g., self-evaluation of goal progress, causal attributions).

Additional evidence of this link is seen in research by Wolters (1998, 1999; Wolters, Yu, & Pintrich, 1996). In these studies, the researchers determined how various strategies designed to maintain optimal task motivation (e.g., expend effort, persist, make the task interesting, self-reward) related to self-regulatory strategy use during learning (e.g., rehearsal, elaboration, planning, monitoring, organization). The results showed that the motivation regulation activities that learners used predicted their self-regulation. Adopting a learning-goal orientation was associated with higher self-efficacy, task value, and achievement.

One aspect of self-regulation that is drawing increased research attention is *volition*, which is discussed in the next section. Some researchers define volition as part of a larger self-regulatory system that includes motivation and other cognitive processes (Corno, 1993, 2001, 2008; Snow, 1989). Many other motivational components are receiving research attention for their role in self-regulation—for example, goal properties, goal orientations, self-efficacy, interest, attributions, values, self-schemas, and help seeking (Schunk & Zimmerman, 2008). We have examined the roles of goal properties (Zimmerman, 2008), goal orientations (Fryer & Elliot, 2008), self-efficacy (Schunk & Pajares, 2009), interest (Hidi & Ainley, 2008), and attributions (Schunk, 2008) in motivation (Chapter 8); the remainder of this section discusses volition and the latter three influences.

Volition

Volition has been of interest for a long time. Early psychologists drew on the writings of Plato and Aristotle (Chapter 1) and conceived of the mind as comprising knowing (cognition), feeling (emotion), and willing (motivation). The will reflected one's desire, want, or purpose; volition was the act of using the will (Schunk et al., 2008).

Philosophers and psychologists have debated whether volition was an independent process or a by-product of other mental processes (e.g., perceptions). Wundt (Chapter 1) thought volition was a central, independent factor in human behavior, which presumably accompanied such processes as attention and perception and helped translate thoughts and emotions into actions. James (1890, 1892) also believed that volition was the process of translating intentions into actions and had its greatest effect when different intentions competed for action. Volition worked to execute intended actions by activating mental representations of them, which served as guides for behavior.

Ach (1910) pioneered the experimental study of volition. Ach considered volition the process of dealing with implementing actions designed to attain goals. This is a narrow view of motivation because it does not address the process whereby people formulate goals and commit themselves to attaining them (Heckhausen, 1991; Schunk et al., 2008). Processes that allow goals to be translated into action are *determining tendencies*; they compete with previously learned association tendencies to produce action even when the action conflicts with prior associations.

The conceptual basis for contemporary work derives from *action control theory* by Heckhausen (1991) and Kuhl (1984). These theorists proposed differentiating *predecisional processing* (cognitive activities involved in making decisions and setting goals) from *postdecisional processing* (activities engaged in subsequent to goal setting). Predecisional analyses involve decision making and are motivational; postdecisional analyses deal with goal implementation and are volitional. Volition mediates the relation between goals and actions to accomplish them. Once students move from planning and goal setting to implementation of plans, they cross a metaphorical Rubicon that protects goals by self-regulatory activities rather than reconsidering or changing them (Corno, 1993, 2001, 2008).

Debate continues over whether motivation and volition are separate constructs or whether the latter is part of the former. Nonetheless, separating pre- from postdecisional processes seems worthwhile. Some motivational indexes used in studies of performance are not useful in learning. Choice of activities is a common index, yet in school students often do not choose to engage in tasks. There often is little predecisional activity by students. In contrast, postdecisional activity offers more latitude, especially if multiple ways are available to accomplish tasks or deal with distractions. Choice is an integral component of self-regulation (Zimmerman, 1994, 1998, 2000), but students still can have many choices available even when they do not choose whether to work on a task. Volitional activities presumably direct and control information processing, affects, and behaviors directed toward accomplishing goals (Corno, 1993).

Corno (1989, 1993, 1994, 2001, 2008; Corno & Kanfer, 1993; Corno & Mandinach, 2004) has written extensively about the role of volition in self-regulation:

> Volition can be characterized as a dynamic system of psychological control processes that protect concentration and directed effort in the face of personal and/or environmental distractions, and so aid learning and performance. (Corno, 1993, p. 16)

It is useful to distinguish two aspects of volitional function with respect to self-regulation: action control and volitional style (Corno, 1994). The *action-control* function refers to potentially modifiable regulatory skills or strategies. This function would include the focus of many interventions aimed at enhancing self-regulation, such as metacognitive monitoring (self-observation), self-arranged contingencies, redesign of tasks, strategies of emotion control, and management of environmental resources. Kuhl (1985) proposed a taxonomy of volitional strategies; Corno (1993) discussed two such strategies with educational examples (Table 9.8). Many examples are available of successful training efforts for action-control strategies (Corno, 1994).

Table 9.8
Examples of volitional control strategies.

Motivation Control

- Set contingencies for performance that can be carried out mentally (e.g., self-reward).
- Escalate goals by prioritizing and imagining their value.
- Visualize doing the work successfully.
- Uncover ways to make the work more fun or challenging.
- Immerse yourself in plans for achieving goals.
- Self-instruct.
- Analyze failure to direct a second try.

Emotion Control

- Count to 10 in your head.
- Control breathing so it is slow, steady, and deep.
- Generate useful diversions (e.g., sing to yourself).
- Visualize doing the work successfully and feeling good about that (change the way you respond emotionally to the task).
- Recall your strengths and your available resources.
- Consider any negative feelings about the experience and ways to make it more reassuring.

Source: From "The Best-Laid Plans: Modern Conceptions of Volition and Educational Research," by L. Corno, 1993, *Educational Researcher, 22* (2), p. 16. Copyright 1993 by American Educational Research Association. Reprinted by permission.

A second function, *volitional style*, refers to stable, individual differences in volition, as opposed to the specific skills and strategies involved in action control. Volitional style includes personality variables that should be less amenable to change through instruction—for example, impulsiveness, conscientiousness, and dependability (Snow, 1989). Corno (1994) cited research showing that these dispositions predict various student academic outcomes.

The case for treating volition as a separate construct has some merit. One problem with separating goal setting from implementation stems from research showing that learners adjust or set new goals during task performance (Locke & Latham, 1990; Zimmerman, 2008). Another concern is how such motivationally germane processes as attributions and self-efficacy relate to volition. Researchers continue to address these issues.

Values

A central component of motivation that relates to self-regulation is the *value* students ascribe to learning (Wigfield, Hoa, & Klauda, 2008). Students who do not value what they are learning are not motivated to improve or exercise self-regulation over their activities (Wigfield et al., 2004).

Wigfield (1994; Wigfield et al., 2008) discussed the process whereby valuing a task can lead to greater self-regulation. Values have a direct link to such achievement behaviors as persistence, choice, and performance. Values may relate positively to many self-regulating processes such as self-observation, self-evaluation, and goal setting. For instance, students who value history are apt to study for history tests diligently, set goals for their learning, monitor their learning progress, not be overcome by obstacles, and adjust their strategies as needed. In contrast, students who do not value history should be less likely to engage in these activities.

Research supports the idea that valuing achievement tasks relates to the productive use of cognitive learning strategies, perceived self-regulation, and academic performance (Pintrich & De Groot, 1990; Wigfield, 1994; Wigfield et al., 2004, 2008). Pokay and Blumenfeld (1990), for example, found that students' valuing of mathematics led to their using different cognitive strategies, and in turn, strategy use influenced mathematics performance. Wigfield (1994) noted that task values may relate positively to the strategies of volitional action control proposed by Kuhl (1985).

Unfortunately, research shows that children often value academic tasks less as they get older (Eccles & Midgley, 1989). Many ways to enhance student motivation relate directly to perceptions of task value, including showing students how tasks are important in their lives and how learning these tasks helps them attain their goals. In the opening scenario, Kim may not value her courses, but Connie tries to encourage her by stressing that using strategies can help her perform better, which may increase how much she values her studies. Linking learning to real-world phenomena improves perceptions of value. Teachers should incorporate methods for enhancing perceived value into their planning to ensure benefits for learning and self-regulation.

Self-Schemas

Self-schemas are "cognitive manifestations of enduring goals, aspirations, motives, fears, and threats" (Markus & Nurius, 1986, p. 954). They include cognitive and affective evaluations of ability, volition, and personal agency. They essentially are conceptions of ourselves in different situations or what we might be. The theoretical importance of self-schemas is that they presumably mediate the link between situations and behavior. Individuals act in part based on their perceptions of themselves. Self-concept includes many self-schemas, only some of which are active at a given time. Those active at any time are *working self-concepts*. Self-schemas have an affective dimension (self-conceptions are positive and negatively valued), a temporal dimension (experiences result in concepts of past, present, and future possible selves), an efficacy dimension (beliefs about what we can do to attain our selves), and a value dimension (importance or centrality of the self to the individual).

As organized knowledge structures, possible selves are ways to network multiple motivational beliefs at a higher level (Garcia & Pintrich, 1994). Thus, goals are important motivational processes, and self-schemas are organized knowledge structures that link multiple goals. Self-schemas may provide a link between motivation and strategy use. If persons have ideas about what they can be and what they can do, then possible selves can serve as guides for action and contain strategies to be implemented.

Possible selves can play an important role in self-regulation because the notion of what one might become underlies use of self-regulatory strategies (Garcia & Pintrich, 1994). Individuals regulate their behaviors to approximate or become their possible selves and to avoid becoming negative possible selves. People must understand what to do to become their possible selves. Garcia and Pintrich discussed motivational strategies that individuals may use to attain selves and protect their sense of self-worth. Research on self-schemas is promising and results support the claim that self-schemas serve to link motivation and self-regulation.

Help Seeking

Help seeking is a way to regulate the social environment to promote learning. Self-regulated learners are likely to ask for assistance when they confront difficult tasks and perceive the need for help (Newman, 1994, 2000, 2002, 2008). In particular, high achievers often seek help from teachers and peers (Zimmerman & Martinez-Pons, 1990).

Newman (1994) proposed a model in which adaptive help seeking:

- Occurs following a student's lack of understanding.
- Includes the student considering the need for help, the content of the request, and the request target.
- Involves expressing the need for help in the most suitable fashion given the circumstances.
- Requires that the help seeker receive and process help in a way that will optimize the probability of success in later help-seeking attempts.

Help seeking is a relatively complex activity that includes more than the verbal request for assistance. Motivational factors come into play. Many motivational processes have been investigated for their relation to help seeking, especially the roles of self-efficacy and goal setting. Students with higher self-efficacy for learning are more apt to seek help than are those with lower efficacy (Ryan, Gheen, & Midgley, 1998). Students with a task goal orientation are more likely to seek assistance to determine the correctness of their work, whereas ego-involved students may seek help to determine how their work compares with that of others (Newman & Schwager, 1992; Ryan et al., 1998).

This research suggests that different motivational patterns can prompt various forms of help seeking. From the perspective of self-regulation, the most adaptive type of help seeking is that which provides feedback on learning and progress. Teachers can work with students to encourage their seeking assistance when it is likely to help them develop their academic skills.

INSTRUCTIONAL APPLICATIONS

Self-regulation, like other skills, can be learned (B. Zimmerman, 2000). Effective methods for teaching self-regulation often include exposing students to social models, teaching them to use learning strategies, giving them practice and corrective feedback, and assisting them to evaluate their learning goal progress (Schunk & Ertmer, 2000). As discussed earlier in this chapter, the key is for students to internalize the various social influences in their environments so that they become part of their self-regulatory processes (Schunk, 1999).

The principles of self-regulation discussed in this chapter lend themselves well to instructional applications. The most effective applications are those in which self-regulatory processes are incorporated into academic learning instruction. Three areas that are especially germane are academic studying, writing, and mathematics.

Academic Studying

Many students have problems studying, and much research has examined students' self-regulated learning during academic studying (Weinstein & Palmer, 1990; Weinstein, Palmer, & Schulte, 1987; Zimmerman, 1998). There are published materials that help students develop better study habits (Kiewra & Dubois, 1998; Weinstein & Hume, 1998; Zimmerman et al., 1996), as well as effective studying courses that are integrated with academic course content (Hofer, Yu, & Pintrich, 1998; Lan, 1998). Research shows that academic studying benefits from instruction on strategies and time management.

Strategy Instruction. Researchers have investigated how strategy instruction affects academic studying. Dansereau (1978; Dansereau et al., 1979) developed a strategy instruction program for college students. These researchers distinguished *primary strategies*, or those applied directly to the content, from *support strategies* that learners use to create and maintain a favorable psychological climate for learning. The latter strategies include affective techniques and those used to monitor and correct ongoing primary strategies.

Effective studying requires that students comprehend, retain, retrieve, and use information. These are the primary elements of the *Survey-Question-Read-Recite (Recall)-Review (SQ3R)* method (Robinson, 1946), later modified to the SQ4R method with the addition of Reflection. When students use the SQ3R method, they first survey a text chapter by reading headings and boldface (or italics) print, after which they develop questions.

Learners then read the text while keeping the questions in mind. After reading, students try to recall what they have read. They then review the material.

In Dansereau's learning strategies program, students comprehend material by highlighting important ideas, recalling material without referring to text, digesting and expanding the information, and reviewing it. Expanding information means relating it to other information in LTM by creating links between memory networks. Students learn to ask themselves questions similar to the following: "Imagine you could talk to the author. What questions would you ask? What criticisms would you raise?" "How can the material be applied?" and "How could you make the material more understandable and interesting to other students?"

This program moves beyond the SQ3R method because it includes support strategies such as goal setting, concentration management, and monitoring and diagnosing. Students learn to set daily, weekly, and longer-term goals by establishing schedules. Learners monitor progress and adjust their work or goals as necessary if their performance does not match expectations. *Concentration management* is developed by helping students deal with frustration, anxiety, and anger. Use of *self-talk* is encouraged, and students can be *desensitized* by imagining anxiety-provoking situations when relaxing (Chapter 3). *Monitoring* and *diagnosing* require that students determine in advance where they will stop in the text to assess their level of comprehension. As they reach each stop point, they *assess understanding* and *take corrective action* (e.g., rereading) as needed. Evaluations of the strategy-instructional program have shown that it improves academic behaviors and attitudes (Dansereau et al., 1979).

Dansereau (1988) modified this program for use in cooperative learning dyads. Each member of the pair took turns reading approximately 500 words of a 2,500-word passage. One member then served as recaller and orally summarized what was read; the other listened, corrected errors in recall, and elaborated knowledge by adding imagery and links to prior knowledge. Dansereau reported that this cooperative arrangement facilitated learning and transfer better than individual studying.

Time Management. Investigators from different theoretical traditions (e.g., social cognitive, information processing) increasingly have focused on the cognitive and behavioral processes that students use to plan and manage academic studying time (Winne, 2001; Zimmerman, Greenberg, & Weinstein, 1994). Effective time management contributes to learning and achievement. Britton and Tesser (1991) found that the time management components of short-range planning and time attitudes were significant predictors of grade point averages among college students. Effective use of time appears partly to be a function of students' use of goal setting and planning (Weinstein & Mayer, 1986). These procedures, in turn, prompt students to engage in other self-regulatory activities such as self-monitoring of progress. Time is an important dimension of self-regulation and can be a performance outcome (e.g., how much time to devote to a task).

Poor time management may reflect problems in several areas (Zimmerman et al., 1994). It can result when students do not properly self-observe, self-evaluate, and self-react to their performance outcomes. It also may occur when students do not adequately use planning aids such as watches, alarms, and appointment books. Unrealistic goals, low self-efficacy, attributions of learning difficulties to low ability, and perceptions that strategies are not all that important also affect time management (Zimmerman, 1998; Zimmerman et al., 1994).

Students can learn to manage time more effectively. Weinstein et al. (1987) included time management as one of the areas of the *Learning and Study Strategies Inventory* (*LASSI*), a diagnostic and prescriptive self-report measure of strategic, goal-directed learning for students that focuses on thoughts, attitudes, beliefs, and behaviors that are related to academic success and can be altered. Completion of the LASSI or a similar instrument usually is necessary to ascertain the extent of a student's study problems.

Programs to facilitate better use of time typically include instruction and practice on topics such as becoming a strategic learner; the roles of goal setting and self-management; time-management planning; various study strategies including note taking, listening, underlining, summarizing, and coping with stress; test-taking strategies; and organizing a setting for learning.

An important study time issue is that students often do not realize how they really spend their time. A good assignment is to have students keep a time log for a week to show how much time they devoted to each task. Often they are surprised at how much time they wasted. Instruction must address ways to eliminate or reduce such waste.

Another common problem is failing to understand how long tasks take to complete. A student once informed me that she thought she would need about two hours to read eight chapters in her educational psychology textbook. At 15 minutes per chapter with no break, that's what you call speed reading! A useful exercise is to have students estimate the amount of time various tasks will take, and then keep a log of the actual times and record these with the estimates to determine the correspondence between estimated and actual times.

Students often need a change in work environment. They may try to study in places with potential distractions such as friends, cell phones, televisions, refrigerators, stoves, video and audio equipment, and so forth. Some students may benefit from light music or noise in the background, but almost everyone has difficulty concentrating when a powerful distraction or many potential distractions are present. It helps for students to complete an inventory of study preferences and present study conditions, after which they can determine whether environmental changes are necessary.

Writing

Like other forms of learning, the development of writing skill is affected by motivation and self-regulation (Graham, 2006). Bruning and Horn (2000) characterized this development as "a highly fluid process of problem solving requiring constant monitoring of progress toward task goals" (p. 25). Cognitive models of writing incorporate self-regulation components (Hayes, 2000; Chapter 7). Students are active information processors who employ cognitive and metacognitive strategies during writing.

Goal setting and self-monitoring of goal progress are key self-regulatory processes (Schunk, 1995). Zimmerman and Kitsantas (1999) found that high school students who shifted their goals from process (following steps in a strategy) to outcomes (number of words in sentences) showed higher writing revision skill, self-efficacy, and interest than did students who pursued only process or only outcome goals. These results suggest that as skills develop, students can shift their focus from following a strategy to the outcomes that strategy use produces (e.g., making fewer errors). Although more research is needed on the effects of instructional procedures on motivation to write, writing motivation can be enhanced by using authentic writing tasks and by creating a supportive context for writing (e.g., the task appears doable with requisite effort).

Klassen (2002) reviewed the literature on self-efficacy for writing. Most studies found that self-efficacy was a significant predictor of writing achievement. Some studies yielded gender differences in self-efficacy with boys' judgments higher than those of girls, although there were no performance differences. Establishing a classroom environment that builds self-efficacy is conducive to improving writing.

Writing is demanding and requires attention control, self-monitoring, and volitional control. Graham and Harris (2000) noted that self-regulation affects writing in two ways. For one, self-regulatory processes (e.g., planning, monitoring, and evaluating) provide building blocks that are assembled to complete a writing task. For another, these processes can lead to strategic adjustments in writing and longer-term effects. Thus, successful planning will increase its likelihood of future use and build self-efficacy for writing, which in turn positively impacts motivation and future writing. Teaching students self-regulatory skills in the context of writing assignments results in higher achievement and motivation (Graham & Harris, 2000; Schunk & Swartz, 1993a, 1993b).

The self-regulated strategy development model has been widely applied to writing (Glaser & Brunstein, 2007; Graham, Harris, MacArthur, & Schwartz, 1998; Harris & Graham, 1996; Zito, Adkins, Gavins, Harris, & Graham, 2007; Chapter 7). This model utilizes teacher modeling of writing strategies, collaborative peer group practice, and independent practice, where assistance (scaffolds) is generally faded out. The model has been used successfully with students with writing problems, learning disabilities, and attention deficit/hyperactivity disorders (Harris et al., 2006; Reid & Lienemann, 2006). The model includes general and genre-specific strategies (as emphasized in the introductory scenario), as well as motivational components (e.g., self-reinforcement). De La Paz (2005) found that the model helped culturally diverse students improve their argumentative essay writing skills.

Given that writing involves language and reflects one's thoughts and cognitive processes, writing has been viewed as a way to improve learning capabilities and academic achievement. This "writing to learn" idea stresses having students write in various disciplines. Bangert-Drowns, Hurley, and Wilkinson (2004) reviewed the research literature on writing-to-learn interventions and found a small positive effect on overall academic achievement. These researchers also found that prompting students during writing to reflect on their knowledge and learning processes was effective in raising achievement. These findings suggest that writing-to-learn has promise as a useful way to augment content-area learning.

Mathematics

Mathematics learning can be enhanced by teaching students effective strategies (general and specific). This approach is followed in the self-regulated strategy development model (Fuchs et al., 2003a; see preceding section). Fuchs et al. worked with third-grade students on mathematical problem solving. Self-regulation strategies included goal setting for individual sessions and self-monitoring and self-assessment of progress toward goal attainment. These general strategies were supplemented with specific strategies to use to solve the problems. Compared with regular teacher instruction, self-regulation instruction increased students' performance and transfer of skills. Other research shows that teaching strategies to children with learning disabilities and those who have experienced difficulties learning mathematical skills improves self-efficacy and achievement (Schunk, 1985; Schunk & Cox, 1986). Jitendra et al. (2007) found with third graders that specific strategy instruction was more effective in promoting word problem-solving skills than was instruction on general strategies, although both types of instruction raised students' computational skills.

Much has been written in recent years on gender and ethnic differences in mathematical achievement (Byrnes, 1996; Halpern, 2006; Meece, 2002). Some evidence shows that boys tend to outperform girls and that Asian Americans and White Americans do better than African Americans and Hispanic Americans; however, the literature is complex, often contradictory, and not subject to easy interpretation. Royer et al. (1999) found that among higher-performing students, boys displayed faster mathematical fact retrieval than did girls. Nonetheless, girls typically earn better mathematics grades than boys (Meece, 2002). Gender differences favoring boys also have been obtained in other cultures (e.g., Germany; Rustemeyer & Fischer, 2005).

Motivational variables (Chapter 8) and self-regulatory skills have been implicated as causes of mathematical performance (Meece, 2002; Schutz, Drogosz, White, & DiStefano, 1998). Among sixth graders, Vermeer, Boekaerts, and Seegers (2000) found that girls reported lower perceived competence (i.e., self-efficacy) than boys on applied problem solving and were more likely to attribute poor performance to low ability and high task difficulty (attributions to uncontrollable variables). Girls often report lower self-efficacy in mathematics than boys (Rustemeyer & Fischer, 2005), although this gender difference is not consistent (Meece, 2002). Self-efficacy, however, is a strong predictor of mathematics performance (Chen, 2003; Pajares & Schunk, 2001; Pietsch, Walker, & Chapman, 2003). Goal setting (McNeil & Alibali, 2000) and self-efficacy enhancing interventions (Schunk & Ertmer, 2000) are effective for promoting motivation in mathematics. The ideas for enhancing self-regulation discussed in this chapter can build motivation and self-efficacy (Schunk, 1995).

Ethnic differences in mathematical achievement are more consistent and pronounced. Based on several research studies, experts draw the following conclusions (Byrnes, 1996):

- White American students perform better than African American and Hispanic American students.
- Asian American students perform better than White Americans.
- Researchers find no significant difference in mathematical achievement between African American and Hispanic American students.

A few caveats are in order. A confounding factor is socioeconomic status (SES); Stevenson, Chen, and Uttal (1990) found that differences between White American, African American, and Hispanic American students disappeared when SES was taken into account. Regardless of ethnicity, mathematics achievement bears a significant and positive relation to SES. Second, differences are most pronounced for formal (curriculum-based) mathematics achievement (Byrnes, 1996). Researchers find little evidence for ethnic differences in children's informal (constructed) knowledge. These findings are consistent with Geary's (1995) contention that biologically primary abilities should be evident across cultures, whereas biologically secondary abilities are more susceptible to cultural influence.

Another variable that has been shown to influence mathematical achievement is the transition between grades. Anderman (1998) studied adolescents with learning disabilities and found higher achievement among those who did not make a transition until the ninth grade compared with students who made an earlier transition. School transitions can lead to declines in motivation and achievement (Chapter 8), and they seem especially problematic for students with learning problems. When teachers who span transition grades (e.g., fifth and sixth grades) work together, they can help ease transition problems and maintain students' motivation for learning. For example, prior to the transition, teachers can teach students self-regulatory skills that will help them in the next grade (e.g., organizing, planning). After the transition, teachers can ensure that students are competent in the mathematical skills and self-regulatory processes they need to be successful.

SUMMARY

Self-regulation (self-regulated learning) refers to processes that learners use to systematically focus their thoughts, feelings, and actions on the attainment of their goals. The application of self-regulation to learning began as an outgrowth of psychological research on the development of self-control by adults and children. Early self-regulation research tended to be conducted in clinics, where researchers taught participants to alter dysfunctional behaviors such as aggression, addictions, sexual disorders, interpersonal conflicts, and behavioral problems at home and in school. In the past several years, researchers have expanded their focus to address academic learning and achievement.

By its very nature, self-regulation involves learners' choices. To engage in self-regulation students must have some choices available to them, such as whether to participate, which method they use, what outcomes they will pursue, and which social and physical setting they will work in. Self-regulation involves behaviors, as individuals regulate their actions to keep them focused on goal attainment. Individuals also regulate their cognitions and affects. While they are engaged in learning, they self-regulate cognitions and affects by maintaining their self-efficacy for learning, valuing the learning, holding expectations for positive outcomes as a result of the learning, evaluating their goal progress, determining how effective their strategies are and altering them as necessary, and maintaining a positive emotional climate.

Self-regulatory processes and strategies that learners apply can be general (apply to many types of learning) or specific (apply only to a particular type of learning). Self-regulatory processes such as setting goals and evaluating goal progress can be employed with different types of learning (e.g., academic skills, motor skills), whereas others pertain only to specific content areas or tasks (e.g., mathematical formulas, grammatical rules).

Self-regulation has been addressed by different theories of learning. Behavioral theories stress the setting of stimuli and conditions to which learners respond, after which they are reinforced for their efforts. Key behavioral subprocesses are self-monitoring, self-instruction, and self-reinforcement. Learners decide which behaviors to regulate, set discriminative stimuli for their occurrence, participate in instruction as needed, monitor performance, and administer reinforcement when it matches the standard. Behavioral principles are useful for self-regulation, but by ignoring cognitive and affective processes they offer an incomplete account of the range of self-regulation possible.

The classical social cognitive theoretical account of self-regulation viewed it as comprising three subprocesses: self-observation, self-judgment, and self-reaction. Students enter learning activities with various goals such as acquiring knowledge and skills and completing assignments. With these goals in mind, they observe, judge, and react to their perceived goal progress. This classical view was broadened to emphasize the cyclical nature of self-regulation and to include activities before and after task engagement. This cyclical process reflects the social cognitive emphasis on reciprocal interactions between personal, behavioral, and social/environmental factors. The forethought phase precedes actual performance and refers to processes that set the stage for action, such as setting goals, deciding on a strategy, and assessing self-efficacy for learning. The performance control phase involves processes that occur during learning and affect attention and action, such as applying strategies and monitoring progress. During the self-reflection phase that occurs during breaks and after task completion, learners respond to their efforts by setting new goals, adjusting their strategies, and making attributions for outcomes.

Information processing theories emphasize that self-regulation reflects metacognitive awareness. Self-regulation requires that learners understand task demands, personal qualities, and strategies for completing the task. Metacognitive awareness also includes procedural knowledge. The basic unit of self-regulation may be a problem-solving system in which the problem is to reach the goal and the monitoring checks progress to determine whether the learning is occurring. Information processing research historically focused on cognitive variables, but increasingly researchers in this tradition are including motivational variables.

Constructivist theories stress that self-regulation involves the coordination of mental functions, such as memory, planning, evaluation, and synthesis. Learners use the tools of their cultures, such as language and symbols, to construct meanings of content and situations. A key feature is the internalization of self-regulatory processes; although learners may acquire self-regulatory strategies from their environments, they alter and adapt them for use in their personal self-regulatory systems.

Self-regulation and motivation are related. Such processes as goal setting, self-efficacy, and outcome expectations are important motivational variables that affect self-regulation. In turn, engaging in successful self-regulated learning can motivate learners to set new goals and continue learning. Researchers increasingly are examining the role of volition in achievement settings and especially as it relates to self-regulation. Other motivational variables involved in self-regulation include values, goal orientations, self-schemas, and help seeking. Collectively, these variables may help to determine how achievement behavior is instigated and sustained as learners engage in choices regarding the content, location, timing, and outcomes of their learning.

Like other skills, learners can be taught self-regulatory skills and can become better self-regulated learners. An effective teaching model begins with social (environmental) influences, such as teacher models explaining and demonstrating self-regulatory strategies. As students practice and become more skillful, they transform these social influences in idiosyncratic ways and internalize them into their personal self-regulatory systems. Self-regulation instruction is most effective when it is linked to academic content. Self-regulation principles have been applied to such areas as academic studying, writing, and mathematics.

FURTHER READING

Corno, L. (2008). Work habits and self-regulated learning: Helping students to find a "will" from a "way." In D. H. Schunk & B. J. Zimmerman (Eds.), *Motivation and self-regulated learning: Theory, research, and applications* (pp. 197–222). New York: Taylor & Francis.

Henderson, R. W., & Cunningham, L. (1994). Creating interactive sociocultural environments for self-regulated learning. In D. H. Schunk & B. J. Zimmerman (Eds.), *Self-regulation of learning and performance: Issues and educational applications* (pp. 255–281). Hillsdale, NJ: Erlbaum.

Mace, F. C., Belfiore, P. J., & Hutchinson, M. M. (2001). Operant theory and research on self-regulation. In B. J. Zimmerman & D. H. Schunk (Eds.), *Self-regulated learning and academic achievement: Theoretical perspectives* (2nd ed., pp. 39–65). Mahwah, NJ: Erlbaum.

Pressley, M., Harris, K. R., & Marks, M. B. (1992). But good strategy instructors are constructivists! *Educational Psychology Review, 4,* 3–31.

Winne, P. H., & Hadwin, A. F. (2008). The weave of motivation and self-regulated learning. In D. H. Schunk & B. J. Zimmerman (Eds.), *Motivation and self-regulated learning: Theory, research, and applications* (pp. 297–314). New York: Taylor & Francis.

Zimmerman, B. J. (2000). Attaining self-regulation: A social cognitive perspective. In M. Boekaerts, P. R. Pintrich, & M. Zeidner (Eds.), *Handbook of self-regulation* (pp. 13–39). San Diego: Academic Press.

Zimmerman, B. J., Bonner, S., & Kovach, R. (1996). *Developing self-regulated learners: Beyond achievement to self-efficacy.* Washington, DC: American Psychological Association.

10

Development

During a lunch break, a group of middle school teachers are discussing why adolescents are so difficult to teach. This issue sparks a lively debate.

Darren says, "Look, I've been teaching these kids a long time, and I think it's just a stage that all adolescents go through. There's not much we can do. I remember when I was their age. As soon as those hormones started to kick in, all I wanted to do was look at girls, play soccer, and hang out with my friends! They'll grow out of it. Meanwhile, we just have to live with them."

Lucia replies, "I may be new at teaching, but I don't think it's that simple. Sure these kids are going through some physical changes, but isn't there more that we could do for them? I think they're just bored with school, and that's why they're so difficult to teach. Maybe there are some ways we can make learning more meaningful to them. I'm going to start using more cooperative learning activities in my classroom. I'm also going to let them have a bigger say in deciding how we do things. They're old enough to take on more responsibility for their own learning."

Frank, a seventh-grade social studies teacher, just shakes his head. "Where have you been? Haven't you read the papers? Kids today need a firm hand. They need discipline. That's the problem. Teachers like you are way too permissive. We can change these kids if we reward the good ones and punish the bad ones. Taxpayers are paying for their education, and they should be expected to learn so they can get jobs when they graduate. Learning isn't fun; it's hard work. You won't find any fooling around in my classes. My students know that they have to finish their work or stay after school. It's that simple." (Meece, 2002, pp. 3–4)

This chapter discusses human development and its relation to learning. *Development* refers to changes over time that follow an orderly pattern and enhance survival (Meece, 2002). These changes are progressive (rather than sudden) and occur over the course of the life span (rather than at only one point in time).

Development is an important educational topic, although (as the above scenario shows) it may be the subject of lively debate. Development often is taken for granted. In earlier chapters several learning principles were explained; however, these do not exist in a vacuum. Each principle of learning could be prefaced with, "Assuming proper level of development . . ." For example, in discussing the formation of memory networks, we noted that students link information in memory. The capability to do this improves with development. Older students have more extensive memory networks and can make connections that younger students cannot.

Development is intimately linked with learning. In Chapter 1, learning was defined as relatively permanent changes in an individual due to experiences, and we contrasted these changes with those arising from maturation. Both learning and maturation may be thought of as components of development. At any given time, developmental level places constraints on learning possibilities: The what, where, when, why, and how of learning. But as the opening scenario shows, educators often disagree on the amount and nature of those constraints. This chapter focuses on cognitive development because this is most relevant to learning, although other types of development (e.g., physical, social, emotional, and moral) can affect learning.

Many developmental theories postulate that cognitive development involves *construction* of knowledge as a function of the individual's experiences (Chapter 6). This contrasts with the behavioral theory view (Chapter 3) that knowledge is received from the environment. Contemporary theories also stress the increasing sophistication of information processing functions as a consequence of development (Chapters 5 and 7).

This chapter begins with material on the historical and philosophical foundations of the scientific study of development to include the important contributions of the Child Study Movement. Various theoretical perspectives on development are explained with an emphasis on cognitive and constructivist perspectives. Bruner's theory of cognitive growth is covered, along with contemporary developmental research on cognitive processes. The related topics of developmentally appropriate instruction and transitions in schooling are addressed. Separate sections are included on home and family influences on development, developmental changes in motivation, and instructional applications. The related topics of brain development (Chapter 2), Piaget's theory (Chapter 6), and Vygotsky's theory (Chapter 6) are covered in other chapters.

When you finish studying this chapter, you should be able to do the following:

- Describe the major influences leading to the scientific study of human development.

- State some of the major contributions and shortcomings of the Child Study Movement.

- Explain developmental issues relevant to learning and major perspectives on human development.

- Compare and contrast structural and functional accounts of development.

- Describe the types of knowledge representation proposed by Bruner and what is meant by the "spiral curriculum."

- Discuss some major changes in cognitive information processing that occur during development.

- Explain what is meant by developmentally appropriate instruction and why transitions in schooling affect learning and teaching.

- Discuss the relation of socioeconomic status, home environment, parental involvement, and media influence to development and learning.

- Describe developmental changes in motivation and their implications for learning.

- Explain some instructional implications of the literature on learning styles, Case's instructional model, and research on teacher–student interactions.

BEGINNINGS OF THE SCIENTIFIC STUDY OF DEVELOPMENT

The beginnings of the scientific study of human development are deeply rooted in history and philosophy. These are examined in turn.

Historical Foundations

Educators acknowledge the influence of development on teaching and learning, but this has not always been the case. During the 1800s, life in the United States and the role of children in society were different than they are today (Mondale & Patton, 2001). Despite the guarantees of the U.S. Constitution, education was not universal, but rather pursued mostly by children of middle- and upper-class families. Many children—especially those from rural and working-class backgrounds—worked to earn money or otherwise helped to support their families. These children attended school sporadically, and many quit at young ages. At the elementary level, the major goal was to teach reading; the "3 Rs" had not yet become standard. Secondary schools were largely preparatory schools for the universities, which were oriented toward the humanities and religion.

The period between the Civil War and World War I, known as the Industrial Revolution, is widely hailed for significant progress, but life was harsh. Economic conditions created an underclass, despite many people working long hours six days per week. Inadequate sanitary conditions gave rise to the spread of diseases in large cities.

Schoolmasters were strict, and lessons often were long and boring. Children were expected to study and learn; if they failed to learn, they (and not society, parents, or teachers) were held responsible. Individualized instruction was nonexistent; students worked on the same lesson at the same time. Schoolmasters lectured and held recitations. They were trained in school subjects, not pedagogy.

Into this picture entered scores of immigrants to the United States, especially between 1880 and 1920. This vast influx necessitated major increases in numbers of schools and teachers. Normal schools and universities were not equipped to produce large numbers of high-quality teachers. Normal schools were the major source of teacher preparation, but increasingly they were perceived as inadequate, especially for the preparation of secondary teachers (Davidson & Benjamin, 1987). In the latter half of the nineteenth century, schools of education were established in greater numbers at major colleges and universities. The challenge was to train teachers to deal with large numbers of students from diverse backgrounds.

Philosophical Foundations

The writings of educational philosophers and critics also helped to establish the scientific study of development and improvement of education. A number of European philosophers, including Rousseau, Pestalozzi, and Froebel, wrote extensively about the nature of children. As their writings became better known in the United States, educators and others increasingly questioned whether U.S. education was appropriate for students.

Rousseau (1712–1778) believed that children were basically good and that the purpose of education was to help develop this propensity. Teachers should establish one-to-one relationships with students (i.e., tutor/tutee) and consider their individual needs and talents in arranging learning activities. Above all, learning should be satisfying and self-directed; children should learn from hands-on experience and not be forced to learn.

Pestalozzi (1746–1827) emphasized that education should be for everyone and that learning should be self-directed rather than rote—the dominant style of learning at the time in U.S. schools. Pestalozzi stressed the emotional development of students, which could be enhanced through close relationships between teachers and learners.

Froebel (1782–1852) believed that children were basically good and needed to be nurtured starting at an early age. He founded the *kindergarten* ("garden for children"), which reflected his belief that children—like young plants—needed to be nurtured.

Recall the Chapter 1 discussion of how psychology underwent a transformation beginning at the end of the nineteenth century from a branch of philosophy to a science of its own. A similar transformation occurred in education. The emergence of psychology, writings on the goodness of children and the need for their nurturing, and pressure for the education of all children triggered by large numbers of immigrants—along with other influences (e.g., social Darwinism, compulsory attendance laws)—led to a call for the scientific study of children.

By the end of the nineteenth century:

> Immigration and industrialization heightened the need for schooling, the increasing enrollment of students sparked a demand from parents and teachers for information about how to teach children; the social Darwinists and individual difference psychologists wanted to know about how adult differences started, and the child welfare workers wanted help in planning programs to help children. The Child Study Movement attempted to meet these diverse needs. (Davidson & Benjamin, 1987, p. 46)

We now turn to a discussion of the Child Study Movement.

The Child Study Movement

Hall's Work. The generally acknowledged founder of the Child Study Movement is G. (Granville) Stanley Hall (1844–1924). After receiving his doctorate from Harvard University, Hall studied in Germany for two years and became enamored with the German educational system and its view of the child's nature (Davidson & Benjamin, 1987). In 1882 he spoke before the National Education Association and called for child study as the core of the study of pedagogy. Subsequently he conducted a large-scale study of Boston children entering school. He administered a lengthy questionnaire designed to determine what they knew about various subjects (e.g., animals, mathematics). The results showed that children were ignorant of many features of U.S. life (e.g., 93% were unaware that leather came from animals).

As a professor of psychology at Johns Hopkins University, Hall was in prime position to establish child study as a scientific discipline. Hall (1894) stated that the new science of psychology had a natural application to education. Unfortunately, Hall did not remain active in the movement because he moved to Clark University as its president; however, he continued to speak publicly on its importance and publish extensively (Hall, 1894, 1896, 1900, 1903). Others became proponents of child study, and active centers were established in universities and normal schools.

From the outset, the Child Study Movement was broad and somewhat ill defined:

> It is a nondescript and . . . unparalleled movement—partly psychology, partly anthropology, partly medico-hygiene. It is closely related at every step to the study of instinct in animals, and to the rites and beliefs of primitive people; and it has a distinct ethico-philosophical aspect . . . with a spice of folk-lore and of religious evolution, sometimes with an alloy of gossip and nursery tradition, but possessing a broad, practical side in the pedagogy of all stages. It has all the advantages and the less grave disadvantages of its many-sidedness. (Hall, 1900, p. 689)

Despite Hall's glowing description, the broad scope of the Child Study Movement eventually contributed to its undoing.

Goals and Methods. The need for child study was felt by teachers, parents, and others who believed that teaching and child raising would improve through proper understanding of children. A major goal of child study was to assist education (Davidson & Benjamin, 1987). Prior to the Child Study Movement, the predominant belief was that knowledge of children could be acquired by teaching. Child study advocates believed that such knowledge should be acquired prior to teaching so that education would be more successful and satisfying. "From this standpoint it is plain that the teacher must know two things: (1) the subject matter to be taught; and (2) the nature and capacity of the minds in which it is to be rooted" (Hall, 1900, p. 699). The Child Study Movement helped to establish schools of education in universities with strong ties to public schools.

Another goal was to discover knowledge that would help parenting (Davidson & Benjamin, 1987). By understanding child development, parents would be in a better position to ensure that children developed to their full potential.

Given its close link with psychology, the Child Study Movement also had a research agenda. Primarily this was to understand children better through testing. Hall developed an extensive questionnaire, and others followed suit. Other research methods used were naturalistic observations, aptitude and ability testing, and psychophysical studies of vision and perception.

Critique. The Child Study Movement contributed in several ways to psychology and education. One contribution was the *baby biography*, which consisted of a series of observations on a single child over a lengthy period. Baby biographies provided detailed accounts of children's actions, responses, and verbalizations and highlighted changes in processes with development. This type of longitudinal research using naturalistic observations is common today, especially by researchers interested in infants and toddlers.

A second contribution was the use of children as research participants. The experimental methods of the new science of psychology were increasingly applied to children. The Child Study Movement helped to create the belief that children could be legitimate participants in research. As research results accumulated, they required outlets for publication and presentation; thus, new journals and professional associations were begun.

The Child Study Movement also affected teacher training. Normal schools and schools of education in universities were charged with providing high-quality preservice training so that graduates could assume teaching duties. As with other professions, teaching benefited from teacher education programs that were firmly rooted in educational theory and research.

Finally, the Child Study Movement filled an important public void. People wanted information about children and child study advocates obliged (Davidson & Benjamin, 1987). Child-care professionals, such as teachers and social workers, felt the need for more information to help them perform their jobs better. The growth in journals led to articles published on ways to teach specific school subjects. With respect to teaching methods, some of the emphasis on drills and recitations lessened as children were increasingly allowed free expression and exploration of interests (including through play). In short, the Child Study Movement had a humanizing effect on educational practice.

Despite these contributions, some psychologists and educators criticized the soundness of the Child Study Movement. Although purportedly research based, many studies of children had suspect validity due to weaknesses in methods and assessment instruments. Parents and teachers often collected data. Such participatory research is common today, but in Hall's time it was opposed by many professionals because they believed that only trained experts should collect data.

Perhaps the major problem with the Child Study Movement was the same one that plagued functionalism (Chapter 1): Its focus was simply too broad to hold it together. The Child Study Movement was an amalgamation of individuals with diverse interests and agendas—researchers, practitioners, parents, child-care providers, and administrators. Because it tried to accomplish too much, it accomplished little very well. Hall's self-imposed dissociation from child study, coupled with his writings on controversial topics (e.g., corporal punishment, role of women in education), created a leadership void. The rise of behaviorism in psychology (Chapters 1 and 3) further contributed to its demise.

Nonetheless, the legacy of child study lives on in several venues, including psychology (educational, developmental, school, experimental child, and mental testing), education (early education, teacher training, physical education, and special education), and counseling (social work, vocational) (Davidson & Benjamin, 1987). As child study became more scientific, new child development centers flourished at universities.

The Child Study Movement touched many individuals who became influential in their own right. John Dewey (Chapter 1) studied with Hall at Johns Hopkins and worked with other child study advocates. Arnold Gesell (discussed later in this chapter) capitalized on child study's emphasis on normative data to produce age-related norms. Edward L. Thorndike (Chapter 3) provided a much-needed methodological sophistication to educational research and attempted to make sense out of findings of child study research studies. Thorndike continued the emphasis on the integration of learning and development (Davidson & Benjamin, 1987).

By the 1920s the Child Study Movement was no longer viable and effectively had been replaced in psychology by behaviorism. We now consider types of developmental theories that have emerged since then.

PERSPECTIVES ON DEVELOPMENT

Many perspectives on human development exist. This section examines those that have the greatest relevance to learning. Initially some issues that are controversial and bear directly on learning are discussed.

Table 10.1
Developmental issues relevant to learning.

- *Nature versus nurture:* Does development depend more on heredity, environment, or a combination?

- *Stability versus change:* Are developmental periods flexible, or do certain critical times exist in which developmental changes must occur for development to proceed normally?

- *Continuity versus discontinuity:* Does development occur continuously through small changes, or do sudden, abrupt changes occur?

- *Passivity versus activity:* Do changes occur regardless of children's actions, or do children play an active role in their development?

- *Structure versus function:* Does development consist of a series of changes in cognitive structures or processes?

Issues Relevant to Learning

Although most investigators could agree with the definition of development presented earlier, theories of development differ in many ways. Table 10.1 shows some issues that theorists disagree about and which have implications for learning (Meece, 2002; Zimmerman & Whitehurst, 1979). These are discussed in turn.

Nature Versus Nurture. This is one of the oldest controversies in behavioral science. It is evident in the opening conversation among the middle school teachers. Theories differ in the weights they assign to heredity, environment, and their combination (interaction) as contributors to development. Psychoanalytic theories stress the role of heredity. As we saw in the preceding section, child study proponents placed a fair amount of emphasis on the child's emerging nature (heredity); however, because they also emphasized good teaching, the implication was that environmental and hereditary influences interacted to affect development. In the opening scenario, Darren comes out strongly for hereditary influence.

Conversely, behavioral theorists take an extreme environmental view. The right conditions produce learning; heredity is important only for providing the necessary physical and mental prerequisites needed to respond to stimuli in the environment. In the opening scenario, Frank seems to espouse a behavioral position.

The implications for learning are clear. If we assume that development primarily is hereditary, then learning will proceed pretty much at its own rate and others cannot do much about it. If we assume that the environment makes a difference, then we can structure it to foster development.

Stability Versus Change. Theories differ in whether they predict that developmental periods are relatively fixed or have more flexibility. *Readiness,* or what children are capable of doing or learning at various points in development, relates directly to this issue. A strict view holds that because developmental periods are relatively fixed, only certain types of learning are possible at a given time. Darren seems to espouse this position. Most school curricula reflect this idea to some degree because they specify content to be taught at particular grade levels.

Other theories contend that because developmental periods have much leeway, children should have more latitude to learn at their own pace. This idea is reflected in Lucia's comments. Thus, most children will develop the prerequisite abilities to learn to read in the first grade, but some will not, and forcing these children to read will create problems. A key issue, therefore, is how to assess readiness.

Continuity Versus Discontinuity. Whether development proceeds in continuous or discontinuous fashion is a subject of debate. Behavioral theories posit continuous development. As behaviors develop, they form the basis for acquiring new ones. Conversely, Piaget's theory (Chapter 6) describes a process of discontinuity. Changes from one mode of thinking to another may occur abruptly, and children will differ in how long they remain at a particular stage.

Educationally speaking, discontinuity is more difficult to plan for because activities that are effective now need to be changed as students' thinking develops. Continuous views allow for a better ordered sequence of curriculum. Although many school curricula are established assuming continuous development, educators readily admit that the process rarely proceeds smoothly.

Passivity Versus Activity. This issue refers to whether development progresses in natural fashion or whether more and varied experiences can promote it. This has important implications for teaching because it speaks to the issue of how active students should be. If activity is important, then lessons need to incorporate hands-on activities. Whether learning can be accelerated through modeling and practice has been the focus of much research with positive results (Rosenthal & Zimmerman, 1978). In the opening scenario, Lucia comes out on the side of activity, whereas Frank promotes a more passive view of learning.

In contrast to behavioral theories that view learning passively, cognitive and constructivist theories believe that learners are active and contribute heavily to their learning. This notion of activity also is seen in the topics of motivation (Chapter 8) and self-regulation (Chapter 9).

Structure Versus Function. *Structural theories of development* assume that human development consists of changes in structures (or schemas). Development proceeds in a fixed, invariant fashion because each structural change follows preceding ones. A common assumption of structural theories is that human learning reflects one's general organization of knowledge (Zimmerman & Whitehurst, 1979). Behavior is given relatively less emphasis because it is assumed that behavior is an incomplete reflection of one's structures. Structural theories often (but not always) label the different periods of development as "stages." Readers should note that the label "stage" is not an explanation of learning but rather a shorthand way of referring to a constellation of activities that tend to occur together. Darren's comments are indicative of a structural position.

In contrast, *functional theories of development* do not employ stages but rather talk in terms of the types of functions or processes that a child is able to do at a particular time. Behavior is given more weight because behavior reflects functions. Although most children end up with the same basic competencies, the order and rate of development of functions can vary. Most contemporary views of development are functional. Lucia's comments reflect a functional view of development. Some combination of these two approaches is possible; for example, a structural theory might include some functional elements.

Types of Developmental Theories

Meece (2002) identified five primary classes of theories: biological, psychoanalytical, behavioral, cognitive, and contextual (Table 10.2). These are discussed next.

Biological Theories. Biological theories cast human development as an *unfolding* process. Children proceed through a set sequence of invariant stages of development in roughly the same time. The environment provides opportunities for growth but exerts no direct influence; rather, development is overwhelmingly determined by genetics. Darren's comment about the hormones kicking in indicates a biological view of development.

A primary proponent was Arnold Gesell, who, together with his colleagues, published age-based norms for growth and behavioral changes (Gesell & Ilg, 1946; Gesell, Ilg, & Ames, 1956). The Gesell norms provide general expectations and may be useful for identifying children who do not fit the age-based expectations (e.g., a child who displays excessive "baby" behavior in the third grade). At the same time, the wide variation in developmental changes between children means that the norms have limited usefulness. When norms are misused and become criteria for learning readiness, they can retard educational progress. Although growth and behavior are correlated with cognitive development, they are not valid reasons for assuming that children cannot learn.

Current biological work focuses on the extent that cognitive, behavioral, and personality characteristics have genetic predispositions (Chapter 2). Thus, the tendency for children to understand counting may be largely inherited (Geary, 1995; Chapter 7), and the capacity for language acquisition seems biologically predisposed (Chomsky, 1957; Chapters 2 and 5). A

Table 10.2
Types of developmental theories.

Type	Key Developmental Processes
Biological	Individuals proceed through an invariant sequence of stages; stage progression is largely determined by genetics.
Psychoanalytic	Development represents a series of changes in personality brought about by need satisfaction. Stages are qualitatively distinct.
Behavioral	Development represents changes in behaviors produced by conditioning; changes are continuous and quantitative.
Cognitive	Development represents changes in mental structures or processes that occur as individuals take in information and mentally construct understandings.
Contextual	Social and cultural factors affect development; changes in persons or situations interact with and influence other changes.

long-standing debate concerns the extent that intelligence is inherited. Researchers continue to explore how genetics and environmental factors interact to influence development (Plomin, 1990).

Psychoanalytic Theories. Psychoanalytic theories emphasize the fulfillment of *needs*, which differ as a function of developmental level (Meece, 2002). Development is viewed as progressive changes in personality, which emerges as children seek to satisfy their needs. Children pass through a series of stages, each of which is qualitatively different from preceding ones. Children interact with their environments to fulfill needs, and their successes in resolving conflicts associated with need fulfillment influence personality.

Two well-known psychoanalytic theorists were Sigmund Freud and Erik Erikson. Freud (1966) believed that the basic structure of a child's personality was established during the first five years of life. Erikson (1963), on the other hand, felt that development was a lifelong process and thus postulated developmental stages into old age. Psychoanalytic theories emphasize the role of innate factors in development. Needs are innate, and how they are resolved affects development. The role of learning in development is downplayed in favor of need resolution.

Psychoanalytic theories have their share of problems. As with other stage theories (e.g., Piaget's; Chapter 6), stage progression from child to child often is so uneven that using theories to explain development is difficult. Although the needs and conflicts described by psychoanalytic theories are well known to parents, caregivers, and teachers, how they can be resolved successfully is left open. Consequently, how significant others in children's lives can best foster development is unclear. For example, should adults provide for all of children's needs or teach children self-regulation skills so they can begin to satisfy their own needs? Theories that offer clearer predictions about development and especially the role of learning have greater applicability to education.

Behavioral Theories. In contrast to biological and psychoanalytical theories that stress innate factors, behavioral theories—while acknowledging developmental capabilities—postulate that development can be explained by the same principles that explain other behaviors. The major developmental changes occur as a result of *conditioning* (Chapters 1 and 3). Behavioral theories represent a continuity position: Small changes occur over time. Developmental changes are best viewed in quantitative terms: Children learn to do more in less time. The primary mechanism of learning is shaping of new behaviors through differential reinforcement of successive approximations to the target behaviors (Chapter 3).

Behavioral theories do not specify critical periods in development. The capacity for learning continues throughout the life span. They also emphasize that the major changes in behavior emanate from the environment, which provides the stimuli to which children respond and the reinforcement and punishment as consequences of their actions. Frank's comments in the opening vignette indicate a behavioral view of development. Behavioral theories downplay the role of personal factors associated with learners (e.g., thoughts, emotions) and the interaction between learners and their environments. Consequently, these theories treat self-regulation largely as the establishment of self-reinforcement contingencies. As noted in Chapter 3, behavioral methods often are useful in teaching and learning, but explanations for learning and development based on conditioning are incomplete because they negate the role of personal influences.

Cognitive Theories. Beginning with the work of Piaget in the early 1960s (Chapter 6), cognitive theories have gained ascendance in the field of human development. Cognitive theories focus on how children construct their understandings of themselves and of the world about them (Meece, 2002). Cognitive theories are constructivist (Chapter 6); they postulate that understanding is not automatic. Others do not convey information that children process rotely; rather, children take in information and formulate their own knowledge. They are active seekers and processors of information. Cognitive theories are interactional because they explain development in terms of interactions between personal, behavioral, and environmental factors. In the opening scenario, Lucia's comment about making learning more meaningful is indicative of a cognitive perspective. Prominent cognitive theories are Piaget's, Bruner's, Vygotsky's, information processing, and social cognitive theory.

This chapter discusses Bruner's theory and contemporary information processing theory. Piaget's and Vygotsky's theories are covered in Chapter 6 as part of constructivism. Bandura's (1986, 1997) social cognitive theory is described in Chapters 4, 8, and 9. With respect to development, the major points of Bandura's theory are that personal functioning represents a process of *triadic reciprocality* in which personal factors, behaviors, and environmental influences interact with and affect each other. Social cognitive theory also stresses that much learning occurs vicariously through observation of others. Research in the social cognitive tradition highlights the importance of modeling and guided practice as facilitators of developmental changes and acquisition of cognitive skills (Rosenthal & Zimmerman, 1978).

Some cognitive theories (e.g., Piaget's and information processing but not Vygotsky's or social cognitive theory) have been criticized because they tend to emphasize the role of the learner and downplay the influence of the social environment. An issue with constructivist theories is their vagueness in explaining how knowledge construction occurs.

Contextual Theories. These theories highlight the roles played by social and cultural factors. Evidence supporting this perspective comes from cross-cultural comparisons showing wide variability in developmental patterns, as well as from studies demonstrating that even within societies there is considerable variation in development (Meece, 2002). Societal practices clearly play a major role in development.

A well-known contextual model was formulated by Bronfenbrenner (1979), who postulated that the child's social world can be conceptualized as a set of concentric circles with the child at the common point of three intersecting circles: school, peers, and family. Outside of these is a larger circle containing neighborhood, extended family, community, church, workplace, and mass media. The outermost circle contains such influences as laws, cultural values, political and economic systems, and social customs. The model assumes that changes in one level can affect other levels. Thus, physical changes in children can alter their social groups, which in turn are affected by cultural values. The model is highly interactional and is useful for understanding the complexity of influences on human development and its effects.

Cognitive and contextual theories stress that children are active constructors of knowledge and that development is a continuous process across the life span. Contextual theories emphasize the altered nature of social patterns and how these lead children into different interactions with peers and adults. Cognitive development occurs largely as a consequence of these interactions. In turn, children's behaviors alter environments. Thus, children may develop new interests that change the peer groups with which they closely associate. Some cognitive theories (e.g., Vygotsky's and social cognitive) also are contextual in nature.

Contextual theories often are vague in their predictions of how changes in some aspects may affect development and vice versa. They also can be very complex, with a host of variables postulated to affect one another. This situation makes it difficult to conduct research. Despite these limitations, contextual theories call our attention to the need to study the many factors that are involved in human development.

Structural Theories

As mentioned earlier, an issue in the study of human development is whether it represents changes in cognitive structures or functions. Most contemporary views posit changes in functions, but structural theories have figured prominently in the discipline.

Structural theories postulate that development involves changes in cognitive structures, or *schemas*. Information that is learned (i.e., enters the structure) can help to alter the structure. These theories do not equate structures with physical locations in the brain; rather, structures are construed as constellations of capabilities or characteristic means of processing information.

Two structural theories with relevance to learning are described in this section: Chomsky's (1957) psycholinguistic theory and classic information processing theory (Atkinson & Shiffrin, 1968). Piaget's theory (Chapter 6) is another prominent structural theory.

Psycholinguistic Theory. Chomsky (1957, 1959) formulated a theory of language acquisition based on a system of *transformational grammar.* According to Chomsky, language can be differentiated into two levels: an overt *surface structure* that involves speech and syntax and a covert *deep structure* that includes meaning. A single deep structure can be represented by multiple surface structures. To illustrate this distinction, assume that Rhonda is playing basketball with Steve. The meaning as it might be represented as propositions in memory is:

Rhonda—playing basketball (with)—Steve

This meaning could be translated in various surface structures (utterances and sentences), such as:

- Rhonda is playing basketball with Steve.
- Steve is playing basketball with Rhonda.
- Rhonda? Playing basketball with Steve.
- Basketball is being played by Rhonda and Steve.

Chomsky's transformational grammar contains a number of rules that people presumably use to transform varying surface structures into the same meaning (deep structure). The deep structures are assumed to be part of the individual's genetic makeup. Language development, then, involves the progressive capability of mapping surface structures onto their corresponding deep structures.

Importantly, the rules do not allow for all transformations. Thus, "Basketball Steve Rhonda playing," maps onto no deep structure, nor could any deep structure generate such a surface structure. Chomsky (1957) postulated the existence of a *language acquisition device* (*LAD*), which has the capability of forming and verifying transformational rules to account for overt language (spoken, written). Presumably the LAD is innate; children are endowed with deep structures and a LAD that can alter the nature of the deep structures but only in fixed ways.

Chomsky's theory accounts for language development in terms of structures that change in predictable ways. Empirical support for the LAD is mixed. Moerk (1989) argued that the LAD was not necessary to explain linguistic development. Moerk summarized research showing that significant others in the child's environment (e.g., parents, siblings, caregivers) fulfilled the LAD's functions by assisting language development. Rather than the LAD being the mediating device between instances of language and development of a formalized grammar, Moerk found evidence that modeling (primarily maternal) related to the speed of language acquisition. Mothers verbalize simple utterances (e.g., "This is a dog") to their children, often in abbreviated form (e.g., mother points to the dog and says "dog"). This type of language, known as *motherese*, breaks down complex ideas into simple utterances and builds up simple utterances into complex sentences.

Furthermore, mothers tend to repeat utterances, and such repetition creates invariant structures in their children's minds. Mothers not only model utterances, they also perform much information processing on children's behalf by maintaining the accessibility of language through repetition and by rephrasing children's utterances into complete sentences (e.g., child says "milk," to which mother replies, "Do you want milk?").

Moerk concluded that mothers (or more generally primary caregivers) performed all of the functions ascribed to the LAD. Consequently, a special language structure was not necessary to explain language learning. Moerk's account is functional rather than structural because it accounts for language acquisition in terms of the functions played by significant others in the environment. This is one example in the developmental literature of structural and functional accounts being applied to explain the same phenomenon.

Classical Information Processing Theory. Classical information processing theory provides another structural account of development. The model presented in Chapter 5 is based largely on the pioneering work of Atkinson and Shiffrin (1968, 1971). This model assumes that the computer is a useful metaphor for the operation of the human mind. The computer (with corresponding information processing) components are: input (sensory registers), immediate processing (working memory—WM), storage (long-term memory—LTM), output (response), and programming (executive, control processes).

The analogy between the structures of the mind and the computer is useful. Although the mind's structures do not necessarily correspond to physical locations (i.e., the operations performed may occur in multiple locations), structures are constrained in terms of what they do. Once information enters the system, it is processed in linear fashion (i.e., it follows a set path determined by its content) and little room exists for environmental impact (Zimmerman & Whitehurst, 1979). The operation of the structures is largely preprogrammed.

Developmental change occurs in the capacity and efficiency of processing. Through the use of strategies such as rehearsal and organization, older learners—compared with younger ones—are able to hold more information in WM, relate it better to information in LTM, and have more extensive memory networks. With development, information processing of routinized activities becomes largely automatic. Teaching can help to improve processing, as when teachers help students learn and use learning strategies (Chapter 9).

Chapter 5 addresses the concerns of the classical model. The model assumes that information is processed in linear, serial fashion; yet experience shows that people are able to process multiple inputs simultaneously (e.g., "multi-tasking"—talk on the phone and work on e-mail at the same time). The notion of "control processes" is vague. Perhaps the most serious concern involves how processing develops. Maturation and learning are important, but the theory does not address adequately many of the critical issues presented earlier in this chapter. A contemporary information processing perspective on development (discussed later) is better positioned to address these issues.

We now turn to Bruner's theory of cognitive growth. It and Piaget's theory are constructivist because they posit that people form or construct much of what they learn and understand.

BRUNER'S THEORY OF COGNITIVE GROWTH

Jerome Bruner, a developmental psychologist, formulated a theory of cognitive growth (Lutkehaus, 2003). Rather than link changes in development to cognitive structures as Piaget did, Bruner highlighted the various ways that children represent knowledge. Bruner's views represent a functional account of human development and have important implications for teaching and learning.

Knowledge Representation

According to Bruner (1964), "The development of human intellectual functioning from infancy to such perfection as it may reach is shaped by a series of technological advances in the use of mind" (p. 1). These technological advances depend on increasing language facility and exposure to systematic instruction (Bruner, 1966). As children develop, their actions are constrained less by immediate stimuli. Cognitive processes (e.g., thoughts, beliefs) mediate the relationship between stimulus and response so that learners can maintain the same response in a changing environment or perform different responses in the same environment, depending on what they consider adaptive.

People represent knowledge in three ways, which emerge in a developmental sequence: enactive, iconic, and symbolic (Bruner, 1964; Bruner, Olver, & Greenfield, 1966). These modes are not structures, but rather involve different forms of cognitive processing (i.e., functions; Table 10.3).

Enactive representation involves motor responses, or ways to manipulate the environment. Actions such as riding a bicycle and tying a knot are represented largely in muscular actions. Stimuli are defined by the actions that prompt them. Among toddlers, a ball (stimulus) is represented as something to throw and bounce (actions).

Iconic representation refers to action-free mental images. Children acquire the capability to think about objects that are not physically present. They mentally transform objects and think about their properties separately from what actions can be performed with the objects. Iconic representation allows one to recognize objects.

Table 10.3
Bruner's modes of
knowledge representation.

Mode	Type of Representation
Enactive	Motor responses; ways to manipulate objects and aspects of the environment
Iconic	Action-free mental images; visual properties of objects and events that can be altered
Symbolic	Symbol systems (e.g., language and mathematical notation); remote and arbitrary

Symbolic representation uses symbol systems (e.g., language, mathematical notation) to encode knowledge. Such systems allow one to understand abstract concepts (e.g., the x variable in $3x - 5 = 10$) and to alter symbolic information as a result of verbal instruction. Symbolic systems represent knowledge with remote and arbitrary features. The word "Philadelphia" looks no more like the city than a nonsense syllable (Bruner, 1964).

The symbolic mode is the last to develop and quickly becomes the preferred mode, although people maintain the capability to represent knowledge in the enactive and iconic modes. One might experience the feel of a tennis ball, form a mental picture of it, and describe it in words. The primary advantage of the symbolic mode is that it allows learners to represent and transform knowledge with greater flexibility and power than is possible with the other modes (Bruner, 1964).

Spiral Curriculum

That knowledge can be represented in different ways suggests that teachers should consider varying instruction depending on learners' developmental levels. Before children can comprehend abstract mathematical notation, they can be exposed to mathematical concepts and operations represented enactively (with blocks) and iconically (in pictures). Bruner emphasized teaching as a means of prompting cognitive development. To say that a particular concept cannot be taught because students will not understand it (i.e., they lack readiness) really is saying that students will not understand the concept the way teachers plan to teach it. Instruction needs to be matched to children's cognitive capabilities.

Bruner (1960) is well known for his controversial proposition that any content can be taught in meaningful fashion to learners of any age:

> Experience over the past decade points to the fact that our schools may be wasting precious years by postponing the teaching of many important subjects on the ground that they are too difficult. . . . The foundations of any subject may be taught to anybody at any age in some form. . . . The basic ideas that lie at the heart of all science and mathematics and the basic themes that give form to life and literature are as simple as they are powerful. To be in command of these basic ideas, to use them effectively, requires a continual deepening of one's understanding of them that comes from learning to use them in progressively more complex forms. It is only when such basic ideas are put in formalized terms as equations or elaborated verbal concepts that they are out of reach of the young child, if he has not first understood them intuitively and had a chance to try them out on his own. (pp. 12–13)

Bruner's proposition can be misinterpreted to mean that learners of any age can be taught anything, which is not true. Bruner recommended that content be revisited: Concepts initially should be taught in a simple fashion so children can understand them and represented in a more complex fashion with development. In literature, children may be able to understand intuitively the concepts of "comedy" and "tragedy" (e.g., "comedies are funny and tragedies are sad") even though they cannot verbally describe them in literary terms. With development, students will read, analyze, and write papers on comedies and tragedies. Students should address topics at increasing levels of complexity as they move through the curriculum, rather than encountering a topic only once.

Bruner's theory is constructivist because it assumes that at any age learners assign meaning to stimuli and events based on their cognitive capabilities and experiences with the social and physical environments. Bruner's modes of representation bear some similarity to the operations that students engage in during Piaget's stages (i.e., sensorimotor—enactive, concrete operational—iconic, formal operational—symbolic; Chapter 6), although Bruner's is not a stage theory. Bruner's theory also allows for concepts to be mentally represented in multiple modes simultaneously: An adolescent knows how to throw a basketball, can visualize its appearance, and can compute its circumference with the formula $c = \pi d$. Application 10.1 gives some examples of Bruner's ideas applied to teaching and learning.

APPLICATION 10.1
Modes of Knowledge Representation

Bruner's theory elaborates ways that students can represent knowledge and recommends revisiting learning through a spiral curriculum. A good application is found in mathematics. Before students can comprehend abstract mathematical notation, teachers must ensure that students understand the concepts enactively and iconically. Kathy Stone works with both the second- and fourth-grade teachers as she prepares her math units for the year. She wants to ensure that students understand previous concepts before tackling new ones, and she introduces ideas that will be further developed during the next year. When introducing multiplication, she first reviews with her third graders addition and counting by multipliers (e.g., 2, 4, 6, 8; 4, 8, 12, 16). Then she has the students work with

manipulatives (enactive representation), and she provides visual (iconic) representation of multiplication. Eventually she presents problems in symbolic mode (e.g., $4 \times 2 = ?$).

Jim Marshall examines curriculum guides and meets with middle school teachers to determine what American history material has been covered prior to the ninth grade. As he develops units, he starts the first lesson with a review of the material that students studied previously and asks students to share what they can recall. Once he evaluates the mastery level of the students, he is able to build on the unit and add new material. He typically employs all modes of knowledge representation in his teaching: enactive—role playing, dramatization; iconic—pictures, videos; symbolic—print materials, websites.

CONTEMPORARY DEVELOPMENTAL THEMES

Over the past several years, information processing has gained priority in the psychological study of human development (Samuelson & Smith, 2000). Information processing focuses on functions rather than on structures. This section summarizes the changes that occur in the functions of attention, encoding and retrieval, and metacognition. These processes improve with development, along with the speed with which children execute them (Kail & Ferrer, 2007). Other contemporary themes that are discussed in this section are developmentally appropriate instruction and transitions in schooling.

Developmental Changes

Attention. Sustained attention is difficult for young children, as is attending to relevant rather than irrelevant information. Children also have difficulty switching attention rapidly from one activity to another. The ability to control attention contributes to the improvement of WM (Swanson, 2008). It behooves teachers to forewarn students of the attentional demands required to learn. Outlines and study guides can serve as advance organizers and cue learners about the types of information that will be important. While students are working, teachers can use prompts, questions, and feedback to help students remain focused on important task aspects (Meece, 2002).

Encoding and Retrieval. A simple way to assess children's information processing is with a *digit-span task.* In this task, a researcher reads a series of digits (e.g., 5—3—8—10—2—9) to a child at a rate of one digit per second, and when the researcher finishes, the child attempts to repeat the sequence. An average 5-year-old can repeat four digits accurately; this increases to six or seven by age 12 (Meece, 2002).

Underlying this developmental improvement are information processing capacities and cognitive processes. In all likelihood these interact: As information processing capacity expands, better cognitive processes can be applied. For example, as children's capacities for attention, encoding, and storage increase, those who employ better strategies for attending, rehearsing, organizing, and retrieving demonstrate enhanced cognitive development.

Most of a child's basic cognitive processes are well in place by early childhood. From this point onward, developmental changes primarily involve learning how to make better and more efficient use of existing perceptual and attentional processes. Some of the more important changes include the ability to make fine discriminations between stimulus objects, the development of automaticity and selective attention, and the ability to exert control over attentional processes (Meece, 2002).

Automaticity is an important function (Chapter 5). Automatic attention means that children gradually eliminate attention as an active cognitive process. When attention becomes automatic, less cognitive effort is needed in the early stages of information processing, and thus children can put forth effort where it is needed. For example, as decoding becomes automatic, more cognitive processing can be shifted to comprehension. Poor readers, for whom decoding is not automatic, expend much effort to decode, with the result that comprehension suffers.

Much developmental research has focused on the strategies that children use in encoding, retention, and retrieval. Chapter 5 discusses the usefulness of having mental representations of often-repeated events, or *scripts* (Wellman, 1988), which create predictability in a child's world and also organize information for quicker processing. With experience, children acquire a larger repertoire of scripts (Flavell, 1985).

Children also improve in their knowledge and use of encoding strategies (Matlin, 2009). Rehearsal appears early and improves as children become older (Flavell, Beach, & Chinsky, 1966). In other areas such as organization and elaboration (Chapter 5), children's use of strategies improves with age. These strategies can be taught and enhance children's memory and understanding (Meece, 2002).

With respect to retrieval, older children use better strategies than younger ones (Flavell, 1985). For example, older children are more likely to conduct an exhaustive memory search and not quit when the needed information does not come to mind immediately. Older children also have learned different ways to access information, such as by thinking about different situations where that information may be useful. Although strategy change often occurs slowly in children, they are likely to adopt new strategies when these lead to consistently more accurate solutions than their present strategies (Siegler & Svetina, 2006).

Metacognition. Much developmental research has explored children's understanding about cognition, or *metacognition* (Flavell, 1999). Metacognitive understanding expands greatly between the ages of 5 and 10 (Siegler, 1991). Metacognitive improvements are a hallmark of development as children acquire methods for monitoring their level of understanding, asking themselves questions about what they have read, and summarizing information. They learn what strategies to use for different tasks, and with development they are more likely to believe that strategy use leads to better performance (Paris et al., 1983).

Children's metacognitive awareness develops gradually. Alexander et al. (1995) found that steady developmental improvements occurred in declarative metacognitive knowledge, as well as in the metacognitive skills of self-monitoring and self-regulation of strategy use (Zimmerman et al., 1996). The development of self-regulation may vary as a function of gender. As early as kindergarten, and continuing into middle school, girls develop and apply better self-regulatory skills in school learning (Keeney-Benson, Pomerantz, Ryan, & Patrick, 2006; Matthews, Ponitz, & Morrison, 2009). Self-monitoring of performance is aided with self-recording, such as with diaries and checklists that contain essential aspects of the task. For example, if students are engaged in reading comprehension, the checklist can contain steps such as reading the passage, determining the main characters, deciding on the main action, and so forth.

Developmentally Appropriate Instruction

Another theme of contemporary cognitive views of human development is developmentally appropriate instruction. *Developmentally appropriate instruction* is matched (compatible) with children's developmental levels. That idea sounds basic, but unfortunately instructional activities and developmental levels often are mismatched. Teaching may involve nothing more than presenting information to students (as apparently is the case in Frank's class), who receive and process it. Not only might the information be presented in such a way that students have difficulty processing it, they also might process it in ways that produce learning different from what the teacher desires.

For example, many students take precalculus in high school. Much of the content of precalculus is highly abstract (e.g., conic sections, trigonometric relations, limits of functions). Although high school students increasingly are able to function at a Piagetian formal operational level and cognitively handle abstract content, many students are primarily concrete operational thinkers. Teachers who make little effort to provide concrete referents for precalculus topics create a mismatch between the content and students' thinking. It is little wonder that so many students have difficulty with precalculus, which in turn can adversely affect their motivation for further study of mathematics.

Developmentally appropriate instruction relies upon several assumptions, which follow from the material discussed in this chapter. First, students construct knowledge based on their prior experiences and present schemas. Knowledge never is transmitted automatically; the construction of knowledge and integration with current mental structures are the means whereby learning proceeds. This requires that instruction be designed to foster such knowledge construction. Piaget recommended active exploration, a notion that is compatible with instructional methods such as discovery learning and small-group projects (Lucia will start using more of these).

Second, the social environment is important. This notion is seen clearly in Vygotsky's theory (Chapter 6). When interacting with others, children receive ideas and opinions that conflict with their own; this sets the Piagetian equilibration process into motion (Meece, 2002). The cognitive conflict that ensues is considered the impetus behind learning in many developmental theories.

Third, conflict is created when the material to be learned is just beyond students' present understandings. This creates the zone of proximal development (ZPD; Chapter 6), within which learning can occur through cognitive conflict, reflection, and conceptual reorganization (Meece, 2002). Little conflict exists when material is too far advanced beyond current understandings; conflict similarly is minimized when learning is at children's current levels.

Finally, developmentally appropriate instruction incorporates active exploration and hands-on activities. Bruner's theory recommends that enactive learning occurs first, followed by iconic and symbolic. Although children's learning is based largely on what they do, hands-on learning is beneficial at all developmental levels. Adults who are learning computer skills benefit from observing teachers demonstrate them (iconic) and explain them (symbolic), as well as by performing the skills themselves (enactive).

What would a developmentally appropriate classroom look like? Meece (2002) suggested several appropriate practices that are summarized in Table 10.4. Some classroom applications of developmentally appropriate instruction are provided in Application 10.2.

Table 10.4
Developmentally appropriate instructional practices.

- Teachers structure the learning environment to include adults, other children, materials, and opportunities for children to engage in active exploration and interaction.

- Children select many of their own activities from a variety.

- Children stay active as they engage in much self-directed learning.

- Children work most of the time in small groups or individually.

- Children work with concrete, hands-on activities.

- Teachers actively monitor children's work to ensure continued involvement.

- Teachers focus on the process children use to arrive at answers and not insist always on one right answer.

Transitions in Schooling

Researchers have explored developmental issues involved during transitions in schooling. In the U.S. educational system, natural transitions occur when children change schools or experience major shifts in curricula and activities; for example, preschool to elementary, elementary to middle/junior high, middle/junior high to senior high, and senior high to college.

APPLICATION 10.2
Developmentally Appropriate Instruction

Students learn best in a classroom where instruction is developmentally appropriate. Even in a primary class, developmental levels will vary. Beginning in preschool and kindergarten, teachers should ensure that students have the opportunity to learn in different ways to address the learning mode that is most appropriate for each child's developmental level.

Betty Thompson is a kindergarten teacher. For a unit on magnets, she designed a learning station where students individually use magnets of different sizes and shapes. She divided the students into small groups and had them work cooperatively to discover the differences

between items that can and cannot be picked up by magnets. She worked with each small group to complete a chart looking at the differences between items attracted by magnets. For story time that day, she read a book about the uses of magnets; while she read, each student had a magnet and items to test. For homework, she asked students to bring two items to class the next day, one of which can be picked up by a magnet and one that cannot. The next day in small groups students tested their items and then discussed why some items were and others were not attracted; she moved around the room and interacted with each group.

Transitions are important because they can produce disruptions in routines and ways of thinking and because of students' developmental levels at the times they occur (Eccles & Midgley, 1989). Thus, the transition from elementary school to middle school/junior high would be disruptive for anyone, but it becomes especially so for students at that age given the bodily changes they are undergoing and their typical insecurities about their sense of self and appearance. Transitional variables and development most likely interact in reciprocal fashion. Developmental variables can make a transition smooth or rough, but in turn factors associated with the transition might affect students' personal, social, and cognitive development (Wigfield & Wagner, 2005).

The transition to middle school/junior high school is especially problematic (Eccles & Midgley, 1989; Wigfield et al., 2006). This transition occurs at a significant period of physical change in young adolescents with its attendant personal and social changes. Furthermore, numerous changes occur in school and class structures and subject areas. In elementary school, children typically are with the same teacher and peers for most of the school day. The teacher often has a warm and nurturing relationship with the children. Instruction frequently is individualized, and teachers track and report individual progress in content areas. Ability-level differences within a class may be wide, with students ranging from those with learning disabilities to gifted.

In contrast, in middle and junior high schools students typically change classes for each subject, which results in different teachers and peers. Teachers develop close relationships with few, if any, students. Instruction is provided to the entire class and rarely individualized. Grades—whether based on absolute or normative standards— do not reflect individual progress, nor is that generally reported. Ability-level within-class differences may be minimal if students are tracked. In general, middle school and junior high classes are more formal, impersonal, evaluative, and competitive (Meece, 2002). Eccles and her colleagues (Eccles & Midgley, 1989; Eccles, Midgley, & Adler, 1984; Wigfield et al., 2006) contended that these structural and curricular changes produce changes in students' achievement-related beliefs and motivation, often in a negative direction. The opening conversation between the three middle school teachers contains statements indicating why middle school is difficult for many students.

School transitions need not be so difficult. In theory, the middle school configuration should help to ease the transition. Although some middle schools resemble junior high schools except for a different grade organization (typically grades 6 to 8 in middle schools and grades 7 to 9 in junior high schools), many middle schools attempt to ease the transition by keeping students together for much of the day and using interdisciplinary teams of teachers (e.g., four teachers, one each for language arts, social studies, mathematics, and science). These teachers work to ensure an integrated curriculum. They rotate in and out of the classroom such that although the teachers change, the peers do not. Alternatively, children may change classes but they have some of the same peers in two or more classes. Greater efforts also may be made to report individual progress. Less emphasis on evaluative comparisons among peers helps to lighten young adolescents' self-concerns so typical at this time. Application 10.3 gives some additional suggestions for ways to ease transitions in schooling.

APPLICATION 10.3
Transitions in Schooling

Making the transition from one school level to another is difficult for many students. Ability and socioemotional levels vary widely, and students differ in their ability to cope with the numerous organizational changes that occur. The transition from elementary to middle school/junior high level can be especially troublesome.

Kay Appleton is a sixth-grade social studies teacher at a middle school. She understands that students become accustomed to having one teacher for most content areas. She works with fifth-grade teachers to suggest activities that they might incorporate (e.g., using assignment notebooks) that will help students when they are faced with changing classes and being responsible for remembering and completing assignments for each class. She also spends time at the start of the school year helping her students set up their assignment books and organize their materials. She makes herself available during lunch and after school to give students assistance they might need about transition issues.

Jim Marshall asks eighth-grade social studies teachers about their policies for assigning class work and homework, giving tests, requiring projects, receiving late work, allowing students to make up missed work, and so forth. He tries to incorporate some of the same approaches in his ninth-grade history classes so that these class procedures will be familiar and will reduce student concerns that could impede learning.

FAMILY INFLUENCES

There are many contextual factors that can influence development, several of which are found in the family environment. Although common sense tells us that families have profound influences on children's development and learning, some critics contend that the family's role has been overstated (Harris, 1998). Research is, however, increasingly showing that families make a difference and often a great one (Collins, Maccoby, Steinberg, Hetherington, & Bornstein, 2000; Masten & Coatsworth, 1998). Some of the key influences on development and learning are socioeconomic status, home environment, parental involvement, and electronic media.

Socioeconomic Status

Definition. *Socioeconomic status (SES)* has been defined in various ways, with definitions typically comprising social status (position, rank) and economic indicators (wealth, education). Many researchers have considered three prime indicators in determining SES: parental income, education, and occupation (Sirin, 2005). Increasingly investigators are stressing the idea of *capital* (resources, assets) (Bradley & Corwyn, 2002). Capital includes such indices as financial or material resources (e.g., income and assets), human or nonmaterial resources (e.g., education), and social resources (e.g., those obtained through social networks and connections) (Putnam, 2000). Each of these would seem to potentially affect children's development and learning.

However SES is defined, it is important to remember that it is a descriptive variable, not an explanatory one (Schunk et al., 2008). To say that children lag in development because they are from poor families does not explain why they lag in development. Rather, the factors that typically accompany poor families may be responsible for the development difficulties. Conversely, not all children from poor families lag in development. There are countless stories of successful adults who were raised in impoverished conditions. It therefore is more meaningful to speak of a relation between SES and development and then look for the responsible factors.

SES and Development. There is much correlational evidence showing that poverty and low parental education relate to poorer development and learning (Bradley & Corwyn, 2002). What is less clear is which aspects of SES are responsible for this relation.

Undoubtedly family resources are critical. Families with less education, money, and social connections cannot provide many resources that help to stimulate children's cognitive development. Compared with wealthier families, poorer families cannot provide their children with computers, books, games, travel, and cultural experiences. Regardless of their perspective, developmental theorists agree that the richness of experiences is central to cognitive development. On this count, then, it is little wonder that SES relates to cognitive development.

Another factor is socialization. Schools and classrooms have a middle-class orientation, and there are accepted rules and procedures that children must follow to succeed (e.g., pay attention, do your work, study, and work cooperatively with others). Socialization influences in lower-SES homes may not match or prepare students for these conditions (Schunk et al., 2008). To the extent that this occurs, lower-SES children may have more discipline and behavior problems in school and not learn as well.

SES also relates to school attendance and years of schooling (Bradley & Corwyn, 2002). SES is related positively to school achievement (Sirin, 2005), and is, unfortunately, one of the best predictors of school dropout. Lower SES children may not understand the benefits of schooling (Meece, 2002); they may not realize that more education leads to better jobs, more income, and a better lifestyle than they have experienced. They may be drawn by immediate short-term benefits of leaving school (e.g., money from working full-time) and not be swayed by potential long-term assets. In their home environments, they may not have positive role models displaying the benefits of schooling or parental encouragement to stay in school.

The relation of SES to cognitive development seems complex, with some factors contributing directly and others serving a moderating influence (Bradley & Corwyn, 2002). Its predictive value also may vary by group. For example, SES is a stronger predictor of academic achievement for White students than for minority students (Sirin, 2005). SES has been implicated as a factor contributing to the achievement gap between White and minority children. Gaps exist when children enter kindergarten. The White–Hispanic American gap narrows in kindergarten and first grade (perhaps because of Hispanic American children's increasing English language proficiency) and then stays steady through fifth grade; however, the White–African American gap continues to widen through fifth grade (Reardon & Galindo, 2009).

While the effects of material, human, and social capital seem clear, the influence of other factors may be indirect. For example, large families are not inherently beneficial or harmful to cognitive development and achievement. But in deprived conditions they may be harmful as already scarce resources are spread among more children.

The literature suggests that early educational interventions for children from low-SES families are critical to ensuring that they are prepared for schooling. One of the best known early intervention efforts is Project Head Start, a federally funded program for pre-school children (3- to 5-year-olds) from low income families across the United States. Head Start programs provide preschool children with intensive educational experiences, as well as social, medical, and nutritional services. Most programs also include a parent education and involvement component (Washington & Bailey, 1995).

Early evaluations of Head Start indicated that programs were able to produce short-term gains in IQ scores. Compared to comparable groups of children who had not attended Head Start, they also performed better on cognitive measures in kindergarten and first grade (Lazar, Darlington, Murray, Royce, & Snipper, 1982). Although Head Start children lost this advantage by ages 10 and 17, other measures of program effectiveness indicated that participants were less likely to be retained, to receive special education, and to drop out of high school than nonparticipants (Lazar et al., 1982). Providing Head Start teachers with training and professional development on practices to enhance children's literacy and socioemotional skills can lead to gains in children's social problem-solving skills (Bierman et al., 2008).

Home and family factors can affect outcomes for Head Start participants. Robinson, Lanzi, Weinburg, Ramey, and Ramey (2002) identified at the end of third grade the top achieving 3% of 5,400 children in the National Head Start/Public School Early Childhood Transition Demonstration Project. Compared with the remaining children, these children came from families that had more resources (capital). These families also endorsed more positive parenting attitudes, more strongly supported and encouraged their children's academic progress, and volunteered more often in their children's schools. Teachers reported these children as more motivated to succeed academically. Although there were not strong differences in children's ratings of motivational variables, fewer children in the top 3% group rated school negatively compared with the remaining children. Thus, among low-income groups as well as the general population, greater parental support and better home resources are associated with achievement and motivational benefits for children.

Encouraged by the success of Head Start, many states today are running prekindergarten programs for 3- and 4-year-olds under the auspices of public schools to reduce the number of children failing in the early grades (Clifford, Early, & Hill, 1999). Most programs are half day and vary with regard to teacher–student ratios, socioeconomic and ethnic diversity, quality, and curricula. Early evaluations of these programs are promising. Children enrolled in prekindergarten programs tend to improve on standardized measures of language and mathematics skills (FPG Child Development Institute, 2005). The long-term benefits of these programs are not yet known.

One highly effective preschool program for low income children was the High/Scope Perry Preschool Project. Initiated in 1962, this program predated Head Start. In this two-year program, 3- and 4-year-old children received a half-day cognitively oriented program based on Piaget's principles (Oden, Schweinhart, & Weikart, 2000). Teachers also made weekly 90-minute home visits to each mother and child to review classroom activities and to discuss similar activities in the home. Longitudinal data collected over 25 years revealed that the High/Scope program improved children's school achievement, reduced their years in special education, reduced the likelihood of grade retention, and increased the years of school completed (Oden et al., 2000; Schweinhart & Weikart, 1997).

Unfortunately, the effects of such early interventions do not always persist over time as children progress in school, but there are promising results. Campbell, Pungello, Miller-Johnson, Burchinal, and Ramey (2001) evaluated the Abecedarian Project, a full-time educational child-care project for children from low-income families. These researchers found that the benefits of the intervention persisted through the last evaluation when many of the children had attained age 21. Given the longitudinal nature of this project (it began when the participants were infants), it is difficult to determine when and how it better prepared them to work in school environments. SES is an active area of developmental research, and we are sure to learn more as researchers attempt to unravel these complexities.

Home Environment

There is much variability in the richness of home environments, and usually (but not always) this richness matches SES. Some homes provide experiences replete with economic capital (computers, games, and books), human capital (parents help children with homework, projects, and studying), and social capital (through social contacts parents get children involved in activities and teams). Other homes lack in one or more of these respects.

The effects of the home environment on cognitive development seem most pronounced in infancy and early childhood (Meece, 2002). Children's social networks expand as they grow older, especially as a consequence of schooling and participation in activities. Peer influence becomes increasingly important with development.

There is much evidence that the quality of children's early home learning relates positively to the development of intelligence (Schunk et al., 2008). Important home factors include mother's responsiveness, discipline style, and child involvement; organization present in the home; availability of stimulating materials; and opportunities for interaction. Parents who provide a warm and responsive home environment tend to encourage children's explorations and stimulate their curiosity and play, which accelerate intellectual development (Meece, 2002). Hoff (2003) found that higher-SES children grew more than middle-SES children in the size of their vocabularies, and this difference was accounted for largely by properties of mothers' speech.

The increasing role of peer influence was found in longitudinal research by Steinberg, Brown, and Dornbusch (1996). Over a 10-year period, these researchers surveyed more than 20,000 adolescents from high schools in different states and interviewed many teachers and parents. These authors found that peer influence rose during childhood and peaked around grades 8 and 9, after which it declined somewhat in high school. A key period of influence is roughly between the ages of 12 and 16. It is noteworthy that this is the period during which parental involvement in children's activities declines. With parental involvement declining and peer involvement rising, early adolescents are especially vulnerable to peer pressures.

These authors also tracked students over a three-year period, from when they entered high school until their senior year. Not surprisingly, students who were part of more academically oriented crowds achieved better in school compared with those in less academically oriented crowds. Those who started high school in the former crowd but moved away from it also showed lower achievement.

Although parents do not have total control over the crowds with which their children associate, they can exert indirect influence by steering them in appropriate directions. For example, parents who urge their children to participate in activities in which the children of other like-minded parents participate steer them toward appropriate peer influence regardless of whom they select as friends. Parents who offer their home as a place where friends are welcome further guide their children in positive directions.

Parental Involvement

Harris (1998) downplayed the influence of parents on children past infancy and concluded that peers exert a much greater effect; however, there is substantial evidence that parental influence continues to be strong well past infancy (Vandell, 2000). This section considers the role of parental involvement in children's activities, which is a key factor influencing cognitive development (Meece, 2002). Such involvement occurs in and away from the home, such as in school and activities.

Research shows that parental involvement in schools has a positive impact on children, teachers, and the school itself (Englund, Luckner, Whaley, & Egeland, 2004; Gonzalez-DeHass, Willems, & Doan Holbein, 2005; Hill & Craft, 2003; Sénéchal & LeFevre, 2002). These effects may vary by group, since parent involvement effects seem stronger among White students than among minority students (Lee & Bowen, 2006).

One effect of parent involvement, as noted above, is that parents can be influential in launching their children onto particular trajectories by involving them in groups and activities (Steinberg et al., 1996). For example, parents who want their children to be academically focused are likely to involve them in activities that stress academics.

Fan and Chen (2001) conducted a meta-analysis of research on the relation of parental involvement to children's academic attainments. The results showed that parents' expectations for their children's academic successes bore a positive relation to their actual cognitive achievements. The relation was strongest when academic attainment was assessed globally (e.g., GPA) than by subject-specific indicators (e.g., grade in a particular class). There also is evidence that parental involvement effects on children's achievement are greatest when there is a high level of parental involvement in the neighborhood (Collins et al., 2000).

Parental involvement is a critical factor influencing children's self-regulation, which is central to the development of cognitive functioning. Research by Stright, Neitzel, Sears, and Hoke-Sinex (2001) found that the type of instruction parents provide and how they provide it relate to children's subsequent self-regulation in school. Children of parents who provided understandable metacognitive information displayed greater classroom monitoring, participation, and metacognitive talk. Children's seeking and attending to classroom instruction also were related to whether parents' instruction was given in an

APPLICATION 10.4
Parental Involvement

Kathy Stone understands the importance of parental involvement for children's learning and self-regulation. Early in the academic year, the school holds an open house for parents. When Kathy meets with her parents, she explains the many ways that parents can become involved. She asks for volunteers for three groups: school learning, out-of-school learning, and planning. School-learning parents volunteer a half-day per week to work in class, assisting with small-group and individual work. Out-of-school-learning parents accompany the class on field trips and organize and work with children on community projects (e.g., a walk through the neighborhood to identify types of trees). Planning-group parents periodically meet as a group with Kathy, where she explains upcoming units and asks parents to help design activities. Kathy's goal is 100% involvement of at least one parent or guardian per child, which she usually is able to attain because of the options available.

Jim Marshall knows what a valuable resource parents are in American history because they have lived through some of the events his students learn about. Jim contacts parents at the start of the year and provides them with a list of events in the past several years that students will study in class (e.g., Vietnam War, fall of the Berlin wall, World Trade Center terrorist attack). Jim seeks the assistance of every family on at least one event, such as by the parent coming to class to discuss it (i.e., what they remember about it, why it was important, how it affected their lives). When several parents volunteer for the same event, he forms them into a panel to discuss the event. If there are living grandparents in the area, Jim asks them to share their experiences about such events as the Great Depression, World War II, and the Eisenhower presidency. Jim's students set up a website containing information about key events and excerpts from parents and grandparents about them.

understandable manner. These authors suggested that parental instruction helps to create the proper conditions for their children to develop self-regulatory competence. Some suggestions for parents working with their children are given in Application 10.4.

Positive effects of parental involvement have been obtained in research with ethnic minority children and those from impoverished environments (Hill & Craft, 2003; Masten & Coatsworth, 1998; Masten et al., 1999). Some forms of parents' involvement that make a difference are contacting the school about their children, attending school functions, communicating strong educational values to their children, conveying the value of effort, expecting children to perform well in school, and monitoring or helping children with homework and projects. Miliotis, Sesma, and Masten (1999) found that after families left homeless shelters, high parent involvement in children's education was one of the best predictors of children's school success.

Researchers have investigated the role of parenting styles on children's development. Baumrind (1989) distinguished three styles: authoritative, authoritarian, permissive.

Authoritative parents provide children with warmth and support. They have high demands (e.g., expectations for achievement), but support these through good communication, explanations, and encouragement of independence. Authoritarian parents are strict and assert power. They are neither warm nor responsive. Permissive parents are moderately responsive but are lax in demands (e.g., expectations) and tolerant of misbehavior. Nor surprisingly, much research shows a positive relation between authoritative parenting and student achievement (Spera, 2005).

One of the strongest advocates of community and parental involvement in education is James Comer. Comer and his colleagues began the *School Development Program* in two schools, and it has now spread to more than 500.

The SDP (or Comer Program) is based on the principles shown in Table 10.5 (Comer, 2001; Comer & Haynes, 1999; Emmons, Comer, & Haynes, 1996). Children need positive interactions with adults because these help to form their behaviors. Planning for child development should be a collaborative effort between professionals and community members.

Three guiding principles of SDP are consensus, collaboration, and no-fault (Schunk et al., 2008). Decisions are arrived at by consensus to discourage taking sides for critical votes. Collaboration means working as part of a team. No-fault implies that everyone is responsible for change.

School staff and community members are grouped into teams. The School Planning and Management Team includes the building principal, teachers, parents, and support staff. This team plans and coordinates activities. The Parent Team involves parents in all school activities. The Student and Staff Support Team is responsible for schoolwide prevention issues and individual student cases.

At the core of the SDP is a comprehensive school plan with such components as curriculum, instruction, assessment, social and academic climate, and information sharing. This plan provides structured activities addressing academics, social climate, staff development, and public relations. The School Planning and Management Team establishes priorities and coordinates school improvement.

Comer and his colleagues report impressive effects on children's cognitive achievement due to implementation of the SDP (Haynes, Emmons, Gebreyesus, & Ben-Avie, 1996). Comer schools often show gains in student achievement and outperform school district averages in reading, mathematical, and language skills. Cook, Murphy, and Hunt

Table 10.5
Principles of the School Development Program (SDP).

- Children's behaviors are determined by their interactions with the physical, social, and psychological environments.

- Children need positive interactions with adults to develop adequately.

- Child-centered planning and collaboration among adults facilitate positive interactions.

- Planning for child development should be done collaboratively by professional and community members.

(Emmons, Comer, and Haynes, 1996)

(2000) evaluated the Comer SDP in 10 inner-city Chicago schools over four years. Using students in grades 5 through 8, these authors found that by the last years, Comer program students showed greater gains in reading and mathematics compared with control students. Cook et al. (1999) found that Comer schools do not always implement all of the program's elements, which can limit gains for children. Regardless of whether schools adopt the Comer program, it contains many points that should aid in children's cognitive development.

Electronic Media

The advent of electronic media began in the middle of the twentieth century when televisions became common household items. In recent years, the potential influence of electronic media has expanded with increased television programming (i.e., cable channels), audio and video players, radios, video game players, computers (e.g., applications, Internet), and handheld devices (e.g., cell phones, iPods). The amount of time that children spend engaged with electronic media daily can seem daunting. In 2005, children age 6 and younger averaged over 2.25 hours per day (Roberts & Foehr, 2008). In 2004, children ages 8 to 18 reported an average of almost 8 hours of daily electronic media exposure that consumed almost 6 hours of their time (i.e., about 25% of the time they were using more than one media source at once—multitasking; Roberts & Foehr, 2008).

Researchers have investigated the potential ways that exposure to electronic media relates to children's cognitive development, learning, and achievement. Most research has investigated the link between children's television viewing and measures of cognitive development and achievement and found no relationship or a negative relationship between the time children spend watching television and their school achievement (Schmidt & Vandewater, 2008). When negative associations are found, they typically are weak. The relation may not be linear. Compared with no television viewing, moderate viewing (1–10 hours) per week is positively associated with achievement, whereas heavier viewing is negatively associated.

The relation between television viewing and achievement is difficult to interpret because the data are correlational and therefore causality cannot be determined. Several causal explanations are possible. It is possible that heavy television viewing lowers achievement because it takes children away from studying and completing assignments. It also is possible that children with academic problems are less motivated to learn academic content and thus are drawn more strongly to television. The link between television viewing and achievement may be mediated by a third variable, such as SES. In support of this possibility, children from lower-class homes tend to watch more television and demonstrate lower achievement (Kirkorian, Wartella, & Anderson, 2008).

Examining the relation between time spent watching television and academic achievement does not consider the content of what children watch. Television programming varies; some programs are educational, whereas others are entertaining or violent. A general finding from research is that watching educational programming is positively related to achievement, whereas watching entertainment is negatively linked (Kirkorian et al., 2008). This varies as a function of amount of television watched, because moderate viewers are more apt to watch educational programming whereas heavier viewers watch extensive entertainment. Correlational research has demonstrated a positive relation between exposure to *Sesame Street* and school readiness (Kirkorian et al., 2008). Ennemoser and Schneider (2007) found a negative association between the amount of entertainment television watched by children at age 6 and reading achievement at age 9, after controlling for intelligence, SES, and prior reading ability. Watching educational television was positively associated with reading achievement.

The findings on the link between interactive media (e.g., video games, Internet) and school achievement are mixed. Some research has obtained a positive relation between computer use and achievement and a negative association between video game use and achievement (Kirkorian et al., 2008). The same result obtained with television also may hold for other media; that is, educational content may link positively with achievement and entertaining content negatively.

With respect to measures of cognitive development, research has identified a *video deficit* among infants and toddlers such that they learn better from real-life experiences than from video. This deficit disappears by around age 3, after which children can learn just as well from video experiences (Kirkorian et al., 2008). It may be that young children are less attentive to dialogue and do not fully integrate content portrayed across different scenes, which may change rapidly. This does not imply that viewing is negatively associated with the development of attention. Again, the critical variable may be the content of the programming. Educational programs have been shown to actually help children develop attention skills, in contrast to entertaining programs (Kerkorian et al., 2008).

Some research has investigated links between electronic media and the development of spatial skills. Most of this research has involved video games. There is some evidence that video games can have short-term benefits on spatial reasoning and problem-solving skills (Schmidt & Vandewater, 2008). However, long-term benefits depend on whether students generalize those skills to learning contexts outside of game play. To date, evidence does not support the point that such transfer occurs (Schmidt & Vandewater, 2008).

Parents and other adults can have important influences on children's learning and cognitive development from electronic media. Adults can control what media children interact with and how much time they do so. This control can help to ensure that children do not spend an excessive amount of time engaged with media, but rather only a moderate amount (1–10 hours per week; Schmidt & Vandewater, 2008). Further, parent coviewing seems to be a critical variable. Adults who interact with media while their children are engaged (e.g., watch television programs together) can enhance benefits from electronic media by pointing out important aspects of the program and linking those with what children previously have learned. Some research has shown obtained benefits from coviewing on children's learning and development of attention (Kirkorian et al., 2008).

In summary, it is clear that use of electronic media is associated with children's learning, achievement, and cognitive development. Determining causal links is difficult because data are correlational and there are potential mediating variables. Content is of utmost importance. Moderate exposure to televised educational content is associated with benefits for children, entertaining content is not, and the same results may hold for other forms of media (Kirkorian et al., 2008). Coviewing adults can further enhance the educational links. While games may have some benefits for spatial and problem-solving skills, evidence does not show transfer to academic learning settings. Although electronic media can be a valuable means of learning, they will be effective to the extent that they are designed with sound instructional principles in mind, just like any other teaching method. Some applications of instructional uses of electronic media are given in Application 10.5.

APPLICATION 10.5
Electronic Media

At the parent meeting at the start of the school year, Kathy Stone spends some time discussing how parents can help their children. She explains research findings showing that children who watch television for a moderate amount of time per week (up to 10 hours) and whose television viewing is primarily educational content actually can benefit from it. Engaging with other educational media (e.g., computers) is similarly beneficial. She advises parents to monitor children's use of electronic media. She also demonstrates how parents might interact with children while they view television programs together. She presents some film clips from children's shows and then demonstrates to parents the types of questions to ask their children. At individual parent meetings later in the school year she follows up by asking parents how they are engaging with their children with media.

Over the course of the school year, Jim Marshall gives his students assignments to watch historical programs on television (e.g., PBS). For each program, they are to write a short essay that answers questions that he gives them in advance. By giving these assignments, he feels that he can help to focus their attention on those aspects of the programs that are most germane to the content of his course and thereby promote students' learning.

MOTIVATION AND DEVELOPMENT

In addition to its role in cognition and learning, development has effects on children's motivation. Motivation is covered in Chapter 8; this section examines its changes with development.

Motivational influences on children may not have much effect on adolescents, and what motivates adolescents may be ineffective with adults. Within any developmental period, not everyone is motivated in the same way. Developmental researchers have identified ways that motivation changes with development (Table 10.6). These are discussed in turn.

Table 10.6
Developmental changes in motivation.

- Children's understanding of motivational processes changes.
- Motivation becomes more differentiated and complex.
- Levels of motivation change.
- Beliefs, values, and goals correspond better with choices and performances.
- Long-term motivation is sustained better.

Developmental Changes

Children's understanding of motivational processes changes with development (Wigfield & Eccles, 2002). For example, young children tend to equate ability with outcome and believe that children who perform better are more able. With development, the concepts of ability and effort are disentangled and children understand that both can affect outcomes. Children's understanding of social comparison also changes. Young children compare on the basis of physical characteristics (e.g., size), whereas as children develop they are able to compare themselves with others on the basis of underlying qualities (e.g., abilities).

A related change is that motivation becomes more differentiated and complex (Wigfield & Eccles, 2002). Young children have a global sense of what they can do. As they develop and progress in school, they begin to focus their interests and develop separate conceptions of their abilities in different domains.

Third, the levels of children's motivation change with development (Wigfield & Eccles, 2002). Young children often are highly confident about what they can do, but these perceptions typically decline with development (Lepper, Corpus, & Iyengar, 2005; Otis, Grouzet, & Pelletier, 2005; Watt, 2004; Wigfield, Eccles, & Rodriguez, 1998). Many factors have been implicated as producing this decrease, including school transitions, norm-referenced achievement feedback, social comparisons, and grading practices. It should be noted that this change is not always problematic. Focusing one's efforts on what one feels confident about learning or doing well can result in successes and a strong sense of self-efficacy (Schunk & Pajares, 2009). Similarly, avoiding what one feels one cannot do well can prevent failures. Still, in some children the decline becomes generalized to all academic areas, with resulting low performance, grades, and motivation.

Fourth, with development, children's beliefs, values, and goals correspond better with their performances and choices (Wigfield & Eccles, 2002). As children develop specific interests and feel competent about them, these are the activities in which they engage. Thus, motivation and behavior bear a closer resemblance to one another. It is not that one causes the other; they undoubtedly affect one another. Whatever children feel competent to do, they work at and develop skills, and their perceptions of better performance increase self-efficacy and motivation (Bandura, 1997).

Finally, children become better able to sustain long-term motivation. Motivation among youngsters is short-term, as elementary teachers well know. With development, students are able to represent long-term goals in thought, subdivide tasks into short-term subgoals, and assess progress. Self-monitoring of progress and changing strategies when they do not work well are hallmarks of higher-performing students in school.

Noted earlier was the research finding that development results in peers becoming more important influences on motivation and parental influence declining in importance (Steinberg et al., 1996); however, parental influence does not disappear. When children are young, parents can be more directive and exert greater control on their children's activities. With development, children seek less parental control. But parents' expectations for and engagement with children continue to be influential. Klauda (2009) reported that parental support for their adolescent children's reading relates positively to adolescents' motivation for reading. Among older children, such parental support may occur as discussing and sharing books with them.

The role of friends seems especially critical. Friends tend to display similar levels of motivation on such indexes as self-perceptions of competence (e.g., self-efficacy), academic standards, importance of meeting standards, and preference for challenges (Altermatt & Pomerantz, 2003). In their study of middle-school students, Wentzel, Barry, and Caldwell (2004) found that students without friends showed lower prosocial behavior and grade-point averages and greater emotional distress compared to students with friends. Thus, friends are important for both learning and motivation.

Implications

The preceding points suggest how motivation strategies might be modified depending on students' developmental levels. With respect to goal setting, the suggestion is that short-term (proximal) and specific goals be used with young children. Given their immediate time frames of reference, a goal beyond the immediate context is apt to have little or no motivational effect.

It is important to work with students on goal setting and help them break long-term goals into subgoals with timelines. When teachers assign projects, they can help students understand the component tasks and formulate completion schedules. Students then can check their progress against the plan to determine whether they are on track to finish on time. Goal setting and self-monitoring of progress are key motivational processes contributing to self-regulation (B. Zimmerman, 2000).

That most young children generally are optimistic about what they can do seems desirable for motivation. The down side, however, is that they may attempt tasks beyond their means and experience failures. Since most work in elementary grades involves basic skills, teachers present tasks to students that they should be able to master. As tasks become tougher, teachers need to prepare students for the added difficulty. Trying hard and not succeeding on a difficult task does not have the negative effects on perceived ability that can result when students perceive a task as easy.

As the capacity to socially compare increases to include internal qualities (e.g., abilities), it behooves teachers to try to focus students' comparisons on their own progress rather than on how their performances compare with those of their peers. In Chapter 4 it was noted that self-evaluations of progress exert important effects on self-efficacy. Even when children know that their performances lag behind those of others, if they believe they have made progress, they also may believe that they can continue to do so and eventually they will be at the higher levels.

Many schools have mottos such as "All children can learn." This type of motto implies that teachers and administrators do not accept excuses for failure. Even if there is a decline in children's perceived capabilities as they grow older, it should not lead to failure so long as the decline is not great and there is an attitude in the school that students should not fail. If the decline results in more accurate correspondence with actual performance, then students are in good position to assess their strengths and weaknesses and help identify areas where they need additional instruction. Keeping capability self-perceptions tied to progress is critical for motivation. Applications based on developmental changes in motivation are given in Application 10.6.

APPLICATION 10.6
Motivation and Development

Research offers several insights into how teachers can appeal to motivational processes at different points in development. Young children are motivated by teacher praise and positive consequences of their actions. Kathy Stone sets the tone for her class by always reminding them that they can learn. She praises students for their learning progress (e.g., "That's great—you really are learning how to do this"). Students earn free time by completing their work and following classroom rules. She also praises desirable behavior (e.g., "I like the way you are working so hard today") and uses social comparative information to change undesirable behavior (e.g., "Tisha, see how well Brianna is working—I know that you can do just as well").

Jim Marshall knows that not all of his students are intrinsically interested in history. He also knows that his students are concerned about perceptions of ability and do not want to be seen as incapable of learning. In class he attempts to minimize activities that highlight ability differences, such as history bees and quick answers to questions. Rather, he has students work on group projects in which each student is responsible for certain tasks contributing to the final product. Group members also share the responsibility for class presentations and dramatizations of

historical events. Although Jim gives grades for tests and assignments, in the public arena he provides a context in which all students can succeed and be perceived positively by others.

Gina Brown capitalizes on her knowledge that as students become older they can evaluate their capabilities more realistically. In preparation for unit tests she has students evaluate their capabilities to perform different tasks, such as "Define key terms in Piaget's theory" and "Explain how peer models might be used in a classroom to teach skills and build observers' self-efficacy." She provides study materials on appropriate topics for students who evaluate themselves low in a particular area. She reviews with the class those topics in which self-evaluations are generally low. In conjunction with students' field placements in schools, she asks them to evaluate their skills for such tasks as "Tutor a child in reading" and "Assist the teacher in designing a lesson on fractions." Working with teachers in the schools, she holds tutorials on topics in which students' self-evaluations and behaviors indicate low perceived capabilities. Allowing students to provide self-evaluations helps them take more responsibility for their learning and inculcates the type of self-reflection on teaching that their academic programs are attempting to foster.

INSTRUCTIONAL APPLICATIONS

Developmental theories and principles suggest many ways to take developmental differences into account in instruction. Earlier in this chapter we examined developmentally appropriate instruction and the instructional implications of Bruner's theory. This section covers learning styles, Case's instructional model, and teacher–student interactions.

Learning Styles

Many researchers interested in learner characteristics have explored *learning styles* (also known as *cognitive* or *intellectual styles*), which are stable individual variations in perceiving, organizing, processing, and remembering information (Shipman & Shipman, 1985). Styles are people's preferred ways to process information and handle tasks (Sternberg & Grigorenko, 1997; Zhang & Sternberg, 2005); they are not synonymous with abilities. Abilities refer to capacities to learn and execute skills; styles are habitual ways of processing and using information.

Styles are inferred from consistent individual differences in organizing and processing information on different tasks (Messick, 1984). To the extent that styles affect cognition, affects, and behavior, they help link cognitive, affective, and social functioning (Messick, 1994). In turn, stylistic differences are associated with differences in learning and receptivity to various forms of instruction (Messick, 1984).

This section discusses three styles (field dependence–independence, categorization, cognitive tempo) that have substantial research bases and educational implications. There are many other styles including *leveling* or *sharpening* (blurring or accentuating differences among stimuli), *risk taking* or *cautiousness* (high or low willingness to take chances to achieve goals), and *sensory modality preference* (enactive or kinesthetic, iconic or visual, symbolic or auditory; Sternberg & Grigorenko, 1997; Tobias, 1994). A popular style inventory is the *Myers-Briggs Type Indicator* (Myers & McCaulley, 1988), which purports to identify individuals' preferred ways of seeking out learning environments and attending to elements in them. Its four dimensions are: extroversion–introversion, sensing–intuitive, thinking–feeling, and judging–perceiving. Readers are referred to Zhang and Sternberg (2005) for in-depth descriptions of other styles.

Styles provide important information about cognitive development. One also can relate styles to larger behavioral patterns to study personality development (e.g., Myers-Briggs). Educators investigate styles to devise complementary learning environments and to teach students more adaptive styles to enhance learning and motivation. Styles also are relevant to brain development and functions (Chapter 2).

Field Dependence–Independence. *Field dependence–independence* (also called *psychological differentiation, global* and *analytical functioning*) refers to the extent that one depends on or is distracted by the context or perceptual field in which a stimulus or event occurs (Sternberg & Grigorenko, 1997). The construct was identified and principally researched by Witkin (1969; Witkin, Moore, Goodenough, & Cox, 1977).

Various measures determine reliance on perceptual context. One is the Rod-and-Frame test, in which the individual attempts to align a tilted luminous rod in an upright position within a tilted luminous frame—inside a dark room with no other perceptual cues. Field independence originally was defined as the ability to align the rod upright using only an internal standard of upright. Other measures are the Embedded Figures test, in which one attempts to locate a simpler figure embedded within a more complex design, and the Body Adjustment test, in which the individual sits in a tilted chair in a tilted room and attempts to align the chair upright. Participants who can easily locate figures and align themselves upright are classified as field independent (Application 10.7).

APPLICATION 10.7
Learning Styles

Elementary teachers must be careful to address the cognitive differences of their children in designing classroom activities, particularly because young children are more field dependent (global) than field independent (analytical). For the primary child, emphasis should be placed on designing activities that address global understanding, while at the same time taking analytical thinking into account.

For example, when Kathy Stone implements a unit on the neighborhood, she and her children might initially talk about the entire neighborhood and all the people and places in it (global thinking). The children might build replicas of their homes, the school, churches, stores, and so forth—which could tap analytical thinking—and place these on a large floor map to get an overall picture of the neighborhood (global). Children could think about people in the neighborhood and their major features (analytical thinking) and then put on a puppet show portraying them interacting with one another without

being too precise about exact behaviors (global). Mrs. Stone could show a real city map to provide a broad overview (global) and then focus on that section of the map detailing their neighborhood (analytical).

Secondary teachers can take style differences into account in lesson planning. In teaching about the Civil War, Jim Marshall should emphasize both global and analytical styles by discussing overall themes and underlying causes of the war (e.g., slavery, economy) and by creating lists of important events and characters (e.g., Lincoln, Grant, Lee, Battle of Fredericksburg, Appomattox). Student activities can include discussions of important issues underlying the war (global style) and making time lines showing dates of important battles and other activities (analytical style). If he were to stress only one type of style, students who process and construct knowledge differently may doubt their ability to understand material, which will have a negative impact on self-efficacy and motivation for learning.

Young children primarily are field dependent, but an increase in field independence begins during preschool and extends into adolescence. Children's individual preferences remain reasonably consistent over time. The data are less clear on gender differences. Although some data suggest that older male students are more field independent than older female students, research on children shows that girls are more field independent than boys. Whether these differences reflect cognitive style or some other construct that contributes to test performance (e.g., activity–passivity) is not clear.

Witkin et al. (1977) noted that field dependent and independent learners do not differ in learning ability but may respond differently to learning environments and content. Because field dependent persons may be more sensitive to and attend carefully to aspects of the social environment, they are better at learning material with social content; however, field independent learners can easily learn such content when it is brought to their attention. Field dependent learners seem sensitive to teacher praise and criticism. Field independent persons are more likely to impose structure when material lacks organization; field dependent learners consider material as it is. With poorly structured material, field dependent learners may be at a disadvantage. They use salient features of situations in learning, whereas field independent learners also consider less-salient cues. The latter students may be at an advantage with concept learning when relevant and irrelevant attributes are contrasted.

These differences suggest ways for teachers to alter instructional methods. If field dependent learners miss cues, teachers should highlight them to help students distinguish relevant features of concepts. This may be especially important with children who are beginning readers as they focus on letter features. Evidence indicates that field dependent learners have more trouble during early stages of reading (Sunshine & DiVesta, 1976).

Categorization Style. *Categorization style* refers to criteria used to perceive objects as similar to one another (Sigel & Brodzinsky, 1977). Style is assessed with a grouping task in which one must group objects on the basis of perceived similarity. This is not a cut-and-dried task because objects can be categorized in many ways. From a collection of animal pictures, one might select a cat, dog, and rabbit and give as the reason for the grouping that they are mammals, have fur, run, and so forth. Categorization style reveals information about how the individual prefers to organize information.

Three types of categorization styles are relational, descriptive, and categorical (Kagan, Moss, & Sigel, 1960). A *relational (contextual) style* links items on a theme or function (e.g., spatial, temporal); a *descriptive (analytic) style* involves grouping by similarity according to some detail or physical attribute; a *categorical (inferential) style* classifies objects as instances of a superordinate concept. In the preceding example, "mammals," "fur," and "run," reflect categorical, descriptive, and relational styles, respectively.

Preschoolers' categorizations tend to be descriptive; however, relational responses of the thematic type also are prevalent (Sigel & Brodzinsky, 1977). Researchers note a developmental trend toward greater use of descriptive and categorical classifications along with a decrease in relational responses.

Style and academic achievement are related, but the causal direction is unclear (Shipman & Shipman, 1985). Reading, for example, requires perception of analytic relations (e.g., fine discriminations); however, the types of discriminations made are as important as the ability to make such discriminations. Students are taught the former. Style and achievement may influence each other. Certain styles may lead to higher achievement, and the resulting rewards, perceptions of progress, and self-efficacy may reinforce one's continued use of the style.

Cognitive Tempo. *Cognitive (conceptual, response) tempo* has been extensively researched by Kagan (1966; Kagan, Pearson, & Welch, 1966). Kagan was investigating categorization when he observed that some children responded rapidly whereas others were more thoughtful and took their time. Cognitive tempo refers to the willingness "to pause and reflect upon the accuracy of hypotheses and solutions in a situation of response uncertainty" (Shipman & Shipman, 1985, p. 251).

Kagan developed the Matching Familiar Figures (MFF) test to use with children. The MFF is a 12-item match-to-standard test in which a standard figure is shown with six possible matches, one of which is perfect. The dependent variables are time to the first response on each item and total errors across all items. Reflective children score above the median on time (longer) but below the median on errors (fewer), whereas impulsive children show the opposite pattern. Two other groups of children are fast-accurate (below the median on both measures) and slow-inaccurate (above the median on both measures).

Children become more reflective with development, particularly in the early school years (Sigel & Brodzinsky, 1977). Evidence suggests different rates of development for boys and girls, with girls showing greater reflectivity at an earlier age. A moderate positive correlation between scores over a 2-year period indicates reasonable stability (Brodzinsky, 1982; Messer, 1970).

Differences in tempo are unrelated to intelligence scores but correlate with school achievement. Messer (1970) found that children not promoted to the next grade were more impulsive than peers who were promoted. Reflective children tend to perform better on moderately difficult perceptual and conceptual problem-solving tasks and make mature judgments on concept attainment and analogical reasoning tasks (Shipman & Shipman, 1985). Reflectivity bears a positive relationship to prose reading, serial recall, and spatial perspective-taking (Sigel & Brodzinsky, 1977). Impulsive children often are less attentive and more disruptive than reflective children, oriented toward quick success, and demonstrate low performance standards and mastery motivation (Sternberg & Grigorenko, 1997).

Given the educational relevance of cognitive tempo, many have suggested training children to be less impulsive. Meichenbaum and Goodman (1971; Chapter 4) found that self-instructional training decreased errors among impulsive children. Modeled demonstrations of reflective cognitive style, combined with student practice and feedback, seem important as a means of change.

Cognitive styles seem important for teaching and learning, and a fair amount of developmental research exists that may help guide attempts by practitioners to apply findings to improve students' adaptive functioning. For example, learners with a visual-spatial style are better able to process and learn from graphical displays (Vekiri, 2002). At the same time, drawing instructional conclusions from the literature can be difficult (Miller, 1987). The distinction between cognitive styles and abilities is tenuous and controversial (Tiedemann, 1989); field independence may be synonymous with aspects of intelligence (Sternberg & Grigorenko, 1997). A continuing issue is whether styles are individual traits (relatively permanent) or states (alterable). If styles are ability driven, then attempts to alter styles may meet with less success than if styles are acquired and subject to change. Recent research has investigated the organization of styles within information processing frameworks and within the structure of human personality (Messick, 1994; Sternberg & Grigorenko, 1997; Zhang & Sternberg, 2005).

Ideally the conditions of instruction will match learners' styles; however, this match often does not occur. Learners may need to adapt their styles and preferred modes of working to instructional conditions involving content and teaching methods. Self-regulation methods help learners adapt to changing instructional conditions.

Instructional conditions can be tailored to individual differences to provide equal learning opportunities for all students despite differences in aptitudes, styles, and so forth (Corno & Snow, 1986; Snow, Corno, & Jackson, 1996). Teachers control many aspects of the instructional environment, which they can tailor to student differences. These aspects include organizational structure (whole-class, small-group, individual), regular and supplementary materials, use of technology, type of feedback, and type of material presented (tactile, auditory, visual). Teachers also make adaptations when they provide remedial instruction to students who have difficulty grasping new material.

Case's Instructional Model

Case (1978a, 1978b, 1981) formulated a structural stage model of development to account for changes in cognitive information processing capabilities. Case's stages (approximate age ranges) and their defining characteristics are (Meece, 2002): sensory motor (birth to 1.5 years)—mental representations linked to physical movements; relational (1.5 to 5 years)—relations coordinated along one dimension (e.g., weight is heavy or light); dimensional (5 to 11 years)—relations coordinated along two dimensions (e.g., height and weight compared); abstract (11 to 18.5 years)—use of abstract reasoning.

Structural changes (i.e., movement to new stages) are linked with the development of cognitive strategies and memory processes. Cognitive development includes the acquisition of efficient strategies for processing information. Development produces an increase in the size of WM. As strategies become more efficient (automatic), they consume less WM space, which frees space for acquiring new strategies.

Case emphasized providing instruction to help students process information more automatically. One first identifies the learning goal and the steps through which learners must proceed to reach the goal. During instruction, demands on WM are reduced by not presenting too much new material at once and by breaking each complex step into simpler steps.

This process can be illustrated with missing addend problems of the form $4 + \_\_ = 7$ (Case, 1978b). The required steps are as follows:

- Read symbols from left to right.
- Note that quantity to be found is one of the two addends.
- Decide that the known addend must be subtracted from the known total.
- Note and store value of the given addend.
- Note and store value of the total.
- Perform the subtraction. (p. 214)

Children commonly make two types of strategy errors in solving the above problem: (a) They give either 4 or 7 as the answer, seemingly by first looking at the symbols and reading one of them, then copying this symbol as the answer; and (b) they add the two given numbers to get 11 by performing the following strategy:

- Look at and store the first symbol.
- Count out that many (on fingers).
- Look at and store the second symbol.
- Count out that many.
- Count out the total number.
- Write this number as the answer.

To show children that their strategies are incorrect, a teacher might use faces. A full face is placed on one side of an equal sign and a half face on the other. Children see that these faces are not the same. Then a full face is portrayed on one side of the equal sign and two half faces on the other side, where one half face has markings on it and the other is blank. Children fill in the markings on the blank half to make it the same as the full face. Eventually numerical symbols are introduced to replace the faces.

Case (1978a) cited evidence showing that the previous method is more effective than either structured practice or traditional instruction. Case's model has been applied to the design of instruction and other areas such as assessment and early childhood education (Case, 1993). One drawback of the theory is the time required to diagnose, analyze, and plan. The model may be most useful for students requiring remedial assistance because they tend to use inefficient strategies and have WM limitations.

Teacher–Student Interactions

Through their interactions with students, teachers can tailor instruction to developmental differences (Meece, 2002). Young children's attention can be captured by novel, interesting displays while minimizing unnecessary distractions. It helps to provide opportunities for physical movement and to keep activities short to maintain children's concentration. Young students also benefit from physical objects and visual displays (e.g., manipulatives, pictures). Teachers may need to point out how the knowledge students are learning relates to what they already know. Children should be encouraged to use outlines and pictures to help them organize information. Making learning meaningful (as Lucia recommended in the opening scenario), such as by relating it to real-life experiences, helps to build children's memory networks. Other important aspects of interactions involve feedback and classroom climate.

Feedback. Rosenshine and Stevens (1986) recommended that teachers provide performance feedback (e.g., "Correct," "Good") and maintain lesson momentum when students make mistakes by giving corrective feedback but not completely re-explaining the process. Reteaching is called for when many students do not understand the material. When leading lessons, teachers should keep interactions with younger students brief (30 or fewer seconds) when such interactions are geared to leading them toward the correct answer with hints or simple questions. Longer contacts lose other students' attention.

Reteaching and leading students to correct answers are effective ways to promote learning (Rosenshine & Stevens, 1986). Asking simpler questions and giving hints are useful when contacts can be kept short. Reteaching is helpful when many students make errors during a lesson. Feedback informing students that answers are correct motivates because it indicates the students are becoming more competent and are capable of further learning (Schunk, 1995). Feedback indicating an error also can build self-efficacy if followed by corrective information on how to perform better. Younger students benefit from frequent feedback.

Similarly, other interactions involving rewards, goals, contracts, and so forth must be linked with student progress. For example, rewards linked to progress build self-efficacy (Schunk, 1983e). With children, progress is best indicated with short-term tasks. Rewards given merely for participation regardless of level of performance actually may convey negative efficacy information. Students may wonder whether they are capable of performing better.

Classroom Climate. Teachers help to establish a *classroom climate* that affects interactions. Emotional aspects of teacher–student interactions are important for children. A positive classroom climate that reflects teacher warmth and sensitivity is associated with higher achievement and better self-regulation among elementary students (Pianta, Belsky, Vandergrift, Houts, & Morrison, 2008).

A classic study by Lewin, Lippitt, and White (1939) showed that a *democratic (collaborative) leadership style* is effective. The teacher works cooperatively with students, motivating them to work on tasks, posing questions, and having them share their ideas. Although an *authoritarian style* (strict with rigid rules and procedures) can raise achievement, high anxiety levels characterize such classrooms and productivity drops off when the teacher is absent. A *laissez-faire style* with the teacher providing little classroom direction results in wasted time and aimless activities. Democratic leadership encourages independence and initiative in students, who continue to work productively in the teacher's absence.

Teacher–student interactions often include praise and criticism. An extensive literature exists on the effects of these variables on student behavior.

Praise goes beyond simple feedback on accuracy of work or appropriateness of behavior because it conveys positive teacher affect and provides information about the worth of students' behaviors (Brophy, 1981). Thus, a teacher who says, "Correct, your work is so good," is providing both performance feedback ("Correct") and praise ("Your work is so good").

Brophy (1981) reviewed research on teacher praise and found that it does not always reinforce desirable behavior (Chapter 3) because teachers often do not give it based on student responses. Rather, it may be infrequent, noncontingent, general, and highly dependent on teachers' perceptions of students' need for praise. Many studies also show that praise is not strongly related to student achievement (Dunkin & Biddle, 1974). The effects of praise seem to depend on developmental level, SES, and ability. In the early elementary grades, praise correlates weakly but positively with achievement among low SES and low-ability students but weakly and negatively or not at all with achievement among high SES and high-ability students (Brophy, 1981).

After the first few grades in school, praise is a weak reinforcer. Up to approximately age 8, children want to please adults, which makes praise effects powerful; but this desire to please weakens with development. Praise also can have unintended effects. Because it conveys information about teachers' beliefs, teachers who praise students for success may convey that they do not expect students to learn much. Students might believe that the teacher thinks they have low ability, and this negatively affects motivation and learning (Weiner et al., 1983).

When linked to progress in learning, praise substantiates students' beliefs that they are becoming more competent and raises self-efficacy and motivation for learning. Praise used indiscriminantly carries no information about capabilities and has little effect on behavior (Schunk et al., 2008).

Criticism provides information about undesirability of student behaviors. Criticism ("I'm disappointed in you") is distinguished from performance feedback ("That's wrong"). Interestingly, research shows criticism is not necessarily bad (Dunkin & Biddle, 1974). We might expect that criticism's effect on achievement will depend on the extent to which it conveys that students are competent and can perform better with more effort or better use of strategies. Thus, a statement such as, "I'm disappointed in you. I know you can do better if you work harder" might motivate students to learn because it contains positive self-efficacy information. As with praise, other variables temper the effects of criticism. Some research shows that criticism is given more often to boys, African American students, students for whom teachers hold low expectations, and students of lower SES status (Brophy & Good, 1974).

As a motivational technique to aid learning, criticism probably is not a good choice because it can have variable effects. Younger children may misinterpret academic criticism to mean that the teacher does not like them or is mean. Some students respond well to criticism. In general, however, teachers are better advised to provide positive feedback about ways to improve performance than to criticize present performance. Application 10.8 offers ways to use praise and criticism in learning settings.

APPLICATION 10.8
Using Praise and Criticism

The praise and criticism teachers use as they interact with their students can affect student performance. Teachers must be careful to use both appropriately and remember that criticism generally is not a good choice because it can have variable effects.

Praise is most effective when it is simple and direct and is linked with accomplishment of specific actions. For example, a teacher who is complimenting a student for sitting quietly, concentrating, and completing his or her work accurately that day should not say, "You really have been good today" (too general). Instead, the teacher might say something such as, "I really like the way you worked hard at your seat and finished all of your math work today. It paid off because you got all of the division problems correct. Great job!"

When a student answers a question in American history class during a discussion about a chapter, it is desirable that Jim Marshall let him or her know why the answer was a good one. Instead of replying, "Good answer," Mr. Marshall adds, "You outlined very well the three points in that chapter."

If criticism is used, it should convey that students are competent and can perform better, which may motivate performance. For example, assume that a capable student submitted a very poor educational psychology project that did not fulfill the assignment. Gina Brown says to her student, "John, I am very disappointed in your project. You are one of the best students in our class. You always share a great deal in class and perform well on all the tests. I know you are capable of completing an outstanding project. Let's work some more on this assignment and try harder as you redo this project."

SUMMARY

Development refers to changes over time that follow an orderly pattern and enhance survival. These changes are progressive and occur during the life span. Development is intimately linked with learning because at any time developmental level places constraints on learning.

The scientific study of human development began in the late 1800s. Major societal changes occurred through technological advances and influxes of immigrants. Society needed teachers and schools to educate many students from diverse backgrounds. Drawing from psychology and philosophy, many educators banded together under the loosely organized Child Study Movement. Early efforts at child study generated research and provided implications of development for teachers and parents, but the broad agenda of the Child Study Movement eventually was replaced by behaviorism and other theories.

Researchers have many perspectives on development: biological, psychoanalytic, behavioral, cognitive, and contextual. Regardless of perspective, certain issues exist that developmental theories address, including the role of heredity, the stability of developmental periods, the continuity of processes, the role of learner activity, and the locus of developmental changes (structures or functions).

Structural theories include Chomsky's psycholinguistic theory, classical information processing theory, and Piaget's theory. These theories postulate that development involves changes in cognitive structures. Information that is learned can help to alter the structures. Piaget's, Vygotsky's, and many other theories of development reflect a constructivist perspective because they postulate that knowledge is not acquired automatically but rather that learners construct their own understandings.

Bruner's theory of cognitive growth discusses the ways that learners represent knowledge: enactively, iconically, and symbolically. He advocated the spiral curriculum, in which subject matter is periodically revisited with increasing cognitive development and student understanding.

Many developmental researchers study how information processing changes as a function of experiences and schooling. Developmental changes are seen especially in the functions of attention, encoding, retrieval, metacognition, and self-regulation. Cognitive developmental theory and research have implications for designing developmentally appropriate instruction and for helping to ease transitions in schooling.

Family influences on development include socioeconomic status (SES), home environment, parental involvement, and electronic media. SES relates to school socialization, attendance, and years of schooling. Higher SES families have greater capital and provide more and richer opportunities for children. Early interventions for low-SES families help prepare children for school. Home environment effects on cognitive development are most pronounced in infancy and early childhood. As children become older, their social networks expand and peers become more important. Parents can launch children onto trajectories by involving them in groups and activities. Parents' expectations for children relate positively to their achievement. Comer's School Development Program involves parents and community members in school planning. Children learn from electronic media, and moderate exposure to educational media is associated with better cognitive development and achievement. Parents and caregivers who view media with children can help to promote children's learning.

With development, motivation becomes more differentiated and complex; children's understanding of motivational processes (e.g., goals, social comparisons) and levels of motivation change; there is better correspondence between children's values, beliefs, and goals and their choices and performances; and long-term motivation becomes important. Children are motivated by short-term, specific goals and comparisons of progress in performance. With development, breaking tasks into subgoals and self-evaluations of progress become more motivating.

Developmental theories suggest that instruction be tailored to take differences into account. Students differ in their preferred learning styles. Teachers can take stylistic differences into account by ensuring that information is conveyed in multiple ways and that student activities are varied. Case's model is a structural account of changes in information processing capabilities. The model emphasizes helping students process information more automatically. After learners' initial knowledge is assessed, learning goals and task sequences are specified to move learners to greater proficiency. Teacher-student interactions should reflect developmental changes. Teachers who structure feedback and provide a positive classroom climate—which includes effectively using praise and criticism—help motivate students and improve their learning.

FURTHER READING

Bradley, R. H., & Corwyn, R. F. (2002). Socioeconomic status and child development. *Annual Review of Psychology, 53,* 371–399.

Bruner, J. S. (1966). *Toward a theory of instruction.* New York: Norton.

Case, R. (1993). Theories of learning and theories of development. *Educational Psychologist, 28,* 219–233.

Comer, J. P. (2001, April 23). Schools that develop children. *The American Prospect,* 30–35.

Davidson, E. S., & Benjamin, L. T., Jr. (1987). A history of the child study movement in America. In J. A. Glover & R. R. Ronning (Eds.), *Historical foundations of educational psychology* (pp. 41–60). New York: Plenum.

Kirkorian, H. L., Wartella, E. A., & Anderson, D. R. (2008). Media and young children's learning. *The Future of Children, 18*(1), 39–61.

Sternberg, R. J., & Grigorenko, E. L. (2005). Are cognitive styles still in style? *American Psychologist, 52,* 700–712.

Glossary

Accommodation The process of changing internal structures to provide consistency with external reality.

Accretion Encoding new information in terms of existing schemata

Achievement Motivation The striving to be competent in effortful activities.

Act A class of movements that produces an outcome.

Action Control Potentially modifiable self-regulatory volitional skills and strategies.

Action Control Theory Theory stressing the role of volitional processes in behavior.

Activation Level Extent that information in memory is being processed or is capable of being processed quickly; information in an active state is quickly accessible.

Actualizing Tendency Innate motive that is a precursor to other motives and is oriented toward personal growth, autonomy, and freedom from external control.

Adaptation See *Equilibration*.

Adapting Instruction Tailoring instructional conditions at the system, course, or individual class level to match important individual differences to ensure equal learning opportunities for all students.

Advance Organizer Device that helps connect new material with prior learning, usually with a broad statement presented at the outset of a lesson.

Affective Learning Technique Specific procedure included in a learning strategy to create a favorable psychological climate for learning by helping the learner cope with anxiety, develop positive beliefs, set work goals, establish a place and time for working, or minimize distractions.

All-or-None Learning View that a response is learned by proceeding from zero or low strength to full strength rapidly (e.g., during one trial).

Amygdala Part of the brain involved in regulating emotion and aggression.

Analogical Reasoning Problem-solving strategy in which one draws an analogy between the problem situation and a situation with which one is familiar, works through the problem in the familiar domain, and relates the solution to the problem situation.

Apprenticeship Situation in which novice works with expert in joint work-related activities.

Archival Record Permanent record that exists independently of other assessments.

Artificial Intelligence Programming computers to engage in human activities such as thinking, using language, and solving problems.

Assessment The process of determining students' status with respect to educational variables.

Assimilation The process of fitting external reality to existing cognitive structures.

Assistive Technology Equipment adapted for use by students with disabilities.

Associative Shifting Process of changing behavior whereby responses made to a particular stimulus eventually are made to a different stimulus as a consequence of altering the stimulus slightly on repeated trials.

Associative Strength Strength of association between a stimulus and a response.

Associative Structure Means of representing information in long-term memory; bits of information that occur close together in time or that otherwise are associated and stored together so that when one is remembered, the other also is remembered.

Associative Writing Writing that reflects one's knowledge of a topic without regard for elements of style.

Asynchronous Learning Nonreal-time interactions.

Attention The process of selecting some environmental inputs for further information processing.

Attribution Perceived cause of an outcome.

Attribution Retraining Intervention strategy aimed at altering students' attributional beliefs, usually from dysfunctional attributions (e.g., failure attributed to low ability) to those conducive to motivation and learning (failure attributed to low effort).

Automaticity Cognitive processing with little or no conscious awareness.

Autonomic Nervous System (ANS) The part of the nervous system that regulates involuntary behaviors involving the heart, lungs, glands, and muscles.

Axon Long thread of brain tissue in a neuron that sends messages.

Baby Biography A report on a single child based on a series of observations over a lengthy period.

Backup Reinforcer A reinforcer that one receives in exchange for a generalized reinforcer.

Balance Theory Theory postulating the tendency for people to balance relations between persons, situations, and events.

Behavior Modification (Therapy) Systematic application of behavioral learning principles to facilitate adaptive behaviors.

Behavior Rating An estimate of how often a behavior occurs in a given time.

Behavioral Objective Statement describing the behaviors a student will perform as a result of instruction, the conditions under which behaviors will be performed, and the criteria for assessing behaviors to determine whether the objective has been accomplished.

Behavioral Theory Theory that views learning as a change in the form or frequency of behavior as a consequence of environmental events.

Biologically Primary Ability An ability that is largely biologically based.

Biologically Secondary Ability An ability that is largely culturally taught.

Blended Model Instruction that combines face-to-face instruction with e-learning.

489

Bottom-Up Processing Pattern recognition of visual stimuli that proceeds from analysis of features to building a meaningful representation.

Brain The primary organ in the nervous system that regulates cognition, motivation, and emotions.

Brainstem That part of the central nervous system that links the lower brain with the middle brain and hemispheres.

Brainstorming Problem-solving strategy that comprises defining the problem, generating possible solutions, deciding on criteria to use in judging solutions, and applying criteria to select the best solution.

Branching Program Type of programmed instruction in which students complete different sequences depending on how well they perform.

Broca's Area Brain part in the left frontal lobe that controls speech production.

Buggy Algorithm An incorrect rule for solving a mathematical problem.

Capital Socioeconomic indicator that includes one's financial, material, human, and social resources.

CAT Scan Computerized axial tomography; technology that provides three-dimensional images used to detect body abnormalities.

Categorical Clustering Recalling items in groups based on similar meaning or membership in the same category.

Categorization Style Cognitive style referring to the criteria used to perceive objects as similar to one another.

Cell Assembly In Hebb's theory, a structure that includes cells in the cortex and subcortical centers.

Central Nervous System (CNS) The part of the nervous system that includes the spinal cord and the brain.

Cerebellum Part of the brain that regulates body balance, muscular control, movement, and body posture.

Cerebral Cortex The thin, outer covering of the cerebrum.

Cerebrum The largest part of the brain that includes left and right hemispheres; involved in cognition and learning.

Chaining The linking of three-term contingencies so that each response alters the environment and that altered condition serves as a stimulus for the next response.

Chameleon Effect Nonconscious mimicking of behaviors and mannerisms of persons in one's social environment.

Chunking Combining information in a meaningful fashion.

Classical Conditioning Descriptive term for Pavlov's theory in which a neutral stimulus becomes conditioned to elicit a response through repeated pairing with an unconditioned stimulus.

Closed-Loop Theory Theory of motor skill learning postulating that people develop perceptual traces of motor movements through practice and feedback.

Cognitive Behavior Modification Behavior modification techniques that incorporate learners' thoughts (overt and covert) as discriminative and reinforcing stimuli.

Cognitive Consistency Idea that people have a need to make behaviors and cognitions consistent.

Cognitive Constructivism See *Dialectical Constructivism.*

Cognitive Dissonance Mental tension that is produced by conflicting cognitions and that has drivelike properties leading to reduction.

Cognitive Map Internal plan comprising expectancies of which actions are required to attain one's goal.

Cognitive Modeling Modeled explanation and demonstration incorporating verbalizations of the model's thoughts and reasons for performing given actions.

Cognitive Style Stable variation among learners in ways of perceiving, organizing, processing, and remembering information.

Cognitive (Response) Tempo Cognitive style referring to the willingness to pause and reflect on the accuracy of information in a situation of response uncertainty.

Cognitive Theory Theory that views learning as the acquisition of knowledge and cognitive structures due to information processing.

Collective Teacher Efficacy Perceptions of teachers in a school that their efforts as a whole will positively affect students.

Comer Program See *School Development Program.*

Comparative Organizer Type of advance organizer that introduces new material by drawing an analogy with familiar material.

Comprehension Attaching meaning to verbal (printed or spoken) information and using it for a particular purpose.

Comprehension Monitoring Cognitive activity directed toward determining whether one is properly applying knowledge to material to be learned, evaluating whether one understands the material, deciding that the strategy is effective or that a better strategy is needed, and knowing why strategy use improves learning. Monitoring procedures include self-questioning, rereading, paraphrasing, and checking consistencies.

Computer-Based (-Assisted) Instruction Interactive instruction in which a computer system provides information and feedback to students and receives student input.

Computer-Based Learning Environment Setting that includes computer technology used for learning in various ways, including with simulations, computer-based instruction, and hypermedia/multimedia.

Computer Learning Learning that occurs with the aid of a computer.

Computer-Mediated Communication (CMC) Technological applications that allow users to communicate with one another (e.g., distance education, computer conferencing).

Concept Labeled set of objects, symbols, or events sharing common characteristics (critical attributes).

Concept Learning Identifying attributes, generalizing them to new examples, and discriminating examples from nonexamples.

Conception of Ability One's belief/theory about the nature of intelligence (ability) and how it changes over time.

Concrete Operational Stage Third of Piaget's stages of cognitive development, encompassing roughly ages 7 to 11.

Conditional Knowledge Knowledge of when to employ forms of declarative and procedural knowledge and why doing so is important.

Conditional Regard Regard that is contingent on certain actions.

Conditioned Response (CR) The response elicited by a conditioned stimulus.

Conditioned Stimulus (CS) A stimulus that, when repeatedly paired with an unconditioned stimulus, elicits a conditioned response similar to the unconditioned response.

Conditioning Theory See *Behavioral Theory*.

Conditions of Learning Circumstances that prevail when learning occurs and that include internal conditions (prerequisite skills and cognitive processing requirements of the learner) and external conditions (environmental stimuli that support the learner's cognitive processes).

Connectionism Descriptive term for Thorndike's theory postulating learning as the forming of connections between sensory experiences (perceptions of stimuli or events) and neural impulses that manifest themselves behaviorally.

Connectionist Model Computer simulation of learning processes in which learning is linked with neural system processing, where impulses fire across synapses to form connections.

Consolidation The process of stabilizing and strengthening neural (synaptic) connections.

Constructivism Doctrine stating that learning takes place in contexts and that learners form or construct much of what they learn and understand as a function of their experiences in situations.

Constructivist Theory See *Constructivism*.

Contiguity (Contiguous Conditioning) The basic principle of Guthrie's theory, which refers to learning that results from a pairing close in time of a response with a stimulus or situation.

Contingency Contract Written or oral agreement between teacher and student specifying what work the student must accomplish to earn a particular reinforcer.

Continuous Reinforcement Reinforcement for every response.

Control (Executive) Processes Cognitive activities that regulate the flow of information through the processing system.

Cooperative Learning Situation in which a group of students work on a task that is too great for any one student to complete and in which an objective is to develop in students the ability to work collaboratively.

Coping Model Model who initially demonstrates the typical fears and deficiencies of observers but gradually demonstrates improved performance and self-confidence in his or her capabilities.

Corpus Callosum Band of fibers in the brain that connects the right and left hemispheres.

Correlational Research A study in which an investigator explores naturally existing relations among variables.

Cortex See *Cerebral Cortex*.

Cortisol Bodily hormone that when elevated in babies can retard their brain development.

Declarative Knowledge Knowledge that something is the case; knowledge of facts, beliefs, organized passages, and events of a story.

Decoding Deciphering printed symbols or making letter-sound correspondences.

Deductive Reasoning Process of deriving specific points from general principles.

Deep Structure The meaning of the speech and syntax of a language.

Dendrite Elongated brain tissue surrounding a neuron that receives messages.

Descriptive Research See *Qualitative Research*.

Development Changes in people over time that follow an orderly pattern and enhance survival.

Developmental Status What an individual is capable of doing given his or her present level of development.

Developmentally Appropriate Instruction Instruction matched to students' developmental levels.

Dialectical Constructivism Constructivist perspective stating that knowledge derives from interactions between persons and their environments.

Dialogue Conversation between two or more persons while engaged in a learning task.

Dichotic Listening Hearing two verbal inputs simultaneously.

Differentiated Task Structure Class situation in which all students work on different tasks and materials or methods are tailored to students' needs.

Digit-Span Task Information processing task in which participants hear a series of digits and then attempt to recall them in the same order.

Direct Observations Instances of behavior that are observed.

Discovery Learning A type of inductive reasoning in which one obtains knowledge by formulating and testing hypotheses through hands-on experiences.

Discrimination Responding differently, depending on the stimulus.

Discriminative Stimulus The stimulus to which one responds in the operant model of conditioning.

Disinhibition See *Inhibition/Disinhibition*.

Distance Learning (Education) Instruction that originates at one site and is transmitted to students at one or more remote sites; it may include two-way interactive capabilities.

Domain Specificity Discrete declarative and procedural knowledge structures.

Dopamine A chemical neurotransmitter that can lead to the brain being more sensitive to the pleasurable effects of drugs and alcohol.

Drive Internal force that energizes and propels one into action.

Dual-Code Theory The view that long-term memory represents knowledge with a verbal system that in cludes knowledge expressed in language and an imaginal system that stores visual and spatial information.

Dual-Memory Model of Information Processing See *Two-Store (Dual) Memory Model of Information Processing.*

Duration Measure Amount of time a behavior occurs during a given period.

Echo Sensory memory for auditory sounds.

EEG Electroencephalograph; measures electrical patterns caused by movement of neurons and used to investigate brain disorders.

Effectance Motivation (Mastery Motivation) Motivation to interact effectively with one's environment and control critical aspects.

Efficacy Expectations See *Self-Efficacy.*

Ego Involvement Motivational state characterized by self-preoccupation, a desire to avoid looking incompetent, and viewing learning as a means to the end of avoiding appearing to lack ability.

Egocentrism Cognitive inability to take the perspective of another person.

Eidetic Imagery Photographic memory in which an image appears and disappears in segments.

Elaboration The process of expanding upon new information by adding to it or linking it to what one already knows.

Elaboration Theory of Instruction Means of presenting instruction in which one begins with a general view of the content, moves to specific details, and returns later to the general view with review and practice.

E-Learning Learning through electronic means.

Electronic Bulletin Board (Conference) Electronic means for posting messages and participating in a discussion (chat group).

Electronic Media Media that operate through electronic means including televisions, cell phones, video games, Web social networks, and e-mail.

Empiricism The doctrine that experience is the only source of knowledge.

Enactive Learning Learning through actual performance.

Enactive Representation Representing knowledge through motor responses.

Encoding The process of putting new, incoming information into the information processing system and preparing it for storage in long-term memory.

Encoding Specificity Hypothesis The idea that retrieval of information from long-term memory is maximized when retrieval cues match those present during encoding.

Endogenous Constructivism Constructivist perspective stating that people construct mental structures out of preexisting structures and not directly from environmental information.

Entity Theory The belief that abilities represent fixed traits over which one has little control.

Episodic Memory Memory of particular times, places, persons, and events, which is personal and autobiographical.

Epistemology Study of the origin, nature, limits, and methods of knowledge.

Equilibration A biological drive to produce an optimal state of equilibrium; it includes the complementary processes of assimilation and accommodation.

Event-Related Potentials Changes in brain waves measured while individuals are engaged in various tasks.

Evoked Potentials, See *Event-Related Potentials.*

Executive Processes See *Control (Executive) Processes.*

Exogenous Constructivism Constructivist perspective stating that the acquisition of knowledge represents a reconstruction of structures that exist in the external world.

Expectancy-Value Theory Psychological theory postulating that behavior is a function of how much one values a particular outcome and one's expectation of obtaining that outcome as a result of performing that behavior.

Experimental Research A study in which an investigator systematically varies conditions (independent variables) and observes changes in outcomes (dependent variables).

Expert A person who has attained a high level of competence in a domain.

Expert System Computer system that is programmed with a large knowledge base and that behaves intelligently by solving problems and providing instruction.

Expository Organizer Type of advance organizer that introduces new material with concept definitions and generalizations.

Expository Teaching Deductive teaching strategy in which material is presented in an organized and meaningful fashion with general ideas followed by specific points.

Extinction Decrease in intensity and disappearance of a conditioned response due to repeated presentations of the conditioned stimulus without the unconditioned stimulus.

Extrinsic Motivation Engaging in a task as a means to the end of attaining an outcome (reward).

Facilitator One who arranges resources and shares feelings and thoughts with students in order to promote learning.

Fatigue Method of Behavioral Change Altering behavior by transforming the cue for engaging in the behavior into a cue for avoiding it through repeated presentation.

Fear of Failure The tendency to avoid an achievement goal that derives from one's belief concerning the anticipated negative consequences of failing.

Feature Analysis Theory of perception postulating that people learn the critical features of stimuli, which are stored in long-term memory as images or verbal codes and compared with environmental inputs.

Field Dependence and Independence Cognitive style referring to the extent that one is dependent on or distracted by the context in which a stimulus or event occurs. Also called global and analytical functioning.

Field Expectancy Perceived relation between two stimuli or among a stimulus, response, and stimulus.

Field Research Study conducted where participants live, work, or go to school.

Figure-Ground Relation See *Gestalt Principles.*

Filter (Bottleneck) Theory Theory of attention contending that information not perceived is not processed beyond the sensory register.

First Signal System See *Primary Signals.*

Flow Total involvement in an activity.

fMRI See *Functional Magnetic Resonance Imaging.*

Forgetting Loss of information from memory or inability to recall information due to interference or improper retrieval cues.

Formal Operational Stage Fourth of Piaget's stages of cognitive development, encompassing roughly ages 11 to adult.

Free Recall Recalling stimuli in any order.

Frequency Count Frequency of a behavior in a given time period.

Frontal Lobe Brain lobe responsible for processing information relating to memory, planning, decision making, goal setting, and creativity; also contains the primary motor cortex regulating muscular movements.

Functional Analysis of Behavior Process of determining the external variables of which behavior is a function.

Functional Fixedness Failure to perceive different uses for objects or new configurations of elements in a situation.

Functional Magnetic Resonance Imaging (fMRI) Technology measuring magnetic flow in the brain caused by performance of mental tasks that fires neurons and causes blood flow; image compared to that of the brain at rest to show responsible regions.

Functional Theories of Development Theories postulating the types of functions or processes that a child is able to perform at a particular time.

Functionalism Doctrine postulating that mental processes and behaviors of living organisms help them adapt to their environments.

Game Activity that creates an enjoyable learning context by linking material to sport, adventure, or fantasy.

General Skill Skill applying to many domains (e.g., goal setting).

Generalization Occurrence of a response to a new stimulus or in a situation other than that present during original learning. See also *Transfer.*

Generalized Reinforcer A secondary reinforcer that becomes paired with more than one primary or secondary reinforcer.

Generate-and-Test Strategy Problem-solving strategy in which one generates (thinks of) a possible problem solution and tests its effectiveness.

Gestalt Principles *Figure-ground relationship*: A perceptual field is composed of a figure against a background. *Proximity*: Elements in a perceptual field are viewed as belonging together according to their closeness in space or time. *Similarity*: Perceptual field elements similar in such respects as size or color are viewed as belonging together. *Common direction*: Elements of a perceptual field appearing to constitute a pattern or flow in the same direction are perceived as a figure. *Simplicity*: People organize perceptual fields in simple, regular features. *Closure*: People fill in incomplete patterns or experiences.

Gestalt Psychology Psychological theory of perception and learning stressing the organization of sensory experiences.

Glial Cell Brain cell that serves to nourish and cleanse neurons.

Global and Analytical Functioning See *Field Dependence and Independence.*

Goal The behavior (outcome) that one is consciously trying to perform (attain).

Goal Orientations Reasons for engaging in academic tasks.

Goal Setting Process of establishing a standard or objective to serve as the aim of one's actions.

Grammar The underlying abstract set of rules governing a language.

Grouping Structure Instructional method for linking attainment of students' goals. *Cooperative*—positive link; *competitive*—negative link; *individualistic*—no link.

Habit Behavior established to many cues.

Hedonism Philosophical position that humans seek pleasure and avoid pain.

Heuristic A method for solving problems in which one employs principles (rules of thumb) that usually lead to a solution.

Higher-Order Conditioning Use of a conditioned stimulus to condition a new, neutral stimulus by pairing the two stimuli.

Hill Climbing See *Working Forward.*

Hippocampus Brain structure responsible for memory of the immediate past and helps to establish information in long-term memory.

Holistic Idea that we must study people's behaviors, thoughts, and feelings together and not in isolation.

Homeostasis Optimal levels of physiological states.

Hope for Success The tendency to approach an achievement goal that derives from one's subjective estimate of the likelihood of succeeding.

Humanistic Theory Theory emphasizing people's capabilities to make choices and seek control over their lives.

Hypermedia See *Multimedia.*

Hypothalamus Part of the autonomic nervous system that controls body functions needed to maintain homeostasis and also is involved in emotional reactions.

Hypothesis Assumption that can be empirically tested.

Icon Sensory memory for visual inputs.

Iconic Representation Representing knowledge with mental images.

Identical Elements View of transfer postulating that application of a response in a situation other than the one in which it was learned depends on the number of features (stimuli) common to the two situations.

Imitation Copying the observed behaviors and verbalizations of others.

Implicit Theories Students' beliefs about themselves, others, and their environments.

Inclusion Process of integrating students with disabilities into regular classroom instruction.

Incompatible Response Method of Behavioral Change Altering behavior by pairing the cue for the undesired behavior with a response incompatible with (i.e., that cannot be performed at the same time as) the undesired response.

Incremental Learning View that learning becomes established gradually through repeated performances (exemplified by Thorndike's theory).

Incremental Theory The belief that abilities are skills that can improve through learning.

Inductive Reasoning Process of formulating general principles based on specific examples.

Information Processing Sequence and execution of cognitive events.

Inhibition In Pavlov's theory, a type of neural excitation that works antagonistically to an excitation producing conditioning and that diminishes the conditioned response in intensity or extinguishes it.

Inhibition/Disinhibition Strengthening/weakening of inhibitions over behaviors previously learned, which results from observing consequences of the behaviors performed by models.

Inquiry Teaching Socratic teaching method in which learners formulate and test hypotheses, differentiate necessary from sufficient conditions, make predictions, and decide when more information is needed.

Insight A sudden perception, awareness of a solution, or transformation from an unlearned to a learned state.

Instinct A natural behavior or capacity.

Instructional Quality The degree to which instruction is effective, efficient, appealing, and economical in promoting student performance and attitude toward learning.

Instructional Scaffolding See *Scaffolding.*

Instructional Self-Efficacy Personal beliefs about one's capabilities to help students learn.

Interference Blockage of the spread of activation across memory networks.

Intermittent Reinforcement Reinforcement for some but not all responses.

Internalization Transforming information acquired from the social environment into mechanisms of self-regulating control.

Internet International collection of computer networks.

Interval Schedule Reinforcement is contingent on the first response being made after a specific time period.

Interview Situation in which interviewer presents questions or points to discuss and respondent answers orally.

Intrinsic Motivation Engaging in a task for no obvious reward except for the activity itself (the activity is the means and the end).

Introspection Type of self-analysis in which individuals verbally report their immediate perceptions following exposure to objects or events.

Irreversibility The cognitive belief that once something is done it cannot be changed.

Keyword Method Mnemonic technique in which one generates an image of a word sounding like the item to be learned and links that image with the meaning of the item to be learned.

Laboratory Research Study conducted in a controlled setting.

Language Acquisition Device (LAD) Mental structure that forms and verifies transformational rules to account for overt language.

Latent Learning Learning that occurs from environmental interactions in the absence of a goal or reinforcement.

Lateralization See *Localization.*

Law of Disuse That part of the Law of Exercise postulating that the strength of a connection between a situation and response is decreased when the connection is not made over a period of time.

Law of Effect The strength of a connection is influenced by the consequences of performing the response in the situation: Satisfying consequences strengthen a connection; annoying consequences weaken a connection. Eventually modified by Thorndike to state that annoying consequences do not weaken connections.

Law of Exercise Learning (unlearning) occurs through repetition (nonrepetition) of a response. Eventually discarded by Thorndike.

Law of Readiness When an organism is prepared to act, to do so is satisfying and not to do so is annoying. When an organism is not prepared to act, forcing it to act is annoying.

Law of Use That part of the Law of Exercise postulating that the strength of a connection between a situation and response is increased when the connection is made.

Learned Helplessness Psychological state involving a disturbance in motivation, cognition, and emotions due to previously experienced uncontrollability (lack of contingency between action and outcome).

Learning An enduring change in behavior or in the capacity to behave in a given fashion resulting from practice or other forms of experience.

Learning Goal A goal of acquiring knowledge, behaviors, skills, or strategies.

Learning Hierarchy Organized set of intellectual skills.

Learning Method Specific procedure or technique included in a learning strategy and used to attain a learning goal.

Learning Strategy Systematic plan oriented toward regulating academic work and producing successful task performance.

Learning Style See *Cognitive Style*.

Levels (Depth) of Processing Conceptualization of memory according to the type of processing that information receives rather than the processing's location.

Linear Program Programmed instructional materials that all students complete in the same sequence.

Localization Control of specific functions by different sides of the brain or in different areas of the brain.

Locus of Control Motivational concept referring to generalized control over outcomes; individuals may believe that outcomes occur independently of how they act (external control) or are highly contingent on their actions (internal control).

Long-Term Memory (LTM) Stage of information processing corresponding to the permanent repository of knowledge.

Mapping Learning technique in which one identifies important ideas and specifies how they are related.

Mastery Learning A systematic instructional plan that has as its objective students demonstrating high achievement and that includes the components of defining mastery, planning for mastery, teaching for mastery, and grading for mastery.

Mastery Model Model who demonstrates faultless performance and high self-confidence throughout the modeled sequence.

Mastery Motivation See *Effectance Motivation*.

Matched-Dependent Behavior Behavior matched to (the same as) that of the model and dependent on (elicited by) the model's action.

Meaningful Reception Learning Learning of ideas, concepts, and principles when material is presented in final form and related to students' prior knowledge.

Means–Ends Analysis Problem-solving strategy in which one compares the current situation with the goal to identify the differences between them, sets a subgoal to reduce one of the differences, performs operations to reach the subgoal, and repeats the process until the goal is attained.

Mediation Mechanism that bridges the link between external reality and mental processes and affects the development of the latter.

Mental Discipline The doctrine that learning certain subjects in school enhances mental functioning better than does studying other subjects.

Mental Imagery Mental representation of spatial knowledge that includes physical properties of the object or event represented.

Mentoring Situation involving the teaching of skills and strategies to students or other professionals within advising and training contexts.

Metacognition Deliberate conscious control of one's cognitive activities.

Method of Loci Mnemonic technique in which information to be remembered is paired with locations in a familiar setting.

Mimesis See *Imitation*.

Min Model Counting method in which one begins with the larger addend and counts in the smaller one.

Mnemonic A type of learning method that makes to-be-learned material meaningful by relating it to information that one already knows.

Modeling Behavioral, cognitive, and affective changes deriving from observing one or more models.

Molar Behavior A large sequence of behavior that is goal directed.

Motherese Speaking to children in simple utterances, often in abbreviated form.

Motivated Learning Motivation to acquire new knowledge, skills, and strategies, rather than merely to complete activities.

Motivation The process of instigating and sustaining goal-directed activities.

Motivational State A complex neural connection that includes emotions, cognitions, and behaviors.

Movement Discrete behavior that results from muscle contractions.

MRI Magnetic resonance imaging; technology in which radio waves cause the brain to produce signals that are mapped, which can detect tumors, lesions, and other abnormalities.

Multidimensional Classroom Classroom having many activities and allowing for diversity in student abilities.

Multimedia Technology that combines the capabilities of computers with other media such as film, video, sound, music, and text.

Myelin Sheath Brain tissue surrounding an axon and facilitating travel of signals.

Naïve Analysis of Action The way that common people interpret events.

Narration Written account of behavior and the context in which it occurs.

Negative Reinforcer A stimulus that, when removed by a response, increases the future likelihood of the response occurring in that situation.

Negative Transfer Prior learning that makes subsequent learning more difficult.

Network A set of interrelated propositions in long-term memory.

Networking Computers in various locations connected to one another and to central peripheral devices.

Neural Assemblies Collections of neurons synoptically connected with one another.

Neuron Brain cell that sends and receives information across muscles and organs.

Neuroscience Science of the relation of the nervous system to learning and behavior.

Neuroscience of Learning See *Neuroscience*.

Neurotransmitter Chemical secretions that travel along a brain axon to dendrites of the next cell.

Nonsense Syllable Three-letter (consonant-vowel-consonant) combination that makes a nonword.

Novice A person who has some familiarity with a domain but performs poorly.

Novice-to-Expert Methodology Means of analyzing learning by comparing behaviors and reported thoughts of skilled individuals (experts) with those of less-skilled persons (novices) and deciding on an efficient means of moving novices to the expert level.

Observational Learning Display of a new pattern of behavior by one who observes a model; prior to the modeling, the behavior has a zero probability of occurrence by the observer even with motivational inducements in effect.

Occipital Lobe Brain lobe primarily concerned with processing visual information.

Operant Behavior Behavior that produces an effect on the environment.

Operant Conditioning Presenting reinforcement contingent on a response emitted in the presence of a stimulus to increase the rate or likelihood of occurrence of the response.

Operational Definition Definition of a phenomenon in terms of the operations or procedures used to measure it.

Oral Responses Verbalized questions or answers to questions.

Outcome Expectation Belief concerning the anticipated outcome of actions.

Overjustification Decrease in intrinsic interest (motivation) in an activity subsequent to engaging in it under conditions that make task engagement salient as a means to some end (e.g., reward).

Paired-Associate Recall Recalling the response of a stimulus–response item when presented with the stimulus.

Paradigm Model for research.

Parietal Lobe Brain lobe responsible for the sense of touch; helps determine body position, and integrates visual information.

Parsing Mentally dividing perceived sound patterns into units of meaning.

Participant Modeling Therapeutic treatment (used by Bandura) comprising modeled demonstrations, joint performance between client and therapist, gradual withdrawal of performance aids, and individual mastery performance by the client.

Pattern Recognition See *Perception.*

Peer Collaboration Learning that occurs when students work together and their social interactions serve an instructional function.

Peer Tutoring Situation in which a student who has learned a skill teaches it to one who has not.

Pegword Method Mnemonic technique in which the learner memorizes a set of objects rhyming with integer names (e.g., one is a bun, two is a shoe, etc.), generates an image of each item to be learned, and links it with the corresponding object image. During recall, the learner recalls the rhyming scheme with its associated links.

Perceived Control Belief that one can influence task engagement and outcomes.

Perceived Self-Efficacy See *Self-Efficacy.*

Perception Process of recognizing and assigning meaning to a sensory input.

Performance Goal A goal of completing a task.

PET Scan Positive emission tomography scan; assesses gamma rays produced by mental activity and provides overall picture of brain activity.

Phase Sequence In Hebb's theory, a series of cell assemblies.

Phi Phenomenon Perceptual phenomenon of apparent motion caused by lights flashing on and off at short intervals.

Phonemes The smallest unit of a speech sound.

Positive Regard Feelings such as respect, liking, warmth, sympathy, and acceptance.

Positive Reinforcer A stimulus that, when presented following a response, increases the future likelihood of the response occurring in that situation.

Positive Self-Regard Positive regard that derives from self-experiences.

Positive Transfer Prior learning facilitates subsequent learning.

Postdecisional Processes Cognitive activities engaged in subsequent to goal setting.

Predecisional Processes Cognitive activities involved in making decisions and setting goals.

Prefrontal Cortex Front part of the frontal lobe of the brain.

Premack Principle A principle stating that the opportunity to engage in a more-valued activity reinforces engaging in a less-valued activity.

Preoperational Stage Second of Piaget's stages of cognitive development, encompassing roughly ages 2 to 7.

Primacy Effect Tendency to recall the initial items in a list.

Primary Motor Cortex. Area of the brain that controls bodily movements.

Primary Qualities Characteristics of objects (e.g., size, shape) that exist in the external world as part of the objects.

Primary Reinforcement Behavioral consequence that satisfies a biological need.

Primary Signals Environmental events that can become conditioned stimuli and produce conditioned responses.

Private Events Thoughts or feelings accessible only to the individual.

Private Speech The set of speech phenomena that has a self-regulatory function but is not socially communicative.

Proactive Interference Old learning makes new learning more difficult.

Problem A situation in which one is trying to reach a goal and must find a means of attaining it.

Problem Solving One's efforts to achieve a goal for which one does not have an automatic solution.

Problem Space The problem-solving context that comprises a beginning state, a goal state, and possible solution paths leading through subgoals and requiring application of operations.

Procedural Knowledge   Knowledge of how to do something: employ algorithms and rules, identify concepts, solve problems.

Process-Product Research   Study that relates changes in teaching processes to student products or outcomes.

Production   Translating visual and symbolic conceptions of events into behaviors.

Production Deficiency   The failure to generate task-relevant verbalizations when they could improve performance.

Production System (Production)   Memory network of condition–action sequences (rules), where the condition is the set of circumstances that activates the system and the action is the set of activities that occurs.

Productive Thinking   See *Problem Solving.*

Programmed Instruction (PI)   Instructional materials developed in accordance with behavioral learning principles.

Proposition   The smallest unit of information that can be judged true or false.

Propositional Network   Interconnected associative structure in long-term memory comprising nodes or bits of information.

Prototype   Abstract form stored in memory that contains the basic ingredients of a stimulus and is compared with an environmental input during perception.

Punishment   Withdrawal of a positive reinforcer, or presentation of a negative reinforcer contingent on a response, which decreases the future likelihood of the response being made in the presence of the stimulus.

Purposive Behaviorism   Descriptive term for Tolman's theory emphasizing the study of large sequences of (molar) goal-directed behaviors.

Qualitative Research   Study characterized by depth and quality of analysis and interpretation of data through the use of methods such as classroom observations, use of existing records, interviews, and think-aloud protocols.

Questionnaire   Situation in which respondents are presented with items or questions asking about their thoughts and actions.

Ratings by Others   Evaluations of students on quality or quantity of performance.

Ratio Schedule   A schedule where reinforcement is contingent on the number of responses.

Rationalism   The doctrine that knowledge derives from reason without the aid of the senses.

Readiness   What children are capable of doing or learning at various points in development.

Reasoning   Mental processes involved in generating and evaluating logical arguments.

Recency Effect   Tendency to recall the last items in a list.

Reciprocal Teaching   Interactive dialogue between teacher and students in which teacher initially models activities, after which teacher and students take turns being the teacher.

Reflective Teaching   Thoughtful teacher decision making that takes into account knowledge about students,

the context, psychological processes, learning and motivation, and self-knowledge.

Rehearsal   Repeating information to oneself aloud or subvocally.

Reinforcement   Any stimulus or event that leads to response strengthening.

Reinforcement History   Extent that an individual has been reinforced previously for performing the same or similar behavior.

Reinforcement Theory   See *Behavioral Theory.*

Reinforcing Stimulus   The stimulus in the operant model of conditioning that is presented contingent on a response and increases the probability of the response being emitted in the future in the presence of the discriminative stimulus.

Relativism   The doctrine that all forms of knowledge are justifiable because they are constructed by learners, especially if they reflect social consensus.

Research   Systematic investigation designed to develop or contribute to generalizable knowledge.

Resource Allocation   Learning model specifying that attention is a limited resource and is allocated to activities as a function of motivation and self-regulation.

Respondent Behavior   Response made to an eliciting stimulus.

Response Facilitation   Previously learned behaviors of observers are prompted by the actions of models.

Response Tempo   See *Cognitive (Response) Tempo.*

Restructuring   Process of forming new schemata.

Retention   Storage of information in memory.

Reticular Formation   Part of the brain that handles autonomic nervous systems functions, controls sensory inputs, and is involved in awareness.

Retroactive Interference   New learning makes recall of old knowledge and skills more difficult.

Reversibility   Cognitive ability to sequence operations in opposite order.

Rhetorical Problem   The problem space in writing, which includes the writer's topic, intended audience, and goals.

Satiation   Fulfillment of reinforcement that results in decreased responding.

Savings Score   Time or trials necessary for relearning as a percentage of time or trials required for original learning.

Scaffolding   Process of controlling task elements that are beyond the learner's capabilities so that the learner can focus on and master those task features that he or she can grasp quickly.

Schedule of Reinforcement   When reinforcement is applied.

Schema   A cognitive structure that organizes large amounts of information into a meaningful system.

Schema Theory   Theory explaining how people develop schemas (organized memory structures composed of related information).

School Development Program   System of community and parental involvement in schools stressing consensus, collaboration, and no-fault.

Scientific Literacy Understanding the meanings, foundations, current status, and problems of scientific phenomena.

Script A mental representation of an often-repeated event.

Second Signal System Words and other features of language that are used by humans to communicate and that can become conditioned stimuli.

Secondary Qualities Characteristics of objects (e.g., color, sound) that depend on individuals' senses and cognitions.

Secondary Reinforcement Process whereby a behavioral consequence (e.g., money) becomes reinforcing by being paired with a primary reinforcer (e.g., food).

Self-Actualization The desire for self-fulfillment or for becoming everything one is capable of becoming; the highest level in Maslow's hierarchy of needs.

Self-Concept One's collective self-perceptions that are formed through experiences with, and interpretations of, the environment and that are heavily influenced by reinforcements and evaluations by significant other persons.

Self-Confidence The extent that one believes one can produce results, accomplish goals, or perform tasks competently (analogous to *Self-Efficacy*).

Self-Determination Motive aimed at developing competence, which begins as undifferentiated but eventually differentiates into specific areas.

Self-Efficacy (Efficacy Expectations) Personal beliefs concerning one's capabilities to organize and implement actions necessary to learn or perform behaviors at designated levels.

Self-Esteem One's perceived sense of self-worth; whether one accepts and respects oneself.

Self-Evaluation Process involving self-judgments of current performance by comparing it to one's goal and self-reactions to these judgments by deeming performance noteworthy, unacceptable, and so forth.

Self-Evaluative Standards Standards people use to evaluate their performances.

Self-Instruction In a learning setting, discriminative stimuli that are produced by the individual and that set the occasion for responses leading to reinforcement.

Self-Instructional Training Instructional procedure that comprises cognitive modeling, overt guidance, overt self-guidance, faded overt self-guidance, and covert self-instruction.

Self-Judgment Comparing one's current performance level with one's goal.

Self-Modeling Changes in behaviors, thoughts, and affects that derive from observing one's own performances.

Self-Monitoring (-Observation, -Recording) Deliberate attention to some aspect of one's behavior, often accompanied by recording its frequency or intensity.

Self-Reaction Changes in one's beliefs and behaviors after judging performance against a goal.

Self-Regulation (Self-Regulated Learning) The process whereby students personally activate and sustain behaviors, cognitions, and affects that are systematically oriented toward the attainment of learning goals.

Self-Reinforcement The process whereby individuals, after performing a response, arrange to receive reinforcement that increases the likelihood of future responding.

Self-Reports People's judgments and statements about themselves.

Self-Schema Manifestation of enduring goals, aspirations, motives, and fears, which includes cognitive and affective evaluations of ability, volition, and personal agency.

Self-Worth Perceptions of one's value, grounded largely in beliefs about ability.

Semantic Memory Memory of general information and concepts available in the environment and not tied to a particular individual or context.

Sensorimotor Stage First of Piaget's stages of cognitive development, encompassing birth to roughly age 2.

Sensory Register State of information processing concerned with receiving inputs, holding them briefly in sensory form, and transferring them to working memory.

Serial Recall Recalling stimuli in the order in which they are presented.

Shaping Differential reinforcement of successive approximations to the desired rate or form of behavior.

Short-Term (Working) Memory (STM or WM) Information processing stage corresponding to awareness, or what one is conscious of at a given moment.

Simulation Real or imaginary situation that cannot be brought into a learning setting.

Situated Cognition (Learning) Idea that thinking is situated (located) in physical and social contexts.

Social Cognitive Theory Cognitive theory that emphasizes the role of the social environment in learning.

Social Comparison Process of comparing one's beliefs and behaviors with those of others.

Social Constructivism Constructivist perspective emphasizing the importance of the individual's social interactions in the acquisition of skills and knowledge.

Socially Mediated Learning Learning influenced by aspects of the sociocultural environment.

Socioeconomic Status (SES) Descriptive term denoting one's capital (resources, assets).

Specific Skill Skill applying only to certain domains (e.g., regrouping in subtraction).

Spinal Cord That part of the central nervous system that connects the brain to the rest of the body.

Spiral Curriculum Building on prior knowledge by presenting the same topics at increasing levels of complexity as students move through schooling.

Spontaneous Recovery Sudden recurrence of the conditioned response following presentation of the conditioned stimulus after a time lapse in which the conditioned stimulus is not presented.

Spreading Activation Activation in long-term memory of propositions that are associatively linked with material currently in one's working memory.

SQ3R Method (Survey-Question-Read-Recite (Recall)-Review) Method of studying text that stands for Survey-Question-Read-Recite-Review; modified to SQ4R with addition of Reflection.

Steroid A type of hormone that can affect various functions including sexual development and stress reactions.

Stimulated Recall Research procedure in which people work on a task and afterward recall their thoughts at various points; the procedure may include videotaping.

Stimulus-Response (S-R) Theory Learning theory emphasizing associations between stimuli and responses.

Strategy Value Information Information linking strategy use with improved performance.

Structural Theories of Development Theories positing that development consists of changes in mental structures.

Structuralism Doctrine postulating that the mind is composed of associations of ideas and that studying the complexities of the mind requires breaking associations into single ideas.

Successive Approximations See *Shaping.*

Sum Model Counting method in which one counts in the first addend and then the second one.

Surface Structure The speech and syntax of a language.

Syllogism Deductive reasoning problem that includes premises and a conclusion containing *all, no,* or *some.*

Symbolic Representation Representing knowledge with symbol systems (e.g., language, mathematical notation).

Synapse Point where axons and dendrites meet in the brain.

Synaptic Gap. Space between axons and dendrites into which neurotransmitters are released.

Synchronous Learning Real-time interactions.

Systematic Desensitization Therapeutic procedure used to extinguish fears by pairing threatening stimuli with cues for relaxation.

Tabula Rasa Native state of a learner (blank tablet).

TARGET Acronym representing classroom motivation variables: task, authority, recognition, grouping, evaluation, time.

Task Involvement Motivational state characterized by viewing learning as a goal and focusing on task demands rather than on oneself.

Technology The designs and environments that engage learners.

Template Matching Theory of perception postulating that people store templates (miniature copies of stimuli) in memory and compare these templates with environmental stimuli during perception.

Temporal Lobe Brain lobe responsible for processing auditory information.

Teratogen A foreign substance that can cause abnormalities in a developing embryo or fetus.

Thalamus Part of the brain that sends sensory inputs (except for smell) to the cortex.

Theory Scientifically acceptable set of principles offered to explain a phenomenon.

Think-Aloud Research procedure in which participants verbalize aloud their thoughts, actions, and feelings while performing a task.

Three-Term Contingency The basic operant model of conditioning: A discriminative stimulus sets the occasion for a response to be emitted, which is followed by a reinforcing stimulus.

Threshold Method of Behavioral Change Altering behavior by introducing the cue for the undesired response at a low level and gradually increasing its magnitude until it is presented at full strength.

Time Needed for Learning Amount of academically engaged time required by a student to learn a task.

Time-Out (From Reinforcement) Removal of an individual from a situation where reinforcement can be obtained.

Time-Sampling Measure Measure of how often a behavior occurs during an interval of a longer period.

Time Spent in Learning Amount of academically engaged time expended to learn.

Tools The objects, language, and social institutions of a culture.

Top-Down Processing Pattern recognition of stimuli that occurs by forming a meaningful representation of the context, developing expectations of what will occur, and comparing features of stimuli to expectations to confirm or disconfirm one's expectations.

Trace Decay Loss of a stimulus from the sensory register over time.

Transfer (Generalization) Application of skills or knowledge in new ways or situations.

Translation Aspect of writing involving putting one's ideas into print.

Triadic Reciprocality Reciprocal interactions (causal relations) among behaviors, environmental variables, and cognitions and other personal factors.

Trial and Error Learning by performing a response and experiencing the consequences.

Tuning Modification and refinement of schemata as they are used in various contexts.

Tutoring A situation in which one or more persons serve as the instructional agents for another, usually in a specific subject or for a particular purpose

Two-Store (Dual) Memory Model of Information Processing Conceptualization of memory as involving stages of processing and having two primary areas for storing information (short- and long-term memory).

Type R Behavior See *Operant Behavior.*

Type S Behavior See *Respondent Behavior.*

Unconditional Positive Regard Attitudes of worthiness and acceptance with no conditions attached.

Unconditioned Response (UCR) The response elicited by an unconditioned stimulus.

Unconditioned Stimulus (UCS) A stimulus that when presented elicits a natural response from the organism.

Undifferentiated Task Structure Class situation in which all students work on the same or similar tasks and instruction uses a small number of materials or methods.

Unidimensional Classroom Classroom having few activities that address a limited range of student abilities.

Unitary Theory Theory postulating that all information is represented in long-term memory in verbal codes.

Unlearning See *Forgetting*.

Utilization The use made of parsed sound patterns (e.g., store in memory, respond if a question, or seek additional information).

Utilization Deficiency Failure to use a strategy of which one is cognitively aware.

Value The perceived importance or usefulness of learning.

Verbal Behavior Vocal responses shaped and maintained by the actions of other persons.

Vicarious Learning Learning that occurs without overt performance, such as by observing live or symbolic models.

Video Deficit Poorer learning by young children from video compared with real-life experiences.

Virtual Reality Computer-based technology that incorporates input and output devices and that allows students to experience and interact with an artificial environment as if it were the real world.

Visual Cortex Occipital lobe of the brain.

Volition The act of using the will; the process of dealing with the implementation of actions to attain goals.

Volitional Style Stable individual differences in volition.

Wernicke's Area Brain part in the left hemisphere that is involved in speech comprehension and use of proper syntax when speaking.

Will That part of the mind that reflects one's desire, want, or purpose.

Worked Example Step-by-step problem solution that may include diagrams.

Working Backward Problem-solving strategy in which one starts with the goal and asks which subgoals are necessary to accomplish it, what is necessary to accomplish these subgoals, and so forth, until the beginning state is reached.

Working Forward Problem-solving strategy in which one starts with the beginning problem state and decides how to alter it to progress toward the goal.

Working Memory (WM) See *Short-Term Memory*.

Working Self-Concept Those self-schemas that are mentally active at any time; currently accessible self-knowledge.

Written Responses Performances on tests, quizzes, homework, term papers, reports, and computer documents.

X-Ray High frequency electromagnetic waves used to determine abnormalities in solid body structures.

Zero Transfer One type of learning has no obvious effect on subsequent learning.

Zone of Proximal Development (ZPD) The amount of learning possible by a student given the proper instructional conditions.

References

Abramson, L. Y., Seligman, M. E. P., & Teasdale, J. D. (1978). Learned helplessness in humans: Critique and reformulation. *Journal of Abnormal Psychology, 87*, 49–74.

Ackerman, S. (1992). *Discovering the brain*. Washington, DC: National Academy Press.

Adams, J. A. (1971). A closed-loop theory of motor learning. *Journal of Motor Behavior, 3*, 111–150.

Akamatsu, T. J., & Thelen, M. H. (1974). A review of the literature on observer characteristics and imitation. *Developmental Psychology, 10*, 38–47.

Alderman, M. K. (1985). Achievement motivation and the preservice teacher. In M. K. Alderman & M. W. Cohen (Eds.), *Motivation theory and practice for preservice teachers* (pp. 37–51). Washington, DC: ERIC Clearinghouse on Teacher Education.

Alderman, M. K. (1999). *Motivation for achievement: Possibilities for teaching and learning*. Mahwah, NJ: Erlbaum.

Alexander, J. E., Carr, M., & Schwanenflugel, P. J. (1995). Development of metacognition in gifted children: Directions for future research. *Developmental Review, 15*, 1–37.

Alexander, P. A., & Murphy, P. K. (1998). Profiling the differences in students' knowledge, interest, and strategic planning. *Journal of Educational Psychology, 90*, 435–447.

Altermatt, E. R., & Pomerantz, E. M. (2003). The development of competence-related and motivational beliefs: An investigation of similarity and influence among friends. *Journal of Educational Psychology, 95*, 1–13.

American Psychological Association (1992). Special issue: Reflections on B. F. Skinner and psychology. *American Psychologist, 47*, 1269–1533.

American Psychological Association Work Group of the Board of Educational Affairs (1997). *Learner-centered psychological principles*. Washington, DC: Author.

Ames, C. (1984). Competitive, cooperative, and individualistic goal structures: A cognitive-motivational analysis. In R. Ames & C. Ames (Eds.), *Research on motivation in education* (Vol. 1, pp. 177–208). New York: Academic Press.

Ames, C. (1985). Attributions and cognitions in motivation theory. In M. K. Alderman & M. W. Cohen (Eds.), *Motivation theory and practice for preservice teachers* (pp. 16–21). Washington, DC: ERIC Clearinghouse on Teacher Education.

Ames, C. (1987). The enhancement of student motivation. In M. L. Maehr & D. A. Kleiber (Eds.), Advances in motivation and achievement (Vol. 5, pp. 123–148). Greenwich, CT: JAI Press.

Ames, C. (1992a). Achievement goals and the classroom motivational climate. In D. H. Schunk & J. L. Meece (Eds.), *Student perceptions in the classroom* (pp. 327–348). Hillsdale, NJ: Erlbaum.

Ames, C. (1992b). Classrooms: Goals, structures, and student motivation. *Journal of Educational Psychology, 84*, 261–271.

Ames, C., & Archer, J. (1988). Achievement goals in the classroom: Student learning strategies and motivation processes. *Journal of Educational Psychology, 80*, 260–267.

Anand, P. G., & Ross, S. M. (1987). Using computer-assisted instruction to personalize arithmetic materials for elementary school children. *Journal of Educational Psychology, 79*, 72–78.

Anderman, E. M. (1998). The middle school experience: Effects on the math and science achievement of adolescents with LD. *Journal of Learning Disabilities, 31*, 128–138.

Anderman, E. M., Austin, C. C., & Johnson, D. M. (2002). The development of goal orientation. In A. Wigfield & J. S. Eccles (Eds.), *Development of achievement motivation* (pp. 197–220). San Diego: Academic Press.

Anderman, E. M., & Maehr, M. L. (1994). Motivation and schooling in the middle grades. *Review of Educational Research, 64*, 287–309.

Anderman, E. M., & Wolters, C. A. (2006). Goals, values, and affects: Influences on student motivation. In P. A. Alexander & P. H. Winne (Eds.), *Handbook of educational psychology* (2nd ed., pp. 369–389). Mahwah, NJ: Erlbaum.

Anderson, J. R. (1980). Concepts, propositions, and schemata: What are the cognitive units? In J. H. Flowers (Ed.), *Nebraska Symposium on Motivation, 1980* (Vol. 28, pp. 121–162). Lincoln, NE: University of Nebraska Press.

Anderson, J. R. (1982). Acquisition of cognitive skill. *Psychological Review, 89*, 369–406.

Anderson, J. R. (1983). A spreading activation theory of memory. *Journal of Verbal Learning and Verbal Behavior, 22*, 261–295.

Anderson, J. R. (1984). Spreading activation. In J. R. Anderson & S. M. Kosslyn (Eds.), *Tutorials in learning and memory: Essays in honor of Gordon Bower* (pp. 61–90). San Francisco: Freeman.

Anderson, J. R. (1990). *Cognitive psychology and its implications* (3rd ed.). New York: Freeman.

Anderson, J. R. (1993). Problem solving and learning. *American Psychologist, 48*, 35–44.

Anderson, J. R. (1996). ACT: A simple theory of complex cognition. *American Psychologist, 51*, 355–365.

Anderson, J. R. (2000). *Learning and memory: An integrated approach* (2nd ed.). New York: Wiley.Ander

Anderson, J. R., Bothell, D., Byrne, M. D., Douglass, S., Lebiere, C., & Qin, Y. (2004). An integrated theory of the mind. *Psychological Review, 111*, 1036–1060.

Anderson, J. R., Fincham, J. M., & Douglass, S. (1997). The role of examples and rules in the acquisition of a cognitive skill. *Journal of Experimental Psychology: Learning, Memory, and Cognition, 23*, 932–945.

Anderson, J. R., Reder, L. M., & Lebiere, C. (1996). Working memory: Activation limitations on retrieval. *Cognitive Psychology, 30*, 221–256.

Anderson, J. R., Reder, L. M., & Simon, H. A. (1996). Situated learning and education. *Educational Researcher, 25*(4), 5–11.

Anderson, L. W. (1976). An empirical investigation of individual differences in time to learn. *Journal of Educational Psychology, 68*, 226–233.

Anderson, L. W. (2003). Benjamin S. Bloom: His life, his works, and his legacy. In B. J. Zimmerman & D. H. Schunk

(Eds.), *Educational psychology: A century of contributions* (pp. 367–389). Mahwah, NJ: Erlbaum.

Anderson, R. C. (1982). Allocation of attention during reading. In A. Flammer & W. Kintsch (Eds.), *Discourse processing* (pp. 292–305). Amsterdam: North Holland Publishing Company.

Anderson, R. C., & Pichert, J. W. (1978). Recall of previously unrecallable information following a shift in perspective. *Journal of Verbal Learning and Verbal Behavior, 17,* 1–12.

Anderson, R. C., Reynolds, R. E., Schallert, D. L., & Goetz, T. E. (1977). Frameworks for comprehending discourse. *American Educational Research Journal, 14,* 367–381.

Andersson, U., & Lyxell, B. (2007). Working memory deficit in children with mathematical difficulties: A general or specific deficit? *Journal of Experimental Child Psychology, 96,* 197–228.

Andre, T. (1986). Problem solving and education. In G. D. Phye & T. Andre (Eds.), *Cognitive classroom learning: Understanding, thinking, and problem solving* (pp. 169–204). Orlando: Academic Press.

Andrews, G. R., & Debus, R. L. (1978). Persistence and the causal perception of failure: Modifying cognitive attributions. *Journal of Educational Psychology, 70,* 154–166.

Armstrong, D. G., & Savage, T. V. (2002). *Teaching in the secondary school: An introduction* (5th ed.). Upper Saddle River, NJ: Merrill/Prentice Hall.

Aronson, E. (1966). The psychology of insufficient justification: An analysis of some conflicting data. In S. Feldman (Ed.), *Cognitive consistency: Motivational antecedents and behavioral consequences* (pp. 109–133). New York: Academic Press.

Asher, J. W. (2003). The rise to prominence: Educational psychology 1920–1960. In B. J. Zimmerman & D. H. Schunk (Eds.), *Educational psychology: A century of contributions* (pp. 189–205). Mahwah, NJ: Erlbaum.

Ashton, P. T. (1985). Motivation and the teacher's sense of efficacy. In C. Ames & R. Ames (Eds.), *Research on motivation in education. Vol. 2: The classroom milieu* (pp. 141–171). Orlando: Academic Press.

Ashton, P. T., & Webb, R. B. (1986). *Making a difference: Teachers' sense of efficacy and student achievement.* New York: Longman.

Assor, A., & Connell, J. P. (1992). The validity of students' self-reports as measures of performance affecting self-appraisals. In D. H. Schunk & J. L. Meece (Eds.), *Student perceptions in the classroom* (pp. 25–47). Hillsdale, NJ: Erlbaum.

Atkinson, J. W. (1957). Motivational determinants of risk-taking behavior. *Psychological Review, 64,* 359–372.

Atkinson, J. W., & Birch, D. (1978). *Introduction to motivation* (2nd ed.). New York: D. Van Nostrand.

Atkinson, J. W., & Feather, N. T. (1966). *A theory of achievement motivation.* New York: Wiley.

Atkinson, J. W., & Raynor, J. O. (1974). *Motivation and achievement.* Washington, DC: Hemisphere.

Atkinson, J. W., & Raynor, J. O. (1978). *Personality, motivation, and achievement.* Washington, DC: Hemisphere.

Atkinson, R. C. (1975). Mnemotechnics in second-language learning. *American Psychologist, 30,* 828–921.

Atkinson, R. C., & Raugh, M. R. (1975). An application of the mnemonic keyword method to the acquisition of a Russian vocabulary. *Journal of Experimental Psychology: Human Learning and Memory, 104,* 126–133.

Atkinson, R. C., & Shiffrin, R. M. (1968). Human memory: A proposed system and its control processes. In K. W. Spence & J. T. Spence (Eds.), *The psychology of learning and motivation: Advances in research and theory* (Vol. 2, pp. 89–195). New York: Academic Press.

Atkinson, R. C., & Shiffrin, R. M. (1971). The control of short-term memory. *Scientific American, 225,* 82–90.

Atkinson, R. K., Derry, S. J., Renkl, A., & Wortham, D. (2000). Learning from examples: Instructional principles from the worked examples research. *Review of Educational Research, 70,* 181–214.

Atkinson, R. K., & Renkl, A. (2007). Interactive example-based learning environments: Using interactive elements to encourage effective processing of worked examples. *Educational Psychology Review, 19,* 375–386.Atkin

Atkinson, R. K., Renkl, A., & Merrill, M. M. (2003). Transitioning from studying examples to solving problems: Effects of self-explanation prompts and fading worked-out steps. *Journal of Educational Psychology, 95,* 774–783.

Austin, J. L. (1962). *How to do things with words.* Oxford, England: Oxford University Press.

Ausubel, D. P. (1963). *The psychology of meaningful verbal learning: An introduction to school learning.* New York: Grune & Stratton.

Ausubel, D. P. (1968). *Educational psychology: A cognitive view.* New York: Holt, Rinehart & Winston.

Ausubel, D. P. (1977). The facilitation of meaningful verbal learning in the classroom. *Educational Psychologist, 12,* 162–178.

Ausubel, D. P. (1978). In defense of advance organizers: A reply to the critics. *Review of Educational Research, 48,* 251–257.

Ausubel, D. P., & Robinson, F. G. (1969). *School learning: An introduction to educational psychology.* New York: Holt, Rinehart & Winston.

Ayllon, T., & Azrin, N. (1968). *The token economy: A motivational system for therapy and rehabilitation.* New York: Appleton-Century-Crofts.

Azevedo, R. (2005a). Computer environments as metacognitive tools for enhancing learning. *Educational Psychologist, 40,* 193–197.

Azevedo, R. (2005b). Using hypermedia as a metacognitive tool for enhancing student learning? The role of self-regulated learning. *Educational Psychologist, 40,* 199–209.

Azevedo, R., & Cromley, J. G. (2004). Does training on self-regulated learning facilitate students' learning with hypermedia? *Journal of Educational Psychology, 96,* 523–535.

Azevedo, R., Greene, J. A., & Moos, D. C. (2007). The effect of a human agent's external regulation upon college students' hypermedia learning. *Metacognition & Learning, 2,* 67–87.

Azevedo, R., Guthrie, J. T., & Seibert, D. (2004). The role of self-regulated learning in fostering students' conceptual understanding of complex systems with hypermedia. *Journal of Educational Computing Research, 30,* 85–109.

Baddeley, A. D. (1978). The trouble with levels: A reexamination of Craik and Lockhart's framework for memory research. *Psychological Review, 85,* 139–152.

Baddeley, A. D. (1992). Working memory. *Science, 255,* 556–559.

Baddeley, A. D. (1998). *Human memory: Theory and practice* (Rev. ed.). Boston: Allyn and Bacon.

Baddeley, A. D. (2001). Is working memory still working? *American Psychologist, 56,* 851–864.

Bailey, T. (1993). Can youth apprenticeship thrive in the United States? *Educational Researcher, 22*(3), 4–10.

Baker, L. (1989). Metacognition, comprehension monitoring, and the adult reader. *Educational Psychology Review, 1,* 3–38.

Baker, L., & Brown, A. L. (1984). Metacognitive skills and reading. In P. D. Pearson (Ed.), *Handbook of reading research* (pp. 353–394). New York: Longman.

Ball, D. L., Lubienski, S. T., & Mewborn, D. S. (2001). Mathematics. In V. Richardson (Ed.), *Handbook of research on teaching* (4th ed., pp. 433–456). Washington, DC: American Educational Research Association.

Bandura, A. (1969). *Principles of behavior modification.* New York: Holt, Rinehart & Winston.

Bandura, A. (1973). *Aggression: A social learning analysis.* Englewood Cliffs, NJ: Prentice Hall.

Bandura, A. (1977a). Self-efficacy: Toward a unifying theory of behavioral change. *Psychological Review, 84,* 191–215.

Bandura, A. (1977b). *Social learning theory.* Englewood Cliffs, NJ: Prentice Hall.

Bandura, A. (1981). Self-referent thought: A developmental analysis of self-efficacy. In J. H. Flavell & L. Ross (Eds.), *Social cognitive development: Frontiers and possible futures* (pp. 200–239). Cambridge, England: Cambridge University Press.

Bandura, A. (1982a). The self and mechanisms of agency. In J. Suls (Ed.), *Psychological perspectives on the self* (Vol. 1, pp. 3–39). Hillsdale, NJ: Erlbaum.

Bandura, A. (1982b). Self-efficacy mechanism in human agency. *American Psychologist, 37,* 122–147.

Bandura, A. (1986). *Social foundations of thought and action: A social cognitive theory.* Englewood Cliffs, NJ: Prentice Hall.

Bandura, A. (1988). Self-regulation of motivation and action through goal systems. In V. Hamilton, G. H. Bower, & N. H. Frijda (Eds.), *Cognitive perspectives on emotion and motivation* (pp. 37–61). Dordrecht, The Netherlands: Kluwer Academic Publishers.

Bandura, A. (1991). Self-regulation of motivation through anticipatory and self-reactive mechanisms. In R. A. Dienstbier (Ed.), *Nebraska Symposium on Motivation, 1990* (Vol. 38, 69–164). Lincoln, NE: University of Nebraska Press.

Bandura, A. (1993). Perceived self-efficacy in cognitive development and functioning. *Educational Psychologist, 28,* 117–148.

Bandura, A. (1994). Social cognitive theory and the exercise of control over HIV infection. In R. DiClemente & J. Peterson (Eds.), *Preventing AIDS: Theories and methods of behavioral interventions* (pp. 25–59). New York: Plenum.

Bandura, A. (1997). *Self-efficacy: The exercise of control.* New York: Freeman.

Bandura, A. (2001). Social cognitive theory: An agentic perspective. *Annual Review of Psychology, 52,* 1–26.

Bandura, A. (2005). The primacy of self-regulation in health promotion. *Applied Psychology: An International Review, 54,* 245–254.

Bandura, A., & Adams, N. E. (1977). Analysis of self-efficacy theory of behavioral change. *Cognitive Therapy and Research, 1,* 287–308.

Bandura, A., Adams, N. E., & Beyer, J. (1977). Cognitive processes mediating behavioral change. *Journal of Personality and Social Psychology, 35,* 125–139.

Bandura, A., Barbaranelli, C., Caprara, G. V., & Pastorelli, C. (1996). Multifaceted impact of self-efficacy beliefs on academic functioning. *Child Development, 67,* 1206–1222.

Bandura, A., Barbaranelli, C., Caprara, G. V., & Pastorelli, C. (2001). Self-efficacy beliefs as shapers of children's aspirations and career trajectories. *Child Development, 72,* 187–206.

Bandura, A., & Bussey, K. (2004). On broadening the cognitive, motivational, and sociostructural scope of theorizing about gender development and functioning: Comment on Martin, Ruble, and Szkrybalo (2002). *Psychological Bulletin, 130,* 691–701.

Bandura, A., & Cervone, D. (1983). Self-evaluative and self-efficacy mechanisms governing the motivational effects of goal systems. *Journal of Personality and Social Psychology, 45,* 1017–1028.

Bandura, A., & Cervone, D. (1986). Differential engagement of self-reactive influences in cognitive motivation. *Organizational Behavior and Human Decision Processes, 38,* 92–113.

Bandura, A., & Jeffery, R. W. (1973). Role of symbolic coding and rehearsal processes in observational learning. *Journal of Personality and Social Psychology, 26,* 122–130.

Bandura, A., & Kupers, C. J. (1964). Transmission of patterns of self-reinforcement through modeling. *Journal of Abnormal and Social Psychology, 69,* 1–9.

Bandura, A., Ross, D., & Ross, S. A. (1963). Imitation of film-mediated aggressive models. *Journal of Abnormal and Social Psychology, 66,* 3–11.

Bandura, A., & Schunk, D. H. (1981). Cultivating competence, self-efficacy, and intrinsic interest through proximal self-motivation. *Journal of Personality and Social Psychology, 41,* 586–598.

Bandura, A., & Walters, R. H. (1963). *Social learning and personality development.* New York: Holt, Rinehart & Winston.

Bangert, R. L., Kulik, J. A., & Kulik, C. C. (1983). Individualized systems of instruction in secondary schools. *Review of Educational Research, 53,* 143–158.

Bangert-Drowns, R. L., Hurley, M. M., & Wilkinson, B. (2004). The effects of school-based writing-to-learn interventions on academic achievement: A meta-analysis. *Review of Educational Research, 74,* 29–58.

Bargh, J. A., & Ferguson, M. J. (2000). Beyond behaviorism: On the automaticity of higher mental processes. *Psychological Bulletin, 126,* 925–945.

Barnett, S. M., & Ceci, S. J. (2002). When and where do we apply what we learn? A taxonomy for far transfer. *Psychological Bulletin, 128,* 612–637.

Bartlett, F. C. (1932). *Remembering: A study in experimental and social psychology.* Cambridge, England: Cambridge University Press.

Basden, B. H., Basden, D. R., Devecchio, E., & Anders, J. A. (1991). A developmental comparison of the effectiveness of encoding tasks. *Genetic, Social, and General Psychology Monographs, 117,* 419–436.

Baumrind, D. (1989). Rearing competent children. In W. Damon (Ed.), *Child development today and tomorrow* (pp. 349–378). San Francisco: Jossey-Bass.

Beal, C. R., & Belgrad, S. L. (1990). The development of message evaluation skills in young children. *Child Development, 61,* 705–712.

Beal, C. R., Garrod, A. C., & Bonitatibus, G. J. (1990). Fostering children's revision skills through training in comprehension monitoring. *Journal of Educational Psychology, 82,* 275–280.

Becker, W. C. (1971). *Parents are teachers: A child management program.* Champaign, IL: Research Press.

Begley, S. (2007, January 29). How the brain rewires itself. *Time, 169,* 72–74, 77, 79.

Belfiore, P. J., & Hornyak, R. S. (1998). Operant theory and application to self-monitoring in adolescents. In D. H. Schunk & B. J. Zimmerman (Eds.), *Self-regulated learning: From teaching to self-reflective practice* (pp. 184–202). New York: Guilford Press.

Bellini, S., & Akullian, J. (2007). A meta-analysis of video modeling and video self-modeling interventions for children and adolescents with autism spectrum disorders. *Exceptional Children, 73,* 264–287.

Belmont, J. M. (1989). Cognitive strategies and strategic learning: The socio-instructional approach. *American Psychologist, 44,* 142–148.

Bempechat, J., London, P., & Dweck, C. S. (1991). Children's conceptions of ability in major domains: An interview and experimental study. *Child Study Journal, 21,* 11–36.

Benight, C. C., & Bandura, A. (2004). Social cognitive theory of posttraumatic recovery: The role of perceived self-efficacy. *Behaviour Research and Therapy, 42,* 1129–1148.

Benjamin, L. T., Jr. (1988). A history of teaching machines. *American Psychologist, 43,* 703–712.

Benjamin, L. T., Jr. (2000). The psychological laboratory at the turn of the 20th century. *American Psychologist, 55,* 318–321.

Benjamin, L. T., Jr., Durkin, M., Link, M., Vestal, M., & Acord, J. (1992). Wundt's American doctoral students. *American Psychologist, 47,* 123–131.

Bereiter, C. (1980). Development in writing. In L. W. Gregg & E. R. Steinberg (Eds.), *Cognitive processes in writing* (pp. 73–93). Hillsdale, NJ: Erlbaum.

Bereiter, C. (1994). Constructivism, socioculturalism, and Popper's World 3. *Educational Researcher, 23*(7), 21–23.

Berk, L. E. (1986). Relationship of elementary school children's private speech to behavioral accompaniment to task, attention, and task performance. *Developmental Psychology, 22,* 671–680.

Berlyne, D. E. (1960). *Conflict, arousal, and curiosity.* New York: McGraw-Hill.

Berlyne, D. E. (1963). Motivational problems raised by exploratory and epistemic behavior. In S. Koch (Ed.), *Psychology: A study of a science* (Vol. 5, pp. 284–364). New York: McGraw-Hill.

Bernard, R. M., Abrami, P. C., Borokhovski, E., Wade, C. A., Tamim, R. M., Surkes, M. A., &

Bethel, E. C. (2009). A meta-analysis of three types of interaction treatments in distance education. *Review of Educational Research, 79,* 1243–1289.

Bernard, R. M., Abrami, P. C., Lou, Y., Borokhovski, E., Wade, A., Wozney, L., Wallet, P. A., Fiset, M., & Huang, B. (2004). How does distance education compare with classroom instruction? A meta-analysis of the empirical literature. *Review of Educational Research, 74,* 379–439.

Bernier, M., & Avard, J. (1986). Self-efficacy, outcome, and attrition in a weight-reduction program. *Cognitive Therapy and Research, 10,* 319–338.

Betz, N. E., & Hackett, G. (1981). The relationship of career-related self-efficacy expectations to perceived career options in college women and men. *Journal of Counseling Psychology, 28,* 399–410.

Betz, N. E., & Hackett, G. (1983). The relationship of mathematics self-efficacy expectations to the selection of science-based college majors. *Journal of Vocational Behavior, 23,* 329–345.

Bierman, K L., Domitrovich, C. E., Nix, R. L., Gest, S. D., Welsh, J. A., Greenberg, M. T., Blair, C., Nelson, K. E., & Gill, S. (2008). Promoting academic and social-emotional school readiness: The Head Start REDI Program. *Child Development, 79,* 1802–1817.

Binney, R., & Janson, M. (Eds.) (1990). *Atlas of the mind and body.* London: Mitchell Beazley Publishers.

Birnbaum, J. C. (1982). The reading and composing behaviors of selected fourth- and seventh-grade students. *Research in the Teaching of English, 16,* 241–260.

Black, J. B. (1984). Understanding and remembering stories. In J. R. Anderson & S. M. Kosslyn (Eds.), *Tutorials in learning and memory: Essays in honor of Gordon Bower* (pp. 235–255). San Francisco: Freeman.

Block, J. H., & Burns, R. B. (1977). Mastery learning. In L. S. Shulman (Ed.), *Review of research in education* (Vol. 4, pp. 3–49). Itasca, IL: Peacock.

Blok, H., Oostdam, R., Otter, M. E., & Overmaat, M. (2002). Computer-assisted instruction in support of beginning reading instruction: A review. *Review of Educational Research, 72,* 101–130.

Bloom, B. S. (1976). *Human characteristics and school learning.* New York: McGraw-Hill.

Bloom, B. S., Hastings, J. T., & Madaus, G. F. (1971). *Handbook on formative and summative evaluation of student learning.* New York: McGraw-Hill.

Blumenfeld, P. C. (1992). Classroom learning and motivation: Clarifying and expanding goal theory. *Journal of Educational Psychology, 84,* 272–281.

Boersma, F. J., & Chapman, J. W. (1981). Academic self-concept, achievement expectations, and locus of control in elementary learning-disabled children. *Canadian Journal of Behavioural Science, 13,* 349–358.

Bong, M., & Clark, R. (1999). Comparisons between self-concept and self-efficacy in academic motivation research. *Educational Psychologist, 34,* 139–154.

Borkowski, J. G. (1985). Signs of intelligence: Strategy generalization and metacognition. In S. Yussen (Ed.), *The growth of reflection in children* (pp. 105–144). New York: Academic Press.

Borkowski, J. G., & Cavanaugh, J. C. (1979). Maintenance and generalization of skills and strategies by the retarded. In N. R. Ellis (Ed.), *Handbook of mental deficiency, psychological theory and research* (2nd ed., pp. 569–617). Hillsdale, NJ: Erlbaum.

Borkowski, J. G., Johnston, M. B., & Reid, M. K. (1987). Metacognition, motivation, and controlled performance. In S. J. Ceci (Ed.), *Handbook of cognitive, social, and neuropsychological aspects of learning disabilities* (Vol. 2, pp. 147–173). Hillsdale, NJ: Erlbaum.

Borowsky, R., & Besner, D. (2006). Parallel distributed processing and lexical-semantic effects in visual word recognition: Are a few stages necessary? *Psychological Review, 113,* 181–195.

Bouffard-Bouchard, T., Parent, S., & Larivee, S. (1991). Influence of self-efficacy on self-regulation and performance among junior and senior high-school age students. *International Journal of Behavioral Development, 14*, 153–164.

Bourne, L. E., Jr. (1992). Cognitive psychology: A brief overview. *Psychological Science Agenda, 5*(5), 5, 20.

Bousfield, W. A. (1953). The occurrence of clustering in the recall of randomly arranged associates. *Journal of General Psychology, 49*, 229–240.

Bousfield, W. A., & Cohen, B. H. (1953). The effects of reinforcement on the occurrence of clustering in the recall of randomly arranged associates. *Journal of Psychology, 36*, 67–81.

Bouton, M. E., Nelson, J. B., & Rosas, J. M. (1999). Stimulus generalization, context change, and forgetting. *Psychological Bulletin, 125*, 171–186.

Bower, G. H., & Hilgard, E. R. (1981). *Theories of learning* (5th ed.). Englewood Cliffs, NJ: Prentice Hall.

Bower, G. H., & Morrow, D. G. (1990). Mental models in narrative comprehension. *Science, 247*, 44–48.

Bowers, J. S. (2009). On the biological plausibility of grandmother cells: Implications for neural network theories in psychology and neuroscience. *Psychological Review, 116*, 220–251.

Braaksma, M. A. H., Rijlaarsdam, G., & van den Bergh, H. (2002). Observational learning and the effects of model-observer similarity. *Journal of Educational Psychology, 94*, 405–415.

Bradford, H. F. (1998). Neurotransmitters and neuromodulators. In R. L. Gregory (Ed.), *The Oxford companion to the mind* (pp. 550–560). Oxford, England: Oxford University Press.

Bradley, R. H., & Corwyn, R. F. (2002). Socioeconomic status and child development. *Annual Review of Psychology, 53*, 371–399.

Brainerd, C. J. (2003). Jean Piaget, learning research, and American education. In B. J. Zimmerman & D. H. Schunk (Eds.), *Educational psychology: A century of contributions* (pp. 251–287). Mahwah, NJ: Erlbaum.

Bransford, J. D., & Johnson, M. K. (1972). Contextual prerequisites for understanding: Some investigations of comprehension and recall. *Journal of Verbal Learning and Verbal Behavior, 11*, 717–726.

Bransford, J. D., & Schwartz, D. L. (1999). Rethinking transfer: A simple proposal with multiple implications. In A. Iran-Nejad & P. D. Pearson (Eds.), *Review of research in education* (Vol. 24, pp. 61–100). Washington, DC: American Educational Research Association.

Bransford, J. D., & Stein, B. S. (1984). *The IDEAL problem solver: A guide for improving thinking, learning, and creativity.* New York: Freeman.

Bransford, J. D., Stein, B. S., Vye, N. J., Franks, J. J., Auble, P. M., Mezynski, K. J., & Perfetto, G. A. (1982). Differences in approaches to learning: An overview. *Journal of Experimental Psychology: General, 111*, 390–398.

Bredo, E. (1997). The social construction of learning. In G. Phye (Ed.), *Handbook of academic learning: The construction of knowledge* (pp. 3–45). New York: Academic Press.

Bredo, E. (2003). The development of Dewey's psychology. In B. J. Zimmerman & D. H. Schunk (Eds.), *Educational psychology: A century of contributions* (pp. 81–111). Mahwah, NJ: Erlbaum.

Bredo, E. (2006). Conceptual confusion and educational psychology. In P. A. Alexander & P. H. Winne (Eds.), *Handbook of educational psychology* (2nd ed., pp. 43–57). Mahwah, NJ: Erlbaum.

Brewer, W. F. (1974). There is no convincing evidence for operant or classical conditioning in adult humans. In W. B. Weimer & D. S. Palermo (Eds.), *Cognition and the symbolic processes* (pp. 1–42). Hillsdale, NJ: Erlbaum.

Brewer, W. F., & Treyens, J. C. (1981). Role of schemata in memory for places. *Cognitive Psychology, 13*, 207–230.

Brigham, T. A. (1982). Self-management: A radical behavioral perspective. In P. Karoly & F. H. Kanfer (Eds.), *Self-management and behavior change: From theory to practice* (pp. 32–59). New York: Pergamon.

Britton, B. K., & Tesser, A. (1991). Effects of time-management practices on college grades. *Journal of Educational Psychology, 83*, 405–410.

Broadbent, D. E. (1958). *Perception and communication.* London: Pergamon.

Broadhurst, P. L. (1957). Emotionality and the Yerkes-Dodson Law. *Journal of Experimental Psychology, 54*, 345–352.

Brody, G. H., & Stoneman, Z. (1985). Peer imitation: An examination of status and competence hypotheses. *Journal of Genetic Psychology, 146*, 161–170.

Brodzinsky, D. M. (1982). Relationship between cognitive style and cognitive development: A 2-year longitudinal study. *Developmental Psychology, 18*, 617–626.

Bronfenbrenner, U. (1979). *The ecology of human development: Experiments by nature and design.* Cambridge, MA: Harvard University Press.

Brooks, J. G., & Brooks, M. G. (1999). *In search of understanding: The case for constructivist classrooms.* Alexandria, VA: Association for Supervision and Curriculum Development.

Brophy, J. E. (1981). Teacher praise: A functional analysis. *Review of Educational Research, 51*, 5–32.

Brophy, J. E. (1985). Teacher-student interaction. In J. B. Dusek (Ed.), *Teacher expectancies* (pp. 303–328). Hillsdale, NJ: Erlbaum.

Brophy, J. E., & Good, T. L. (1974). *Teacher-student relationships: Causes and consequences.* New York: Holt, Rinehart & Winston.

Brown, A. L. (1980). Metacognitive development and reading. In R. J. Spiro, B. C. Bruce, & W. F. Brewer (Eds.), *Theoretical issues in reading comprehension* (pp. 453–481). Hillsdale, NJ: Erlbaum.

Brown, A. L., Palincsar, A. S., & Armbruster, B. B. (1984). Instructing comprehension-fostering activities in interactive learning situations. In H. Mandl, N. L. Stein, & T. Trabasso (Eds.), *Learning and comprehension of text* (pp. 255–286). Hillsdale, NJ: Erlbaum.

Brown, G. D. A., Neath, I., & Chater, N. (1007). A temporal ratio model of memory. *Psychological Review, 114*, 539–576.

Brown, I., Jr., & Inouye, D. K. (1978). Learned helplessness through modeling: The role of perceived similarity in competence. *Journal of Personality and Social Psychology, 36*, 900–908.

Brown, J. (1968). Reciprocal facilitation and impairment of free recall. *Psychonomic Science, 10*, 41–42.

Brown, J. S. (2006, September/October). New learning environments for the 21st century: Exploring the edge. *Change, 38*, 18–24.

Brown, J. S., & Burton, R. R. (1978). Diagnostic models for procedural bugs in basic mathematical skills. *Cognitive Science, 2*, 155–192.

Brown, S. C., & Craik, F. I. M. (2000). Encoding and retrieval of information. In E. Tulving & F. I. M. Craik (Eds.), *The Oxford handbook of memory* (pp. 93–108). New York: Oxford University Press.

Bruner, J. S. (1960). *The process of education*. New York: Vintage.

Bruner, J. S. (1961). The act of discovery. *Harvard Educational Review, 31*, 21–32.

Bruner, J. S. (1964). The course of cognitive growth. *American Psychologist, 19*, 1–15.

Bruner, J. S. (1966). *Toward a theory of instruction*. New York: Norton.

Bruner, J. S. (1984). Vygotsky's zone of proximal development: The hidden agenda. In B. Rogoff & J. V. Wertsch (Eds.), *Children's learning in the "zone of proximal development"* (pp. 93–97). San Francisco: Jossey-Bass.

Bruner, J. S. (1985). Models of the learner. *Educational Researcher, 14*(6), 5–8.

Bruner, J. S., Goodnow, J., & Austin, G. A. (1956). *A study of thinking*. New York: Wiley.

Bruner, J. S., Olver, R. R., & Greenfield, P. M. (1966). *Studies in cognitive growth*. New York: Wiley.

Bruning, R. H., & Horn, C. (2000). Developing motivation to write. *Educational Psychologist, 35*, 25–37.

Bruning, R. H., Schraw, G. J., Norby, M. M., & Ronning, R. R. (2004). *Cognitive psychology and instruction* (4th ed.). Upper Saddle River, NJ: Merrill/Prentice Hall.

Brunton, M. (2007, January 29). What do babies know? *Time, 169*, 94–95.

Bryan, J. H., & Bryan, T. H. (1983). The social life of the learning disabled youngster. In J. D. McKinney & L. Feagans (Eds.), *Current topics in learning disabilities* (Vol. 1, pp. 57–85). Norwood, NJ: Ablex.

Bryan, J. H., & Walbek, N. H. (1970). Preaching and practicing generosity: Children's actions and reactions. *Child Development, 41*, 329–353.

Bryan, T., Cosden, M., & Pearl, R. (1982). The effects of cooperative goal structures and cooperative models on LD and NLD students. *Learning Disability Quarterly, 5*, 415–421.

Butkowsky, I. S., & Willows, D. M. (1980). Cognitive-motivational characteristics of children varying in reading ability: Evidence for learned helplessness in poor readers. *Journal of Educational Psychology, 72*, 408–422.

Butler, D. L. (1998a). The strategic content learning approach to promoting self-regulated learning: A report of three studies. *Journal of Educational Psychology, 90*, 682–697.

Butler, D. L. (1998b). A strategic content learning approach to promoting self-regulated learning by students with learning disabilities. In D. H. Schunk & B. J. Zimmerman (Eds.), *Self-regulated learning: From teaching to self-reflective practice* (pp. 160–183). New York: Guilford Press.

Butler, R. (1992). What young people want to know when: Effects of mastery and ability goals on interest in different kinds of social comparisons. *Journal of Personality and Social Psychology, 62*, 934–943.

Butler, R. (1998). Age trends in the use of social and temporal comparison for self-evaluation: Examination of a novel developmental hypothesis. *Child Development, 69*, 1054–1073.

Byrnes, J. P. (1996). *Cognitive development and learning in instructional contexts*. Boston: Allyn and Bacon.

Byrnes, J. P. (2001). *Minds, brains, and learning: Understanding the psychological and educational relevance of neuroscientific research*. New York: Guilford Press.

Byrnes, J. P., & Fox, N. A. (1998). The educational relevance of research in cognitive neuroscience. *Educational Psychology Review, 10*, 297–342.

Calfee, R. (1981). Cognitive psychology and educational practice. In D. C. Berliner (Ed.), *Review of research in education* (Vol. 9, pp. 3–73). Washington, DC: American Educational Research Association.

Calfee, R., & Drum, P. (1986). Research on teaching reading. In M. C. Wittrock (Ed.), *Handbook of research on teaching* (3rd ed., pp. 804–849). New York: Macmillan.

Cameron, J., & Pierce, W. D. (1994). Reinforcement, reward, and intrinsic motivation: A meta-analysis. *Review of Educational Research, 64*, 363–423.

Cameron, J., & Pierce, W. D. (2002). *Rewards and intrinsic motivation: Resolving the controversy*. Westport, CT: Bergin & Garvey.

Campbell, F. A., Pungello, E. P., Miller-Johnson, S., Burchinal, M., & Ramey, C. T. (2001). The development of cognitive and academic abilities: Growth curves from an early childhood educational experiment. *Developmental Psychology, 37*, 231–242.

Campbell, G. (2006, September/October). Education, information technologies, and the augmentation of human intellect. *Change, 38*, 26–31.

Campione, J. C., Brown, A. L., Ferrara, R. A., & Bryant, N. R. (1984). The zone of proximal development: Implications for individual differences and learning. In B. Rogoff & J. V. Wertsch (Eds.), *Children's learning in the "zone of proximal development"* (pp. 77–91). San Francisco: Jossey-Bass.

Cantor, N., & Kihlstrom, J. F. (1987). *Personality and social intelligence*. Englewood Cliffs, NJ: Prentice Hall.

Caprara, G. V., Barbaranelli, C., Borgogni, L., & Steca, P. (2003). Efficacy beliefs as determinants of teachers' job satisfaction. *Journal of Educational Psychology, 95*, 821–832.

Caprara, G. V., Fida, R., Vecchione, M., Del Bove, G., Vecchio, G. M., Barbaranelli, C., & Bandura, A. (2008). Longitudinal analysis of the role of perceived self-efficacy for self-regulated learning in academic continuance and achievement. *Journal of Educational Psychology, 100*, 515–534.

Carlson, R., Chandler, P., & Sweller, J. (2003). Learning and understanding science instructional material. *Journal of Educational Psychology, 95*, 629–640.

Carney, R. N., & Levin, J. R. (2002). Pictorial illustrations *still* improve students' learning from text. *Educational Psychology Review, 14*, 5–26.

Carpenter, P. A., Miyake, A., & Just, M. A. (1995). Language comprehension: Sentence and discourse processing. *Annual Review of Psychology, 46*, 91–120.

Carroll, J. B. (1963). A model of school learning. *Teachers College Record, 64*, 723–733.

Carroll, J. B. (1965). School learning over the long haul. In J. D. Krumboltz (Ed.), *Learning and the educational process* (pp. 249–269). Chicago: Rand McNally.

Carroll, J. B. (1989). The Carroll model: A 25-year retrospective and prospective view. *Educational Researcher, 18*(1), 26–31.

Carroll, W. R., & Bandura, A. (1982). The role of visual monitoring in observational learning of action patterns: Making the unobservable observable. *Journal of Motor Behavior, 14*, 153–167.

Carver, C. S., & Scheier, M. F. (1990). Origins and functions of positive and negative affect: A control-process view. *Psychological Review, 97*, 19–35.

Carver, C. S., & Scheier, M. F. (1998). *On the self-regulation of behavior.* New York: Cambridge University Press.

Carver, C. S., & Scheier, M. F. (2000). On the structure of behavioral self-regulation. In M. Boekaerts, P. R. Pintrich, & M. Zeidner (Eds.), *Handbook of self-regulation* (pp. 41–84). San Diego: Academic Press.

Case, R. (1978a). A developmentally based theory and technology of instruction. *Review of Educational Research, 48,* 439–463.

Case, R. (1978b). Piaget and beyond: Toward a developmentally based theory and technology of instruction. In R. Glaser (Ed.), *Advances in instructional psychology* (Vol. 1, pp. 167–228). Hillsdale, NJ: Erlbaum.

Case, R. (1981). Intellectual development: A systematic reinterpretation. In F. H. Farley & N. J. Gordon (Eds.), *Psychology and education: The state of the union* (pp. 142–177). Berkeley, CA: McCutchan.

Case, R. (1993). Theories of learning and theories of development. *Educational Psychologist, 28,* 219–233.

Ceci, S. J. (1989). On domain specificity . . . More or less general and specific constraints on cognitive development. *Merrill-Palmer Quarterly, 35,* 131–142.

Cervone, D., Jiwani, N., & Wood, R. (1991). Goal setting and the differential influence of self-regulatory processes on complex decision-making performance. *Journal of Personality and Social Psychology, 61,* 257–266.

Chan, W., Lau, S., Nie, Y., Lim, S., & Hogan, D. (2008). Organizational and personal predictors of teacher commitment: The mediating role of teacher efficacy and identification with school. *American Educational Research Journal, 45,* 597–630.

Chapin, M., & Dyck, D. G. (1976). Persistence in children's reading behavior as a function of N length and attribution retraining. *Journal of Abnormal Psychology, 85,* 511–515.

Chapman, J. W. (1988). Learning disabled children's self-concepts. *Review of Educational Research,* 58, 347–371.

Chapman, J. W., & Tunmer, W. E. (1995). Development of young children's reading self-concepts: An examination of emerging subcomponents and their relationship with reading achievement. *Journal of Educational Psychology, 87,* 154–167.

Chartrand, T. L., & Bargh, J. A. (1999). The Chameleon Effect: The perception-behavior link and social interaction. *Journal of Personality and Social Psychology, 76,* 893–910.

Chen, P. P. (2003). Exploring the accuracy and predictability of the self-efficacy beliefs of seventh-grade mathematics students. *Learning and Individual Differences, 14,* 77–90.

Chen, Z. (1999). Schema induction in children's analogical problem solving. *Journal of Educational Psychology, 91,* 703–715.

Cherry, E. C. (1953). Some experiments on the recognition of speech with one and two ears. *Journal of the Acoustical Society of America, 25,* 975–979.

Chi, M. T. H., Bassok, M., Lewis, M. W., Reimann, P., & Glaser, R. (1989). Self-explanations: How students study and use examples in learning to solve problems. *Cognitive Science, 13,* 145–182.

Chi, M. T. H., Feltovich, P. J., & Glaser, R. (1981). Categorization and representation of physics problems by experts and novices. *Cognitive Science, 5,* 121–152.

Chi, M. T. H., & Glaser, R. (1985). Problem-solving ability. In R. J. Sternberg (Ed.), *Human abilities: An information-processing approach* (pp. 227–250). New York: Freeman.

Chi, M. T. H., Glaser, R., & Farr, M. J. (Eds.). (1988). *The nature of expertise.* Hillsdale, NJ: Erlbaum.

Chi, M. T. H., Glaser, R., & Rees, E. (1982). Expertise in problem solving. In R. J. Sternberg (Ed.), *Advances in the psychology of human intelligence* (Vol. 1, pp. 7–75). Hillsdale, NJ: Erlbaum.

Chiesi, H. L., Spilich, G. J., & Voss, J. R. (1979). Acquisition of domain-related information in relation to high and low domain knowledge. *Journal of Verbal Learning and Verbal Behavior, 18,* 257–274.

Childs, C. P., & Greenfield, P. M. (1981). Informal modes of learning and teaching: The case of Zincanteco weaving. In N. Warren (Ed.), *Studies in cross-cultural psychology* (Vol. 2, pp. 269–319). London: Academic Press.

Chinn, C. A., & Samarapungavan, A. (2009). Conceptual change—multiple routes, multiple mechanisms: A commentary on Ohlsson (2009). *Educational Psychologist, 44,* 48–57.

Chomsky, N. (1957). *Syntactic structures.* The Hague: Mouton.

Chomsky, N. (1959). Review of *Verbal Behavior* by B. F. Skinner. *Language, 35,* 26–58.

Clark, H. H., & Clark, E. V. (1977). *Psychology and language: An introduction to psycholinguistics.* New York: Harcourt Brace Jovanovich.

Clark, H. H., & Haviland, S. E. (1977). Psychological processes as linguistic explanation. In R. O. Freedle (Ed.), *Discourse production and comprehension* (pp. 1–40). Norwood, NJ: Ablex.

Clark, J. M., & Paivio, A. (1991). Dual coding theory and education. *Educational Psychology Review, 3,* 149–210.

Clark, K. (2008, January 21). New answers for e-learning. *U. S. News & World Report, 144,* 46, 48–50.

Clark, R. E., & Salomon, G. (1986). Media in teaching. In M. C. Wittrock (Ed.), *Handbook of research on teaching* (3rd ed., pp. 464–478). New York: Macmillan.

Cleary, T. J., Zimmerman, B. J., & Keating, T. (2006). Training physical education students to self-regulate during basketball free throw practice. *Research Quarterly for Exercise and sport, 77,* 251–262.

Clifford, R. M., Early, D. M., & Hill, T. (1999). About a million children in school before kindergarten. *Young Children, 54,* 48–51.

Coates, B., & Hartup, W. W. (1969). Age and verbalization in observational learning. *Developmental Psychology, 1,* 556–562.

Cobb, P. (1994). Where is the mind? Constructivist and sociocultural perspectives on mathematical development. *Educational Researcher, 23*(7), 13–20.

Cobb, P., & Bowers, J. (1999). Cognitive and situated learning perspectives in theory and practice. *Educational Researcher, 28*(2), 4–15,

Cofer, C. N., Bruce, D. R., & Reicher, G. M. (1966). Clustering in free recall as a function of certain methodological variations. *Journal of Experimental Psychology, 71,* 858–866.

Cohen, E. G. (1994). Restructuring the classroom: Conditions for productive small groups. *Review of Educational Research, 64,* 1–35.

Collins, A. (1977). Processes in acquiring knowledge. In R. C. Anderson, R. J. Spiro, & W. E. Montague (Eds.), *Schooling and the acquisition of knowledge* (pp. 339–363). Hillsdale, NJ: Erlbaum.

Collins, A., & Loftus, E. F. (1975). A spreading-activation theory of semantic processing. *Psychological Review, 82,* 407–428.

Collins, A., & Quillian, M. R. (1969). Retrieval time from semantic memory. *Journal of Verbal Learning and Verbal Behavior, 8,* 240–247.

Collins, A., & Stevens, A. L. (1983). A cognitive theory of inquiry teaching. In C. M. Reigeluth (Ed.), *Instructional-design theories and models: An overview of their current status* (pp. 247–278). Hillsdale, NJ: Erlbaum.

Collins, J. L. (1982, March). *Self-efficacy and ability in achievement behavior.* Paper presented at the annual meeting of the American Educational Research Association, New York.

Collins, W. A., Maccoby, E. E., Steinberg, L., Hetherington, E. M., & Bornstein, M. H. (2000). Contemporary research on parenting: The case for nature and nurture. *American Psychologist, 55,* 218–232.

Comer, J. P. (2001, April 23). Schools that develop children. *The American Prospect,* 30–35.

Comer, J. P., & Haynes, N. M. (1999). The dynamics of school change: Response to the article, "Comer's School Development Program in Prince George's County, Maryland: A theory-based evaluation," by Thomas D. Cook et al. *American Educational Research Journal, 36,* 599–607.

Cook, T. D., Habib, F., Phillips, M., Settersten, R. A., Shagle, S. C., & Degirmencioglu, S. M. (1999). Comer's School Development Program in Prince George's County, Maryland: A theory-based evaluation. *American Educational Research Journal, 36,* 543–597.

Cook, T. D., Murphy, R. F., & Hunt, H. D. (2000). Comer's School Development Program in Chicago: A theory-based evaluation. *American Educational Research Journal, 37,* 535–597.

Cooper, A. J. R., & Monk, A. (1976). Learning for recall and learning for recognition. In J. Brown (Ed.), *Recall and recognition* (pp. 131–156). London: Wiley.

Cooper, H. M., & Good, T. L. (1983). *Pygmalion grows up: Studies in the expectation communication process.* New York: Longman.

Cooper, H. M., Robinson, J. C., & Patall, E. A. (2006). Does homework improve academic achievement? A synthesis of research, 1987–2003. *Review of Educational Research, 76,* 1–62.

Cooper, H. M., & Tom, D. Y. H. (1984). Teacher expectation research: A review with implications for classroom instruction. *Elementary School Journal, 85,* 77–89.

Cooper, L. A., & Shepard, R. N. (1973). Chronometric studies of the rotation of mental images. In W. G. Chase (Ed.), *Visual information processing* (pp. 95–176). New York: Academic Press.

Cooper, R. P., & Shallice, T. (2006). Hierarchical schemas and goals in the control of sequential behavior. *Psychological Review, 113,* 887–916.

Cooper, W. H. (1983). An achievement motivation nomological network. *Journal of Personality and Social Psychology, 44,* 841–861.

Corballis, M. C. (2006). Language. In K. Pawlik & G. d'Ydewalle (Eds.), *Psychological concepts: An international historical perspective* (pp. 197–221). New York: Psychology Press.

Corno, L. (1989). Self-regulated learning: A volitional analysis. In B. J. Zimmerman & D. H. Schunk (Eds.), *Self-regulated learning and academic achievement: Theory, research, and practice* (pp. 111–142). New York: Springer-Verlag.

Corno, L. (1993). The best-laid plans: Modern conceptions of volition and educational research. *Educational Researcher, 22*(2), 14–22.

Corno, L. (1994). Student volition and education: Outcomes, influences, and practices. In D. H. Schunk & B. J. Zimmerman (Eds.), *Self-regulation of learning and performance: Issues and educational applications* (pp. 229–251). Hillsdale, NJ: Erlbaum.

Corno, L. (2001). Volitional aspects of self-regulated learning. In B. J. Zimmerman & D. H. Schunk (Eds.), *Self-regulated learning and academic achievement: Theoretical perspectives* (2nd ed., pp. 191–225). Mahwah, NJ: Erlbaum.

Corno, L. (2008). Work habits and self-regulated learning: Helping students to find a "will" from a "way." In D. H. Schunk & B. J. Zimmerman (Eds.), *Motivation and self-regulated learning: Theory, research, and applications* (pp. 197–222). New York: Taylor & Francis.

Corno, L., & Kanfer, R. (1993). The role of volition in learning and performance. In L. Darling-Hammond (Ed.), *Review of research in education* (Vol. 19, pp. 301–341). Washington, DC: American Educational Research Association.

Corno, L., & Mandinach, E. B. (2004). What we have learned about student engagement in the past twenty years. In D. M. McInerney & S. Van Etten (Eds.), *Big theories revisited* (pp. 299–328). Greenwich, CT: Information Age Publishing.

Corno, L., & Snow, R. E. (1986). Adapting teaching to individual differences among learners. In M. C. Wittrock (Ed.), *Handbook of research on teaching* (3rd ed., pp. 605–629). New York: Macmillan.

Courage, M. L., & Setliff, A. E. (2009). Debating the impact of television and video material on very young children: Attention, learning, and the developing brain. *Child Development Perspectives, 3,* 72–78.

Covey, S. R. (1989). *The seven habits of highly effective people: Restoring the character ethic.* New York: Simon and Schuster.

Covington, M. V. (1983). Motivated cognitions. In S. G. Paris, G. M. Olson, & H. W. Stevenson (Eds.), *Learning and motivation in the classroom* (pp. 139–164). Hillsdale, NJ: Erlbaum.

Covington, M. V. (1984). The self-worth theory of achievement motivation: Findings and implications. *Elementary School Journal, 85,* 5–20.

Covington, M. V. (1992). *Making the grade: A self-worth perspective on motivation and school reform.* Cambridge, England: Cambridge University Press.

Covington, M. V. (2004). Self-worth theory goes to college: Or do our motivation theories motivate? In D. M. McInerney & S. Van Etten (Eds.), *Big theories revisited* (pp. 91–114). Greenwich, CT: Information Age Publishing.

Covington, M. V. (2009). Self-worth theory: Retrospection and prospects. In K. R. Wentzel & A. Wigfield (Eds.), *Handbook of motivation at school* (pp. 141–169). New York: Routledge.

Covington, M. V., & Beery, R. G. (1976). *Self-worth and school learning.* New York: Holt, Rinehart & Winston.

Covington, M. V., & Dray, E. (2002). The developmental course of achievement motivation: A need-based approach. In A. Wigfield & J. S. Eccles (Eds.), *Development of achievement motivation* (pp. 33–56). San Diego: Academic Press.

Covington, M. V., & Omelich, C. L. (1979). Effort: The double-edged sword in school achievement. *Journal of Educational Psychology, 71,* 688–700.

Cowey, A. (1998). Localization of brain function and cortical maps. In R. L. Gregory (Ed.), *The Oxford companion to the mind* (pp. 436–438). Oxford, England: Oxford University Press.

Cox, B. D. (1997). The rediscovery of the active learner in adaptive contexts: A developmental-historical analysis of transfer of training. *Educational Psychologist, 32*, 41–55.

Craik, F. I. M. (1979). Human memory. *Annual Review of Psychology, 30*, 63–102.

Craik, F. I. M., & Lockhart, R. S. (1972). Levels of processing: A framework for memory research. *Journal of Verbal Learning and Verbal Behavior, 11*, 671–684.

Craik, F. I. M., & Tulving, E. (1975). Depth of processing and the retention of words in episodic memory. *Journal of Experimental Psychology: General, 104*, 268–294.

Crisafi, M. A., & Brown, A. L. (1986). Analogical transfer in very young children: Combining two separately learned solutions to reach a goal. *Child Development, 57*, 953–968.

Crouse, J. H. (1971). Retroactive interference in reading prose materials. *Journal of Educational Psychology, 52*, 39–44.

Crowley, K., & Siegler, R. S. (1999). Explanation and generalization in young children's strategy learning. *Child Development, 70*, 304–316.

Csikszentmihalyi, M. (1975). *Beyond boredom and anxiety.* San Francisco: Jossey-Bass.

Csikszentmihalyi, M., & Rathunde, K. (1993). The measurement of flow in everyday life: Toward a theory of emergent motivation. In J. E. Jacobs (Ed.), *Nebraska symposium on motivation 1992* (Vol. 40, pp. 57–97). Lincoln, NE: University of Nebraska Press.

Cummins, D. D., Kintsch, W., Reusser, K., & Weimer, R. (1988). The role of understanding in solving word problems. *Cognitive Psychology, 20*, 405–438.

Cuny, H. (1965). *Pavlov: The man and his theories* (P. Evans, Trans.). New York: Paul S. Eriksson.

Dansereau, D. F. (1978). The development of a learning strategies curriculum. In H. F. O'Neil, Jr. (Ed.), *Learning strategies* (pp. 1–29). New York: Academic Press.

Dansereau, D. F. (1988). Cooperative learning strategies. In C. E. Weinstein, E. T. Goetz, & P. A. Alexander (Eds.), *Learning and study strategies: Issues in assessment, instruction, and evaluation* (pp. 103–120). San Diego: Academic Press.

Dansereau, D. F., McDonald, B. A., Collins, K. W., Garland, J., Holley, C. D., Diekhoff, G. M., & Evans, S. H. (1979). Evaluation of a learning strategy system. In H. F. O'Neil, Jr., & C. D. Spielberger (Eds.), *Cognitive and affective learning strategies* (pp. 3–43). New York: Academic Press.

Darwin, C. J., Turvey, M. T., & Crowder, R. G. (1972). An auditory analogue of the Sperling partial report procedure: Evidence for brief auditory storage. *Cognitive Psychology, 3*, 255–267.

Daugherty, M., & White, C. S. (2008). Relationships among private speech and creativity in Head Start and low-socioeconomic status preschool children. *Gifted Child Quarterly, 52*, 30–39.

Davelaar, E. J., Goshen-Gottstein, Y., Ashkenazi, A., Haarmann, H. J., & Usher, M. (2005). The demise of short-term memory revisited: Empirical and computational investigations of recency effects. *Psychological Review, 112*, 3–42.

Davidson, E. S., & Benjamin, L. T., Jr. (1987). A history of the child study movement in America. In J. A. Glover & R. R. Ronning (Eds.), *Historical foundations of educational psychology* (pp. 41–60). New York: Plenum.

Davidson, E. S., & Smith, W. P. (1982). Imitation, social comparison, and self-reward. *Child Development, 53*, 928–932.

de Beaugrande, R. (1984). *Text production: Toward a science of composition.* Norwood, NJ: Ablex.

de Charms, R. (1968). *Personal causation: The internal affective determinants of behavior.* New York: Academic Press.

de Charms, R. (1976). *Enhancing motivation: Change in the classroom.* New York: Irvington.

de Charms, R. (1984). Motivation enhancement in educational settings. In R. Ames & C. Ames (Eds.), *Research on motivation in education* (Vol. 1, pp. 275–310). Orlando: Academic Press.

Deci, E. L. (1975). *Intrinsic motivation.* New York: Plenum.

Deci, E. L. (1980). *The psychology of self-determination.* Lexington, MA: D. C. Heath.

Deci, E. L., Koestner, R., & Ryan, R. M. (1999). A meta-analytic review of experiments examining the effects of extrinsic rewards on intrinsic motivation. *Psychological Bulletin, 125*, 627–668.

Deci, E. L., Koestner, R., & Ryan, R. M. (2001). Extrinsic rewards and intrinsic motivation in education: Reconsidered once again. *Review of Educational Research, 71*, 1–27.

Deci, E. L., & Moller, A. C. (2005). The concept of competence: A starting place for understanding intrinsic motivation and self-determined extrinsic motivation. In A. J. Elliot & C. S. Dweck (Eds.), *Handbook of competence and motivation* (pp. 579–597). New York: Guilford Press.

Deci, E. L., & Ryan, R. M. (1991). A motivational approach to self: Integration in personality. In R. A. Dienstbier (Ed.), *Nebraska symposium on motivation 1990* (Vol. 38, pp. 237–288). Lincoln, NE: University of Nebraska Press.

DeGrandpre, R. J. (2000). A science of meaning: Can behaviorism bring meaning to psychological science? *American Psychologist, 55*, 721–739.

de Jong, P. F. (1998). Working memory deficits of reading disabled children. *Journal of Experimental Child Psychology, 70*, 75–96.

de Jong, T., & van Joolingen, W. R. (1998). Scientific discovery learning with computer simulations of conceptual domains. *Review of Educational Research, 68*, 179–201.

De La Paz, S. (2005). Effects of historical reasoning instruction and writing strategy mastery in culturally and academically diverse middle school classrooms. *Journal of Educational Psychology, 97*, 139–156.

DeLeeuw, K. E., & Mayer, R. E. (2008). A comparison of three measures of cognitive load: Evidence for separable measures of intrinsic, extraneous, and germane load. *Journal of Educational Psychology, 100*, 223–234.

Dempster, F. N., & Corkill, A. J. (1999). Interference and inhibition in cognition and behavior: Unifying themes for educational psychology. *Educational Psychology Review, 11*, 1–88.

Denney, D. R. (1975). The effects of exemplary and cognitive models and self-rehearsal on children's interrogative strategies. *Journal of Experimental Child Psychology, 19*, 476–488.

Denney, N. W., & Turner, M. C. (1979). Facilitating cognitive performance in children: A comparison of strategy modeling and strategy modeling with overt self-verbalization. *Journal of Experimental Child Psychology, 28*, 119–131.

Dermitzaki, I. (2005). Preliminary investigation of relations between young students' self-regulatory strategies and their metacognitive experiences. *Psychological Reports, 97,* 759–768.

Derry, S. J. (1996). Cognitive schema theory in the constructivist debate. *Educational Psychologist, 31,* 163–174.

Dewey, J. (1896). The reflex arc concept in psychology. *Psychological Review, 3,* 357–370.

Dewey, J. (1900). Psychology and social practice. *Psychological Review, 7,* 105–124.

Dewsbury, D. A. (2000). Introduction: Snapshots of psychology circa 1900. *American Psychologist, 55,* 255–259.

Dick, W., & Carey, L. (1985). *The systematic design of instruction* (2nd ed.). Glenview, IL: Scott, Foresman.

DiClemente, C. C. (1981). Self-efficacy and smoking cessation maintenance: A preliminary report. *Cognitive Therapy and Research, 5,* 175–187.

DiClemente, C. C. (1986). Self-efficacy and the addictive behaviors. *Journal of Social and Clinical Psychology, 4,* 302–315.

DiClemente, C. C., Prochaska, J. O., & Gilbertini, M. (1985). Self-efficacy and the stages of self-change in smoking. *Cognitive Therapy and Research, 9,* 181–200.

Diener, C. I., & Dweck, C. S. (1978). An analysis of learned helplessness: Continuous changes in performance, strategy, and achievement cognitions following failure. *Journal of Personality and Social Psychology, 36,* 451–462.

Diener, C. I., & Dweck, C. S. (1980). An analysis of learned helplessness: II. The processing of success. *Journal of Personality and Social Psychology, 39,* 940–952.

Dillon, A., & Gabbard, R. (1998). Hypermedia as an educational technology: A review of the quantitative research literature on learner comprehension, control, and style. *Review of Educational Research, 68,* 322–349.

Dinsmore, D. L., Alexander, P. A., & Loughlin, S. M. (2008). Focusing the conceptual lens on metacognition, self-regulation, and self-regulated learning. *Educational Psychology Review, 20,* 391–409.

DiPardo, A., & Freedman, S. W. (1988). Peer response groups in the writing classroom: Theoretic foundations and new directions. *Review of Educational Research, 58,* 119–149.

Dowrick, P. W. (1983). Self-modelling. In P. W. Dowrick & S. J. Biggs (Eds.), *Using video: Psychological and social applications* (pp. 105–124). Chichester, England: Wiley.

Dowrick, P. W. (1999). A review of self modeling and related interventions. *Applied & Preventive Psychology, 8,* 23–39.

Dragoi, V., & Staddon, J. E. R. (1999). The dynamics of operant conditioning. *Psychological Review, 106,* 20–61.

Driver, R., Asoko, H., Leach, J., Mortimer, E., & Scott, P. (1994). Constructing scientific knowledge in the classroom. *Educational Researcher, 23*(7), 5–12.

Duchastel, P., & Brown, B. R. (1974). Incidental and relevant learning with instructional objectives. *Journal of Educational Psychology, 66,* 481–485.

Duda, J. L., & Nicholls, J. G. (1992). Dimensions of achievement motivation in schoolwork and sport. *Journal of Educational Psychology, 84,* 290–299.

Duell, O. K. (1986). Metacognitive skills. In G. D. Phye & T. Andre (Eds.), *Cognitive classroom learning: Understanding, thinking, and problem solving* (pp. 205–242). Orlando: Academic Press.

Duncan, R. M. (1995). Piaget and Vygotsky revisited: Dialogue or assimilation? *Developmental Review, 15,* 458–472.

Duncker, K. (1945). On problem-solving (L. S. Lees, Trans.). *Psychological Monographs, 58*(5, Whole No. 270).

Dunham, P. (1977). The nature of reinforcing stimuli. In W. K. Honig & J. E. R. Staddon (Eds.), *Handbook of operant behavior* (pp. 98–124). Englewood Cliffs, NJ: Prentice Hall.

Dunkin, M. J., & Biddle, B. J. (1974). *The study of teaching.* New York: Holt, Rinehart and Winston.

Dusek, J. B. (Ed.) (1985). *Teacher expectancies.* Hillsdale, NJ: Erlbaum.

Dweck, C. S. (1975). The role of expectations and attributions in the alleviation of learned helplessness. *Journal of Personality and Social Psychology, 31,* 674–685.

Dweck, C. S. (1986). Motivational processes affecting learning. *American Psychologist, 41,* 1040–1048.

Dweck, C. S. (1991). Self-theories and goals: Their role in motivation, personality, and development. In R. A. Dienstbier (Ed.), *Nebraska Symposium on Motivation, 1990* (Vol. 38, pp. 199–235). Lincoln, NE: University of Nebraska Press.

Dweck, C. S. (1999). *Self-theories: Their role in motivation, personality, and development.* Philadelphia: Taylor & Francis.

Dweck, C. S. (2002). The development of ability conceptions. In A. Wigfield & J. S. Eccles (Eds.), *Development of achievement motivation* (pp. 57–88). San Diego: Academic Press.

Dweck, C. S. (2006). *Mindset: The new psychology of success.* New York: Random House.

Dweck, C. S., & Bempechat, J. (1983). Children's theories of intelligence: Consequences for learning. In S. G. Paris, G. M. Olson, & H. W. Stevenson (Eds.), *Learning and motivation in the classroom* (pp. 239–256). Hillsdale, NJ: Erlbaum.

Dweck, C. S., & Leggett, E. L. (1988). A social-cognitive approach to motivation and personality. *Psychological Review, 95,* 256–273.

Dweck, C. S., & Master, A. (2008). Self-theories motivate self-regulated learning. In D. H. Schunk & B. J. Zimmerman (Eds.), *Motivation and self-regulated learning: Theory, research, and applications* (pp. 31–51). New York: Taylor & Francis.

Dweck, C. S., & Molden, D. C. (2005). Self-theories: Their impact on competence motivation and acquisition. In A. J. Elliot & C. S. Dweck (Eds.), *Handbook of competence and motivation* (pp. 122–140). New York: Guilford Press.

Dweck, C. S., & Repucci, N. D. (1973). Learned helplessness and reinforcement responsibility in children. *Journal of Personality and Social Psychology, 25,* 109–116.

Eccles, J. S. (1983). Expectancies, values, and academic behaviors. In J. T. Spence (Ed.), *Achievement and achievement motivation* (pp. 75–146). San Francisco: Freeman.

Eccles, J. S. (2005). Subjective task value and the Eccles et al. model of achievement-related choices. In A. J. Elliot & C. S. Dweck (Eds.), *Handbook of competence and motivation* (pp. 105–121). New York: Guilford Press.

Eccles, J. S., & Midgley, C. (1989). Stage-environment fit: Developmentally appropriate classrooms for young adolescents. In C. Ames & R. Ames (Eds.), *Research on motivation in education* (Vol. 3, pp. 139–186). San Diego: Academic Press.

Eccles, J. S., Midgley, C., & Adler, T. F. (1984). Grade-related changes in the school environment: Effects on achievement motivation. In J. Nicholls (Ed.), *Advances in motivation and achievement* (Vol. 3, pp. 283–311). Greenwich, CT: JAI Press.

Eccles, J. S., & Wigfield, A. (1985). Teacher expectations and student motivation. In J. B. Dusek (Ed.), *Teacher expectancies* (pp. 185–226). Hillsdale, NJ: Erlbaum.

Elkind, D. (2004). The problem with constructivism. *The Educational Forum, 68,* 306–312.

Elliot, A. J. (2005). A conceptual history of the achievement goal construct. In A. J. Elliot & C. S. Dweck (Eds.), *Handbook of competence and motivation* (pp. 52–72). New York: Guilford Press.

Elliot, A. J., & Church, M. A. (1997). A hierarchical model of approach and avoidance achievement motivation. *Journal of Personality and Social Psychology, 72,* 218–232.

Elliot, A. J., & Harackiewicz, J. M. (1996). Approach and avoidance achievement goals and intrinsic motivation: A mediational analysis. *Journal of Personality and Social Psychology, 70,* 461–475.

Elliot, A. J., & McGregor, H. A. A 2 ¥ 2 achievement goal framework. Journal of Personality and Social Psychology, 80, 501–519.

Elliot, A. J., & Thrash, T. M. (2001). Achievement goals and the hierarchical model of achievement motivation. *Educational Psychology Review, 13,* 139–156,

Elliott, E. S., & Dweck, C. S. (1988). Goals: An approach to motivation and achievement. *Journal of Personality and Social Psychology, 54,* 5–12.

Ellis, S., & Rogoff, B. (1982). The strategies and efficacy of child versus adult teachers. *Child Development, 53,* 730–735.

Elstein, A. S., Shulman, L. S., & Sprafka, S. A. (1978). *Medical problem solving.* Cambridge, MA: Harvard University Press.

Emmons, C. L., Comer, J. P., & Haynes, N. M. (1996). Translating theory into practice: Comer's theory of school reform. In J. P. Comer, N. M. Haynes, E. T. Joyner, & M. Ben-Avie (Eds.), *Rallying the whole village: The Comer process for reforming education* (pp. 27–41). New York: Teachers College Press.

Englert, C. S., Raphael, T. E., Anderson, L. M., Anthony, H. M., & Stevens, D. D. (1991). Making strategies and self-talk visible: Writing instruction in regular and special education classrooms. *American Educational Research Journal, 28,* 337–372.

Englund, M. M., Luckner, A. E., Whaley, G. J. L., & Egeland, B. (2004). Children's achievement in early elementary school: Longitudinal effects of parental involvement, expectations, and quality of assistance. *Journal of Educational Psychology, 96,* 723–730.

Ennemoser, M., & Schneider, W. (2007). Relations of television viewing and reading: Findings from a 4-year longitudinal study. *Journal of Educational Psychology, 99,* 349–368.

Ennis, R. H. (1987). A taxonomy of critical thinking dispositions and abilities. In J. B. Baron & R. J. Sternberg (Eds.), *Teaching thinking skills: Theory and practice* (pp. 9–26). New York: Freeman.

Epstein, J. L. (1989). Family structures and student motivation: A developmental perspective. In C. Ames & R. Ames (Eds.), *Research on motivation in education* (Vol. 3, pp. 259–295). San Diego: Academic Press.

Erickson, F. (1986). Qualitative methods in research on teaching. In M. C. Wittrock (Ed.), *Handbook of research on teaching* (3rd ed., pp. 119–161). New York: Macmillan.

Ericsson, K. A., & Charness, N. (1994). Expert performance: Its structure and acquisition. *American Psychologist, 49,* 725–747.

Ericsson, K. A., Krampe, R. T., & Tesch-Römer, C. (1993). The role of deliberate practice in the acquisition of expert performance. *Psychological Review, 100,* 363–406.

Erikson, E. (1963). *Childhood and society* (2nd ed.). New York: Norton.

Ertmer, P. A. (1999). Addressing first- and second-order barriers to change: Strategies for technology integration. *Educational Technology Research & Development, 47,* 47–61.

Ertmer, P. A., Driscoll, M. P., & Wager, W. W. (2003). The legacy of Robert Mills Gagné. In B. J. Zimmerman & D. H. Schunk (Eds.), *Educational psychology: A century of contributions* (pp. 303–330). Mahwah, NJ: Erlbaum.

Estes, W. K. (1970). *Learning theory and mental development.* New York: Academic Press.

Estes, W. K. (1997). Processes of memory loss, recovery, and distortion. *Psychological Review, 104,* 148–169.

Evans, R. B. (2000). Psychological instruments at the turn of the century. *American Psychologist, 55,* 322–325.

Evenson, D. H., Salisbury-Glennon, J. D., & Glenn, J. (2001). A qualitative study of six medical students in a problem-based curriculum: Toward a situated model of self-regulation. *Journal of Educational Psychology, 93,* 659–676.

Fabos, B., & Young, M. D. (1999). Telecommunication in the classroom: Rhetoric versus reality. *Review of Educational Research, 69,* 217–259.

Falmagne, R. J., & Gonsalves, J. (1995). Deductive inference. *Annual Review of Psychology, 46,* 525–559.

Fan, X., & Chen, M. (2001). Parental involvement and students' academic achievement: A meta-analysis. *Educational Psychology Review, 13,* 1–22.

Farnham-Diggory, S. (1992). *Cognitive processes in education* (2nd ed.). New York: HarperCollins.

Faw, H. W., & Waller, T. G. (1976). Mathemagenic behaviours and efficiency in learning from prose materials: Review, critique and recommendations. *Review of Educational Research, 46,* 691–720.

Feltz, D. L., Chase, M. A., Moritz, S. E., & Sullivan, P. J. (1999). A conceptual model of coaching efficacy: Preliminary investigation and instrument development. *Journal of Educational Psychology, 91,* 765–776.

Ferster, C. S., & Skinner, B. F. (1957). *Schedules of reinforcement.* New York: Appleton-Century-Crofts.

Festinger, L. (1954). A theory of social comparison processes. *Human Relations, 7,* 117–140.

Festinger, L. (1957). *A theory of cognitive dissonance.* Stanford, CA: Stanford University Press.

Fillmore, L. W., & Valadez, C. (1986). Teaching bilingual learners. In M. W. Wittrock (Ed.), *Handbook of research on teaching* (3rd ed., pp. 648–685). New York: Macmillan.

Fincham, F. D., & Cain, K. M. (1986). Learned helplessness in humans: A developmental analysis. *Developmental Review, 6,* 301–333.

Fischler, M. A., & Firschein, O. (1987). *Intelligence: The eye, the brain, and the computer.* Reading, MA: Addison-Wesley.

Fish, M. C., & Pervan, R. (1985). Self-instruction training: A potential tool for school psychologists. *Psychology in the Schools, 22,* 83–92.

Fitts, P. M., & Posner, M. I. (1967). *Human performance.* Belmont, CA: Brooks/Cole.

Fitzgerald, J. (1987). Research on revision in writing. *Review of Educational Research, 57,* 481–506.

Fitzgerald, J., & Markham, L. (1987). Teaching children about revision in writing. *Cognition and Instruction, 4,* 3–24.

Flavell, J. H. (1985). *Cognitive development* (2nd ed.). Englewood Cliffs, NJ: Prentice Hall.

Flavell, J. H. (1999). Cognitive development: Children's knowledge about the mind. *Annual Review of Psychology, 50,* 21–45.

Flavell, J. H., Beach, D. R., & Chinsky, J. M. (1966). Spontaneous verbal rehearsal in a memory task as a function of age. *Child Development, 37,* 283–299.

Flavell, J. H., Friedrichs, A. G., & Hoyt, J. D. (1970). Developmental changes in memorization processes. *Cognitive Psychology, 1,* 324–340.

Flavell, J. H., Green, F. L., & Flavell, E. R. (1995). Young children's knowledge about thinking. *Monographs of the Society for Research in Child Development, 60*(1) (Serial No. 243).

Flavell, J. H., & Wellman, H. M. (1977). Metamemory. In R. B. Kail, Jr., & J. W. Hagen (Eds.), *Perspectives on the development of memory and cognition* (pp. 3–33). Hillsdale, NJ: Erlbaum.

Floden, R. E. (2001). Research on effects of teaching: A continuing model for research on teaching. In V. Richardson (Ed.), *Handbook of research on teaching* (4th ed., pp. 3–16). Washington, DC: American Educational Research Association.

Flower, L., & Hayes, J. R. (1980). The dynamics of composing: Making plans and juggling constraints. In L. W. Gregg & E. R. Steinberg (Eds.), *Cognitive processes in writing* (pp. 31–50). Hillsdale, NJ: Erlbaum.

Flower, L., & Hayes, J. R. (1981a). A cognitive process theory of writing. *College Composition and Communication, 32,* 365–387.

Flower, L., & Hayes, J. R. (1981b). The pregnant pause: An inquiry into the nature of planning. *Research in the Teaching of English, 15,* 229–243.

FPG Child Development Institute. (2005). *Early developments. NCEDL pre-kindergarten study, 9(1).* Chapel Hill, NC: Author. Available online at: http://www.fpg.unc.edu/~ncdel.

Franks, J. J., & Bransford, J. D. (1971). Abstraction of visual patterns. *Journal of Experimental Psychology, 90,* 65–74.

Frauenglass, M. H., & Diaz, R. M. (1985). Self-regulatory functions of children's private speech: A critical analysis of recent challenges to Vygotsky's theory. *Developmental Psychology, 21,* 357–364.

Freud, S. (1966). *The complete introductory lectures on psychoanalysis* (J. Strachey, Trans.). New York: Norton.

Friedman, D. E., & Medway, F. J. (1987). Effects of varying performance sets and outcome on the expectations, attributions, and persistence of boys with learning disabilities. *Journal of Learning Disabilities, 20,* 312–316.

Friend, R., & Neale, J. (1972). Children's perceptions of success and failure: An attributional analysis of the effects of race and social class. *Developmental Psychology, 7,* 124–128.

Frieze, I. H. (1980). Beliefs about success and failure in the classroom. In J. H. McMillan (Ed.), *The social psychology of school learning* (pp. 39–78). New York: Academic Press.

Frieze, I. H., Francis, W. D., & Hanusa, B. H. (1983). Defining success in classroom settings. In J. M. Levine & M. C. Wang (Eds.), *Teacher and student perceptions: Implications for learning* (pp. 3–28). Hillsdale, NJ: Erlbaum.

Fryer, J. W., & Elliot, A. J. (2008). Self-regulation of achievement goal pursuit. In D. H. Schunk & B. J. Zimmerman (Eds.), *Motivation and self-regulated learning: Theory, research, and applications* (pp. 53–75). New York: Taylor & Francis.

Fuchs, D., Fuchs, L. S., Mathes, P. G., & Simmons, D. C. (1997). Peer-assisted learning strategies: Making classrooms more responsive to diversity. *American Educational Research Journal, 34,* 174–206.

Fuchs, L. S., Fuchs, D., Finelli, R., Courey, S. J., & Hamlett, C. L. (2004). Expanding schema-based transfer instruction to help third graders solve real-life mathematical problems. *American Educational Research Journal, 41,* 419–445.

Fuchs, L. S., Fuchs, D., Prentice, K., Burch, M., Hamlett, C. L., Owen, R., Hosp, M., & Jancek, D. (2003a). Explicitly teaching for transfer: Effects on third-grade students' mathematical problem solving. *Journal of Educational Psychology, 95,* 293–305.

Fuchs, L. S., Fuchs, D., Prentice, K., Burch, M., Hamlett, C. L., Owen, R., & Schroeter, K. (2003b). Enhancing third-grade students' mathematical problem solving with self-regulated learning strategies. *Journal of Educational Psychology, 95,* 306–315.

Furth, H. G. (1970). *Piaget for teachers.* Englewood Cliffs, NJ: Prentice Hall.

Fuson, K. C. (1979). The development of self-regulating aspects of speech: A review. In G. Zivin (Ed.), *The development of self-regulation through private speech* (pp. 135–217). New York: Wiley.

Fuson, K. C., & Willis, G. B. (1989). Second graders' use of schematic drawings in solving addition and subtraction word problems. *Journal of Educational Psychology, 81,* 514–520.

Gaa, J. P. (1973). Effects of individual goal-setting conferences on achievement, attitudes, and goal-setting behavior. *Journal of Experimental Education, 42,* 22–28.

Gaa, J. P. (1979). The effects of individual goal-setting conferences on academic achievement and modification of locus of control orientation. *Psychology in the Schools, 16,* 591–597.

Gage, N. L. (1978). *The scientific basis of the art of teaching.* New York: Teachers College Press.

Gagné, E. D., Yekovich, C. W., & Yekovich, F. R. (1993). *The cognitive psychology of school learning* (2nd ed.). New York: HarperCollins.

Gagné, R. M. (1984). Learning outcomes and their effects: Useful categories of human performance. *American Psychologist, 39,* 377–385.

Gagné, R. M. (1985). *The conditions of learning* (4th ed.). New York: Holt, Rinehart & Winston.

Gagné, R. M., & Briggs, L. J. (1979). *Principles of instructional design* (2nd ed.). New York: Holt, Rinehart & Winston.

Gagné, R. M., & Dick, W. (1983). Instructional psychology. *Annual Review of Psychology, 34,* 261–295.

Gagné, R. M., & Glaser, R. (1987). Foundations in learning research. In R. M. Gagné (Ed.), *Instructional technology: Foundations* (pp. 49–83). Hillsdale, NJ: Erlbaum.

Galbreath, J. (1992). The educational buzzword of the 1990's: Multimedia, or is it hypermedia, or interactive multimedia, or … ? *Educational Technology, 32*(4), 15–19.

Garcia, J., & Garcia y Robertson, R. (1985). Evolution of learning mechanisms. In B. L. Hammonds (Ed.), *Psychology and learning: Master lecture series* (Vol. 4, pp. 191–243). Washington, DC: American Psychological Association.

Garcia, J., & Koelling, R. A. (1966). Relation of cue to consequence in avoidance learning. *Psychonomic Science, 4,* 123–124.

Garcia, T., & Pintrich, P. R. (1994). Regulating motivation and cognition in the classroom: The role of self-schemas and self-regulatory strategies. In D. H. Schunk & B. J. Zimmerman (Eds.), *Self-regulation of learning and performance: Issues and educational applications* (pp. 127–153). Hillsdale, NJ: Erlbaum.

Gazzaniga, M., Bogen, J., & Sperry, R. (1962). Some functional effects of sectioning the cerebral commissures in man. *Proceedings of the National Academy of Science, USA, 48,* 1765–1769.

Gazzaniga, M., Ivry, R., & Mangun, R. (1998) *Cognitive neuroscience.* New York: Norton.

Geary, D. C. (1995). Reflections of evolution and culture in children's cognition: Implications for mathematical development and instruction. *American Psychologist, 50,* 24–37.

Geary, D. C., Hoard, M. K., Byrd-Craven, J., Nugent, L., & Numtee, C. (2007). Cognitive mechanisms underlying achievement deficits in children with mathematical learning disability. *Child Development, 78,* 1343–1359.

Gelman, R., & Gallistel, C. R. (1978). *The child's understanding of number.* Cambridge, MA: Harvard University Press.

Gentner, D., Loewenstein, J., & Thompson, L. (2003). Learning and transfer: A general role for analogical encoding. *Journal of Educational Psychology, 95,* 393–408.

George, T. R., Feltz, D. L., & Chase, M. A. (1992). Effects of model similarity on self-efficacy and muscular endurance: A second look. *Journal of Sport and Exercise Psychology, 14,* 237–248.

Gersten, R., Chard, D. J., Jayanthi, M., Baker, S. K., Morphy, P., & Flojo, J. (2009). Mathematics instruction for students with learning disabilities: A meta-analysis of instructional components. *Review of Educational Research, 79,* 1202–1242.

Geschwind, N. (1998). Language areas in the brain. In R. L. Gregory (Ed.), *The Oxford companion to the mind* (pp. 425–426). Oxford, England: Oxford University Press.

Gesell, A., & Ilg, F. (1946). *The child from five to ten.* New York: Harper Brothers.

Gesell, A., Ilg, F., & Ames, L. (1956). *Youth: The years from ten to sixteen.* New York: Harper Brothers.

Gibson, S., & Dembo, M. H. (1984). Teacher efficacy: A construct validation. *Journal of Educational Psychology, 76,* 569–582.

Gick, M. L., & Holyoak, K. J. (1980). Analogical problem solving. *Cognitive Psychology, 12,* 306–355.

Gick, M. L., & Holyoak, K. J. (1983). Schema induction and analogical transfer. *Cognitive Psychology, 15,* 1–38.

Ginsburg, H., & Opper, S. (1988). *Piaget's theory of intellectual development* (2nd ed.). Englewood Cliffs, NJ: Prentice Hall.

Ginsburg-Block, M. D., Rohrbeck, C. A., & Fantuzzo, J. W. (2006). A meta-analytic review of social, self-concept, and behavioral outcomes of peer-assisted learning. *Journal of Educational Psychology, 98,* 732–749.

Gitomer, D. H., & Glaser, R. (1987). If you don't know it work on it: Knowledge, self-regulation and instruction. In R. E. Snow & M. J. Farr (Eds.), *Aptitude, learning, and instruction* (Vol. 3, pp. 301–325). Hillsdale, NJ: Erlbaum.

Glaser, C., & Brunstein, J. C. (2007). Improving fourth-grade students' composition skills: Effects of strategy instruction and self-regulation procedures. *Journal of Educational Psychology, 99,* 297–310.

Glaser, R. (1990). The reemergence of learning theory within instructional research. *American Psychologist, 45,* 29–39.

Glaser, R., & Bassok, M. (1989). Learning theory and the study of instruction. *Annual Review of Psychology, 40,* 631–666.

Glasgow, K. L., Dornbusch, S. M., Troyer, L., Steinberg, L., & Ritter, P. L. (1997). Parenting styles, adolescents' attributions, and educational outcomes in nine heterogeneous high schools. *Child Development, 68,* 507–529.

Glass, D. C., & Singer, J. E. (1972). *Urban stress: Experiments on noise and social stressors.* New York: Academic Press.

Glover, J. A., Plake, B. S., Roberts, B., Zimmer, J. W., & Palmere, M. (1981). Distinctiveness of encoding: The effects of paraphrasing and drawing inferences on memory from prose. *Journal of Educational Psychology, 73,* 736–744.

Glover, J. A., Ronning, R. R., & Bruning, R. H. (1990). *Cognitive psychology for teachers.* New York: Macmillan.

Goble, F. G. (1970). *The third force: The psychology of Abraham Maslow.* New York: Grossman.

Goddard, R. D., Hoy, W. K., & Woolfolk Hoy, A. (2000). Collective teacher efficacy: Its meaning, measure, and impact on student achievement. *American Educational Research Journal, 37,* 479–507.

Goddard, R. D., Hoy, W. K., & Woolfolk Hoy, A. (2004). Collective efficacy beliefs: Theoretical developments, empirical evidence, and future directions. *Educational Researcher, 33*(3), 3–13.

Godden, D. R., & Baddeley, A. D. (1975). Context-dependent memory in two natural environments: On land and underwater. *British Journal of Psychology, 66,* 325–332.

Godding, P. R., & Glasgow, R. E. (1985). Self-efficacy and outcome expectations as predictors of controlled smoking status. *Cognitive Therapy and Research, 9,* 583–590.

Goldin-Meadow, S., Alibali, M. W., & Church, R. B. (1993). Transitions in concept acquisition: Using the hand to read the mind. *Psychological Review, 100,* 279–297.

Gollub, L. (1977). Conditioned reinforcement: Schedule effects. In W. K. Honig & J. E. R. Staddon (Eds.), *Handbook of operant behavior* (pp. 288–312). Englewood Cliffs, NJ: Prentice Hall.

Gonzalez-DeHass, A. R., Willems, P. P., & Doan Holbein, M. F. (2005). Examining the relationship between parental involvement and student motivation. *Educational Psychology Review, 17,* 99–123.

Good, T. L., & Brophy, J. E. (1984). *Looking in classrooms* (3rd ed.). New York: Harper & Row.

Gottfried, A. E. (1985). Academic intrinsic motivation in elementary and junior high school students. *Journal of Educational Psychology, 77,* 631–645.

Gottfried, A. E. (1990). Academic intrinsic motivation in young elementary school children. *Journal of Educational Psychology, 82,* 525–538.

Gottfried, A. E., Fleming, J. S., & Gottfried, A. W. (1998). Role of cognitively stimulating home environment in children's academic intrinsic motivation: A longitudinal study. *Child Development, 69,* 1448–1460.

Gould, D., & Weiss, M. (1981). The effects of model similarity and model talk on self-efficacy and muscular endurance. *Journal of Sport Psychology, 3,* 17–29.

Grabe, M. (1986). Attentional processes in education. In G. D. Phye & T. Andre (Eds.), *Cognitive classroom learning: Understanding, thinking, and problem solving* (pp. 49–82). Orlando: Academic Press.

Grabe, M., & Grabe, C. (1998). *Learning with Internet tools: A primer.* Boston: Houghton Mifflin.

Graham, S. (1991). A review of attribution theory in achievement contexts. *Educational Psychology Review, 3,* 5–39.

Graham, S. (1994). Motivation in African Americans. *Review of Educational Research, 64,* 55–117.

Graham, S. (2006). Writing. In P. A. Alexander & P. H. Winne (Eds.), *Handbook of educational psychology* (2nd ed., pp. 457–478). Mahwah, NJ: Erlbaum.

Graham, S., & Golan, S. (1991). Motivational influences on cognition: Task involvement, ego involvement, and depth of information processing. *Journal of Educational Psychology, 83,* 187–194.

Graham, S., & Harris, K. R. (2000). The role of self-regulation and transcription skills in writing and writing development. *Educational Psychologist, 35,* 3–12.

Graham, S., & Harris, K. R. (2003). Students with learning disabilities and the process of writing: A meta-analysis of SRSD studies. In H. L. Swanson, K. R. Harris, & S. Graham (Eds.), *Handbook of learning disabilities* (pp. 323–344). New York: Guilford Press.

Graham, S., Harris, K. R., MacArthur, C. A., & Schwartz, S. S. (1998). Writing instruction. In B. Y. L. Wong (Ed.), *Learning about learning disabilities* (2nd ed., pp. 391–424). New York: Academic Press.

Graham, S., & Hudley, C. (2005). Race and ethnicity in the study of motivation and competence. In A. J. Elliot & C. S. Dweck (Eds.), *Handbook of competence and motivation* (pp. 392–413). New York: Guilford Press.

Graham, S., & Long, A. (1986). Race, class, and the attributional process. *Journal of Educational Psychology, 78,* 4–13.

Graham, S., & Taylor, A. Z. (2002). Ethnicity, gender, and the development of achievement values. In A. Wigfield & J. S. Eccles (Eds.), *Development of achievement motivation* (pp. 121–146). San Diego: Academic Press.

Graham, S., & Williams, C. (2009). An attributional approach to motivation in school. In K. R. Wentzel & A. Wigfield (Eds.), *Handbook of motivation at school* (pp. 11–33). New York: Routledge.

Gray, C. R., & Gummerman, K. (1975). The enigmatic eidetic image: A critical examination of methods, data, and theories. *Psychological Bulletin, 82,* 383–407.

Gredler, M. E. (2009). Hiding in plain sight: The stages of mastery/self-regulation in Vygotsky's cultural-historical theory. *Educational Psychologist, 44,* 1–19.

Green, C. D. (2009). Darwinian theory, functionalism, and the first American psychological revolution. *American Psychologist, 64,* 75–83.

Greene, J. A., & Azevedo, R. (2007). A theoretical review of Winne and Hadwin's model of self-regulated learning: New perspectives and directions. *Review of Educational Research, 77,* 334–372.

Greene, J. A., & Azevedo, R. (2009). A macro-level analysis of SRL processes and their relations to the acquisition of a sophisticated mental model of a complex system. *Contemporary Educational Psychology, 34,* 18–29.

Greeno, J. G. (1980). Trends in the theory of knowledge for problem solving. In D. Tuma & F. Reif (Eds.), *Problem solving and education: Issues in teaching and research* (pp. 9–23). Hillsdale, NJ: Erlbaum.

Greeno, J. G. (1989). A perspective on thinking. *American Psychologist, 44,* 134–141.

Greeno, J. G., & the Middle School Mathematics Through Applications Project Group (1998). The situativity of knowing, learning, and research. *American Psychologist, 53,* 5–26.

Griffin, M. M. (1995). You can't get there from here: Situated learning, transfer, and map skills. *Contemporary Educational Psychology, 20,* 65–87.

Groen, G., & Parkman, J. M. (1972). A chronometric analysis of simple addition. *Psychological Review, 79,* 329–343.

Grolnick, W. S., Gurland, S. T., Jacob, K. F., & Decourcey, W. (2002). The development of self-determination in middle childhood and adolescence. In A. Wigfield & J. S. Eccles (Eds.), *Development of achievement motivation* (pp. 147–171). San Diego: Academic Press.

Grossen, B. (1991). The fundamental skills of higher order thinking. *Journal of Learning Disabilities, 24,* 343–353.

Gunnar, M. R. (1996). *Quality of care and buffering of stress physiology: Its potential for protecting the developing human brain.* Minneapolis: University of Minnesota Institute of Child Development.

Gupta, P., & Cohen, N. J. (2002). Theoretical and computational analysis of skill learning, repetition priming, and procedural memory. *Psychological Review, 109,* 401–448.

Guskey, T. R., & Passaro, P. D. (1994). Teacher efficacy: A study of construct dimensions. *American Educational Research Journal, 31,* 627–643.

Guthrie, E. R. (1930). Conditioning as a principle of learning. *Psychological Review, 37,* 412–428.

Guthrie, E. R. (1938). *The psychology of human conflict.* New York: Harper & Brothers.

Guthrie, E. R. (1940). Association and the law of effect. *Psychological Review, 47,* 127–148.

Guthrie, E. R. (1942). Conditioning: A theory of learning in terms of stimulus, response, and association. In N. B. Henry (Ed.), *The psychology of learning: The forty-first yearbook of the National Society for the Study of Education* (Part II, pp. 17–60). Chicago: University of Chicago Press.

Guthrie, E. R. (1952). *The psychology of learning* (Rev. ed.). New York: Harper & Brothers.

Guthrie, E. R. (1959). Association by contiguity. In S. Koch (Ed.), *Psychology: A study of a science* (Vol. 2, pp. 158–195). New York: McGraw-Hill.

Guthrie, E. R., & Horton, G. P. (1946). *Cats in a puzzle box.* New York: Rinehart & Company.

Guthrie, J. T., Wigfield, A., Barbosa, P., Perencevich, K. C., Taboada, A., Davis, M. H., Scafiddi, N. T., & Tonks. S. (2004). Increasing reading comprehension and engagement through concept-oriented reading instruction. *Journal of Educational Psychology, 96,* 403–423.

Guthrie, J. T., Wigfield, A., & Perencevich, K. C. (Eds.) (2004). *Motivating reading comprehension: Concept-oriented reading instruction.* Mahwah, NJ: Erlbaum.

Guthrie, J. T., Wigfield, A., & VonSecker, C. (2000). Effects of integrated instruction on motivation and strategy use in reading. *Journal of Educational Psychology, 92,* 331–341.

Hackett, G., & Betz, N. E. (1981). A self-efficacy approach to the career development of women. *Journal of Vocational Behavior, 18,* 326–339.

Halgren, E., & Marinkovic, K. (1995). Neurophysiological networks integrating human emotions. In M. S. Gazzaniga (Ed.),

The cognitive neurosciences (pp. 1137–1151). Cambridge, MA: MIT Press.

Hall, G. S. (1894). The new psychology as a basis of education. *The Forum, 17,* 710–720.

Hall, G. S. (1896). The case of the public schools. *Atlantic Monthly, 77,* 402–413.

Hall, G. S. (1900). Child study and its relation to education. *The Forum, 29,* 688–702.

Hall, G. S. (1903). Child study at Clark University. *American Journal of Psychology, 14,* 96–106.

Hall, V., Howe, A., Merkel, S., & Lederman, N. (1986). Behavior, motivation, and achievement in desegregated junior high school science classes. *Journal of Educational Psychology, 78,* 108–115.

Hall, V. C. (2003). Educational psychology from 1890 to 1920. In B. J. Zimmerman & D. H. Schunk (Eds.), *Educational psychology: A century of contributions* (pp. 3–39). Mahwah, NJ: Erlbaum.

Hallahan, D. P., Kneedler, R. D., & Lloyd, J. W. (1983). Cognitive behavior modification techniques for learning disabled children: Self-instruction and self-monitoring. In J. D. McKinney & L. Feagans (Eds.), *Current topics in learning disabilities* (Vol. 1, pp. 207–244). Norwood, NJ: Ablex.

Halliday, A. M. (1998). Evoked potential. In R. L. Gregory (Ed.), *The Oxford companion to the mind* (pp. 231–233). Oxford, England: Oxford University Press.

Halpern, D. F. (2006). Assessing gender gaps in learning and academic achievement. In P. A. Alexander & P. H. Winne (Eds.), *Handbook of educational psychology* (2nd ed., pp. 635–653). Mahwah, NJ: Erlbaum.

Halpern, D. F., & Hakel, M. D. (2003). Applying the science of learning to the university and beyond: Teaching for long-term retention and transfer. *Change, 35*(4), 36–41.

Halpern, D. F., Hansen, C., & Riefer, D. (1990). Analogies as an aid to understanding and memory. *Journal of Educational Psychology, 82,* 298–305.

Hamilton, R. J. (1985). A framework for the evaluation of the effectiveness of adjunct questions and objectives. *Review of Educational Research, 55,* 47–85.

Hancock, C. R. (2001). The teaching of second languages: Research trends. In V. Richardson (Ed.), *Handbook of research on teaching* (4th ed., pp. 358–369). Washington, DC: American Educational Research Association.

Hannafin, M. J., & Peck, K. L. (1988). *The design, development, and evaluation of instructional software.* New York: Macmillan.

Hannus, M., & Hyönä, J. (1999). Utilization of illustrations during learning of science textbook passages among low- and high-ability children. *Contemporary Educational Psychology, 24,* 95–123.

Harackiewicz, J. M., Barron, K. E., Tauer, J. M., Carter, S. M., & Elliot, A. J. (2000). Short-term and long-term consequences of achievement goals: Predicting interest and performance over time. *Journal of Educational Psychology, 92,* 316–330.

Harari, O., & Covington, M. V. (1981). Reactions to achievement behavior from a teacher and student perspective: A developmental analysis. *American Educational Research Journal, 18,* 15–28.

Hardiman, P. T., Dufresne, R., & Mestre, J. P. (1989). The relation between problem categorization and problem solving among experts and novices. *Memory & Cognition, 17,* 627–638.

Harlow, S., Cummings, R., & Aberasturi, S. M. (2006). Karl Popper and Jean Piaget: A rationale for constructivism. *The Educational Forum, 71,* 41–48.

Harris, B. (1979). Whatever happened to Little Albert? *American Psychologist, 34,* 151–160.

Harris, J. A. (2006). Elemental representations of stimuli in associative learning. *Psychological Review, 113,* 584–605.

Harris, J. R. (1998). *The nurture assumption: Why children turn out the way they do.* New York: Free Press.

Harris, K. R., & Graham, S. (1996). *Making the writing process work: Strategies for composition and self-regulation.* Cambridge, MA: Brookline Books.

Harris, K. R., Graham, S., & Mason, L. H. (2006). Improving the writing, knowledge, and motivation of struggling young writers: Effects of self-regulated strategy development with and without peer support. *American Educational Research Journal, 43,* 295–340.

Harris, K. R., & Pressley, M. (1991). The nature of cognitive strategy instruction: Interactive strategy construction. *Exceptional Children, 57,* 392–404.

Harter, S. (1978). Effectance motivation reconsidered: Toward a developmental model. *Human Development, 21,* 34–64.

Harter, S. (1981). A model of mastery motivation in children: Individual differences and developmental change. In W. A. Collins (Ed.), *Aspects on the development of competence: The Minnesota symposia on child psychology* (Vol. 14, pp. 215–255). Hillsdale, NJ: Erlbaum.

Harter, S., & Connell, J. P. (1984). A comparison of children's achievement and related self-perceptions of competence, control, and motivational orientation. In J. G. Nicholls (Ed.), *Advances in motivation and achievement* (Vol. 3, pp. 219–250). Greenwich, CT: JAI Press.

Hartley, E. T., Bray, M. A., & Kehle, T. J. (1998). Self-modeling as an intervention to increase student classroom participation. *Psychology in the Schools, 35,* 363–372.

Hattie, J. (1992). *Self-concept.* Hillsdale, NJ: Erlbaum.

Hattie, J., Biggs, J., & Purdie, N. (1996). Effects of learning skills interventions on student learning: A meta-analysis. *Review of Educational Research, 66,* 99–136.

Hattie, J., & Timperley, H. (2007). The power of feedback. *Review of Educational Research, 77,* 81–112.

Haviland, S. E., & Clark, H. H. (1974). What's new? Acquiring new information as a process in comprehension. *Journal of Verbal Learning and Verbal Behavior, 13,* 512–521.

Hayes, J. R. (1996). A new framework for understanding cognition and affect in writing. In C. M. Levy & S. Ransdell (Eds.), *The science of writing: Theories, methods, individual differences, and applications* (pp. 1–27). Mahwah, NJ: Erlbaum.

Hayes, J. R. (2000). A new framework for understanding cognition and affect in writing. In R. Indrisano & J. R. Squire (Eds.), *Perspectives on writing: Research, theory, and practice* (pp. 6–44). Newark, DE: International Reading Association.

Hayes, J. R., & Flower, L. (1980). Identifying the organization of writing processes. In L. W. Gregg & E. R. Steinberg (Eds.), *Cognitive processes in writing* (pp. 3–30). Hillsdale, NJ: Erlbaum.

Hayes-Roth, B., & Thorndyke, P. W. (1979). Integration of knowledge from text. *Journal of Verbal Learning and Verbal Behavior, 18,* 91–108.

Haynes, N. M., Emmons, C. L., Gebreyesus, S., & Ben-Avie, M. (1996). The School Development Program evaluation process. In J. P. Comer, N. M. Haynes, E. T. Joyner, & M. Ben-Avie (Eds.), *Rallying the whole village: The Comer process for reforming education* (pp. 123–146). New York: Teachers College Press.

Hebb, D. O. (1949). *The organization of behavior: A neuropsychological theory.* New York: Wiley.

Heckhausen, H. (1991). *Motivation and action.* Berlin: Springer-Verlag.

Hegarty, M., Mayer, R. E., & Monk, C. A. (1995). Comprehension of arithmetic word problems: A comparison of successful and unsuccessful problem solvers. *Journal of Educational Psychology, 87,* 18–32.

Heidbreder, E. (1933). *Seven psychologies.* New York: Appleton-Century-Crofts.

Heider, F. (1946). Attitudes and cognitive organization. *Journal of Psychology, 21,* 107–112.

Heider, F. (1958). *The psychology of interpersonal relations.* New York: Wiley.

Henderson, J. G. (1996). *Reflective teaching: The study of your constructivist practices* (2nd ed.). Englewood Cliffs, NJ: Merrill/Prentice Hall.

Henderson, R. W., & Cunningham, L. (1994). Creating interactive sociocultural environments for self-regulated learning. In D. H. Schunk & B. J. Zimmerman (Eds.), *Self-regulation of learning and performance: Issues and educational applications* (pp. 255–281). Hillsdale, NJ: Erlbaum.

Henson, R. K. (2002). From adolescent angst to adulthood: Substantive implications and measurement dilemmas in the development of teacher efficacy research. *Educational Psychologist, 37,* 137–150.

Hidi, S. E. (1995). A reexamination of the role of attention in learning from text. *Educational Psychology Review, 7,* 323–350.

Hidi, S. E., & Ainley, M. (2008). Interest and self-regulation: Relationships between two variables that influence learning. In D. H. Schunk & B. J. Zimmerman (Eds.), *Motivation and self-regulated learning: Theory, research, and applications* (pp. 77–109). New York: Taylor & Francis.

Higgins, E. T. (1981). Role taking and social judgment: Alternative developmental perspectives and processes. In J. H. Flavell & L. Ross (Eds.), *Social cognitive development: Frontiers and possible futures* (pp. 119–153). Cambridge, England: Cambridge University Press.

Highet, G. (1950). *The art of teaching.* New York: Vintage.

Hilgard, E. R. (1956). *Theories of learning* (2nd ed.). New York: Appleton-Century-Crofts.

Hilgard, E. R. (1996). Perspectives on educational psychology. *Educational Psychology Review, 8,* 419–431.

Hill, N. E., & Craft, S. A. (2003). Parent-school involvement and school performance: Mediated pathways among socioeconomically comparable African American and Euro-American families. *Journal of Educational Psychology, 95,* 74–83.

Hirsch, E. D., Jr. (1987). *Cultural literacy: What every American needs to know.* New York: Houghton Mifflin.

Hirt, E. R., Erickson, G. A., & McDonald, H. E. (1993). Role of expectancy timing and outcome consistency in expectancy-guided retrieval. *Journal of Personality and Social Psychology, 65,* 640–656.

Hitchcock, C. H., Dowrick, P. W., & Prater, M. A. (2003). Video self-modeling intervention in school-based settings. *Remedial and Special Education, 24,* 36–45, 56.

Hmelo-Silver, C. E. (2004). Problem-based learning: What and how do students learn? *Educational Psychology Review, 16,* 235–266.

Hofer, B. K., Yu, S. L., & Pintrich, P. R. (1998). Teaching college students to be self-regulated learners. In D. H. Schunk & B. J. Zimmerman (Eds.), *Self-regulated learning: From teaching to self-reflective practice* (pp. 57–85). New York: Guilford Press.

Hogan, D. M., & Tudge, J. R. H. (1999). Implications of Vygotsky's theory for peer learning. In A. M. O'Donnell & A. King (Eds.), *Cognitive perspectives on peer learning* (pp. 39–65). Mahwah, NJ: Erlbaum.

Holland, J. G. (1992). Obituary: B. F. Skinner (1904–1990). *American Psychologist, 47,* 665–667.

Holland, J. G., & Skinner, B. F. (1961). *The analysis of behavior.* New York: McGraw-Hill.

Holley, C. D., Dansereau, D. F., McDonald, B. A., Garland, J. C., & Collins, K. W. (1979). Evaluation of a hierarchical mapping technique as an aid to prose processing. *Contemporary Educational Psychology, 4,* 227–237.

Hollis, K. L. (1997). Contemporary research on Pavlovian conditioning: A "new" functional analysis. *American Psychologist, 52,* 956–965.

Holyoak, K. J. (1984). Mental models in problem solving. In J. R. Anderson & S. M. Kosslyn (Eds.), *Tutorials in learning and memory: Essays in honor of Gordon Bower* (pp. 193–218). San Francisco: Freeman.

Holyoak, K. J., & Thagard, P. (1997). The analogical mind. *American Psychologist, 52,* 35–44.

Hom, H. L., Jr., & Murphy, M. D. (1985). Low need achievers' performance: The positive impact of a self-determined goal. *Personality and Social Psychology Bulletin, 11,* 275–285.

Homme, L., Csanyi, A. P., Gonzales, M. A., & Rechs, J. R. (1970). *How to use contingency contracting in the classroom.* Champaign, IL: Research Press.

Hooper, S., & Hannafin, M. J. (1991). Psychological perspectives on emerging instructional technologies: A critical analysis. *Educational Psychologist, 26,* 69–95.

Hopkins, S. L., & Lawson, M. J. (2002). Explaining the acquisition of a complex skill: Methodological and theoretical considerations uncovered in the study of simple addition and the moving-on process. *Educational Psychology Review, 14,* 121–154.

Horner, S. L. (2004). Observational learning during shared book reading: The effects on preschoolers' attention to print and letter knowledge. *Reading Psychology, 25,* 1–22.

Horner, S. L., & Gaither, S. M. (2004). Attribution retraining instruction with a second-grade class. *Early Childhood Education Journal, 31,* 165–170.

Horowitz, F. D. (1992). John B. Watson's legacy: Learning and environment. *Developmental Psychology, 28,* 360–367.

Hosford, R. E. (1981). Self-as-a-model: A cognitive social learning technique. *The Counseling Psychologist, 9*(1), 45–62.

Hull, C. L. (1943). *Principles of behavior: An introduction to behavior theory.* New York: Appleton-Century-Crofts.

Humphrey, G. (1921). Imitation and the conditioned reflex. *Pedagogical Seminary, 28,* 1–21.

Hunt, E. (1989). Cognitive science: Definition, status, and questions. *Annual Review of Psychology, 40,* 603–629.

Hunt, J. McV. (1963). Motivation inherent in information processing and action. In O. J. Harvey (Ed.), *Motivation and social interaction* (pp. 35–94). New York: Ronald.

Hunt, M. (1993). *The story of psychology.* New York: Doubleday.

Hyslop-Margison, E. J., & Strobel, J. (2008). Constructivism and education: Misunderstandings and pedagogical implications. *The Teacher Educator, 43,* 72–86.

Isaksen, S. G., & Gaulin, J. P. (2005). A reexamination of brainstorming research: Implications for research and practice. *Gifted Child Quarterly, 49,* 315–329.

Jacoby, L. L., Bartz, W. H., & Evans, J. D. (1978). A functional approach to levels of processing. *Journal of Experimental Psychology: Human Learning and Memory, 4,* 331–346.

Jagacinski, C. M., & Nicholls, J. G. (1984). Conceptions of ability and related affects in task involvement and ego involvement. *Journal of Educational Psychology, 76,* 909–919.

Jagacinski, C. M., & Nicholls, J. G. (1987). Competence and affect in task involvement and ego involvement: The impact of social comparison information. *Journal of Educational Psychology, 79,* 107–114.

James, W. (1890). *The principles of psychology* (Vols. I & II). New York: Henry Holt.

James, W. (1892). *Psychology: Briefer course.* New York: Henry Holt.

Jensen, E. (2005). *Teaching with the brain in mind* (2nd ed.). Alexandria, VA: Association for Supervision and Curriculum Development.

Jitendra, A. K., Griffin, C. C., Haria. P., Leh, J., Adams, A., & Kaduvettoor, A. (2007). A comparison of single and multiple strategy instruction on third-grade students' mathematical problem solving. *Journal of Educational Psychology, 99,* 115–127.

Johnson, C. I., & Mayer, R. E. (2009). A testing effect with multimedia learning. *Journal of Educational Psychology, 101,* 621–629.

Johnson, D. S. (1981). Naturally acquired learned helplessness: The relationship of school failure to achievement behavior, attributions, and self-concept. *Journal of Educational Psychology, 73,* 174–180.

Johnson, W. B. (2006). *On being a mentor: A guide for higher education faculty.* Mahwah, NJ: Erlbaum.

Johnson-Laird, P. N. (1972). The three-term series problem. *Cognition, 1,* 57–82.

Johnson-Laird, P. N. (1985). Deductive reasoning ability. In R. J. Sternberg (Ed.), *Human abilities: An information-processing approach* (pp. 173–194). New York: Freeman.

Johnson-Laird, P. N. (1999). Deductive reasoning. *Annual Review of Psychology, 50,* 109–135.

Johnson-Laird, P. N., Byrne, R. M. J., & Schaeken, W. (1992). Propositional reasoning by model. *Psychological Review, 99,* 418–439.

Johnson-Laird, P. N., Byrne, R. M. J., & Tabossi, P. (1989). Reasoning by model: The case of multiple quantification. *Psychological Review, 96,* 658–673.

Jonassen, D. H. (1996). *Computers in the classroom: Mind tools for critical thinking.* Englewood Cliffs, NJ: Merrill/Prentice Hall.

Jonassen, D. H., & Hung, W. (2006). Learning to troubleshoot: A new theory-based design architecture. *Educational Psychology Review, 18,* 77–114.

Jonassen, D. H., Peck, K. L., & Wilson, B. G. (1999). *Learning with technology: A constructivist perspective.* Upper Saddle River, NJ: Merrill/Prentice Hall.

Jourden, F. J., Bandura, A., & Banfield, J. T. (1991). The impact of conceptions of ability on self-regulatory factors and motor skill acquisition. *Journal of Sport and Exercise Psychology, 8,* 213–226.

Jussim, L., Robustelli, S. L., & Cain, T. R. (2009). Teacher expectations and self-fulfilling prophecies. In K. R. Wentzel & A. Wigfield (Eds.), *Handbook of motivation at school* (pp. 349–380). New York: Routledge.

Just, M. A., & Carpenter, P. A. (1992). A capacity theory of comprehension: Individual differences in working memory. *Psychological Review, 99,* 122–149.

Justice, E. M., Baker-Ward, L., Gupta, S., & Jannings, L. R. (1997). Means to the goal of remembering: Developmental changes in awareness of strategy use-performance relations. *Journal of Experimental Child Psychology, 65,* 293–314.

Kagan, J. (1966). Reflection-impulsivity: The generality and dynamics of conceptual tempo. *Journal of Abnormal Psychology, 71,* 17–24.

Kagan, J., Moss, H. A., & Sigel, I. E. (1960). Conceptual style and the use of affect labels. *Merrill-Palmer Quarterly, 6,* 261–278.

Kagan, J., Pearson, L., & Welch, L. (1966). Modifiability of an impulsive tempo. *Journal of Educational Psychology, 57,* 359–365.

Kail, R. (2002), Developmental change in proactive interference. *Child Development, 73,* 1703–1714.

Kail, R. B., Jr., & Hagen, J. W. (1982). Memory in childhood. In B. B. Wolman (Ed.), *Handbook of developmental psychology* (pp. 350–366). Englewood Cliffs, NJ: Prentice Hall.

Kail, R. V., & Ferrer, E. (2007). Processing speed in childhood and adolescence: Longitudinal models for examining developmental change. *Child Development, 78,* 1760–1770.

Kanfer, F. H., & Gaelick, L. (1986). Self-management methods. In F. H. Kanfer & A. P. Goldstein (Eds.), *Helping people change: A textbook of methods* (3rd ed., pp. 283–345). New York: Pergamon.

Kanfer, R., & Ackerman, P. L. (1989). Motivation and cognitive abilities: An integrative/aptitude-treatment interaction approach to skill acquisition. *Journal of Applied Psychology, 74,* 657–690.

Kanfer, R., & Kanfer, F. H. (1991). Goals and self-regulation: Applications of theory to work settings. In M. L. Maehr & P. R. Pintrich (Eds.), *Advances in motivation and achievement* (Vol. 7, pp. 287–326). Greenwich, CT: JAI Press.

Kardash, C. A. M., Royer, J. M., & Greene, B. A. (1988). Effects of schemata on both encoding and retrieval of information from prose. *Journal of Educational Psychology, 80,* 324–329.

Karoly, P., & Harris, A. (1986). Operant methods. In F. H. Kanfer & A. P. Goldstein (Eds.), *Helping people change: A textbook of methods* (3rd ed., pp. 111–144). New York: Pergamon.

Karpov, Y. V., & Haywood, H. C. (1998). Two ways to elaborate Vygotsky's concept of mediation: Implications for instruction. *American Psychologist, 53,* 27–36.

Katona, G. (1940). *Organizing and memorizing.* New York: Columbia University Press.

Katzir, T., & Paré-Blagoev, J. (2006). Applying cognitive neuroscience research to education: The case of literacy. *Educational Psychologist, 41,* 53–74.

Keeney, T. J., Cannizzo, S. R., & Flavell, J. H. (1967). Spontaneous and induced verbal rehearsal in a recall task. *Child Development, 38,* 953–966.

Keeney-Benson, G. A., Pomerantz, E. M., Ryan, A. M., & Patrick, H. (2006). Sex differences in math performance: The role of children's approach to schoolwork. *Developmental Psychology, 42,* 11–26.

Keller, F. S., & Ribes-Inesta, E. (1974). *Behavior modification: Applications to education.* New York: Academic Press.

Kempermann, G., & Gage, F. (1999, May). New nerve cells for the adult brain. *Scientific American, 280*(6), 48–53.

Kerst, S. M., & Howard, J. H., Jr. (1977). Mental comparisons for ordered information on abstract and concrete dimensions. *Memory & Cognition, 5,* 227–234.

Kiewra, K. A., & Dubois, N. F. (1998). *Learning to learn: Making the transition from student to life-long learner.* Boston: Allyn & Bacon.

King, J., & Just, M. A. (1991). Individual differences in syntactic processing: The role of working memory. *Journal of Memory and Language, 30,* 580–602.

Kintsch, W. (1974). *The representation of meaning in memory.* Hillsdale, NJ: Erlbaum.

Kintsch, W. (1979). On modeling comprehension. *Educational Psychologist, 14,* 3–14.

Kintsch, W., & van Dijk, T. A. (1978). Toward a model of text comprehension and production. *Psychological Review, 85,* 363–394.

Kirkland, K., & Hollandsworth, J. G. (1980). Effective test taking: Skills-acquisition versus anxiety-reduction techniques. *Journal of Consulting and Clinical Psychology, 48,* 431–439.

Kirkorian, H. L., Wartella, E. A., & Anderson, D. R. (2008). Media and young children's learning. *The Future of Children, 18*(1), 39–61.

Kirschner, F., Paas, F., & Kirschner, P. A. (2009). A cognitive load approach to collaborative learning: United brains for complex tasks. *Educational Psychology Review, 21,* 31–42.

Kirschner, P. A., Sweller, J., & Clark, R. E. (2006). Why minimal guidance during instruction does not work: An analysis of the failure of constructivist, discovery, problem-based, experiential, and inquiry-based teaching. *Educational Psychologist, 41,* 75–86.

Kitsantas, A., & Zimmerman, B. J. (1998). Self-regulation of motoric learning: A strategic cycle view. *Journal of Applied Sport Psychology, 10,* 220–239.

Klahr, D., & Simon, H. A. (1999). Studies of scientific discovery: Complementary approaches and convergent findings. *Psychological Bulletin, 125,* 524–543.

Klassen, R. (2002). Writing in early adolescence: A review of the role of self-efficacy beliefs. *Educational Psychology Review, 14,* 173–203.

Klauda, S. L. (2009). The role of parents in adolescents' reading motivation and activity. *Educational Psychology Review, 21,* 325–363.

Klauer, K. J., & Phye, G. D. (2008). Inductive reasoning: A training approach. *Review of Educational Research, 78,* 85–123.

Klausmeier, H. J. (1990). Conceptualizing. In B. F. Jones & L. Idol (Eds.), *Dimensions of thinking and cognitive instruction* (pp. 93–138). Hillsdale, NJ: Erlbaum.

Klausmeier, H. J. (1992). Concept learning and concept teaching. *Educational Psychologist, 27,* 267–286.

Koffka, K. (1922). Perception: An introduction to the Gestalttheorie. *Psychological Bulletin, 19,* 531–585.

Koffka, K. (1924). *The growth of the mind* (R. M. Ogden, Trans.). London: Kegan Paul, Trench, Trubner.

Koffka, K. (1926). Mental development. In C. Murchison (Ed.), *Psychologies of 1925* (pp. 129–143). Worcester, MA: Clark University Press.

Köhler, W. (1925). *The mentality of apes* (E. Winter, Trans.). New York: Harcourt, Brace & World.

Köhler, W. (1926). An aspect of Gestalt psychology. In C. Murchinson (Ed.), *Psychologies of 1925* (pp. 163–195). Worcester, MA: Clark University Press.

Köhler, W. (1947). *Gestalt psychology: An introduction to new concepts in modern psychology.* New York: Liveright. (Reprinted 1959, New American Library, New York)

Kolodner, J. L. (1997). Educational implications of analogy: A view from case-based reasoning. *American Psychologist, 52,* 57–66.

Kopp, C. B. (1982). Antecedents of self-regulation: A developmental perspective. *Developmental Psychology, 18,* 199–214.

Kosiewicz, M. M., Hallahan, D. P., Lloyd, J., & Graves, A. W. (1982). Effects of self-instruction and self-correction procedures on handwriting performance. *Learning Disability Quarterly, 5,* 71–78.

Kosslyn, S. M. (1980). *Image and mind.* Cambridge, MA: Harvard University Press.

Kosslyn, S. M. (1984). Mental representation. In J. R. Anderson & S. M. Kosslyn (Eds.), *Tutorials in learning and memory: Essays in honor of Gordon Bower* (pp. 91–117). San Francisco: Freeman.

Kosslyn, S. M. (1988). Aspects of a cognitive neuroscience of mental imagery. *Science, 240,* 1621–1626.

Kosslyn, S. M., & Pomerantz, J. P. (1977). Imagery, propositions, and the form of internal representations. *Cognitive Psychology, 9,* 52–76.

Kovalchick, A., & Dawson, K. (Eds.) (2004a). *Education and technology: An encyclopedia* (Vol. 1). Santa Barbara, CA: ABC-CLIO.

Kovalchick, A., & Dawson, K. (Eds.) (2004b). *Education and technology: An encyclopedia* (Vol. 2). Santa Barbara, CA: ABC-CLIO.

Kozulin, A. (1986). The concept of activity in Soviet psychology: Vygotsky, his disciples and critics. *American Psychologist, 41,* 264–274.

Kramarski, B., & Mevarech, Z. R. (2003). Enhancing mathematical reasoning in the classroom: The effects of cooperative learning and metacognitive training. *American Educational Research Journal, 40,* 281–310.

Kubovy, M., & van den Berg, M. (2008). The whole is equal to the sum of its parts: A probabilistic model of grouping by proximity and similarity in regular patterns. *Psychological Review, 115,* 131–154.

Kuhl, J. (1984). Volitional aspects of achievement motivation and learned helplessness: Toward a comprehensive theory of action control. In B. A. Maher (Ed.), *Progress in experimental personality research* (Vol. 13, pp. 99–171). New York: Academic Press.

Kuhl, J. (1985). Volitional mediators of cognition-behavior consistency: Self-regulatory processes and action versus state orientation. In J. Kuhl & J. Beckmann (Eds.), *Action control: From cognition to behavior* (pp. 101–128). New York: Springer-Verlag.

Kuhl, J., & Blankenship, V. (1979a). Behavioral change in a constant environment: Shift to more difficult tasks with constant probability of success. *Journal of Personality and Social Psychology, 37,* 549–561.

Kuhl, J., & Blankenship, V. (1979b). The dynamic theory of achievement motivation: From episodic to dynamic thinking. *Psychological Review, 86,* 141–151.

Kuhn, D. (1999). A developmental model of critical thinking. *Educational Researcher, 28*(2), 16–25, 46.

Kulik, C. C., Kulik, J. A., & Bangert-Drowns, R. L. (1990). Effectiveness of mastery learning programs: A meta-analysis. *Review of Educational Research, 60,* 265–299.

Kulik, J. A., Kulik, C. C., & Cohen, P. A. (1980). Effectiveness of computer-based college teaching: A meta-analysis of findings. *Review of Educational Research, 50,* 525–544.

Lajoie, S. P. (2003). Transitions and trajectories for studies of expertise. *Educational Researcher, 32*(8), 21–25.

Lampert, M. (1990). When the problem is not the question and the solution is not the answer: Mathematical knowing and teaching. *American Educational Research Journal, 27,* 29–63.

Lan, W. Y. (1998). Teaching self-monitoring skills in statistics. In D. H. Schunk & B. J. Zimmerman (Eds.), *Self-regulated learning: From teaching to self-reflective practice* (pp. 86–105). New York: Guilford Press.

Lange, P. C. (1972). What's the score on: Programmed instruction? *Today's Education, 61,* 59.

Langer, J. A., & Applebee, A. N. (1986). Reading and writing instruction: Toward a theory of teaching and learning. In E. Z. Rothkopf (Ed.), *Review of research in education* (Vol. 13, pp. 171–194). Washington, DC: American Educational Research Association.

Larkin, J. H., McDermott, J., Simon, D. P., & Simon, H. A. (1980). Models of competence in solving physics problems. *Cognitive Science, 4,* 317–345.

Larrauri, J. A., & Schmajuk, N. A. (2008). Attentional, associative, and configural mechanisms in extinction. *Psychological Review, 115,* 640–676.

Larreamendy-Joerns, J., & Leinhardt, G. (2006). Going the distance with online education. *Review of Educational Research, 76,* 567–605.

Lattal, K. A. (1992). B. F. Skinner and psychology: Introduction to the special issue. *American Psychologist, 47,* 1269–1272.

Lauer, P. A., Akiba, M., Wilkerson, S. B., Apthorp, H. S., Snow, D., & Martin-Glenn, M. L. (2006). Out-of-school-time programs: A meta-analysis of effects for at-risk students. *Review of Educational Research, 76,* 275–313.

Lazar, I., Darlington, R., Murray, H., Royce, J., & Snipper, A. (1982). Lasting effects of early education: A report from the Consortium for Longitudinal Studies. *Monograph of the Society for Research in Child Development* (Serial no. 195).

Leask, J., Haber, R. N., & Haber, R. B. (1969). Eidetic imagery in children: II. Longitudinal and experimental results. *Psychonomic Monograph Supplement, 3* (3, Whole No. 35).

Lee, F. J., & Anderson, J. R. (2001). Does learning a complex task have to be complex? A study in learning decomposition. *Cognitive Psychology, 42,* 267–316.

Lee, J., & Bowen, N. K. (2006). Parent involvement, cultural capital, and the achievement gap among elementary school children. *American Educational Research Journal, 43,* 193–218.

Leeper, R. (1935). A study of a neglected portion of the field of learning—The development of sensory organization. *Pedagogical Seminary and Journal of Genetic Psychology, 46,* 41–75.

Lefcourt, H. M. (1976). *Locus of control: Current trends in theory and research.* Hillsdale, NJ: Erlbaum.

Lemonick, M. D. (2003, February 17). A twist of fate. *Time, 161,* 48–58.

Lemonick, M. D. (2007, January 29). The flavor of memories. *Time, 169,* 102–104.

Lemonick, M. D., & Dorfman, A. (2006, October 9). What makes us different? *Time, 168,* 44–50, 53.

Lent, R. W., Brown, S. D., & Hackett, G. (2000). Contextual supports and barriers to career choice: A social cognitive analysis. *Journal of Counseling Psychology, 47,* 36–49.

Lepper, M. R. (1983). Extrinsic reward and intrinsic motivation: Implications for the classroom. In J. M. Levine & M. C. Wang (Eds.), *Teacher and student perceptions: Implications for learning* (pp. 281–317). Hillsdale, NJ: Erlbaum.

Lepper, M. R. (1985). Microcomputers in education: Motivational and social issues. *American Psychologist, 40,* 1–18.

Lepper, M. R., Corpus, J. H., & Iyengar, S. S. (2005). Intrinsic and extrinsic motivational orientations in the classroom: Age differences and academic correlates. *Journal of Educational Psychology, 97,* 184–196.

Lepper, M. R., & Greene, D. (1978). Overjustification research and beyond: Toward a means-ends analysis of intrinsic and extrinsic motivation. In M. R. Lepper & D. Greene (Eds.), *The hidden costs of reward: New perspectives on the psychology of human motivation* (pp. 109–148). Hillsdale, NJ: Erlbaum.

Lepper, M. R., Greene, D., & Nisbett, R. E. (1973). Undermining children's intrinsic interest with extrinsic rewards: A test of the "overjustification" hypothesis. *Journal of Personality and Social Psychology, 28,* 129–137.

Lepper, M. R., & Gurtner, J. (1989). Children and computers: Approaching the twenty-first century. *American Psychologist, 44,* 170–178.

Lepper, M. R., Henderlong, J., & Gingras, I. (1999). Understanding the effects of extrinsic rewards on intrinsic motivation—uses and abuses of meta-analysis: Comment on Deci, Koestner, and Ryan (1999). *Psychological Bulletin, 125,* 669–676.

Lepper, M. R., & Hodell, M. (1989). Intrinsic motivation in the classroom. In C. Ames & R. Ames (Eds.), *Research on motivation in education* (Vol. 3, pp. 73–105). San Diego: Academic Press.

Lepper, M. R., & Malone, T. W. (1987). Intrinsic motivation and instructional effectiveness in computer-based education. In R. E. Snow & M. J. Farr (Eds.), *Aptitude, learning, and instruction: Cognitive and affective process analysis* (Vol. 3, pp. 255–286). Hillsdale, NJ: Erlbaum.

Lepper, M. R., Sethi, S., Dialdin, D., & Drake, M. (1997). Intrinsic and extrinsic motivation: A developmental perspective. In S. S. Luthar, J. A. Burack, D. Cicchetti, & J. R. Weisz (Eds.), *Developmental psychopathology: Perspectives on adjustment, risk, and disorder* (pp. 23–50). New York: Cambridge University Press.

Lesgold, A. M. (1984). Acquiring expertise. In J. R. Anderson & S. M. Kosslyn (Eds.), *Tutorials in learning and memory: Essays in honor of Gordon Bower* (pp. 31–60). San Francisco: Freeman.

Lesgold, A.M. (2001). The nature and methods of learning by doing. *American Psychologist, 56,* 964–973.

Lewin, K., Lippitt, R., & White, R. K. (1939). Patterns of aggressive behavior in experimentally created "social climates." *Journal of Social Psychology, 10,* 271–299.

Licht, B. G., & Kistner, J. A. (1986). Motivational problems of learning-disabled children: Individual differences and their implications for treatment. In J. K. Torgesen & B. W. L. Wong (Eds.), *Psychological and educational perspectives on learning disabilities* (pp. 225–255). Orlando: Academic Press.

Linn, M. C., & Eylon, B. (2006). Science education: Integrating views of learning and instruction. In P. A. Alexander & P. H. Winne (Eds.), *Handbook of educational psychology* (2nd ed., pp. 511–544). Mahwah, NJ: Erlbaum.

Linnenbrink, E. A., & Pintrich, P. R. (2002). Achievement goal theory and affect: An asymmetrical bi-directional model. *Educational Psychologist, 37*, 69–78.

Lirgg, C. D., & Feltz, D. L. (1991). Teacher versus peer models revisited: Effects on motor performance and self-efficacy. *Research Quarterly for Exercise and Sport, 62*, 217–224.

Littleton, K., Light, P., Joiner, R., Messer, D., & Barnes, P. (1998). Gender, task scenarios and children's computer-based problem solving. *Educational Psychology, 18*, 327–338.

Locke, E. A., Frederick, E., Lee, C., & Bobko, P. (1984). Effect of self-efficacy, goals, and task strategies on task performance. *Journal of Applied Psychology, 69*, 241–251.

Locke, E. A., & Latham, G. P. (1990). *A theory of goal setting and task performance.* Englewood Cliffs, NJ: Prentice Hall.

Locke, E. A., & Latham, G. P. (2002). Building a practically useful theory of goal setting and task motivation: A 35-year odyssey. *American Psychologist, 57*, 705–717.

Locke, E. A., Shaw, K. N., Saari, L. M., & Latham, G. P. (1981). Goal setting and task performance: 1969–1980. *Psychological Bulletin, 90*, 125–152.

Lockhart, R. S., Craik, F. I. M., & Jacoby, L. (1976). Depth of processing, recognition and recall. In J. Brown (Ed.), *Recall and recognition* (pp. 75–102). London: Wiley.

Logan, G. D. (2002). An instance theory of attention and memory. *Psychological Review, 109*, 376–400.

Lovaas, O. I. (1977). *The autistic child: Language development through behavior modification.* New York: Irvington.

Love, S. Q. (1983). *Prediction of bulimic behaviors: A social learning analysis.* Unpublished doctoral dissertation, Virginia Polytechnic Institute and State University.

Luchins, A. S. (1942). Mechanization in problem solving: The effect of Einstellung. *Psychological Monographs, 54*(6, Whole No. 248).

Luiten, J., Ames, W., & Ackerson, G. (1980). A meta-analysis of the effects of advance organizers on learning and retention. *American Educational Research Journal, 17*, 211–218.

Luria, A. R. (1961). *The role of speech in the regulation of normal and abnormal behavior* (J. Tizard, Trans.). New York: Liveright.

Lutkehaus, N. C., & Greenfield, P. (2003). From *The process of education* to *The culture of education*: An intellectual biography of Jerome Bruner's contributions to education. In B. J. Zimmerman & D. H. Schunk (Eds.), *Educational psychology: A century of contributions* (pp. 409–430). Mahwah, NJ: Erlbaum.

Maag, J. W. (2001). Rewarded by punishment: Reflections on the disuse of positive reinforcement in schools. *Exceptional Children, 67*, 173–186.

Mabbott, D. J., & Bisanz, J. (2003). Developmental change and individual differences in children's multiplication. *Child Development, 74*, 1091–1107.

Maccoby, E. E., & Jacklin, C. N. (1974). *The psychology of sex differences.* Stanford, CA: Stanford University Press.

MacDonald, M. C., Just, M. A., & Carpenter, P. A. (1992). Working memory constraints on the processing of syntactic ambiguity. *Cognitive Psychology, 24*, 56–98.

Mace, F. C., Belfiore, P. J., & Hutchinson, J. M. (2001). Operant theory and research on self-regulation. In B. J. Zimmerman & D. H. Schunk (Eds.), *Self-regulated learning and academic achievement: Theoretical perspectives* (2nd ed., pp. 39–65). Mahwah, NJ: Erlbaum.

Mace, F. C., Belfiore, P. J., & Shea, M. C. (1989). Operant theory and research on self-regulation. In B. J. Zimmerman & D. H. Schunk (Eds.), *Self-regulated learning and academic achievement: Theory, research, and practice* (pp. 27–50). New York: Springer-Verlag.

Mace, F. C., & Kratochwill, T. R. (1988). Self-monitoring: Applications and issues. In J. Witt, S. Elliott, & F. Gresham (Eds.), *Handbook of behavior therapy in education* (pp. 489–502). New York: Pergamon.

Mace, F. C., & West, B. J. (1986). Unresolved theoretical issues in self-management: Implications for research and practice. *Professional School Psychology, 1*, 149–163.

Maddux, J. E. (1993). Social cognitive models of health and exercise behavior: An introduction and review of conceptual issues. *Journal of Applied Sport Psychology, 5*, 116–140.

Maddux, J. E., Brawley, L., & Boykin, A. (1995). Self-efficacy and healthy behavior: Prevention, promotion, and detection. In J. E. Maddux (Ed.), *Self-efficacy, adaptation, and adjustment: Theory, research, and application* (pp. 173–202). New York: Plenum.

Maehr, M. L., & Zusho, A. (2009). Achievement goal theory: The past, present, and future. In K. R. Wentzel & A. Wigfield (Eds.), *Handbook of motivation at school* (pp. 77–104). New York: Routledge.

Maes, S., & Gebhardt, W. (2000). Self-regulation and health behavior: The health behavior goal model. In M. Boekaerts, P. R. Pintrich, & M. Zeidner (Eds.), *Handbook of self-regulation* (pp. 343–368). San Diego: Academic Press.

Maes, S., & Karoly, P. (2005). Self-regulation assessment and intervention in physical health and illness: A review. *Applied Psychology: An International Review, 54*, 245–277.

Mager, R. (1962). *Preparing instructional objectives.* Palo Alto, CA: Fearon.

Mahoney, J. L., Lord, H., & Carryl, E. (2005). An ecological analysis of after-school program participation and the development of academic performance and motivational attributes for disadvantaged children. *Child Development, 76*, 811–825.

Maier, S. F., & Seligman, M. E. P. (1976). Learned helplessness: Theory and evidence. *Journal of Experimental Psychology, 105*, 3–46.

Manderlink, G., & Harackiewicz, J. M. (1984). Proximal versus distal goal setting and intrinsic motivation. *Journal of Personality and Social Psychology, 47*, 918–928.

Mandler, J. M. (1978). A code in the node: The use of a story schema in retrieval. *Discourse Processes, 1*, 14–35.

Mandler, J. M., & Johnson, N. S. (1976). Some of the thousand words a picture is worth. *Journal of Experimental Psychology: Human Learning and Memory, 2*, 529–540.

Mandler, J. M., & Ritchey, G. H. (1977). Long-term memory for pictures. *Journal of Experimental Psychology: Human Learning and Memory, 3*, 386–396.

Markman, A. B. (1999). *Knowledge representation*. Mahwah, NJ: Erlbaum.

Markus, H., & Nurius, P. (1986). Possible selves. *American Psychologist, 41*, 954–969.

Markus, H., & Wurf, E. (1987). The dynamic self-concept: A social psychological perspective. *Annual Review of Psychology, 38*, 299–337.

Marsh, H. W., & Hau, K. (2003). Big-fish-little-pond effect on academic self-concept: A cross-cultural (26-country) test of the negative effects of academically selective schools. *American Psychologist, 58*, 364–376.

Marsh, H. W., & Shavelson, R. (1985). Self-concept: Its multifaceted, hierarchical structure. *Educational Psychologist, 20*, 107–123.

Marshall, H. H., & Weinstein, R. S. (1984). Classroom factors affecting students' self-evaluations: An interactional model. *Review of Educational Research, 54*, 301–325.

Martin, J. (1980). External versus self-reinforcement: A review of methodological and theoretical issues. *Canadian Journal of Behavioural Science, 12*, 111–125.

Martin, J. (2004). Self-regulated learning, social cognitive theory, and agency. *Educational Psychologist, 39*, 135–145.Martin, J

Mashburn, A. J., Justice, L. M., Downer, J. T., & Pianta, R. C. (2009). Peer effects on children's language achievement during pre-kindergarten. *Child Development, 80*, 686–702.

Maslow, A. H. (1968). *Toward a psychology of being* (2nd ed.). New York: Van Nostrand Reinhold.

Maslow, A. H. (1970). *Motivation and personality* (2nd ed.). New York: Harper & Row.

Mason, L. H. (2004). Explicit self-regulated strategy development versus reciprocal questioning: Effects on expository reading comprehension among struggling readers. *Journal of Educational Psychology, 96*, 283–296.

Masten, A. S., & Coatsworth, J. D. (1998). The development of competence in favorable and unfavorable environments: Lessons from research on successful children. *American Psychologist, 53*, 205–220.

Masten, A. S., Hubbard, J. J., Gest, S. D., Tellegen, A., Garmezy, N., & Ramirez, M. (1999). Competence in the context of adversity: Pathways to resilience and maladaptation from childhood to late adolescence. *Development and Psychopathology, 11*, 143–169.M

Matlin, M. W. (2009). *Cognition* (7th ed.). Hoboken, NJ: Wiley.

Matthews, J. S., Ponitz, C. C., & Morrison, F. J. (2009). Early gender differences in self-regulation and academic achievement. *Journal of Educational Psychology, 101*, 689–704.

Mautone, P. D., & Mayer, R. E. (2001). Signaling as a cognitive guide in multimedia learning. *Journal of Educational Psychology, 93*, 377–389.

Mautone, P. D., & Mayer, R. E. (2007). Cognitive aids for guiding graph comprehension. *Journal of Educational Psychology, 99*, 640–652.

Mayer, R. E. (1979). Can advance organizers influence meaningful learning? *Review of Educational Research, 49*, 371–383.

Mayer, R. E. (1984). Aids to text comprehension. *Educational Psychologist, 19*, 30–42.

Mayer, R. E. (1985). Mathematical ability. In R. J. Sternberg (Ed.), *Human abilities: An information-processing approach* (pp. 127–150). New York: Freeman.

Mayer, R. E. (1992). *Thinking, problem solving, cognition* (2nd ed.). New York: Freeman.

Mayer, R. E. (1996). Learners as information processors: Legacies and limitations of educational psychology's second metaphor. *Educational Psychologist, 31*, 151–161.

Mayer, R. E. (1997). Multimedia learning: Are we asking the right questions? *Educational Psychologist, 32*, 1–19.

Mayer, R. E. (1999). *The promise of educational psychology: Learning in the content areas*. Upper Saddle River, NJ: Merrill/Prentice Hall.

Mayer, R. E. (2003). E. L. Thorndike's enduring contributions to educational psychology. In B. J. Zimmerman & D. H. Schunk (Eds.), *Educational psychology: A century of contributions* (pp. 113–154). Mahwah, NJ: Erlbaum.

Mayer, R. E. (2004). Should there be a three-strikes rule against pure discovery learning? The case for guided methods of instruction. *American Psychologist, 59*, 14–19.

Mayer, R. E., & Chandler, P. (2001). When learning is just a click away: Does simple user interaction foster deeper understanding of multimedia messages? *Journal of Educational Psychology, 93*, 390–397.

Mayer, R. E., Dow, G. T., & Mayer, S. (2003). Multimedia learning in an interactive self-explaining environment: What works in the design of agent-based microworlds? *Journal of Educational Psychology, 95*, 806–813.

Mayer, R. E., Fennell, S., Farmer, L., & Campbell, J. (2004). A personalization effect in multimedia learning: Students learn better when words are in conversational style rather than formal style. *Journal of Educational Psychology, 96*, 389–395.

Mayer, R. E., & Moreno, R. (2003). Nine ways to reduce cognitive load in multimedia learning. *Educational Psychologist, 38*, 43–52.

Mayer, R. E., Moreno, R., Boire, M., & Vagge, S. (1999). Maximizing constructivist learning from multimedia communications by minimizing cognitive load. *Journal of Educational Psychology, 91*, 638–643.

Mayer, R. E., Sobko, K., & Mautone, P. D. (2003). Social cues in multimedia learning: Role of speaker's voice. *Journal of Educational Psychology, 95*, 419–425.

McClelland, D. C., Atkinson, J. W., Clark, R. A., & Lowell, E. L. (1953). *The achievement motive*. New York: Appleton-Century-Crofts.

McCloskey, M., & Kaiser, M. (1984). The impetus impulse: A medieval theory of motion lives on in the minds of children. *The Sciences, 24*(6), 40–45.

McCullagh, P. (1993). Modeling: Learning, developmental, and social psychological considerations. In R. N. Singer, M. Murphey, & L. K. Tennant (Eds.), *Handbook of research on sport psychology* (pp. 106–126). New York: Macmillan.

McCutchen, D. (2000). Knowledge, processing, and working memory: Implications for a theory of writing. *Educational Psychologist, 35*, 13–23.

McCutchen, D., & Perfetti, C. A. (1982). Coherence and connectedness in the development of discourse production. *Text, 2*, 113–139.

McDougall, W. (1926). *An introduction to social psychology* (Rev. ed.). Boston: John W. Luce.

McGregor, G., & Vogelsberg, R. T. (1998). *Inclusive schooling practices: Pedagogical and research foundations*. Baltimore: Paul H. Brookes.

McKeachie, W. J. (1990). Learning, thinking, and Thorndike. *Educational Psychologist, 25*, 127–141.

McNeil, J. D. (1987). *Reading comprehension: New directions for classroom practice* (2nd ed.). Glenview, IL: Scott, Foresman.

McNeil, N. M., & Alibali, M. W. (2000). Learning mathematics from procedural instruction: Externally imposed goals influence what is learned. *Journal of Educational Psychology, 92*, 734–744.

McVee, M. B., Dunsmore, K., & Gavelek, J. R. (2005). Schema theory revisited. *Review of Educational Research, 75,* 531–566.

Medin, D. L., Lynch, E. B., & Solomon, K. O. (2000). Are there kinds of concepts? *Annual Review of Psychology, 51,* 121–147.

Meece, J. L. (1991). The classroom context and students' motivational goals. In M. L. Maehr & P. R. Pintrich (Eds.), *Advances in motivation and achievement* (Vol. 7, pp. 261–285). Greenwich, CT: JAI Press.

Meece, J. L. (1994). The role of motivation in self-regulated learning. In D. H. Schunk & B. J. Zimmerman (Eds.), *Self-regulation of learning and performance: Issues and educational applications* (pp. 25–44). Hillsdale, NJ: Erlbaum.

Meece, J. L. (2002). *Child and adolescent development for educators* (2nd ed.). New York: McGraw-Hill.

Meece, J. L., Blumenfeld, P. C., & Hoyle, R. H. (1988). Students' goal orientations and cognitive engagement in classroom activities. *Journal of Educational Psychology, 80*, 514–523.

Meece, J. L., & Courtney, D. P. (1992). Gender differences in students' perceptions: Consequences for achievement-related choices. In D. H. Schunk & J. L. Meece (Eds.), *Student perceptions in the classroom* (pp. 209–228). Hillsdale, NJ: Erlbaum.

Meece, J. L., & Miller, S. D. (2001). A longitudinal analysis of elementary school students' achievement goals in literacy activities. *Contemporary Educational Psychology, 26,* 454–480.

Meece, J. L., Parsons, J. E., Kaczala, C. M., Goff, S. B., & Futterman, R. (1982). Sex differences in math achievement: Towards a model of academic choice. *Psychological Bulletin, 91*, 324–348.

Meichenbaum, D. (1977). *Cognitive behavior modification: An integrative approach.* New York: Plenum.

Meichenbaum, D. (1986). Cognitive behavior modification. In F. H. Kanfer & A. P. Goldstein (Eds.), *Helping people change: A textbook of methods* (3rd ed., pp. 346–380). New York: Pergamon.

Meichenbaum, D., & Asarnow, J. (1979). Cognitive-behavior modification and metacognitive development: Implications for the classroom. In P. C. Kendall & S. D. Hollon (Eds.), *Cognitive behavioral interventions: Theory, research, and procedures* (pp. 11–35). New York: Academic Press.

Meichenbaum, D., & Goodman, J. (1971). Training impulsive children to talk to themselves: A means of developing self-control. *Journal of Abnormal Psychology, 77*, 115–126.

Merrill, P. F. (1987). Job and task analysis. In R. M. Gagné (Ed.), *Instructional technology: Foundations* (pp. 141–173). Hillsdale, NJ: Erlbaum.

Messer, S. (1970). Reflection-impulsivity: Stability and school failure. *Journal of Educational Psychology, 61*, 487–490.

Messick, S. (1984). The nature of cognitive styles: Problems and promise in educational practice. *Educational Psychologist, 19*, 59–74.

Messick, S. (1994). The matter of style: Manifestations of personality in cognition, learning, and teaching. *Educational Psychologist, 29*, 121–136.

Meyer, D. E., & Schvaneveldt, R. W. (1971). Facilitation in recognizing pairs of words: Evidence of a dependence between retrieval operations. *Journal of Experimental Psychology, 90*, 227–234.

Meyer, D. K., & Turner, J. C. (2002). Discovering emotion in classroom motivation research. *Educational Psychologist, 37*, 107–114.

Mickelson, R. (1990). The attitude-achievement paradox among Black adolescents. *Sociology of Education, 63*, 44–61.

Miliotis, D., Sesma, A., Jr., & Masten, A. S. (1999). Parenting as a protective process for school success in children from homeless families. *Early Education & Development, 10*, 111–133.

Miller, A. (1987). Cognitive styles: An integrated model. *Educational Psychology, 7*, 251–268.

Miller, G. A. (1956). The magical number seven, plus or minus two: Some limits on our capacity for processing information. *Psychological Review, 63*, 81–97.

Miller, G. A. (1988). The challenge of universal literacy. *Science, 241*, 1293–1299.

Miller, G. A., Galanter, E., & Pribham, K. H. (1960). *Plans and the structure of behavior.* New York: Holt, Rinehart & Winston.

Miller, N. E., & Dollard, J. (1941). *Social learning and imitation.* New Haven, CT: Yale University Press.

Moerk, E. L. (1989). The LAD was a lady and the tasks were ill-defined. *Developmental Review, 9*, 21–57.

Molfese, D. L., Key, A. F., Kelly, S., Cunningham, N., Terrell, S., Ferguson, M., Molfese, V. J., & Bonebright, T. (2006). Below-average, average, and above-average readers engage different and similar brain regions while reading. *Journal of Learning Disabilities, 39,* 352–363.

Moll, L. C. (2001). Through the mediation of others: Vygotskian research on teaching. In V. Richardson (Ed.), *Handbook of research on teaching* (4th ed., pp. 111–129). Washington, DC: American Educational Research Association.

Mondale, S., & Patton, S. B. (Eds.) (2001). *School: The story of American public education.* Boston: Beacon Press.

Montemayor, R., & Eisen, M. (1977). The development of self-conceptions from childhood to adolescence. *Developmental Psychology, 13*, 314–319.

Monty, R. A., & Perlmuter, L. C. (1987). Choice, control, and motivation in the young and aged. In M. L. Maehr & D. A. Kleiber (Eds.), *Advances in motivation and achievement* (Vol. 5, pp. 99–122). Greenwich, CT: JAI Press.

Moore, M. T. (1990). Problem finding and teacher experience. *Journal of Creative Behavior, 24*, 39–58.

Moors, A., & De Houwer, J. (2006). Automaticity: A theoretical and conceptual analysis. *Psychological Bulletin, 132*, 297–326.

Moos, D. C., & Azevedo, R. (2009). Learning with computer-based learning environments: A literature review of computer self-efficacy. *Review of Educational Research, 79*, 576–600.

Moray, N., Bates, A., & Barnett, T. (1965). Experiments on the four-eared man. *Journal of the Acoustical Society of America, 38*, 196–201.

Moreno, R., & Mayer, R. E. (2000). Engaging students in active learning: The case for personalized multimedia messages. *Journal of Educational Psychology, 92,* 724–733.

Moreno, R., & Mayer, R. E. (2004). Personalized messages that promote science learning in virtual environments. *Journal of Educational Psychology, 96,* 165–173.

Moreno, R., & Mayer, R. E. (2007). Interactive multimodal learning environments. *Educational Psychology Review, 19,* 309–326.

Morgan, P. L., & Fuchs, D. (2007). Is there a bidirectional relationship between children's reading skills and reading motivation? *Exceptional Children, 73,* 165–183.

Morris, C. D., Bransford, J. D., & Franks, J. J. (1977). Levels of processing versus transfer-appropriate processing. *Journal of Verbal Learning and Verbal Behavior, 16,* 519–533.

Morris, E. K. (2003). B. F. Skinner: A behavior analyst in educational psychology. In B. J. Zimmerman & D. H. Schunk (Eds.), *Educational psychology: A century of contributions* (pp. 229–250). Mahwah, NJ: Erlbaum.

Morse, W. H., & Kelleher, R. T. (1977). Determinants of reinforcement and punishment. In W. K. Honig & J. E. R. Staddon (Eds.), *Handbook of operant behavior* (pp. 174–200). Englewood Cliffs, NJ: Prentice Hall.

Mosatche, H. S., & Bragonier, P. (1981). An observational study of social comparison in preschoolers. *Child Development, 52,* 376–378.

Moscovitch, M., & Craik, F. I. M. (1976). Depth of processing, retrieval cues, and uniqueness of encoding as factors in recall. *Journal of Verbal Learning and Verbal Behavior, 15,* 447–458.

Moshman, D. (1982). Exogenous, endogenous, and dialectical constructivism. *Developmental Review, 2,* 371–384.

Motl, R. W., Dishman, R. K., Saunders, R. P., Dowda, M., & Pate, R. R. (2007). Perceptions of physical and social environment variables and self-efficacy as correlates of self-reported physical activity among adolescent girls. *Journal of Pediatric Psychology, 32,* 6–12.

Mueller, C. G. (1979). Some origins of psychology as science. *Annual Review of Psychology, 30,* 9–29.

Mullen, C. A. (2005). *Mentorship primer.* New York: Peter Lang.

Mullen, C. A. (in press). Facilitating self-regulatory learning using mentoring approaches with doctoral students. In B. J. Zimmerman & D. H. Schunk (Eds.), *Handbook of self-regulation of learning and performance.* New York: Routledge.

Muller, U., Sokol, B., & Overton, W. F. (1998). Reframing a constructivist model of the development of mental representation: The role of higher-order operations. *Developmental Review, 18,* 155–201.

Multon, K. D., Brown, S. D., & Lent, R. W. (1991). Relation of self-efficacy beliefs to academic outcomes: A meta-analytic investigation. *Journal of Counseling Psychology, 38,* 30–38.

Murdock, T. B., & Anderman, E. M. (2006). Motivational perspectives on student cheating: Toward an integrated model of academic dishonesty. *Educational Psychologist, 41,* 129–145.

Murray, D. J., Kilgour, A. R., & Wasylkiw, L. (2000). Conflicts and missed signals in psychoanalysis, behaviorism, and Gestalt psychology. *American Psychologist, 55,* 422–426.

Murray, H. A. (1936). Techniques for a systematic investigation of fantasy. *Journal of Psychology, 3,* 115–143.

Murray, H. A. (1938). *Explorations in personality.* New York: Oxford University Press.

Muth, K. D., Glynn, S. M., Britton, B. K., & Graves, M. F. (1988). Thinking out loud while studying text: Rehearsing key ideas. *Journal of Educational Psychology, 80,* 315–318.

Myers, I. B., & McCaulley, M. H. (1988). *Manual: A Guide to the Development and Use of the Myers-Briggs Type Indicator.* Palo Alto, CA: Consulting Psychologists.

Myers, M., II, & Paris, S. G. (1978). Children's metacognitive knowledge about reading. *Journal of Educational Psychology, 70,* 680–690.

Nairne, J. S. (2002). Remembering over the short-term: The case against the standard model. *Annual Review of Psychology, 53,* 53–81.

National Research Council (2000). *How people learn: Brain, mind, experience, and school.* Washington, DC: National Academy Press.

Neisser, U. (1967). *Cognitive psychology.* Englewood Cliffs, NJ: Prentice Hall.

Nelson, R. O., & Hayes, S. C. (1981). Theoretical explanations for reactivity in self-monitoring. *Behavior Modification, 5,* 3–14.

Nelson, T. O. (1977). Repetition and depth of processing. *Journal of Verbal Learning and Verbal Behavior, 16,* 151–171.

Nesbit, J. C., & Adesope, O. O. (2006). Learning with concept and knowledge maps: A meta-analysis. *Review of Educational Research, 76,* 413–448.

Neumeister, K. L. S., & Finch, H. (2006). Perfectionism in high-ability students: Relational precursors and influences on achievement motivation. *Gifted Child Quarterly, 50,* 238–251.

Newcombe, N. S., Ambady, N., Eccles, J., Gomez, L., Klahr, K., Linn, M., Miller, K., & Mix, K. (2009). Psychology's role in mathematics and science education. *American Psychologist, 64,* 538–550.

Newell, A., & Simon, H. A. (1972). *Human problem solving.* Englewood Cliffs, NJ: Prentice Hall.

Newman, R. S. (1994). Adaptive help seeking: A strategy of self-regulated learning. In D. H. Schunk & B. J. Zimmerman (Eds.), *Self-regulation of learning and performance: Issues and educational applications* (pp. 283–301). Hillsdale, NJ: Erlbaum.

Newman, R. S. (2000). Social influences on the development of children's adaptive help seeking: The role of parents, teachers, and peers. *Developmental Review, 20,* 350–404.

Newman, R. S. (2002). What do I need to do to succeed … when I don't understand what I'm doing!?: Developmental influences on students' adaptive help seeking. In A. Wigfield & J. S. Eccles (Eds.), *Development of achievement motivation* (pp. 285–306). San Diego: Academic Press.

Newman, R. S. (2008). The motivational role of adaptive help seeking in self-regulated learning. In D. H. Schunk & B. J. Zimmerman (Eds.), *Motivation and self-regulated learning: Theory, research, and applications* (pp. 315–337). New York: Taylor & Francis.

Newman, R. S., & Schwager, M. T. (1992). Student perceptions and academic help-seeking. In D. H. Schunk & J. L. Meece (Eds.), *Student perceptions in the classroom* (pp. 123–146). Hillsdale, NJ: Erlbaum.

Nicholls, J. G. (1978). The development of the concepts of effort and ability, perception of academic attainment, and the understanding that difficult tasks require more ability. *Child Development, 49,* 800–814.

Nicholls, J. G. (1979). Development of perception of own attainment and causal attribution for success and failure in reading. *Journal of Educational Psychology, 71*, 94–99.

Nicholls, J. G. (1983). Conceptions of ability and achievement motivation: A theory and its implications for education. In S. G. Paris, G. M. Olson, & H. W. Stevenson (Eds.), *Learning and motivation in the classroom* (pp. 211–237). Hillsdale, NJ: Erlbaum.

Nicholls, J. G. (1984). Achievement motivation: Conceptions of ability, subjective experience, task choice, and performance. *Psychological Review, 91*, 328–346.

Nicholls, J. G., Cobb, P., Wood, T., Yackel, E., & Patashnick, M. (1990). Assessing students' theories of success in mathematics: Individual and classroom differences. *Journal for Research in Mathematics Education, 21*, 109–122.

Nicholls, J. G., & Miller, A. T. (1984). Reasoning about the ability of self and others: A developmental study. *Child Development, 55*, 1990–1999.

Nicholls, J. G., Patashnick, M., & Nolen, S. B. (1985). Adolescents' theories of education. *Journal of Educational Psychology, 77*, 683–692.

Nicholls, J. G., & Thorkildsen, T. A. (1989). Intellectual conventions versus matters of substance: Elementary school students as curriculum theorists. *American Educational Research Journal, 26*, 533–544.

Nielsen, M. (2006). Copying actions and copying outcomes: Social learning through the second year. *Developmental Psychology, 42*, 555–565.

Nokes, J. D., Dole, J. A., & Hacker, D. J. (2007). Teaching high school students to use heuristics while reading historical texts. *Journal of Educational Psychology, 99*, 492–504.

Nolen, S. B. (1988). Reasons for studying: Motivational orientations and study strategies. *Cognition and Instruction, 5*, 269–287.

Nolen, S. B. (1996). Why study? How reasons for learning influence strategy selection. *Educational Psychology Review, 8*, 335–355.

Nolen-Hoeksema, S., Girgus, J. S., & Seligman, M. E. P. (1986). Learned helplessness in children: A longitudinal study of depression, achievement, and explanatory style. *Journal of Personality and Social Psychology, 51*, 435–442.

Norman, D. A. (1976). *Memory and attention: An introduction to human information processing* (2nd ed.). New York: Wiley.

Norman, D. A., & Rumelhart, D. E. (1975). *Explorations in cognition*. San Francisco: Freeman.

Nussbaum, E. M., & Kardash, C. M. (2005). The effects of goal instructions and text on the generation of counterarguments during writing. *Journal of Educational Psychology, 97*, 157–169.

Nussbaum, J., & Novick, N. (1982). Alternative frameworks, conceptual conflict, and accommodation: Toward a principled teaching strategy. *Instructional Science, 11*, 183–200.

Oberauer, K., & Lewandowsky, S. (2008). Forgetting in immediate serial recall: Decay, temporal distinctiveness, or interference? *Psychological Review, 115*, 544–576.

O'Day, E. F., Kulhavy, R. W., Anderson, W., & Malczynski, R. J. (1971). *Programmed instruction: Techniques and trends*. New York: Appleton-Century-Crofts.

Oden, S., Schweinhart, L., & Weikart, D. (2000). *Into adulthood: A study of the effects of Head Start*. Ypsilanti, MI: High/Scope Educational Research Foundation.

O'Donnell, A. M. (2006). The role of peers and group learning. In P. A. Alexander & P. H. Winne (Eds.), *Handbook of educational psychology* (2nd ed., pp. 781–802). Mahwah, NJ: Erlbaum.

O'Donnell, A. M., Dansereau, D. F., & Hall, R. H. (2002). Knowledge maps as scaffolds for cognitive processing. *Educational Psychology Review, 14*, 71–86.

Ohlsson, S. (1993). The interaction between knowledge and practice in the acquisition of cognitive skills. In S. Chipman & A. L. Meyrowitz (Eds.), *Foundations of knowledge acquisition: Cognitive models of complex learning* (pp. 147–208). Boston: Kluwer.

Ohlsson, S. (1996). Learning from performance errors. *Psychological Review, 103*, 241–262.

O'Leary, K. D., & Drabman, R. (1971). Token reinforcement programs in the classroom: A review. *Psychological Bulletin, 75*, 379–398.

O'Leary, S. G., & Dubey, D. R. (1979). Applications of self-control procedures by children: A review. *Journal of Applied Behavior Analysis, 12*, 449–466.

Ollendick, T. H., & Hersen, M. (1984). *Child behavioral assessment: Principles and procedures*. New York: Pergamon.

O'Mara, A. J., Marsh, H. W., Craven, R. G., & Debus, R. L. (2006). Do self-concept interventions make a difference? A synergistic blend of construct validation and meta-analysis. *Educational Psychologist, 41*, 181–206.

Oppenheimer, T. (1997, July). The computer delusion. *The Atlantic Monthly, 285*, 45–48, 50–56, 61–62.

Ornstein, R. (1997). *The right mind*. Orlando: Harcourt Brace.

Osborn, A. F. (1963). *Applied imagination*. New York: Scribner's.

Otis, N., Grouzet, F. M. E., & Pelletier, L. G. (2005). Latent motivational change in an academic setting: A 3-year longitudinal study. *Journal of Educational Psychology, 97*, 170–183.

Overskeid, G. (2007). Looking for Skinner and finding Freud. *American Psychologist, 62*, 590–595.

Packer, M. J., & Goicoechea, J. (2000). Sociocultural and constructivist theories of learning: Ontology, not just epistemology. *Educational Psychologist, 35*, 227–241.

Padilla, A. M. (2006). Second language learning: Issues in research and teaching. In P. A. Alexander & P. H. Winne (Eds.), *Handbook of educational psychology* (2nd ed., pp. 571–591). Mahwah, NJ: Erlbaum.

Paivio, A. (1970). On the functional significance of imagery. *Psychological Bulletin, 73*, 385–392.

Paivio, A. (1971). *Imagery and verbal processes*. New York: Holt, Rinehart & Winston.

Paivio, A. (1978). Mental comparisons involving abstract attributes. *Memory & Cognition, 6*, 199–208.

Paivio, A. (1986). *Mental representations: A dual-coding approach*. New York: Oxford University Press.

Pajares, F. (1996). Self-efficacy beliefs in achievement settings. *Review of Educational Research, 66*, 543–578.

Pajares, F. (1997). Current directions in self-efficacy research. In M. Maehr & P. R. Pintrich (Eds.), *Advances in motivation and achievement* (Vol. 10, pp. 1–49). Greenwich, CT: JAI Press.

Pajares, F. (2003). William James: Our father who begat us. In B. J. Zimmerman & D. H. Schunk (Eds.), *Educational psychology: A century of contributions* (pp. 41–64). Mahwah, NJ: Erlbaum.

Pajares, F. (2008). Motivational role of self-efficacy beliefs in self-regulated learning. In D. H. Schunk & B. J. Zimmerman (Eds.), *Motivation and self-regulated learning: Theory, research, and applications* (pp. 111–139). New York: Taylor & Francis.

Pajares, F., & Miller, M. D. (1994). The role of self-efficacy and self-concept beliefs in mathematical problem-solving: A path analysis. *Journal of Educational Psychology, 86*, 193–203.

Pajares, F., & Miller, M. D. (1995). Mathematics self-efficacy and mathematics performances: The need for specificity of assessment. *Journal of Counseling Psychology, 42*, 190–198.

Pajares, F., & Schunk, D. H. (2001). Self-beliefs and school success: Self-efficacy, self-concept, and school achievement. In R. J. Riding & S. G. Rayner (Eds.), *Self-perception* (pp. 239–265). Westport, CT: Ablex.

Pajares, F., & Schunk, D. H. (2002). Self and self-belief in psychology and education: A historical perspective. In J. Aronson (Ed.), *Improving academic achievement: Impact of psychological factors on education* (pp. 3–21). San Diego, CA: Academic Press.

Palincsar, A. S., & Brown, A. L. (1984). Reciprocal teaching of comprehension-fostering and comprehension-monitoring activities. *Cognition and Instruction, 1*, 117–175.

Palmer, D. J., Drummond, F., Tollison, P., & Zinkgraff, S. (1982). An attributional investigation of performance outcomes for learning-disabled and normal-achieving pupils. *Journal of Special Education, 16*, 207–219.

Papini, M. R., & Bitterman, M. E. (1990). The role of contingency in classical conditioning. *Psychological Review, 97*, 396–403.

Paris, S. G., & Byrnes, J. P. (1989). The constructivist approach to self-regulation and learning in the classroom. In B. J. Zimmerman & D. H. Schunk (Eds.), *Self-regulated learning and academic achievement: Theory, research, and practice*, (pp. 169–200). New York: Springer-Verlag.

Paris, S. G., Byrnes, J. P., & Paris, A. H. (2001). Constructing theories, identities, and actions of self-regulated learners. In B. J. Zimmerman & D. H. Schunk (Eds.), *Self-regulated learning and academic achievement: Theoretical perspectives* (2nd ed., pp. 253–287). Mahwah, NJ: Erlbaum.

Paris, S. G., Lipson, M. Y., & Wixson, K. K. (1983). Becoming a strategic reader. *Contemporary Educational Psychology, 8*, 293–316.

Paris, S. G., & Oka, E. R. (1986). Children's reading strategies, metacognition, and motivation. *Developmental Review, 6*, 25–56.

Paris, S. G., & Paris, A. H. (2001). Classroom applications of research on self-regulated learning. *Educational Psychologist, 36*, 89–101.

Paris, S. G., Wixson, K. K., & Palincsar, A. S. (1986). Instructional approaches to reading comprehension. In E. Z. Rothkopf (Ed.), *Review of research in education* (Vol. 13, pp. 91–128). Washington, DC: American Educational Research Association.

Pavlov, I. P. (1927). *Conditioned reflexes* (G. V. Anrep, Trans.). London: Oxford University Press.

Pavlov, I. P. (1928). *Lectures on conditioned reflexes* (W. H. Gantt, Trans.). New York: International Publishers.

Pavlov, I. P. (1932a). Neuroses in man and animals. *Journal of the American Medical Association, 99*, 1012–1013.

Pavlov, I. P. (1932b). The reply of a physiologist to psychologists. *Psychological Review, 39*, 91–127.

Pavlov, I. P. (1934). An attempt at a physiological interpretation of obsessional neurosis and paranoia. *Journal of Mental Science, 80*, 187–197.

Pearl, R. A., Bryan, T., & Donahue, M. (1980). Learning disabled children's attributions for success and failure. *Learning Disability Quarterly, 3*, 3–9.

Péladeau, N., Forget, J., & Gagné, F. (2003). Effect of paced and unpaced practice on skill application and retention: How much is enough? *American Educational Research Journal, 40*, 769–801.

Pellegrino, J. W. (1985). Inductive reasoning ability. In R. J. Sternberg (Ed.), *Human abilities: An information-processing approach* (pp. 195–225). New York: Freeman.

Pellegrino, J. W., Baxter, G. P., & Glaser, R. (1999). Addressing the "two disciplines" problem: Linking theories of cognition and learning with assessment and instructional practice. In A. Iran-Nejad & P. D. Pearson (Eds.), *Review of Research in Education* (Vol. 24, pp. 307–353). Washington, DC: American Educational Research Association.

Perfetti, C. A., & Lesgold, A. M. (1979). Coding and comprehension in skilled reading and implications for reading instruction. In L. B. Resnick & P. A. Weaver (Eds.), *Theory and practice of early reading* (pp. 57–84). Hillsdale, NJ: Erlbaum.

Perkins, D. N., & Salomon, G. (1989). Are cognitive skills context-bound? *Educational Researcher, 18*(1), 16–25.

Perry, D. G., & Bussey, K. (1979). The social learning theory of sex differences: Imitation is alive and well. *Journal of Personality and Social Psychology, 37*, 1699–1712.

Perry, N. E. (1998). Young children's self-regulated learning and contexts that support it. *Journal of Educational Psychology, 90*, 715–729.

Peterson, C. (2000). The future of optimism. *American Psychologist, 55*, 44–55.

Peterson, L. R., & Peterson, M. J. (1959). Short-term retention of individual verbal items. *Journal of Experimental Psychology, 58*, 193–198.

Petri, H. L. (1986). *Motivation: Theory and research* (2nd ed.). Belmont, CA: Wadsworth.

Phares, E. J. (1976). *Locus of control in personality.* Morristown, NJ: General Learning Press.

Phelps, E. A. (2006). Emotion and cognition: Insights from studies of the human amygdale. *Annual Review of Psychology, 57*, 27–53.

Phillips, D. C. (1995). The good, the bad, and the ugly: The many faces of constructivism. *Educational Researcher, 24*(7), 5–12.

Phillips, J. L., Jr. (1969). *The origins of intellect: Piaget's theory.* San Francisco: Freeman.

Phye, G. D. (1989). Schemata training and transfer of an intellectual skill. *Journal of Educational Psychology, 81*, 347–352.

Phye, G. D. (1990). Inductive problem solving: Schema inducement and memory-based transfer. *Journal of Educational Psychology, 82*, 826–831.

Phye, G. D. (1992). Strategic transfer: A tool for academic problem solving. *Educational Psychology Review, 4*, 393–421.

Phye, G. D. (1997). Inductive reasoning and problem solving: The early grades. In G. D. Phye (Ed.), *Handbook of academic learning: The construction of knowledge* (pp. 451–471). San Diego: Academic Press.

Phye, G. D. (2001). Problem-solving instruction and problem-solving transfer: The correspondence issue. *Journal of Educational Psychology, 93,* 571–578.

Phye, G. D., & Sanders, C. E. (1992). Accessing strategic knowledge: Individual differences in procedural and strategy transfer. *Contemporary Educational Psychology, 17,* 211–223.

Phye, G. D., & Sanders, C. E. (1994). Advice and feedback: Elements of practice for problem solving. *Contemporary Educational Psychology, 19,* 286–301.

Piaget, J. (1952). *The origins of intelligence in children.* New York: International Universities Press.

Piaget, J. (1962). *Play, dreams and imitation.* New York: Norton.

Piaget, J. (1970). Piaget's theory. In P. Mussen (Ed.), *Carmichael's manual of child psychology* (3rd ed., Vol. 1, pp. 703–732). New York: Wiley.

Piaget, J., & Inhelder, B. (1969). *The psychology of the child.* New York: Basic Books.

Pianta, R. C., Belsky, J., Vandergrift, N., Houts, R., & Morrison, F. J. (2008). Classroom effects on children's achievement trajectories in elementary school. *American Educational Research Journal, 45,* 365–397.

Pianta, R.C., & Hamre, B. K. (2009). Conceptualization, measurement, and improvement of classroom processes: Standardized observation can leverage capacity. *Educational Researcher, 38,* 109–119.

Pietsch, J., Walker, R., & Chapman, E. (2003). The relationship among self-concept, self-efficacy, and performance in mathematics during secondary school. *Journal of Educational Psychology, 95,* 589–603.

Pintrich, P. R. (2000a). Multiple goals, multiple pathways: The role of goal orientation in learning and achievement. *Journal of Educational Psychology, 92,* 544–555.

Pintrich, P. R. (2000b). The role of goal orientation in self-regulated learning. In M. Boekaerts, P. R. Pintrich, & M. Zeidner (Eds.), *Handbook of self-regulation* (pp. 451–502). San Diego: Academic Press.

Pintrich, P. R. (2003). A motivational science perspective on the role of student motivation in learning and teaching contexts. *Journal of Educational Psychology, 95,* 667–686.

Pintrich, P. R. (2004). A conceptual framework for assessing motivation and self-regulated learning in college students. *Educational Psychology Review, 16,* 385–407.

Pintrich, P. R., Cross, D. R., Kozma, R. B., & McKeachie, W. J. (1986). Instructional psychology. *Annual Review of Psychology, 37,* 611–651.

Pintrich, P. R., & De Groot, E. V. (1990). Motivational and self-regulated learning components of classroom academic performance. *Journal of Educational Psychology, 82,* 33–40.

Pintrich, P. R., & Garcia, T. (1991). Student goal orientation and self-regulation in the college classroom. In M. L. Maehr & P. R. Pintrich (Eds.), *Advances in motivation and achievement* (Vol. 7, pp. 371–402). Greenwich, CT: JAI Press.

Pintrich, P. R., Marx, R. W., & Boyle, R. A. (1993). Beyond cold conceptual change: The role of motivational beliefs and classroom contextual factors in the process of conceptual change. *Review of Educational Research, 63,* 167–199.

Pintrich, P. R., & Schrauben, B. (1992). Students' motivational beliefs and their cognitive engagement in classroom academic tasks. In D. H. Schunk & J. L. Meece (Eds.), *Student perceptions in the classroom* (pp. 149–183). Hillsdale, NJ: Erlbaum.

Pintrich, P. R., & Zusho, A. (2002). The development of academic self-regulation: The role of cognitive and motivational factors. In A. Wigfield & J. S. Eccles (Eds.), *Development of achievement motivation* (pp. 249–284). San Diego: Academic Press.

Plomin, R. (1990). *Nature and nurture.* Pacific Grove, CA: Brooks/Cole.

Poag-DuCharme, K. A., & Brawley, L. R. (1993). Self-efficacy theory: Use in the prediction of exercise behavior in the community setting. *Journal of Applied Sport Psychology, 5,* 178–194.

Pokay, P., & Blumenfeld, P. C. (1990). Predicting achievement early and late in the semester: The role of motivation and use of learning strategies. *Journal of Educational Psychology, 82,* 41–50.

Polk, T. A., & Newell, A. (1995). Deduction as verbal reasoning. *Psychological Review, 102,* 533–566.

Polya, G. (1945). *How to solve it.* Princeton, NJ: Princeton University Press. (Reprinted 1957, Doubleday, Garden City, NY)

Popham, W. J. (2008). *Classroom assessment: What teachers need to know* (5th ed.). Boston: Pearson Education.

Popkewitz, T. S. (1998). Dewey, Vygotsky, and the social administration of the individual: Constructivist pedagogy as systems of ideas in historical spaces. *American Educational Research Journal, 35,* 535–570.

Posner, M. I., & Keele, S. W. (1968). On the genesis of abstract ideas. *Journal of Experimental Psychology, 77,* 353–363.

Postman, L. (1961). The present status of interference theory. In C. N. Cofer (Ed.), *Verbal learning and verbal behavior* (pp. 152–179). New York: McGraw-Hill.

Postman, L., & Stark, K. (1969). Role of response availability in transfer and interference. *Journal of Experimental Psychology, 79,* 168–177.

Premack, D. (1962). Reversibility of the reinforcement relation. *Science, 136,* 255–257.

Premack, D. (1971). Catching up with common sense or two sides of a generalization: Reinforcement and punishment. In R. Glaser (Ed.), *The nature of reinforcement* (pp. 121–150). New York: Academic Press.

Pressley, M., & Harris, K. R. (2006). Cognitive strategy instruction: From basic research to classroom instruction. In P. A. Alexander & P. H. Winne (Eds.), *Handbook of educational psychology* (2nd ed., pp. 265–286). Mahwah, NJ: Erlbaum.

Pressley, M., Harris, K. R., & Marks, M. B. (1992). But good strategy instructors are constructivists! *Educational Psychology Review, 4,* 3–31.

Pressley, M., Levin, J. R., & Delaney, H. D. (1982). The mnemonic keyword method. *Review of Educational Research, 52,* 61–91.

Pressley, M., & McCormick, C. B. (1995). *Advanced educational psychology for educators, researchers, and policymakers.* New York: HarperCollins.

Pressley, M., Woloshyn, V., Lysynchuk, L. M., Martin, V., Wood, E., & Willoughby, T. (1990). A primer of research on cognitive strategy instruction: The important issues and how to address them. *Educational Psychology Review, 2,* 1–58.

Pugh, K. J., & Bergin, D. A. (2006). Motivational influences on transfer. *Educational Psychologist, 41,* 147–160.

Puntambekar, S., & Hübscher, R. (2005). Tools for scaffolding students in a complex learning environment: What have we gained and what have we missed? *Educational Psychologist, 40*, 1–12.

Purdie, N., Hattie, J., & Douglas, G. (1996). Student conceptions of learning and their use of self-regulated learning strategies: A cross-cultural comparison. *Journal of Educational Psychology, 88*, 87–100.

Putnam, R. D. (2000). *Bowling alone: The collapse and revival of American community*. New York: Simon & Schuster.

Pylyshyn, Z. W. (1973). What the mind's eye tells the mind's brain: A critique of mental imagery. *Psychological Bulletin, 80*, 1–24.

Quellmalz, E. S. (1987). Developing reasoning skills. In J. B. Baron & R. J. Sternberg (Eds.), *Teaching thinking skills: Theory and practice* (pp. 86–105). New York: Freeman.

Rachlin, H. (1991). *Introduction to modern behaviorism* (3rd ed.). New York: Freeman.

Radziszewska, B., & Rogoff, B. (1991). Children's guided participation in planning imaginary errands with skilled adult or peer partners. *Developmental Psychology, 27*, 381–389.

Ramsel, D., & Grabe, M. (1983). Attentional allocation and performance in goal-directed reading: Age differences in reading flexibility. *Journal of Reading Behavior, 15*, 55–65.

Ratelle, C. F., Guay, F., Larose, S., & Senécal, C. (2004). Family correlates of trajectories of academic motivation during a school transition: A semiparametric group-based approach. *Journal of Educational Psychology, 96*, 743–754.

Ratner, H. H., Foley, M. A., & Gimpert, N. (2002). The role of collaborative planning in children's source-monitoring errors and learning. *Journal of Experimental Child Psychology, 81*, 44–73.

Ray, J. J. (1982). Achievement motivation and preferred probability of success. *Journal of Social Psychology, 116*, 255–261.

Reardon, S. F., & Galindo, C. (2009). The Hispanic-White achievement gap in math and reading in the elementary grades. *American Educational Research Journal, 46*, 853–891.

Reder, L. M. (1979). The role of elaborations in memory for prose. *Cognitive Psychology, 11*, 221–234.

Reder, L. M. (1982). Plausibility judgment versus fact retrieval: Alternative strategies for sentence verification. *Psychological Review, 89*, 250–280.

Redish, A. D., Jensen, S., Johnson, A., & Kurth-Nelson, Z. (2007). Reconciling reinforcement learning models with behavioral extinction and renewal: Implications for addiction, relapse, and problem gambling. *Psychological Review, 114*, 784–805.

Reed, S. K. (2006). Cognitive architectures for multimedia learning. *Educational Psychologist, 41*, 87–98.

Reeve, J., Deci, E. L., & Ryan, R. M. (2004). Self-determination theory: A dialectical framework for understanding sociocultural influences on student motivation. In D. M. McInerney & S. Van Etten (Eds.), *Big theories revisited* (pp. 31–60). Greenwich, CT: Information Age Publishing.

Reid, R., & Lienemann, T. O. (2006). Self-regulated strategy development for written expression with students with attention deficit/hyperactivity disorder. *Exceptional Children, 73*, 53–68.

Reid, R., Trout, A. L., & Schartz, M. (2005). Self-regulation interventions for children with attention deficit/hyperactivity disorder. *Exceptional Children, 71*, 361–377.

Reigeluth, C. M. (Ed.) (1999). *Instructional design theories and models*. Mahwah, NJ: Erlbaum.

Relich, J. D., Debus, R. L., & Walker, R. (1986). The mediating role of attribution and self-efficacy variables for treatment effects on achievement outcomes. *Contemporary Educational Psychology, 11*, 195–216.

Renkl, A., & Atkinson, R. K. (2003). Structuring the transition from example study to problem solving in cognitive skill acquisition: A cognitive load perspective. *Educational Psychologist, 38*, 15–22.

Renkl, A., Hilbert, T., & Schworm, S. (2009). Example-based learning in heuristic domains: A cognitive load theory account. *Educational Psychology Review, 21*, 67–78.

Rescorla, R. A. (1972). Informational variables in conditioning. In G. H. Bower (Ed.), *The psychology of learning and motivation* (Vol. 6, pp. 1–46). New York: Academic Press.

Rescorla, R. A. (1976). Pavlovian excitatory and inhibitory conditioning. In W. K. Estes (Ed.), *Handbook of learning and cognitive processes* (Vol. 2, pp. 7–35). Hillsdale, NJ: Erlbaum.

Rescorla, R. A. (1987). A Pavlovian analysis of goal-directed behavior. *American Psychologist, 42*, 119–129.

Resnick, L. B. (1981). Instructional psychology. *Annual Review of Psychology, 32*, 659–704.

Resnick, L. B. (1985). Cognition and instruction: Recent theories of human competence. In B. L. Hammonds (Ed.), *Psychology and learning: The master lecture series* (Vol. 4, pp. 127–186). Washington, DC: American Psychological Association.

Resnick, L. B. (1989). Developing mathematical knowledge. *American Psychologist, 44*, 162–169.

Reynolds, R., & Anderson, R. (1982). Influence of questions on the allocation of attention during reading. *Journal of Educational Psychology, 74*, 623–632.

Riccio, D. C., Rabinowitz, V. C., & Axelrod, S. (1994). Memory: When less is more. *American Psychologist, 49*, 917–926.

Richland, L. E., Morrison, R. G., & Holyoak, K. J. (2006). Children's development of analogical reasoning: Insights from scene analogy problems. *Journal of Experimental Child Psychology, 94*, 249–273.

Richter, C. P. (1927). Animal behavior and internal drives. *Quarterly Review of Biology, 2*, 307–343.

Rilling, M. (1977). Stimulus control and inhibitory processes. In W. K. Honig & J. E. R. Staddon (Eds.), *Handbook of operant behavior* (pp. 432–480). Englewood Cliffs, NJ: Prentice Hall.

Rips, L. J., Shoben, E. J., & Smith, E. E. (1973). Semantic distance and the verification of semantic relations. *Journal of Verbal Learning and Verbal Behavior, 12*, 1–20.

Rittle-Johnson, B. (2006). Promoting transfer: Effects of self-explanation and direct instruction. *Child Development, 77*, 1–15.

Rittle-Johnson, B., & Alibali, M. W. (1999). Conceptual and procedural knowledge of mathematics: Does one lead to the other? *Journal of Educational Psychology, 91*, 175–189.

Rittle-Johnson, B., & Star, J. (2007). Does comparing solution methods facilitate conceptual and procedural knowledge? An experimental study on learning to solve equations. *Journal of Educational Psychology, 99*, 561–574.

Roberts, D. F., & Foehr, U. G. (2008). Trends in media use. *The Future of Children, 18*(1), 11–37.

Robertson, J. S. (2000). Is attribution training a worthwhile classroom intervention for K-12 students with learning difficulties? *Educational Psychology Review, 12,* 111–134.

Robinson, D. R., Schofield, J. W., & Steers-Wentzell, K. L. (2005). Peer and cross-age tutoring in math: Outcomes and their design implications. *Educational Psychology Review, 17,* 327–362.

Robinson, F. P. (1946). *Effective study.* New York: Harper.

Robinson, N. M., Lanzi, R. G., Weinberg, R. A., Ramey, S. L., & Ramey, C. T. (2002). Family factors associated with high academic competence in former Head Start children at third grade. *Gifted Child Quarterly, 46,* 278–290.

Robinson, T. R., Smith, S. W., Miller, M. D., & Brownell, M. T. (1999). Cognitive behavior modification of hyperactivity-impulsivity and aggression: A meta-analysis of school-based studies. *Journal of Educational Psychology, 91,* 195–203.

Roblyer, M. D. (2006). *Integrating educational technology into teaching* (4th ed.). Upper Saddle River, NJ: Merrill/Prentice Hall.

Roeser, R. D., & Chi, M. T. H. (2007). Understanding tutor learning: Knowledge-building and knowledge-telling in peer tutors' explanations and questions. *Review of Educational Research, 77,* 534–574.

Roeser, R. W., Urdan, T. C., & Stephens, J. M. (2009). School as a context of student motivation and achievement. In K. R. Wentzel & A. Wigfield (Eds.), *Handbook of motivation at school* (pp. 381–410). New York: Routledge.

Rogers, C. R. (1959). A theory of therapy, personality, and interpersonal relationships, as developed in the client-centered framework. In S. Koch (Ed.), *Psychology: A study of a science* (Vol. 3, pp. 184–256). New York: McGraw-Hill.

Rogers, C. R. (1963). The actualizing tendency in relation to "motives" and to consciousness. In M. R. Jones (Ed.), *Nebraska symposium on motivation* (Vol. 11, pp. 1–24). Lincoln, NE: University of Nebraska Press.

Rogers, C. R. (1969). *Freedom to learn.* Columbus, OH: Merrill.

Rogers, C. R., & Freiberg, H. J. (1994). *Freedom to learn* (3rd ed.). Columbus, OH: Merrill/Prentice Hall.

Rogoff, B. (1986). Adult assistance of children's learning. In T. E. Raphael (Ed.), *The contexts of school-based literacy* (pp. 27–40). New York: Random House.

Rogoff, B. (1990). *Apprenticeship in thinking: Cognitive development in the social context.* New York: Oxford University Press.

Rohrbeck, C. A., Ginsburg-Block, M. D., Fantuzzo, J. W., & Miller, T. R. (2003). Peer-assisted learning interventions with elementary school students: A meta-analytic review. *Journal of Educational Psychology, 95,* 240–257.

Rohrkemper, M. M. (1989). Self-regulated learning and academic achievement: A Vygotskian view. In B. J. Zimmerman & D. H. Schunk (Eds.), *Self-regulated learning and academic achievement: Theory, research, and practice* (pp. 143–167). New York: Springer-Verlag.

Romberg, T. A., & Carpenter, T. P. (1986). Research on teaching and learning mathematics: Two disciplines of scientific inquiry. In M. C. Wittrock (Ed.), *Handbook of research on teaching* (3rd ed., pp. 850–873). New York: Macmillan.

Root-Bernstein, R. S. (1988). Setting the stage for discovery. *The Sciences, 28*(3), 26–34.

Rosch, E. (1973). Natural categories. *Cognitive Psychology, 4,* 328–350.

Rosch, E. (1975). Cognitive representations of semantic categories. *Journal of Experimental Psychology: General, 104,* 192–233.

Rosch, E. (1978). Principles of categorization. In E. Rosch & B. Lloyd (Eds.), *Cognition and categorization* (pp. 9–31). Hillsdale, NJ: Erlbaum.

Rose, S. P. R. (1998). Memory: Biological basis. In R. L. Gregory (Ed.), *The Oxford companion to the mind* (pp. 456–460). Oxford, England: Oxford University Press.

Rosen, B., & D'Andrade, R. C. (1959). The psychosocial origins of achievement motivation. *Sociometry, 22,* 185–218.

Rosenberg, M., & Kaplan, H. B. (1982). *Social psychology of the self-concept.* Arlington Heights, IL: Harlan Davidson.

Rosenholtz, S. J., & Rosenholtz, S. H. (1981). Classroom organization and the perception of ability. *Sociology of Education, 54,* 132–140.

Rosenholtz, S. J., & Simpson, C. (1984). The formation of ability conceptions: Developmental trend or social construction? *Review of Educational Research, 54,* 31–63.

Rosenshine, B., & Stevens, R. (1986). Teaching functions. In M. C. Wittrock (Ed.), *Handbook of research on teaching* (3rd ed., pp. 376–391). New York: Macmillan.

Rosenstock, I. M. (1974). The health belief model and preventive health behavior. *Health Education Monographs, 2,* 354–386.

Rosenthal, R. (1974). *On the social psychology of the self-fulfilling prophecy: Further evidence for Pygmalion effects and their mediating mechanisms.* New York: MSS Modular Publications.

Rosenthal, R. (2002). Covert communication in classrooms, clinics, courtrooms, and cubicles. *American Psychologist, 57,* 839–849.

Rosenthal, R., & Jacobson, L. (1968). *Pygmalion in the classroom.* New York: Holt, Rinehart & Winston.

Rosenthal, T. L., & Bandura, A. (1978). Psychological modeling: Theory and practice. In S. L. Garfield & A. E. Bergin (Eds.), *Handbook of psychotherapy and behavior change: An empirical analysis* (2nd ed., pp. 621–658). New York: Wiley.

Rosenthal, T. L., & Zimmerman, B. J. (1978). *Social learning and cognition.* New York: Academic Press.

Ross, S. M., McCormick, D., Krisak, N., & Anand, P. (1985). Personalizing context in teaching mathematical concepts: Teacher-managed and computer-assisted models. *Educational Communication and Technology Journal, 33,* 169–178.

Rotter, J. B. (1966). Generalized expectancies for internal versus external control of reinforcement. *Psychological Monographs, 80*(1, Whole No. 609).

Royer, J. M. (1986). Designing instruction to produce understanding: An approach based on cognitive theory. In G. D. Phye & T. Andre (Eds.), *Cognitive classroom learning: Understanding, thinking, and problem solving* (pp. 83–113). Orlando: Academic Press.

Royer, J. M., Tronsky, L. N., Chan, Y., Jackson, S. J., & Marchant, H., III. (1999). Math-fact retrieval as the cognitive mechanism underlying gender differences in math test performance. *Contemporary Educational Psychology, 24,* 181–266.

Ruble, D. N. (1983). The development of social-comparison processes and their role in achievement-related self-socialization. In E. T. Higgins, D. N. Ruble, & W. Hartup (Eds.),

Social cognition and social development (pp. 134–157). New York: Cambridge University Press.

Ruble, D. N., Boggiano, A. K., Feldman, N. S., & Loebl, J. H. (1980). Developmental analysis of the role of social comparison in self-evaluation. *Developmental Psychology, 16,* 105–115.

Ruble, D. N., Feldman, N. S., & Boggiano, A. K. (1976). Social comparison between young children in achievement situations. *Developmental Psychology, 12,* 191–197.

Rumelhart, D. E. (1975). Notes on a schema for stories. In D. G. Bobrow & A. M. Collins (Eds.), *Representation and understanding: Studies in cognitive science* (pp. 211–236). New York: Academic Press.

Rumelhart, D. E. (1977). Understanding and summarizing brief stories. In D. Laberge & S. J. Samuels (Eds.), *Basic processes in reading* (pp. 265–303). Hillsdale, NJ: Erlbaum.

Rumelhart, D. E., & McClelland, J. L. (1986). *Parallel distributed processing: Explorations in the microstructure of cognition.* Cambridge, MA: MIT Press.

Rumelhart, D. E., & Norman, D. A. (1978). Accretion, tuning, and restructuring: Three modes of learning. In J. W. Cotton & R. L. Klatzky (Eds.), *Semantic factors in cognition* (pp. 37–53). Hillsdale, NJ: Erlbaum.

Rundus, D. (1971). Analysis of rehearsal processes in free recall. *Journal of Experimental Psychology, 89,* 63–77.

Rundus, D., & Atkinson, R. C. (1970). Rehearsal processes in free recall: A procedure for direct observation. *Journal of Verbal Learning and Verbal Behavior, 9,* 99–105.

Rustemeyer, R., & Fischer, N. (2005). Sex- and age-related differences in mathematics. *Psychological Reports, 97,* 183–194.

Ryan, A. M., Gheen, M. H., & Midgley, C. (1998). Why do some students avoid asking for help? An examination of the interplay among students' academic efficacy, teachers' social-emotional role, and the classroom goal structure. *Journal of Educational Psychology, 90,* 528–535.

Ryan, R. M., Connell, J. P., & Deci, E. L. (1985). A motivational analysis of self-determination and self-regulation in education. In C. Ames & R. Ames (Eds.), *Research on motivation in education* (Vol. 2, pp. 13–51). Orlando: Academic Press.

Ryan, R. M., & Deci, E. L. (2000). Self-determination theory and the facilitation of intrinsic motivation, social development, and well-being. *American Psychologist, 55,* 68–78.

Ryan, R. M., & Deci, E. L. (2009). Promoting self-determined school engagement: Motivation, learning, and well-being. In K. R. Wentzel & A. Wigfield (Eds.), *Handbook of motivation at school* (pp. 171–195). New York: Routledge.

Sagotsky, G., Patterson, C. J., & Lepper, M. R. (1978). Training children's self-control: A field experiment in self-monitoring and goal-setting in the classroom. *Journal of Experimental Child Psychology, 25,* 242–253.

Sakitt, B. (1976). Iconic memory. *Psychological Review, 83,* 257–276.

Sakitt, B., & Long, G. M. (1979). Spare the rod and spoil the icon. *Journal of Experimental Psychology: Human Perception and Performance, 5,* 19–30.

Salatas, H., & Flavell, J. H. (1976). Retrieval of recently learned information: Development of strategies and control skills. *Child Development, 47,* 941–948.

Salomon, G. (1984). Television is "easy" and print is "tough": The differential investment of mental effort in learning as a function of perceptions and attributions. *Journal of Educational Psychology, 76,* 647–658.

Salomon, G., & Perkins, D. N. (1989). Rocky roads to transfer: Rethinking mechanisms of a neglected phenomenon. *Educational Psychologist, 24,* 113–142.

Samuelson, L. K., & Smith, L. B. (2000). Grounding development in cognitive processes. *Child Development, 71,* 98–106.

Sandoval, J. (1995). Teaching in subject matter areas: Science. *Annual Review of Psychology, 46,* 355–374.

Scardamalia, M., & Bereiter, C. (1982). Assimilative processes in composition planning. *Educational Psychologist, 17,* 165–171.

Scardamalia, M., & Bereiter, C. (1983). The development of evaluative, diagnostic, and remedial capabilities in children's composing. In M. Martlew (Ed.), *The psychology of written language: A developmental approach* (pp. 67–95). London: Wiley.

Scardamalia, M., & Bereiter, C. (1986). Research on written composition. In M. C. Wittrock (Ed.), *Handbook of research on teaching* (3rd ed., pp. 778–803). New York: Macmillan.

Scheiter, K., & Gerjets, P. (2007). Learner control in hypermedia environments. *Educational Psychology Review, 19,* 285–307.

Schiefele, U. (1996). Topic interest, text representation, and quality of experience. *Contemporary Educational Psychology, 21,* 3–18.

Schiefele, U. (2009). Situational and individual interest. In K. R. Wentzel & A. Wigfield (Eds.), *Handbook of motivation at school* (pp. 197–222). New York: Routledge.

Schmidt, M. E., & Vandewater, E. A. (2008). Media and attention, cognition, and school achievement. *The Future of Children, 18*(1), 63–85.

Schmidt, R. A. (1975). A schema theory of discrete motor skill learning. *Psychological Review, 82,* 225–260.

Schnotz, W., & Kürschner, C. (2007). A reconsideration of cognitive load theory. *Educational Psychology Review, 19,* 469–508.

Schoenfeld, A. H. (2006). Mathematics teaching and learning. In P. A. Alexander & P. H. Winne (Eds.), *Handbook of educational psychology* (2nd ed., pp. 479–510). Mahwah, NJ: Erlbaum.

Schraw, G., & Moshman, D. (1995). Metacognitive theories. *Educational Psychology Review, 7,* 351–371.

Schuh, K. L. (2003). Knowledge construction in the learner-centered classroom. *Journal of Educational Psychology, 95,* 426–442.

Schultz, W. (2006). Behavioral theories and the neurophysiology of reward. *Annual Review of Psychology, 57,* 87–115.

Schunk, D. H. (1981). Modeling and attributional effects on children's achievement: A self-efficacy analysis. *Journal of Educational Psychology, 73,* 93–105.

Schunk, D. H. (1982a). Effects of effort attributional feedback on children's perceived self-efficacy and achievement. *Journal of Educational Psychology, 74,* 548–556.

Schunk, D. H. (1982b). Verbal self-regulation as a facilitator of children's achievement and self-efficacy. *Human Learning, 1,* 265–277.

Schunk, D. H. (1983a). Ability versus effort attributional feedback: Differential effects on self-efficacy and achievement. *Journal of Educational Psychology, 75,* 848–856.

Schunk, D. H. (1983b). Developing children's self-efficacy and skills: The roles of social comparative information and goal setting. *Contemporary Educational Psychology, 8,* 76–86.

Schunk, D. H. (1983c). Goal difficulty and attainment information: Effects on children's achievement behaviors. *Human Learning, 2,* 107–117.

Schunk, D. H. (1983d). Progress self-monitoring: Effects on children's self-efficacy and achievement. *Journal of Experimental Education, 51,* 89–93.

Schunk, D. H. (1983e). Reward contingencies and the development of children's skills and self-efficacy. *Journal of Educational Psychology, 75,* 511–518.

Schunk, D. H. (1984a). Enhancing self-efficacy and achievement through rewards and goals: Motivational and informational effects. *Journal of Educational Research, 78,* 29–34.

Schunk, D. H. (1984b). Sequential attributional feedback and children's achievement behaviors. *Journal of Educational Psychology, 76,* 1159–1169.

Schunk, D. H. (1985). Participation in goal setting: Effects on self-efficacy and skills of learning disabled children. *Journal of Special Education, 19,* 307–317.

Schunk, D. H. (1986). Verbalization and children's self-regulated learning. *Contemporary Educational Psychology, 11,* 347–369.

Schunk, D. H. (1987). Peer models and children's behavioral change. *Review of Educational Research, 57,* 149–174.

Schunk, D. H. (1990). Goal setting and self-efficacy during self-regulated learning. *Educational Psychologist, 25,* 71–86.

Schunk, D. H. (1991). Self-efficacy and academic motivation. *Educational Psychologist, 26,* 207–231.

Schunk, D. H. (1994). Self-regulation of self-efficacy and attributions in academic settings. In D. H. Schunk & B. J. Zimmerman (Eds.), *Self-regulation of learning and performance: Issues and educational applications* (pp. 75–99). Hillsdale, NJ: Erlbaum.

Schunk, D. H. (1995). Self-efficacy and education and instruction. In J. E. Maddux (Ed.), *Self-efficacy, adaptation, and adjustment: Theory, research, and applications* (pp. 281–303). New York: Plenum.

Schunk, D. H. (1996). Goal and self-evaluative influences during children's cognitive skill learning. *American Educational Research Journal, 33,* 359–382.

Schunk, D. H. (1998). Teaching elementary students to self-regulate practice of mathematical skills with modeling. In D. H. Schunk & B. J. Zimmerman (Eds.), *Self-regulated learning: From teaching to self-reflective practice* (pp. 137–159). New York: Guilford Press.

Schunk, D. H. (1999). Social-self interaction and achievement behavior. *Educational Psychologist, 34,* 219–227.

Schunk, D. H. (2001). Social cognitive theory and self-regulated learning. In B. J. Zimmerman & D. H. Schunk (Eds.), *Self-regulated learning and academic achievement: Theoretical perspectives* (2nd ed., pp. 125–151). Mahwah, NJ: Erlbaum.

Schunk, D. H. (2008). Attributions as motivators of self-regulated learning. In D. H. Schunk & B. J. Zimmerman (Eds.), *Motivation and self-regulated learning: Theory, research, and applications* (pp. 245–266). New York: Taylor & Francis.

Schunk, D. H., & Cox, P. D. (1986). Strategy training and attributional feedback with learning disabled students. *Journal of Educational Psychology, 78,* 201–209.

Schunk, D. H., & Ertmer, P. A. (1999). Self-regulatory processes during computer skill acquisition: Goal and self-evaluative influences. *Journal of Educational Psychology, 91,* 251–260.

Schunk, D. H., & Ertmer, P. A. (2000). Self-regulation and academic learning: Self-efficacy enhancing interventions. In M. Boekaerts, P. R. Pintrich, & M. Zeidner (Eds.), *Handbook of self-regulation* (pp. 631–649). San Diego: Academic Press.

Schunk, D. H., & Gunn, T. P. (1986). Self-efficacy and skill development: Influence of task strategies and attributions. *Journal of Educational Research, 79,* 238–244.

Schunk, D. H., & Hanson, A. R. (1985). Peer models: Influence on children's self-efficacy and achievement. *Journal of Educational Psychology, 77,* 313–322.

Schunk, D. H., & Hanson, A. R. (1989a). Influence of peer-model attributes on children's beliefs and learning. *Journal of Educational Psychology, 81,* 431–434.

Schunk, D. H., & Hanson, A. R. (1989b). Self-modeling and children's cognitive skill learning. *Journal of Educational Psychology, 81,* 155–163.

Schunk, D. H., Hanson, A. R., & Cox, P. D. (1987). Peer-model attributes and children's achievement behaviors. *Journal of Educational Psychology, 79,* 54–61.

Schunk, D. H., & Miller, S. D. (2002). Self-efficacy and adolescents' motivation. In F. Pajares & T. Urdan (Eds.), *Academic motivation of adolescents* (pp. 29–52). Greenwich, CT: Information Age Publishing.

Schunk, D. H., & Pajares, F. (2002). The development of academic self-efficacy. In A. Wigfield & J. S. Eccles (Eds.), *Development of academic motivation* (pp. 15–31). San Diego: Academic Press.

Schunk, D. H., & Pajares, F. (2005). Competence perceptions and academic functioning. In A. J. Elliot & C. S. Dweck (Eds.), *Handbook of competence and motivation* (pp. 85–104). New York: Guilford Press.

Schunk, D. H., & Pajares, F. (2009). Self-efficacy theory. In K. R. Wentzel & A. Wigfield (Eds.), *Handbook of motivation at school* (pp. 35–53). New York: Routledge.

Schunk, D. H., Pintrich, P. R., & Meece, J. L. (2008). *Motivation in education: Theory, research, and applications* (3rd ed.). Upper Saddle River, NJ: Pearson Education.

Schunk, D. H., & Rice, J. M. (1986). Extended attributional feedback: Sequence effects during remedial reading instruction. *Journal of Early Adolescence, 6,* 55–66.

Schunk, D. H., & Rice, J. M. (1987). Enhancing comprehension skill and self-efficacy with strategy value information. *Journal of Reading Behavior, 19,* 285–302.

Schunk, D. H., & Rice, J. M. (1989). Learning goals and children's reading comprehension. *Journal of Reading Behavior, 21,* 279–293.

Schunk, D. H., & Rice, J. M. (1991). Learning goals and progress feedback during reading comprehension instruction. *Journal of Reading Behavior, 23,* 351–364.

Schunk, D. H., & Rice, J. M. (1993). Strategy fading and progress feedback: Effects on self-efficacy and comprehension among students receiving remedial reading services. *Journal of Special Education, 27,* 257–276.

Schunk, D. H., & Swartz, C. W. (1993a). Goals and progress feedback: Effects on self-efficacy and writing achievement. *Contemporary Educational Psychology, 18,* 337–354.

Schunk, D. H., & Swartz, C. W. (1993b). Writing strategy instruction with gifted students: Effects of goals and feedback on self-efficacy and skills. *Roeper Review, 15,* 225–230.

Schunk, D. H., & Zimmerman, B. J. (Eds.) (1994). *Self-regulation of learning and performance: Issues and educational applications.* Hillsdale, NJ: Erlbaum.

Schunk, D. H., & Zimmerman, B. J. (1996). Modeling and self-efficacy influences on children's development of self-regulation. In J. Juvonen & K. R. Wentzel (Eds.), *Social motivation: Understanding children's school adjustment* (pp. 154–180). Cambridge, England: Cambridge University Press.

Schunk, D. H., & Zimmerman, B. J. (1997). Social origins of self-regulatory competence. *Educational Psychologist, 32,* 195–208.

Schunk, D. H., & Zimmerman, B. J. (Eds.) (1998). *Self-regulated learning: From teaching to self-reflective practice.* New York: Guilford Press.

Schunk, D. H., & Zimmerman, B. J. (2006). Competence and control beliefs: Distinguishing the means and ends. In P. A. Alexander & P. H. Winne (Eds.), *Handbook of educational psychology* (2nd ed., pp. 349–367). Mahwah, NJ: Erlbaum.

Schunk, D. H., & Zimmerman, B. J. (Eds.) (2008). *Motivation and self-regulated learning: Theory, research, and applications.* New York: Taylor & Francis.

Schutz, P. A., Drogosz, L. M., White, V. E., & DiStefano, C. (1998). Prior knowledge, attitude, and strategy use in an introduction to statistics course. *Learning and Individual Differences, 10,* 291–308.

Schweinhart, L. J., & Weikart, D. (1997). *Lasting differences: The High/Scope Perry Preschool curriculum comparison study through age 23.* (Monographs of the High/Scope Educational Research Foundation, 12). Ypsilanti, MI: High/Scope Press.

Schwenck, C., Bjorklund, D. F., & Schneider, W. (2007). Factors influencing the incidence of utilization deficiencies and other patterns of recall/strategy-use relations in a strategic memory task. *Child Development, 78,* 1771–1787.

Searle, J. R. (1969). *Speech acts.* Cambridge, England: Cambridge University Press.

Seidel, T., & Shavelson, R. J. (2007). Teaching effectiveness research in the past decade: The role of theory and research design in disentangling meta-analysis results. *Review of Educational Research, 77,* 454–499.

Seligman, M. E. P. (1975). *Helplessness: On depression, development, and death.* San Francisco: Freeman.

Seligman, M. E. P. (1991). *Learned optimism.* New York: Knopf.

Sénéchal, M., & LeFevre, J. (2002). Parental involvement in the development of children's reading skill: A five-year longitudinal study. *Child Development, 73,* 445–460.

Shaul, M. S., & Ganson, H. C. (2005). The No Child Left Behind Act of 2001: The Federal Government's role in strengthening accountability for student performance. In L. Parker (Ed.), *Review of Research in Education* (Vol. 29, pp. 151–165). Washington, DC: American Educational Research Association.

Shavelson, R. J., & Bolus, R. (1982). Self-concept: The interplay of theory and methods. *Journal of Educational Psychology, 74,* 3–17.

Shell, D. F., Murphy, C. C., & Bruning, R. H. (1989). Self-efficacy and outcome expectancy mechanisms in reading and writing achievement. *Journal of Educational Psychology, 81,* 91–100.

Shepard, R. N. (1978). The mental image. *American Psychologist, 33,* 125–137.

Shepard, R. N., & Cooper, L. A. (1983). *Mental images and their transformations.* Cambridge, MA: MIT Press.

Shipman, S., & Shipman, V. C. (1985). Cognitive styles: Some conceptual, methodological, and applied issues. In E. W. Gordon (Ed.), *Review of research in education* (Vol. 12, pp. 229–291). Washington, DC: American Educational Research Association.

Shore, N. (1997). *Rethinking the brain: New insights into early development.* New York: Families and Work Institute.

Short, E. J., Friebert, S. E., & Andrist, C. G. (1990). Individual differences in attentional processes as a function of age and skill level. *Learning and Individual Differences, 2,* 389–403.

Shuell, T. J. (1986). Cognitive conceptions of learning. *Review of Educational Research, 56,* 411–436.

Shuell, T. J. (1988). The role of the student in learning from instruction. *Contemporary Educational Psychology, 13,* 276–295.

Shuell, T. J. (1990). Phases of meaningful learning. *Review of Educational Research, 60,* 531–547.

Shuell, T. J. (1996). Teaching and learning in a classroom context. In D. C. Berliner & R. C. Calfee (Eds.), *Handbook of educational psychology* (pp. 726–764). New York: Macmillan.

Shultz, T. R., & Lepper, M. R. (1996). Cognitive dissonance reduction as constraint satisfaction. *Psychological Review, 103,* 219–240.

Shute, N. (2009, February). The amazing teen brain. *U. S. News & World Report, 146,* 37–39.

Siegler, R. S. (1989). Mechanisms of cognitive development. *Annual Review of Psychology, 40,* 353–379.

Siegler, R. S. (1991). *Children's thinking* (2nd ed.). Englewood Cliffs, NJ: Prentice Hall.

Siegler, R. S. (2000). The rebirth of children's learning. *Child Development, 71,* 26–35.

Siegler, R. S. (2005). Children's learning. *American Psychologist, 60,* 769–778.

Siegler, R. S., & Svetina, M. (2006). What leads children to adopt new strategies? A microgenetic/cross-sectional study of class inclusion. *Child Development, 77,* 997–1015.

Sigel, I. E., & Brodzinsky, D. M. (1977). Individual differences: A perspective for understanding intellectual development. In H. Hom & P. Robinson (Eds.), *Psychological processes in early education* (pp. 295–329). New York: Academic Press.

Silver, E. A. (1981). Recall of mathematical problem information: Solving related problems. *Journal for Research in Mathematics Education, 12,* 54–64.

Simon, H. A. (1974). How big is a chunk? *Science, 183,* 482–488.

Simon, H. A. (1979). Information processing models of cognition. *Annual Review of Psychology, 30,* 363–396.

Simpson, T. L. (2002). Dare I oppose constructivist theory? *The Educational Forum, 66,* 347–354.

Sirin, S. R. (2005). Socioeconomic status and academic achievement: A meta-analytic review of research. *Review of Educational Research, 75,* 417–453.

Sivan, E. (1986). Motivation in social constructivist theory. *Educational Psychologist, 21,* 209–233.

Skinner, B. F. (1938). *The behavior of organisms.* New York: Appleton-Century-Crofts.

Skinner, B. F. (1953). *Science and human behavior.* New York: Free Press.

Skinner, B. F. (1954). The science of learning and the art of teaching. *Harvard Educational Review, 24*, 86–97.

Skinner, B. F. (1958). Teaching machines. *Science, 128*, 969–977.

Skinner, B. F. (1961). Why we need teaching machines. *Harvard Educational Review, 31*, 377–398.

Skinner, B. F. (1968). *The technology of teaching*. New York: Appleton-Century-Crofts.

Skinner, B. F. (1970). B. F. Skinner An autobiography. In P. B. Dews (Ed.), *Festschrift for B. F. Skinner* (pp. 1–21). New York: Appleton-Century-Crofts.

Skinner, B. F. (1971). *Beyond freedom and dignity*. New York: Knopf.

Skinner, B. F. (1978). *Reflections on behaviorism and society*. Englewood Cliffs, NJ: Prentice Hall.

Skinner, B. F. (1984). The shame of American education. *American Psychologist, 39*, 947–954.

Skinner, B. F. (1987). Whatever happened to psychology as the science of behavior? *American Psychologist, 42*, 780–786.

Skinner, B. F. (1990). Can psychology be a science of mind? *American Psychologist, 45*, 1206–1210.

Skinner, E. A., Wellborn, J. G., & Connell, J. P. (1990). What it takes to do well in school and whether I've got it: A process model of perceived control and children's engagement and achievement in school. *Journal of Educational Psychology, 82*, 22–32.

Slavin, R. E. (1994). *Using team learning* (4th ed.). Baltimore: Johns Hopkins University, Center for Research on Elementary Schools.

Slavin, R. E. (1995). *Cooperative learning* (2nd ed.). Boston: Allyn & Bacon.

Slavin, R. E., & Cheung, A. (2005). A synthesis of research on language of reading instruction for English language learners. *Review of Educational Research, 75*, 247–284.

Smith, E. E., & Medin, D. L. (1981). *Categories and concepts*. Cambridge, MA: Harvard University Press.

Smith, E. R. (1996). What do connectionism and social psychology offer each other? *Journal of Personality and Social Psychology, 70*, 893–912.

Smith, P. L., & Fouad, N. A. (1999). Subject-matter specificity of self-efficacy, outcome expectancies, interests, and goals: Implications for the social-cognitive model. *Journal of Counseling Psychology, 46*, 461–471.

Smith, R. E. (1989). Effects of coping skills training on generalized self-efficacy and locus of control. *Journal of Personality and Social Psychology, 56*, 228–233.

Snow, R. E. (1989). Toward assessment of cognitive and conative structures in learning. *Educational Researcher, 18*(9), 8–14.

Snow, R. E., Corno, L., & Jackson, D., III. (1996). Individual differences in affective and cognative functions. In D. C. Berliner & R. C. Calfee (Eds.), *Handbook of educational psychology* (pp. 243–310). New York: Macmillan.

Snowman, J. (1986). Learning tactics and strategies. In G. D. Phye & T. Andre (Eds.), *Cognitive classroom learning: Understanding, thinking, and problem solving* (pp. 243–275). Orlando: Academic Press.

Spence, J. T. (1984). Gender identity and its implications for the concepts of masculinity and femininity. In T. B. Sonderegger (Ed.), *Nebraska Symposium on Motivation, 1984* (Vol. 32, pp. 59–95). Lincoln, NE: University of Nebraska Press.

Spence, K. W. (1936). The nature of discrimination learning in animals. *Psychological Review, 43*, 427–449.

Spera, C. (2005). A review of the relationship among parenting practices, parenting styles, and adolescent school achievement. *Educational Psychology Review, 17*, 125–146.

Sperling, G. (1960). The information available in brief visual presentations. *Psychological Monographs, 74*(Whole No. 498).

Sperling, M., & Freedman, S. W. (2001). Research on writing. In V. Richardson (Ed.), *Handbook of research on teaching* (4th ed., pp. 379–389). Washington, DC: American Educational Research Association.

Spilich, G. J., Vesonder, G. T., Chiesi, H. L., & Voss, J. F. (1979). Text-processing of domain-related information for individuals with high and low domain knowledge. *Journal of Verbal Learning and Verbal Behavior, 18*, 275–290.

Springer, L., Stanne, M. E., & Donovan, S. S. (1999). Effects of small-group learning on undergraduates in science, mathematics, engineering, and technology: A meta-analysis. *Review of Educational Research, 69*, 21–51.

Stein, B. S., Littlefield, J., Bransford, J. D., & Persampieri, M. (1984). Elaboration and knowledge acquisition. *Memory & Cognition, 12*, 522–529.

Stein, M., & Carnine, D. (1999). Designing and delivering effective mathematics instruction. In R. J. Stevens (Ed.), *Teaching in American schools* (pp. 245–269). Upper Saddle River, NJ: Merrill/Prentice Hall.

Stein, N. L., & Glenn, C. G. (1979). An analysis of story comprehension in elementary school children. In R. O. Freedle (Ed.), *New directions in discourse processing* (pp. 53–120). Norwood, NJ: Ablex.

Stein, N. L., & Trabasso, T. (1982). What's in a story: An approach to comprehension and instruction. In R. Glaser (Ed.), *Advances in instructional psychology* (Vol. 2, pp. 213–267). Hillsdale, NJ: Erlbaum.

Steinberg, L., Brown, B. B., & Dornbusch, S. M. (1996). *Beyond the classroom: Why school reform has failed and what parents need to do*. New York: Simon & Schuster.

Stenhoff, D. M., & Lignugaris/Kraft, B. (2007). A review of the effects of peer tutoring on students with mild disabilities in secondary settings. *Exceptional Children, 74*, 8–30.

Sternberg, R. J. (1986). Cognition and instruction: Why the marriage sometimes ends in divorce. In R. F. Dillon & R. J. Sternberg (Eds.), *Cognition and instruction* (pp. 375–382). Orlando: Academic Press.

Sternberg, R. J., & Grigorenko, E. L. (1997). Are cognitive styles still in style? *American Psychologist, 52*, 700–712.

Sternberg, R. J., & Horvath, J. A. (1995). A prototype view of expert teaching. *Educational Researcher, 24*(6), 9–17.

Sternberg, S. (1969). Memory-scanning: Mental processes revealed by reaction-time experiments. *American Scientist, 57*, 421–457.

Stevenson, H. W., Chen, C., & Uttal, D. H. (1990). Beliefs and achievement: A study of black, white, and Hispanic children. *Child Development, 61*, 508–523.

Stipek, D. J. (1996). Motivation and instruction. In D. C. Berliner & R. C. Calfee (Eds.), *Handbook of educational psychology* (pp. 85–113). New York: Macmillan.

Stipek, D. J. (2002). Good instruction is motivating. In A. Wigfield & J. S. Eccles (Eds.), *Development of achievement motivation* (pp. 309–332). San Diego: Academic Press.

Stipek, D. J., & Kowalski, P. S. (1989). Learned helplessness in task-orienting versus performance-orienting testing conditions. *Journal of Educational Psychology, 81*, 384–391.

Stipek, D. J., & Ryan, R. H. (1997). Economically disadvantaged preschoolers: Ready to learn but further to go. *Developmental Psychology, 33*, 711–723.

Strain, P. S., Kerr, M. M., & Ragland, E. U. (1981). The use of peer social initiations in the treatment of social withdrawal. In P. S. Strain (Ed.), *The utilization of classroom peers as behavior change agents* (pp. 101–128). New York: Plenum.

Strecher, V. J., DeVellis, B. M., Becker, M. H., & Rosenstock, I. M. (1986). The role of self-efficacy in achieving health behavior change. *Health Education Quarterly, 13*(1), 73–91.

Stright, A. D., Neitzel, C., Sears, K. G., & Hoke-Sinex, L. (2001). Instruction begins in the home: Relations between parental instruction and children's self-regulation in the classroom. *Journal of Educational Psychology, 93*, 456–466.

Stull, A. T., & Mayer, R. E. (2007). Learning by doing versus learning by viewing: Three experimental comparisons of learner-generated versus author-provided graphic organizers. *Journal of Educational Psychology, 99*, 808–820.

Sun, R., Slusarz, P., & Terry, C. (2005). The interaction of the explicit and the implicit in skill learning: A dual-process approach. *Psychological Review, 112*, 159–192.

Sunshine, P. M., & DiVesta, F. J. (1976). Effects of density and format on letter discrimination by beginning readers with different learning styles. *Journal of Educational Psychology, 68*, 15–19.

Suppes, P. (1974). The place of theory in educational research. *Educational Researcher, 3*(6), 3–10.

Swanson, H. L. (2008). Working memory and intelligence in children: What develops? *Journal of Educational Psychology, 100*, 581–602.

Swanson, H. L., Howard, C. B., & Sáez, L. (2006). Do different components of working memory underlie different subgroups of reading disabilities? *Journal of Learning Disabilities, 39*, 252–269.

Sweller, J., van Merriënboer, J. J. G., & Paas, F. (1998). Cognitive architecture and instructional design. *Educatioinal Psychology Review, 10*, 251–296.

Tallent-Runnels, M. K., Thomas, J. A., Lan, W. Y., Cooper, S., Ahern, T. C., Shaw, S. M., & Liu, X. (2006). Teaching courses online: A review of the research. *Review of Educational Research, 76*, 93–135.

Tarde, G. (1903). *The laws of imitation.* New York: Henry Holt.

Taylor, A. M., Josberger, M., & Whitely, S. E. (1973). Elaboration instruction and verbalization as factors facilitating retarded children's recall. *Journal of Educational Psychology, 64*, 341–346.

Tennyson, R. D. (1980). Instructional control strategies and content structure as design variables in concept acquisition using computer-based instruction. *Journal of Educational Psychology, 72*, 525–532.

Tennyson, R. D. (1981). Use of adaptive information for advisement in learning concepts and rules using computer-assisted instruction. *American Educational Research Journal, 18*, 425–438.

Tennyson, R. D., & Park, O. (1980). The teaching of concepts: A review of instructional design research literature. *Review of Educational Research, 50*, 55–70.

Tennyson, R. D., Steve, M. W., & Boutwell, R. C. (1975). Instance sequence and analysis of instance attribute repre-sentation in concept acquisition. *Journal of Educational Psychology, 67*, 821–827.

Terry, W. S. (2009). *Learning and memory: Basic principles, processes, and procedures* (4th ed.). Boston: Allyn & Bacon.

Tharp, R. G. (1989). Psychocultural variables and constants: Effects on teaching and learning in schools. *American Psychologist, 44*, 349–359.

Tharp, R. G., & Gallimore, R. (1988). *Rousing minds to life: Teaching, learning, and schooling in social context.* New York: Cambridge University Press.

Thelen, M. H., Fry, R. A., Fehrenbach, P. A., & Frautschi, N. M. (1979). Therapeutic videotape and film modeling: A review. *Psychological Bulletin, 86*, 701–720.

Thomson, D. M., & Tulving, E. (1970). Associative encoding and retrieval: Weak and strong cues. *Journal of Experimental Psychology, 86*, 255–262.

Thorndike, E. L. (1906). *The principles of teaching: Based on psychology.* New York: A. G. Seiler.

Thorndike, E. L. (1911). *Animal intelligence: Experimental studies.* New York: Macmillan.

Thorndike, E. L. (1912). *Education: A first book.* New York: Macmillan.

Thorndike, E. L. (1913a). *Educational psychology: Vol. 1. The original nature of man.* New York: Teachers College Press.

Thorndike, E. L. (1913b). *Educational psychology: Vol. 2. The psychology of learning.* New York: Teachers College Press.

Thorndike, E. L. (1914). *Educational psychology: Vol. 3. Mental work and fatigue and individual differences and their causes.* New York: Teachers College Press.

Thorndike, E. L. (1924). Mental discipline in high school studies. *Journal of Educational Psychology, 15*, 1–22, 83–98.

Thorndike, E. L. (1927). The law of effect. *American Journal of Psychology, 39*, 212–222.

Thorndike, E. L. (1932). *The fundamentals of learning.* New York: Teachers College Press.

Thorndike, E. L., & Gates, A. I. (1929). *Elementary principles of education.* New York: Macmillan.

Thorndike, E. L., & Woodworth, R. S. (1901). The influence of improvement in one mental function upon the efficiency of other functions. *Psychological Review, 8*, 247–261, 384–395, 553–564.

Thorndyke, P. W., & Hayes-Roth, B. (1979). The use of schemata in the acquisition and transfer of knowledge. *Cognitive Psychology, 11*, 82–106.

Tiedemann, J. (1989). Measures of cognitive styles: A critical review. *Educational Psychologist, 24*, 261–275.

Timberlake, W., & Farmer-Dougan, V. A. (1991). Reinforcement in applied settings: Figuring out ahead of time what will work. *Psychological Bulletin, 110*, 379–391.

Titchener, E. B. (1909). *Lectures on the experimental psychology of the thought processes.* New York: Macmillan.

Tobias, C. U. (1994). *The way they learn: How to discover and teach your child's strengths.* Colorado Springs: Focus on the Family Publishing.

Tollefson, N., Tracy, D. B., Johnsen, E. P., Farmer, A. W., & Buenning, M. (1984). Goal setting and personal responsibility training for LD adolescents. *Psychology in the Schools, 21*, 224–233.

Tolman, E. C. (1932). *Purposive behavior in animals and men.* New York: Appleton-Century-Crofts. (Reprinted 1949, 1951, University of California Press, Berkeley, CA)

Tolman, E. C. (1942). *Drives toward war*. New York: Appleton-Century-Crofts.

Tolman, E. C. (1949). There is more than one kind of learning. *Psychological Review, 56,* 144–155.

Tolman, E. C. (1951). *Collected papers in psychology*. Berkeley, CA: University of California Press.

Tolman, E. C. (1959). Principles of purposive behavior. In S. Koch (Ed.), *Psychology: A study of a science* (Vol. 2, pp. 92–157). New York: McGraw-Hill.

Tolman, E. C., & Honzik, C. H. (1930). Introduction and removal of reward, and maze performance in rats. *University of California Publications in Psychology, 4,* 257–275.

Tolman, E. C., Ritchie, B. F., & Kalish, D. (1946a). Studies in spatial learning. I. Orientation and the short-cut. *Journal of Experimental Psychology, 36,* 13–24.

Tolman, E. C., Ritchie, B. F., & Kalish, D. (1946b). Studies in spatial learning. II. Place learning versus response learning. *Journal of Experimental Psychology, 36,* 221–229.

Tolson, J. (2006, October 23). Is there room for the soul? New challenges to our most cherished beliefs about self and the human spirit. *U. S. News & World Report, 141,* 56–63.

Tracey, T. J. G. (2002). Development of interests and competency beliefs: A 1-year longitudinal study of fifth- to eighth-grade students using the ICA-R and structural equation modeling. *Journal of Counseling Psychology, 49,* 148–163.

Trappl, R. (1985). Artificial intelligence: A one-hour course. In R. Trappl (Ed.), *Impacts of artificial intelligence: Scientific, technological, military, economic, societal, cultural, and political* (pp. 5–30). Amsterdam: Elsevier Science Publishers.

Trautwein, U., Lüdtke, O., Marsh, H. W., & Nagy, G. (2009). Within-school social comparison: How students perceive the standing of their class predicts academic self-concept. *Journal of Educational Psychology, 101,* 853–866.

Trawick-Smith, J. (2003). *Early childhood development: A multicultural perspective* (3rd ed.). Upper Saddle River, NJ: Merrill/Prentice Hall.

Treffinger, D. J. (1985). Review of the Torrance Tests of Creative Thinking. In J. Mitchell (Ed.), *Ninth Mental Measurements Yearbook* (pp. 1633–1634). Lincoln, NE: Buros Institute of Mental Measurement.

Treffinger, D. J. (1995). Creative problem solving: Overview and educational implications. *Educational Psychology Review, 7,* 301–312.

Treffinger, D. J., & Isaksen, S. G. (2005). Creative problem solving: The history, development, and implications for gifted education and talent development. *Gifted Child Quarterly, 49,* 342–353.

Treisman, A. M. (1960). Contextual cues in selective listening. *Quarterly Journal of Experimental Psychology, 12,* 242–248.

Treisman, A. M. (1964). Verbal cues, language, and meaning in selective attention. *American Journal of Psychology, 77,* 206–219.

Treisman, A. M., & Gelade, G. (1980). A feature-integration theory of attention. *Cognitive Psychology, 12,* 97–136.

Treisman, A. M. (1992). Perceiving and re-perceiving objects. *American Psychologist, 47,* 862–875.

Trevarthen, C. (1998). Brain development. In R. L. Gregory (Ed.), *The Oxford companion to the mind* (pp. 101–110). Oxford, England: Oxford University Press.

Tschannen-Moran, M., Hoy, A. W., & Hoy, W. K. (1998). Teacher efficacy: Its meaning and measure. *Review of Educational Research, 68,* 202–248.

Tudge, J. R. H., & Scrimsher, S. (2003). Lev S. Vygotsky on education: A cultural-historical, interpersonal, and individual approach to development. In B. J. Zimmerman & D. H. Schunk (Eds.), *Educational psychology: A century of contributions* (pp. 207–228). Mahwah, NJ: Erlbaum.

Tudge, J. R. H., & Winterhoff, P. A. (1993). Vygotsky, Piaget, and Bandura: Perspectives on the relations between the social world and cognitive development. *Human Development, 36,* 61–81.

Tulving, E. (1972). Episodic and semantic memory. In E. Tulving & W. Donaldson (Eds.), *Organization of memory* (pp. 381–403). New York: Academic Press.

Tulving, E. (1974). Cue-dependent forgetting. *American Scientist, 62,* 74–82.

Tulving, E. (1983). *Elements of episodic memory*. Oxford, England: Clarendon Press.

Tuovinen, J. E., & Sweller, J. (1999). A comparison of cognitive load associated with discovery learning and worked examples. *Journal of Educational Psychology, 91,* 334–341.

Tweney, R. D., & Budzynski, C. A. (2000). The scientific status of American psychology in 1900. *American Psychologist, 55,* 1014–1017.

Ullmann, L. P., & Krasner, L. (1965). *Case studies in behavior modification*. New York: Holt, Rinehart & Winston.

Ulrich, R., Stachnik, T., & Mabry, J. (1966). *Control of human behavior*. Glenview, IL: Scott, Foresman.

Underwood, B. J. (1961). Ten years of massed practice on distributed practice. *Psychological Review, 68,* 229–247.

Underwood, B. J. (1983). *Attributes of memory*. Glenview, IL: Scott, Foresman.

Unsworth, N., & Engle, R. W. (2007). The nature of individual differences in working memory capacity: Active maintenance in primary memory and controlled search from secondary memory. *Psychological Review, 114,* 104–132.

Valentine, C. W. (1930a). The innate base of fear. *Journal of Genetic Psychology, 37,* 394–419.

Valentine, C. W. (1930b). The psychology of imitation with special reference to early childhood. *British Journal of Psychology, 21,* 105–132.

Valentine, J. C., DuBois, D. L., & Cooper, H. (2004). The relation between self-beliefs and academic achievement: A meta-analytic review. *Educational Psychologist, 39,* 111–133.

Vandell, D. L. (2000). Parents, peer groups, and other socializing influences. *Developmental Psychology, 36,* 699–710.

van Gog, T., Paas, F., Marcus, N., Ayres, P., & Sweller, J. (2009). The mirror neuron system and observational learning: Implications for the effectiveness of dynamic visualizations. *Educational Psychology Review, 21,* 21–30.

van Laar, C. (2000). The paradox of low academic achievement but high self-esteem in African American students: An attributional account. *Educational Psychology Review, 12,* 33–61.

VanLehn, K. (1996). Cognitive skill acquisition. *Annual Review of Psychology, 47,* 513–539.

van Merriënboer, J. J. G., Kirschner, P. A., & Kester, L. (2003). Taking the load off a learner's mind: Instructional design for complex learning. *Educational Psychologist, 38,* 5–13.

van Merriënboer, J. J. G., & Sweller, J. (2005). Cognitive load theory and complex learning: Recent developments and future directions. *Educational Psychology Review, 17,* 147–177.

Varma, S., McCandliss, B. D., & Schwartz, D. L. (2008). Scientific and pragmatic challenges for bridging education and neuroscience. *Educational Researcher, 37,* 140–152.

Vekiri, I. (2002). What is the value of graphical displays in learning? *Educational Psychology Review, 14,* 261–312.

Vellutino, F. R., & Denckla, M. B. (1996). Cognitive and neuropsychological foundations of word identification in poor and normally developing readers. In R. Barr, M. L. Kamil, P. B. Mosenthal, & P. D. Pearson (Eds.), *Handbook of reading research* (Vol. 2, pp. 571–608). Mahwah, NJ: Erlbaum.

Verdi, M. P., & Kulhavy, R. W. (2002). Learning with maps and texts: An overview. *Educational Psychology Review, 14,* 27–46.

Vermeer, H. J., Boekaerts, M., & Seegers, G. (2000). Motivational and gender differences: Sixth-grade students' mathematical problem-solving behavior. *Journal of Educational Psychology, 92,* 308–315.

Veroff, J. (1969). Social comparison and the development of achievement motivation. In C. P. Smith (Ed.), *Achievement-related motives in children* (pp. 46–101). New York: Russell Sage Foundation.

Vispoel, W. P. (1995). Self-concept in artistic domains: An extension of the Shavelson, Hubner, and Stanton (1976) model. *Journal of Educational Psychology, 87,* 134–153.

Vollmeyer, R., & Rheinberg, F. (2006). Motivational effects on self-regulated learning with different tasks. *Educational Psychology Review, 18,* 239–253.

Voss, J. F., Vesonder, G. T., & Spilich, G. J. (1980). Text generation and recall by high-knowledge and low-knowledge individuals. *Journal of Verbal Learning and Verbal Behavior, 19,* 651–657.

Voss, J. F., Wiley, J., & Carretero, M. (1995). Acquiring intellectual skills. *Annual Review of Psychology, 46,* 155–181.

Vygotsky, L. (1962). *Thought and language.* Cambridge, MA: MIT Press.

Vygotsky, L. (1978). *Mind in society: The development of higher psychological processes.* Cambridge, MA: Harvard University Press.

Vygotsky, L. (1987). *The collected works of L. S. Vygotsky: Vol. 1. Problems of general psychology* (R. W. Rieber & A. S. Carton, Vol. Eds.; N. Minick, Trans.). New York: Plenum.

Wadsworth, B. J. (1996). *Piaget's theory of cognitive and affective development* (5th ed.). White Plains, NY: Longman.

Wallas, G. (1921). *The art of thought.* New York: Harcourt, Brace, & World.

Wallis, C. (2004, May 10). What makes teens tick. *Time, 163,* 56–62, 65.

Washington, V., & Bailey, U. J. O. (1995). *Project Head Start: Models and strategies for the twenty-first century.* New York: Garland.

Wason, P. C. (1966). Reasoning. In B. M. Foss (Ed.), *New horizons in psychology* (pp. 135–151). Harmondsworth, England: Penguin.

Wason, P. C., & Johnson-Laird, P. N. (1972). *The psychology of deduction: Structure and content.* Cambridge, MA: Harvard University Press.

Watson, J. B. (1916). The place of the conditioned-reflex in psychology. *Psychological Review, 23,* 89–116.

Watson, J. B. (1924). *Behaviorism.* New York: Norton.

Watson, J. B. (1926a). Experimental studies on the growth of the emotions. In C. Murchison (Ed.), *Psychologies of 1925* (pp. 37–57). Worcester, MA: Clark University Press.

Watson, J. B. (1926b). What the nursery has to say about instincts. In C. Murchison (Ed.), *Psychologies of 1925* (pp. 1–35). Worcester, MA: Clark University Press.

Watson, J. B., & Rayner, R. (1920). Conditioned emotional reactions. *Journal of Experimental Psychology, 3,* 1–14.

Watt, H. M. G. (2004). Development of adolescents' self-perceptions, values, and task perceptions according to gender and domain in 7th- through 11th-grade Australian students. *Child Development, 75,* 1556–1574.

Weiner, B. (1979). A theory of motivation for some classroom experiences. *Journal of Educational Psychology, 71,* 3–25.

Weiner, B. (1985). An attributional theory of achievement motivation and emotion. *Psychological Review, 92,* 548–573.

Weiner, B. (1990). History of motivational research in education. *Journal of Educational Psychology, 82,* 616–622.

Weiner, B. (1992). *Human motivation: Metaphors, theories, and research.* Newbury Park, CA: SAGE Publications.

Weiner, B. (2000). Intrapersonal and interpersonal theories of motivation from an attributional perspective. *Educational Psychology Review, 12,* 1–14.

Weiner, B. (2004). Attribution theory revisited: Transforming cultural plurality into theoretical unity. In D. M. McInerney & S. Van Etten (Eds.), *Big theories revisited* (pp. 13–29). Greenwich, CT: Information Age Publishing.

Weiner, B. (2005). Motivation from an attributional perspective and the social psychology of perceived competence. In A. J. Elliot & C. S. Dweck (Eds.), *Handbook of competence and motivation* (pp. 73–84). New York: Guilford Press.

Weiner, B., Frieze, I. H., Kukla, A., Reed, L., Rest, S., & Rosenbaum, R. M. (1971). *Perceiving the causes of success and failure.* Morristown, NJ: General Learning Press.

Weiner, B., Graham, S., Taylor, S. E., & Meyer, W. (1983). Social cognition in the classroom. *Educational Psychologist, 18,* 109–124.

Weiner, B., & Kukla, A. (1970). An attributional analysis of achievement motivation. *Journal of Personality and Social Psychology, 15,* 1–20.

Weiner, B., & Peter, N. (1973). A cognitive-developmental analysis of achievement and moral judgments. *Developmental Psychology, 9,* 290–309.

Weinstein, C. E. (1978). Elaboration skills as a learning strategy. In H. F. O'Neil, Jr. (Ed.), *Learning strategies* (pp. 31–55). New York: Academic Press.

Weinstein, C. E., & Hume, L. M. (1998). *Study strategies for lifelong learning.* Washington, DC: American Psychological Association.

Weinstein, C. E., & Mayer, R. E. (1986). The teaching of learning strategies. In M. C. Wittrock (Ed.), *Handbook of research on teaching* (3rd ed., pp. 315–327). New York: Macmillan.

Weinstein, C. E., & Palmer, D. R. (1990). *LASSI-HS: Learning and Study Strategies Inventory—High School Version.* Clearwater, FL: H & H Publishing Company.

Weinstein, C. E., Palmer, D. R., & Schulte, A. C. (1987). *LASSI: Learning and Study Strategies Inventory.* Clearwater, FL: H & H Publishing Company.

Weiss, M. R. (1983). Modeling and motor performance: A developmental perspective. *Research Quarterly for Exercise and Sport, 54,* 190–197.

Weiss, M. R., Ebbeck, V., & Wiese-Bjornstal, D. M. (1993). Developmental and psychological factors related to children's observational learning of physical skills. *Pediatric Exercise Science, 5,* 301–317.

Weiss, M. R., & Klint, K. A. (1987). "Show and tell" in the gymnasium: An investigation of developmental differences in modeling and verbal rehearsal of motor skills. *Research Quarterly for Exercise and Sport, 58*, 234–241.

Wellman, H. M. (1977). Tip of the tongue and feeling of knowing experiences: A developmental study of memory monitoring. *Child Development, 48*, 13–21.

Wellman, H. M. (1988). The early development of memory strategies. In F. Weinert & M. Perlmutter (Eds.), *Memory development: Universal changes and individual differences* (pp. 3–29). Hillsdale, NJ: Erlbaum.

Wellman, H. M. (1990). *The child's theory of mind.* Cambridge, MA: MIT Press.

Wentzel, K. R. (1992). Motivation and achievement in adolescence: A multiple goals perspective. In D. H. Schunk & J. L. Meece (Eds.), *Student perceptions in the classroom* (pp. 287–306). Hillsdale, NJ: Erlbaum.

Wentzel, K. R. (1996). Social goals and social relationships as motivators of school adjustment. In J. Juvonen & K. R. Wentzel (Eds.), *Social motivation: Understanding children's school adjustment* (pp. 226–247). Cambridge, England: Cambridge University Press.

Wentzel, K. R., Barry, C. M., & Caldwell, K. A. (2004). Friendships in middle school: Influences on motivation and school adjustment. *Journal of Educational Psychology, 96*, 195–203.

Wertheimer, M. (1945). *Productive thinking.* New York: Harper & Row.

Wertsch, J. V. (1979). From social interaction to higher psychological processes: A clarification and application of Vygotsky's theory. *Human Development, 22*, 1–22.

Wertsch, J. V. (1984). The zone of proximal development: Some conceptual issues. In B. Rogoff & J. V. Wertsch (Eds.), *Children's learning in the "zone of proximal development"* (pp. 7–18). San Francisco: Jossey-Bass.

Wertsch, J. V. (1985). *Culture, communication, and cognition: Vygotskian perspectives.* New York: Cambridge University Press.

Wheeler, L., & Suls, J. (2005). Social comparison and self-evaluations of competence. In A. J. Elliot & C. S. Dweck (Eds.), *Handbook of competence and motivation* (pp. 566–578). New York: Guilford Press.

White, P. H., Kjelgaard, M. M., & Harkins, S. G. (1995). Testing the contribution of self-evaluation to goal-setting effects. *Journal of Personality and Social Psychology, 69*, 69–79.

White R. (2001). The revolution in research on science teaching. In V. Richardson (Ed.), *Handbook of research on teaching* (4th ed., pp. 457–471). Washington, DC: American Educational Research Association.

White, R. T., & Tisher, R. P. (1986). Research on natural sciences. In M. C. Wittrock (Ed.), *Handbook of research on teaching* (3rd ed., pp. 874–905). New York: Macmillan.

White, R. W. (1959). Motivation reconsidered: The concept of competence. *Psychological Review, 66*, 297–333.

Whitely, S. E., & Taylor, A. M. (1973). Overt verbalization and the continued production of effective elaborations by EMR children. *American Journal of Mental Deficiency, 78*, 193–198.

Wickelgren, W. A. (1979). *Cognitive psychology.* Englewood Cliffs, NJ: Prentice Hall.

Wigfield, A. (1994). The role of children's achievement values in the self-regulation of their learning outcomes. In D. H. Schunk & B. J. Zimmerman (Eds.), *Self-regulation of learning and performance: Issues and educational applications* (pp. 101–124). Hillsdale, NJ: Erlbaum.

Wigfield, A., Byrnes, J. P., & Eccles, J. S. (2006). Development during early and middle adolescence. In P. A. Alexander & P. H. Winne (Eds.), *Handbook of educational psychology* (2nd ed., pp. 87–113). Mahwah, NJ: Erlbaum.

Wigfield, A., & Eccles, J. S. (1992). The development of achievement task values: A theoretical analysis. *Developmental Review, 12*, 265–310.

Wigfield, A., & Eccles, J. S. (2000). Expectancy-value theory of motivation. *Contemporary Educational Psychology, 25*, 68–81.

Wigfield, A., & Eccles, J. S. (2002). The development of competence beliefs, expectancies for success, and achievement values from childhood through adolescence. In A. Wigfield & J. S. Eccles (Eds.), *Development of achievement motivation* (pp. 91–120). San Diego: Academic Press.

Wigfield, A., Eccles, J. S., & Rodriguez, D. (1998). The development of children's motivation in school contexts. In P. D. Pearson (Ed.), *Review of Research in Education* (Vol. 23, pp. 73–118). Washington, DC: American Educational Research Association.

Wigfield, A., Hoa, L. W., & Klauda, S. L. (2008). The role of achievement values in the regulation of achievement behaviors. In D. H. Schunk & B. J. Zimmerman (Eds.), *Motivation and self-regulated learning: Theory, research, and applications* (pp. 169–195). New York: Taylor & Francis.

Wigfield, A., Tonks, S., & Eccles, J. S. (2004). Expectancy value theory in cross-cultural perspective. In D. M. McInerney & S. Van Etten (Eds.), *Big theories revisited* (pp. 165–198). Greenwich, CT: Information Age Publishing.

Wigfield, A., Tonks, S., & Klauda, S. L. (2009). Expectancy-value theory. In K. R. Wentzel & A. Wigfield (Eds.). *Handbook of motivation at school* (pp. 55–76). New York: Routledge.

Wigfield, A., & Wagner, A. L. (2005). Competence, motivation, and identity development during adolescence. In A. J. Elliot & C. S. Dweck (Eds.), *Handbook of competence and motivation* (pp. 222–239). New York: Guilford Press.

Williams, J. M., & Tolmie, A. (2000). Conceptual change in biology: Group interaction and the understanding of inheritance. *British Journal of Developmental Psychology, 18*, 625–649.

Windholz, G. (1997). Ivan P. Pavlov: An overview of his life and psychological work. *American Psychologist, 52*, 941–946.

Windschitl, M. (2002). Framing constructivism in practice as the negotiation of dilemmas: An analysis of the conceptual, pedagogical, cultural, and political challenges facing teachers. *Review of Educational Research, 72*, 131–175.

Windschitl, M., & Thompson, J. (2006). Transcending simple forms of school science investigation: The impact of preservice instruction on teachers' understandings of model-based inquiry. *American Educational Research Journal, 43*, 783–835.

Winett, R. A., & Winkler, R. C. (1972). Current behavior modification in the classroom: Be still, be quiet, be docile. *Journal of Applied Behavior Analysis, 5*, 499–504.

Winn, W. (2002). Current trends in educational technology research: The study of learning environments. *Educational Psychology Review, 14*, 331–351.

Winne, P. H. (2001). Self-regulated learning viewed from models of information processing. In B. J. Zimmerman & D. H. Schunk (Eds.), *Self-regulated learning and academic achievement: Theoretical perspectives* (2nd ed., pp. 153–189). Mahwah, NJ: Erlbaum.

Winne, P. H., & Hadwin, A. F. (1998). Studying as self-regulated learning. In D. J. Hacker, J. Dunlosky, & A. C. Graesser (Eds.), *Metacognition in educational theory and practice* (pp. 277–304). Hillsdale, NJ: Erlbaum.

Winne, P. H., & Hadwin, A. R. (2008). The weave of motivation and self-regulated learning. In D. H. Schunk & B. J. Zimmerman (Eds.), *Motivation and self-regulated learning: Theory, research, and applications* (pp. 297–314). New York: Taylor & Francis.

Winsler, A., & Naglieri, J. (2003). Overt and covert verbal problem-solving strategies: Developmental trends in use, awareness, and relations with task performance in children aged 5 to 17. *Child Development, 74,* 659–678.

Witkin, H. A. (1969). Social influences in the development of cognitive style. In D. A. Goslin (Ed.), *Handbook of socialization theory and research* (pp. 687–706). Chicago: Rand McNally.

Witkin, H. A., Moore, C. A., Goodenough, D. R., & Cox, P. W. (1977). Field-dependent and field-independent cognitive styles and their educational implications. *Review of Educational Research, 47,* 1–64.

Wolfe, P. (2001). *Brain matters: Translating research into classroom practice.* Alexandria, VA: Association for Supervision and Curriculum Development.

Wolleat, P. L., Pedro, J. D., Becker, A. D., & Fennema, E. (1980). Sex differences in high school students' causal attributions of performance in mathematics. *Journal for Research in Mathematics Education, 11,* 356–366.

Wolpe, J. (1958). *Psychotherapy by reciprocal inhibition.* Stanford, CA: Stanford University Press.

Wolters, C. A. (1998). Self-regulated learning and college students' regulation of motivation. *Journal of Educational Psychology, 90,* 224–235.

Wolters, C. A. (1999). The relation between high school students' motivational regulation and their use of learning strategies, effort, and classroom performance. *Learning and Individual Differences, 11,* 281–299.

Wolters, C. A. (2003). Regulation of motivation: Evaluating an underemphasized aspect of self-regulated learning. *Educational Psychologist, 38,* 189–205.

Wolters, C. A., Yu, S. L., & Pintrich, P. R. (1996). The relation between goal orientation and students' motivational beliefs and self-regulated learning. *Learning and Individual Differences, 8,* 211–238.

Wood, D. A., Rosenberg, M. S., & Carran, D. T. (1993). The effects of tape-recorded self-instruction cues on the mathematics performance of students with learning disabilities. *Journal of Learning Disabilities, 26,* 250–258, 269.

Wood, D. J., Bruner, J. S., & Ross, G. (1976). The role of tutoring in problem solving. *Journal of Child Psychology and Psychiatry, 17,* 89–100.

Wood, G., & Underwood, B. J. (1967). Implicit responses and conceptual similarity. *Journal of Verbal Learning and Verbal Behavior, 6,* 1–10.

Wood, R., & Bandura, A. (1989). Impact of conceptions of ability on self-regulatory mechanisms and complex decision-making. *Journal of Personality and Social Psychology, 56,* 407–415.

Wood, W., & Neal, D. T. (2007). A new look at habits and the habit-goal interface. *Psychological Review, 114,* 843–863.

Woodward, J., Carnine, D., & Gersten, R. (1988). Teaching problem solving through computer simulations. *American Educational Research Journal, 25,* 72–86.

Woodworth, R. S. (1918). *Dynamic psychology.* New York: Columbia University Press.

Woodworth, R. S., & Schlosberg, H. (1954). *Experimental psychology* (Rev. ed.). New York: Holt, Rinehart & Winston.

Woolfolk, A. E., & Hoy, W. K. (1990). Prospective teachers' sense of efficacy and beliefs about control. *Journal of Educational Psychology, 82,* 81–91.

Wouters, P., Paas, F., & van Merriënboer, J. J. G. (2008). How to optimize learning from animated models: A review of guidelines based on cognitive load. *Review of Educational Research, 78,* 645–675.

Wurtele, S. K. (1986). Self-efficacy and athletic performance: A review. *Journal of Social and Clinical Psychology, 4,* 290–301.

Wylie, R. C. (1979). *The self-concept* (Vol. 2). Lincoln, NE: University of Nebraska Press.

Yerkes, R. M., & Dodson, J. D. (1908). The relation of strength of stimulus to rapidity of habit-formation. *Journal of Comparative Neurology and Psychology, 18,* 459–482.

Zeiler, M. (1977). Schedules of reinforcement: The controlling variables. In W. K. Honig & J. E. R. Staddon (Eds.), *Handbook of operant behavior* (pp. 201–232). Englewood Cliffs, NJ: Prentice Hall.

Zepeda, S. J., & Mayers, R. S. (2006). An analysis of research on block scheduling. *Review of Educational Research, 76,* 137–170.

Zhang, L., & Sternberg, R. J. (2005). A threefold model of intellectual styles. *Educational Psychology Review, 17,* 1–53.

Zimmerman, B. J. (1977). Modeling. In H. Hom & P. Robinson (Eds.), *Psychological processes in children's early education* (pp. 37–70). New York: Academic Press.

Zimmerman, B. J. (1986). Becoming a self-regulated learner: Which are the key subprocesses? *Contemporary Educational Psychology, 11,* 307–313.

Zimmerman, B. J. (1989). Models of self-regulated learning and academic achievement. In B. J. Zimmerman & D. H. Schunk (Eds.), *Self-regulated learning and academic achievement: Theory, research, and practice* (pp. 1–25). New York: Springer-Verlag.

Zimmerman, B. J. (1990). Self-regulating academic learning and achievement: The emergence of a social cognitive perspective. *Educational Psychology Review, 2,* 173–201.

Zimmerman, B. J. (1994). Dimensions of academic self-regulation: A conceptual framework for education. In D. H. Schunk & B. J. Zimmerman (Eds.), *Self-regulation of learning and performance: Issues and educational applications* (pp. 3–21). Hillsdale, NJ: Erlbaum.

Zimmerman, B. J. (1998). Developing self-fulfilling cycles of academic regulation: An analysis of exemplary instructional models. In D. H. Schunk & B. J. Zimmerman (Eds.), *Self-regulated learning: From teaching to self-reflective practice* (pp. 1–19). New York: Guilford Press.

Zimmerman, B. J. (2000). Attaining self-regulation: A social cognitive perspective. In M. Boekaerts, P. R. Pintrich, & M. Zeidner (Eds.), *Handbook of self-regulation* (pp. 13–39). San Diego: Academic Press.

Zimmerman, B. J. (2001). Theories of self-regulated learning and academic achievement: An overview and analysis. In

B. J. Zimmerman & D. H. Schunk (Eds.), *Self-regulated learning and academic achievement: Theoretical perspectives* (2nd ed., pp. 1–38). Mahwah, NJ: Erlbaum.

Zimmerman, B. J. (2008). Goal setting: A key proactive source of academic self-regulation. In D. H. Schunk & B. J. Zimmerman (Eds.), *Motivation and self-regulated learning: Theory, research, and applications* (pp. 267–295). New York: Taylor & Francis.

Zimmerman, B. J., & Bandura, A. (1994). Impact of self-regulatory influences on writing course achievement. *American Educational Research Journal, 31,* 845–862.

Zimmerman, B. J., Bandura, A., & Martinez-Pons, M. (1992). Self-motivation for academic attainment: The role of self-efficacy beliefs and personal goal setting. *American Educational Research Journal, 29,* 663–676.

Zimmerman, B. J., & Blom, D. E. (1983a). On resolving conflicting views of cognitive conflict. *Developmental Review, 3,* 62–72.

Zimmerman, B. J., & Blom, D. E. (1983b). Toward an empirical test of the role of cognitive conflict in learning. *Developmental Review, 3,* 18–38.

Zimmerman, B. J., Bonner, S., & Kovach, R. (1996). *Developing self-regulated learners: Beyond achievement to self-efficacy.* Washington, DC: American Psychological Association.

Zimmerman, B. J., & Cleary, T. J. (2009). Motives to self-regulate learning: A social cognitive account. In K. R. Wentzel & A. Wigfield (Eds.), *Handbook of motivation at school* (pp. 247–264). New York: Routledge.

Zimmerman, B. J., Greenberg, D., & Weinstein, C. E. (1994). Self-regulating academic study time: A strategy approach. In D. H. Schunk & B. J. Zimmerman (Eds.), *Self-regulation of learning and performance: Issues and educational applications* (pp. 181–199). Hillsdale, NJ: Erlbaum.

Zimmerman, B. J., & Kitsantas, A. (1996). Self-regulated learning of a motoric skill: The role of goal setting and self-monitoring. *Journal of Applied Sport Psychology, 8,* 60–75.

Zimmerman, B. J., & Kitsantas, A. (1997). Developmental phases in self-regulation: Shifting from process goals to outcome goals. *Journal of Educational Psychology, 89,* 29–36.

Zimmerman, B. J., & Kitsantas, A. (1999). Acquiring writing revision skill: Shifting from process to outcome self-regulatory goals. *Journal of Educational Psychology, 91,* 241–250.

Zimmerman, B. J., & Kitsantas, A. (2005). The hidden dimension of perceived competence: Self-regulated learning and practice. In A. J. Elliot & C. S. Dweck (Eds.), *Handbook of competence and motivation* (pp. 509–526). New York: Guilford Press.

Zimmerman, B. J., & Koussa, R. (1975). Sex factors in children's observational learning of value judgments of toys. *Sex Roles, 1,* 121–132.

Zimmerman, B. J., & Martinez-Pons, M. (1990). Student differences in self-regulated learning: Relating grade, sex, and giftedness to self-efficacy and strategy use. *Journal of Educational Psychology, 82,* 51–59.

Zimmerman, B. J., & Martinez-Pons, M. (1992). Perceptions of efficacy and strategy use in the self-regulation of learning. In D. H. Schunk & J. L. Meece (Eds.), *Student perceptions in the classroom* (pp. 185–207). Hillsdale, NJ: Erlbaum.

Zimmerman, B. J., & Ringle, J. (1981). Effects of model persistence and statements of confidence on children's self-efficacy and problem solving. *Journal of Educational Psychology, 73,* 485–493.

Zimmerman, B. J., & Schunk, D. H. (Eds.) (2001). *Self-regulated learning and academic achievement: Theoretical perspectives* (2nd ed.). Mahwah, NJ: Erlbaum.

Zimmerman, B. J., & Schunk, D. H. (2003). Albert Bandura: The scholar and his contributions to educational psychology. In B. J. Zimmerman & D. H. Schunk (Eds.), *Educational psychology: A century of contributions* (pp. 431–457). Mahwah, NJ: Erlbaum.

Zimmerman, B. J., & Schunk, D. H. (2004). Self-regulating intellectual processes and outcomes: A social cognitive perspective. In D. Y. Dai & R. J. Sternberg (Eds.), *Motivation, emotion, and cognition: Integrative perspectives on intellectual functioning and development* (pp. 323–350). Mahwah, NJ: Erlbaum.

Zimmerman, B. J., & Tsikalas, K. E. (2005). Can computer-based learning environments (CBLEs) be used as self-regulatory tools to enhance learning? *Educational Psychologist, 40,* 267–271.

Zimmerman, B. J., & Whitehurst, G. J. (1979). Structure and function: A comparison of two views of the development of language and cognition. In G. J. Whitehurst & B. J. Zimmerman (Eds.), *The functions of language and cognition* (pp. 1–22). New York: Academic Press.

Zimmerman, C. (2000). The development of scientific reasoning skills. *Developmental Review, 20,* 99–149.

Zito, J. R., Adkins, M., Gavins, M., Harris, K. R., & Graham, S. (2007). Self-regulated strategy development: Relationship to the social-cognitive perspective and the development of self-regulation. *Reading & Writing Quarterly, 23,* 77–95.

Author Index

Hallahan, D. P., 102, 249, 404
Halliday, A. M., 55
Halpern, D. F., 307, 323, 440
Hamilton, R. J., 104
Hamlett, C. L., 322
Hamre, B. K., 18, 19
Hancock, C. R., 204
Hannafin, M. J., 326, 330
Hannus, M., 299
Hansen, C., 307
Hanson, A. R., 137, 150, 409, 412
Hanusa, B. H., 368
Harackiewicz, J. M., 141, 361, 378
Harari, O., 365, 395
Hardiman, P. T., 310
Harkins, S. G., 413
Harlow, S., 230
Harris, A., 88
Harris, J. A., 79, 382
Harris, J. R., 465
Harris, K., 439
Harris, K. R., 248, 290, 292, 334, 426, 439
Harter, S., 378, 386–388
Hartley, E. T., 137
Hartup, W. W., 250
Hastings, J. T., 107
Hattie, J., 142, 149, 378, 383, 425
Hau, K., 384
Haviland, S. E., 202, 208
Hayes, J. R., 334, 336, 438
Hayes, S. C., 403
Hayes-Roth, B., 193, 211
Haynes, N. M., 471
Haywood, H. C., 242, 245, 252
Hebb, D. O., 46, 47, 62
Heckhausen, H., 432
Hegarty, M., 340
Heidbreder, E., 4, 6, 9, 72
Heider, F., 349, 367–369
Henderlong, J., 389
Henderson, J. G., 272
Henderson, R. W., 252, 428
Henson, R. K., 153
Hersen, M., 402
Hetherington, E. M., 465
Hidi, S. E., 174, 432
Higgins, E. T., 373
Highet, G., 18
Hilbert, T., 333
Hilgard, E. R., 4, 46, 73, 75, 76
Hill, N. E., 469, 470
Hill, T., 467
Hippocrates, 37
Hirsch, E. D., Jr., 318
Hirt, E. R., 201

Hitchcock, C. H., 137
Hitler, A., 305
Hmelo-Silver, C. E., 268, 316, 317
Hoa, L. W., 434
Hoard, M. K., 339
Hodell, M., 326, 389, 390
Hofer, B. K., 436
Hoff, 468
Hogan, D., 153
Hogan, D. M., 270
Hoke-Sinex, L., 469
Holland, J. G., 89, 109
Hollandsworth, J. G., 425
Holley, C. D., 423
Hollis, K. L., 81, 82
Holyoak, K. J., 303, 307, 308
Hom, H. L. Jr., 141
Homme, L., 112
Honzik, C. H., 122
Hooper, S., 330
Hopkins, S. L., 339
Horn, C., 438
Horner, S. L., 129, 393
Hornyak, R. S., 402, 403
Horowitz, F. D., 72
Horton, G. P., 85
Horvath, J. A., 282
Hosford, R. E., 137
Houts, R., 484
Howard, C. B., 184, 293
Howard, J. H. Jr., 216
Howe, A., 371
Hoy, W. K., 153, 154
Hoyle, R. H., 377
Hoyt, J. D., 288
Hübscher, R., 243, 245, 246
Hudley, C., 371
Hull, C. L., 348
Hume, D., 6
Hume, L. M., 436
Humphrey, G., 125
Hung, W., 321
Hunt, E., 196, 198, 311, 313
Hunt, H. D., 471
Hunt, J., 388
Hunt, M., 4, 72, 78
Hurley, M. M., 439
Hutchinson, J. M., 102
Hyönä, J., 299
Hyslop-Margison, E. J., 230

Ilg, F., 452
Inhelder, B., 236
Inouye, D. K., 147, 149
Isaksen, S. G., 303, 308

Ivry, R., 35
Iyengar, S. S., 389, 475

Jacklin, C. N., 136
Jackson, D., III, 481
Jackson, S. J., 339
Jacob, K. F., 389
Jacobson, L., 258, 259
Jacoby, L., 168
Jacoby, L. L., 169
Jagacinski, C. M., 366, 379
James, W., 7, 9, 124, 432
Jannings, L. R., 289
Janson, M., 37
Jensen, E., 31, 33, 37, 43, 51–55, 58, 59, 66
Jensen, S., 79
Jitendra, A. K., 440
Jiwani, N., 412
Johnsen, E. P., 142
Johnson, A., 79, 376
Johnson, C. I., 327
Johnson, M. K., 194
Johnson, W. B., 159
Johnson-Laird, P. N., 311, 313–315
Johnston, M. B., 426
Joiner, R., 330
Jonassen, D. H., 110, 322, 324, 325
Josberger, M., 250
Jourden, F. J., 379
Jussim, L., 258, 259
Just, M. A., 204, 207
Justice, E. M., 289
Justice, L. M., 4

Kaczala, C. M., 371
Kagan, J., 480
Kail, R., 210
Kail, R. B., Jr., 287
Kail, R. V., 460
Kaiser, M., 283
Kalish, D., 143, 144
Kanfer, F. H., 123, 172, 407, 409, 411, 412
Kanfer, R., 172, 409, 412, 433
Kant, I., 5–6
Kaplan, H. B., 383
Kardash, C. A. M., 190
Kardash, C. M., 139
Karoly, P., 88, 156
Karpov, Y. V., 242, 245, 252
Katona, G., 187, 300
Katzir, T., 64
Keating, T., 412
Keele, S. W., 180
Keeney, T. J., 250

Marsh, H. W., 384, 385
Marshall, H. H., 254
Martin, J., 405, 430
Martinez-Pons, M., 257, 289, 412–414, 435
Marx, R. W., 298
Mashburn, A. J., 4
Maslow, A., 351–353
Mason, L. H., 292, 334
Masten, A. S., 465, 470
Master, 431
Mathes, P. G., 270
Matlin, M. W., 164, 165, 168, 172, 179, 180, 187–189, 196, 198, 201, 204, 213, 214, 286, 306, 461
Matthews, J. S., 461
Mautone, P. D., 218, 327
Mayer, R. E., 73, 76, 164, 165, 199, 200, 203, 218, 223, 224, 268, 298, 306, 308, 310, 326, 327, 333, 334, 337, 340, 417, 418, 420, 422, 425, 437
Mayer, S., 327
Mayers, R. S., 106
McCandliss, B. D., 42
McCarthy, J., 331
McCaulley, M. H., 478
McClelland, D. C., 358
McClelland, J. L., 199
McCloskey, M., 283
McCormick, C. B., 279, 426
McCormick, D., 112
McCullagh, P., 131, 132
McCutchen, D., 334–336
McDermott, J., 283
McDonald, B. A., 423
McDonald, H. E., 201
McDougall, W., 124
McGregor, G., 395
McGregor, H. A., 376, 378
McKeachie, W. J., 22, 73
McNeil, J. D., 131, 290, 423
McNeil, N. M., 440
McVee, M. B., 189
Medin, D. L., 293
Medway, F. J., 383
Meece, J. L., 203, 236, 237, 239, 243, 255, 292, 358, 362, 366, 371, 376–378, 440, 444, 450, 452–454, 460–462, 464, 466, 468, 469, 482, 483
Meichenbaum, D., 102, 129–131, 249, 250, 404, 424, 481
Merkel, S., 371
Merrill, M. M., 316

Merrill, P. F., 221
Messer, D., 330
Messer, S., 481
Messick, S., 478, 481
Mestre, J. P., 310
Mevarech, Z. R., 342
Mewborn, D. S., 337
Meyer, D. E., 195
Meyer, D. K., 378, 389
Meyer, W., 368
Mickelson, R., 145
Midgley, C., 434, 435, 464
Miliotis, D., 470
Mill, J. S., 6–7
Miller, A. T., 378, 395
Miller, G. A., 166, 183, 187, 209, 416, 481
Miller, M. D., 102, 371
Miller, N. E., 118, 125
Miller, S. D., 135, 292
Miller, T. R., 158
Miller-Johnson, S., 468
Miyake, A., 204
Moerk, E. L., 456
Molden, D. C., 257, 379
Molfese, D. L., 55
Moll, L. C., 245, 246, 252, 257
Moller, A. C., 389
Mondale, S., 446
Monk, A., 182
Monk, C. A., 340
Montemayor, R., 384
Monty, R. A., 370
Moore, C. A., 478
Moore, M. T., 311
Moors, A., 197
Moos, D. C., 148, 427
Moray, N., 179
Moreno, R., 224, 326, 327
Morgan, P. L., 292
Moritz, S. E., 153
Morris, C. D., 169
Morris, E. K., 89
Morrison, F. J., 461, 484
Morrison, R. G., 308
Morse, W. H., 99
Mortimer, E., 233
Moscovitch, M., 169
Moshman, D., 232, 286, 289
Moss, H. A., 480
Mostache, H. S., 374
Motl, R. W., 152
Mueller, C. G., 7
Mullen, C. A., 159, 247
Muller, U., 235
Multon, K. D., 148

Murdock, T. B., 379
Murphy, C. C., 144
Murphy, M. D., 141
Murphy, P. K., 386
Murphy, R. F., 471
Murray, D. J., 72
Murray, H., 467
Murray, H. A., 358
Muth, K. D., 105
Myers, I. B., 478
Myers, M. II, 288
Myers-Briggs, 478

Naglieri, J., 424
Nagy, G., 384
Nairne, J. S., 168, 170, 184, 212
National Research Council, 47, 56
Neal, D. T., 85
Neale, J., 371
Neath, I., 211
Neisser, U., 172, 178
Neitzel, C., 469
Nelson, J. B., 81
Nelson, R. O., 403
Nelson, T. O., 169
Nesbit, J. C., 296
Neumeister, K. L. S., 361
Newcombe, N. S., 337
Newell, A., 186, 303, 304, 310, 314, 315
Newman, R. S., 435, 436
Nicholls, J. G., 257, 258, 365, 366, 376, 378, 379, 395, 396
Nie, Y., 153
Nisbett, R. E., 390
Nokes, J. D., 315
Nolen, S. B., 258, 378
Nolen-Hoeksma, S., 382
Norby, M. M., 183
Norman, D. A., 172, 186, 191, 198
Novick, N., 298
Nugent, L., 339
Numtee, C., 339
Nurius, P., 384, 434
Nussbaum, E. M., 139
Nussbaum, J., 298

Oberauer, K., 211
O'Day, E. F., 109
Oden, S., 468
O'Donnell, A. M., 216, 246, 296
Ohlsson, S., 281
Oka, E. R., 424
O'Leary, K. D., 97
O'Leary, S. G., 405
Ollendick, T, H, 402

Subject Index